Praise for *The Presidents vs. The Press*

"[*The Presidents vs. The Press*] gives us a panoramic survey of the most contentious president-on-press brawls from the past two and a quarter centuries, providing both the scholar and the general reader with valuable perspective on the current bout between Trump and reporters."

—*The New York Times Book Review*

"A lively, deeply researched history of the roller-coaster relationships between presidents and journalists, from George Washington to Donald Trump . . . Holzer recounts all this and much more in considerable colorful detail."

—*The Washington Post*

"A perceptive and readable account." —*The Wall Street Journal*

"An immensely informative account of the perennial struggle between presidents and the fourth estate." —*Minneapolis Star Tribune*

"A shrewd history of the fight to convey and repress objective truth."

—*Kirkus Reviews*

"A lively and informative work that will appeal to anyone interested in American history, politics, and journalism." —*Library Journal*

"While this fascinating book doesn't ease the pain and anxiety of witnessing the elevated battle between Trump and reporters, it does provide an essential historical perspective."

—*Booklist*

"Timely and informative." —*Washington Independent Review of Books*

"Harold Holzer has brought us a sweeping, groundbreaking, and important history of the conflict between American presidents and the press, and it could not arrive at a more crucial moment."

—Michael Beschloss, NBC News presidential historian and *New York Times* bestselling author of *Presidents of War*

"Harold Holzer's fascinating new book beautifully narrates the long history of contention between the press and the White House, but it does more than that. Presidential politics were born at the dawn of popular newspaper writing, and the fighting, seducing, and conniving on both sides has continued ever since. Presidents and reporters can't really exist without each other, and Holzer, a historian of the presidency with the eye of a reporter, expertly explains why."

—Sean Wilentz, Pulitzer Prize finalist and author of *The Rise of American Democracy: Jefferson to Lincoln*

"Harold Holzer is a master in telling us exactly what we need to know—no more, no less—on a critical and obsessive relationship spanning 200 years. With a gimlet eye, Holzer shows how some of our best presidents—from George Washington to Abraham Lincoln to Barack Obama—were the most resistant to press scrutiny."

—Jonathan Alter, *New York Times* bestselling author of *His Very Best: Jimmy Carter, a Life*

"Not surprisingly, George Washington was the first president to protest 'the malicious falsehoods' and 'violent abuse' he'd suffered from the press. In this vivid, anecdotal history, Harold Holzer, himself a shrewd veteran of political press relations as well as a fine historian, chronicles the ways in which Washington and eighteen of his most important successors have sought to seduce and cajole, defy, and sometimes conspire with the men and women who cover them. No one interested in the presidency—or in the long history of 'fake news'—should miss it."

—Geoffrey C. Ward, *New York Times* bestselling author of *A First Class Temperament: The Emergence of Franklin Roosevelt*

"From George Washington railing against 'infamous scribblers' to the ravings of Donald Trump against 'fake news,' there is an inherent tension between presidents and the press. Harold Holzer brings this centuries-long struggle to life in a brisk, enjoyable and authoritative book that offers valuable perspective on the art of governing while shining a light on how the free press is still the ultimate guarantor of freedom."

—John Avlon, CNN Senior Political Analyst and author of *Washington's Farewell: The Founding Father's Warning to Future Generations*

THE PRESIDENTS vs. THE PRESS

Authored, co-authored, or edited by Harold Holzer

Monument Man

The Annotated Lincoln

A Just and Generous Nation

1865

Exploring Lincoln

President Lincoln Assassinated!

Lincoln and the Power of the Press

The Civil War in 50 Objects

1863: Lincoln's Pivotal Year

Emancipating Lincoln

Hearts Touched by Fire

Lincoln on War

The New York Times Complete Civil War

Lincoln: How Abraham Lincoln Ended Slavery in America

Lincoln and New York

Lincoln President-Elect

The Lincoln Assassination Conspirators

The Lincoln Anthology

In Lincoln's Hand

Lincoln and Freedom

Lincoln's White House Secretary

The Emancipation Proclamation: Three Views

The Battle of Hampton Roads

Lincoln in the Times

Lincoln at Cooper Union

Prang's Civil Pictures

Lincoln Seen and Heard

Lincoln as I Knew Him

The Lincoln Forum

The Lincoln Mailbag

Dear Mr. Lincoln

Washington and Lincoln Portrayed

Mine Eyes Have Seen the Glory

The Lincoln-Douglas Debates

Lincoln on Democracy

The Union Image

The Lincoln Family Album

The Confederate Image

The Lincoln Image

THE PRESIDENTS
—VS.—
THE PRESS

The Endless Battle Between the White House and the Media—
from the Founding Fathers to Fake News

HAROLD HOLZER

DUTTON

DUTTON
An imprint of Penguin Random House LLC
penguinrandomhouse.com

Previously published as a Dutton hardcover in August 2020

First Dutton trade paperback printing: August 2021

Jacket photographs: (cover) President Kennedy and members of the press at the signing of the Cuba Quarantine, October 23, 1962. (Photo by © CORBIS/Corbis via Getty Images)
(spine, top to bottom) Theodore Roosevelt delivering a speech on the preparation of the U.S. military, 1917. (Snark/Art Resource NY)
Democratic presidential candidate (AR Gov.) Bill Clinton reading newspaper aboard airplane, probably on campaign trail. (Photo by Steve Liss/The LIFE Images Collection via Getty Images/Getty Images)
Picture taken on November 22, 1960 at Paris showing American Vice President Lyndon Johnson talking to journalists after his meeting with French President Charles de Gaulle. (Photo by AFP via Getty Images)
U.S. President Ronald Reagan and First Lady Nancy Reagan relax in the 3rd Floor Solarium at the White House, October 15, 1981 in Washington, DC. (Photo by David Hume Kennerly/Getty Images)
U.S. President Barack Obama (C) speaks about the Affordable Care Act as U.S. Vice President Joe Biden (R) watches in the Rose Garden of the White House on April 1, 2014 in Washington, DC.
(Photo by Win McNamee/Getty Images)
American President Franklin Delano Roosevelt (1882–1945) addresses America over a nationwide hook up in a speech on the Neutrality Bill, October 12, 1939 (Photo by Topical Press Agency/Getty Images)

THE LIBRARY OF CONGRESS HAS CATALOGED THE HARDOVER EDITION OF THIS BOOK AS FOLLOWS:

Names: Holzer, Harold, author.
Title: The presidents vs. the press: the endless battle between the White House and the media—from the founding fathers to fake news / Harold Holzer.
Other titles: Presidents versus the press
Description: New York: Dutton, 2020. | Includes bibliographical references and index.
Identifiers: LCCN 2020000679 (print) | LCCN 2020000680 (ebook) |
ISBN 9781524745264 (hardcover) | ISBN 9781524745271 (ebook)
Subjects: LCSH: Presidents—Press coverage—United States—History. |
Press and politics—United States—History. | Mass media—Political aspects—United States—History.
Classification: LCC JK554 .H65 2020 (print) | LCC JK554 (ebook) |
DDC 070.4/4935230973—dc23
LC record available at https://lccn.loc.gov/2020000679
LC ebook record available at https://lccn.loc.gov/2020000680

Dutton trade paperback ISBN: 9781524745288

Printed in the United States of America
1st Printing

BOOK DESIGN BY LAURA K. CORLESS

To Edith

With enormous love and much gratitude for the first 49 years

CONTENTS

PART FIVE: "TRUTH IS THE GLUE"

I read only the *Richmond Enquirer*, and in that chiefly the advertisements, for they contain the only truths to be relied on in a newspaper.

—THOMAS JEFFERSON

Newspapers villainously mislead the public through ignorance but more frequently from dishonest design.

—ANDREW JACKSON

[T]ake possession by military force, of the printing establishments of the "New York World," and "Journal of Commerce," and hold the same until further order, and prevent any further publication therefrom.

—ABRAHAM LINCOLN

There is great anger in our Country caused in part by inaccurate, and even fraudulent, reporting of the news. The Fake News Media, the true Enemy of the People, must stop the open & obvious hostility & report the news accurately & fairly.

—DONALD TRUMP

PREFACE TO THE PAPERBACK EDITION

To pretend that the historic relationship between the presidency and the press did not change dramatically after this book originally appeared would be tantamount to, well, spreading fake news. That's why I am grateful to my publisher for allowing me to update the story with this preface to the paperback edition. I'll admit, too, that the opportunity gives me the chance to present some of the anecdotes that did not make it into the original. Now they seem too relevant to ignore, considering the experiences that the White House, the press corps, and American media consumers have lived through since—including the most fraught presidential transition in centuries.

I argue in this book, and still believe, that presidential hostility toward the press is not a new or inherently dangerous phenomenon, nor is tough, even highly partisan, press scrutiny of our presidents. That fundamental tension dates to the founding era. Yet Donald Trump managed to escalate it into an outright, unrelenting war against the media and truth itself, especially during the final year of his term, doing inestimable, but hopefully not permanent, damage.

As readers will note, the book's narrative ends in early 2020, with Trump about to face a rocky path to re-election, but by no means doomed to failure, however much he had antagonized the media. Then, as we know, something unexpected and transformational rocked the country: a global pandemic that required a nationwide lockdown and triggered a severe economic slump—and a new opportunity for Trump to try dominating news coverage, only to wilt under scrutiny.

Within months came his attempt to discredit, and ultimately resist, the results of his election defeat, and his surreally muted final days in office, out of the media spotlight he always craved. And finally, to use words that were once deployed to mourn Lincoln—by way of Shakespeare—came the "deep damnation of his taking-off." If we judge presidents, and their relationships with the press and public, in part by the grace they show during the transition to their successors, Trump may forever stand condemned.

Other presidential farewells have been quite different. Shortly before George W. Bush departed the White House after more than 2,900 days in the presidency—many of them spent in combat of his own with the media—he hosted his 210th and final press conference. Perhaps animated by a mutual sense of relief, it proved almost convivial. "We have been through a lot together," Bush began his opening statement that day in 2009, addressing both the "new faces" populating the press corps and the old hands who had traveled with him "around the world."

"Through it all," he told them, ". . . I respected you. Sometimes didn't like the stories that you wrote or reported on. Sometimes you 'misunderestimated' me. But always the relationship I have felt has been professional. And I appreciate it." Bush concluded by turning the tables on news conference protocol, posing a question of his own, and then providing a somewhat garbled, but heartfelt, answer: "My friends say, what is it like to deal with the press corps? I said, these are just people trying to do the best they possibly can . . . so thank you for the job."*

Unknowingly, Bush had launched what promised to become a valuable new ritual: the presidential farewell to the White House press, highlighted by a reaffirmation of the media's right to ask even disobliging questions in order to keep the public informed. Eight years later, in his own final session with correspondents, Barack Obama not only embraced the tradition, but sounded many of the themes his predecessor had. "I want . . . to thank all of you," he began his 2017 farewell press session, and then, unconsciously echoing Bush, added: "Some of you have been covering me for a long time. . . . Some of you I've just gotten to know. We have traveled the world together . . . and even when you complained about my long answers, I just want you to know that the only reason they were long was because you asked six-part questions."

When the laughter subsided, Obama, like Bush, turned nostalgic—with an edge: "I have enjoyed working with all of you. That does not, of course, mean that I've enjoyed every story that you have ever filed, but that's the point of the

---

* "President Bush's Final News Conference," *New York Times* transcript, January 12, 2009, online at https://www.nytimes.com/2009/02/12/us/politics/12text-bush.html.

relationship. You're not supposed to be fans, you're supposed to be skeptics. You're supposed to ask me tough questions. You're not supposed to be complimentary, but you're supposed to cast a critical eye on folks who hold enormous power and make sure that we are accountable to the people who sent us here, and you have done that . . . in ways that I could appreciate for fairness, even if I didn't always agree with your conclusions. And having you in this building has made this place work better. It keeps us honest. It makes us work harder."*

But there the tradition would die. By the time Obama's successor belatedly and begrudgingly signaled he would leave the White House four years later, it was no longer possible to imagine an exit interview overflowing with bonhomie and punctuated by re-affirmation of press freedom. By then, Donald Trump had demonized what Obama had called the virtue of media skepticism. As president, Trump's press strategy consisted of flattering sycophants and libeling critics. Using social media to unleash "alternative facts" beyond the scrutiny of professional journalists, Trump unleashed insults, accusations, and baseless conspiracy theories, climaxing a four-year onslaught on the truth with the most gargantuan lie of all: that the 2020 election was rigged and stolen.†

At the end of his term, in the irony of all ironies, the bully pulpit's most garrulous bully found himself "de-platformed"—banned by the very online megaphones he had weaponized for so long. Via Twitter in particular, Trump became purveyor-in-chief of the "fake news" for which he long blamed others. By its final count—a tally it began recording on Trump's first full day in the presidency—the *Washington Post* calculated that the forty-fifth president had told 30,573 lies in office. Trump ended with an average thirty-nine fabrications daily during his final year in office, and nearly 500 in his last hundred days—a staggering 10,000 more untruths than had been counted at the time I finished the hardcover edition of this book in early 2020.‡

No one can doubt that the America Trump left in his wake is more skeptical than ever about journalism and more dubious about indisputable facts, not to mention frighteningly susceptible to outright falsehoods, especially when

---

* "Obama's Last News Conference: Full Transcript," *New York Times*, January 18, 2017, online at https://www.nytims.com/2017/01/18/us/politics/obama-fina-news-conference.html.

† Historian Kathryn Olmsted

‡ Glenn Kessler, "Trump made 30,573 false or misleading claims as president. Nearly half came in his final year," *Washington Post*, January 23, 2021.

repeated often enough. Examples include Trump's claims that Mexico paid for his border wall (a lie he repeated on more than 200 occasions); his early guarantees that the COVID-19 epidemic would quickly fade or be mitigated by quack cures; and of course the 800 times he insisted he had won a landslide victory in the 2020 election, even after he lost by seven million votes and failed to overturn the results in some sixty court challenges.*

To be fair, not all experts assign sole blame to the ex-President for the decline of truth. Some assert that the press might have tried harder to understand the grievances that Trump's rise laid bare or, failing that, should have shamed and disqualified him the moment he told his first whopper. Instead, eager for good copy, especially a sustained story as difficult to ignore as a highway wreck, the media long gave Trump's bogus claims, conspiracy theories, and Islamophobia a free ride. Indeed, CBS Executive Chairman Les Moonves had admitted of Trump's first presidential candidacy: "It may not be good for America, but it's damn good for CBS."† Only in 2020 did CNN and MSNBC finally recover from their addiction to telecasting Trump campaign rallies live in their entirety.

Did journalists also ignore the white supremacist undertones lurking within Trump's messaging? "That crazed content has always been there," says Kathleen Hall Jamieson, co-founder of FactCheck.org. "But it becomes dangerous when it is legitimized and when it has the power of the state behind it."‡ Were enough objections raised not only to what was covered but to who covered it? Veteran journalist Karen Attiah chastises some of her colleagues for "willful moral malpractice" by "coddling . . . those who attack racial and religious minorities." But Attiah doubts that standards will rebound simply with Trump's defeat, arguing that recovery also requires "newsroom diversity and anti-racist coverage."§

The free press may have survived the Trump era—barely—but it operates now in a climate of pervasive doubt as well as physical threat from radicalized

---

* Ibid.

† Pete Vernon, "Media's Day of Reckoning: Don's antics were reviled by most news outlets even as he made them rich; now they must chart a new course," New York *Daily News*, January 24, 2021. For criticism of press, see for example Kathleen Parker, "If we're to unite as a country again, we need the media's cooperation," *Washington Post*, November 27, 2020.

‡ Quoted in Jose A. Del Real, "The Trump presidency was marked by battles over truth itself. Those aren't over," *Washington Post*, January 18, 2021.

§ Karen Attiah, "The media had a role to play in the rise of Trump. It's time to hold ourselves accountable," *Washington Post*, January 20, 2021.

news consumers. The domestic terrorists who invaded the U.S. Capitol on January 6, 2021, not only targeted Vice President Mike Pence and House Speaker Nancy Pelosi, but also the correspondents Trump had so often vilified as traitors. Evidence could be found in the message rioters scrawled on one of the Capitol doors that day: "MURDER THE MEDIA."*

Not since defenders of slavery murdered abolitionist editor Elijah P. Lovejoy in 1837 have journalists faced what young Abraham Lincoln characterized, in the wake of Lovejoy's violent death, as "the ravages of mob law . . . scenes becoming more and more frequent in this land so lately famed for the love of law and order." As Lincoln presciently warned, "whenever the vicious portion of population shall be permitted to gather in bands . . . shoot editors, and hang and burn obnoxious persons at pleasure, and with impunity; depend on it, this Government cannot last." And when "the perpetrators of such acts" go "unpunished," he added, "the lawless in spirit, are encouraged to become lawless in practice, and having been used to no restraint . . . have become absolutely unrestrained. Having ever regarded Government as their deadliest bane, they make a jubilee of the suspension of its operations; and pray for nothing so much, as its total annihilation."†

Few could have been surprised that Donald Trump hosted no farewell press give-and-take before leaving office. He had already abandoned the custom, after hosting eighty-eight formal news conferences (and countless daily briefings) during his four-year term. Trump blamed even his withdrawal from media interrogation on the media. Reporters were, he said, unfair to him.

Yet during the spring and summer of 2020, Trump had put himself on seemingly constant display, appearing almost daily at times in the White House briefing room, alongside his medical advisors, to update the nation on the pandemic. This opportunity he bungled by spouting junk science and taking umbrage at skeptical questions. The president deflected one probing inquiry from a CNN correspondent by blustering, "You're fake news . . . you

---

* Wendy Melillo, "The Free Press and Democracy in a 'Murder the Media' Age," History News Network, January 17, 2021, online at: https://historynewsnetwork.org/article/178792,

† Abraham Lincoln, "The Perpetuation of Our Political Institutions," address before the Young Men's Lyceum, Springfield, Illinois, January 27, 1838, in Roy P. Basler, ed., *The Collected Works of Abraham Lincoln*, 8 vols. (New Brunswick, NJ: Rutgers University Press, 1953-55), 1:110-111.

don't have the brains you were born with." (Just a few days earlier, he had publicly boasted—yet again, and as readers of this book will learn, inaccurately—"I think I came up with the term, 'Fake News.'") When another reporter questioned his prediction that the disease would vanish by Easter, Trump roared: "It's corrupt news . . . The press is very dishonest—they're siding with China, they are doing things they shouldn't be doing." Asked if he was giving Americans false hope about quick-fix COVID cures, Trump shot back, "I think you're a terrible reporter, that's what I say. I think it's a very nasty question."*

Almost mercifully, the answers ceased altogether when bad news became as incurable as the virus and when Trump, felled by COVID himself, vanished from the podium. By the time he prepared to storm out of office, he had been silent for weeks except for pre-taped messages as sincere as hostage videos. But he could not quite resist one last faceoff with the media. It came not in the manner of Bush's or Obama's final absolutions, but in a format Trump had long fancied. Throughout his term, just before boarding the presidential helicopter, he had made it his habit to stride toward the media gaggle gathered on the White House lawn to parry with reporters.

Now heading toward the chopper for his last flight on January 20, 2021, Trump detoured to the press pen one more time and there offered a surprisingly subdued version of the media farewell. "It has been something very special," Trump shouted over the din of the whirling blades of Marine One. "And I just want to say goodbye, but hopefully not a long-term goodbye." What followed could be interpreted either as a promise or a threat, depending on the reporters' tolerance for further bullying: "We'll see each other again."†

At the time this book was completed, the Coronavirus pandemic had not yet exploded. I well remember considering for inclusion in the book—but ultimately discarding—a yarn about President Woodrow Wilson's 1918 visit to Paris to negotiate the formal end to World War I. In light of recent events, it is

* Exchange published in Harold Holzer, "Pressing the Issue: Why Trump's attack on the media is more corrosive than other presidents'," New York *Daily News*, September 6, 2020.

† Jill Colvin, "Donald Trump leaves White House for last time as president, says his departure 'not a long term goodbye,'" Associated Press, January 20, 2021, reprinted online at https://abc7/com/trump/farewell-speech-inauguration-day-2021-biden/9837405/.

worth relating here. Wilson did not exactly keep journalists well-informed during that trip, and in the months to come his Administration would lie blatantly about his declining health. In Paris, suspicious reporters noticed at one point that, without explanation, he simply vanished from sight. No one would tell correspondents why or where the president had disappeared, and an official explanation never came. Unbeknownst to the press, Wilson had been laid low by blinding headaches, a hacking cough, and a fever that spiked to 103 degrees—enough to send any man into seclusion. It turned out to be a likely case of "Spanish Flu," the 1918 pandemic that would claim up to fifty million lives worldwide.* Writing this book a century later (but before COVID), I convinced myself that no one would want to read an episode that took place during a long-forgotten epidemic. Especially since we had endured none since—and surely never would, certainly not on a scale sufficient to infect another president.

When the clothbound edition of this book first appeared in late summer 2020, Trump still awaited his reckoning in the upcoming presidential election. When writing about a sitting chief executive, it is impossible to guess, much less craft, an ending to the story. And few observers could have predicted the tumult that followed: a race conducted amidst a dystopian outbreak of disease that altered the way conventions and campaigns are staged, yet somehow inspired a record turnout, a substantial victory for Joe Biden, and a violent insurrection at the U.S. Capitol.

After the transition from hell, the saga of Trump and the press finally ended—or at least paused—and the Joe Biden chapter commenced. In his inaugural address, the new president promised to resume frank dealings with the media and public. "We must reject a culture," he declared, "in which facts themselves are manipulated and even manufactured." He pledged his administration would be devoted to "yes, the truth."† And so commenced one of those idyllic press honeymoons described throughout this book, which seldom last as long as incoming presidents hope.

With Biden came, too, the resumption of daily briefings in the White House press room—another tradition that Trump had upended long before CNN's lead Washington anchor Jake Tapper complained that Trump's press secretary

---

* A. Scott Berg, *Wilson* (New York: G. P. Putnam's Sons, 2013), 568.

† "President Biden's Inaugural Address, Annotated," *New York Times*, January 21, 2021.

Kayleigh McEnany "lies the way that most people breathe."* At her debut, Biden's new spokesperson Jen Psaki channeled Jimmy Carter by assuring the press corps: "I will never lie to you."† After years spent "on the receiving end of offensive or hostile remarks"—particularly women correspondents—the White House press corps seemed eager to move past Trump's "predictably unpredictable nature" and from press conferences that had become a "theater for conflict."‡

But as history has taught us, presidents and their press secretaries often do not—sometimes cannot—live up to pledges of transparency and comity, however sincere. Thomas Jefferson once insisted he would prefer newspapers without government to government without newspapers—then feuded with press critics throughout his White House tenure and took his distrust of newspapers to the grave. As noted, Lincoln decried violence against editors as a local politician, but during the Civil War, as president, allowed his administration and army to jail hundreds of opposition editors.

Just two days after Germany attacked Poland to start World War II, Franklin D. Roosevelt extolled the free flow of information in America and promised it would continue. "You, the people of this country, are receiving news through your radios and your newspapers at every hour of the day," Roosevelt all but boasted in a Fireside Chat broadcast on September 3, 1939. "You are, I believe, the most enlightened and the best-informed people in all the world at this moment. You are subjected to no censorship of news, and I want to add that your government has no information which it withholds or which it has any thought of withholding from you."§

But two days after the Japanese attacked Pearl Harbor in 1941, bringing the United States into the global conflict, Roosevelt used another Fireside Chat to caution the public (and the press): "If you feel that your government is not

---

* Justin Baragona, "Kayleigh McEnany Proves Jake Tapper Right, Effortlessly Lies on Fox [Can't Stop, Won't Stop]," *Daily Beast*, December 28, 2020, https://www.thedailybeast.com/kayleigh-mcenany-proves-jake-tapper-right-effortlessly-lies-on-fox.

† Katie Rogers and Annie Karni, "Biden's New Press Secretary Debuts With Dodges, Parries and a Sense of Normalcy," *New York Times*, January 22, 2021.

‡ Olivia Nuzzi, "A Beleaguered White House Press Corps: Four years of history, day after day after day," *New York Magazine*, January 4-17, 2021.

§ Franklin D. Roosevelt, transcript of Fireside chat, September 3, 1939 ("On the European War"), Franklin D. Roosevelt Presidential Library & Museum, www.docs.fdrlibrary.marist.edu. See also Russell D. Buhite and David W. Levy, *FDR's Fireside Chats* (Norman: University of Oklahoma Press, 1992), 148-149.

disclosing enough of the truth, you have every right to say so. But—in the absence of all the facts, as revealed by official sources—you have no right in the ethics of patriotism, to deal out unconfirmed reports in such a way as to make people believe that they are gospel truth."*

A generation later, in December 1962, President John F. Kennedy sat down for an interview with NBC-TV correspondent Sander Vanocur, who had heard that the president, renowned for devouring information, was now so irked by negative press coverage that he was reading more and enjoying it less." Asked Vanocur: "Are you still as avid a newspaper reader?"

"Oh, yes," Kennedy replied. ". . . I think it's invaluable, even though . . . it is never pleasant to be reading things that are not agreeable news. But I would say that it is an invaluable arm of the presidency, as a check really on what is going on in the administration." Totalitarian systems may block press criticism, JFK went on to say, but ended up at "a terrific disadvantage not having the abrasive quality of the press applied to you daily." This had always been the case, he added, as if speaking not just for himself but for all presidents. "Even though we never like it, and even though we wish they didn't write it, and even though we disapprove, there isn't any doubt that we could not do the job at all in a free society without a very, very active press."† Of course, Kennedy had recently reminded the country's newspaper publishers that patriotism (even when it required the suppression of news) remained a higher calling than press freedom.

On the brief stroll Joe Biden undertook amidst tight security toward the end of his truncated inaugural parade, a knot of journalists near Lafayette Park, the only onlookers at the scene, tried lobbing a few questions at the man making his way toward the White House for the first time as president. Biden was not about to offer a response that deflected from the main news of the day. But he did shout in their direction: "Keep doing your job."

What will be fascinating to observe—and will surely become clear before

---

* Roosevelt Fireside Chat, December 9, 1941 ("On the Declaration of War with Japan"), FDR Presidential Library & Museum; Buhite and Levy, *FDR's Fireside Chats*, 201.

† "John F. Kennedy and the Press," transcript in the John F. Kennedy Presidential Library, online at https://www.jfklibrary.org/learn/about-jfk/jfk-in-history/john-f-kennedy-and-the-press,

this edition comes off the press—is how long Biden will continue encouraging journalists to do so. If history is any guide, the inevitable frost will arrive sooner rather than later. As early as February 2021, reporters groused when press secretary Psaki asked them to advise her in advance on subjects they planned to raise during briefings. "In a non-COVID environment," onetime Obama press officer Eric Schulz tried explaining, "this would happen in casual conversations throughout the day." That did not inhibit one correspondent from saying he was "pissed off."* And so it began. Encouragement will eventually yield to tolerance, and likely descend into resistance and perhaps resentment. The only thing open to question is whether the press and the president can at least restore and maintain the long-reigning understanding that separates news and hype, access and secrecy, the right to know and the power to withhold. That healthy tension prevailed before the Trump era, and once made John Kennedy believe that free society could not survive without it.

Which atmosphere will dominate the latest incarnation of the centuries-old relationship? Expect either the rancor JFK blamed on "the "abrasive quality of the press" or the essential scrutiny he lauded as an "invaluable arm of the presidency?" Or a combination of both.

As Bill Clinton reminded me after the first edition of this book appeared, "The truth is, most reporters want to do a good job. But most presidents want to do a good job, too."†

George W. Bush took an almost Jeffersonian tone when he sent me his reaction to the book. Noting he was all too "familiar" with its subject, he reiterated what he had said to reporters back in 2009. "I believe that an independent press is indispensable to democracy. It is important to hold those in power to account."‡

Harold Holzer
Rye, New York
March 1, 2021

---

* Maxwell Tani, "White House Reporters: Biden Team Wanted Our Questions in Advance," *Daily Beast*, February 1, 2021.

† Phone conversation, January 12, 2021.

‡ George W. Bush to Harold Holzer, December 16, 2020.

INTRODUCTION

In the summer of 1793, five months into his second term as the unanimously elected president of the United States, George Washington caught sight of a gruesome caricature just published in a local newspaper. The crudely drawn "pasquinade," meant to taunt him for tilting to Britain over France in foreign affairs, depicted the president with his head "placed on a Guillotine," ready for execution in the manner of disgraced French royalty. The typically stoic Washington was incensed. His blood rising, he stormed into a cabinet meeting and, as his secretary of state, Thomas Jefferson, observed, "got into one of those passions when he cannot command himself"—in other words, flew into a rage.

As all his cabinet ministers looked on in astonishment, recalled Jefferson, Washington hurled the offending cartoon to the floor of the executive mansion and launched into a tirade "on the personal abuse which had been bestowed on him" by opposition journalists. The president "[d]efied any man on earth to produce one single act of his since he had been in the government which was not done on the purest motives." Angrily repenting that he had not resigned the presidency earlier, he shouted that "by god he had rather be in his grave than his present situation."[1]

First in war, first in peace, and first in the hearts of his countrymen George Washington may have been, but he was also the first president to rant against negative press coverage, and anything but the last to believe himself egregiously maltreated by journalists. Even Jefferson, a staunch defender of the press's freedom to criticize presidents as long as Washington led the country, would endure—and decry—similar attacks once he occupied the White House.

The most recent president to respond angrily to press criticism is the most recent president. Donald Trump's relentless attacks on the journalists he brands "enemies of the people" fill—many opponents say, pollute—both social and mainstream media. Yet, in a way, Trump rails against the press much as his predecessors did—just more publicly, more often, and with faster and wider reach. Nearly all presidents, from Washington to Trump, have reacted to press criticism in this manner: treating what we now call "the media" as the enemy. Today's critics often complain that Trump circumvents the press to deploy his messages directly to the people through technologically advanced media, but so did Abraham Lincoln, Franklin D. Roosevelt, John F. Kennedy, and Barack Obama. Or that Trump obsesses about his press coverage; but so did Washington, Jefferson, Jackson, Theodore Roosevelt, and Lyndon B. Johnson. Or that Trump expects coverage of his personal life to remain off limits, as did FDR, JFK, and Bill Clinton.

In fact, no American president has ever counted himself fully satisfied with his press coverage. Their belief that they are better than their bad press, and that they bear a nearly sacred obligation to counter or control criticism, has remained fixed since the age of bewigged chief executives and hand-screwed printing presses. Most presidents have believed that unfriendly journalists cover their campaigns and administrations predisposed to assail their policies, misconstrue their motives, misunderstand their sincerity, and injure their reputations. What has changed far more than this basic antipathy is the technology that conveys it. The modern high-speed media has expanded the frequency, the timeliness, and abundance of presidential news—whether the presidents or the public like it or not.

By the same token, just as presidents have always convinced themselves of their own wisdom and virtue, the journalists who cover them have consistently believed that by working to uncover the presidents' errors and transgressions, they protect the country from danger. It is no wonder that administrations have often tried restricting access while journalists have consistently demanded more transparency. Fulfilling its ideal function as sentinel, the press has come to be considered, even in the age of the so-called imperial presidency, almost a fourth branch of government—or, in a term borrowed from the British, "the fourth estate"—and like guests who have stayed too long at the manor, never quite as welcome as the other three.

Whether the unavoidable tensions between chief executives and the journalists who cover them protect democracy or threaten it has remained a major bone of contention in American political culture for nearly a quarter of a millennium, without producing anything approaching consensus. That, in essence, is the unresolved debate animating this book.

From colonial times onward, advocates of unfettered journalism have argued that vigorous inquiry is essential to keep a free people free.

The earliest newspapers on this continent concerned themselves primarily with encouraging commerce and keeping new residents apprised of local and foreign news, often reprinting stories from the European papers arriving (slowly) by ship. The very first American paper, a Boston weekly called *Publick Occurrences Both Forreign and Domestick*, reported in its maiden edition on such "news" as an epidemic of smallpox, the suicide of a disconsolate widower, and the recent Christianization of Indians near Plymouth, Massachusetts.[2]

In the 1720s, Benjamin Franklin established the *Pennsylvania Gazette* in Philadelphia, and William Bradford founded the *New York Gazette* on Manhattan Island, launching the era of modern domestic journalism. Like other papers of the period, these journals strove to educate and amuse as well as inform. Politics was barely covered. Within half a century, however, editors split dramatically, and in print, over the question of separation from England. With the supply of imported paper cut off, pro-independence newspapers took to recycling rags and old ledger books to keep their struggling journals and radical views alive. Few journalists have equaled the bravery of the editors who defied the Crown to spread the revolutionary spirit among the colonists. But when America finally won its independence, its war casualties included the press: as many newspapers had failed as had been launched. The subsequent recovery of the decimated vocation—it could not yet be called an enterprise—constituted one of the commercial miracles of the early republic.

But the first colonial journalists enjoyed no automatic right to print "fake news." Doing so in defiance of local statutes might even earn them condemnation as "enemies" of the people. The 1682 *Great Law of Pennsylvania,* in fact, specified that "all Scandalous and Malicious reporters Defamers and Spreaders of false News whether against Magistrates or Private Persons being convicted thereof Shall be accordingly Severely punisht as Enemys to the Peace & Concord of the Province."[3] After ratification of the Constitution, the First Amendment codified the recent experience of journalistic independence by guaranteeing that "Congress shall make no law . . . abridging the freedom of speech, or of the press." But tellingly, Congress itself did not quite unite on the proposition, with Federalists calling the amendment "unnecessary," instead arguing, "The power of Congress does not extend to the Press."[4] Even the opposition Republicans who advocated for a bill of rights did not contend that the press should be entirely shielded from scrutiny, but merely that the national government should enjoy no defined power to oversee newspapers. State authorities, they believed, should judge libel and slander for themselves. Hence came the negative construction of the final First Amendment: not that the press was entitled to write what it pleased, but that Congress had no constitutional power to restrict it.

Yet even this compromised interpretation would not prevent Congress, or future presidents, from abridging such freedoms anyway.

This book attempts to tell the turbulent story of the presidents and the press, exploring in tandem two bedrock institutions of the republic, through the lenses of both action and reaction, from the Age of the Founding to the Age of the Donald. It chronicles disputes and truces; mutual distrust as well as occasional collaboration; sanitized news and fake news; and the efforts that both sides have undertaken over many generations to dominate the other, either by granting or withholding access, by remaining aloof or striking back.

How much this relationship has shifted over time, or whether it has truly shifted at all, remains the overarching focus of this work. As the book will show, the more things have changed, the more they have in some key ways remained the same, even if press independence has often required what the nineteenth-century abolitionist Wendell Phillips once called "eternal vigilance." As Phillips also acknowledged, "We live under a government of men and morning newspapers."[5]

This study has grown out of long experience and deep interest. Nearly fifty years ago, at age twenty, I miraculously landed my dream job right out of college as a cub reporter for a weekly newspaper called the *Manhattan Tribune*. At first, its editors sent me to cover the most local of local beats, but when senior writers began melting away (the publisher did not pay us regularly), I landed a plum assignment: asking leading historians whether, soon after Chappaquiddick, Ted Kennedy still had a viable path to the presidency. Pay heed to what the White House correspondents say, several of my interview subjects urged me. These ideally placed journalists write the first draft of presidential history, sometimes with indelible ink. Indeed, these seers proved right. The press remained unsympathetic to Kennedy through the 1970s, and unforgiving when he finally sought the White House in earnest in 1980.[6]

After my brief career in journalism, I became a political press secretary, working for two legendary public figures from the mid-1970s through the mid-'90s. I had the honor of handling (and occasionally mishandling) tough journalists as a spokesman for Congresswoman Bella Abzug in her campaigns for the U.S. Senate in 1976 and mayor of New York City in 1977. And I took on similar responsibilities for Mario Cuomo in his own 1977 race for mayor, and later in promoting his economic development initiatives during his years as governor of New York. I still believe I inadvertently launched the "Cuomo for president" boom in late 1991 when, in Tokyo, I tried to paraphrase something Cuomo had just told a reporter asking him, for about the hundredth time that trip, whether he would seek the White House the following year. I ended up blurting out, "Anything is possible!" Cuomo raised no objections and the quote went viral (for its day); not the best, but not the worst, way to launch an exploratory campaign for the presidency.[7]

Over the years, I have also enjoyed precious opportunities to discuss press coverage with several American presidents face-to-face. In his private second-floor White House office, Bill Clinton confided to me in 1999 that journalists—maybe even their secret listening devices—had made his recent life hell. A handwritten sign on the desk in that private office read "Shhhh. Ken Starr may be listening." Following an event for his new Houston library, George H. W. Bush invited my wife and me to dinner at his country club, bringing along veteran White House correspondent Hugh Sidey to discuss the press hostility that had pervaded the nation's capital from the age of the sixteenth president to that of the forty-first—yet had not prevented presidents from befriending certain journalists, allowing men like Bush and Sidey, for example, to forge close personal friendships.

I do not attempt to place every one of our forty-four presidents under scrutiny here—such a tome would prove far too long and much too redundant. What I try to do on the following pages is revisit the most epochal presidencies and the most transformative milestones in presidential press coverage.

The question of which institution has emerged from their 250 years of combat the more powerful—the presidency or the press—has yet fully to be decided. The press surely helped bring down John Adams and Richard Nixon. It helped elevate Abraham Lincoln and Barack Obama, to name two, by emphasizing their inspiring personal stories. Yet the press has done little to inhibit Donald Trump, either because of his own mastery of nontraditional media, the establishment media's declining influence, a public inured to presidential misbehavior, or all of the above.

Whereas presidents once remained remote, above the political fray, and removed from day-to-day involvement with the press, they now make news as often as they please. They summon journalists into their confidence for exclusive coverage and daily place themselves before cameras, microphones, and personal devices. From Thomas Jefferson to Donald Trump, they have optimized the media platforms of the day to advance their arguments—Jefferson by pioneering "official" administration newspapers, FDR through Fireside Chats, Kennedy with his charismatic presence on television, and Trump by dominating an entirely new medium to transport his unfiltered views: in his case, Twitter.

The term "press" once described weekly newspapers set laboriously in wooden or metal type, printed by handpresses, and distributed only as quickly as the early postal system could carry them. Information moves today with breathtaking speed and ubiquity—though even the most modern platforms will no doubt seem sluggish when the next technology again, inevitably, transforms communications in the future.

Today a president can easily conflate his roles as newsmaker and news purveyor by posting his messages directly on the Internet. But how less revolutionary is this technique when compared with the Founders' unprecedented efforts to plant stories in the triweekly gazettes that published their era's version of rapid news in the late eighteenth century? Or Abraham Lincoln's appropriation of the military telegraph to dispatch news from the front at the end of the Civil War? Or Franklin Roosevelt's ingenious mastery of radio to reassure a country brought to its knees by the Great Depression; or John Kennedy's use of televised news conferences to charm his way out of crises during his two brief years in office?

This book is designed to alert readers to historical traditions, original principles, and ominous trends by charting the evolution of the most powerful and profound newsmaker–observer relationship in the world: the parallel pursuits of American presidents and the American press.

Does traditional press coverage remain the proverbial first draft of American history, or has it been discredited forever by the mantra of "fake news"?

How has the reputation of the press corps we now call "White House correspondents" changed—and how crucial is it to restore faith in their objectivity and respect for their toughness? Do facts still matter in an era in which a president's thousands of false statements have been exposed without ramification?

Indeed, how vital is press coverage today—in whatever form it has taken or may take—to the best practices of executive administration and the best interests of the American people? How hard should we—must we—fight to preserve its independence? And in an age of so-called news deserts, those large swaths of the country that increasingly lack regional newspapers, what form of media can and should replace them, and with what kind of constraints, if any, when free speech so often borders on hate speech?

If the past is prologue, history is where the debate ought to begin; not just in protest over the demonization of the press or the vilification of a chief executive, but with an understanding of how a free press is truly meant to cover our duly elected leaders.

So much has altered since the Founding Era, in terms of access and expectation, literacy and technology, that it is almost impossible to compare either the executive branch or the news environment of the eighteenth century with those of the twenty-first. This book will nonetheless endeavor to do so, if only to demonstrate the crucial importance of the ongoing relationship between presidents and those who cover them, and to emphasize the contribution the rivalry at its best makes to encouraging both righteous leadership and civil discourse.

EDITORIAL NOTE

Early American newspapers often burdened themselves—and their readers—with long, cumbersome names that reflected city of origin, frequency of publication, and preference in politics. In this book, for simplicity's sake, such titles are abbreviated. In many cases, I have for example removed the word "daily" from the names of nineteenth-century papers: thus, for example, Springfield's *Illinois Daily State Journal* and *Daily Illinois State Register* (no one knows why the world "daily" appeared in different places in the mastheads of each) are simplified to *Illinois State Journal* and *Illinois State Register.* Finally, the quaint hyphens that once appeared in the names of the *New-York Times,* the *New-York Tribune*, and newspapers from New-Orleans to New-Haven, have been removed altogether. It is hoped that these editorial tweaks will make the text of this book more coherent.

THE PRESIDENTS vs. THE PRESS

PART ONE

"MALIGNANT INDUSTRY"

1

GEORGE WASHINGTON

George Washington entered the presidency in 1789 with no particular animus toward the press, though he already had ample reason to be on his guard. During the Revolutionary War, he had grown alarmed by the publication of "injurious" bulletins reporting the movements of his army. The commanding general feared these reports might fall into enemy hands and place his men in peril. Yet the closest he came to censure was to express his mild wish "that our Printers were more discreet."[1]

Six months before his first election, Washington still optimistically regarded newspapers as "vehicles of knowledge more happily calculated than any other to preserve liberty, stimulate the industry, and meliorate the morals of an enlightened and free people." Washington hoped the "common Gazettes," as he called them without irony, "might be spread through every city, town and village in America."[2] As president, he would subscribe to five different daily papers and devour all of them hungrily.[3]

Once in office, Washington even weighed an economic stimulus for newspapers by exempting them from prohibitive federal postal rates. This burden he regarded as a "tax on the transportation of public prints."[4] For a young industry dependent on mail subscriptions, such relief would have provided a boon. Free postage never materialized, but a grateful press remained for a time relatively free of complaint about the nation's first chief executive—for reasons that of course went beyond his magnanimous gesture regarding postal rates. Washington remained a living icon; to question him was akin to criticizing the new nation itself. But the state of mutual admiration did not last.

Toward the end of Washington's first term, Americans, once relatively unified in the quest for independence, began splitting into warring political factions devoted to markedly different aspirations. Pro-Washington, pro–Alexander Hamilton Federalists pledged to strengthen the new national government, regulate fiscal policy, and reestablish ties with Great Britain. The emerging Democratic-Republicans, led by Secretary of State Thomas Jefferson and the father of the Constitution, James Madison, advocated smaller government and states' rights. Infatuated by the French Revolution, Jeffersonians favored shunning America's mother country and embracing Enlightenment France. Federalists viewed recent upheavals there as a mobocratic threat to global stability, while populist Republicans regarded the French uprising as an inspirational outgrowth of America's successful revolt against England. Jeffersonians feared the imposition of a British-style class system here; Hamiltonians in turn dreaded a Jacobin-style reign of terror.[5]

As the chasm widened, newspapers aligned with one or the other party ratcheted up their criticism of the respective opposition. In openly choosing sides, some editors abandoned original commitments to objectivity and embraced new roles as propagandists. Others established their journals under the direct auspices of party leaders, fully committed to their platforms from the start. Whether a divided America emboldened the rise of a partisan press, or the partisan press widened an existing political gulf, remains open to debate. In either case, most newspaper readers seemed to enjoy the lively new journalism. Colorfully written vitriol deflected subscribers' attention from cheap paper, coarse printing, and an overabundance of dull advertising. For his part, Washington "lamented" when "the Editors of the different Gazettes in the Union" first began "stuffing their papers with scurrility and nonsensical declamation."[6]

The escalating editorial invective coincided with a revolution in printing technology. Ever-faster presses meant that more papers could be produced more rapidly. As biweeklies matured into weeklies, and weeklies morphed into dailies, readership skyrocketed. Only one hundred papers existed in the United States at the dawn of Washington's presidency in 1790. Within ten years, that number more than doubled, and the press began attracting two million readers per month.[7] Remarkably, this explosive growth occurred in a nation where half the population was sixteen years old or younger, a fifth were enslaved African

Americans discouraged or forbidden by law from reading, and most subscribers shared their newspapers with as many as twenty relatives and friends. As the future lexicographer Noah Webster marveled, "In no other country on earth, not even in Great Britain, are Newspapers so generally circulated among the body of the people, as in America."[8] Thirteen years before publishing his first dictionary, Webster secured a $1,500 loan from none other than Alexander Hamilton and in 1793 established his own pro-Federalist newspaper in New York: the *American Minerva*. It was the first, but not the last, investment Hamilton would make in partisan journalism.

By then, the secretary of the treasury had become not only Washington's closest policy advisor but also his chief press strategist, the forerunner of the modern White House communications director—and more. Hamilton not only devised and implemented policy; he transmitted Washington's instructions to friendly editors, contributed his own anti-Republican screeds under a variety of noms de plume, and, as the Webster episode demonstrates, helped finance pro-administration journals.

Webster's new *American Minerva* did not long go unanswered. Envisioning political advantage if they could sully the most deified Federalist of all, Jefferson's press allies commenced a frontal assault on the once-sacrosanct Washington. As a consequence, the initial and, as it turned out, longest-ever press honeymoon in the history of the American presidency came to a halt. Beginning in late 1792, at the end of his first term, Republican editors subjected Washington to wholesale disparagement, some of it based on genuine differences over issues, but much of it personal, and some close to libelous.

He did count many defenders. Among them were Webster in New York and, in Boston, onetime stonemason and Revolutionary War veteran Benjamin B. Russell, who wholeheartedly devoted his biweekly, the *Columbian Centinel*, to supporting the Federalist agenda. Russell defended Federalists on the streets as well. In 1793, he spat in the face of pro-Republican editor Benjamin Austin Jr. The transgression cost Russell a twenty-shilling fine and did nothing to thaw partisan rancor.

Serving from the early years of Washington's presidency as a quasi-official administration mouthpiece was a newspaper called the *Gazette of the United States*. Edited by schoolmaster-turned-journalist John Ward Fenno, a loyal Hamiltonian, it debuted in New York just six weeks after Washington's inauguration. Although the paper's early articles evinced restraint, from the outset it advocated controlling "the turbulent passions of men"—meaning Jeffersonians—and strengthening "the tone of government," in other words, the ruling Federalists.[9] When the national capital moved from New York to Philadelphia, Fenno took his printing press and followed, and there cemented the paper's status as a government organ. Hamilton made sure Fenno secured enough government printing orders to keep his presses busy and his new operation solvent.[10] Such subsidies fell comfortably within the loose ethical standards of the age. By then, readers expected their newspapers to be political, and in turn editors like Fenno expected the political parties they backed to support them.

Launched only as a biweekly, Fenno's paper never reached more than 1,400 subscribers and consistently lost money. For it to survive, Fenno at one point pleaded for a new loan from Hamilton along with cash contributions from readers.[11] Yet the *Gazette* exerted outsize national influence. Fenno obtained and exclusively published government news—the equivalent of modern-day press releases—which other editors then reprinted (and praised, in precursors of political spin) in like-minded journals across the republic. Simultaneously, Fenno lobbed attacks at Jefferson and the Democratic-Republicans. Some came pseudonymously from the pen of Hamilton himself, encouraging the belief that Washington authorized such assaults and stimulating bitter counterattacks. Washington may have come to rue the advent of politically motivated press attacks, but in truth many originated in a newspaper founded to support him.

The growing power of the *Gazette of the United States* made it inevitable that an opposition journal would emerge to counter it. Behind the scenes, launching a decades-long practice in stealth journalism, Jefferson himself proved crucial in this development. As adroit as his rival Hamilton at promoting a party agenda, and equally bold when it came to securing financial emoluments for press allies, Jefferson encouraged another gifted writer, known as the "poet of the American Revolution," Philip Morin Freneau, to move from New York to Philadelphia to launch his own national paper there. To be called the *National Gazette*, it would of course prove sympathetic to France and Jeffersonians and hostile to England and Hamiltonians—"written in a contrary spirit to that of Fenno," in Jefferson's own words.[12]

By birth and experience alike, the "slight," "muscular," and "engaging" thirty-eight-year-old Freneau seemed an ideal choice for the task.[13] Not only was he descended from French Huguenots, but he nursed a seething hatred for the British, having suffered near-fatal hardships aboard an enemy prison ship during the American Revolution. Moreover, Freneau had attended Princeton, where James Madison was his roommate.[14] Believing a new paper would provide "an antidote" to "discourses circulated in favor of Monarchy and Aristocracy," Madison now joined Jefferson in urging Freneau to establish a Republican sheet in the national capital.[15]

But Freneau was not wealthy. So, to provide financial security for his new venture, Jefferson obtained for the editor a $250-per-year government job as a State Department translator, though Freneau knew no foreign language except French, which Jefferson himself spoke fluently. This was a bold move even in an age when government ethics, like government itself, was a new concept, and Jefferson's effort hardly escaped criticism. One letter in Fenno's rival paper, signed only "T. L." but clearly authored by Hamilton, pondered sarcastically whether Freneau was being paid "for *translations* or for *publications*, the design of which is to vilify those to whom the voice of the people has committed the administration of our public affairs."[16]

Jefferson saw no conflict at all in the arrangement. To be fair, no expectation then existed that cabinet members must be loyal to the political party of the president they served. Describing Freneau as "a man of genius," Jefferson supplied his new clerk with foreign newspapers and, some whispered, State Department documents to enhance reporting that targeted Hamilton and the supposed cabal around Washington. Later, Jefferson vowed "in the presence of heaven"—at least to his diary—that he never uttered "a syllable" of political instruction to his handpicked press advocate, admitting only to procuring him a few subscriptions. He also encouraged Madison and other followers to contribute articles to the paper, prompting one Federalist writer to insist that Freneau's journal was "published under the eye of" Jefferson himself.[17] In justification, Jefferson argued, "No government ought to be free of censors: & where the press is free, no one ever will."[18] At its launch, the new *National Gazette* declared its goal was "to energize the spirit of democracy," a coded warning to Federalists ever fearful of the rabble.[19] It came as little surprise that Freneau hailed Jefferson in his October 31, 1791, maiden issue as a "colossus of liberty."[20]

Under Fenno and Freneau, Philadelphia now boasted rival newspapers bearing similar titles, run by editors with like-sounding names of their own, pledged to rival political parties, and openly backed by a member of Washington's cabinet. It was a recipe for bedlam. From 1792 onward, the two papers attacked each other as often, and as viciously, as they assailed political foes. Their political differences could be discerned not only from what they wrote but also from what they ignored. When a financial panic struck the country in April 1792, Jefferson observed that Federalist newspapers refused to cover it, much less place blame at Washington's doorstep. "Notwithstanding the magnitude of this calamity," he complained, "every newspaper almost is silent on it, Freneau's excepted."[21]

As Fenno drew fire from the Jeffersonians for shielding the president, Freneau aroused Federalist ire, particularly when he shifted course and began attacking the president himself for the first time. Washington rebuked such "indecently" communicated missives, worried that "the complexion of some of our News-Papers" might persuade "Foreigners . . . that inveterate political dissensions existed among us, and that we are on the very verge of disunion." Still, Washington clung to the belief that Freneau's hostility was "an evil w[hi]ch. must be placed in opposition to the infinite benefits resulting from a free Press."[22]

Vice President John Adams was less sanguine. "The hell-hounds," he warned in early 1793, "are now in full cry in the newspapers against the President." Adams feared Washington would not bear up well to further criticism, "as his skin is thinner than mine."[23] Jefferson, who bore considerable blame for the harshening journalistic tone, at least acknowledged that the president seemed "extremely afflicted by the attacks made & kept up on him in the public papers." Jefferson added, as if to blame the victim and excuse himself: "I think he feels these things more than any person I ever yet met with."[24]

At that dramatic August 1793 cabinet meeting, at which Washington lost his temper over the "guillotine" caricature, the "much-inflamed" president railed that "he had rather be on his farm than to be made emperor of the world"; yet here was the *National Gazette* "charging him with wanting to be a king." That the "*rascal Freneau* sent him 3 of his papers every day, as if he thought he would become the distributor of his papers," the president bellowed, amounted to "an impudent design to insult him."[25]

"He was evidently sore & warm" is how Jefferson described the outburst with understated, if disingenuous, acuity. But when Washington urged him to "interpose in some way with Freneau, perhaps withdraw his appointment of translating clerk to my office," the secretary of state demurred. "His paper," Jefferson truly believed, "has saved our constitution which was galloping into monarchy."[26] The president insisted otherwise. "These articles tend to produce a separation of the Union, the most dreadful of calamities," he warned, "and whatever tends to produce anarchy, tends, of course, to produce a resort to anarchical government."[27] With both party newspapers stoking the fire, the rift could hardly continue unrepaired. In December 1793, Jefferson quit the cabinet, marking the final split between Federalists and Democratic-Republicans, who until then, policy differences and personal rivalries notwithstanding, had somehow managed to govern together under Washington.

Its own resources and readership dwindling, Freneau's anti-Washington *National Gazette* vanished around the same time, in one sense a casualty of a yellow fever epidemic that killed more than 10 percent of Philadelphia's population in late 1793 and sent thousands more fleeing into the countryside.[28] By then, however, primary responsibility for Republican press opposition had already shifted to another newspaper.

The most relentless anti-Washington hostility came from a newer journal: Philadelphia's *Aurora*, founded by the young Francophile Benjamin Franklin Bache. Adding insult to injury for George Washington was the embarrassment that Bache was the grandson and namesake of his late partner in the American founding, Benjamin Franklin. As Washington well knew, newspaper publishing coursed incurably through the Franklin family's DNA: old Ben had founded the *Pennsylvania Gazette* fifty years before the Revolution, and Bache had all but learned the printing trade at his grandfather's knee.

Back in 1776, Franklin had taken his seven-year-old grandson along with him on his first diplomatic mission to France. Franklin educated "Benny" in both Paris and Geneva. Additional training under master printer François-Ambrose Didot helped build the boy's skills in the family vocation. When the slim, well-mannered teenager returned to Philadelphia in 1785, he furthered his education at the University of Pennsylvania. In the summers, he resumed his practical schooling by apprenticing at Franklin's Market Street printing house.

The ancient polymath died in April 1790, and within five months his twenty-one-year-old grandson revived the family tradition by launching a newspaper of his own. Bearing the cumbersome title *Aurora General Advertiser, and Political, Commercial, Agricultural, and Literary Journal*, it debuted October 1 with subscriptions at five dollars per annum. In 1791, Bache abbreviated the unwieldy name to the *Aurora General Advertiser*, and by 1794 it came to be known simply as the *Aurora*—as if, like Aurora, the Roman goddess of the dawn, the paper guaranteed to shed new light on the world each morning.[29]

At the outset, Bache vowed that his would be an "impartial" gazette "whose object is to inform."[30] Soon enough, that goal shifted tectonically. One decisive factor may have been the appearance in Fenno's rival *Gazette* of a particularly ardent defense of the president that included a gratuitous denunciation of Franklin. Alerted to the article, a horrified Washington had informed his cabinet that "such a mode of defense would be peculiarly painful to him, and he wished it could be stopped." Hamilton in turn advised Fenno "to suppress it, without mentioning it as the President's wish."[31] Bache, unaware that Washington had tried intervening to head off the criticism of his beloved ancestor, never forgave him. By 1794, the *Aurora* editor had become Washington's most aggressive critic. In unmistakable reference to Dr. Franklin, whose myriad achievements had included experiments in electricity, his combative grandson soon became known as "Lightning Rod Junior."

Increasingly hostile toward what he regarded as Washington's aristocratic bearing and allegiance to all things British, Bache's attacks grew virulent and occasionally ludicrous. In the *Aurora*'s view, Washington was a dotard. He was a thief. He yearned to be a monarch. He presided over ostentatious soirées and demanded annual birthday tributes. He grandly rode the streets of Philadelphia in a gaudy carriage. By January 1794, John Adams observed, "Bache's paper, which is nearly as bad as Freneau's, begins to join in concert with it to maul the President for his drawing rooms, levees, declining to accept invitations to dinners and tea parties, his birthday odes, visits, compliments, &c."[32] Far worse was yet to come.

In October 1794, the *Aurora* denounced Washington for supposedly abandoning Philadelphia—shirking his executive duties, the paper charged—the previous month. In fact, the old general had headed off to western Pennsylvania to help suppress the Whiskey Rebellion, which he believed was in part ignited by Francophiles. At the front, by most accounts, Washington only added to his luster, becoming the first (and to date, only) sitting president to lead troops into battle.[33] Insisting the Constitution forbade him from commanding the army while Congress sat in session, Bache excoriated Washington for "stately journeying through the American continent in search of personal incense."[34] The aggrieved commander in chief, who took that title seriously, condemned "the impertinence of Mr. Bache"—but only in a private note to Jefferson.[35] The armed challenge to the federal whiskey excise had been enough to spur the old warrior to a new front, but the attack in the *Aurora* proved insufficient to provoke an equally militant public rejoinder. Back in the capital, Washington gritted his false teeth and stayed mute.

To be sure, the president remained the darling of painters, sculptors, and a large slice of the public, still lionized, in the words of an adoring caption to one period engraving, as "Sacred to Patriotism."[36] But that never inhibited Bache, whose attacks established a new tradition of contentious and occasionally insolent political journalism. However outrageous some of its tactics, the *Aurora* did at least successfully test the boundaries of free speech. It helped create the tradition of subjecting even the most exalted figures to challenge. Ultimately, its editor sacrificed his claim to a higher niche in journalistic history by too often breaching the boundaries of taste and truth.

To the administration, Bache came to be regarded not as an observer but as an enemy. Once, when Philadelphians asked Washington to lend his presence to a local festival, the president declined simply because he spied Bache's name among the organizers. Washington refolded the invitation and scrawled on the back: "*Intended as an Insult* It is perceived."[37]

A true reckoning came in mid-1795, when Washington sent Chief Justice John Jay's recently negotiated treaty with Great Britain to the U.S. Senate for ratification. In theory, the pact offered to put belated closure on the American Revolution and avoid renewed armed conflict with the far mightier power. Its terms at least provided that the British would finally abandon the North American forts they had occupied since the war. But the flawed treaty also imposed insulting limits on American maritime trade in the West Indies. Washington summoned the Senate into special session in June to consider the agreement and somehow persuaded its solons to conduct their debate in the same secrecy under which the new nation's leaders had once hammered out the Constitution.

The news blackout fueled suspicion among Republican editors, stoking their thirst for revenge against Washington. When treaty details finally emerged, matters only got worse. Appalled to find the pact included neither an affirmation of American neutrality in French–British affairs nor compensation for the British seizure of slaves during the Revolution, Jeffersonians worked hard to kill it in the Senate. Ultimately, the Jay Treaty prevailed without a single vote to spare, 20–10, the bare two-thirds needed to ratify it. Then, before Washington could sign the treaty, Bache obtained and leaked an error-laden summary of its terms, triggering a nationwide uproar with his scoop.[38] Fanning the anger, Bache editorialized that Washington had not only ordered the pact "crammed down the throats of the Republicans by point of bayonet" but "violated our Constitution and made a treaty with a nation abhorred by our people.[39] Pro-administration journals countered that the treaty would end the threat of

British aggression—and in this prediction they proved correct, at least for the next few years.

One result of so ferocious a battle—refought on the pages of party-aligned newspapers as heatedly as it had been waged on the Senate floor—was a further escalation in national disharmony. When Bache and Fenno each published the official text of the treaty on July 1, street demonstrations—some marked by violence—erupted across the country. Riding the wave, Bache issued a pamphlet edition and further inflamed his followers by undertaking a kind of anti–Jay Treaty book tour into New York and New England. He became nothing less than the country's first celebrity journalist—that is, since his grandfather.[40]

Escalating its anti-Washington cannonade that fall, the *Aurora* launched a direct assault on the president's character by accusing him of having accepted "more money than he was legally entitled for his first term of service"—in short, stealing from the federal treasury.[41] Washington, who had always declined a salary but requested periodic reimbursements for expenses, refused to respond to what he regarded as an outright calumny. The attack surely wounded a leader who had built his reputation on integrity.

Next the *Aurora* struck at the vulnerable underbelly of the entire American experiment, casting the president of an ostensibly free country as a hypocrite for owning slaves. Yet in expressing indignation that "Liberty's Apostle should be seen with chains in his hands, holding men in bondage," Bache conveniently neglected to mention an equally culpable opposition leader. His own benefactor, Thomas Jefferson, author of the founding principle that "all men are created equal," was no less guilty of "holding men in bondage."[42] Washington reacted with fury at being singled out. Jefferson was on hand to witness another outburst from the frustrated president, watching him "throw the *Aurora* hastily on the floor with a 'damn' of the author."[43]

By March 1796, with the next presidential election approaching, Bache intensified his efforts "to destroy undue impressions in favor of Mr. Washington."[44] Not until summer, perhaps inspired by the twentieth anniversary of the Declaration of Independence, did Washington finally respond in kind—even if he still refused to protest beyond private correspondence. In a July letter to his new secretary of state, Timothy Pickering, the president anguished: "The continual attacks which have been made and [they] are still making on the administration, in Bache's and other papers of that complexion, indecent as they are void of truth and fairness . . . resort to misrepresentation and mutilated authorities; and oftentimes to unfounded and round assertions."[45]

"Under these circumstances," the president wondered, as ever muffling his emotions under suffocating syntax, "it were to be wished that the enlightened public could have a clear and comprehensive view of facts. But how to give it lies the difficulty." Briefly, Washington did weigh one counteroffensive: to thwart Bache and "his numerous correspondents and communicants," he considered publicly releasing a slew of documents attesting to his administration's latest peace overtures to France.[46] Perhaps if the facts about recent diplomacy were made public, the Jeffersonian press would lose credibility. In the end, Washington could not bring himself to authorize even this modest rebuttal.

To be sure, the first president never lacked for press support. He could always count on validation (and commensurate anti-Jeffersonian venom) from loyal Federalists like Fenno, Webster, and others. Yet in the wake of incessant criticism by Freneau, Bache, and pro-Jefferson editors outside the capital, Washington perpetually felt outgunned. He would be "stupid," he sputtered one day, to believe that "little sugar plumbs [*sic*] here & there" could make up for all the abuse.[47] That July, when Andrew Brown's Philadelphia *National Gazette and Universal Daily Advertiser* merely alerted its readers that Washington had gone home to Mount Vernon for his annual summer vacation, the exasperated president harbored, he said, "little doubt, but the insertion in Brown's Paper, of my sudden return, was put there to answer some insidious purpose."[48]

Two days after Independence Day 1796, weary of so long being castigated as both "the enemy of one Nation, and subject to the influence of another," Washington dispatched a strongly worded letter to Thomas Jefferson, focused in part on the worsening plague of press abuse. Once more, Washington insisted he had been targeted for "the grossest, and most insidious misrepresentations . . . in such exaggerated and indecent terms as could scarcely be applied to a Nero; a notorious defaulter; or even to a common pickpocket."[49] If he nurtured any resentment that Jefferson himself had incubated the attacks, Washington still refrained from saying so, either to his former secretary of state or to the public. But he would never write to Jefferson again.

Long resigned to opprobrium, and stoically committed to ignoring it, Washington nonetheless worried more than ever about its cumulative and corrosive effect on both his reputation and his country. "That Mr. Bache will continue his attacks on the Government, there can be no doubt," he sourly predicted in a letter that same July 6 to Alexander Hamilton, "but that they will make no Impression on the public mind is not so certain, for drops of Water will Impress (in time) the hardest Marble."[50]

After surviving this avalanche of press assaults, Washington concluded in 1796 that he had endured enough. Feeling elderly at sixty-four, he yearned for a quiet retirement. To be sure, he harbored other reasons for stepping down. He had always planned to serve briefly, establish the presidential office, and bequeath it to others. Now he hoped a two-term tradition would discourage dictatorial impulses in his successors.

Yet the relentless press attacks surely contributed equally to his decision to retreat from the public sphere. Columns by "Mr. Bache and his correspondents" had both injured and tarnished him, he admitted, and he felt "a disinclination to be longer buffited [*sic*] in the public prints by a set of infamous scribblers."[51] His friend Dr. Benjamin Rush, a signer of the Declaration of Independence, maintained that the volleys from the *Aurora* alone convinced Washington "to retire from the President's chair."[52]

Although the next election contest was fast approaching, Washington chose to keep his plans quiet for as long as possible, worried that news of his departure might stir pandemonium. Even his preferred successor, John Adams, did not learn of Washington's decision until late March.[53] With no desire to give his press enemies one more opportunity to assail him, Washington kept the newspapers in the dark for as long as he could. Then, ironically, the press became central to the story's unveiling—once Washington determined that his retirement called for an expansive public accounting of his achievements and aspirations. For years he had planned to issue such a magnum opus whenever he stepped down. Now this "master of farewells" determined to conclude his career by communicating with the American people one last time—as it would turn out, through the newspapers.[54]

With nearly a year to go before the next inauguration, he resumed work on a state paper designed to influence American policy far into the future.[55] Madison had contributed to a draft discarded four years earlier, when Washington reluctantly agreed to stand for reelection.[56] The final document that became known as Washington's Farewell Address was largely drafted by Hamilton, who had left the cabinet in 1795 and returned to New York to resume his legal practice. Washington did extensive work of his own on the message in spring 1796. On May 15, he sent a rewrite back to Hamilton for further review. What Hamilton read must have astonished him: the draft featured a stunning passage devoted entirely to Washington's long-unexpressed chagrin over press criticism.

At last the president intended to reveal his dissatisfaction with newspaper partisanship, perhaps in the hope of reversing it.

Yet even now, eight years of indignation could not liberate him from the strangulating literary style through which he had expressed (or concealed) himself for so long. The draft offered no direct criticism. Washington would "take note" of press "abuse" without exacting revenge, and in the bargain seek vindication for his long silence. As he expressed himself in this extraordinary passage:

> As this Address, Fellow citizens will be the last I shall ever make you, and as some of the Gazettes of the United States have teemed with all the Invective that disappointment, ignorance of facts, and malicious falsehoods could invent, to misrepresent my politics and affections; to wound my reputation and feelings; and to weaken, if not entirely destroy that confidence you had been pleased to repose in me; it might be expected at the parting scene of my public life that I should take some notice of such virulent abuse. But, as heretofore, I shall pass them over in utter silence; never having myself, nor by any other with my participation or knowledge, written, or published a scrap in answer to any of them.[57]

Had even these indirect words survived subsequent revisions, they would have marked the first and only time Washington publicly aired his grievances against what he viewed as scurrilous journalism. As it turned out, even this muted "scrap" failed to survive Hamilton's editorial hand. Urging his mentor to avoid self-pity—he even suggested Washington delete a charming reference to his increasing "gray hairs"—Hamilton cut the entire press section from the rewrite he sent back to the president.[58] There, the opportunity to settle old scores with the press died without further insistence from Washington.[59] Except for vague references to "irregular oppositions" and the "baneful effects of the spirit of party," he would publish his "Address to the People of the United States" on September 19, 1796, shorn of its comments on press malediction.[60]

In an impressive show of tactical ingenuity, however, Washington deployed his farewell so that he might at least dominate the newspapers one last time, even those he abhorred. For despite the informal title soon attached to it, the "address" was crafted to be delivered not in public as a speech, but as a text to be printed in the press. Washington so envisioned it from the start, fretting a month before its release over "the length of it for a News Paper publication," worried that "all the columns of a large Gazette would scarcely, I conceive contain the present draught" (he proved correct). Yet Washington could not imagine his valedictory appearing "in any other form."[61]

Then, long before the term was invented, came a stroke of public relations genius. At Hamilton's urging, Washington chose to bypass the obvious choice for exclusive publication, John Fenno's *Gazette*, surely a blow to its long-loyal editor. Instead, having asked Hamilton "which Editor in this City do you think it had best be sent for Publication," the president chose Philadelphia editor David Claypoole's apolitical *American Daily Advertiser*. In doing so, Washington wisely anointed a paper "never stained with the ribaldry and violence of party recriminations."[62] The choice elevated the Farewell Address above the realm of faction.

Until then, editors had been unwelcome at the executive mansion. Now, to arrange this exclusive release, Washington summoned a stunned Claypoole there on Friday, September 16, 1796. As the editor remembered, the president confided that he intended to retire and "had some Thoughts and Reflections on the Occasion, which he deemed proper to communicate to the People of the United States . . . and which he wished to appear in the Daily Advertiser." Claypoole profusely thanked him "for having preferred that Paper as the channel of his Communications with the People," and the two arranged to issue the address the following Monday.[63]

Claypoole rallied his staff to typeset the opus quickly, then allowed Washington to review the proofs, and incorporated his last-minute changes. In return, Claypoole asked the president if he might retain the original manuscript as a souvenir. More interested in its dissemination than in its talismanic value, Washington obliged him. That it took the public by storm became evident just hours after its initial publication, when it reappeared in several other Philadelphia newspapers. Eventually it adorned every gazette in the country—even if it took months for the most remote western papers to catch up with it. With advertising still granted front-page prominence, the message typically filled two broad interior sheets.

Its appearance did not, however, assuage Benjamin Franklin Bache or the other anti-Federalist editors who now castigated Washington for encouraging idolatry. Bache had come too far in opposition to allow a sentimental retreat just because Washington planned to retire. Besides, the presidency itself remained at stake. Bache knew he must summon all his power if Jefferson were to succeed Washington. Since presidential aspirants in the Founding Era did not declare their candidacies in advance, much less campaign for the office, the *Aurora* resumed its attacks on the outgoing president.

A major opening came when the French minister to the United States, Pierre Auguste Adet, penned a series of audacious letters threatening a diplomatic breach unless American voters rejected the Federalists. The *Aurora* published the missives, seconding the motion that only Jefferson's election could avert war with France. Washington may have used his Farewell Address to caution against "foreign entanglements," but it had not inhibited Adet from attempting, and Bache from colluding in, the very first effort by a foreign government to interfere with an American presidential election. In the end, the Adet letters backfired against the Republicans. Their publication unleashed such outrage that James Madison worried the episode would poison Americans permanently against France.[64] Armed with Washington's still-valuable, if only tacit, backing, Adams, and not Jefferson, would narrowly win America's first contested presidential election.

Washington's stormy relations with the opposition press did not end with his Farewell Address—or even Adams's victory. Continuing, in Washington's estimate, to print "exaggerated and odious" articles,[65] Bache hounded the president all the way back to Mount Vernon, opening a fresh line of attack at the end of 1796 by publishing a brutal letter recently dispatched to Washington by fellow Founder Thomas Paine.

Long in self-imposed exile in Paris, the author of *Common Sense* had been arrested there without eliciting protest or sympathy from America's outgoing president. Infuriated, Paine berated Washington as both "treacherous in private friendship" and "a hypocrite in public life," melodramatically demanding to know if the president was "an *apostate* or an *imposter*—whether you have abandoned your principles, or whether you ever had any."[66] Washington regarded the missive as "the most insulting letter he ever received," but wished to believe, as he expressed it in his almost regal fashion, that there remained "too much confidence, and perhaps personal regard for, the present chief magistrate" for its publication to prove injurious.[67]

Still hoping to leave office as he had entered it—above the fray—Washington only grudgingly expressed gratitude when the British-born satirist William Cobbett, editor of the prickly, aptly named *Porcupine's Gazette and Advertiser*, came to his defense. "Peter Porcupine" labeled Bache "an ill-looking devil" dressed as if he "has been about a week or ten days in a gibbett [*sic*]."[68] Washington, "making allowances for the asperity of an Englishman" and for Porcupine's "strange and coarse expressions," at least conceded of Cobbett's lacerating response that "it is not a bad thing."[69]

Unrepentant, the *Aurora* unleashed a farewell message of its own two days before Christmas 1796. It was likely the work of a newly hired, pro-Republican pamphleteer named James Thomson Callender, then in the early stages of a brief but impactful career as a scandalmonger: "If ever a nation was debauched by a man, the American nation has been debauched by WASHINGTON" went the salvo. ". . . Let his conduct then be an example to future ages. Let it serve as a warning that no man may be an idol, and that a people may confide in themselves rather than in an individual."[70] Even now, Washington would react but privately, still in the remote third person, regretting that "although he is soon to become a private citizen, his opinions are to be knocked down, and his character reduced as low as they are capable of sinking it, even by resorting to absolute falsehoods."[71]

Then the *Aurora* mounted its most odious attack yet, exhuming twenty-year-old "Washington" letters that supposedly called into question the general's loyalty during the Revolution. The purported correspondence had long before been exposed as a clumsy fraud. "If you read the Aurora of this City, or those Gazettes which are under the same influence," the aggrieved president bemoaned their reappearance, "you cannot but have perceived with what malignant industry, and persevering falsehoods I am assailed, in order to weaken, if not destroy, the confidence of the Public."[72]

To Washington, the republication of the 1777 correspondence was the last straw—a slander calculated "to attach principles to me that which every action of my life have given the lie to. But *that* is no stumbling block," he knew, "with the Editors of these Papers and their supporters. And now, *perceiving* as disinclination on my part, perhaps *knowing*, that I had determined not to take notice of such attacks, they are pressing this matter upon the public mind with more avidity than usual; urging, that my silence, is a proof of their genuineness." As he forced himself to reiterate, "I never wrote, or even saw, one of the letters until they issued from New York, in Print."[73] Still he offered no public denial.

Thus when Jeremiah Wadsworth, a Connecticut legislator who had once served as commissary general of Washington's army, offered to expose the letters as fakes, the outgoing president rejoiced. "I shall thank you (when republished)," he replied, "for the refutation of the impudent forgeries of letters, carrying my signature, which Mr. Bache has taken so much pains to impose on the public as genuine proclamations." Only then did Washington offer a rare glimpse into his bottled-up resentment toward his most persistent and pernicious press critic. In a coda that came close to a quip, he observed of Bache, "This man has celebrity in a certain way, for His calumnies are to be exceeded only by his Impudence, and both stand unrivalled."[74] Even in the terse future medium of Twitter, no future chief executive would ever dismiss a journalist so bitingly in so few words.

On March 3, 1797, with only hours left in his presidency, Washington decided he could no longer restrain himself after all. He had "suffered every attack that was made upon my Executive conduct . . . to pass unnoticed while I remained in office," but "such immense pains has [*sic*] been taken by this said Mr Bache . . . to dissiminate [*sic*] these counterfeit letters" that he had no choice now but to break his long silence. A reply, however long delayed, would be "a piece of justice due to my own character and to Posterity." Of course, he could still not bring himself to speak out directly. Instead, he sent Secretary of State Pickering a detailed recapitulation of the wartime scheme to "wound my character and deceive the people." Again characterizing the old letters as "a base forgery," Washington authorized Pickering to use the explanation when he saw fit as a rebuttal for "the present generation and to posterity.[75] To Washington's satisfaction, his disavowal was indeed "published in the Gazettes"—soon after he returned to private life.[76] His remarkable record of patient silence during his years in office remained unblemished.

But not before the battle for the last word reignited. The ex-president had barely reached Mount Vernon when, on March 6, the *Aurora* launched a final torrent of invective. Labeling him "the source of all the misfortunes of our country," the paper exulted that Washington was "no longer possessed of power to multiply his evils in the United States," adding, "if ever there was a period for rejoicing, this is the moment."[77] Soon thereafter, Bache sunk even lower by resuscitating a long-discredited libel that during the French and Indian War forty years earlier, Washington had "fired on a flag of truce," killing an officer. In furious rebuttal, John Fenno charged that Bache "seems to take a kind of hellish pleasure in defaming the name of WASHINGTON." Exchanging pity for scorn, he concluded: "That a man who was born in America and is part of the Great Family of the United States should thus basely aim his poisoned dagger at the FATHER OF HIS COUNTRY is sorely to be lamented."[78]

Had he been a vindictive man, Washington might have taken some pleasure from what befell his press nemesis only a month later. In April 1797, a shipbuilder's son assaulted Benjamin Franklin Bache at a Philadelphia dockyard, in full view of jeering spectators. Not long thereafter, John Fenno's son encountered Bache on a nearby street and lunged at him for insulting his father. Bache got the best of things that time, striking young Fenno over the head with his cane.[79] But a year later, incensed veterans of Washington's old army hurled a rock through Bache's office window and menaced his home and family.[80] Whether these outbursts foreshadowed a violent escalation in tensions between newspapers and their readers only time would tell.

For his part, Washington could honestly maintain that he had never fueled the rancor. Lesser men might easily have fallen into the temptation to strike back at criticism and critics. Conscious of his unique responsibility for establishing presidential tradition, Washington admirably refrained from publicizing his dismay over press scurrility and never attempted while serving as president to censor it. Conducting research for the first Washington biography, John Marshall marveled at the absence of his complaints against the press: "Of the sensibility of the President to the calumnies against his Administration with which the press abounded, and of their new direction against him personally, his correspondence furnishes but few evidences."[81]

Even if none of his successors chose to emulate his exemplary restraint, Washington deserves credit in history for patiently allowing the press to establish, and perhaps even exceed, its boundaries. As if conscious of what permanent damage his own criticism might exact on freedom of expression, Washington never attempted as president to turn the public against the newspapers, thereby safeguarding the press as an independent institution. Even though he would waver during Adams's presidency, while in office he set a high bar for tolerance that future presidents found difficult, if not impossible, to reach.[82]

Six months into his retirement, Washington dismissed Benjamin Franklin Bache as "no more than the Agent or tool of those who are endeavoring to destroy the confidence of the people in the officers of Government."[83] Even that reappraisal Washington never shared with any but his confidants. He ended his life still believing that "a Newspaper vindication would be of little avail."[84] Among the most sensitive of all presidents to criticism, he unleashed the least indignation to the people. This was one precedent his successors declined to follow.

Washington no doubt found at least some consolation merely by outliving the far younger Bache. When news of the first president's own 1799 passing reached the American people—through the press, of course—Washington would be elevated almost by acclamation into the realm of secular sainthood, the rancor that had marked his final years in office forgotten in the mists of mourning. In the end, even the most rabidly anti-Federalist newspapers of the late eighteenth century proved unable to degrade the reputation of the man eulogized as "first in war, first in peace, and first in the hearts of his countrymen." General "Light Horse" Harry Lee, who coined that memorable phrase, might well have added that Washington was also the first to stand in the crosshairs of the press, but the last to turn the other cheek.

Washington's remarkable strength of character may provide one explanation for his ability to withstand so much press criticism without responding in kind. As he put it in a rare moment of self-reflection back in 1793, he possessed "a consolation within" that inured him against abuse. "The arrows of malevolence . . . however barbed and well pointed," he almost boasted, "never can reach the most vulnerable part of me; though whilst I am *up* as a *mark*, they will be continually aimed. The publications in Freneau's and Bache's papers are outrages on common decency; and they progress in that style, in proportion as their pieces are treated with contempt, and are passed by in silence, by those at whom they are aimed."[85]

He loathed the press, but to the end of his life, he could not resist it. A visitor to Mount Vernon during Washington's final illness discovered the weakened ex-president sitting in his parlor, trying hoarsely to read aloud—from a newspaper.

2

JOHN ADAMS

When the presidency passed to the genuinely thin-skinned John Adams, editor Benjamin Franklin Bache of the *Aurora*, George Washington's most relentless press nemesis, seemed poised to continue the vituperative coverage to which he had subjected the Father of His Country. As far as anyone knew, young Bache had a long future ahead of him, and no inclination to reform his habit of traducing Federalists even when it meant stretching or disregarding the truth.

Adams made for a truly inviting target. Vain and choleric—albeit hardworking and incorruptible—the new president seemed in many ways a caricature awaiting a lampoon. In appearance and accomplishment, he was certainly no Washington, and, unfairly or not, suffered in the inevitable comparison. Opponents dubbed him "His Rotundity." Adding to his vulnerability, Adams had but barely won the new nation's first contested presidential election—prevailing against Thomas Jefferson by just three electoral votes. Lacking military glory to burnish his image and saddled with a testy nature that alienated him even from those who shared his politics, Adams seemed destined to incite newspaper opprobrium from the moment he took office.

Instead, astonishingly, the second president enjoyed a press honeymoon entirely free of hostility (although Jefferson accurately prophesied that "its moments of extasy would be ransomed by years of torment & hatred").[1] The same Republican editors who had unleashed relentless assaults against Washington—and even continued assailing him after he left office (Bache among them)—completely restrained themselves once Adams took over in March 1797.

It remains difficult to unravel the web of motives that animated this abrupt shift in journalistic tone. But Republicans did consider Adams a moderate within his party, less hostile to their beloved France than "High Federalists" like Alexander Hamilton were. Republican editors likely calculated that a grace period for Adams might encourage his tolerance for the French while widening the long-standing rift between the new president and Hamilton, whom Republicans reviled even more than Adams did. And if Adams himself harbored monarchical aspirations, at least he knew how to conceal them. The new president was conspicuous for his plain dress—a sharp contrast to Washington, who could not help appearing splendid. As long as Adams refrained from overtly tilting toward the British, Bache and his fellow Jeffersonian editors gave him the benefit of the doubt and fed his ego with a shower of unanticipated praise.

The ever-suspicious Adams, no naïf when it came to press relations, harbored no illusions about either the newspaper truce or the latent enmity he believed most opposition editors harbored for him. Unlike his predecessor, he had long tried to manage the press directly. For decades he had personally contributed opinion pieces, which he modestly called "flickerings in the newspapers," to the *Boston Gazette* and other journals, sometimes under the pseudonym Davila, but often proudly under his own name.[2] "The public service and my duty," he justified one such submission, "require of me that I should communicate to the public."[3] Over the years, his articles had enjoyed widespread republication.

Just after taking office as vice president back in 1789, he urged Washington to open direct communications of his own with friendly editors. Such outreach, Adams argued, might sway "the public mind" toward the Federalists.[4] Washington preferred to remain above the fray. Direct outreach to "printers" seemed unthinkable. So Adams tried emulating Washington's resolve to countenance press criticism without responding. The effort only frustrated Adams further; for unlike Washington, he relished a good brawl even if he was more overtly sensitive to criticism. After five years in the vice presidency, Adams came not only to loathe "anti-federalist scribblers" but eventually to imagine himself—and not Washington—as their principal target. As he declared at one point, "I have held the office of Libellee-General long enough."[5] Adams assumed the presidency fully expecting he would remain the chief victim of Republican press attacks, even if he had only imagined himself so until then.

That is why the subsequent truce proved so shocking. On the eve of his swearing-in, Bache cooed that "Republicans are well satisfied with the election of Mr. Adams." The *Aurora* hailed him as "a firm and upright patriot" and reminded readers of the new president's earnest desire for "peace with France."[6] That this particular encomium appeared in print on Washington's birthday, February 22, a date the general's admirers already celebrated as a holiday, amounted to a subtle barb against Adams's predecessor—a comparison likely to appeal to one who had long remained in Washington's shadow.

The new president sounded a conciliatory note of his own, expressing "a resolution to do justice," in what Bache hailed as an "honorable" inaugural address on March 4, 1797.[7] Unimpressed, many Federalist papers reprinted the speech without comment, while Republican editors followed Bache's lead and added hosannas. The unexpected approbation might have turned a less jaundiced politician's head. Adams remained wary of support from perennial foes and hungry for accolades from longtime allies. "All the Federalists seem to be afraid to approve anybody but Washington," he groused to his wife, Abigail, a few weeks after his swearing-in. "The Jacobin papers damn with faint praise, and undermine with misrepresentation and insinuation."[8] Abigail confirmed that applause for her husband from long-hostile editors "mortified him, much more, than all their impudent abuse does."[9] Her husband seemed certain he would quickly reclaim his familiar place in Republican crosshairs, predicting, "I shall soon be acquitted of the crime of *Chronicle*, *Argus*, and *Aurora* praise."[10] His suspicions turned out to be well founded.

In the end, the détente between Adams and the Jeffersonian press lasted just three months—for all its brevity, still a remarkably long armistice in such a hotly partisan age. And it was upended only by a diplomatic crisis that had originated during the previous administration: the so-called XYZ Affair. That episode began during Washington's final year in office, when he named moderate Federalist Charles Cotesworth Pinckney as U.S. minister to France. Pinckney's assignment was to smooth over the resentments generated by America's recent Jay Treaty with Great Britain. Its ratification so infuriated the French that their ships had begun menacing American merchant vessels on the high seas. Pinckney's mission, however, was not accomplished. The French, convinced that all Federalists bore a pro-England bias, not only refused to accept his credentials, they eventually expelled him from the country.

When Adams assumed the presidency, he appointed two additional American envoys, Elbridge Gerry and John Marshall, to join Pinckney in Paris to make another attempt at ending the discord. Matters only got worse once the commissioners arrived in early October. When the trio sought an official meeting with the new French foreign minister, Charles de Talleyrand, the wily Frenchman dispatched three of his own emissaries to inform the Americans he would negotiate only if they agreed to guarantee France an enormous loan—along with a £50,000 inducement for Talleyrand himself. Apparently this constituted business as usual in European diplomacy, but the Americans indignantly refused the bribe demand and reported the outrage to President Adams.

The ensuing crisis was aggravated by the glacial pace of communications across the Atlantic. It still took seven weeks (in good weather) for news to reach America from Europe. "On the tiptoe of expectation the American public must stand," one newspaper described the fraught situation. Only "fresh arrivals will afford the pleasure of relieving the pain of anxiety."[11] By the time news of the French affront finally reached Philadelphia five months after it occurred, Adams had already delivered a message to Congress castigating France for its original insult to Pinckney and recommending a buildup in American armed forces to resist a rumored French invasion.

That message alone proved enough to terminate Adams's honeymoon with the Republican press even as it enhanced the president's standing with his Federalist base. Quickly reverting to form, Bache condemned Adams as "a man divested of his reason, and wholly under the domination of his passions." Just a few days later, the *Aurora* demanded he step down from the presidency altogether, "before it is too late to retrieve our deranged affairs."[12] Hastening to Adams's defense, John Fenno's friendly *Gazette of the United States* earned Abigail Adams's gratitude for reporting on the crisis, she cheered, "with accuracy."[13] As the uproar grew, the old lines of press demarcation reemerged and hardened. Bache not only resumed his attacks on Adams; he actually went on record yearning for the days of Washington. At least the first president, he sneered, "knew that *those who have neither strength nor weapons to defend themselves, ought at least to be civil.*"[14]

Official reports of Talleyrand's demands finally arrived in Philadelphia in March 1798. "Millions for defense," Federalist congressman Robert Goodloe Harper famously erupted in defiance, "but not one cent for tribute." When the House and Senate demanded access to the actual dispatches Talleyrand's agents had submitted to the Americans in Paris, Adams first redacted the three Frenchmen's names and substituted "X," "Y," and "Z"—thus giving the popular name to the affair.[15] Newspapers of both parties soon published the sensational correspondence, with Federalist editors denouncing the notion that any foreign power could hold peace hostage for money.[16]

Although France and America now intensified their hostilities at sea—a conflict that came to be called the Quasi-War—publication of the XYZ papers gained Adams the greatest acclaim he had ever enjoyed. Fenno, in particular, poured on the praise, noting in one news item that when an orchestra struck up "The President's March" at a Philadelphia theater, the tune elicited "uproar and applause from all quarters of the house." Orchestras quickly began playing the tune in playhouses across the republic, transforming the ditty into a Founding Era version of a hit song. Such puffery delighted Abigail, but even at this moment of glory she astutely recognized that the laudation no longer crossed party lines. "In short we are now wonderfully popular," she confided to her sister, "except with Bache & Co. who in his paper calls the President Old, querulous, Bald, blind, crip[p]led, Toothless Adams. Thus in scripture was the Prophet mocked."[17] From retirement, George Washington condemned the Republican papers for renewing their "cowardly, illiberal, and assassin like" attacks.[18] The honeymoon over, the war of words resumed. And it was anything but "quasi."

Surging acclaim provided insufficient solace for the perennially vexed John Adams. At the high point of his popularity, he came to regard the resumption of press criticism as a danger to national security amid the worsening tensions with France. So he determined to put a stop to it.

In 1798, Adams put his signature to a set of emergency bills passed by the Federalist-controlled Congress, designed to both curtail immigration and criminalize opposition journalism. What became known as the Alien and Sedition Acts emanated from neither a presidential initiative nor the moderate wing of the Federalist Party most likely to back Adams for reelection in 1800. Yet as soon as he approved the obnoxious statutes, Adams became the living symbol of their constitutionally dubious restrictions against the freedom of the press. The question of whether dissent should ever be regarded as disloyalty roiled America for the first—but not the last—time.[19]

The new laws were, to put it mildly, heavy-handed. Stoking irrational fears that French and Irish Catholics plotted to swarm into the country and tilt American politics toward the Jacobins, the Federalists put an end to free-flowing immigration. Blocking the foreign-born from a path to citizenship (and voting rights) was another of the bill's aims. The law restricted the movements of resident aliens as well; violations could result in deportation.

The companion sedition statutes made it a federal crime to "write, print, utter or publish . . . any false, scandalous, or malicious" criticism designed to place the government or its leaders "into contempt or disrepute." Wary Republicans surely noticed, as historian Merrill D. Peterson has pointed out, that the vice president—meaning Jefferson—was "omitted from the officers of the government placed under the mantle of protection."[20] What inflamed Republicans most was the prospect that violations would be adjudicated in federal courts whose judges had all been appointed by the first two Federalist presidents and likely harbored a predisposition to inhibit press opposition. The law set harsh penalties for seditious journalism: up to two years in prison and a $2,000 fine. But what exactly separated criticism from sedition? No one knew for sure. Benjamin Bache sarcastically cautioned that "good citizens . . . had better hold their tongues and make tooth picks of their pens."[21] Reinforcing the concerns that the measure was meant principally to shield the current administration from disparagement, the Sedition Act was written to sunset on March 3, 1801—the final day of Adams's current term.[22]

To be fair, Adams was not the only prominent leader to support the overwrought press crackdown. George Washington, too, bought into fears that the French were plotting to disrupt the United States, and he raised no objections to sedition laws. He not only told the secretary of war, "I highly approve," but expressed his wish that the bills could be "more energetic."[23] Republican outrage he dismissed as whining. "The Alien and Sedition Laws, are now the desideratum in the opposi[t]ion," he commented the day after Christmas 1798. "But any thing else would have done; and something there would always be, for them to torture, and to disturb the public mind with their unfounded and ill-favored forebodings."[24]

Even Jefferson had no ideological quarrels with the notion of holding journalists accountable for slander. He maintained, however, that while the crime could indeed be prosecuted locally, under common law, and after the fact, legislation that made press criticism unlawful in advance (and under federal law) flew "palpably in the teeth of the Constitution."[25] Summoning all his rhetorical flair, he declared himself "for freedom of the press, & against all violations of the Constitution to silence by force & not by reason" all "complaints and criticism, just or unjust."[26]

Together with Madison, Jefferson now ghostwrote a set of challenges known as the Virginia and Kentucky Resolutions. These documents argued that the sedition law violated not only First Amendment guarantees that "Congress shall make no law . . . abridging the freedom of speech, or the press," but also the

Tenth Amendment reserving to states alone the power to enact and enforce such statutes.[27] Dangerously, the resolves implied that the Union itself might require dissolution should federal tyranny continue to run roughshod over state and individual rights.[28] The consequences of this new argument would unleash agitation among the press and the public for the next half century.

Adams ultimately—and deservedly—bore much of the blame for the onerous new sedition law. Yet he seldom convincingly defended it.[29] In one feeble attempt at justification, quickly published in the press, he argued, "Unless the spirit of libeling and sedition shall be controlled by an execution of the laws, that spirit will again increase."[30] What specific dangers such a rising "spirit" posed, however, Adams failed to articulate. His opponents continued to infer that he meant principally to chill his own press foes. As it happened, no challenge to the sedition law ever reached the all-Federalist Supreme Court.[31] But in the court of public opinion, Adams earned a resounding guilty verdict for dictatorial impulses and censorious overreach.

It did little to enhance the president's reputation that he assumed a direct role in two Sedition Act prosecutions, both brought against outspoken critics of his administration. He not only approved the arrest of Thomas Cooper, whose anti-Adams denunciations had appeared in the *Northumberland Gazette*, he seemed to revel in it. Adams believed a "meaner, more artful, or more malicious libel has not appeared," insisting that "it ought to be prosecuted."[32] Samuel Chase, the associate justice of the Supreme Court who presided over the ensuing trial, flagrantly prejudged the case by arguing that Cooper's was "the boldest attempt I have known to poison the minds of the people."[33] Convicted by a jury, Cooper was given six months in prison and ordered to pay a $500 fine plus court costs.[34] The freedom of the press to question the president—any president—faced the likelihood of an even grimmer sentence: death.

To no one's surprise, another victim of the crackdown was the outspoken journalist whom, Republicans insisted, the repressive law had been mainly designed to silence: *Aurora* editor Benjamin Bache. Ben Franklin's grandson had been railing against Washington and Adams for nearly ten years—save for the brief honeymoon at the beginning of the latter's presidency—inviting rage but never prosecution. As Abigail Adams now saw matters, Bache had begun spouting "the malice & falsehood of Satin [*sic*]."[35]

In this attitude Abigail was perfectly in sync with her husband, or at least privy to the president's own escalating irritation. Between winter 1797 and late spring 1798, Abigail grew increasingly eager to see Bache silenced and punished. Once viewed merely as "saussy," the editor had become in her view a "lying wretch" and a "vile" libeler prone to the "most wicked and base, violent & calumnating abuse." Abigail warned that "nothing will have an Effect until congress pass a Sedition Bill." By June she added that "in any other Country Bache & all his papers would have been seazed [sic]."[36] She did not have to wait long to see her lust for censorship fulfilled.

Arrested that same month, and kept out of prison only by posting bond, Bache vowed to continue advocating for "truth and republicanism . . . to the best of his abilities, while life remains."[37] He could not have known how little life he had left. Before he could stand trial, another yellow fever epidemic engulfed Philadelphia and claimed Bache as one of its thousands of victims. He was only twenty-nine when he died. To the very end, the daring, habitually irreverent, and frequently reckless editor blamed England for nearly all America's ills, including the pestilence now crippling the capital. In one of his final editorials, he labeled the yellow fever outbreak that would soon kill him "a present from the British."[38]

Determined to pursue a highly symbolic prosecution, the administration pursued Bache's successor, assistant editor William Duane, after he resumed publishing the *Aurora* and married Bache's widow. Within months, Duane, too, faced prosecution for what the pro-Federalist *Porcupine's Gazette* characterized as "base misrepresentations . . . intended to urge on the democrats to open rebellion."[39] In Duane's case, the government acted under the Alien Enemies law, labeling the native-born but Irish-raised editor eligible for deportation under a technicality: his birth had occurred before American independence, and thus he could be treated as a foreigner.[40] Of course, so had the president's.*

Secretary of State Thomas Pickering, charged with pursuing sedition indictments for the administration, believed Duane guilty of publishing "an uninterrupted stream of slander on the American Government." This included, as Pickering advised the president, the calumny "that you had asserted the influence of the British government in affairs of our own" in return for bribes.[41] Adams exploded: "Is there anything evil in the regions of actuality that the Aurora has not suggested of me[?]" In the president's judgment, "the matchless effrontery of this Duane merits the execution of the alien law. I am willing to

---

* Ironically, Duane had once been deported from India for the anti-royalist editorials he published in a Calcutta newspaper.

try its strength upon him."[42] America's only ex-president echoed the hope that officials would "probe this matter to the bottom." As George Washington put it: "There can be no medium between the reward and punishment of an Editor, who shall publish such things as Duane has been doing for sometime past. Can hardihood itself be so great, as to stigmatize characters in the Public Gazettes for the most heinous offenses?"[43] Washington would die a few months later without the chance to observe or comment on the law's full impact.

Federal marshals arrested Duane on August 2, 1799, but the editor posted a $3,000 bond and remained at liberty. While awaiting his day in court, he continued lobbing invectives against the Adams administration. Speaking of himself in the third person, he boasted: "Neither persecution nor any other peril to which bad men may expose him can make him swerve from the cause of republicanism, or prove himself unworthy to be the successor of the descendant of Franklin."[44] Worthy, or at the very least elusive, he indeed proved to be. Despite three separate attempts to silence him—including a charge of contempt of the Senate—he managed to avoid conviction without abandoning his attacks on Adams. The charges against Duane eventually evaporated, but not before a Federalist mob soundly thrashed him.

The Cooper and Duane cases were but the show trials in a widespread campaign of presidentially sanctioned press intimidation that lasted until 1801. In all, the government issued some seventeen indictments for sedition, twelve of them against publishers and printers.[45] (Other opposition journalists answered similar charges under local laws.) Not coincidentally, four of the five leading Republican newspapers faced prosecution, including the *Boston Independent Chronicle*, James Callender's *Richmond Examiner*, and the *New York Argus*, whose owner, Thomas Greenleaf, also died before he could be tried. When Greenleaf's widow, Anne, continued publishing the paper, she herself was indicted—the only woman ever prosecuted under the Sedition Act.[46]

Ironically, the sedition law also brought unanticipated consequences to some of the Federalist editors who supported it. The junior John Ward Fenno, who took over the *Gazette of the United States* after his namesake father perished in the same Philadelphia epidemic that claimed Bache, ended up paying a $2,500 libel fine of his own. In a separate case, when the acidulous William Cobbett charged Dr. Benjamin Rush with malpractice during the Philadelphia fever outbreak, the physician-patriot sued and won a $5,000 judgment. After years of mischief-making, Cobbett, alias "Peter Porcupine," had no recourse but to close down *Porcupine's Gazette*, sell off his printing press, and sail back to his native England.[47]

Surely it was no accident that the government brought most of its sedition cases during the presidential election year of 1800. The administration clearly meant the campaign-season crackdown to inhibit Republican electioneering in an era in which national campaigns were still largely waged by journalists, not candidates. By spring, Adams even fantasized about filling the void with a "gazette in the service of the government."[48] With no time to establish such an official organ, he braced himself for a tough challenge from Jefferson and his press allies. In the coming months, Republican editors risked prosecution to condemn Adams as a militarist. Meanwhile pro-Adams editors had a field day assailing Jefferson (without fear of reprisals) as an infidel. In one typical exchange, James Callender characterized the race as a choice between "Adams, war and beggary, and Jefferson, peace and competency." From the opposite side, and with equal hyperbole, John Ward Fenno labeled it a contest between "God—and a religious President" and "Jefferson—and no God."[49]

To Adams's chagrin, a number of "High Federalist" editors—those loyal to Hamilton—proposed that he yield to a stronger candidate. While Noah Webster and other moderate party journalists rushed to the president's defense, Hamilton launched a newspaper and handbill campaign designed to undermine Adams in New York even if it meant throwing the White House—the freshly built executive mansion now adorning the new federal capital of Washington—to Jefferson.

That fall, facing likely defeat and already searching for scapegoats, Adams expressed as much resentment toward press critics from his own party as from the opposition's. "Porcupine's gazette and Fenno's gazette," he roared, "from the moment of the mission to France, aided, countenanced and encouraged by the *soi-disant* Federalists in Boston, New York, and Philadelphia, have done more to shuffle the cards into the hands of the Jacobin leaders, than all the acts of the administration." With no shortage of self-pity he added, "For myself, age, infirmities, family misfortunes, have conspired with the unreasonable conduct of jacobins and insolent Federalists, to make me too indifferent to whatever can happen."[50]

Adams very nearly won a second term in spite of himself. A few hundred switched votes in New York might have turned the entire contest in his favor.[51] Instead, the two leading Republicans, Jefferson and Aaron Burr, finished in a dead heat nationally—each with eight more electoral votes than Adams—thus sending the contest between the top two finishers to the House of Representatives. Only after thirty-six ballots there did Jefferson emerge the victor, with runner-up Burr installed as vice president.[52] The result promised an end, the incoming chief executive vowed, to an era of newspaper repression that he called the "reign of witches."[53] Exulted Bache's *Aurora*, "The Revolution of 1776 is now, and for the first time, arrived at its completion."[54]

Adams blamed his defeat on the press. Once he returned home to Massachusetts (after skipping his successor's inauguration), he bitterly complained that he had been "overthrown by Philip Freneau, Duane, Callender," and other "foreign liars" who had "discomfited the education, the talents, the virtues, and the property of the country."[55] Adams took no responsibility for arousing unprecedented newspaper wrath by so imprudently attempting to silence opposition editors.

Adams never got over his defeat or his sense of victimization at the hands of journalists. "I have been disgraced and degraded, and I have a right to complain," he indeed complained in one of his many letters to Thomas Jefferson after both men had retired from public life. "But, as I have always expected it, I have always submitted to it, perhaps with too much tameness."[56] Self-awareness was never one of Adams's virtues.

He got much closer to the truth in 1815, when at age seventy-nine he perceptively identified a genuine and seemingly intractable problem: party-aligned newspapers never gave equal space to both sides of a political issue, so their respective subscribers seldom found contrary viewpoints in their gazettes. "One party reads the newspapers and pamphlets of its own church, and interdicts all writings of the opposite complexion," Adams observed. "The other party condemns all such as heresy, and will not read or suffer to be read, as far as its influence extends, anything but its own libels. 'The avenue to the public ear is shut.'"

Yet Adams's only proposed remedy remained "the regulation of the press," however "difficult" and "dangerous." As the old man stubbornly insisted, "Mankind cannot now be governed without it, nor at present with it."[57] The correspondent with whom he shared this recommendation would have proved a receptive audience: James Lloyd, the onetime U.S. senator from Maryland who had first proposed a sedition law so draconian that his fellow Federalists had been compelled to soften it.[58] Not enough, as it turned out, to spare Adams from the first reelection defeat ever handed to a sitting president, along with the stern judgment of history for his ill-advised efforts to control history's so-called first draft: the free flow of journalism.

Unlike George Washington, of whom he remained jealous for the remainder of his long life, John Adams loved politics and, much as he groused, rather enjoyed sparring with the press. He proved unable, however, to dismiss past slights, tending instead to catalog them in a mental file of resentments he could neither forget nor forgive. His enemies almost enjoyed taunting him.

Nor did Adams ever give his press supporters much reason to care deeply about him. He lacked the charm required to transform followers into admirers. Even those who embraced Federalist policies found Adams to be, at best, a mercurial and often petulant advocate for party goals. He briefly gained stature and acclaim when he stood up to France over the XYZ Affair, but he paid a steep price among his most Francophobic fellow Federalists by subsequently advocating peace over war. Unquestionably, his biggest mistake ever was cracking down on the press. In signing and enforcing the sedition laws, Adams chose repression over persuasion. He forfeited reelection, squandered his reputation, and helped hasten the demise of the Federalist Party itself.

Bluster alone—whether in the cause of sound policy or bad—seldom charms either journalists or the reading public for very long. At least such counted for common wisdom at the end of America's first century.

3

THOMAS JEFFERSON

"The press," Thomas Jefferson continued to maintain a year and a half into his presidency, provided "the only tocsin of a nation"—its only reliable alarm bell against the danger of tyranny.[1] That he so believed after enduring the slings and arrows of his sharpest newspaper critic, friend-turned-foe James Thomson Callender, constituted a miracle of idealism over injury.

Perhaps no editor of the Founding Era outraged more readers or vilified more politicians than Callender. A hard-drinking, tough-talking provocateur—perhaps the most unsympathetic victim of the sedition law prosecutions—Callender also proved a uniquely unreliable figure in the transition between Adams and Jefferson. In an age in which partisan editors seldom switched political allegiances, this Republican mouthpiece not only turned against his party and began vigorously promoting the Federalists he had formerly attacked, he made life hell for his longtime hero and patron, Thomas Jefferson. It was as if Callender chose to heed one of his own early warnings (originally leveled against the Federalists): "It is time for Americans to cast aside that trimming tide of sycophancy which is too well calculated to oil the wheels of despotism."[2]

Born in Scotland around 1758, Callender earned early notoriety there as a pamphleteer. He published his scathing *Deformities of Samuel Johnson* in 1782 and followed it with *An Impartial Account of the Excise Tax*—which proved anything but. After accusing the Crown of abuses against its Scottish subjects, he fled to America one step ahead of the law, leaving a wife and children behind. Making his way to Philadelphia, he found employment at the Republican *Aurora*, writing at first under the pseudonym "A correspondent just arrived from

Europe." Utilizing his skills as a stenographer, he earned supplemental income transcribing congressional proceedings.[3] For all his efforts, Callender's luck never really returned in Philadelphia. After finally amassing enough funds to send for his family, his wife died here, leaving him with three youngsters to raise alone. In 1798, he tried relaunching himself in Virginia as coeditor of the pro-Republican *Richmond Examiner.*

The following year, after labeling President Adams "a professed aristocrat" whose reign amounted to "one continued tempest of *malignant* passions," Callender went on trial for seditious communication.[4] Found guilty, he was ordered to pay a $200 fine and spend nine months in prison—less than the maximum, but still harsh.[5] After serving his full sentence in a dank Richmond jail—made more onerous to the racist editor because its prison population included inmates of color—Callender regained his freedom on March 2, 1801, just two days before Jefferson's inauguration. Anticipating a fresh start, he turned to the newly installed president for the rewards to which he thought a martyred journalist entitled: funds to pay his fine, a financial subvention to launch a new paper, and a well-paying government job, in his case appointment as U.S. postmaster of the Virginia capital. Callender believed he had earned all this and more.

At first sympathetic, Jefferson hailed Callender as "a man of genius suffering under persecution" and suggested that Republicans "refund his fine by private contributions." He not only issued a retrospective presidential pardon, he wrote a $50 check to cover a quarter of Callender's debt. "I think it essentially just and necessary," the president told James Monroe, "that Callender should be substantially defended."[6] But after the editor journeyed to Washington to undertake what Jefferson regarded as "high-toned" lobbying on his own behalf—which may have included outright blackmail threats—the president cut him off from further support. Jefferson bristled that Callender seemed to believe additional funds "due, in fact, as hush money," adding: "Such a misconstruction of my charities puts an end to them forever."[7] Livid, Callender protested, "By the cause, I have lost five years of labour; gained five thousand personal enemies; [and] got my name insulted in five hundred libels."[8] Callender had a point. The incumbent Richmond postmaster was a Federalist; how difficult would it be for the administration to replace him with a deserving Republican?

Indeed, Jefferson had it well within his power to placate Callender. Merely by replicating his historic support for Republican journals and journalists, he might have spared his legacy enormous damage. Instead, Jefferson turned

Callender down, insisting, "He knows nothing of me which I am not willing to declare to the world myself."[9] Few presidents have ever made such a delusional observation about a newspaperman. In response, Callender switched allegiances and became associate editor of the *Richmond Recorder*, a pro-Federalist journal. There, he resumed his venomous attacks—now directed against the man and party he had once championed.

His ultimate revenge was yet to come. The following autumn, it was Callender who published the first scandalous exposé of Jefferson's purported longtime sexual relationship with his late wife's half sister: his own enslaved African American servant Sally Hemings. As Callender snickered in the biggest scoop of the new century: "It is well known that the man *whom it delighteth the people to honor*, keeps, and for many years past, has kept, as his concubine, one of his own slaves. Her name is SALLY. The name of her eldest son is TOM. His features are said to bear a striking although sable resemblance to those of the president himself. . . . The delicacy of this arrangement must strike every person of common sensibilities. What a sublime pattern for an American ambassador."[10]

Jefferson paid a steep price for rebuking Callender, at least in history. Widely republished then and periodically since, the story of his liaison with Sally Hemings haunted Jefferson without quite hurting him—at least not in his own time. But the explosive charges percolated beneath the surface for generations, at first regarded as rumor more than accepted fact. Contemporary admirers and reverential biographers long denied it, until the scholarship of Fawn M. Brodie and, more recently, Annette Gordon Reed, left no doubt that Jefferson's DNA indeed endures in Hemings's many descendants.[11] Perhaps tellingly, Jefferson never publicly refuted the allegation, although by then his silence in the face of all manner of press hostility had become the habit of a lifetime. "It has been so impossible to contradict all their lies," he piously declared of opposition editors, ". . . that I have determined to contradict none; for while I should be engaged with one, they would publish twenty new ones."[12]

As for James Callender, he soon, and almost predictably, met with an untimely end. On July 17, 1803, after staggering through the streets of Richmond in a state of inebriation, the dissipated Republican-turned-Federalist seemed to vanish from sight. A few hours later, residents discovered his inert body in the James River. Authorities ruled Callender's death by drowning an accident caused by drunkenness. Whether he was the last of the scathing mudslingers or the first of the modern muckrakers remains a matter of debate to this day.

Certainly Callender represented partisan presidential coverage at its fiercest—and least tethered to principle or loyalty.

The editor's death did little to calm the storm of controversy he had instigated, or the fierce style of attack he brought to the coverage of the presidency. Abigail Adams, for one, long found it hard to absolve her husband's successor from the sin of once embracing Callender—not so much because he had gone on to tarnish Jefferson, but because he had unleashed his earlier poison against her husband. "The Serpent you cherished and warmed," she almost gloated a year after the editor's death, "bit the hand that nourished him, and gave you Sufficient Specimins [*sic*] of his talents, his gratitude, his justice and his truth. When such vipers are let loose upon Society all distinction between virtue and vice are levelld [*sic*] all respect for character is lost in the overwhelming deluge of calumny."[13]

Conceding that he had misjudged Callender as "a man of genius, unjustly persecuted," Jefferson insisted in his reply that the editor had "told some useful truths in his coarse way" and never deserved persecution under the unjust sedition law. "[M]y charities to him," he maintained, "were no more meant as encouragements to his scurrilities than those I give to the beggar at my door are meant as rewards for the vices of his life. . . . With respect to the calumnies and falsehoods which writers and printers at large published against mr Adams, I was as far from stooping to any concern or approbation of them as mr Adams was respecting those of Porcupine, Fenno, or Russell, who published volumes against me for every sentence vended by their opponents against mr Adams. But I never supposed mr Adams had any participation in the atrocities of these editors or their writers."[14]

If Jefferson learned any lessons from flirting with combustible editors, he never so admitted. In fact, just as he first embraced and then subsequently discarded Callender, this steadfast opponent of Sedition Act crackdowns on Republican editors raised no known objections when state authorities began prosecuting Federalist critics of his own administration. A Pennsylvania court went after Joseph Dennie, editor of the anti-Republican Philadelphia *Port Folio*, and in late 1802 the New York bench brought libel charges against Harry Croswell, editor of a Hudson-based sheet called *The Wasp*.[15] The president remained silent.

Ironically, Croswell, who wrote under the pseudonym Robert Rusticoat, had invited prosecution by lambasting Jefferson over the Callender affair. Like Abigail Adams, Croswell wondered how Jefferson could have considered as "an object of charity" a journalist "who presented a face bloated with vices, a heart black as hell—one who could be guilty of such foul falsehoods, such vile aspersions. . . . No! He is the very man, that an aspiring mean and hollow hypocrite would press into the service of crime . . . to spit the venom and scatter the malicious, poisonous slanders of his employer."[16] For good measure, Croswell charged that before Jefferson had married, he had tried to seduce the wife of a friend—another charge the president never denied. Croswell, convicted at his initial trial, attracted the attention of no less than Alexander Hamilton, who took the editor's case on appeal. After a dazzling summation, during which Hamilton argued that truth was an absolute defense against libel, the court split on granting Croswell a new trial. But as the state legislature was already moving to reform its libel laws in harmony with Hamilton's arguments, Croswell escaped further prosecution.

Explaining his inconsistent position on censorship to Abigail Adams the following September, Jefferson made it clear, despite "the overwhelming torrent of slander which is confounding all vice and virtue," that he objected to press constraints only when imposed by federal authorities and not out of a moral commitment to absolute press liberty. "While we deny that Congress have a right to controul the freedom of the press," he insisted, "we have ever asserted the right of the states, and their exclusive right, to do so."[17]

Above all, Thomas Jefferson was a states' rights man, not a press-freedom man.

More than either of his two predecessors, Thomas Jefferson came to office having practiced and perfected the art of cultivating, encouraging, and, in some cases, financing friendly newspapers. John Adams enviously declared him "their great patron and protector."[18] Yet Jefferson also supported, in theory at least, the notion of unshackling even hostile editors to publish what they believed. "The basis of our government being the opinion of the people," he had memorably declared back in 1787, "were it left to me to decide whether we should have a government without newspapers, or newspapers without government, I should not hesitate a moment to prefer the latter. But I should mean that every man should receive those papers, and be capable of reading them."[19]

Unlike Adams, Jefferson largely left actual editorializing to surrogates such as James Madison. "I never in my life had directly or indirectly written one sentence for a newspaper," he commended himself in his diary, making a virtue of his reluctance to communicate directly with the people.[20] In truth, by restraining himself, this great American writer denied his cause a potent weapon in the battle for public opinion. Meantime, his behind-the-scenes efforts on behalf of Republican journalists, starting with his ethically dubious move to hire propagandist Philip Freneau at the State Department, had helped nourish partisan journalism anyway. Under the system Jefferson helped create, newspapers became participants in, not merely observers of, politics and government. Policy debates descended into personal malignity, with the partisan press extravagantly lauding presidents as saints or acrimoniously vilifying them as sinners.

Following the brutal 1800 presidential campaign, Jefferson entered the White House with no expectation that he would enjoy the same kind of grace period from Federalist journals as Adams had earlier earned from Republican ones. From the time the Constitution itself had been debated, Jefferson anticipated he would thereafter "have his peace of mind . . . disturbed by any individual who shall think proper to arraign him in a newspaper." In theory, he considered the inevitable onslaught "an evil for which there is no remedy," conceding that "our liberty depends on the freedom of the press, and that cannot be limited without being lost."[21] Withstanding the onslaught would test that faith.

Not that Jefferson allowed himself to become an undefended target. To counter the opposition, he adroitly reengineered the ideologically driven network of pro-Republican newspapers he had previously helped forge when the capital had first moved from New York to Philadelphia. With the government now located in Washington, Jefferson encouraged the establishment of a new gazette there that would remain reliably favorable to his administration. Its reward would be first access to official news, along with lucrative government printing contracts to keep otherwise idle presses busy between editions. Meanwhile Jefferson urged William Duane to continue operating the pro-administration *Aurora* from Philadelphia, still the most populous city in the nation. The president encouraged Abijah Adams (no relation to the former president) to maintain his *Boston Independent Chronicle*, and by 1804 persuaded Thomas Ritchie to found the *Richmond Enquirer*. In the Boston case, the administration resurrected an editor once convicted of libel for supporting the Virginia and Kentucky Resolutions; in Ritchie's, it launched the career of a gifted journalist who would remain influential for the next fifty years.[22]

Most consequential of all was Jefferson's 1800 role in persuading Samuel Harrison Smith to establish the new Washington *National Intelligencer*, the first official government newspaper in American history. As a reward, Jefferson favored its twenty-eight-year-old editor with "official" printing orders for passports, patent applications, and pamphlet versions of newly passed laws, not to mention the first edition of the president's own 1801 treatise, *A Manual of Parliamentary Practice*. The alliance raised few eyebrows at the time. In March 1801, the *Intelligencer* published Jefferson's first inaugural address with such alacrity that it was assumed the new president supplied Smith with its text in advance so that he could typeset it for the public first. This was an unheard-of exclusive arrangement. To secure his own belated access to the manuscript, the president's longtime ally William Dunne even had to wait until Smith expressed a copy to Philadelphia for his use.[23]

If all these favors were not enough to make Smith a Republican loyalist for life, Jefferson also ushered the editor and his bride into his social circle, another first for the executive mansion, where editors had seldom been welcomed as guests. Flattered, Mrs. Smith came to regard Jefferson as not only "the champion of human rights" and "reformer of abuses" but also her personal "friend."[24] Her husband repaid the president's solicitude and patronage with glowing reports of his own. At the White House, Smith once observed a Prussian diplomat reading a newspaper that featured a damning attack on the administration. The astonished envoy wondered why Jefferson did not suppress it. "Put that paper in your pocket," came the president's reply, ". . . and should you ever hear the reality of our liberty, the freedom of the press questioned, show them the paper—*and tell them where you found it*."[25] Smith made sure the noble quote reached thousands.

Of course, in this so-called Dark Age of American journalism, Jefferson's ascent did not please all the newspapers covering him. In fact, his presidency inspired the debut and growth of Federalist papers, too, which continued to outnumber Republican journals throughout Jefferson's eight years in the White House. Back in Philadelphia, Enos Bronson took over the *Gazette of the United States* and kept it churning out criticism of the new president. And in Manhattan, a onetime Massachusetts lawyer named William Coleman used generous investments by Alexander Hamilton and other anti-administration backers to establish the *New York Evening Post*, whose debut in 1801 elicited widespread admiration for its handsome printing. In his final months, even James Callender had taken to calling Coleman the "Field-Marshal of the Federalist editors."[26]

Enemies whispered that Coleman often rendezvoused with Hamilton on New York's noisy streets to slavishly take down the former treasury secretary's anti-Jefferson screeds so they could be printed in the *Post* verbatim.

The first press controversy to roil the new administration and excite newspapers on both sides of the partisan divide began in a sense even before Jefferson's election. It took many months, however, for the brouhaha to erupt, owing again to slow communication across the ocean. It would not much matter that the issue itself was symbolic and inconsequential. It reopened the divide between admirers of England and France and provided a fresh opportunity for Federalists to attack Jefferson, and they seized it.

The contretemps involved sixty-five-year-old expatriate Thomas Paine, the still-controversial author of the 1776 treatise *Common Sense*. In 1800, he confided to Jefferson his desire to leave France and at last return to the United States. But Paine worried that if captured by a British ship while sailing aboard an ordinary passenger vessel, he might be dragooned to his native England, where he had remained a condemned man since the Revolutionary War. Paine asked Jefferson if he might instead provide safe passage on "any American frigate" anchored near France.[27] On March 18, 1801, just two weeks after his inauguration, the new president replied in the affirmative. Paine would be welcomed aboard the U.S. warship *Maryland*, transported west, and afforded a warm welcome home. "I am in hopes you will find us returned generally to sentiments worthy of former times," Jefferson said, no doubt referring to his own recent ascendancy. Then he effusively, and in retrospect unwisely, added: "In these it will be your glory to have steadily laboured with as much effect as any man living. That you may long live to continue your useful labours and to reap the reward in the thankfulness of nations is my sincere prayer."[28]

As it turned out, hostilities between France and England ceased just a few weeks later under the terms of the Treaty of Amiens, and Paine concluded he no longer required American naval protection to cross the Atlantic safely. In a bald effort at self-promotion, however, he shared Jefferson's warm letter with the French press. It was only a matter of time before copies of those Paris newspapers made their way to Washington. On April 27, the *National Intelligencer* innocently republished Jefferson's text, triggering an uproar. While Duane's *Aurora* rushed to Jefferson's defense, endorsing his generous hospitality without question, the rival *Gazette of the United States* erupted: "When the story arrived here, that the President of the United States had written a *very affectionate letter* to that living opprobrium of humanity, TOM PAINE, the infamous scavenger of all the filth which could be raked from the dirty paths which have been hitherto trodden by all the revilers of Christianity, Duane, instead of attempting to refute the scandalous charge upon the President admits that it may be true, and even endeavours to justify it."[29]

The outrage was unsurprising. Although Paine deserved credit for, in a sense, philosophizing American independence into existence, it was also true that he had invited much controversy during his lengthy exile. Many Americans remembered with disgust Paine's widely publicized attack on George Washington at the end of the late president's second term, and few sympathized with Paine's well-reported hostility toward organized religion or his alleged indifference to the Reign of Terror in France. As a pro-Federalist newspaper in Boston exaggerated: "What! Invite to the United States that lying, drunken, brutal infidel, who rejoiced in the opportunity of basking and wallowing in the confusion, devastation, bloodshed, rapine, and murder in which his soul delights?"[30]

Paine did not set foot back in the United States until October 30, 1802, and then only as a commercial traveler. But the uproar over Jefferson's year-old offer of free transport on a government vessel plagued the president from the time his invitation hit the American press virtually until Paine's death (and Jefferson's own retirement) in 1809. The press would not let go of it. To his credit as a gentleman if not a politician, Jefferson never tempered his original embrace. When Paine visited Washington, the president could be seen strolling the White House grounds, arm in arm with a figure who still aroused both admiration and revulsion in America.

For all his theoretical belief in press freedom, Jefferson soon came to revile opposition journalists as passionately as Washington and Adams had. He complained that "the printers can never leave us in a state of perfect rest and union of opinion." He deplored "the malignant & long-continued efforts which the federalists exerted in their newspapers," and he considered himself "the single object of their accumulated hatred," a "fair mark for every man's dirt."[31] On one occasion Jefferson complained of Federalist editors, "They never utter a truth." And he protested that "every syllable from me is distorted" by the opposition. "Like the clergy," he once jeered, the press "live by the zeal they can kindle and the schemes they can create."[32] As if to prove his point, the Federalist press in

1802 circulated the fiction that an enfeebled Jefferson was either preparing to resign or wasting away on his deathbed.[33] In fact, he would last another twenty-four years.

The juicy Thomas Paine affair wasn't the only Jefferson administration initiative to trigger press indignation. Although Republican editors cheered his efforts to rescind Adams's lame-duck, last-minute appointments to the Federal courts—the "midnight judges"—Federalist journals pilloried Jefferson for challenging his predecessor's right to flood the bench with allies, even on the eve of his departure.[34] The *Gazette of the United States* actually reprimanded Jefferson for seeking to oust jurists "upon whose independence and uprightedness . . . the security of our rights and liberties absolutely and wholly depend"—an absurdity contradicted by the politicized decisions made by Federalist judges on sedition prosecutions.[35] As further proof, when Jeffersonian editor Samuel Smith stepped forward to condemn the entire federal judiciary for "destroying all freedom of opinion," the D.C. Circuit Court, still dominated by Federalists, recommended that the president's favorite editor be prosecuted. Fortunately for Smith, a grand jury declined to indict.[36]

Even the 1803 Louisiana Purchase, which not only doubled the size of the country but seemed in theory a perfect expression of Federalist-style nationalism, unleashed attacks from opposition editors determined to deride anything the president accomplished. In this case, they flogged Jefferson for hypocrisy, charging that in making the deal, he had abandoned his once-strict belief in limited presidential powers. Other newspaper critics denounced the pact for bringing the United States into closer alignment with ever-suspect France. The acquisition would diminish the political power of the original states, they argued, while inviting war with Spain, which harbored claims of its own on the western lands. One Federalist paper in Boston mocked the new territory as "a great waste, a wilderness unpeopled with any being except wolves and wandering Indians," warning it would eventually "be cut up into States without number, but each with *two votes in the Senate*"—tilting that body permanently to Jefferson's own party.

The city's rival Republican sheet countered, not without justification, "The more successful, & the more eminently beneficial to the country, the measures of the present administration are hourly becoming, the more virulent becomes the abuse and outrage which is daily displayed in the federal papers."[37] In the end, the *New York Evening Post* could summon no better argument against the Louisiana Purchase than that the deal had been achieved "solely owing to a fortuitous concurrence of unforeseen and unexpected circumstances, and not to any wise or vigorous measures on the part of the American government."[38]

This latest criticism left Jefferson convinced that the press printed "only the caricatures of disaffected minds." Yet in the same breath he reiterated to a French scientist his reluctance to strike back, either with comment or censorship: "It is so difficult to draw a clear line of separation between the abuse and the wholesome use of the press," he told Marc-Auguste Pictet, "that as yet we have found it better to trust the public judgment, rather than the magistrate, with the discrimination between truth & falsehood. And hitherto the public judgment has performed that office with wonderful correctness."[39]

Not every major news event exposed Jefferson to partisan attack. In 1804, he surprisingly escaped rebuke when his own vice president, Aaron Burr, killed Federalist icon Alexander Hamilton on a Weehawken, New Jersey, dueling field—following an argument precipitated by a newspaper article. Hamilton was not yet fifty years old. No doubt Jefferson had inured himself from criticism by marginalizing Burr while they served in the same administration. He had also made clear before the duel that he wanted a different vice president when he sought a second term. Even his most rabid enemies could not stretch facts enough to make the president the villain in a rogue act perpetrated by a political outcast.

Meanwhile, the Federalist press ushered Hamilton into the realm of martyrdom. In one tribute, the newspaper he had helped create, the *New York Evening Post*, beribboned its front page in thick black borders for nine successive days—a marvel of printing, not to mention devotion.[40] Not since Washington's death five years earlier had a statesman earned such a flood of laudation. Republican editors gritted their teeth and contained themselves as Federalist editors conducted the canonization largely unopposed. For the most part, Jeffersonians respectfully, if insincerely, lamented Hamilton's passing, too. Only occasionally did some let their cynicism get the better of them, as when the Republican *Boston Independent Chronicle* blasted the protracted mourning as "pagan toil for an Apotheosis."[41] When James Cheetham, editor of the pro-Republican *New York American Citizen*, countered by praising Hamilton anyway, the *Chronicle* charged him with "out Herod[ing] Herod."[42] Incensed, Cheetham followed Callender's example, recanting his alliance with the Jeffersonians and pledging himself to the Federalists.[43]

Even though journalists mercifully exempted Jefferson from their Hamilton coverage, he stood ready to make his overall dissatisfaction with the press clear to the public once safely reelected. In his March 4, 1805, inaugural address he broke his own long-standing rule and at last took direct public aim at the newspapers. "During the course of administration, and in order to disturb it," he complained, "the artillery of the press has been levelled against us, charged with whatever its licentiousness could devise or dare. These abuses of an institution so important to freedom and science, are deeply to be regretted, inasmuch as they tend to lessen its usefulness, and to sap its safety." Once again, Jefferson raised the threat of using local libel laws to discourage "falsehood and defamation." But, as he sardonically concluded, "public duties more urgent press on the time of public servants, and the offenders have therefore been left to find their punishment in the public indignation."[44]

Two years later, in 1807, Jefferson stirred yet another round of attacks by imposing an ill-conceived embargo on American goods shipped to England. Meant to pressure the British by depriving its consumers, the ban ended up hurting New England commercial interests more, backfiring on the president and earning condemnation in Federalist gazettes. While the ever-faithful Samuel Smith applauded Jefferson for his "watchful preservation of our resources," the *New York Evening Post* more convincingly lamented "the sacrifice of all the pride, and all the liberty, and all the good sense of the nation."[45]

A year before he finished his second term, Jefferson confided his anger toward the press in a unique fashion. He conceived a tongue-in-cheek guide to the establishment of an ideal newspaper—one that would openly label both facts and its falsehoods. Here was a satirical volley worthy of Voltaire. Predictably, Jefferson cautioned the correspondent to whom he shared these amusing instructions to keep them to himself and out of the press:

> To your request of my opinion of the manner in which a newspaper should be conducted, so as to be most useful, I should answer, "by restraining it to true facts & sound principles only." Yet I fear such a paper would find few subscribers. It is a melancholy truth, that a suppression of the press could not more compleatly deprive the nation of it's benefits, than is done by it's abandoned prostitution to falsehood. . . . General facts may indeed be collected from them . . . but no details can be relied on. . . .
>
> Perhaps an editor might begin a reformation in some such way as this. Divide his paper into 4. chapters, heading the 1st. Truths. 2d. Probabilities.

> 3d. Possibilities. 4th. Lies. The 1st. chapter would be very short, as it would contain little more than authentic papers, and information from such sources as the editor would be willing to risk his own reputation for their truth. The 2d. would contain what, from a mature consideration of all circumstances, his judgment should conclude to be probably true. This however, should rather contain too little than too much. The 3d. & 4th. should be professedly for those readers who would rather have lies for their money than the blank paper they would occupy.[46]

Jefferson approached the end of his presidency certain that, as he put it, "Nothing can now be believed which is seen in a newspaper. Truth itself becomes suspicious by being put into that polluted vehicle. . . . I will add that the man who never looks into a newspaper is better informed than he who reads them; inasmuch as he who knows nothing is nearer to truth than he whose mind is filled with falsehoods & errors."[47] By then the laws in his home state of Virginia codified the "ancient" tradition of "punishing *divulgers of false news.*"[48]

Buffeted by violent newspaper criticism throughout his presidency, Jefferson spent his long retirement at Monticello endeavoring to ignore the press altogether. At least he so claimed when he told John Adams in 1812 that he had abandoned the habits of a lifetime and turned instead to more serious reading. "I have given up newspapers in exchange for Tacitus & Thucydides, for Newton & Euclid," he reported, "and I find myself much the happier."[49] In his final years, Jefferson insisted that the only journal he still consulted was Thomas Ritchie's *Richmond Enquirer*, "and in that chiefly the advertisements." As he caustically explained, "they contain the only truths to be relied on in a newspaper."[50]

As he aged, his anti-press fury only grew. "I deplore, with you, the putrid state into which our newspapers have passed," he told his neighbor Walter Jones in 1814, "and the malignity, the vulgarity, and the mendacious spirit of those who write for them. . . . These ordures are rapidly depraving the public taste and lessening its relish for sound food." Writing to former attorney general Richard Rush six years later, Jefferson began: "I have no news to give you; for I have none but from the newspapers, and believing little of that myself, it would be an unworthy present to my friends."[51]

Yet when he generously decided to donate his vast personal library to the government, he turned to his longtime Washington newspaper ally Samuel

Harrison Smith to handle the arrangements.* The collection that would seed what became the Library of Congress included, along with its thousands of books, some sixty years' worth of newspapers that Jefferson had amassed, presumably read, and long refused to discard. As he admitted of the trove: "I cherish it."[52]

Often put to the test on freedom of the press, even before it secured constitutional protection, Thomas Jefferson to his immense credit consistently defended the right of opposition voices to make themselves heard free of federal oversight—even if he endorsed the prosecution of slander under local statutes. He pardoned editors convicted under Adams's sedition laws and even encouraged the impeachment of jurists who had sentenced the offenders.

Yet earlier, this enigmatic leader had done as much as anyone in the Founding Era to inspire and finance the kind of virulent journalism he later came to rue. Shrouding such efforts in implausible denial, he remained eternally reluctant to admit his key role in promoting partisan journalism. As president, Jefferson felt the wrath of press vilification keenly and answered it by sponsoring America's first official administration newspaper. He granted its editor the status of confidant, armed him with the right to learn and print news first and disseminate it nationally, and made him the well-paid de facto public printer. But by the time he left office and returned to his Monticello home, the nation of readers was no closer to an era of nonpartisan journalism than it was when Washington first felt the sting of attack journalism midway through his first term.

A week before Jefferson's death, on July 4, 1826—the same milestone Independence Day John Adams coincidentally breathed his last—Jefferson received an invitation to celebrate that golden anniversary in Washington, D.C. The eighty-three-year-old Founding Father was by then far too weak to travel. But in the last letter this prolific master of democratic gospel ever composed, he proved he remained fully capable of reminding new generations about a key blessing that America granted its citizens: "the free right to the unbounded exercise of reason and freedom of opinion."[53]

As he had told the Marquis de Lafayette three years earlier: "[T]he only

---

*By then the founding editor of the *National Intelligencer* had gone on to serve Republican administrations in such patronage posts as commissioner of revenue and interim secretary of the treasury, and Jefferson had helped raise funds to keep his paper afloat.

security of all, is in a free press. The force of public opinion cannot be resisted, when permitted freely to be expressed. The agitation it produces must be submitted to. It is necessary to keep the waters pure."[54]

Convinced he had been subjected to far more press abuse than either Washington or Adams, Jefferson never abandoned his core belief that under no circumstances could the federal government prevent a newspaper from printing opinions, even if they provoked distress. As he had famously put it in 1816, "[W]here the press is free, and every man able to read, all is safe."[55]

If he never fully practiced what he preached, neither did any other president—and certainly none ever expressed the ideal of press liberty more memorably or more often.

PART TWO

"A GOVERNMENT OF NEWSPAPERS"

4

ANDREW JACKSON

Andrew Jackson became an American hero during the presidency of James Madison, who had fled Washington, D.C., in August 1814, leaving British invaders to seize the city and burn the White House.

Five months later, on a fog-shrouded January morning a thousand miles southwest, Jackson's army of local militiamen, regulars, and free African Americans miraculously repulsed a superior British force at New Orleans, inflicting two thousand casualties while losing fewer than seventy men. The general's achievement struck one newspaper of the day as both "gallant" and "extraordinary"; to another, it "covered him with glory" that would "bloom for ages."[1] It would hardly matter that, as it turned out, Jackson won the battle in a conflict that had already ended. Unbeknownst to either side, the War of 1812 had been settled under a pact negotiated by diplomat John Quincy Adams in Belgium two weeks previously.[2]

When news of the Treaty of Ghent finally reached American shores a few weeks afterward, it may quickly have occurred to some observers that Adams, the son of a New England president, and Jackson, the frontier general already regarded as another George Washington by his admirers, might one day square off in a battle of their own—for high office: the peacemaker versus the warrior. It took nine more years for that fight to get underway, with journalists serving as foot soldiers, in a field that must have seemed nearly as crowded as New Orleans. The other 1824 contenders for president included rising-star Speaker of the House Henry Clay of Kentucky, along with Senator John C. Calhoun of

South Carolina and Secretary of War William H. Crawford (though he had suffered a stroke months earlier).

After twenty-four consecutive years of one-party Jeffersonian rule—the last sixteen under Presidents Madison and James Monroe—the 1824 candidates found themselves competing without the backing of traditional political organizations. The old Federalist Party cofounded by Adams's father—still alive at age eighty-eight—was now in its death throes, with the future Democratic and Whig Parties yet unborn. In the void, newspaper editors scrambled to realign themselves with emerging leaders while politicians maneuvered to enlist a new generation of press supporters. Corruption and the proper role of the central government emerged as major issues. And for a time, Americans would define their political affiliations not by party label but according to their visceral reactions to the dominant public figure of the age: they were either pro-Jackson or anti-Jackson.

In the heated campaign that ensued, warriors were armed not with rifles and Congreve rockets but with pens and printing presses. And as one unsurprising part of the anti-Jackson strategy, pro-Adams newspapers undertook a new war to diminish the general's record at New Orleans—particularly his harsh grip on the city leading up to and after the battle. "What might be expected of his . . . fierce and vindictive spirit, when clothed with the immense power?" worried the *New York Advertiser*.[3] Other critics reminded voters that the battle had established Jackson's reputation for toughness against both military foes and civilian ones, including the press.

Not long after that triumph, a local newspaper had published an article by a politician named Louis Louaillier criticizing the general's decision to place the town under martial law. The editorial acknowledged a debt to Jackson "for the preservation of our city," but a disinclination, "through gratitude, to sacrifice any of our privileges."[4] Jackson, who saw danger in unbridled press criticism, responded by ordering Louaillier imprisoned without trial. When Louaillier's attorney, Pierre L. Morel, appeared before federal judge Dominick A. Hall to seek a writ of habeas corpus, the general ordered the lawyer and jurist jailed, too. Only when news of the Ghent Treaty finally arrived in the Crescent City a few weeks later did Jackson allow civilian rule restored—after which Judge Hall slapped him with a $1,000 judgment for contempt of court.[5]

Other presidents had suppressed, and would suppress, the authors of disobliging newspaper articles; yet none but Andrew Jackson ever restrained a writer, his attorney, and the judge before whom they sought redress. Now his press critics exhumed the Louaillier episode and added it to what they called Jackson's "catalogue of outrages."[6]

Adams began his 1824 White House bid with only regional support. No one doubted his qualifications: weaned on public service as his father's chief aide, he had been a U.S. senator, an ambassador, a secretary of state, and a chief negotiator at Ghent. But JQA was his father's child in ways other than prodigious accomplishment. "I am a man of reserved, cold, austere, and forbidding manners," he conceded, "my adversaries say, a gloomy misanthropist, and my personal enemies, an unsocial savage."[7] Adams's personality repelled more journalists than it attracted. Rather than share his aspirations with editors who might promote them, Adams confided his thoughts to a private diary that ultimately filled fifteen thousand handwritten pages.

Looming largest in 1824 was the already iconic Andrew Jackson of Tennessee. The military chieftain could trace his career in uniform back to the Revolutionary War; he had served in the Continental Army as a teenage orderly. After New Orleans, Jackson had waged hard—some said merciless—war against the Indians in Florida. Not everyone expressed admiration. The general's impulsiveness and hair-trigger temper had gained him notoriety as well: for killing a man in an 1806 duel over a mere forfeited horse race, for executing six court-martialed militiamen for seemingly minor infractions, for mistreating Native Americans, and, above all, for marrying a woman still technically wed to another man.[8]

By now occupying the epicenter of American culture through sheer force of personality—exalted by a growing cadre of worshipful journalists—Jackson was either adored or abhorred: to some a valiant warrior and to others a bloodthirsty tyrant; either a friend of the common man or an aristocrat; a populist or a plantation master; a cunning politician or the quintessential outsider; a nationalist or a racist; a disrupter or a traditionalist. John Quincy Adams spoke for all the general's 1824 rivals by branding Jackson "incompetent both by his ignorance and by the fury of his passions."[9]

Despite all the newspaper ink spilled in assailing him, the general earned the highest number of popular votes among that year's candidates, earning 42 percent of the total, 10 percent more than runner-up Adams. Still, Jackson secured only ninety-nine electoral votes, thirty-two short of the majority needed for election. As the Constitution prescribed, the contest headed to the House of

Representatives, with only the top three vote-getters—Jackson, Adams, and Crawford—eligible to compete.

Before House votes could be cast, Clay (who loathed Jackson) threw his support to Adams, guaranteeing JQA a first-ballot victory. Returning the favor, Adams nominated Clay to be his secretary of state, unleashing charges of a "corrupt bargain" hatched to block the controversial general. The accusation would haunt Adams throughout his presidency and pave the way for Jackson to renew his campaign for the White House almost immediately. Jackson's home state officially renominated him for president in 1825, three full years before the next scheduled election. From his Nashville plantation, the Hermitage, the general impatiently waited for his next chance, poring over as many as twenty newspapers a day to keep current with political intelligence.

Adams endured a turbulent presidency, bereft of major conflicts but plagued by frequent clashes with hostile journalists, refusing to respond to what he called "continual streams of slander." As he rather grandly explained, "The tongue of falsehood can never be silenced, and I have not time to spare from public business to the vindication of myself."[10] This proved to be a fatal miscalculation. As the *Washington Gazette* had already observed, "[T]he government of our union is so much swayed by the press, that it has not been inappropriately styled a government of newspapers."[11]

Occasionally, Adams did invite editors to White House levees he dubbed "drawing-rooms." The invitations gave journalists greater access but did little to grow support for their unapproachable host. Peter Force, founder of Washington's *National Journal*, attended one levee but remained partial to Henry Clay.[12] After enjoying himself at another soirée, William Winston Seaton, editor of the *National Intelligencer*, stayed in Clay's camp, too.[13] Inexplicably appearing on yet another election-year guest list was Russell Jarvis, the hot-tempered associate editor of the openly pro-Jackson *United States Telegraph*. When Jarvis turned up at an event in April 1828, the president's son and private secretary, John Adams II, was overheard objecting to the presence of a man who, as his father put it, "lives by the detail of daily slander upon me."[14]

A few days later, young Adams was striding through the Capitol Rotunda to hand-deliver his father's latest message to Congress when Jarvis "approached him from behind, accosted him by name," and demanded that he account for his recent comments. Receiving no reply, Jarvis "struck him on the face," according to the apoplectic president.[15] Young Adams managed to land only one glancing blow in retaliation before startled onlookers separated the combatants.

The president entertained no hope that his son's assailant would be held accountable. "They brought him here for the purpose of assassination," he melodramatically complained, "and they cannot punish him for laboring in the very vocation to which they called him."[16] Just as the president expected, John Adams II faced far more aggressive questioning at the ensuing congressional inquiry than did Russell Jarvis. To conduct the interrogation, Congress assigned the Senate's official printer Duff Green, a flamboyantly rustic pro-Jackson newspaperman regarded by Adams as the "editor of . . . a scurrilous and abusive print set up by and for the opposition."[17] This was no exaggeration. Jackson himself had provided Green with a $3,000 loan two years earlier to launch his daily—the very paper that now employed Russell Jarvis.[18] Just as Adams predicted, Congress declined to press charges against him.

While this squabble played itself out, the public braced for the main event: the 1828 rematch between Adams and the challenger who had outpolled him in their first presidential showdown four years earlier. Two men of such contrasting background and personality never before faced off as presidential antagonists—much less twice. Breeding, superior education, and a preference for negotiation over confrontation still characterized the chilly Adams. Courage, unbridled aggressiveness, and an undeniable popular touch continued to mark the volcanic Jackson.

No one welcomed the approaching fray more eagerly than newspaper editors anticipating spikes in both subscriptions and advertising if they could fan public interest in the contest. As if the Jarvis incident portended further violence, the ensuing one-on-one campaign would prove the most rancorous since the Jefferson-Adams race in 1800.

Per tradition, the 1828 candidates did no public electioneering on their own behalf. Instead, the bitter contest played out on the pages of the nation's newspapers, including "campaign extras"—temporary papers devoted exclusively, and heatedly, to current politics—all of them unapologetically filled with exaggeration and libel. To great effect, Jacksonian papers reminded voters of the "corrupt bargain" that had elevated the incumbent four years earlier. Now in full campaign mode, Duff Green excoriated Adams for sins ranging from monarchical ambition to runaway federalism.[19] Other Jackson allies warned that a reelected Adams would likely revive his father's notorious alien and sedition laws. Reporting took a turn for the salacious when pro-Jackson New Hampshire editor Isaac Hill alleged that Adams, back in his days as minister to Russia, had pimped his housekeeper to Czar Alexander.

With equal abandon, pro-Adams newspapers countered that Jackson's mother had once been, in the general's own incredulous recounting of the slander, "a prostitute who intermarried with a Negro"; that Jackson himself was therefore "a Mulatto."[20] With the general labeled almost daily as "a murderer, a swindler, an adulterer, and a traitor," Jacksonian editors protested that the Adams press had "lost sight of every decent regard for public reputation and private feelings."[21] Love for Adams did not inspire such passion; hatred for Jackson proved sufficient motivation.

In perhaps the most brutal of the 1828 press attacks, John Binns, editor of Philadelphia's anti-Jackson *Democratic Press*, reignited long-standing concerns about Jackson's violent nature with an audacious, widely distributed handbill: *Some Accounts of the Bloody Deeds OF GENERAL JACKSON*. To dramatize its litany of alleged atrocities, it featured illustrations of eighteen black coffins representing the civilians and soldiers, foreigners and Native Americans, allegedly put to death by Jackson over the years.[22] The print packed the emotional wallop of a mass funeral.

Acknowledging Binns's broadside as "terrifying," one Jacksonian condemned its publisher as "the corrupt fountain" feeding a "great torrent of invective."[23] Isaac Hill's *New Hampshire Patriot* made a bold effort to discredit it; if Jackson had murdered anyone, Hill nimbly countered, it had been the "1500 British soldiers" who attacked New Orleans in 1815 "in search of Booty and Beauty."[24]

The unseemly back-and-forth ensnared the candidates' wives as well. Jackson had instructed one press supporter that "female character never should be introduced or touched by my friends."[25] But Jacksonians began circulating the "absurdity" that Louisa Adams was not even an American citizen.[26] (The First Lady had indeed been born in England, but at the time her father, a Marylander, was serving as U.S. consul to London, a circumstance that made her as American as her husband.) The publicity reportedly sent Mrs. Adams into a depression that drove her to compulsive silk-spinning.

Rachel Donelson Jackson, meanwhile, endured renewed reminders that her marriage had been illegal. In this case, the accusations could not be easily dismissed. The Jacksons had wed in 1791 believing that Rachel's brief union to another man had been legally dissolved. As they later discovered, her first husband had filed for divorce but never obtained a final decree. The Jacksons had been obliged to remarry once Rachel's original spouse belatedly completed the process. In a desperate rejoinder, Duff Green charged that Mr. and Mrs. Adams had enjoyed premarital sex. "Let Mrs. Jackson rejoice," Green trumpeted his sordid scoop to the general; "her vindication is complete."[27]

For all its tumult, the campaign ended with an unsurprising Jackson landslide. The challenger swept into office with 56 percent of the popular vote, amassing 178 electoral votes to Adams's 83. Thus JQA joined his recently deceased father as the only presidents to lose bids for reelection in the first half century of the Republic. Perhaps it was not lost on the incoming president that both the Adamses had paid a steep price for failing to endear themselves to journalists.

From the start, by contrast, President Jackson determined to reach out aggressively to friendly editors and to make sure they were organized into a tight network disseminating puffery and propaganda.[28] The new president would not be content to welcome journalists to drawing-rooms. He would place them in government posts and host them in his private office—even if they were required to enter the executive mansion furtively through the kitchen. The first beneficiary of Jackson's largesse was Adams's particular nemesis, Duff Green, whose "vigilance and industry, patriotic ardor and indomitable courage," another editor openly acknowledged, had helped put Jackson in the White House.[29]

Tragically, the general's wife would not join him there. Repeatedly branded an adulteress and bigamist during the campaign, Rachel sank into a depression of her own, compromising her fragile heath. In December 1828, just weeks after Jackson's election, she died of a sudden heart attack at the Hermitage. Plunged into mourning, her embittered husband vowed never to forgive those who had mauled her in print. Jackson entered the presidency hot for revenge. His libelers might "suppose when the elections [are] over all things will die away," Jackson cautioned one editor. "—*Not so*," he warned. ". . . The day of retribution must come."[30]

"It was a proud day for the people," cheered Amos Kendall's *Argus of Western America* in reporting the March 4, 1829, inauguration. "General Jackson is *their own* President."[31]

As if to prove the point, hordes of Jackson's frenzied admirers crammed into the White House for the post-inaugural reception and uninhibitedly ripped souvenirs from drapes, moldings, and upholstery, smashed expensive crystal, and nearly crushed the new president into a corner. The throng might well have remained inside the mansion in perpetuity had the servants not hauled the punch bowls outside onto the lawn.

By no means did every Washington journalist embrace this new wave of populism—or its chief symbol. To critics, the "people's inauguration" more accurately heralded the "Reign of King Mob."[32] Appalled by what he called "the evil effects of General Jackson's election," the *National Intelligencer*'s William Seaton branded Jackson's ascent the "triumph of demagoguism, ignorance, and radicalism in its worst form . . . sweeping away Conservative and Tory gentlemen, and the highest standard of honor, in the tide of unlettered, unmannered vulgarity."[33]

Sincere the editor may have been, but some of the "sweeping away" that he lamented involved the justifiable ouster of anti-Jackson scribblers who had enjoyed favor during the previous administration. To the victor belonged the spoils, and although the new president ultimately replaced only 10 percent of the federal workforce, he would set records for generous patronage for journalists, rewarding as many as fifty-six partisan editors, printers, and publishers by 1830.[34] At this, Adams professed indignation of his own. "The appointments without exception," he grumbled six weeks after Jackson's swearing-in, "are conferred upon the vilest purveyors of slander during the late electioneering campaign, and an excessive disproportion of places is given to editors of the foulest presses."[35]

At first, even pro-Jackson editor Thomas Ritchie worried that the president meant to "bribe the Press to support his measures," adding, "We wish the Executive would let the Press alone."[36] When yet another editor charged that "the public press have been openly and opulently rewarded out of the public treasury," Jackson self-servingly defended his largesse. "It is the object of all who really take an interest in the honor and welfare of our country to elevate the character of the press and make it the vehicle of truth and useful knowledge," he told John Randolph. Jackson actually declared himself proud that by refusing "to consider the editorial calling as unfit to offer a candidate for office," he was helping "elevate" journalists "to some higher character in life."[37]

More accurately, Jackson wanted friendly editors close by, and in his debt, both to promote his administration and offer advice as needed. Jackson became the first president to use journalists as counselors, a tectonic adjustment in the historically remote relationship between presidents and the press. Duff Green of the *United States Telegraph*, Isaac Hill of the *New Hampshire Patriot*, and

Amos Kendall of Kentucky's *Argus of Western America* had all loyally backed the general—belatedly in the case of Kendall, who had questioned Jackson's "tyrannical disposition" until the general's supporters helped him erase a nagging business debt (Adams branded Kendall "one of those authors to be let").[38] Now all three cheerleaders assumed major roles in Jackson's orbit.

Their financial security would come from government jobs. Hill became second comptroller of the United States, while Kendall landed a $3,000-per-year post as auditor of the Treasury Department. But both men spent much time at the White House, eventually rising to celebrity status as members of an influential coterie of unappointed presidential advisors that by 1831 became known as the "Kitchen Cabinet." Introduced as a derogatory sobriquet because its members at first entered the White House clandestinely through the cook's door, the term eventually came to acknowledge privileged access to the president. Legends to the contrary, the Kitchen Cabinet never met regularly as a group or dominated the purportedly doddering chief executive. Always firmly in control, Jackson called on its "members" individually, as needed, even before they were described as a shadow government.

Originally, Jackson set up his team of writers in the belief that his official department heads should function primarily as managers, not counselors—especially once the "parlor Cabinet" broke into rival factions loyal to either Vice President John C. Calhoun or Secretary of State Martin Van Buren, both of whom aspired one day to succeed Jackson (in Calhoun's case sooner rather than later). Reluctant to schedule cabinet meetings once internecine distractions erupted, Jackson turned increasingly to his shadow council, inviting a number of old friends as well as the "big three" journalists: Kendall, Hill, and Green. Jackson appreciated the company of talented professionals who could massage his solecisms into phrases suitable for official documents and newspaper tracts.

Among them, it was Amos Kendall who emerged as his most influential advisor—"the moving spring of the Administration," according to one White House visitor, "the thinker, planner, and doer."[39] Kendall performed the actual work of organizing pro-Jackson newspapers into a nationwide network that spread administration news items and reprinted one another's editorials—the first press syndicate in American history. The chain came to include, along with Kendall's old paper in Kentucky, Thomas Ritchie's *Richmond Enquirer*, Nathaniel Greene's *Boston Statesman*, James Watson Webb's *New York Morning Courier*, and Edwin Croswell's newly launched *Albany Argus*.

Growing into an alter ego, Kendall also composed most of Jackson's state papers, including annual messages to Congress, the 1832 Nullification Proclamation, and the president's historic veto of the bill rechartering the Second Bank of the United States.[40] One dazzled contemporary described Kendall as Jackson's "chief scribe and amanuensis," explaining of the president: "He could think, but could not write; he knew what nerve to touch but he was no surgeon skilled in the instrument of dissection. Kendall was."[41] To a more cynical observer, Kendall became "the President's *thinking* machine, and his *writing* machine—ay, and his *lying* machine."[42]

John Quincy Adams would derisively refer to both Jackson and Van Buren as "the tool[s] of Amos Kendall, the ruling mind of their dominion."[43] In truth, each of the three original editor-advisors performed distinct and useful service to a president secure enough to know he benefited from their aid. Kendall supplied organizational acumen and intellectual heft, Hill devised catchphrases, and Green provided access to his large readership.

Green functioned as chief administration mouthpiece, faithfully echoing Jackson on tariff policy, hatred for the national bank, opposition to the proposed federally funded infrastructure project known as the Maysville Road, and even support for the dubious philanthropic benefits of Indian removal. Before the end of Jackson's first term, the editor was serving as the official printer to both Congress and the executive departments, designations "worth $50,000 per annum," according to Green's own boasts.[44]

But problems in their relationship arose by 1830. To Jackson's mind, Green began going soft on the bank. What was worse, Green's daughter had married Calhoun's son, and the editor and vice president now shared a grandchild, tightening their intimate connection. Green openly described himself as Calhoun's "ardent admirer and warm personal friend,"[45] but in a blunter vein the president worried that Calhoun "controles him as much as the showman does his puppits [*sic*]." Convinced "we must get another organ to announce the policy, & defend the administration," the old general returned to battle mode and plotted a surprise attack.[46]

In a brilliant flanking move, Jackson encouraged Francis Preston Blair, a thirty-nine-year-old Kentucky-based journalist long associated with Kendall's *Argus of Western America*, to hasten to the capital to establish an entirely new journal, the *Washington Globe*. Kendall sweetened the president's offer by promising Blair he would earn $4,000 a year just from government printing orders.[47] As Blair readied for his journey, Jackson misleadingly assured Green that the new paper was meant not to compete with the *Telegraph* but to complement it. Blair meanwhile raced east so quickly that, on his final sprint, his carriage overturned. The skeletally thin, hatchet-faced, shabbily dressed editor reported to the White House with a bandage conspicuously adorning his wounded head. Impressed by Blair's lack of ostentation, Jackson took an immediate liking to him.

By December 7, 1830—just days after his arrival—Blair began publishing his new paper. Lacking both funds and a press of his own, he resorted to parceling out work to job printers, whom he occasionally proved unable to pay. At first the *Globe* appeared only once a week. But Jackson supporters soon generated enough new subscriptions for the editor to purchase a high-speed Napier press and convert his journal into a daily. In short order, the *Globe* established itself as the administration's official voice, and more. As the historian James Schouler accurately put it in 1885, "Never, until the Globe was established, did a President's organ become an institution of government; for Jackson was the first of Presidents who ruled the country by means of the newspaper press."[48] After a while, Jackson, long a voracious newspaper consumer, was reading nothing "except the *Daily Globe* and his private correspondence."[49]

Together with his new business partner William C. Rives, the president's unofficial spokesman of record also founded the *Congressional Globe*, forerunner of the *Congressional Record*, and began profitably publishing House and Senate proceedings.[50] Blair joined the Kitchen Cabinet as well, and soon the *Globe* began raking in lucrative government printing contracts once reserved for the *Telegraph*. "Rough Green," as his critics called the dethroned editor, found himself outside the White House looking in. Jackson, reveling in the swift decapitation, snarled of Green and Calhoun: "They are as completely prostrate as any two Gentlemen ever were. They have cut their own throats & destroyed themselves in a shorter space of time than any two men I ever knew."[51]

While a vengeful Green joined the opposition, Blair became one of Jackson's most trusted confidants. Emaciated but energetic, he seemed the ideal counterpoint to the craggy, white-haired president, now sixty-three years old and slowed by a host of debilitating infirmities. Jackson could often be seen reclining on his office sofa, smoking his long-stemmed clay pipe while he and Blair exchanged a volley of ideas. On other occasions, in the editor's absence, the president might be heard drawling when a problem arose, "Take it to Bla'r," "Give it to Bla'r," or "Go to Frank Bla'r—he knows everything."[52] Jackson gave the editor free access to his correspondence and made him his literary executor.

Not surprisingly, it was Blair who earned the opportunity to announce

Jackson's availability for reelection in January 1831—a full eighteen months in advance of the next canvass. "We are permitted to say," the *Globe* trumpeted in its exclusive, "that if it should be the will of the Nation to call on the President to serve a second term as the Chief Magistrate, he will not decline the summons."[53] The early notice quashed speculation that the chief executive might retire. Duly impressed, anti-Jackson editor William Seaton conceded that Blair had become "intimate at the palace."[54]

Later that same year, the "palace" reeled in the wake of a breathlessly reported crisis that became known as the Petticoat Affair. The scandal centered on an innkeeper's daughter named Margaret "Peggy" O'Neale Timberlake Eaton. Finding herself shunned by Washington society following the death of her husband overseas, she rather quickly married John Eaton, a Tennessean recently named by Jackson as secretary of war. Rumors flew that Eaton had arranged for Timberlake's foreign posting just so he and Peggy could conduct a sexual affair out of his gaze. Timberlake, the gossips whispered, had taken his own life after he discovered his wife's infidelity.

The situation proved too unsavory for Floride Calhoun, spouse of the vice president (and mother of ten), who convinced cabinet wives (and their husbands) to ostracize both of the Eatons from the capital's social life. Rachel Jackson's own niece Emily Donelson, then serving as official White House hostess, reportedly joined the boycott, disappointing the president, who sympathized with women subjected, as his late wife had been, to cruel whispers. Only Secretary of State Martin Van Buren, like Jackson a widower, maintained contact with the Eatons, a development that increased Van Buren's standing in the White House even as Calhoun's further eroded.[55]

The Peggy Eaton imbroglio provided the anti-Jackson press irresistible fodder for scurrility, but ultimately offered a political silver lining. It gave Jackson a convenient opportunity to dissolve his entire cabinet, ridding the administration entirely of Calhoun allies. Even niece Emily Donelson, purged as well, departed Washington for Tennessee. In the void, Jackson turned increasingly to the Kitchen Cabinet, which strengthened its influence and visibility.

For the rest of his presidency, Jackson continued to call on his close newspaper confidants for ideas and support, proffered them exclusive stories, and made sure government jobs and printing contracts sustained their loyalty. Ever a master manipulator, Jackson kept a remarkably tight grip on national news even as the industry more than doubled in size, growing from 359 papers in

1810 to a seemingly ungovernable 1,000 by 1830, with readership tripling from 22 million to 68 million.[56]

The proliferation of newspapers provided fertile ground from which to conduct Jackson's campaign for reelection. In another race marked by personal vitriol, the president's supporters tried emphasizing policy issues: his resistance to states' rights run amok and his distrust of the powerful Bank of the United States and its elitist president, Nicholas Biddle.

In an attempt to gain political advantage, Jackson's enemies had sought to recharter the bank four years earlier than required, and Congress had so legislated. Jackson, who thought the bank too powerful and its paper-money policy too risky, called the bluff and issued the veto message composed by Amos Kendall. In response, acting against the advice of many allies, Biddle sent thousands of dollars in bank funds to help finance Jackson's 1832 White House opponent, Henry Clay. The Jackson press network blasted Biddle for "buying men and votes as cattle in the market" while Congress considered a bill to outlaw "all business connexion [*sic*]" between newspapers and banks.[57] A Clay paper reminded readers, "Has no *patronage* been given to the Press, as a *douceur*, or a reward" by Jackson?[58] Yet Blair and his fellow Jacksonians kept the salvos coming until another pro-Clay paper howled, "The disgusting stuff put forth in the Globe about the U.S. Bank, must nauseate even the rankest Jackson man."[59]

With the Jackson campaign in full swing, the last remaining barriers separating the press from presidential politics crumbled, with Amos Kendall in the role of Joshua. Assuming the role of campaign chairman, Kendall pressured pro-Jackson newspapers nationwide to keep "rousing the patriotic enthusiasm of the people."[60]

When Blair began publishing a campaign edition called the *Extra Globe*, Kendall commanded him "to throw the paper into every neighborhood in the United States." As far away as Maine, a pro-Jackson editor soon reported "Extra Globes . . . sent in bundles" were pouring into "every town where a Jackson man can be found to distribute them."[61] Bitter exchanges only intensified. When a Clay paper chided Blair for working "to begrime whatever is supposed to get in the way of the President's wishes, or the designs of the back-stairs cabinet,"[62] Blair merely gloated: "The Globe is considered by the aristocracy as more mischievous to them, than the coffin hand-bills were to the President."

The well-oiled collaboration between party operatives and newspaper editors worked to Jackson's advantage. With Van Buren in place of Calhoun as his running mate, Jackson handily defeated Clay in 1832, this time earning a 150,000-vote popular majority and winning 219 of the 286 electoral votes. And he earned his victory without the once-crucial support of Duff Green, who had turned against him with a vengeance. Jackson, Green sputtered to little avail, "had violated almost every principle upon which his platform was advocated."[63] The voters judged otherwise. And Jackson would get to enjoy the "retribution" he had promised himself four years earlier.

On Christmas Eve, an oversize pro-Jackson congressman from South Carolina, James Blair (no relation to editor Francis), stole up behind Green as the editor walked along Pennsylvania Avenue and struck him from behind with his cane. A second blow broke the prostrate Green's arm as he lay sprawled in the street. Then the 350-pound congressman launched himself onto the helpless editor, shattering Green's collarbone.[64] John Quincy Adams, back in Washington now as a congressman from Massachusetts, could barely suppress his glee that the "prince of slanderers" who had once labored to "overthrow" him had been taken down by a member of "the race of giants."[65] Undoubtedly Jackson joined in the laughter.

The battle between the president and the bank remained deadly serious. In a move eerily premonitory of the twenty-first-century standoffs between Donald Trump and the Federal Reserve, Biddle responded to Jackson's veto by hiking interest rates. His move unnerved financial markets and sent the economy spiraling toward a recession. The feud continued for the next several years until the bank's charter lapsed in 1836.

Andrew Jackson's second term began as contentiously as his first had ended. Soon after Election Day, South Carolina voted to declare null and void a recently passed compromise tariff, claiming the constitutional right of a state to defy federal law. Ironically, Jackson's new, lower tariffs had supplanted the Adams-era "Tariff of Abominations," which South Carolinians, led by now-senator John C. Calhoun, believed unfairly disadvantaged Southern states. Mocking the nullification argument as "a metaphysical subtlety, in pursuit of an impractical theory," Jackson prepared to dispatch troops to Charleston to prevent what he regarded as an existential threat to national authority.[66] On Inauguration Day, Jackson signed the Force Bill authorizing military intervention. That morning, an infuriated Green draped his front page with black borders and grimly declared that "the constitution is dead."[67] In the end, the crisis cooled without secession or bloodshed. Jackson's tough stance may have preserved the Union, if only for a time.

The constant atmosphere of roiling crisis, however, may have nearly cost Jackson his life. In January 1835, leaving the U.S. Capitol following a funeral service, Jackson came under attack by a pistol-toting would-be assassin. The president escaped death only because the derringers aimed at his chest twice misfired. Though the assailant was clearly deranged, Jackson blamed the bank and its press supporters for inciting violence. When his daily mailbag began swelling with new murder threats, the president instructed Blair to print them all in the *Globe*, relishing his new role as the target of aristocracy.[68]

Later that year, Jackson made Amos Kendall postmaster general. The link between journalism and the White House was now complete. Although he would work diligently to reform the department, Kendall devoted a portion of his energy to effecting speedier mail delivery of western newspapers (likely to support Jackson) and impeding the prompt arrival of eastern ones that tended to back the president's opponents. Kendall responded to the rise of Abolitionist papers by banning their delivery altogether from the solidly Democratic South.

After eight stormy years in the White House, Andrew Jackson headed home to Tennessee on a wave of adulation. At each stop along the long journey west, adoring crowds surrounded and cheered him toward retirement. To the *Cincinnati Republican*, one of many sympathetic journals that reported lavishly on his return voyage, it seemed clear that his admirers had massed "for the last time, perhaps, to look upon, and take by the hand, the brave defender and protector of his country."[69]

William Cullen Bryant of the *New York Evening Post*—the paper founded by Alexander Hamilton—spoke for many editors in acknowledging Jackson's "faults" while hailing him as "precisely the man for the period in which he well and nobly served."[70] Only later would Bryant and the *Post* abandon Jacksonian democracy for antislavery Republicanism.

The seventh president has undergone significant reassessment since. Often remembered now as an unapologetic slaveholder and merciless enemy of Native peoples, Old Hickory recently slid further into reputational decline when the even more controversial Donald Trump made a pilgrimage to the Hermitage and professed admiration for Jackson's unpredictable, authoritarian style. Jackson's once high ranking in historians' surveys has been slipping, too: from sixth-best president in a 1948 survey by Harvard historian Arthur M. Schlesinger Sr. to eighteenth in a 2017 C-SPAN poll. In his own day, few leaders were loved as ardently, despised as strongly, or covered in the press as relentlessly as Old Hickory. For certain, none before him had more astutely understood, or more adroitly corralled, the immense and growing power of the press.

Jackson's presidency overlapped with the explosive growth of newspapers, including the rise of the so-called penny press—cheaper, more vividly written papers sold not only through the mail by subscription but also by newsboys hawking them on city streets. The Jackson machine seized on this revolution to widen Jackson's appeal further, but it erred badly in refusing to reward one particular journalist: Scottish-born James Gordon Bennett. After laboring faithfully on Jackson's behalf, Bennett craved either a foreign posting or funds to launch a pro-administration paper. But the president's inner circle judged him too hard to control. Bennett responded by founding the independent *New York Herald*.[71] Within a few years it became the most widely read daily in the United States—and the first major newspaper in years unaligned with a party or a president. Only later would it begin tipping decidedly to the Democrats.

Even after Andrew Jackson returned to the Hermitage for what would turn out to be an eight-year-long retirement—he died in 1845—his extraordinary quartet of journalistic consorts continued peddling influence and ideas in Washington for decades to come.

Isaac Hill left Jackson's inner circle in 1831, when his home state elected him to the U.S. Senate. After serving five years, Hill headed back to New Hampshire as governor. Later he returned to journalism, founding *Hill's New Hampshire Patriot*, which he handed over to his sons to manage. Hill died a wealthy man in 1851, two weeks shy of his sixty-second birthday.

Amos Kendall stayed on as postmaster general under Jackson's handpicked successor, Martin Van Buren, then resigned for health reasons in 1840. That fall he somehow summoned the energy to contribute pro-Democratic editorials to the *Washington Extra Globe* in a failed effort to elect Van Buren to a second term. Jackson chose his onetime confidant as his official biographer, but Kendall hardly made a dent in the proposed multivolume project before abandoning it. Two attempts to launch new papers in Washington failed as well. To avoid financial ruin, Kendall resumed the practice of law and leased out his home and grounds north of Washington. An unlikely comeback began when one of his legal clients, Samuel F. B. Morse, chose Kendall as his business manager. The old editor made a new fortune by investing in Morse's invention: the telegraph. A generous philanthropist in his final years, Kendall converted his mansion and grounds into a school for the deaf that ultimately became Gallaudet College. He died in 1869 at age eighty.

Francis Preston Blair founded a Washington dynasty. One of his sons, Frank Jr., became a Missouri congressman and Union general; while another, Montgomery, served as Lincoln's postmaster general. Increasingly opposed to slavery expansion though he owned slaves himself, the elder Blair abandoned Jacksonian Democracy in 1848 to support the Free Soil movement, then in the 1850s helped found the new Republican Party.

In the early days of his own presidency, Lincoln designated the now-sepulchral Blair to offer command of the federal army to Robert E. Lee, who refused and pledged allegiance to the Confederacy—one of the few men able to resist Blair's powers of persuasion. Blair continued to advise Lincoln informally from his home opposite the White House, and in early 1865 persuaded the president to make an attempt to end the Civil War through negotiations. At age seventy-four, Blair undertook a journey to Richmond, where he convinced Confederate vice president Alexander H. Stephens to head toward Washington to talk armistice. Blair's bold initiative ended with the failed Hampton Roads Peace Conference, but the old man's ability to arrange the summit testified to his enduring prestige.[72] As a biographer accurately put it, the only family in nineteenth-century Washington that rivaled the Blairs for longevity of influence were the Adamses.[73] Francis Preston Blair Sr. died in Maryland in 1876 at age eighty-five.

The most colorful of the foursome, Duff Green, lived a long life, too. His influence may have declined after Jackson discarded him, but his ambitions and eccentricities remained undimmed. Over the years Green established three more newspapers—in Washington, Baltimore, and New York—though none succeeded. He also performed occasional if ill-defined service for Presidents John Tyler and Zachary Taylor. In December 1860, Green visited Springfield, Illinois, to urge President-elect Lincoln (his brother-in-law's brother-in-law) to conciliate the South by guaranteeing the preservation of slavery. By then the onetime editor sported a long white beard and toted a trademark wooden staff nearly as tall as he was. Unsatisfied with Lincoln's response, Green chided him: "I regret your unwillingness to recommend an amendment to the constitution which will arrest the progress of secession."[74] Green thereupon pledged his loyalty to the Confederacy and spent the war years manufacturing iron to supply the Rebel army.[75]

Audaciously, Green sought out Lincoln one last time, just six days before the war's end, limping aboard the president's steamer, the USS *Malvern*, as it lay anchored off City Point, Virginia. Green was in a foul temper, but the president, fresh from an exhilarating tour of conquered Richmond, where he had been greeted as a Moses by the city's liberated African Americans, was in no mood for an argument. When Green refused Lincoln's hand and berated him for "the notorious crime of setting the niggers free," the enraged president by one account branded Green a "political tramp," a "miserable imposter," and a "vile intruder," and ordered him off the vessel. Another eyewitness remembered only that Lincoln endured Green's outburst in silence, then sent him on his way once the old firebrand had "exhausted himself."[76] Lincoln's successor, Andrew Johnson, who assumed the presidency less than two weeks later, pardoned Green for betraying the Union but exacted a $20,000 fine. Green died at age eighty-three in 1875—outliving Old Hickory by thirty years and Old Abe by ten.

Together with Blair, who endured another sixteen months, the two renowned editors were the last surviving newspapermen who had served Andrew Jackson both in the press and behind the scenes, not just covering but helping to operate the government, permanently blurring the lines between presidents and journalists.

5

ABRAHAM LINCOLN

During a social gathering at the Civil War White House one day, Abraham Lincoln overheard the artist-in-residence Francis B. Carpenter cautioning Mary Jane Welles, wife of the secretary of the navy, that newspapers of the day could often be unreliable. Ever ready to unleash a pun, Lincoln begged to differ. Newspapers were indeed "reliable," he insisted. "That is to say, Mrs. Welles, they '*lie*,' and then they '*re-lie!*'"[1]

Carpenter, who spent six months in the White House executing a large painting celebrating the Emancipation Proclamation, was also on hand to witness another of the sixteenth president's amusing—but no doubt sincerely felt—comments on the Civil War–era press. A delegation had filed into Lincoln's office to promote a newfangled "repeating gun" designed to "prevent the escape of gas." After dutifully examining the weapon, the commander in chief remarked: "Well, I believe this really does what it is represented to do. Now have any of you heard of any machine, or invention, for preventing the escape of 'gas' from newspaper establishments?"[2]

Both these incidents took place in 1864, by which time Lincoln had already endured decades of scorn from opposition journalists, and he was anticipating more, and worse, in that year's upcoming presidential campaign. In some regards, newspapers had treated him no differently than they had his predecessors. But "in a larger sense," as Lincoln might have put it, press hostility toward him in the 1860s ranked as unique because it emanated from not one but three sources: first, from traditional partisan foes in the North (in his case, Democratic editors); second, from European opinion makers who detested Lincoln for blockading their ships from Confederate ports; and third, from press critics united rancorously against him in the rebellious South. Often the criticism proved brutally personal. And much of it was now transported rapidly on the wires of the telegraph invented in 1844.

A Richmond paper set the tone from the start, greeting Lincoln's 1861 arrival in Washington by dubbing him "the Illinois ape."[3] In the same vein, James Gordon Bennett's pro-Democratic *New York Herald* charged him with a "lamentable degree of ignorance."[4] Not even Lincoln's greatest oratory could change such early impressions. The London *Times* correspondent covering the Gettysburg cemetery dedication in November 1863 would charge that the "imposing ceremony" had been rendered "ludicrous by some of the luckless sallies of that poor President Lincoln, who seems determined to play . . . the part of the famous Governor of the Isle of Barataria"—meaning Cervantes's oft-ridiculed Sancho Panza.[5]

To Lincoln, press relations were never really a laughing matter. His often humorous asides helped mask the fact that when it came to dealing with newspapers, he had become by 1864 the harshest, indeed the most repressive, presidential censor yet. Even John Adams's Sedition Act prosecutions could not match, for ferocity and scope, the undeclared, unlegislated, unlitigated, and largely unchallenged war the Lincoln administration began waging against hostile domestic newspapers within months of his inauguration.[6] Starting later that year, his army and administration arrested and imprisoned scores of editors, banned disobliging news from the telegraph wires, stymied war correspondents embedded on the battlefront, seized and confiscated printing presses, tossed newspapers from trains before they could reach subscribers, and barred them from post offices so they could not be mailed. With the writ of habeas corpus under suspension, editors had no real path for recourse. Altogether, nearly two hundred papers would face federally initiated subjugation during the Civil War. While avoiding direct involvement in the unprecedented and arguably unconstitutional crackdown when he could, Lincoln firmly believed the repression necessary to preserve the very freedoms to which he laid siege.

Long before he entered the White House, Lincoln had, like most rising politicians of his day, genuinely "relied" on friendly editors to both promote him and rebut attacks from opposition papers. For years he had courted Whig, later

Republican, editors and seen to the publication of his important speeches in their papers to expand the reach of his oratory.

Before he even entered elective politics, Lincoln began writing pseudonymous anti-Democratic editorials for the hometown, pro-Whig *Sangamo Journal*. Eventually he began treating its Springfield, Illinois, office as his political headquarters; it was in his favorite armchair there that he received the news that he had been nominated for the presidency in 1860.[7] And it was another newspaper ally, Charles H. Ray of the *Chicago Tribune*, who first urged Lincoln to emphasize not his antislavery views but his inspiring log cabin roots—including his "adventures in rail-splitting"—in quest of higher office. "[Y]ou occupy a position, present and prospectively," argued the astute Ray, "that need not shrink from the declaration of an origin ever so humble. . . . The best part of the Lincoln family is not, like potatoes, under the ground."[8] The head of the census bureau noted in 1860 that of four thousand papers circulating in the United States that year, more than three thousand "were political in their character," the *Chicago Tribune* included.[9]

Politics, ethnic politics included, never strayed far from the candidate's mind. In the run-up to the 1860 presidential election, Lincoln actually purchased a newspaper of his own, a weekly he could not read himself because it was printed in German, a language he had tried to learn without success. Before investing, he stipulated only that it feature exclusively pro-Republican editorials, which it faithfully produced for its German-speaking readers. Not a single copy survives, probably because, before departing for Washington, the grateful president-elect repaid its editor's loyalty by convincing the Illinois legislature to buy up all the leftover editions.

Except for the fact it was printed in a tongue he did not comprehend, Lincoln's investment actually fit well into the prevailing culture in which journalism and politics worked in tandem. Other newspapermen had become politicians, including several men destined to join Lincoln's own cabinet.[10] But Lincoln became the first newspaper publisher—albeit a part-time one—to become president of the United States.

Perhaps that explains his later belief that he could control the press, if not by persuasion, investment, and patronage then by intimidation when necessary. This was especially so during a Civil War "testing" whether the nation "conceived and dedicated" to liberty could "long endure" even if its preservation required temporary forfeiture of liberty of the press. Whether or not

Lincoln overreacted and overreached in authorizing wartime press crackdowns has been a matter of historical and constitutional debate for 150 years—with no resolution in sight.

By the time he commenced his pre-inaugural journey to Washington in February 1861, Lincoln could count on the Republican press to report favorably on his speeches and activities.

Before he left Springfield, he had dabbled one more time in anonymous journalism, drafting an editorial for his hometown Republican paper, the *Illinois State Journal*, saluting himself for resisting the temptation to placate secessionists by naming a Southerner to his cabinet ("Does he surrender to Mr. Lincoln, or Mr. Lincoln to him, on the political difference between them?").[11] At the same time, in a remarkable demonstration of audacity, he declined all requests to send the slave states updates on his policies by directing anxious correspondents to those of his speeches that had previously been published in the newspapers ("I could say nothing which is not already . . . in print, and open for the inspection of all").[12]

Opposition Democratic editors, on the other hand, granted Lincoln no honeymoon as he made his way east to the capital.[13] Not even his magnificent first inaugural address—universally admired now for summoning the "better angels of our nature"—escaped regional and partisan scorn at the time.[14] To the *Charleston Mercury*, the speech was the product of "perversity of thought"; to the *Chicago Times*, it was "a loose, disjointed, rambling affair."[15]

Lincoln began his presidency braced for further criticism from Democratic sheets and ready to respond in kind. To arm itself, the White House subscribed to several daily papers and began receiving many others it never ordered. Before long, the office abounded with essential and unsolicited newspapers alike. Clerk William O. Stoddard tried providing a daily press digest for the overburdened president, but Lincoln so seldom found the time to review it that Stoddard abandoned the practice.[16] The president soon confessed he had "no time to read any papers."[17] Two of Lincoln's staff aides had once served as newspaper editors and at least brought a keen publicity sense of their own to the operation. A third, the gifted John Hay, ghostwrote newspaper articles praising administration policy, the precursors of modern-day press releases. In a sense, Hay functioned as presidential press secretary before the title—and the job—became part of White House culture.

Nonetheless, the onset of armed rebellion against the legally elected government triggered an occasionally uncivil war against journalists themselves, at least those who sympathized with Southern independence or opposed Northern military recruitment. The leader who later gained fame as the "Great Emancipator" began his presidency as the "Great Censor."

At first, Lincoln's government clamped down on newspaper criticism in an uncoordinated, ad hoc manner. However scattershot, the repression did chill dissent, especially when mobs and local grand juries began doing the work even the executive branch at first proved unwilling to do. Lincoln tried remaining above the fray, arguing only that the rebellion authorized him to exercise a "war power" to limit free speech and freedom of the press if necessary to preserve the Union. He never made an effort to codify this interpretation. Instead he handled the press, he told Congress, as if confronting a "fatal weakness" in the American system: "Must a government, of necessity be too *strong* for the liberties of its own people, or too *weak* to maintain its own existence?" What Lincoln called "extreme tenderness" might temporarily preserve press freedom, but in the process "put an end to free government upon the earth."[18]

In border states still teetering between loyalty and secession, including Maryland, Missouri, and Kentucky, Lincoln's armies moved aggressively against anti-Union newspapers, confiscating printing presses and imprisoning editors without trial in an effort to choke off Confederate sentiment and maintain loyalty to the Union. One victim of the border-state crackdown, Francis Key Howard of the pro-secession *Baltimore Exchange*, ironically ended up confined at Fort McHenry, the same citadel where the 1814 British attack on the star-spangled banner had inspired his grandfather, Francis Scott Key, to write the national anthem.[19] Nostalgia provided no defense.

The first major crackdown in the North occurred in late summer 1861, as the initial ninety-day enlistment period for Union volunteers neared an end. The Union's humiliating defeat that July at Bull Run—in the war's first battle—raised fears in the federal high command that dispirited soldiers would refuse to reenlist. A number of Democratic journals editorialized against recruitment. Such papers were the first to feel the brunt of Union suppression after federal authorities equated their advice with treason. The Post Office Department, the State Department, and other agencies all worked in their own ways to make sure these papers could not reach their readers. The government closed down the most outspoken antiwar journals entirely and held some editors in custody without trial. In New York and New Jersey, federal grand juries recommended indictments against several.[20] When the pro-Democratic New York *Daily News* bristled at "the dictatorship of 'Honest Old Abe' and his Bloody Administration,"[21] detectives dragged its managing editor to Washington for questioning.

These widely reported incidents did not entirely curtail newspaper dissent, but the federal takeover of the North's telegraph lines tightened the vise. Thereafter, censors regulated, and in countless cases entirely banned unfavorable news emanating from Washington. For a time, Frederick Seward, Secretary of State William H. Seward's son and chief aide, acted as principal regulator. The younger Seward cast an absurdly wide net, prohibiting "all telegraphic dispatches from Washington, intended for publication, which relate to the civil or military operations of the government."[22] Government telegraph superintendent H. Emmons Thayer later freely admitted to censoring reports he thought might "embarrass the Gov't."[23]

The press faced even thornier challenges once the iron-fisted Edwin M. Stanton took over as Lincoln's secretary of war on January 20, 1862. Stanton promptly moved all telegraph operations into a room adjoining his own office, where communications would be easy to oversee. Lincoln himself began frequenting the place to get battlefront news "morning, afternoon, and evening . . . with unvaried regularity."[24] If that situation was not enough to inhibit the free flow of information—and criticism—Stanton issued official orders giving the administration total control over "all the telegraph lines in the United States." He then installed Edward S. Sanford, president of the Atlantic Telegraph Company, as "military supervisor of telegraphic lines"—in other words, the nation's chief censor.[25]

At one point, the crackdowns did provoke a congressional investigation, which has received surprisingly little attention from historians. In the early weeks of 1862, Washington's leading newspaper correspondents made their way up to Capitol Hill, one after another, to offer the House Judiciary Committee anguished evidence of press suppression at the administration's hands. One witness, D. W. Bartlett of the pro-Republican *New York Evening Post*, complained of being "interfered with" as early as Bull Run, when the Union high command ordered that stark reports of the federal rout be kept off the wires. "I made up my mind in a short time," Bartlett joked, ". . . that the best plan was to be on good terms with the censor."[26] Suppression applied to more than military news. Another witness, Samuel Wilkeson of the *New York Tribune*, testified that censors had refused to transmit his scoop detailing cabinet dissension over how to handle the administration's first diplomatic crisis in December 1861.[27] These accounts must have startled congressmen, as they came from writers whose papers supported the administration and the war.

Then there was the case of Henry J. Raymond, the equally pro-Republican *New York Times* editor who had campaigned for Lincoln in 1860 and still hoped the president would grant him influence over federal appointments in his home city. Raymond did not testify before Congress personally, but the *Post*'s Bartlett, who had written the first major Lincoln campaign biography two years earlier, told the committee that even the powerful *Times* had once run afoul of censorship. Raymond had covered Bull Run himself, a rarity for a newspaperman of his prominence. But when he tried to wire his report on the disaster back to New York, the Washington-based telegraph operator suppressed it, replacing it with "a false account of the fight, by the Government." Recalled Bartlett, "I know that Mr. Raymond made a long and loud complaint about it," convinced the substitution had been made "for the purpose of cheating the public."[28]

Yet Raymond responded to the damning testimony with an editorial endorsing the "propriety" of silencing administration critics. Such was his fealty to the Republican administration—from whom he was seeking jobs for his friends—that he insisted the government remained innocent of gross "interference with the freedom of the Press."[29] Raymond clung to that rosy view even after Union general George B. McClellan, a Democrat in politics, accused the *Times* of publishing a battle map that revealed top-secret information to the enemy. An indignant Raymond protested that he had merely copied a chart on open sale at Willard's Hotel, with "no treasonable intent."[30] He went unprosecuted.

As Raymond's otherwise complacent reaction to censorship indicates, one of the most remarkable aspects of the Lincoln administration's early press crackdowns is how earnestly pro-Republican editors fell into line in its defense. The *New York Times* was not alone in condoning the suppression of antiwar journals. Delighted that the "list of killed or wounded among the Democratic newspapers is constantly swelling," an equally ardent administration voice, the *Philadelphia Evening Bulletin*, charged that unpatriotic editors did more to hasten "destruction of the Union than a dozen Bull Run defeats."[31] Raymond, insisting he was not advocating that freedom of the press be totally abandoned, nonetheless expressed willingness "to waive those rights for a time, in order to save the Constitution and the Government."[32]

As the *Times* editor reminded his readers, "The United States is now AT WAR WITH Secessionism," and "whatever stands in the pathway of our triumph must be overthrown," including the "vague notion afloat that freedom of speech carries with it some special and peculiar sanctity."[33] Besides, Raymond confidently predicted, "When the exigency which compels their suppression has passed away, the people will demand their restoration."[34] This view Lincoln himself soon adopted to defend the repression he thereafter insisted was temporary.

As events transpired, the 1862 congressional investigation foundered on the shoals of a sensational side story. Back in December, the president's annual message to Congress had been leaked and published in advance by the most widely read daily in the land, the *New York Herald*, an unheard-of breach of protocol at the time. As the Capitol Hill hearings progressed, House inquisitors grew increasingly sidetracked by this episode.

The story grew especially hot when one witness implicated the president's wife as a possible source for the leak, in return, it was whispered, for a cash payout from the *Herald*'s flamboyant and widely despised publisher, James Gordon Bennett. An alleged coconspirator did face intense questioning, and later imprisonment, for refusing to cooperate with the committee, and Mary Lincoln herself narrowly escaped public censure. Yet the near-catastrophe may have proved worth the risk. One result of the affair was that the *Herald* tamped down its anti-Lincoln criticism so noticeably that Mary was soon privately thanking Bennett for "the kind support and consideration, extended towards the Administration."[35]

The emphasis on White House leaks sucked the wind out of the censorship inquiry. By the time the Judiciary Committee reported a tepid regulatory bill to the full House of Representatives, the war had intensified and the Lincoln administration had solidified its grip over the press. One legislative proposal meant at least to monitor executive censorship went nowhere.[36] Neither did an effort at self-regulation initiated by New York editors, who predictably let long-standing rivalries get in the way of consensus. The group of fifteen editors claimed the constitutional right to criticize the administration and military "freely and fearlessly," but acknowledged that journalists had no more right "to incite, advocate, abet, or uphold or justify treason" than any other citizen. The editor of the anti-Lincoln *New York Argus* sent the defanged manifesto to the president, who ignored it.[37]

With military tribunals now routinely claiming legal jurisdiction in place of civil courts, press crackdowns thereafter went largely unchecked by the other branches of government. Only the boldest Democratic press and political foes voiced objections, often feeling the military heel in response. Where the army failed to silence such critics, violent mobs sometimes performed the work of suppression. (In one particularly ugly incident, rioters in Haverhill, Massachusetts, tarred and feathered Democratic editor Ambrose Kimball; the journalist pledged to write no more critical editorials and then fled to Iowa.)[38] Lincoln meanwhile continued to sidestep direct involvement. When a group of prominent Washington journalists descended on the White House to protest the "annoying . . . surveillance of the press," Lincoln "listened in his dreamy way" and then replied with a funny story.[39] To one plea for mercy for a jailed editor, Lincoln replied, "it would be improper for me to intervene."[40]

What prevented the Civil War press crackdown from spiraling into a reign of terror—though some Lincoln critics maintained that such indeed became the case[41]—was the president's repeatedly demonstrated willingness to tolerate newspaper criticism during election cycles.[42] In the 1862 campaign, he did nothing to quash Democratic attacks on Republicans, and partly as a result of them, his party endured significant off-year losses in state capitals and in the House of Representatives.

Seeking a second term two years later, Lincoln himself absorbed, without retaliation, furious denunciation from Democratic newspapers. The *New York World*, for one, circulated—and even illustrated—the canard that if reelected, the president planned a policy of "miscegenation" to amalgamate the white and black races—in other words, forced race-mixing, a dog whistle to skittish voters.[43] Lincoln merely shrugged off the charge. Only when the *World* added the calumny that the "indecent" president had once called for comic songs on a battlefield strewn with dead and wounded soldiers did Lincoln draft a reply (for someone else to send) denying the charge.[44] But after letting off steam, he left the letter to the editor unsent. "I dislike to appear as an apologist," he remarked, a reaction consistent with his long silence on the issue of press suppression.[45] As sincerely as he believed that only traitors discouraged soldiers from enlisting, or worse, encouraged them to desert, he regarded robust, even rowdy campaign journalism as the holy grail of what he had once called America's "*political religion*."[46] And in its protection he remained almost evangelical.

Lincoln's forbearance when it came to the *World*'s 1864 campaign assaults seems especially tolerant (and the *World*'s attacks themselves particularly bold), considering that only a few weeks earlier he had issued his one and only direct order closing down two newspapers—including the very same *New York World*. Back in May, the *World* had either innocently or maliciously published a spurious presidential proclamation lamenting recent military setbacks and calling for three hundred thousand new Union volunteers or conscripts.[47]

Coincidentally, Lincoln was at the time contemplating just such a recruitment drive, and the *World* story sparked renewed fears that a porous White House was again leaking confidential information. For once, Lincoln affixed his own name to a harsh shutdown order drafted by Stanton. "Whereas there has been wickedly and traitorously published this morning in the '*New York World*' . . . a false and spurious proclamation . . . of a treasonable nature, designed to give aid and comfort to . . . the rebels now at war against the Government," Union general John A. Dix was ordered "to arrest and imprison in any fort or military prison in your command, the editors, proprietors and publishers" and "take possession by military force, of the printing establishments."[48] Accordingly, Union troops escorted *World* editor Manton Marble from his office and readied to send him to Fort Lafayette in Brooklyn harbor, a fate he was spared only when the real impetus for the forgery came to light.

The bogus proclamation turned out to be the handiwork of a *Republican* newspaperman who plotted its publication to depress the financial markets long enough for him to buy low and then sell high once the fraud was uncovered and prices rebounded.[49] One Democratic paper wittily responded to the administration's overreaction by predicting that the dictatorial Lincoln would "be punished for his crimes "in the 'World' to come."[50] In no laughing mood even once liberated, Marble issued a furious public letter excoriating Lincoln for "arbitrary, illegal, and unconstitutional" acts worthy of "impeachment, trial, conviction, and judgment." The editor lectured the president, "For the purpose of gratifying ignoble partisan resentment you have struck down the rights of the press . . . attempting to crush the organs of free discussion."[51] As usual, Lincoln had nothing to say in reply. He had already released his one and only pronouncement on the subject.

Not until 1863 did Lincoln feel any real need to justify his censorship policies to the public. That June, politician Erastus Corning and his fellow Albany, New York, Democrats held a public meeting and condemned the administration for its widening suspension of civil liberties. The protest followed the military arrest and trial of Clement Laird Vallandigham, a former Democratic congressman from Ohio accused of inflaming his former constituents against the new military draft. When Lincoln's longtime press nemesis, the *Chicago Times*, defended Vallandigham, the Union army shut the paper down and arrested its editor.

The Albany rebuke gave Lincoln a perfect opportunity to explain himself. In a long letter to Corning, but released to the daily press and soon reissued as a pamphlet, Lincoln insisted that the crackdowns remained "indispensable to public safety." As he reminded his critics, "under cover of . . . 'Liberty of the Press' . . . a most efficient corps of spies, informers, supplyers [*sic*], and aiders and abettors of treason" had injured the nation "in a thousand ways." In the most famous line of his rebuttal he asked: "Must I shoot a simple-minded soldier boy who deserts, while I must not touch the hair of a wiley [*sic*] agitator who induces him to desert? . . . I think that in such a case, to silence the agitator, and save the boy, is not only constitutional, but, withal, a great mercy."

Echoing editor Henry Raymond's earlier assurances that suppression was but a temporary remedy, Lincoln reminded readers that following the Battle of New Orleans, General Andrew Jackson had not only suspended press freedom there but jailed a judge who had objected. Authorities had eventually lifted that ban without permanent "detriment" to "liberty of speech and the press."[52] Lincoln had spent half his political career castigating Democrat Jackson, but war made for strange bedfellows: now Old Hickory presented a useful example of almost gentle censorship, not to mention tough opposition to secession.[53] Lincoln did not believe that "the American people will, by means of military arrests during the rebellion, lose the right of public discussion, the liberty of speech and the press . . . throughout the indefinite peaceful future which I trust lies before them, any more than I am able to believe that a man could contract so strong an appetite for emetics during temporary illness, as to persist in feeding upon them through the remainder of his healthful life."[54]

In what became known as his "Corning Letter," Lincoln even insisted, "I think the time not unlikely to come, when I shall be blamed for having made too few arrests rather than too many." Aid and comfort to the rebel enemy would not be tolerated—not even, in Lincoln's colloquial reminder, when it came in the form of "'buts' and 'ifs' and 'ands.'"[55] Tellingly, Lincoln authorized the reopening of the *Chicago Times* and *New York World* only when Republican editors and politicians advised him he had gone too far. In the case of the Chicago paper, Lincoln never quite satisfied himself "that the revocation was not right."[56]

When his government was not focusing on censorship, Lincoln proved one of the ablest presidential press manipulators ever, fully as adept at generating press coverage as he was at preventing it. Although he held no news conferences and sat for no real interviews as we now understand them, Lincoln adroitly pulled wires on his own behalf behind the scenes, confiding news to press allies, providing them with copies of his letters for publication (they became known as "public letters"), and periodically misleading newspaper critics. To relate all his efforts to manage the Union message would require a separate book, but some of the highlights cannot be overlooked even in a brief chapter.

For example, when he first took office, Lincoln found himself the first chief executive since Jackson without the ability to designate one loyal newspaper as his "official Administration organ"—at least as that plum had long been defined, as a billboard for administration propaganda. Newly passed federal legislation had established the first U.S. Government Printing Office, so politically appointed newspapers would no longer be needed to transcribe and publish congressional debates at a profit, and, in return, carry flattering presidential news to the nation. (Lincoln did name an "official" administration journal, but the designation now carried none of the benefits that had accompanied it, say, during the Jackson presidency.)

To maintain influence, Lincoln instead saw to it that lucrative government advertising continued flowing to many Republican papers, and he named friendly journalists to well-paid federal posts. The editor of the *Chicago Tribune* became his city's postmaster general, and the *New York Tribune* sacrificed so many editorial hands to government service that one wag wondered whether the understaffed daily could continue to publish. Lincoln's onetime partner in his now-disbanded Illinois German weekly quietly headed to Vienna as the handsomely remunerated American consul. Lincoln outdid even Jackson in rewarding friendly journalists. The new printing law actually liberated Lincoln to dole out favors and scoops to any number of Republican papers over the next four years.

In an early behind-the-scenes power play, Lincoln soon thereafter outflanked newly named Secretary of State Seward along with Seward's longtime press champion Henry Raymond of the *Times* when the two tried to wrest power from the president in something of a coup. Raymond laid the groundwork by editorializing in April 1861 that the new government lacked both "a policy" and "a leader," charges Lincoln regarded as "villainous,"[57] particularly after he had called for one hundred thousand volunteers after the Confederate attack on Fort Sumter. But rather than retaliate in anger, the president composed an irrefutable memorandum asserting his constitutional authority to set the national agenda. Seward lost his nerve and, along with Raymond, pledged loyalty to Lincoln. Neither man ever again wavered in his support for the president.

Shortly thereafter, Lincoln granted one of his few on-the-record audiences to a journalist. Whether he somehow sensed that this particular writer would later gain worldwide acclaim we can only guess. But Nathaniel Hawthorne, a Democrat whose notion of an ideal president began and ended with his old friend and fellow New Englander Franklin Pierce, arrived at the White House with a delegation of visitors in 1862. After submitting his observations to the *Atlantic Monthly*, Hawthorne became incensed when editors balked at printing his frank description of the president. "Chiefly About War-Matters by a Peaceable Man" offered charming recollections to spare, but in an atmosphere of real or implied censorship, the *Atlantic Monthly* would not risk including some of Hawthorne's colorful comments. "By-and-by," he had written after a half hour's wait while the president finished his breakfast, "there was a little stir on the staircase and in the passage-way; and in lunged a tall, loose-jointed figure, of an exaggerated Yankee port and demeanor, whom, (as being about the homeliest man I ever saw, yet by no means repulsive or disagreeable,) it was impossible not to recognize as Uncle Abe. . . ."

"There is no describing his lengthy awkwardness, nor the uncouthness of his movement," Hawthorne continued, before proceeding to do so anyway. "He had shabby slippers on his feet, his hair was black, still unmixed with gray, stiff, somewhat bushy; and had apparently been acquainted with neither brush nor comb, that morning, after the arrangements of the pillow. . . . And yet," Hawthorne concluded his word picture, "I liked this sallow, queer, sagacious visage, with the homely human sympathies that warmed it; and for my small share in the matter, would as life have Uncle Abe for a ruler as any man whom it would have been practicable to put in his place."

One of the tragedies of government censorship—or the mere specter of it—was that such vivid writing was deemed disrespectful and kept from the public while Lincoln lived. As Hawthorne meekly protested to editor James Fields in agreeing to cut the excerpt to save the piece, his Lincoln section was "the only part of the article really worth publishing. Upon my honor," he added, "it seemed to me to have historical value—but let it go."[58]

That summer, Lincoln launched an audacious disinformation campaign to prepare the North's white voters (nearly half of whom were Democrats) for the Emancipation Proclamation he had already drafted. Lincoln believed he had ample reason to tread surreptitiously. He expected resistance from the crucial Border slave states, even though they would be exempt from his executive order. He feared opposition from Democratic generals who had warned they would fight only for the Union, not for black freedom. And he anticipated hostility from poor whites fearful of an influx of newly liberated African Americans competing for jobs. Thus, Lincoln determined to frame emancipation in terms of "military necessity" rather than social philanthropy. His wire-pulling may have made emancipation palatable for whites, but it almost certainly contributed to the lingering suspicion among many modern Americans, especially those of color, that Lincoln was an insincere emancipator.

Delaying the order until his army could boost national morale with a battlefield victory, Lincoln used the time to convince the public, via the press, that if and when he did act against slavery, it would be for the purpose of winning the war, not elevating black people. In one such move, on July 22, he welcomed a delegation of free African Americans to the White House, a first. But then he bluntly told his visitors they should support a plan for their mass emigration to Africa or the Caribbean, insisting: "We should be separated."[59] That the president brought an Associated Press stenographer along with him to record and distribute these harsh remarks was no accident. It was not his finest moment. When abolitionist leader Frederick Douglass read the account, he took to his own newspaper to condemn the president for "his pride of race and blood, his contempt for Negroes and his canting hypocrisy."[60] But Lincoln knew that such criticism might not matter; by and large, black people did not yet enjoy the right to vote. His false leads were aimed at soothing white people who did.

Just a few weeks after his blunt lecture to the black delegation, the nettlesome but influential Horace Greeley published a scathing *New York Tribune* editorial condemning the administration as "strangely and disastrously remiss" for delaying emancipation.[61] Lincoln and Greeley, though both antislavery, had been wrestling each other for preeminence ever since they had both served as

Whig congressmen in the late 1840s. Although evidence exists to suggest Greeley knew that a proclamation was imminent and timed his attack to win credit for inspiring it, Lincoln deftly outmaneuvered him. He composed a cunning but luminous reply asserting that future antislavery initiatives would be deployed only to save the Union, making Greeley appear self-righteous and shortsighted. Twisting the knife, Lincoln made sure his letter landed on the desk of another newspaper before it reached Greeley. Though addressed to the editor and crafted as a private response, the president gave the text not to the *Tribune* but to the Washington *National Intelligencer.* Greeley would be denied not only credit but an exclusive story. Lincoln's disingenuous reply trumped Greeley's self-righteousness and paved the way for the emancipation order he had already prepared. "I can't trust your 'honest old Abe,'" the editor was heard to comment. "He is too smart for me."[62]

Nevertheless, few of Lincoln's appeals to the people through the press ever earned such widespread approbation at the time, or such criticism in the future (for its seeming indifference to the fate of enslaved people). It said in part:

> My paramount object in this struggle *is* to save the Union, and is *not* either to save or destroy slavery. If I could save the Union without freeing *any* slave I would do it, and if I could save it by freeing *all* the slaves I would do it; and if I could save it by freeing some and leaving others alone I would also do that. What I do about slavery and the colored race, I do because I believe it helps to save the Union; and what I forbear, I forbear because I do *not* believe it would help to save the Union. I shall do *less* whenever I shall believe what I am doing hurts the cause, and I shall do *more* whenever I shall believe doing more will help the cause.[63]

Although he added a humane and universal coda—"I intend no modification of my oft-expressed *personal* wish that all men every where could be free"—Lincoln's declaration served overall to complement his tough recent remarks on colonization. Now he had introduced the idea of freeing "some" slaves if such a policy would defeat the Rebels and colonizing others to assuage dubious Northern whites whose support he still required. That Lincoln later embraced a plan to end slavery everywhere by means of a constitutional amendment, and declined to spend much federal funding to resettle African Americans overseas, as authorized by Congress, suggests that his summer of tactical obfuscation was purely diversionary.

Not surprisingly, the proclamation itself unleashed a withering barrage of press criticism from Democratic and Confederate journals, with Lincoln's old nemesis, the *Chicago Times*, labeling it an act of "utter desperation" by a tyrant "cut loose from the constitution."[64] But the president's manipulative run-up to its announcement undoubtedly softened the impact of such attacks and kept his government, and its boldest act and actor, viable. The proclamation's society-altering wallop may well have been blunted by Douglass's harsh advance criticism, too. Douglass reacted with a new editorial: "We shout for joy that we live to record this righteous decree."[65] The final proclamation followed in January 1863.

One thing is certain: Lincoln never doubted himself or his document. As he told witnesses on New Year's Day—pausing before affixing his name to it because his right arm was "almost paralyzed," as he put it, from three hours of unrelenting holiday handshaking—"If my name ever goes into history it will be for this act, and my whole soul is in it."[66] Yet clearly he did not offer the endeavor his whole supply of literary skill. Devoid of his usual rhetorical flourishes, the document attracted few analyses in the United States.

But the preliminary document had inspired a particularly incisive commentary from overseas, and it is intriguing to wonder if Lincoln ever read it. Its author, a Lincoln admirer and sometime contributor to the *New York Tribune* named Karl Marx, complained that the dry document called to mind "the trite summonses that one lawyer sends to an opposing lawyer, the legal chicaneries and pettifogging stipulations of an *actiones juris*"—a court case. Marx found it perfectly astonishing that what he called "the most significant document in American history since the founding of the Union and one which tears up the old American Constitution, bears the same character," although its literary shortcomings did not alter its "historic content."

Marx came amazingly close to the truth when he offered this assessment of Lincoln as a writer: "He always presents the most important act in the most insignificant form possible. Others, when dealing with square feet of land, proclaim it a 'struggle for ideas.' Lincoln, even when he is dealing with ideas, proclaims their 'square feet.' Hesitant, resistant, unwilling, he sings the bravura aria of his role as though he begged pardon for the circumstances that force him 'to be a lion.'"[67]

A few months later, in another sterling example of the new "public letter" genre, Lincoln boldly took on the issue of black military enlistment, which even some pro-Emancipation Republicans opposed. Lincoln had come to believe the new "U.S. Colored Troops" might well tip military momentum to the Union.

Invited back to his Springfield hometown to address a patriotic rally, Lincoln composed a long message defending the new policy. "You say you will not fight to free Negroes," he chided his old neighbors. "Some of them seem willing to fight for you. . . . Why should they do any thing for us, if we will do nothing for them?"[68] In the end unwilling to devote time to cross-country travel, the president designated an old neighbor, James C. Conkling, to read his inspiring text aloud in Springfield. Then Lincoln used reverse psychology to stoke advance press interest, telling the Washington AP he would not release the message until Conkling actually recited it. Unfortunately, Conkling sneaked an imperfect advance text to local reporters, and early reprints garbled the manuscript. "I am mortified this morning to find the letter to you, botched up, in the Eastern papers," Lincoln testily wrote to Conkling. "How did this happen?"[69] Sometimes even the ingenious Lincoln could not control all aspects of his messaging. The press ultimately corrected and reprinted the mangled speech, and it exerted its intended impact.

Lincoln won a second term in 1864 almost in spite of the press. With the war going badly, his old nemesis Horace Greeley, who despite a shared hatred of slavery, had found fault with Lincoln for years, fiercely opposed the president's renomination. Even after Lincoln locked down the nod, the editor beseeched party leaders to rescind it and call a new convention. When that outrageous gambit failed, too, Greeley promoted a third-party candidate. Then the *Tribune* editor presumptuously demanded the authority to negotiate peace with so-called Confederate emissaries willing to meet with him in Canada. Backed into a corner, Lincoln allowed the talks to proceed but made clear in advance that he would tolerate no armistice that rescinded emancipation. Not surprisingly, the talks foundered in the wake of the president's precondition, and a chagrined Greeley published what Lincoln called "injurious reports" of the failed truce talks, including transcripts of his private correspondence with Lincoln.[70] To make matters worse, Lincoln's most loyal press supporters worried that his line-in-the-sand defense of black freedom had put the lie to his longtime assertion that his "paramount object" was to save the Union, not to free the slaves.[71]

An exasperated Lincoln never spoke to Greeley again, but then Henry Raymond wavered, too—a far more threatening development. Raymond not only still edited the *New York Times*, but in the starkest example yet of the interlocking connections between the press and politics, now served as chairman of the

Republican (temporarily renamed "National Union") Party.* Raymond was actually standing for Congress as well, not to mention preparing a volume of presidential speeches to boost Lincoln's campaign. Fearing that "the tide is setting strongly against us," Raymond beseeched Lincoln to open his own peace negotiations with the Confederate president Jefferson Davis.[72] Raymond composed this lament on the second anniversary of Lincoln's triumphant public letter to Greeley on emancipation, but the downtrodden president had no similar trick up his sleeve now. At the low point of his entire presidency, he submissively authorized Raymond to arrange such a conference if he could.[73]

This close call with desperation abruptly ended a few days later when Union general William T. Sherman captured the Confederate stronghold of Atlanta. News of the conquest totally upended the presidential campaign and switched momentum to the Republicans. It was surely not lost on Lincoln that the cantankerous Sherman had long ranked among the most oppressive of military press censors, or that when he might have countermanded the general's brutal crackdowns, he had instead shielded him. Now Sherman had done more than turn the tide of war; he had helped Lincoln snatch likely political victory from almost certain political defeat.

Unknown to all but a handful of his closest advisors, Lincoln arranged one more secret public relations deal to secure reelection, particularly in vote-rich New York. Through trusted emissaries he made clear that in return for assuming a pox-against-all houses neutrality, rather than outright editorial opposition, James Gordon Bennett of the *Herald* would be rewarded with a major presidential appointment—one he would thereafter refuse, satisfied merely with the long-withheld honor of recognition. The president went on to win the November race by a wide margin, the first man to earn a second term since Jackson. And as agreed, Lincoln duly offered the newspaperman known to critics as "His Satanic Majesty" the coveted post of American minister to Paris. As expected, Bennett declined. Pennsylvania editor Alexander K. McClure called the arrangement "one of the shrewdest of Lincoln's great political schemes."[74]

In the closing days of the Civil War the following spring, Lincoln returned almost nostalgically to his salad days as a sometime newspaper correspondent, using a final trip to the Union front in Virginia to file his own press dispatches

---

* This was no mere rebranding. The Lincoln campaign aimed to significantly expand its appeal by attracting pro-war Democrats to the ticket.

about General Ulysses S. Grant's final thrusts against Robert E. Lee's disintegrating rebel army. For days, Lincoln's crisp, optimistic reports filled northern newspapers and cheered their war-weary readers. The communiqués signaled imminent triumph for the Union cause while subtly reminding readers that the commander in chief deserved his share of the honor for the approaching victory. At this point Lincoln neither wanted nor needed third-party filtering of his outreach to the public.

Yet all but unnoticed to observers at the time and to historians since, the administration never totally abandoned its policy of aggressive press suppression, even when Union success seemed assured. A month after Election Day, Union troops closed down the *Louisville True Presbyterian* and banished its pro-South editor, Rev. Stuart Robinson, to Canada. Robinson responded with an indignant public letter of his own in late January 1865, lashing the administration "for its tyrannical contempt for personal liberty, freedom of speech and of the press, liberty of conscience and freedom of religion." To Robinson, Lincoln's "minions" had for too long terrorized the "mystified, terrified, dejected, wasted tenants" of his American "bastilles."[75] Had Robinson's brutal manifesto been published in, say, New York rather than distant Toronto, or appeared before Election Day, not after, it might have revived fears of the permanent forfeiture of civil liberties under Lincoln and damaged his chances for a second term. But Robinson's protests proved too little, and too late, to dampen northern joy over its impending triumph.

Just how and when Lincoln would have relaxed his wartime grip on the press remains unknowable. Four days after Lee surrendered, the president fell victim to an assassin's bullet. We do know that when Lincoln's pockets were emptied after his death, his wallet was found stuffed with newspaper clippings, most expressing praise for his recent efforts. As that evidence suggests, Lincoln to his last day continued focusing on press coverage and never relaxed his alternating efforts to stimulate, control, or repress it.

Yet he was not perfect; he missed opportunities. When he met Confederate "peace commissioners" in February 1865 to receive, and reject, their terms for a cease-fire—recognition of Confederate independence and abandonment of the Emancipation Proclamation—Lincoln knew the constitutional amendment abolishing slavery was already en route to the states for ratification. It must have been a sweet moment for the exhausted Civil War president when he told this to the enemy negotiators, yet he neglected to bring a journalist or clerk to the meeting to record the conversation for posterity—or even for the period newspapers.

Although he mastered the art of public relations such as it existed in the 1850s and '60s, Lincoln always preferred to let his own words speak for themselves.

"[P]ublic sentiment is everything," Lincoln once declared. "With public sentiment, nothing can fail; without it nothing can succeed. Consequently he who moulds public sentiment goes deeper than he who enacts statutes or pronounces decisions."[76] No president ever controlled public opinion more firmly than Abraham Lincoln did. His press policies aroused heated controversy and, retrospectively, legal rebuke.

In 1866, a year after his murder, the Supreme Court ruled in the case of *Ex Parte Milligan* that the government never has the right to subject civilians to military justice, journalists included, and even during wartime, where civil courts still operate. Lincoln did not live to comment on that judicial ruling. But he might have countered that his sometimes-harsh tactics against the opposition press had helped preserve the Union, destroy slavery, and perpetuate the freedoms he had for a time felt the need to suspend.

It remains almost too easy for modern observers to condemn Abraham Lincoln for going overboard on press subjugation. Such facile analysis employs hindsight that the sixteenth president never enjoyed. Although modern Americans know who won the Civil War, Lincoln had no assurance when the rebellion erupted that it would be crushed, secession thwarted, majority rule defended, and slavery eradicated. And he had no foreknowledge of the sacrifice it would take to achieve all those objectives: 750,000 lives lost, landscape devastated, and the Constitution itself temporarily forsaken so that it could be permanently secured. Lincoln abrogated press rights in the sincere belief that "public safety" required him to repress the very liberties that made the government worth saving—but only until such time as they could be restored.

And Lincoln always tried to impose his own limits on that aggressive posture. Midway through the war, Union general John M. Schofield imprisoned an editor merely for publishing advance information about the general's own upcoming promotion. On that occasion, Lincoln felt Schofield had crossed a bridge too far. Generals could "suppress newspapers," Lincoln made clear, only "when they may be working *palpable* injury to the Military" itself. In no other cases, the president scolded Schofield, "will you interfere with the expression of opinion in any form, or allow it to be interfered with violently by others."[77]

On this occasion, Lincoln may have been asking a general to exercise more judgment than he had at his command. At least the commander in chief supplied Schofield with guidelines that may constitute as precise a definition as

Abraham Lincoln ever provided about when to interfere with the press—and when not to: "Let your military measures be strong enough to repel the invader and keep the peace, and not so strong as to unnecessarily harass and persecute the people."[78]

That is precisely how Lincoln treated the Civil War press: with a remarkable incongruity. No president ever expanded communication more, or tolerated hostile coverage less. That he emerged the hero of a history whose proverbial first draft came from the very community of writers he had once suppressed makes his enduringly high reputation all the more remarkable.

PART THREE

FROM THE BULLY PULPIT TO THE FIRESIDE

6

THEODORE ROOSEVELT

One afternoon early in his presidency, Theodore Roosevelt summoned journalists to his White House office and gave them a special opportunity to hear and jot down his latest thoughts—provided they could keep up with his galloping mind. What made the session unique was not just that it offered the correspondents spontaneous access. It was that the president conducted the entire briefing while his barber, an African American Treasury Department messenger named Delaney, gave him his regular midday shave.

Finding that he enjoyed the opportunity to accomplish (at least) two tasks at once, the hyperenergetic TR decided that the casual gathering should become as routine as the daily shaves themselves. The sessions became known to the correspondents as "the barber's hour."[1] Near one o'clock each afternoon, reporters would crowd into the narrow room connecting the president's office to that of his private secretary. There they would find TR seated in a "large armchair . . . with his face covered with lather and Delaney's razor sweeping over it." At first the journalists hoped that, cheeks soaped, the garrulous TR "would be at a disadvantage as to talking." But whenever a particular inquiry aroused him, the "writhing" president would leap from his chair clutching his towel and hold forth until he calmed down.[2] "Steady, Mr. President," Delaney would plead, blade in hand, struggling to hold Roosevelt down for fear an unexpected gesture would slit his throat.[3]

"A more skillful barber never existed," sympathized Louis Brownlow, a Washington correspondent for the *Nashville Banner* and a witness to many of the "barber's hours" that commenced in 1901. Just as "the razor would descend toward his face, someone would ask a question. The President would wave both arms, jump up, speak excitedly, and then drop again into the chair and grin at the barber, who would begin all over. Sometimes these explosions interrupted a shave ten or a dozen times. It was more fun to see than a circus."[4]

Lincoln Steffens recalled that the only time TR fell mute during these briefings was "when the barber bent over the presidential head and began to shave the lower lip." Steffens, who devoted an entire chapter of his autobiography to the ritual, titling it "The President Is Shaved," developed a special strategy for making the most of the opportunities: since TR "would pour forth at your first suggestion, I always came into the room primed with a question that I fired quick; and he went off." Steffens likened the president to "a mighty dam which would break and drown you at your first word."[5]

Such extraordinary displays of informality might have shocked even Andrew Jackson, who gave instructions to journalists while lying on a sofa, or TR's idol, the incurably casual Abraham Lincoln, who sometimes greeted visiting reporters wearing his carpet slippers. More than any of his predecessors, Teddy Roosevelt treated journalists as friends, allies, captive audiences, and fellow warriors in common cause. What made TR's bold style so impactful is that its introduction coincided with a sea change in the culture of the news business itself.

The age of partisan—and administration "organ"—journalism was by Roosevelt's time buried. So were the once-powerful newspaper publishers like Greeley and Bennett who had either competed with presidents for influence or slavishly done their bidding. In the words of one journalist of the period, editors now grew "more apt to follow public opinion than to lead it."[6] In the new era of bold-headline front pages meant to stimulate street sales, reporters with stories to break, rather than editors with axes to grind, emerged as the most important members of the press corps. And by 1900, 171 of them were toiling in the capital as Washington correspondents, their scoops magnified via syndicates, wire services, and newspaper chains.

The Roosevelt administration did not secure newspaper loyalty by doling out government printing contracts like Jackson, Lincoln, and their predecessors had. TR secured reporters' attention and admiration through the sheer force of his ebullient personality and his unrestrainable eagerness to share news, gossip, and sometimes even secrets. TR was simply great copy. While admitting that "Roosevelt was not a god," William Allen White, editor of the *Emporia* (Kansas) *Gazette*, marveled that the president "vitalized everything he touched."[7] To the crusading magazine writer Ray Stannard Baker, TR was as "wholesome" as "a gust of wind."[8]

For Roosevelt, press management—sharing information at a whim, steering press coverage in directions he desired, squashing stories when it suited him, and using what he called the "bully pulpit" to galvanize public support through newspapers and magazines—became as crucial a presidential responsibility as administering the federal bureaucracy and commanding the armed forces.

As historian Doris Kearns Goodwin has evocatively detailed, Roosevelt would forge a historic, almost collaborative relationship with the generation of progressive, long-form investigative journalists who became known as "muckrakers"—a term Roosevelt himself would introduce. When TR arrived at the White House in 1901, as one such muckraker, Lincoln Steffens, testified, "many reformers went there to see the first reformer president take charge." The big-game-hunter-turned-president exulted, "It was just as if we had shot some big animal and the carcass lay there exposed for a feast."[9]

Steffens, Ray Baker, and their colleague Ida Tarbell together proceeded to turn the magazine for which they toiled, *McClure's*, into a virtual soapbox for TR and his reform agenda. Steffens brought attention to the misery of urban slums in his influential columns, "Shame of the Cities;" Tarbell produced a meticulously researched exposé of Standard Oil; and Baker undertook an investigation into U.S. Steel. These revelatory articles laid bare the corrupt stranglehold big corporations held over consumers as well as a subservient federal government. The widely read pieces evoked outrage and built public support for Roosevelt's crackdown on industrial trusts.

Yet Roosevelt did not come to power armed with complete trust of his own in the reform ethos beginning to dominate American journalism. Rather, he worried that showboating reformers might morph into radical zealots, requiring him to answer their self-righteous overreach with rationality—just as Abraham Lincoln had resisted radicals of his own era who (as TR viewed history) favored the precipitant abolition of slavery.

In June 1900, while still governor of New York, TR produced an article of his own for *Century Magazine*, warning against "unhealthy extremists who like to take half of any statement and twist it into an argument in favor of themselves or against their opponents." Such reformers, he taunted, must either be "low moral types" or "slightly disordered mentally." At the very least they were "cursed with a moral twist which makes them champion reforms less from a desire to do good than as a kind of tribute to their own righteousness."[10]

"We must not be misled at any time," TR's article warned, "by the cheap assertion . . . that the editor of a degraded newspaper is to be excused because the public want the degradation."[11] And then, adopting a Lincolnian phrase to characterize what later became known as "public opinion," he added, "It is a dreadful thing that public sentiment should condone misconduct in a public man; but this is no excuse for the public man, if by his conduct he degrades public sentiment."[12] At heart, TR did not really believe journalists needed to conduct exhaustive inquiries or compose thousands of words to reach the inevitable conclusion that he was right and his critics were wrong.

Governor Roosevelt likely designed his 1900 *Century* piece primarily to assure conservative Republicans that he was no radical himself and deserved a chance to run on that year's national ticket with William McKinley. If so, his effort proved a success. The convention nominated him for vice president later that very month. In November, Republicans triumphed at the polls, and then, with McKinley's September 1901 assassination, Roosevelt unexpectedly vaulted to the nation's highest office.

TR became the youngest president in history, and his sheer vitality at once transformed the political—and press—culture. As surely as the late chief executive had seemed a relic of the nineteenth century, TR exuded the boundary-breaking energy of the twentieth. Noting that Roosevelt possessed "the knack of doing things, and doing them noisily, clamorously," journalist-turned-historian Mark Sullivan joked that whenever TR was "in the neighborhood the public can no more look the other way than the small boy can turn his head away from a circus parade followed by a steam calliope."[13] In the equally colorful assessment of historian Dixon Wecter, Roosevelt became to government "what Buffalo Bill had been to the big top."[14] To achieve and sustain the high level of fascination he provoked, TR courted journalists more ardently than any of his predecessors. Until Roosevelt, no president of the United States had ever handled the press as skillfully, frequently, aggressively, and informally—or presented to them such an exhausting array of opportunities and contradictions. As correspondent David Barry attested, Roosevelt "knew the value and importance of a news paragraph written as he wanted . . . better than any man who ever occupied the White House."[15]

Over the thirty-six years that separated Lincoln's presidency from Roosevelt's, the world of journalism, in terms of power, reach, and partisanship, had dramatically shifted.

In the wake of Lincoln's 1865 murder, the influential Republican press had split over black rights and the impeachment of Andrew Johnson. Henry Raymond, editor of the *New York Times* (and by then a sitting congressman) took the more conservative stance and backed the cautious president, while Horace Greeley of the *Tribune* denounced Lincoln's successor, yet caused a "tumult," he admitted, by ill-advisedly extending sympathy to onetime Confederate president Jefferson Davis.[16] Johnson escaped Senate conviction, and removal from office, by a single vote.

Newspapers that cheered the subsequent ascent of Ulysses S. Grant proved fickle as well. They soon commenced lambasting the man they had once lauded as the Union's greatest military hero, blaming him for scandals that, at worst, he seemed unable to manage. At one point, Grant felt compelled to defend himself from charges of complicity in a Wall Street scam by assuring a sympathetic editor—for the record: "I had no more to do with the late gold excitement . . . than yourself, or any other innocent party."[17] Such direct explanations to the press were at the time considered undignified, if not degrading. Yet Grant easily won a second term in 1872, aided by the fact that the one man foolhardy enough to run against him was Greeley, the only time a full-time, working journalist ever sought the job.[18]

Except for the two nonconsecutive presidencies of Democrat Grover Cleveland—enlivened by lurid coverage of his early love life and his White House marriage to a woman less than half his age—a succession of Gilded Age Republican presidents ushered in an era of anodyne reporting. One-party government meanwhile helped enrich privileged Americans while reconciling the post–Civil War North and South at the expense of the citizenship rights Republicans had once promised African Americans. The nation matured and further industrialized without imposing regulations to protect ordinary citizens. Newspapers dramatically modernized as well. By the time the century came to a close, journalism—once crafted in hot type from hand-scrawled manuscripts—was being pounded out on typewriters, fact-checked over the telephone, and printed by electrically powered presses.

For a time, however, access to presidents remained as hidebound as in the days of Lincoln. Under McKinley, press corps "privileges" at least became "well-defined and generally recognized." But even invited for the first time to holiday receptions and granted a small corner of the presidential residence from which to work, correspondents continued to keep their traditional distance.[19] It was "part of the unwritten law of the White House," *McClure's Magazine* noted, "that newspaper men shall never approach the President as he passes to and fro near their alcove or crosses the portico to his carriage, unless he himself stops and talks to them." McKinley was said either to read twenty papers a day or glance over a digest prepared by his staff, depending on which tale one believed, always sentimentally reserving time for his hometown daily, Canton, Ohio's *Repository*.[20]

The patina of restraint shattered when McKinley seemingly allowed two rival purveyors of a newer "yellow journalism"—Joseph Pulitzer of the *New York World* and William Randolph Hearst of the *New York Journal*—to goad him into armed conflict with Spain after the USS *Maine* exploded in Havana Harbor with the loss of 260 lives. The "splendid little" Spanish–American War might never have occurred, some journalists later almost boasted, had the "blood guilty" sensationalist papers not outdone one another with giant, inflammatory headlines that charged that the battleship had been blown up intentionally.[21] No proof of sabotage was ever found, but it did not matter; as one modern writer has put it: "fake news helped start a war."[22]

But then, had the rallying cry "Remember the *Maine*" never entered the national vocabulary, Teddy Roosevelt could not have burnished his growing legend by volunteering for the fight. He would never have left the comforts of Washington to take his "Rough Riders" to Cuba, where the regiment's charge up San Juan Hill in May 1898 catapulted their colonel to the status of folk hero.[23] Less than three years later, Roosevelt became vice president. Although McKinley's death elevated Roosevelt to the presidency more quickly than anyone could have anticipated, TR had long operated in an aura of inevitability. He entered the White House suddenly, and at a very young age, but he had been courting press attention for a long time—and surely could never imagine allowing newspapers, as McKinley had, to lead an entire nation into war.[24]

At the very beginning of his political career, serving in the New York State legislature while still in his early twenties, TR had fought against a proposal to subject newspapers to libel suits in any jurisdiction where they circulated. Recognizing the measure as "a bill for gagging journalists," Roosevelt countered, "I think it is a good deal better to err a little bit on the side of having too much discussion and having too virulent language used by the press, rather than to err on the side of having them not say what they ought to say, especially with reference to public men and measures."[25]

The anti-press bill went down to defeat, and Roosevelt's support for free expression earned the gratitude of crusading reporters like James Bucklin Bishop, a onetime Horace Greeley employee who became a Roosevelt enthusiast for life. Later an influential editor and a TR biographer, Bishop was one of many working journalists who forged lasting and useful friendships with this restless, ambitious politician.[26]

As he climbed the political ladder double-quick, TR continued assiduously cultivating press attention, even if it sometimes required peppering the newspapers with letters to the editor. During his tenure as New York City police commissioner from 1895 to 1897, he made sure that journalists—among them Lincoln Steffens—were on hand to witness his dramatic nighttime raids and on board to endorse his crusades against corruption. Elected governor in 1898, TR routinely held not one but two daily press briefings for Albany's legislative correspondents, devoting fifteen minutes at each of them to questions and answers. Invariably, the sessions yielded far more answers than questions, as biographer Edmund Morris has pointed out, owing to the governor's incurable "loquacity."[27]

TR proved no less energetic as vice president, no less devoted to making himself available to journalists, and no less shrewd about how best to generate publicity. After McKinley's death in September 1901, it was said by some that TR refused to take the presidential oath in the parlor of his friend Ansley Wilcox in Buffalo until a sufficient number of reporters had gathered to observe the scene.

The veteran press manipulator literally began his accidental presidency by reaching out to corral Washington's leading wire service correspondents into his orbit. As David S. Barry of the *New York Sun* Press Service remembered, TR defied tradition and summoned him—together with representatives of the Associated Press and Scripps-McRae Press Association (later rebranded United Press International)—just after the newly sworn chief executive returned from the McKinley funeral.

"This being my first day in the White House as President of the United States," Roosevelt briskly informed the group assembled around the cabinet table, "I desired to have a little talk with you gentlemen who are responsible for the collection and dissemination of the news, as to the relations that should, and will, exist between the White House and your organizations." TR vowed to remain "accessible to them, to keep them posted, and trust to their discretion as to publication." But if any dared to "violate a confidence or publish news that the President thought ought not to be published," Roosevelt warned, "he should be punished by having legitimate news withheld from him." When Barry countered that no chief executive could lay down such a rule, the confident TR seemed only amused.[28]

Soon thereafter, strolling the streets of Washington with Lincoln Steffens and William Allen White, Roosevelt not only seemed insensitive to the prevailing gloom that still gripped a nation mourning its fallen leader; he could barely contain his excitement at assuming office. Steffens remembered that TR "laughed at his luck . . . laughed with glee at the power that had come to him," while White grew "pop-eyed with wonder" in the wake of TR's "dynamic, burning candor."[29]

Candor had its limits. No matter how much he talked, TR expected his highly quotable remarks to remain off the record unless otherwise specified—a restriction still considered standard procedure at the time. During his White House years, writers violating this rule faced banishment from TR's convivial inner circle. "I never knew Colonel Roosevelt to do a mean or underhand thing in connection with the press," insisted correspondent Henry S. Brown, "but I have known him to hit hard. He never scorned to use brass knuckles, if brass knuckles were being used on him."[30]

Leaks were deemed offensive, and lies and mischaracterizations intolerable. Violators earned symbolic membership in TR's so-called Ananias Club, a purgatory of ostracism named for the biblical character struck dead before Saint Peter for lying to God.[31] Conversely, "fair-haired" (loyal) reporters secured a favored place in Roosevelt "Paradise," an imaginary Eden inhabited by writers who reflected what TR called the "Oyster Bay atmosphere" (in tribute to his Long Island home), defined by "mutual respect, confidence and friendliness."[32] Especially friendliness.

One of the *New York Times* correspondents who covered Roosevelt conceded, "The standing White House rule, that the President is never quoted, was, of course, enforced strictly. Any violation of that terminated a correspondent's usefulness to his paper, so far as the White House was concerned. Also, it got him immediately elected to the Ananias Club. Mr. Roosevelt trusted a confidant until something happened to cause him to think his confidence had been misplaced. Then he ceased entirely to give his confidence to the man who had not respected it. It was all or nothing with him."[33]

Roosevelt proved especially sensitive when it came to coverage of his family.

The president himself may have yearned to be, in his daughter Alice's memorable judgment, "the corpse at every funeral, the bride at every wedding, and the baby at every christening"; but that did not mean that the publicity-hungry chief executive craved ink for his wife and children. Their activities, he tried insisting, must remain out of bounds.[34]

One Thanksgiving season, however, Jesse Carmichael of Pulitzer's *New York World* glimpsed two of Roosevelt's young sons chasing a frightened turkey around the White House lawn. In a comical attempt to capture it, the boys repeatedly lunged at the poor creature's tail feathers, while the president boisterously encouraged them from the South Portico. Carmichael's somewhat embellished report appeared in the *World* the next day. The item was meant as innocent holiday fare, but an "incensed" TR hotly denied the entire story and cut off not only the reporter but also his entire newspaper—going so far as to issue an executive order barring Carmichael from receiving White House press announcements.[35] In this instance, Carmichael's press colleagues came to the rescue, filling his desk each day with copies of withheld administration reports. Eventually, TR had no choice but to relax his ban, though he never formally rescinded the overwrought official order.[36]

In the end, little Teddy, Kermit, Ethel, and Archie simply proved too adorable and rambunctious to escape reporters' attention. As for Alice Roosevelt, the independent and unpredictable daughter of the president's first marriage, she broke so many rules that the press insisted on the right to cover her colorful antics. A proud, self-proclaimed "individualist," Alice smoked in public, enlivened parties, and unapologetically embarked on a New England motor trip unchaperoned—inspiring headline after headline. According to her father's old Harvard classmate, novelist Owen Wister, when a worried ally begged TR to "look after Alice more," Roosevelt famously replied, "I can be President of the United States—or I can attend to Alice. I cannot possibly do both."[37] Alice would confess in her autobiography: "My 'publicity value' was, I fear, at times a trial to the family."[38] Yet coverage of her expoits kept the Roosevelt name in the news even on those rare occasions when the president had nothing to say. And for TR, almost any kind of press could be interpreted as good press.

One test of that belief came in the wake of Roosevelt's decision, just a few weeks after taking office, to invite the prominent African American educator Booker T. Washington to meet with him at the White House to discuss race relations, and once their session ran late, to stay and join him for dinner. The two men shared many interests, including a passion for newspaper reading, a reverence for Abraham Lincoln, and a cautious approach to extending black rights.[39] The head of the Tuskegee Institute, born enslaved in pre–Civil War Virginia, Washington became the first African American to sit down for a meal in the president's house as a guest. What TR considered a social courtesy ignited a firestorm.[40]

The nation's black newspapers—that is, those that supported the conservative educator—cheered both the event and its host. Edward Elder Cooper's *Colored American* spoke for many with the salute "Well done thou good and faithful servant, thou hast been faithful in ruling over the whole people without respect to race, color or creed, therefore enter thou upon a second term."[41]

Predictably, Southern newspapers spewed venom, with the *Memphis Scimitar* exclaiming, "The most damnable outrage which has ever been perpetrated by any citizen of the United States was committed yesterday by the President when he invited a nigger to dine with him at the White House."[42] Not only had the president invited a man of color to his White House table, critics fumed, TR's wife and teenage daughter had been present, too. The white supremacist senator Benjamin Tillman of South Carolina snarled, "We shall have to kill a thousand niggers to get them back in their places."[43]

To the *Daily Arkansas Gazette*, the "ill-considered, impetuous, sensational" event simply ranked as yet further proof of Roosevelt's "outré" nature. "There are some things in this world of which we can be sure," sneered the Little Rock paper: "One, that a man who has one leg will always limp; another, that a megalomaniac will periodically make an ass of himself."[44] It took a progressive black weekly, the *Chicago Broad Ax*, no supporter of the "Wizard of Tuskegee," to come closest to the sad truth by predicting that "lynching, mobbing, burning Negroes at the stake and disenfranchising them by white Christians, will not cease, but will go bravely on regardless of the fact that Professor Washington was accorded the privilege of resting his feet under President Roosevelt's dinner table."[45]

For weeks, the controversy dominated the press, black and white, North and South, so rattling the administration that the White House tried denying that the dinner had actually taken place—despite having circulated a statement announcing it. Roosevelt, whose civil rights record can only be called mixed, never invited Washington or any other black leaders to dine with him again, though the original event proved enough to rank as a historic milestone.[46] Here was one occasion where TR might have used his powers of persuasion to rally the press both to his own defense and to the symbolic importance of Washington's visit. He did neither.

Despite the clumsy cover-up attempt, Charles Willis Thompson, Washington correspondent for the *New York Times*, continued to insist that Roosevelt never "used" White House reporters. "He never flattered or palavered or went out of his way," Thompson remembered. ". . . But no Man could use that magic as Roosevelt could. Men loved to be put under that spell."[47] As for charges that TR acted impetuously, Thompson insisted "that he never said a public word or did a public act from impulse. . . . The thousand reporters who have tried to catch Roosevelt off guard and make him say something he did not expect to say will laugh at that idea."[48]

TR occasionally showed journalists a softer side. When he noticed reporters clustered outside the executive mansion gates, rain or shine, hoping to question official visitors as they exited, a sympathetic TR established what became the first official White House press room both to shelter reporters and provide them easier access to his callers—as well as himself. Under TR, the newsmen at last graduated from the status of barely tolerated guests to that of resident professionals. When the new West Wing opened in 1902 and Roosevelt moved into the first Oval Office, the press corps encamped at new headquarters specially designated for their own use. White House correspondents have been working from official space there ever since.

With the journalists' path eased, the president became an almost constant object of their attention—always available, consistently newsworthy, usually forthright and occasionally outrageous. He called his favorite reporters by their first names and made a grandiose fuss when any of them took sick. Always unpredictable, TR might pass information without attribution to two or three favorites or call in "forty to fifty reporters at a time, as he did when he launched his first conservation congress." The result, as J. Frederick Essary of the *Baltimore Sun* testified, "was that there were more scoops of White House origin during the Roosevelt period than before or since." Most journalists came to love him if only because he seldom avoided them or told them untruths. In fact, as an astonished David Barry testified, TR "went so far on more than one occasion . . . to write out with his own hand what he wanted sent over the wires."[49]

More than one correspondent expressed shock that the president revealed as much as he did. Kentucky-born Isaac F. Marcosson, an editor at the business magazine *World's Work*, could hardly believe "what sometimes seemed an almost incredible frankness" in Roosevelt's comments to reporters.[50] Once, William Allen White overheard Roosevelt intentionally bellowing "state secrets in a loud voice to statesmen in the Presidential workroom, so that reporters could clearly hear" him from their own nearby quarters.[51] Senator Henry Cabot Lodge admitted of his friend the president: "He has no secrets. The truth that is in him rises unclouded from his lips."[52]

On the other hand, mere access did not mean reporters could get all their questions answered—or even asked. Lincoln Steffens observed of TR that while "it was easy to make him talk, even about a State secret . . . to reverse the process and make him listen was well-nigh impossible."[53] The *New York Times*' David Willis Thompson added: "He gave out many statements, some of them in the form of interviews, and sometimes, too, he was actually interviewed, but in such cases he always directed the form the interview would take. . . . No one ever heard of an interview being given by Roosevelt as he got off a train or entered a hotel corridor—unless it was something he had determined to say."[54] Nor did Roosevelt always wait for journalists to pose questions; he often instigated his own news copy, in much the manner Abraham Lincoln had once released public letters. When, for example, a Standard Oil lobbyist tried to influence a crucial senate vote—a strong-arm tactic one solon promptly reported to the Administration—TR not only informed White House reporters of the outrage; he personally "wrote the preliminary item that was sent to the afternoon papers."[55]

Roosevelt's informality occasionally led him into trouble—especially when he mistook the Washington correspondents for collaborators rather than professionals assigned to cover the news. Often, TR insisted that he had never uttered words quoted by newspapers—even when he had said for the record precisely what they printed. The president denied stories even as he was confiding them. On one such occasion, Roosevelt shared his disdain for the Republican old guard to Scripps syndicate correspondent Ed Keen, clearly hoping the reporter would write something about their intransigence—but without quoting him. TR concluded his harangue by warning Keen, "If you even hint where you got it, I'll say you are a damned liar."[56] Similarly, when Sumner Curtis of the *Chicago Record-Herald* "politely asked" the president whether some comments he had just heard him utter might be treated as "on the record," TR exploded.

"Turning savagely upon Curtis," a witness remembered, "Colonel Roosevelt literally roared his response, demanding that not a word of what had been said should be printed," adding that "if Curtis dared to disregard that order, he, Roosevelt, would repudiate the story within twenty-four hours."[57]

On yet another occasion, William Bayard Hale, Washington bureau chief of the *New York Times*, published an article about William Randolph Hearst's alleged, unsavory ties to railroad tycoon E. H. Harriman—based on material relayed to Hale off the record by TR. Hearst sued the *Times* for libel, demanding $500,000. To protect his status as an unnamed source, Roosevelt had to endure the indignity of being deposed in the White House by the *Times*' defense attorney.[58] Yet later, TR initiated a libel action of his own against another press foe, Pulitzer's *New York World*, going so far as to brand Pulitzer "wantonly and wickedly . . . guilty." The ensuing lawsuit was destined to end in a dismissal; it remained almost impossible to win such cases.[59]

Such episodes did little to cool the president's feverish efforts to keep his name before the public. It was as if he expected to appear on page one of every paper in the country every day. And, often enough, the dailies gratified his ambition. He made it easy for them. "No President ever lived on better terms with the newspaper men than Roosevelt," remarked Washington correspondent Gus J. Karger of the *Cincinnati Times-Star*. ". . . Roosevelt of all the Presidents best understood the uses of publicity. He had a genius for it."[60] The resulting torrent of news helped both the press and the president.

Aside from granting unheard-of access, Roosevelt remained unbeatably quotable when he spoke on the record, displaying a knack for introducing catchphrases that struck a chord with the public. His presidency, for example, provided a "bully pulpit," and when he toured the country, he made "swings around the circle." Reformers who wanted to break up big business were "trustbusters," but do-gooders were "goo-goos," and radicals, part of the "lunatic fringe." TR vowed to "speak softly and carry a big stick" and live a "strenuous life." He would offer the people "a Square Deal" (though Lincoln Steffens took credit for coining that particular slogan).[61] And when TR tried to regain the office in 1912, he threw his "hat in the ring." These Rooseveltisms entered the national vernacular, along with the popular "Teddy Bears" introduced in tribute.

To TR's further advantage, he boasted a face made for caricature: squinting eyes adorned by thick pince-nez glasses; a drooping, walrus-size mustache; a "big, pugnacious nose;" and "a double row of glittering teeth" he loved to bare, gnash, and, during public speeches, loudly click.[62] Lampoonists made him their favorite subject, often depicting him grinning demonically, wearing a broad-brimmed cowboy hat, and wielding an emblematic big stick. Not since Lincoln had a president inspired so many illustrated satires in the press. To the "Dean of American Cartoonists," John T. McCutcheon of the *Chicago Tribune*, Roosevelt proved "an inexhaustible Golconda of inspiration."[63] Although more cartoons mocked TR than lauded him, all of them contributed to making his visage the best-known in the nation, and to his admirers, an emblem of progressive-minded energy.

As spot photography grew into a form of journalism, too, TR seized every chance to create memorable photo opportunities—and sometimes delayed events until lensmen were on hand to record them. When an AP photographer, for example, failed to appear for the signing of his annual Thanksgiving proclamation, Roosevelt simply postponed it until a lensman could be dispatched. When he finally arrived, TR abruptly left a meeting with Secretary of State John Hay to pose at the delayed ceremony. An eyewitness cited the incident as an example of Roosevelt's considerate behavior toward the press, but the delay served TR equally well. Why, after all, sign a Thanksgiving proclamation if the nation's biggest wire service could not be on hand to immortalize it? One iconic photograph showing TR astride a horse leaping over a fence is actually the second of two takes; when the photographer failed to capture his first jump, the president was more than willing to restage it for the camera. On the other hand, TR banned photographs of him playing tennis on the White House courts; voters, he feared, might find that particular form of exercise effete.[64]

Journalists often traveled with the president on his whirlwind tours, doggedly reporting his speeches, but found it understandably hard to explain in words the hypnotic impact TR exerted on audiences. In truth, Roosevelt had a high-pitched staccato voice and a highbrow accent, as the few surviving recordings made late in his life reveal. Such deficiencies mattered little in the era before radio and talking pictures. The earliest newsreels of Roosevelt orating in public show him almost perilously leaning forward from speakers' platforms toward his audiences, pounding his fist into his palm for emphasis. The crowds appear enthralled. Not even faded celluloid can mask the burning charisma.

Being highly quotable and artistically inspiring never provided sufficient reward for the insatiable TR. So he pioneered additional techniques to keep his name dominant before the public. From Roosevelt came "feelers" to gauge press interest in forthcoming news; "leaks" to advance information without attribution; "trial balloons" to float policy initiatives in order to test their viability with the public; and the novel ploy of "swamping" or "blanketing" the press with diversionary stories to deflect attention from bad news. It was TR who developed the art of dropping major news on Sunday afternoons to make sure he dominated newsprint on the first morning of the workweek. Once, learning that Charles Evans Hughes was to declare his candidacy for the Republican nomination to succeed him, the president undercut the New York governor by issuing a message to Congress that same day. Of course, the White House story received wider coverage. Reporters later asked Roosevelt if he had not timed his own announcement simply to "swamp" the opposition, but TR merely shrugged: "If Hughes is going to play the game, he must learn the tricks."[65] Roosevelt not only learned the tricks; he invented them. Isaac Marcosson of *World's Work* judged the president "the master press agent of all time."[66]

Although critics like H. L. Mencken of the *Baltimore Sun* assailed Roosevelt for "facile and meaningless banzais," TR was never just about hype.[67] His first term produced a formidable list of accomplishments. He helped settle a potentially crippling national coal strike, curtailed the railroad monopoly, strengthened the Interstate Commerce Commission, busted the beef trust, and dedicated Yellowstone National Park as the crowning jewel of his campaign to preserve the natural environment. By the time Roosevelt stood for election in his own right in 1904, his victory was widely regarded as an inevitability. "The personality of President Roosevelt was the leading issue," noted the English newspapers.[68] If such was the case, the American public registered its firm admiration. TR won 56 percent of the popular vote that year and swamped his Democratic opponent, Alton B. Parker, in the electoral college.

On election night itself, as returns pointed to his big victory, Roosevelt strode into the press room clutching a statement he wished Charles A. Boynton of the AP to rush out on the wires. It declared that the president would under no circumstances stand for a third term in 1908. Though it was clearly "a great story," Boynton allowed his affection for TR to overcome his "news sense." He turned to Roosevelt and "pleaded with tears in his eyes that the declaration not be issued. But the pleading was of no avail." The "third-term pronouncement" went out via the AP wire, and as Frederick Essary remembered, it "plagued Colonel Roosevelt to his dying day."[69]

In an equally bracing second term, TR continued to find precedent-setting ways to make news—along with unexpected causes to champion. For all his availability to reporters, TR also seized occasional opportunities to bypass them entirely and write for the press himself. He did so in 1907 after developing an almost obsessive distaste for the genre of sentimental nature-writing. Roosevelt and fellow realists loathed literary works that anthropomorphized animals—such as Jack London's popular *Call of the Wild*, which made a hero of the dog Buck. As far as TR was concerned, wild beasts existed solely to supply food and sport for humans. As if he did not already have a sufficiency of causes to promote, the president embraced the Darwinian countermovement led by naturalist John Burroughs. In a cudgel of a magazine article denouncing "'Uncle Remus' wolves" and "story-book beasts," TR damned the "Nature Fakers" as "yellow journalists of the woods."[70]

The following year, in the wake of a fierce exposé of alleged Senate corruption by the Hearst chain, coupled with reports that *McClure's Magazine* was about to lose some of its vaunted writers to rival publications, TR produced an even bigger surprise. At the annual Gridiron Club dinner in Washington, he unleashed a speech castigating investigative journalism as a whole for its excessive focus on negativity. Only a man of Roosevelt's pugnacious self-confidence would have directed such a lecture to newspapermen who had served his cause so well, and at their own private lair. (Despite a name that conjures up an association with football, the Gridiron Club is a gathering place for leading capital journalists. Its annual dinner had been attracting off-the-record presidential orations since the days of Benjamin Harrison.)

In his blunt March 17, 1906, address, Roosevelt dramatically broke ranks with his reform brethren in the press, likening the investigative journalist to "the Man with the Muck-rake" in John Bunyan's novel *Pilgrim's Progress*, "who could look no way but downward." The modern muckraker, he declared in his ferocious attack, focused "only on that which is vile and debasing," providing "not an incitement to good, but one of the most potent forces of evil."[71] This was the first time the "muck-rake" label had been attached to the journalistic crusaders, and TR did not deploy it as a compliment.

"Hysterical sensationalism," Roosevelt lectured his audience that night, "is the very poorest weapon wherewith to fight for lasting righteousness. The men who, with stern sobriety and truth, assail the many evils of our time, whether in the public press, or in magazines, or in books, are the leaders and allies of all engaged in the work for social and political betterment. But if they give good reason for distrust of what they say, if they chill the ardor of those who demand truth as a primary virtue, they thereby betray the good cause, and play into the hands of the very men against whom they are nominally at war."[72] It was TR's six-year-old *Century Magazine* argument revived and repurposed, this time directed more furiously than ever against those he labeled "the wild agitators against the entire existing order."[73]

Once again, mitigating circumstances may have inspired the startling retrenchment. Above all, TR meant his remarks as an indictment of one particular writer: David Graham Phillips, commissioned to produce the "Treason of the Senate" series for the Hearst chain's newly acquired magazine *The Cosmopolitan*. To the president's further chagrin, the opening article muddied his longtime ally Senator Chauncey Depew of New York, who could trace his record of public service back to the Civil War. But the Gridiron outburst served a corollary political purpose as well, distancing Roosevelt from *McClure's* increasingly radical point of view.

Whatever its true motives, the oration terminated TR's once-intimate working relationship with the cadre of journalists who had so reliably provided ballast for his early initiatives. *New York Times* correspondent Charles Willis Thompson, a Gridiron member on hand for the stem-winder, thought the president not only added the new word "muckraker" to the language that night but effectively "smashed muckraking as an industry."[74]

Lincoln Steffens could only agree. "Well," Steffens sourly greeted Roosevelt the next morning at the White House, "you have put an end to all these journalistic investigations that have made you." To Steffens, "T. R. had called the close of a chapter."[75]

Roosevelt not only ended the "chapter"; in typically aggressive fashion he provided his own epilogue. Realizing his off-the-record speech had pleased many of the reporters who heard it at the Gridiron Club, he promptly found another venue at which to deliver it again: the cornerstone-laying for a new congressional office building on April 14. For good measure, he saw to its publication in *Putnam's Magazine*. A defiant TR declared in an appendix to the printed text, "Five months have gone by since I made this speech. . . . I believe more strongly than ever, if that is possible, in all that I have therein said."[76]

Little changed inside the busy White House press room during Roosevelt's second term, not even when Charles Willis Thompson jumped from the mildly critical *New York Times* to Pulitzer's violently anti-TR *New York World*—during a period the latter paper was "trying to convince its readers that [TR] had gone mad and was headed straight for an insane asylum." Valuing his friendship with Thompson more than he nursed hatred for the reporter's new employer, TR continued to provide him with "the most confidential revelations."[77] Besides, as David Barry put it, Roosevelt knew "that editorial articles do not mold public opinion now as they did in the days of Horace Greeley."[78]

The *Times*' new Washington bureau chief, Oscar King Davis, believed similarly and forged an especially close, on-the-ground relationship with the president. TR called his new friend "O.K." and granted him wide access. King first endeared himself to Roosevelt by defending him against belated charges that his brother-in-law had profited from the earlier U.S. purchase of land for the Panama Canal. In the midst of this "hot controversy," Davis became "the only newspaperman to take up the President's challenge for an examination" of the documents relating to the sale.[79] Though the originals proved unobtainable, Davis did manage to secure convincing-enough evidence of TR's honest dealings. The resulting *Times* exclusive proved so thorough an exoneration that Whitelaw Reid, publisher of the rival *New York Tribune* who was then serving as American ambassador to Great Britain, "reorganized his Washington bureau" in response. (Oscar Davis was already a favorite of his own boss, *Times* publisher Adolph Ochs, who had given him a gold watch in recognition of his work.)[80]

Davis acknowledged that the Panama papers affair "helped my relations with the White House so much that within the next twelve days I had nine stories from the President." Although Ochs and the *Times* continued "constantly criticizing Mr. Roosevelt editorially, and steadily opposing many of his policies," TR remained "eager to get in its news columns anything from or about him." Roosevelt's "keen understanding of publicity values," Davis believed, "made him infinitely prefer the news columns to the editorial page." Echoing Barry, he said of TR: "He would rather have one column of news a week than a page of editorials a day." In turn, notwithstanding its editorial opposition, the *Times* believed that "anything the President said, or did, that emanated from him, was worth printing."[81]

Davis earned access beyond the now-traditional midday shave. "I had found that the evening hour, when he signed the day's mail, was by far the best time to see him. He would come back to the Executive offices directly from his exercise, clear up his desk, and then go over to 'the big house' for dinner." Seeing him "two to three times a week, for private talks," Davis marveled at TR's ability to multitask: "He had amazing facility for carrying on conversation while he was going over the mail. He would glance over a letter, make an addition or alteration with his pen, and sign his name at the same time that he was keeping up a steady fire of talk about whatever subject happened to be under discussion."[82]

Davis's detailed recollections not only describe the perils and rewards of news-gathering at the highest levels, but suggest that TR's methods for dealing with reporters had changed little since his days as governor—or even New York City police commissioner. "Mr. Roosevelt was a great news-maker and a great news-giver," Davis attested. "At the same time he was a stickler for the exact proprieties in handling news that came from him. When he gave his confidence to a correspondent, he gave it completely, and trusted to the correspondent's judgment and sense of propriety as to the use that was made of it. I have had many confidential talks with him, and doubt if there were half a dozen times when he uttered any word of caution as to the use to be made of what he had said."[83]

As Davis concluded: "The life of a Washington correspondent who was on terms of confidence at the White House in those days was always full of interest and activity. You might have an hour with the President, and talk all around the horizon, politics, diplomatic affairs, military, naval or congressional situation, money trust, labor, undesirable citizens, or what not, and yet not get a word out of it all that you could write that day. Then, within a week, something might happen that would be trivial and unimportant to one who had not had such a talk with the President, but which furnished a good story to one who did."[84]

In this assessment, Davis unknowingly found himself in agreement with "Pitchfork Ben" Tillman, the racist South Carolina senator who had earlier responded so sickeningly to TR's dinner with Booker T. Washington. "I tell you in all seriousness," Tillman railed on the Senate floor in mid-January 1906, "that Theodore Roosevelt owes more of his success as a public man to the newspaper men of this country than any other one instrumentality. . . . Speaking allegorically, the actual condition at the White House has been for many, many months that of a quack doctor who has certain pills which he wishes to prescribe for the public. The newspapers have been the spoon."[85]

After Roosevelt had advocated and signed both the 1906 Pure Food and Drug Act and the Meat Inspection Act, and further championed the conservation of public lands; after he had launched construction of the Panama Canal, extended the reach of the Monroe Doctrine to authorize U.S. military intervention anywhere in the world, and negotiated the end of the Russo-Japanese War—for which he earned the Nobel Peace Prize—journalists at first doubted he would voluntarily surrender the White House in 1908, notwithstanding his earlier pledge. He had discarded so many other traditions that the long-standing two-term limit (and his own vow not to run) seemed almost irrelevant. Yet Roosevelt confounded expectations once again and urged that the Republican nomination go instead to his handpicked successor, Secretary of War William Howard Taft.

In November, Taft handily defeated William Jennings Bryan and became the twenty-seventh president. Although only a few months remained in his presidency, Roosevelt could not resist a final effort to do battle with the one form of journalism he had been unable to cajole or conquer: the sensationalist "yellow" press. With the charges of corruption surrounding the Panama Canal venture still unresolved, a seething TR sent a lengthy special message to Congress in mid-December 1908 demanding that the attorney general prosecute Joseph Pulitzer and the *New York World* for what the lame duck president considered slander against both himself and the entire nation. What followed was as venomous attack as any president had ever unleashed publicly against any journalist. TR declared it "a high national duty to bring to justice this vilifier of the American people, this man who wantonly and wickedly and without one shadow of justification seeks to blacken the character of reputable private citizens and to convict the Government of his own country in the eyes of the civilized world."[86]

After a lifetime of fighting corruption, TR had now reached the conclusion that the "most corrupt financiers, the most corrupt politicians are no greater menace to this country than the newspaper men of the type I have . . . discussed. Whether they belong to the yellow press or to the purchased press, whatever may be the stimulating cause of their slanderous mendacity . . . matter but little. In any event they represent one of the potent forces for evil in the community."[87]

A defiant Pulitzer responded in kind with a stinging editorial rebuke titled "The Persecution of the Press," in which he insisted that no president could "muzzle the World." As the publisher further warned: "The persecution, if it succeeds, will place every newspaper in the country . . . completely at the mercy of any autocratic, vainglorious president who is willing to prostitute his authority for the glorification of his personal malice."[88] Not since the presidencies of Adams and Lincoln has such battle-lines been drawn.

Although a New York-based grand jury eventually issued a fourteen-count libel indictment against Pulitzer, the charge rested on an absurd technicality:

that in mailing copies of the *World* to West Point, Pulitzer had violated a century-old federal law that protected "fortifications" from "malicious injury." The flawed case languished for two years, until the U.S. Supreme Court ruled unanimously in 1911 that, notwithstanding Roosevelt's fury, the government had no case against Joseph Pulitzer.

By then, the ex-president, seemingly condemned to retirement far too early, had grown more frustrated by his party's seeming retrenchment than by the press's perceived outrages.

Roosevelt did not stay idle for long. After a prolonged African safari and European tour (widely publicized even though TR denied a request from the AP to assign a reporter to the voyage), he returned home in 1910 to a hero's welcome. He had already soured on Taft. As TR saw matters, his successor had abandoned progressive principles and now threatened to unravel his record of accomplishments.

In 1912, Roosevelt challenged Taft for the Republican nomination. Following a series of unprecedented but indecisive primary election contests, TR fell short at the national convention. His flair for drama undiminished, he and his supporters simply staged a convention of their own, from which TR emerged as the Progressive (or "Bull Moose") Party candidate, launching the most formidable third-party presidential run in history.[89] The effort provoked predictable editorial attacks—and worse. The *New York Times* charged that "the Colonel or his friends are attempting to take by disorderly methods the property of another." And when Roosevelt agreed to a contemptible deal to exclude black Southern delegates from the Bull Moose gathering just to placate white ones, the *Times* reacted with further invective: "What Mr. Lincoln would say about this can be imagined but not expressed; but the Reincarnated should have pondered long and seriously before determining thus to cut up by the roots the men who have been so loyal and useful to him all these years."[90] TR may have told several reporters that editorials mattered less to him than news items, but the *Times* opinion pieces surely hurt him badly.

They marked only one discouraging element in what proved a brutal campaign. At one point during the race, TR felt compelled to file criminal and civil libel actions against a small Michigan newspaper called the *Iron Ore*, which claimed that he "lies and curses in a most disgusting way" and "gets drunk, too, and that not infrequently."[91] Not for another year did Roosevelt prevail in the case—earning all of six cents in the symbolic judgment, roughly a refund on the cost of a single copy of the paper.

"Any man familiar with public life realizes the foul gossip which ripples just under the surface about almost every public man," he said in trying to justify the effort, "and especially about every President. It is only occasionally printed in reputable papers and set forth in explicit form; but it is hinted at in the press and set forth with circumstantial mendacity in private; and if left unrefuted until after the man's death it lasts as a stain which is then too late to remove."[92]

TR did find joy on the campaign trail, especially from traveling again with a train full of adoring reporters. To help them separate repetition from real news (and get some rest, which he seldom needed himself), Roosevelt thoughtfully advised the correspondents in advance whenever he was merely to repeat "the usual thing" at one of his trackside talks, and alerted them when they had "better be on the job" because he had "some new stuff" to say. Among the crew was a newsreel cameraman whom TR nicknamed "Movie," and for whose staged productions he emoted with "the most furious gesticulation."[93] Precisely how many people saw these primitive silents no one quite knows. A surviving clip filmed at his Sagamore Hill estate that summer showed a surprisingly bloated TR doing paperwork outdoors and riding his horse.

Roosevelt could still be tough on perceived transgressors. When a rookie correspondent jokingly asked him at Sagamore Hill, "Going to vote the Democratic ticket on election day, Colonel?" Roosevelt replied, his eyes ablaze: "I have come here to answer any sensible questions that may be put to me, but I have not come here to answer any idiotic questions." Then he walked out of a group news session. It reconvened later without the offending reporter. "I felt creepy as soon as I saw him," TR told the AP's Lucius Curtis of the ostracized offender. "I knew right away he didn't have the Oyster Bay atmosphere."[94]

"Spirits soared" when the Roosevelt entourage at last headed home from a final Southern swing. On the last lap, after the candidate had retreated to his private car for the night, one of the reporters "assumed the Colonel's voice and manner, imitated his gestures," and launched into a dead-on impersonation of one of TR's "stock speeches." After the correspondents laughed "uproariously," another journalist tried out his own Roosevelt imitation, followed by a third, then a fourth. Suddenly, TR emerged from his compartment, wagged his finger at the journalists in mock fury, then "crowned the performance by giving a speech in imitation of himself . . . a screamingly funny burlesque of his own style."[95]

Good cheer notwithstanding, Roosevelt went down to defeat on Election Day 1912—losing to Democrat Woodrow Wilson, with Taft running a distant third—but not before inspiring a new chapter in his already legendary life story. Just before entering a Milwaukee venue for an October 12 campaign appearance, Roosevelt came under attack by a deranged gunman. The would-be assassin's bullet crashed into Roosevelt's chest, but not before passing through both an eyeglass case and the thick manuscript folded inside his pocket in readiness for that day's oration. Although blood began trickling through his topcoat, TR rejected entreaties that he seek immediate medical attention, insisting, "I will deliver this speech or die, one or the other."[96] Roosevelt made it through the event and only reluctantly checked into a hospital afterward. The bullet would remain lodged in his body for the rest of his life—a memento of the last major press story TR generated before losing his comeback bid.

Roosevelt did find himself embroiled in one final battle with the press during his forced retirement: defending himself in the spring of 1915 against a libel suit, this time brought against *him* by a political boss he had criticized as corrupt. The party official who had felt TR's sting was William Barnes, grandson of the onetime newspaper editor (and political leader) Thurlow Weed, an Albany powerhouse known in Abraham Lincoln's day as the "Wizard of the Lobby." Roosevelt had accused Barnes of assembling an "invisible government" based on an "alliance between crooked business and crooked politics."[97]

For weeks, as the trial dragged on in Syracuse, New York, his allies feared TR might lose the case and suffer yet another public humiliation. But once he took the witness stand and began playing to the jury as if it were a crowd attending one of his old-time political rallies—testifying for more than thirty-five hours spread over eight days—Roosevelt turned the tide. In the end, the jury not only found for the former president but asked the judge if they could award a financial judgment to the defendant instead of the plaintiffs. It was a pyrrhic victory; the man who had once jousted with key Washington correspondents from the barber's chair in the White House ended his long relationship with the press trying to impress regional reporters outside an upstate New York courtroom.

It has been said that TR ranked as but a near-great president because no major crisis ever arose during his tenure to truly test his enormous talent and indomitable will. Oscar King Davis found the courage to ask him, a few years after he left the White House, what did Roosevelt himself consider "his greatest accomplishment"?

"The Panama Canal, of course," came the swift reply. "It is the greatest fact in my career. Don't you think so?"

Davis begged to differ. His choice was "the example you have set to youth." By building himself from a sickly physical weakling into "the great burly man that you are to-day," TR had come to exemplify, Davis believed, "self-reliance and hard work."

TR shot back that he was really "just an ordinary man." He was "about average" in most things, "a little under" average in others. If there was anything that set him apart, he argued, it was his determination to stick to a decision once made. His critics might regard him as prone to "go off half-cocked." But had he not stayed the course on the Panama Canal, America might have forfeited its dominant position in global trade, gone undefended against future attack from foreign enemies, and at the very least lost its influence among world powers. He would stick with the canal as his greatest achievement, perhaps hoping, even knowing, that Davis would one day quote him in an article or a book for the record—as he did.[98]

TR enjoyed bantering about his legacy, but what would he do next? He was not yet fifty-five. Oscar King Davis and his boss, *New York Times* editor Carr Van Anda, thought they had an answer: the perfect post-presidential career move for this still-energetic, still-ambitious man. TR had already signed a contract to serve as associate editor of and contributor to the reform-minded New York weekly *The Outlook*. "I believe in the kind of American journalism for which the Outlook stands," Roosevelt had declared. It was "as far removed as the poles from the apostles of that hideous yellow journalism which makes a cult of the mendacious, the sensational, and the inane."[99]

But Van Anda and Davis believed the assignment would not prove challenging enough to occupy the former president's far-flung attention. Roosevelt, they argued, should get even *more* involved with journalism: he should become editor of some daily newspaper—and several New York journals might well be on the market, ripe for revival. Listening to the suggestion during a barber's hour at home one day, TR burst out laughing, leapt from his armchair in the old manner, waved his shaving towel in the air, and cried out, "I couldn't edit a paper. It's ridiculous." For one thing, he was under contract to *The Outlook*; and besides, he considered himself only a fair-to-middling writer. Davis reminded him that Horace Greeley had been no writer, either. He had simply attracted great writers and directed them to express his own views. TR could do precisely the same; think of how many able journalists remained in his thrall.

No, TR continued to insist: “I want to preach. I have a good many sermons in me that I want to deliver, and the ‘Outlook’ will furnish me with a bully pulpit.”

Over the years, as prolific as ever, he would write a staggering 190 articles for the magazine—as well as contributions to other publications, for which he amassed a small fortune.[100]

Only late in his abbreviated life—he would succumb to an embolism at age sixty in 1919—did TR admit of the hastily discarded idea of becoming the first ex-president to serve as a full-time newspaper editor: “It would have been great fun.”[101]

7

WOODROW WILSON

As one veteran Washington correspondent observed, the task of shifting attention from the Roosevelt to the Wilson eras was like transferring "from a foundry into a convent." To put it mildly, the press felt a "distinct change of air."[1]

"No two occupants of the White House ever expressed such extremes of personality and point of view," explained *Saturday Evening Post* editor Isaac F. Marcosson. Roosevelt was "all animation . . . the master press agent of all time . . . the most accessible and approachable of all Presidents"—and one from whom "flowed an almost incessant stream of opinion about every conceivable subject." Wilson, by contrast, was "precise, dignified, agreeable" and, unlike TR, both "calm" and "imperturbable."[2]

Accustomed to being entertained as well as briefed, the press found Wilson "cold and remote."[3] As *Baltimore Sun* reporter J. Frederick Essary expressed it, the new president seemed "impartial" yet "impersonal."[4] William Howard Taft, Wilson's immediate predecessor, had "tried to be everybody's friend, and as usual in such cases," did not succeed "in fully pleasing anybody."[5] Wilson decided not to try at all.

Journalists seemed especially to resent Wilson's formality. Although, like Roosevelt, Wilson often "talked much," he would never dream of doing so before journalists in such informal settings as a "barber's hour." Isaac Marcosson noted of the former educator, "He never quite forgets that he is a professional historian and the writer of history does not like a crowd"—least of all a crowd that peppered him with questions.[6]

Nor was Wilson willing to ruminate on issues he had not thoroughly studied, answering one premature inquiry: "My mind is to let on that subject," a response unimaginable from a predecessor so given to spontaneity. Otherwise, "Mr. Wilson met every query with precise and ready response," Isaac Marcosson acknowledged. While TR allowed few interviewers to conduct genuine interviews, drowning out questions with an "avalanche of speech" during which "no one could get in a word edge-wise," Wilson pondered questions carefully, often ruminating aloud on the pros and cons of each topic.[7]

This Socratic style only irked reporters further. While claiming to keep "strictly to the truth," Charles Thompson observed, Wilson often stated things "as to give an opposite impression." The president's "Jesuitical" approach "made things difficult" for journalists "accustomed, from their daily experience with public men, to expect perfect frankness." Almost expecting to be misled, those who covered Wilson stayed "on their guard; and whenever he told them anything, they did not accept it without first turning it inside out to see what hidden counter-meaning might lie in it."[8] Unable or unwilling to charm reporters, Wilson remained under close scrutiny, if not outright suspicion.

Wilson reciprocated with a condescending tolerance that discouraged close professional, much less personal, relationships. All he would admit of the press—and somewhat grudgingly—is that "without thinking too highly of newspapermen, I do realize that they are men who, when you get close to them, can understand more things in five minutes than most other men can understand in half an hour."[9] Those sentiments came at the opening of a 1912 speech to the New York Press Club, and may have constituted what Wilson believed would pass for a joke. Long a prolific freelance writer, Wilson was himself a member of the Press Club, a circumstance that failed to persuade journalists that he was one of them.[10]

In fact, testified *Baltimore Sun* correspondent Frederick Essary, "President Wilson entertained a curious prejudice against the press as a whole. Although he appointed more newspaper men to high public office during his two administrations than did any of his predecessors, he had a feeling that most American journals were hostile to him." Essary could not explain the president's "prejudice against the profession." But he speculated that it arose from a lifetime of aversion to any kind of public exposure.[11] Ultimately it encouraged the reporters' prejudice against the president. Wilson could never convince them, as he once tried assuring the Press Club, that he "like[d] human beings." Wilson not only resisted advice and guidance, recalled Charles W. Thompson of the *New York Times*, "he did not desire information."[12]

Like TR the author of books, articles, and an endless stream of letters to the editor, Wilson—unlike Roosevelt—came of age in the cloister of academia, not the maelstrom of politics. Not that Wilson's years as a college official lacked for news-generating drama. His bold but unsuccessful efforts to transform campus life at Princeton attracted broad coverage outside the arena of higher education. While the barrage of newspaper accounts made him a celebrity, it failed to impress his Princeton trustees, and may have hardened him against self-promotion.

Again like Roosevelt, Wilson particularly bristled at coverage of his family. A report unfavorably comparing one of his wife's first White House receptions to the dazzling soirées hosted by previous First Lady Nellie Taft, "wounded" Mrs. Wilson so deeply that "she wept over it," infuriating her husband. Articles about their three unmarried daughters "irritated" Wilson even more; one "so enraged him" that he confided that "if he could reach him, he would thrash the writer with his own hands."[13]

That was not the only "thrashing" this unlikely pugilist threatened against a journalist. Soon after his election as president in 1912, Wilson took his family on what he hoped would be a press-free vacation to Bermuda. There, reporters instead hounded him. One day, a photographer ignored Wilson's admonitions against taking informal pictures of his daughter Jessie and snapped the young woman astride a bicycle. His face turning "the color of a strawberry," the president-elect lunged toward the photographer, stopping short only when he imagined a headline blaring, "President Knocks Down Cameraman." But he could not restrain himself from blurting out: "You're no gentleman! I want to give you the worst thrashing you ever had in your life; and what's more, I'm perfectly able to do it."[14] Only because writers did not consider photographers to be members of their press fraternity did journalists covering the getaway withhold potentially damaging reports of the flare-up.

Wilson's youngest daughter and future biographer, Eleanor, convinced herself that her father's protective attitude toward the family injured his overall standing with the press. "Father was very courteous and patient" when questioned by reporters on public issues, she insisted, "but he resented almost fiercely the attempts to pry into family affairs and tried to protect us as much as he could. I have always believed that the first rumors of his 'aloofness' and 'unfriendliness' were the result of his annoyance at this first onslaught against us.

The newspaper people could not understand the sensitive shyness and delicacy which were an essential part of his character."[15]

Nursing his grievances, Wilson spent the next eight years holding himself aloof from most newspapermen "as individuals." On the other hand, he made history by hosting the first regular White House news conferences, although Frederick Essary complained that he "abandoned" them "as soon as he could find a suitable pretext."[16] Essary failed to mention that the "pretext" was World War I.

By virtue of ancestry alone, Wilson should have established an easygoing camaraderie with the press, for political journalism was in his DNA. Although his paternal grandfather, James Wilson, died before the future president was born, he had notably worked as a young printer for William Duane's pro-Thomas Jefferson mouthpiece, the *Philadelphia Aurora*. Eventually James rose to the editorship of that boisterous paper and even named his firstborn son for its publisher: William Duane Wilson. Later in life, Grandfather Wilson ran both the *Western Herald* and the *Pennsylvania Advocate*, and pioneered the family tradition in politics by serving as a state legislator. As for young William Duane Wilson, he grew up to become publisher of the *Chicago Tribune*.

The youngest of James's ten children, Woodrow Wilson's father, Joseph Ruggles Wilson, became a theologian, but maintained the family's link to journalism by serving eleven years as editor of the *North Carolina Presbyterian*. In turn, his son Joseph Jr., Woodrow's younger brother, became a newspaperman, too. And in his own undergraduate days at Princeton, Woodrow himself served as managing editor of the college paper, the *Princetonian*, going on to contribute articles to the *New York Evening Post*, *Century Magazine*, and the *Atlantic Monthly*. "I could wish to be a journalist myself if such a place were open to me," he confided to a friend soon after his graduation.[17] Yet in his own attitudes, Woodrow more closely resembled the clergymen who also populated both branches of his family tree.

Geography played as central a role as genealogy in molding the young man's attitudes. The future president, born in Virginia to slave-owning parents in 1856, remained culturally a Southerner. His attitude on race could be traced to his upbringing in Augusta, Georgia, and Columbia, South Carolina—the latter, a town once battered into submission by General Sherman. Wilson was only four years old when the Civil War began, but he long remembered overhearing adults angrily greeting the news of Lincoln's 1860 election with vows of secession. Wilson accepted Union victory but clung to a nostalgic affection for his Confederate heritage and an ineluctable belief in white supremacy.

Abandoning an early foray into the legal profession for a career in higher education, Wilson rose quickly and by age forty-five was serving as president of Princeton. There, he kept a wary eye on press overreach. In 1906, just weeks after TR famously excoriated runaway muckrakers at the Gridiron Club, Wilson similarly admonished journalism students at Princeton to avoid telling falsehoods, "a habit into which many newspapers have fallen."[18] For a time, like John Adams a century earlier, Wilson naively embraced the idea of creating a national newspaper immune from partisan and commercial pressures—and presumably reluctant to question reformers like himself.

In 1910, at the urging of George Harvey, the publisher of *Harper's Weekly*, Wilson ran for governor of New Jersey as an un-bossed Democrat.[19] Although a novice in politics, Wilson was an experienced hand at the kind of public oratory he had long deployed to hold the attention of restless undergraduates. He proved equally mesmerizing on the political stump. Journalist A. R. Groh, who observed Wilson on the campaign trail that fall, dubbed him nothing less than "the most remarkable speaker I ever heard."[20] Also hearing him for the first time that year, onetime muckraker Ray Stannard Baker exulted, "I felt that here was the kind of thinking statesman the country needed and could trust."[21] Newspaper caricatures might mock the bespectacled, lantern-jawed candidate as a stern schoolmaster attired in a billowing cap and gown, but his professorial image proved an appealing contrast to that of his scandal-scarred Republican foe. The press in New Jersey as well as neighboring states flocked to support Wilson.

Not every branch of journalism fell under his spell. The labor press harbored skepticism based on Wilson's occasional criticism of union organizing. And the black press expressed suspicions aroused by what the influential *New York Age* called "the color-line that disgraced Princeton," as well as the "many public occasions" when the Southern-born Wilson allegedly "took a shot at the Negro"—although the paper provided no examples of such remarks.[22] Criticism from these sectors failed to halt Wilson's momentum but would haunt his presidency.

Wilson's resounding 1910 gubernatorial victory sparked immediate press speculation that he might seek the nation's highest office two years later. By now he had enlisted an effective lieutenant: a Jersey City–born political savant named Joseph Patrick Tumulty. Abandoning his own promising career as a state legislator, Tumulty agreed to serve as Wilson's gubernatorial (and, later, White House) chief of staff with responsibilities that included management of the press operation. They grew close: in memoranda, Wilson often addressed his aide as "my dear boy."[23]

Under Tumulty's guidance, the new governor began meeting regularly, if uneasily, with statehouse reporters. Tumulty was soon functioning not only as Wilson's "political advisor" but also as his "sounding board."[24] No doubt with Tumulty's help, Wilson scored a coveted speaking role at the quaint annual "Hobby Night" sponsored by Washington's National Press Club in 1911. There, Wilson vowed to end "privacy and concealment" in government and "drive everything into the open," a direct appeal for press support. "That is the reason why my hobby, if I have any, is the hobby of publicity," he cleverly added. "I cannot imagine anything legitimate that a man is doing that he need be afraid to talk about."[25]

Neither Wilson's pledge of transparent government nor Tumulty's back-room sagacity could lock up the 1912 Democratic presidential nod without a protracted fight for delegate support. It took forty-six exhausting roll calls before the New Jersey governor amassed the required two-thirds majority. The once-divided party nonetheless emerged well positioned to win back the White House against divided opposition from two Republicans: President William Howard Taft and ex-president Theodore Roosevelt.

Tumulty would not reign as Wilson's sole press guru that fall. To oversee campaign publicity, the party turned to North Carolina newspaper editor Josephus Daniels, who had earned notoriety by advocating for the disenfranchisement of black voters in his home state. With the aid of the nominee's own brother, *Nashville Banner* editor Joseph Wilson Jr., Daniels mounted an effort to "reach every newspaper in the country" on Wilson's behalf, with a focus on small- and medium-size dailies. "Your fight for me delights me," Wilson praised Daniels that year. "You are certainly a friend worth having."[26] As for his "kid brother," the candidate jokingly told the New York Press Club in September that "he trembled in the anticipation of what might be revealed" by his sibling, quickly adding: "But the Wilsons are discreet."[27]

Wilson presented himself in 1912 as a thoughtful progressive committed to a reform agenda, which one of his savviest new campaign advisors, editor George Creel, dubbed the "New Freedom." Some liberal journalists remained dubious. To reassure *New York Evening Post* editor Oswald Garrison Villard—grandson of abolitionist William Lloyd Garrison—Wilson had to work particularly hard.[28] Villard fretted over Wilson's white supremacist reputation, which his growing reliance on Josephus Daniels did nothing to overcome.

To Villard, Wilson pledged he would "seek to be President of the whole Nation and would know no differences of race or creed or section." Even if Congress went Democratic—owing its usual debt to Dixie—the candidate vowed that "the negroes had nothing to fear in the way of inimical legislation." Wilson offered to issue a public statement to that effect, though he gratuitously added: "I want these people to be reassured, though I have never said that I needed their support or was giving the assurances I have mentioned for the sake of obtaining it."[29] As for "these people," many remained unconvinced. As the *New York Age* put it in July, "It is perfectly clear to us that the Negro in the United States cannot support Woodrow Wilson without proving a traitor to himself and to his race."[30] Yet the official NAACP magazine, *The Crisis*, endorsed Wilson that year, while Baltimore's *Afro-American* urged its readers to abandon the party of Lincoln. The long-impoverished black voter, it argued, had been "too long on one side of the boat . . . the Democratic Party should receive his support."[31]

Further doubts about Wilson came from foreign-language newspapers widely read by the nation's swelling population of immigrant voters. Ten years earlier, in his *History of the American People*, Wilson had disdained the recent wave of immigrants from eastern and southern Europe. Now the head of the American Association of Foreign Language Newspapers reminded editors and readers alike: "No man who has an iron heart like Woodrow Wilson, and who slanders his fellowmen, because they are poor and many of them without friends when they come to this country seeking honest work and wishing to become good citizens, is fit to be President of the United States."[32] Wilson offered a professorial defense attempting to differentiate between voluntary and commercially sponsored immigration, but it failed to douse the firestorm.

Meanwhile, though the effort made him uncomfortable, Wilson tried to make himself more accessible to reporters. "They must move as I move, go where I go," he complained privately that summer to his friend (and rumored paramour) Mary Allen Hulbert Peck. "If there is anything they are not told, they will spy, must spy it out. I must be under observation without intermission. All eyes are watchful of my slightest action. I have lost all freedom of all privacy. It is all but intolerable."[33] Teddy Roosevelt, who chortled when he first heard rumors of Wilson's infidelities and refused to invoke them in the campaign, instead emphasized Wilson's bloodless image by remarking: "He can't get away from the academic manner. And that is why he doesn't get under the skin of people."[34]

Candidate Wilson found it especially difficult to embrace the latest communications technologies. Inexplicably lacking confidence in his fine speaking voice, he only reluctantly made a series of six campaign recordings in 1912. Josephus Daniels remembered that Wilson "went at it as if he was going to the stake."[35] Equally dubious about the infant medium of film, the nominee likewise had to be pushed into allowing *Pathé's Weekly* and other fledgling newsreel companies to produce silent movies of his campaign stops. In this increasingly important genre, Wilson felt himself at an enormous disadvantage to the photogenic TR. Roosevelt, Wilson candidly admitted, "appeals to their imagination; I do not. He is a real, vivid person, whom they have seen and shouted themselves hoarse over and voted for, millions strong; I am a vague, conjectural personality, more made of opinions and academic prepossessions than of human traits and red corpuscles. We shall see what will happen!"[36]

Just as he feared, Wilson at first came across on celluloid as stiff, grim, and ill at ease. He concluded the race fretting about "what the people are thinking . . . whose opinions do not get into the newspapers," confessing, "I am by no means confident."[37] Yet on Election Day, owing at least in part to the most professionally managed press operation in American campaign history, Wilson easily prevailed over his fractured opposition. Although he tallied only 42 percent of the popular ballots, he amassed 435 of the 531 electoral votes, winning forty of the forty-eight states. Less charismatic than Roosevelt he well may have been, but Wilson and not TR would be the next president. Significantly, the Wilson campaign had authorized the production of a film called *The Old Way and the New*, in which backroom, boss-controlled politics are amusingly compared to fresh appeals to small donors. At one point, an old-line Republican is shown trying to hang a politician's portrait on his wall, and falls off his settee, flat onto his face. Wilson himself does not appear in the eight-minute production, but is represented by a modern-looking election banner. A burlesque it may have been, but the film is now considered the first campaign commercial in American history.[38]

In the months leading up to his inauguration, Wilson remained on his guard with the press. When one reporter defied his arbitrary ban on speculation about cabinet appointments, pressing him on who might become attorney general, Wilson flushed with rage. "Unable to control himself," he actually "sprang out of his chair and ran around his desk," approaching the reporter and menacingly demanding, "[A]re you trying to insult me?" No, came the reply. "Only trying to get the news." To which Wilson "growled, 'You're taking the wrong way to get it.'" Correspondent Charles Willis Thompson, who observed this extraordinary scene, believed it at least confirmed that Wilson was "full of hot blood." Yet, as Thompson admitted, "For all that, people continued to talk of him as a glacial, forbidding, inhuman sort of monstrosity."[39]

"The public man who fights the daily press won't be a public man very long," Wilson had admitted early in the 1912 presidential campaign.[40]

Hewing to that conviction, the new president launched a bold and historic innovation within the first three weeks of his inauguration: the regular White House press conference. At 12:45 P.M. on March 15, 1913, Wilson strode into the Oval Office to find not the twenty to thirty correspondents he had expected for the maiden session, but a crowd four times that size. "The President's amazement was written in his face," reported the *New York Times*. Standing upright at his desk with Tumulty just behind him, Wilson told the throng that while he had intended no formal speech, he now felt obliged to offer opening remarks.

He began by proffering gratitude to the press corps: "I don't suppose any one who has entered this office has been as generously treated as I have." Then he vowed unlimited access to the White House, wanting "it understood that there were no doors to his offices, and that he was always willing and ready to see everybody." Finally, Wilson rebutted the "impression which has spread all over the country to the effect that he was prejudiced against newspaper men." Only then did he turn to questions. When the event ended, he cordially shook hands with every reporter in the room.[41]

In a story headlined "Wilson Wins Newspapermen," the pro-Wilson *Times* pronounced the event a triumph. "As he went on talking, the big hit he was making with the crowd became evident," Charles Thompson commented. "There was something so unaffected and honest about his way of talking . . . that it won everybody, despite the fact that many of the men there had become prejudiced against him"—an acknowledgment of precisely what Wilson believed.[42]

Other journalists came away with a markedly different impression. Branding Wilson's opening speech a "chill and correct performance," correspondent Edward G. Lowry observed: "There was a pause, a cool silence, and presently some one ventured a tentative question. It was answered crisply, politely, and in the fewest possible words. A pleasant time was not had by all."[43] *Trenton Evening*

Times publisher James Kerney concurred that Wilson's "very cool reserve" left the impression "that he was the best judge of what was good for the newspapers to have."[44]

As if in agreement with these dimmer assessments, the president launched his second press conference a week later by admitting his disappointment with the first. For this session, Tumulty cannily shook things up, moving the venue to the vast East Room, ostensibly to accommodate the growing number of "newspaper boys" who clamored for access, but conceivably to add grandeur to the occasion as well.[45] Here, Wilson blamed his initial performance on "the fatigue of the morning" and the fact that "I did not feel that I had anything to say." Adding, "I feel that this gathering has a degree of formality which I wish it might not have," Wilson urged reporters to treat future comments "as just between ourselves"—in other words, off the record—"because I want an opportunity to open some part of my mind to you, that you may know my point of view a little better than perhaps you have had an opportunity to know it so far."[46]

He was not done yet. "I feel that a large part of the success of public affairs depends on the newspapermen," he went on, "not so much on the editorial writers, because we can live down what they say, as upon the news writers, because the news is the atmosphere of public affairs. Unless you . . . disperse the right impressions—things go wrong." Here he echoed TR's faith in the preeminent value of news reporting. But what followed was decidedly Wilsonian—an appeal not to professionalism but to patriotism. In an evangelizing mood, Wilson implored correspondents "to write from the country in and not from Washington out"—to "help me and help everybody else just by swathing my mind and other people's minds in the atmosphere of the thought of the United States."[47]

That plea revealed a fundamental misconception about the role of the White House press corps. Washington reporters were specifically assigned to report "out" rather than write "in"—to tell the nation what the president was thinking, not the other way around.[48] Wilson magnified his skewed expectations by adding an overt warning: "If you play up, every morning, differences of opinion and predict difficulties . . . you are not so much doing an injury to an individual . . . as impeding the public business."[49] By admitting that his own success depended on journalists focusing on "good things," the rookie president ceded far too much power to the press. He would pay a steep price for confiding such vulnerability.

Wilson biographer A. Scott Berg has argued that Wilson's "witty interplay with the press" ultimately charmed many skeptical reporters.[50] Indeed, at the dozens of press sessions that followed, Wilson eventually did display a more human side. Certainly he never backed away from exposure: over the next nine months alone, he subjected himself to sixty press conferences, the following year, another sixty-eight. Although their frequency slowed to just nineteen by 1915 and trickled off altogether in the midst of war, Wilson would take questions from the White House press corps a total of 168 times during his presidency, setting expectations that would endure ever after. Yet Wilson came to regard these events as "intellectual combat" designed to test his skill at withholding, rather than sharing, information.[51] As Wilson freely admitted to reporters, "I could tell you sometimes more than I do . . . but I try to keep a grip on myself."[52]

Still, Wilson did pepper some news conferences with amusing comments. While the repartee did not rise to the level of rapier wit, it occasionally revealed a president willing to engage in lively if sometimes testy back-and-forth with his interlocutors. Asked once, for example, why he seemed willing to voice an early opinion on proposed currency legislation, he answered, "I never play with my hands under the table." When a reporter followed up by suggesting, "Well, it doesn't always do to show your hand," the president insisted, "I am perfectly willing to play with the cards face up."[53] Wilson could be tart. Pressed at one of his early news sessions to discuss ongoing Senate hearings, he replied that they were "none of my business."[54] Asked if he sympathized with House members stuck in an exhaustingly long session, he retorted, "I don't know that it's any less hard on the President than it is on Congress, but I seem to be able to stand it."[55]

At one 1914 press conference, Wilson proved virtually Lincolnesque in illustrating a point with an amusing story—an endearing habit he should have demonstrated to reporters more often. Asked that day if he had considered potential replacements for a recently deceased Supreme Court justice, Wilson replied that the premature query "reminded me of the widow who was proposed to just as soon as she reached the house after attending her husband's funeral, and she said she was sorry but a man had proposed at the grave."[56] As Ray Stannard Baker wrote regretfully: "People don't know Wilson as a story teller. He is full of them."[57]

Wilson's press conferences might be limited on any given day to but half a dozen inquiries or extended to handle fifteen or twenty. From the outset, by mutual consent, none of his responses could be published. When the agreement was quickly violated, the *New York Times*' Washington correspondent, R. V. Oulahan, had to assure Joseph Tumulty that "there shall be no further quotation of the president."[58] On or off the record, whether replying with only a terse yes or no or volunteering lengthier responses, Wilson seldom provided the definitive answers for which the press yearned. Invited in 1913 to comment on proposed Panama Canal tolls, he teased, "I had better not tell you where I began or you might guess where I am going to land." Pushed to compare his vision for antitrust legislation with "accounts in the papers" of a proposed congressional remedy, he conceded only that the draft legislation "had a strong family resemblance."[59]

To sensitive questions he might reply, "You may ask but I can't answer." In that vein, asked in 1914 if he had expressed an opinion on an upcoming immigration bill, he answered, "Very often. Not in public though."[60] Correspondent David Barry concluded that Wilson intended to "sidestep" all legitimate inquiry and treat reporters like "a class of students at Princeton."[61] Yet the feisty president never shied away from challenging what he viewed as false news. On one such occasion, he dismissed a story claiming that an important diplomat was being recalled to Washington, barking, "The whole thing was a fake." Another disputed report irked him into remarking, "I read some interesting fiction in the papers this morning." Yet another newspaper, he scolded, published "nothing but yarns" without "a word of truth in them." Asked in 1915 to comment on a *Washington Post* report that the United States might ask the pope to negotiate world peace, Wilson sneered, "I took that as one of the many ways in which the *Post* amuses itself."[62] It remained difficult to predict what might set the president off.

Several early press conferences focused on surging unrest in Mexico. With tensions growing in Europe, some journalists, including Oswald Garrison Villard, cautioned against American intervention south of the border. Wilson, who seldom encouraged advice, even from famous journalists, curtly informed Villard that his views "distressed" him.[63] Then another press celebrity, Lincoln Steffens, headed to the White House to counsel the president similarly against American involvement. But Steffens reported, "The President would not see me."[64] When the *Princeton Alumni Weekly* merely ran a mild critique of pacifism, Wilson, ever sensitive to perceived insults, canceled his three-dollar-a-year subscription.[65]

Yet when the onetime pro-Roosevelt writer Ray Stannard Baker visited Wilson in the White House for the first time that September, he found the president both "affable and frank." Added Baker, disputing most journalists of his generation: "I used to think that T. R. was often dangerously open in his conversation—but W. W. when he really gives his confidence is fully as free." Baker seemed pleased "with the man himself—his forthrightness, the sense of inner discipline he gave." The flattering article that he subsequently published, he later conceded, may have been "too enthusiastic to be objective."[66] But Baker's exclusive set a pattern: even as Wilson reduced access for Washington correspondents, he remained available for one-on-one interviews with friendly journalists like Baker, Samuel G. Blythe of the *Saturday Evening Post*, and *New York World* editor Frank I. Cobb.

Wilson's contentious relationship with the White House press corps deteriorated further once Germany declared war on France on August 3, 1914. Six weeks later, an American newspaper reported that the United States intended to "call a world congress," and, as the president carped at a September press conference, "do a lot of foolish things." Infuriated, Wilson demanded to know "who understood that, and from whom?" Receiving no reply, he exploded: "I am not as big a fool as I look, and if you will just go on the assumption that I am not a fool, it would correct a good many news items." One journalist tried assuring him, "we are wholly acting on that assumption," but Wilson angrily shot back: "This is no child's play. We may make it impossible for the United States to do the right thing by constantly saying that she thinks of silly things to do. . . . Please, do your best not to let that happen again." Only when another reporter asked the president whether the attitude of the press had otherwise been "satisfactory" did Wilson grumble, "I haven't anything to complain of." Still, he seethed that "mischief may be done without intending it."[67]

In a portent of future restrictions, Wilson confided that he was already weighing the idea of censoring cable and wireless messages. "I am consulting now with international lawyers and the Department of Justice as to what the power of the administration in that matter is," he admitted in August 1914.[68] Around this same time he first considered establishing a government "publicity bureau which would handle the real facts"—another hint of things to come—abandoning the idea only because, as he sarcastically put it, newspapers would not find "real facts . . . to their taste."[69] Wilson's blunt comments laid the foundation for the policies his administration would pursue once the United States entered the Great War.

The foreign and domestic crises of his first term notwithstanding, the longest and sharpest statement Wilson ever offered at a press conference came on March 19, 1914, when once again he flew into a fury over aggressive coverage of his family. "I am a public character for the time being," he lectured the correspondents, "but the ladies of my household are not servants of the government." Then he bristled: "I deeply resent the treatment they are receiving at the hands of the newspapers at this time. I am going to be perfectly frank with you. Take the case of my oldest daughter [Margaret] . . . constantly represented as being engaged to this, that, or the other man in different parts of the country, in some instances to men she has never even met in her life. It is a constant and intolerable annoyance. These things are printed without any attempt to verify them by communications with the White House." Honor bound "to defend the women," Wilson ended the barrage by demanding that future "rumors be checked" with White House spokesmen.[70]

One brave reporter then asked the president if correspondents could obtain transcribed copies of his statement so they might forward it to editors and encourage enforcement. Much as he wanted coverage of his daughters curtailed, Wilson wisely balked. Publication of his off-the-record rant, he sensed, might make a bad situation worse. Moreover, Wilson already seemed presciently aware of the limits of the published word. Even though he believed he had "laid my mind bare" to the press corps, he now sensed that such pleas could no longer be adequately conveyed in print. "You men see me twice a week and you know what my attitude is, and you know . . . the tones of voice in which I say things," he explained. "That could not be conveyed with the written page."[71] In this understanding, Wilson was ahead of his time. But his impassioned plea failed to inhibit press scrutiny of his family. Instead, the episode presaged a future in which presidential press conferences would rise or fall as much on appearance, tone, and attitude as on actual questions and answers.

In all, Wilson's press conferences—particularly the once- or twice-weekly scrums of 1913 and 1914—deserve reappraisal. Although many revealed Wilson at his worst—crabby, nitpicking, suspicious, and chilly—at his best, Wilson proved patient, droll, fully informed, and often informative. He might have possessed no natural gift for conducting such sessions, much less enjoying them. Yet not until FDR would Wilson's presidential news conferences be rivaled for frequency and candor.

To be sure, not all his contemporaries appreciated Wilson's occasionally abrupt way of handling journalists. Columbia University president Nicholas Murray Butler, who disliked his fellow academic from Princeton, recoiled at Wilson's peremptory way with a question. Butler wickedly described him as a man capable of proposing marriage early in the day and then responding to an afternoon inquiry about his romantic intentions by replying: "I married her at ten o'clock this morning. The incident is closed."[72]

By late 1915, with rare exceptions, so was access to Wilson. "We told him the importance of making himself clear to those who had elected him, and placed our services at his command," admitted the *Times*' Charles Willis Thompson, who wanted Wilson to continue meeting the press. "I'd do what I could," came Wilson's plaintive reply. ". . . But it's not my nature. . . . *I can't make myself over*."[73]

Wilson did continue to write both official and private letters to influential editors, telling one Chicago journalist who had published the editorial "Stand Up for the President" that "It has made my heart very warm." He allowed a few reporters to interview him in the White House, though he insisted their discussions be kept out of print. And in April 1917, yearning for "a friend to talk to," Wilson summoned Frank I. Cobb of the *New York World* to a 1:00 A.M. sit-down on war preparation.[74] Yet Wilson stubbornly declined to meet with his powerful nemesis William Randolph Hearst. And when Oswald Garrison Villard asked in 1915 for a face-to-face meeting to discuss his recent articles on military preparedness, "two requests of mine for interviews," Villard complained, ". . . were denied me."[75] A public relations innovator Woodrow Wilson may have been, but by increasingly shunning journalists, he did injury to his own causes. He seemed to take pleasure in boasting to his Princeton class reunion in mid-1914, "I have stopped reading the newspapers."[76] He did so at his peril.

Woodrow Wilson sought a second term in 1916 by arguing he had kept America out of war and notched a formidable record of domestic reforms. In his first four years alone, he pushed Congress to enact lower tariffs and replace the lost revenue with an income tax, established the Federal Trade Commission, signed the Clayton Antitrust Act, advocated for an eight-hour workday, signed a child labor law, nominated the first Jewish justice of the U.S. Supreme Court, and created the Federal Reserve System. American newspaper readers had also followed with sympathy the tragic illness and death of First Lady Ellen Wilson in 1914, and generally rejoiced at the president's remarriage to Edith Bolling Galt, a formidable widow sixteen years his junior, in December of the following year.

Yet Wilson aroused justifiable outrage from liberal journalists by turning back the clock on civil rights. Despite his 1912 pledge to do nothing to curtail African American opportunity, Wilson oversaw the resegregation of the federal bureaucracy, doing particular injury to Washingtonians of color who had slowly but steadily risen in the ranks of the civil service system.[77] Now black employees faced systematic demotions and pay cuts, along with humiliating banishment to separate dining facilities, locker rooms, and toilets at the Post Office and Treasury Departments (each run by Southern-born cabinet officers).[78] Warning that "the colored press . . . harps upon it in every issue," a disenchanted Oswald Garrison Villard, who now chaired the executive committee of the NAACP, fired off an angry protest to the president and demanded a White House meeting to discuss the new restrictions. Reminding Wilson of his 1912 pledge to place no barriers in the way of black rights, Villard charged that African American workers were now being treated "as if they were lepers to be set apart."[79]

Refusing at first to see Villard—his customary response to press critics—Wilson tried suggesting in a letter that segregation actually made African American civil servants "less likely to be discriminated against" by "rendering them more safe in their possession of office" and "exempting them from friction and criticism." Unpersuaded, Villard proposed that the White House host a formal session with the full NAACP leadership. That proved enough to secure Villard his long-sought one-on-one meeting. Hastening to Washington in October 1913, the editor berated the president until Wilson threw up his hands and claimed he was in a "cruel position." He was "at heart working for these people," he insisted, but could not risk offending the racist Southern legislators whose support he needed to pass his reform agenda on Capitol Hill. Resegregation was the ironic price Wilson agreed to pay to enact his New Freedom.[80]

Wilson offered this explanation "with shame and humiliation," Villard recalled unsympathetically. After he warned the president that his harsh policies constituted "a social blunder of the worst kind," Wilson claimed: "I see no way out. It will take a very big man to solve this thing." He was not that man. The discriminatory policies remained in place, and as Villard later acknowledged bitterly, "[N]ot one thing was done by Woodrow Wilson or his Administration to ameliorate the condition of the Negro."[81]

A year later, with what the NAACP branded as the "humiliating" and "hateful" segregation policy still in place, African American editor William Monroe Trotter somehow secured his own White House meeting with the president.[82] We may safely assume that Wilson did not know that Trotter published his *Boston Guardian* from the same building where William Lloyd Garrison had once produced the abolitionist paper the *Liberator*. The Wilson–Trotter session quickly overheated. When the editor protested the new resegregation policy, as expected, Wilson defensively replied, "If the colored people made a mistake in voting for me, they ought to correct it by voting against me." Arguing that it "takes the world generations to outlive all its prejudices," Wilson maintained that immediate integration would "hurt" African Americans "more than it would help them." Trotter tried reminding Wilson that "we are not looking for charity" but simply "equal rights as citizens." Feeling provoked, Wilson bristled, "[Y]our tone, sir, offends me," petulantly adding: "You have spoiled the whole cause for which you came." When Trotter attempted to pursue the subject further, Wilson had him ushered out of the White House.[83]

Wilson engaged white journalists more frequently that campaign season, but often no less rancorously. Addressing the Associated Press at New York's Waldorf Astoria Hotel in April 1915, he warned against news "that turns out to be falsehood," declaring, "We ought not to permit that sort of thing to use up the electrical energy of the wires, because its energy is malign."[84] The following June he tried a friendlier approach before the New York Press Club.[85] "I am sure," cheered Herbert Bayard Swope, city editor of *New York World* after that appearance, "that a few more talks, such as you made to us, will remove any doubts as to your re-election."[86]

Yet with America bitterly divided, the 1916 vote proved heart-stoppingly close. At 9:30 P.M. on election night, "a galaxy of newspaper men" converged on Wilson to share the news of his likely defeat. The president's admirers at the *New York Times* and *World* reached the same conclusion, as their early-edition headlines screamed. When his daughter phoned him the next morning to report he had somehow snared victory with late-breaking support from the West, a skeptical Wilson replied, according to Tumulty, "Tell that to the Marines!"[87] In the final count, Wilson defeated Republican Charles Evans Hughes by only 49–46 percent, and won 277 electoral votes to Hughes's 254.

The second Woodrow Wilson administration would usher in an even more fraught relationship with the press. In his initial term, Wilson had at least engaged journalists to promote his agenda. In his next, as a war president, he would not only ignore the correspondents; he would curtail their freedom to report.

When America finally went to war in 1917, Wilson entirely shut himself off from the press corps, limiting its access to news of the war's horrors, stifling criticism of American participation, arresting Socialist labor leader Eugene V. Debs and others who opposed the military draft, and flooding the press and public with government propaganda.

Even before the United States officially declared war, Wilson publicly doubted the wisdom of maintaining open communication with reporters. Labeling continued access "a difficult question," he tried explaining: "In ordinary times, when our affairs are domestic affairs, we could exercise a great deal of freedom about that, but just now . . . such excessive importance is attached to the President's opinions that a thing said offhand may have an effect that was not contemplated." Admitting that press "fiction" still made him "a little hot under the collar," he pointed out that fake news no longer reached only domestic audiences. "These impressions get to other parts of the water . . . then the foreigner says, 'Well, what in thunder is this man going to do next? Isn't he ever going to mind his own business?'"[88] Wilson offered these comments at a White House press conference on January 15, 1917. Over the next two weeks he hosted two more such sessions. Then they ceased altogether.

Instead Wilson made media history again—just as he had by inaugurating presidential news conferences four years earlier—with an April 4 executive order creating a new federal Committee on Public Information (CPI).[89] Its unprecedented mission would be twofold: first, to oversee restrictions against sensitive press coverage of the conflict; and second, to barrage both home-front and foreign audiences with agitprop villainizing the Hun along with publicity aggrandizing American virtues.[90] Never before had the government created its own official news agency, and the initiative did not lack for critics. Not even Lincoln, who imposed press crackdowns during the Civil War, had thought that the government itself should generate messaging while at the same time curtailing dissent.

To run the new CPI operation as its Civilian Chairman, Wilson tapped the handsome, cleft-chinned former newspaper editor and political supporter George Creel. The Missouri-born forty-one-year-old had grown up believing in both Lost Cause mythology and civic reform.[91] He had first heard Wilson speak at a Kansas City high school back in 1905; by 1912, Creel was working for the educator's election as president.

Since then, the art of managing public opinion had changed much. Professional public relations specialists like Ivy Lee and Edward Bernays had introduced sophisticated techniques to influence consumers.[92] In his own efforts on Wilson's behalf during the 1916 race, Creel had mimicked one of their innovations—the celebrity endorsement—by convincing one of the nation's most admired men, lifelong Republican Thomas Alva Edison, to praise Wilson publicly.[93] Like most of Wilson's backers that year, Creel hailed the president for maintaining American neutrality. In his new role as head of the CPI, Creel effortlessly transformed himself into an enthusiastic advocate for war—and for suppression as well. When America entered the conflict, Creel had made it known in his bid for a job in wartime Washington: "If a censor is to be appointed, I want to be it." The *New York Times* declared itself "unable to discover in his turbulent career . . . any evidence of the ability, the experience, or the judicial temperament required to 'gain the understanding and cooperation of the press.'"[94]

Freedom of expression did not go down without a vigorous and partly successful fight. When Congress, with Wilson's encouragement, first began considering new restrictions—"Wilson Demands Censorship," declared a *New York Times* headline in May 1917—the Hearst newspapers attacked the president for his "invasion of the rights of a free press." Equally appalled, the *Washington Post* insisted that "newspapers, to succeed, must print all the news available."[95] Congress did weigh legislation to make it a federal crime (with harsh penalties) to "print, write, or publish any disloyal, profane, scurrilous, or abusive language about the form of government of the United States," its "military or naval forces . . . or the flag."[96] This draconian bill went down to defeat, but a still-onerous, albeit softer, proposal became law by amendment.

While Creel later took credit for preventing Wilson from imposing more "autocratic" press censorship, the president went on to sign the June 1917 Espionage Act, October's Trading with the Enemy prohibition, and the May 1918 Sedition Act—the first since the John Adams era—all calculated to restrict dissent.[97] Under the espionage law alone, "false reports . . . in time of war" became punishable by twenty years in prison and a $10,000 fine.[98] Journalists did little to push back. Just as pro-Lincoln editors had once counterintuitively backed Civil War crackdowns, modern editors were soon urging Wilson to jail William Randolph Hearst, citing his allegedly "treasonable utterances" as "the strongest reason why there should be a censor."[99] Resistance to new, self-monitored suppression evaporated, and thereafter the press rarely criticized either the war abroad or government overreach at home. Even the *New York Tribune* announced that "it welcomes a sensible censorship."[100]

Although the CPI commenced its work with a small staff, it eventually attracted one hundred thousand volunteers. Creel surrounded himself with a superb leadership team, including veteran journalists and advertising men. To reach wide audiences, he also enlisted the circulation manager of *Cosmopolitan*, Carl Byoir, destined later to found one of the nation's foremost advertising agencies.[101] Attempting to prod the press into self-regulation, Creel began with a statement of principles alerting correspondents, "It will be necessary at times to keep information from our own people in order to keep it from the enemy." Leaks providing aid and comfort to Germany would be scuttled; those likely to agitate the home front would be left to patriotic editors to suppress.[102]

When editors raised concerns about this vague directive, Creel followed with a more specific eighteen-point policy guide mandating secrecy on such matters as troop movements, the arrival and departure of merchant vessels, the sites of antiaircraft positions, and the shipment of munitions. Enforcement, Creel re-emphasized, would remain "a matter for the press itself."[103] But he chillingly warned that "the term traitor is not too harsh in application to the publisher, editor, or writer who wields . . . power without full or even solemn recognition of responsibilities."[104]

Then there was the relentless CPI propaganda campaign. Among his many innovations, Creel deployed journalists to embed themselves with American combat forces overseas and report home with inspiring yarns. The war correspondents soon included Hearst byliner Damon Runyon, who provided a stirring account of New York's heroic "Lost Battalion," a multiethnic unit whose heroic survivors endured both enemy and friendly fire in the Argonne Forest.[105]

Many of the CPI's subsequent initiatives were the products of improvisation. When "Gibson Girl" illustrator Charles Dana Gibson volunteered to craft a war poster, Creel launched an entire Division of Pictorial Publicity and urged Gibson to enlist fellow artists to contribute morale-boosting graphics of their own. James Montgomery Flagg soon obliged with his iconic 1917 Uncle Sam recruiting poster "I Want You."[106] Ultimately, artists produced some two thousand different posters, some so effective that Joseph Goebbels was said to have adapted them years later for Nazi propaganda.

The CPI not only produced its own morale-boosting film documentaries, like *Pershing's Crusaders*; it recruited an army of "Four Minute Men" to deliver pro-war speeches in the nation's movie theaters during the 240-second intervals that projectionists then needed to change film reels. By war's end, 75,000 volunteer orators had delivered 755,000 such pep talks.[107] Creel also established bureaus to design magazine and newspaper ads and urge publishers to place them free of charge. A Division of Syndicate Features churned out human interest stories that reached twenty-three million readers each month. And a Department of Slides sold inspiring, projectable images to schools and churches.[108]

Most tireless of all was the Division of News, which bombarded the country's papers and wire services with mimeographed press releases (sometimes ten a day, six thousand in all), along with photos, opinion pieces, pamphlets, and leaflets designed to penetrate mainstream and specialty audiences alike. Not unimportantly, the Creel Committee also made sure President Wilson's speeches "circulated by the millions," verbatim and unchallenged.[109] The CPI augmented all this by publishing its own official bulletin, which soon swelled to thirty-six pages per issue and often boasted exclusive communiqués from the battlefront. Creel brushed off complaints from newspaper publishers that the free bulletins put them at a competitive disadvantage, and he made sure that bundles continued pouring into post offices nationwide. Circulation reached 115,000.

Meanwhile, the CPI's Foreign Section restricted information traveling in and out of the country via the wireless and cable. The unit also broadly disseminated American publications overseas, establishing reading rooms in foreign countries where patrons could peruse American newspapers and magazines. Edward Bernays, who joined the Foreign Section, strongly defended its work. "The advocacy of what we don't believe in is propaganda," he maintained. "The advocacy of what we believe in is education."[110]

"There was no part of the great war machinery that we did not touch," Creel proudly attested, "no medium of appeal that we did not employ. The printed word, the spoken word, the motion picture, the telegraph, the cable, the wireless, the poster, the sign board—all these were used in our campaign to make our own people and all the other people understand the crisis that compelled America to take arms."[111]

On the darker side, fearing a Bolshevik as well as a German threat to America, the CPI also worked with the Justice and Post Office Departments to ban "suspect" journals from the mails. These included the left-leaning *Milwaukee Journal*, the openly socialist newspaper *The Call*, and the progressive Yiddish-language *Jewish Daily Forward*. Another target was the magazine *The Masses*, whose editor, Max Eastman, was arrested and tried under the Espionage Act. Against this backdrop, Creel gave speeches to press associations around the country claiming the United States had imposed no censorship at all.[112]

Walter Lippmann of the *New Republic*, by then an advisor to Secretary of

War Newton Baker, strongly objected to this aspect of the CPI mission, worried that arbitrary crackdowns would divide "the country's articulate opinion into fanatical jingoism and fanatical pacifism." No admirer of Creel's, Lippmann tried counseling the president that censorship should "never be entrusted to anyone who is not himself tolerant, nor to anyone who is unacquainted with the long record of folly which is the history of suppression."[113]

Wilson made no effort to rein in Creel; instead, he occasionally complained that the CPI was not cracking down hard enough. When a rogue admiral boasted in print that the new Navy Air Corps might soon be capable of destroying the entire German fleet, Wilson scolded Creel, "I wonder how this 'got past' the censors?"[114] Eager to impose even further oversight, Wilson encouraged War Secretary Baker to establish his own propaganda unit with Walter Lippmann in charge. Captain Lippmann would be assisted in this venture by a bearded Yale School of Drama teacher destined to achieve future fame in show business: Monty Woolley.[115]

As for Creel, he would remain a powerful force throughout the war, his advice to Wilson seldom rejected, whether it concerned overall press censorship or such details as the ideal hour at which to release presidential statements for maximum overseas impact. Only when Creel proposed reaching out to African Americans did Wilson resist. "I have received several delegations of Negroes," he lectured his CPI chairman when Creel suggested a meeting, "and I am under the impression that they have gone away dissatisfied." A new effort, Wilson concluded, would "do no good."[116]

To his enormous credit, Wilson dismantled the CPI's domestic operations just three days after the armistice of November 11, 1918. Supporting the swift shutdown, Creel agreed that the CPI had been "a *war organization* only . . . without proper place in the national life in time of peace."[117] And he would always insist: "In no degree was the Committee an agency of Censorship, a machinery of concealment or repression. Its emphasis throughout the war was on the open and positive."[118] Others have disagreed.

To a surprising outpouring of criticism, President Wilson personally led the American delegation to the postwar Paris Peace Conference of 1919, marking the first time a sitting U.S. president had ever journeyed to Europe. Once there, he surprised friends as well as foes by insisting that the press be permitted to cover the proceedings. "Even [French prime minister Georges] Clemenceau, himself a journalist, opposed him," reported Isaac Marcosson, who accompanied Wilson to France, "but the President held out and won."[119]

With hundreds of international correspondents converging on Paris, including Ray Stannard Baker, Wilson also recognized that the conference needed a professional press office to supply official news and handle inquiries. Just as he had turned to George Creel in wartime, Wilson now offered the peacetime job to Baker. The old muckraker "accepted the task with many misgivings," and only after Wilson appealed to his patriotism, reminding him, "[W]e're over here to do one of the most difficult tasks ever entrusted to American leadership."[120]

Journalists on the ground would soon complain that Wilson thereafter neglected to keep American correspondents informed, reneging on his pledge of transparency by attending some two hundred private meetings with the Allies.[121] Even George Creel admitted that his boss's "absurd reticence" angered the very people he needed to boost whatever agreement emerged.[122] As the renowned Kansas editor William Allen White put it, the president was not only guilty of "ignoring his press relations"; White charged that Wilson "believed in the white light of publicity chiefly for the other fellow."[123]

With the Treaty of Versailles triumphantly in hand notwithstanding the renewed wave of press hostility, Wilson headed back to America to secure its ratification. Baker, who joined him on the crossing, recalled the president as "witty and genial" on the voyage, yet, even in his hour of glory, as remote as ever. "If the President was ever fearful of anything in his life," Baker tried explaining, "it was of publicity: he was afraid, I think, not so much of the facts themselves, but of the way they were presented. As a highly cultivated scholar he disliked exaggeration, distrusted sensationalism. And yet he recognized the need of publicity and often seemed irritated and offended if the clear stream of news was fouled at its sources or muddied with propaganda."[124] In the coming fight to sell the nation on the peace treaty, Wilson faced the greatest publicity challenge of his career. Even as he steamed home, the long-critical *Chicago Tribune* suggested that Wilson had taken upon himself a challenge "beyond . . . any man."[125]

The complex agreement hammered out in 1919 harshly punished Germany for waging a horrific world war, but more crucially to Wilson, it established a League of Nations he believed would secure world peace. The pact was subject to ratification by the U.S. Senate, where isolationism had survived the global conflict undimmed. Wilson arrived back in Washington to find opposition mushrooming. Though physically drained, he quickly launched a whistle-stop campaign to rally public support. Plagued by headaches and fatigue, Wilson still managed to deliver pro-League speeches in twenty-nine cities over the course of three grueling weeks.

Doing battle for his legacy, Wilson at last seemed transformed. According to Joseph Tumulty, who joined him on the tour, the president was "full of anecdotes and repartee," spending leisure time with journalists in the dining cars and, on one occasion, squeezed into "one of the little compartments of the train, seated at the bed of a newspaper man . . . who had taken ill." The ever-loyal Tumulty wished that enemies who thought Wilson guilty of "aloofness and exclusiveness" could observe such scenes.[126]

Before audiences could behold the transfiguration, Wilson collapsed in Pueblo, Colorado, the victim of a hemorrhage, an asthmatic attack, or both. Under a cloud of secrecy, his staff whisked the ailing president back to Washington. Only a few days later, on October 2, Wilson suffered a crippling stroke at the White House and for a time, buffeted by complications, hovered between life and death. Long after the danger passed, the patient remained in seclusion, unable to speak or walk. Edith Wilson assumed the role of intermediary—de facto president, some later charged—shielding him from visitors and keeping the press in the dark about her husband's grave condition.

Inevitably, word of the president's paralysis leaked out to those who reported from the White House. Frederick Essary called it "the most difficult story which Washington correspondents have had to cover"—or in this case, conceal. While the White House issued "cryptic bulletins" vaguely describing the president's illness as a "nervous breakdown," the press corps itself was "driven almost to madness by editors who doubted if the real truth were being told."[127]

It was not. Essary and a few other journalists knew that Wilson had suffered an "alarming stroke" in Washington and that his physicians feared that another attack "in all probability would be fatal." But this information remained "confidential." Reporters, accustomed to years of wartime censorship, reflexively joined the conspiracy to hide the truth.[128] Not until October 13 did Wilson's physician issue a bulletin dubiously declaring that the patient's "mind is as 'clear as a bell'" and that "nothing in his condition . . . renders it impossible for him to act" as president.[129] Long critical of fake news, Wilson's White House now unashamedly generated it. Essary claimed that Vice President Thomas R. Marshall did not learn that "at any hour he might be called upon to assume the Presidency" until Tumulty asked him to give Marshall the genuine "story of the whole case." The *Sun* eventually got a "scoop on the Wilson sickness," but no one at the White House admitted the president was incapacitated, and no one in the press corps asked who, if anyone, was running the country.[130]

Gossip loves a vacuum. With countless "fictions" swirling about Washington, one keen-eyed visitor noticed bars on the president's bedroom window, spiking rumors that Wilson "had become violently insane." It took Essary to quash that tale by pointing out that the guardrails had been installed years earlier when the Roosevelts converted the space into a nursery for their younger children. "I hated to spoil a good story," Essary confessed, "but what else was one to do?"[131]

With the president out of circulation, unable to press his case, the U.S. Senate voted down the armistice treaty by seven votes. The *New York Tribune* blamed the defeat on Wilson's "assumption that his word must be accepted as law."[132] To keep the issue before the people, the loyal Ray Stannard Baker proposed a series of celebratory articles about the recent peace conference (later collected for a book, *What Wilson Did in Paris*). Mrs. Wilson tried sealing the arrangement with a luncheon invitation, but when Baker arrived at the White House on November 5, 1919, the president could not summon the strength to make an appearance. "The plain fact," Baker concluded, was that Wilson now "had a 600 horsepower motor in a frail, light, delicate chassis."[133]

For the final year of his term, Wilson remained a virtual recluse. As his own isolation increased, his remaining contacts with press allies dwindled. "The poor President!" Baker confided to his diary in February 1920, "so nearly a friendless man."[134] For the rest of his time in office, a few trusted journalists gained access—and only if they earned clearance from both Tumulty and Mrs. Wilson. One was the *World*'s Louis Siebold, whom Wilson received on the South Portico of the White House in mid-June wearing a broad-rimmed panama hat to shield his still-distorted face. Throughout what historian Patricia O'Toole vividly described as a "staged" event, Edith Wilson hovered forbiddingly behind her seated husband.[135] Siebold's June 18, 1920, article obligingly depicted Wilson as hale and lucid.

By then, Wilson had deluded himself into believing he had recovered enough to seek a third term. Astonishingly, he drafted preliminary notes for not only a convention acceptance speech but an inaugural address.[136] But when Democrats assembled in San Francisco a few weeks later, delegates nominated Ohio governor James A. Cox for president. Cox lost badly in November to Republican Warren G. Harding, even with Wilson's vigorous assistant secretary of the navy, Franklin D. Roosevelt, as his running mate. Joseph Tumulty had dared not only to back Cox but to hint to convention delegates that Wilson preferred him as his successor. He then compounded his offense by publishing a 1921 memoir in defiance of its own opening line: "Woodrow Wilson prefers not to be written about."[137] The Wilsons reacted by banishing him. After a few failed attempts to make amends, Tumulty tried assuring his offended boss that hereafter, "You will find me as a mere private in the ranks, deferring to your unselfish leadership and defending your policies at every turn of the long road which lies ahead of us."[138] It was to no avail. Wilson refused ever to see his long-time press aide again.

Retiring to a comfortable brick home not far from Washington's Dupont Circle, Wilson lived on, making brief public appearances to mark Veterans Day or attend local vaudeville shows, invariably drawing sympathetic crowds. Yearning once more to offer his arguments in print, he tried writing a magazine piece but needed the help of two aides just to massage it into shape for publication. Rejecting a $150,000 offer to prepare his memoirs, he instead agreed to let Ray Stannard Baker produce an authorized biography, granting him access to his presidential papers.[139] Although Baker for a time did his research from a workroom in the ex-president's new home, Wilson's interactions with journalists otherwise ebbed. Traces of the old combativeness did occasionally emerge.[140] In 1922, Wilson blasted the *Washington Evening Star* for "prejudice and jealousy against me." And that April, in a letter he dictated but did not send, Wilson told the *Washington Post* that the recent flood of specially designated "weeks" convinced him there should be a "Mind Your Own Business Week."[141]

One of Wilson's final press visitors, the ever-sympathetic R. V. Oulahan of the *New York Times*, tried to convince readers in June 1923 that the ex-president had not only made a marvelous recovery but also reemerged as "a foremost figure in the capital . . . a dramatic personality in whom there is intense interest."[142] In truth, Wilson was by then in steep decline. Yet he summoned the strength to deliver his first-ever radio broadcast on Armistice Day 1923. Listeners could hear the ex-president hoarsely, but still defiantly, advocating for the League of Nations and condemning "selfish isolationists." Curiously, he pronounced the word, "izzolationists."[143]

A few weeks later, Wilson declined to receive Baker, who had proposed a new "first-class interview" to "help along the principles you have at heart—in which I also believe deeply."[144] Wilson could not help reminding his longtime press ally—by way of a confessional or a final complaint, or both—that the interview format had "never been for me a successful method of utterance."[145] Still believing himself "the spiritual leader of a cause only temporarily lost," Wilson did nothing to discourage rumors that he "might again become the standard bearer of his party" in 1924.[146] Before he could face another inevitable rejection, his broken body finally gave out. Wilson died on February 3.

David Lawrence of the AP and later the *New York Evening Post*, who had covered Wilson for years, always believed that journalists had misjudged him, and vice versa. "Considering the ability of Woodrow Wilson by the printed word to reach into the hearts of men and women everywhere and stimulate liberal ideals," Lawrence lamented a year after the former president's death, "nothing seems so surprising as the relationship between Woodrow Wilson and the press. From the beginning of his public career until the end, they constituted a series of misunderstandings and unfortunate clashes." Their quarrel was never "personal," Lawrence maintained. Wilson simply "disagreed with the methods of American journalism."[147] And, as Lawrence might have added, stubbornly refused to adapt to them.

For his own part, Wilson never accepted responsibility, much less blame, for the frosty image the press presented of him. "I have never read an article about myself in which I recognized myself," he once claimed. Though he wanted to believe that these "cold and removed impressions" had been reported "in absolute good faith," he reiterated that the press consistently misjudged him. He was anything but cold, he insisted to the National Press Club in 1914. Rather, he struggled to "restrain the emotions that are inside of me."

"You may not believe it," he told what must have been an astonished audience of journalists that evening, "but I sometimes feel like a fire from a far from extinct volcano, and if the lava does not seem to spill over it is because you are not high enough to see into the basin and see the cauldron boil."[148]

The press never glimpsed the "lava" burning within Woodrow Wilson because Wilson never recognized the need to lower his "cauldron" to enhance the view.

8

FRANKLIN D. ROOSEVELT–I

Early on the afternoon of November 9, 1932—just one day after winning the presidency in a landslide—Franklin D. Roosevelt, dressed in a dark double-breasted suit, rolled his wheelchair into the second-floor parlor of the family town house on Manhattan's Upper East Side.[1] There, someone—probably his twenty-three-year-old son, James—lifted him into an armchair set before the room's western fireplace, facing a small wooden table adorned with an NBC microphone.[2] Whether or not the fire was lit on this autumn day for what would essentially be the first of FDR's famous Fireside Chats,* no one thought to note. Comfortably seated, Roosevelt awaited his cue. When the signal came, he would not only reassure a nation but launch a revolution in presidential communications.

Few incoming presidents were more gifted, or better prepared, in the art of public persuasion and press relations. It surely helped that Roosevelt had once edited the *Harvard Crimson*. Of course, Woodrow Wilson had run his college paper, too, without ever fully absorbing what journalists expected of those they covered.

Unlike Wilson, through both family and political connections, FDR later enjoyed the unique opportunity to observe presidents as they dealt with the

---

* Their full impact is treated in the next chapter.

press. His cousin and hero, Theodore, who gave the bride away at Franklin and Eleanor Roosevelt's 1905 wedding, introduced easy accessibility and gregarious informality to White House press relations. In turn, FDR's World War I–era boss, Woodrow Wilson, routinized press access while infusing solemnity into the interactions—arguably too much so. FDR learned from each leader's successes—and failures. TR's rise but his inability to rise again exposed the limits of personality-driven public relations and overt favoritism. And Wilson's ineffective final years laid bare the limits of policy without affability.

A minor episode during Wilson's presidency may have played a major role in kindling FDR's own aggressive style of press outreach. In 1914, while serving as assistant secretary of the navy, Roosevelt proposed boosting fellow New York Democrats in upcoming off-year elections. Tantalizingly, the pro-Democratic *New York World* had invited him "to write an article on the New York situation." Reminding Wilson he had thus far "steadfastly refused to be quoted about N. Y. politics in spite of considerable pressure," FDR now asked the president if a good story "might help rather than embarrass the administration." Wilson starchily rejected the idea: "My judgment is that it would be best if members of the administration should . . . say as little as possible on the politics of their several states."[3] Roosevelt obediently muzzled himself but soon came to the realization that leaders can fail when withholding rather than making news: his home state went Republican that November. Determined to chart a more proactive course, Roosevelt began summoning journalists to the Navy Department for regular press briefings, sometimes twice a day. His career-long PR offensive had begun.

Years later, as New York governor from 1929 to 1933, Roosevelt would follow his cousin Teddy's Albany example and host frequent news conferences. In honing this approach he took useful counsel from an asthmatic, gnomelike public relations guru who had begun serving him in 1912. Louis McHenry Howe, the son of a newspaper publisher, had risen no higher in his own journalistic career than freelance reporter for the *New York Herald*.[4] A chance assignment to cover Albany politics brought him into the proximity of then-freshman state senator Franklin Roosevelt. The two became friends. When FDR came down with typhus during his reelection campaign, he asked Howe to oversee the final lap of the race. The Dutchess County Democrat won a second term with a larger majority than before.

Under Howe's tutelage, Roosevelt went on to snag the 1920 Democratic vice presidential nomination. But FDR's presence on the ticket failed to tilt the only White House race ever to pit one former newspaper editor against another:

Republican Warren G. Harding easily outpolled Democrat James M. Cox. The following year, polio struck the athletic FDR while he was vacationing on Campobello Island in Canada. Back in New York, Howe and Eleanor slowly nursed Roosevelt back to health. Eventually, FDR rebuilt his physical strength and emotional independence, and at Howe's urging, he decided to keep the depths of his disability from the public.

Just three years later, Howe convinced FDR to attempt a do-or-die comeback by addressing the 1924 Democratic National Convention. Roosevelt trained for the test by crawling across his library floor for hours at a time to build upper-body strength. On June 26 at Madison Square Garden, he took his first public steps on crutches, his withered legs reinforced by steel braces. Clinging with both hands to the lectern for fear of falling, FDR delivered a rousing speech that reignited his political career. It was an astonishing performance. Although the national ticket went down to defeat that November, by the time FDR appeared to address the convention four years afterward in Houston, he seemed even surer on his feet. "With a cane and my right arm," his son Elliott recalled, "he *walked* to the platform, no longer crippled, merely lame." Or so it seemed. "For a moment," reported the *New York World* in a neat turn of phrase, "we are lifted up."[5] That fall, defying another Republican tide nationwide, FDR eked out a nail-biting victory for governor of New York.

A huge reelection triumph in 1930 made him, in the words of Arthur Krock of the *New York Times*, "inevitably" and "formidably eligible" to seek the presidency in 1932. But his candidacy unleashed powerful editorial opposition.[6] Although incumbent Herbert Hoover had proved helpless in the wake of the Great Depression, Roosevelt failed to earn—that year, or subsequently—majority editorial support from the nation's newspapers. Those long aligned with the Republican Party kept faith with the GOP despite Hoover's inertia. Had Roosevelt sought the presidency a hundred years earlier, such editorial hostility might have doomed him. But by the 1930s, as FDR himself observed, voters had become "less and less influenced by the red fire and the hard cider ballyhoo of newspaper owners . . . who adhere to the practices of a century ago." Somewhat disingenuously, he added that voters had "learned to go behind the glittering headlines and behind the leads and behind the generalities . . . before we make up our own minds."[7]

In truth, no one benefited from "glittering headlines" more than FDR. And few politicians more closely scrutinized the columns of type that appeared "behind the leads," especially criticism. "Franklin reserved certain times for the study of the press," his wife confirmed years later, "particularly the opposition press."[8] Eleanor did not mention it, but FDR went a step further; he tried to render the print press irrelevant.

The remedy was radio. "Sometimes I think we are driving so wholly into a radio future," he prophetically told his son, "that we shall get even our detective stories over the air, instead of through the printed page." With this transformation in mind, Roosevelt pioneered a broadcast-centric strategy for overcoming the animus of newspaper publishers. Shattering tradition at the 1932 convention, he flew to Chicago to claim the presidential nod in person—with reporters, on-air commentators, and newsreel cameras in tow. Because it was aired on radio, no acceptance speech to date made so huge an impression as FDR's stirring call for a "New Deal for the American people."[9] Roosevelt trounced Hoover that fall, winning 57 percent of the popular vote and carrying forty-two of the forty-eight states.

Few voters knew it at the time, but FDR had never regained physical mobility below his waist. When he had returned to politics back in 1920, the once-vital Roosevelt appeared in public propped up on the well-concealed braces that locked his useless legs into place. Clutching a son's arm, dragging one foot in front of the other by heaving his hips successively forward, FDR conveyed the illusion that he could walk again.

Not that he fooled the press. Every journalist who covered the 1932 presidential race knew that FDR remained disabled. But few of their readers learned the full extent of his handicap—then or later. That was because, under what contemporaries described as an "unwritten rule"—in fact one of the most rigorously enforced gentlemen's agreements in American political history—journalists kept FDR's true condition secret. "News stories seldom, if ever, mentioned that he was a cripple," reporter John Gunther bluntly admitted, "and the fact that he used a wheelchair was never printed at all."[10] Ironically, members of President Hoover's informal "Medicine Ball Cabinet"—a group that gathered with him every morning to take vigorous exercise together—had convinced themselves that FDR would be the incumbent's weakest possible 1932 challenger, as his disability was certain to be revealed to his detriment during a long campaign.[11]

Even friendly silence was not enough for Roosevelt. Preparing to run for the presidency, he grandiosely "challenged" writer Earle Looker (a onetime friend of Teddy Roosevelt's) to unearth, if he could, any evidence of his physical incapacity to serve. Then FDR produced rose-colored letters from three handpicked physicians attesting to his sound health. The conspiracy extended all the way to Earle Looker. "Well sir," the author wrote after the clean bill of health appeared in a *Liberty Magazine* whitewash, "we got away with the *Liberty* article."[12] His report brushed off Roosevelt's inability to walk and failed to mention his dangerously high blood pressure.

A small handful of magazine stories did eventually allude to FDR's handicap—including a *New Yorker* magazine profile—but most journalists kept the truth to themselves.[13] They believed, as did Roosevelt and his advisors, that any sign of "weakness" would unfairly hurt him politically and impair his ability to lead.[14] *Christian Science Monitor* correspondent Richard Strout justified the conspiracy to ignore FDR's disability by explaining, "We just took it for granted. . . . It was common knowledge."[15]

Although FDR lost his balance and tumbled on several public occasions—once, at the 1936 Democratic National Convention in Philadelphia, pitching forward and scattering a sheaf of papers while reaching to shake someone's hand—the press never reported these alarming incidents.[16] The moment FDR fell in Philadelphia, aides formed a protective shield around him as he lay on the floor, then quickly hoisted him to his feet before the thousands of spectators noticed or the press cameras could capture the mishap on film.

Photographers imposed a blackout of their own. By mutual understanding, cameramen put down their equipment whenever Roosevelt's wheelchair came into view or aides lifted his inert body into and out of automobiles. "No pictures of me getting out of the machine, boys," a cheerful Roosevelt often reminded them when arriving by car.[17] Early in FDR's presidency, when a New York *Daily News* photographer snapped him gamely descending the granite steps outside his New York home, editors voluntarily declined to publish the result; inadvertently, the picture had revealed the metal stirrups encircling FDR's shoes.[18]

Technically, insisted Murray Alvey of RKO Pathé News, "you were requested, not ordered, to refrain from taking pictures of this type."[19] But later, when rogue press photographers tried defying the tacit ban, Secret Service agents intervened, stepping protectively in front of the president to shield him from intrusive lenses or, in extreme cases, yanking film from cameras. "By what right they do this I don't know," Richard Strout confessed, "but I have never seen the right questioned."[20] Persistent offenders risked losing their press credentials. When *Life* magazine defied the ban and in June 1937 published a distant shot showing FDR being rolled along in his wheelchair to visit his ailing advisor Harold Ickes at Bethesda Naval Hospital, the White House retaliated by banning all photographers from any naval property whenever the president was on the premises.[21]

The policy worked—at least for FDR. Disability rights advocate Hugh G. Gallagher later examined thirty-five thousand surviving photographs of President Roosevelt and found only two showing him in a wheelchair. Gallagher, himself a polio victim, termed the camouflage "FDR's splendid deception."[22] Correspondent Merriman Smith preferred calling it "a friendly conspiracy . . . based on basic principles of American sportsmanship."[23] Roosevelt-era photographer Sammy Shulman never second-guessed the arrangement. "He treated us well, so we treated him well," he maintained. ". . . To have done anything to tear him down in the eyes of the public would have been unthinkable."[24]

In retrospect, the embargo should perhaps have been challenged. On the one hand, it is tempting to be grateful that the press refused to report on FDR's disability since, had they done so, America might never have elected him, much less benefited from the leadership that helped it survive both the Great Depression and World War II. But the masquerade exacted a cost: loss of confidence in the press as a dependably unbiased institution. In times of challenge to the freedom of the press, total honesty makes the strongest argument for protecting its absolute liberty. Whether or not history will yet judge the generous conspiracy to protect FDR as worth its potential permanent damage to the reputation of the press, no one can yet say.

Ironically, shielding Roosevelt from unfiltered coverage was never a professional or patriotic obligation. What may be the most remarkable thing about the reporters' and photographers' acquiescence to it was that it always remained more personal than official. As Sammy Schulman put it, "He was a decent human being, we genuinely liked him, and we didn't want to embarrass him."[25]

Paralysis could not be detected on the radio. For the 1932 post-election speech broadcast from his Manhattan home, a relaxed FDR remained comfortably seated. When the signal came, he began talking into the microphone in measured, almost intimate tones, as if conducting a private conversation rather than delivering a public address. In parlors across the nation, rapt families gathered around their furniture-size radios to listen as the newly elected leader attempted not to claim victory but to calm fears. It took only 153 words:

> I am glad of this opportunity to extend my deep appreciation to the electorate of this country which gave me yesterday such a great vote of confidence. It is a vote that had more than mere party significance; it transcended party lines, and became a national expression of liberal thought. It seems, I am sure, that the masses of the people of this nation firmly believe that there is great and actual possibility in an orderly recovery through a well conceived and actively directed plan of action. Such a plan has been presented to you and you have expressed approval of it. This, my friends, is most reassuring to me. It shows that there is in this country unbounded confidence in the future of sound agriculture and of honorable industry. This clear mandate shall not be forgotten, and I pledge you this and I invite your help in the happy task of restoration.[26]

The remarks lasted barely a minute. Then came an equally brief encore. With a basket of flowers now concealing the tabletop microphone, FDR flawlessly repeated his performance for Fox Movietone News. Within days, the result hit screens at theaters nationwide, in many cases providing a refreshing antidote to *Payment Deferred* and *I Am a Fugitive from a Chain Gang*, two newly released features that grimly dramatized the country's economic desperation.[27] In but sixty seconds on air, and another sixty on film, Roosevelt became a radio and movie star in his own right.

As it turned out, Roosevelt's post-election address also became the first in a sensational series of live broadcasts that recommenced at the White House five months later as Fireside Chats. Although his pioneering Manhattan broadcast never entered the record books as the initial example, it has long deserved such recognition.

The press corps holding vigil outside Roosevelt's East Sixty-Fifth Street house that day might not immediately have grasped the historic irony in this milestone. The leader they had so generously shielded had just sidestepped the print press on which presidents had relied for a century and a half to convey their messages, and on which this president-elect in particular had depended to cloak his physical limitations. By addressing millions of people live on radio, FDR had made news without newspapers, forever upending relations between presidents and the press.

No longer would the public be required to wait a day to learn what a leader was thinking, or depend on party-affiliated print journalism to filter his messages. Beginning with Roosevelt, Americans would be in on news as it was being made by a president bold enough to bypass traditional media yet warm enough to address the people as "my friends." The most that the journalists huddled outside 49 East Sixty-Fifth Street could do that November afternoon was ask that FDR deliver his brief talk a third time for their benefit. He did.[28] Not long afterward, Eleanor Roosevelt invited the reporters to camp in the front parlor. By the time Frances Perkins visited in February to be interviewed for a cabinet post, "the press had established a base of operations" on the "disorderly" premises. "Furniture was broken. Rugs were rolled up and piled in a corner," and the chairs, tables, and floor overflowed "with overcoats, hats, umbrellas, briefcases, notebooks, sheafs of paper . . . smoking stands, ash trays, [and] cigarette stubs."[29] In other words, it had become a typical press room.

Absent the introduction of new technologies like radio and talking pictures (then only five years old), FDR's breakthrough moment on the airwaves would not have shifted the long-standing communications paradigm so tectonically. The new president and the new mediums of radio and sound newsreels came of age together, and each proved ideally suited for the other. It mattered little that Roosevelt enunciated in a patrician Eastern accent and lacked the ability to supply motion for motion pictures. With a mellifluous voice, an optimistic smile, and an electric tilt-of-the-head for occasional emphasis, FDR cast a mesmeric spell. As many observers of the day put it, he was "a natural."[30]

While reporters continued suppressing the truth about Roosevelt's disability when he entered office, some fellow politicians proved more indiscreet. One was Eugene Talmadge, a fellow Democrat elected as governor of Georgia the same year Roosevelt won the White House, who blurted to the *New York Times* that the "greatest calamity to this country is that President Roosevelt can't walk around and hunt up people to talk to."[31]

Gestures of sympathy similarly endangered FDR's well-protected image. Within days of his inauguration—also broadcast live, and highlighted by his assurance that Americans had "nothing to fear but fear itself"—the New York *Daily News* conceived a project to keep the new president in sound health. Publishing a front-page photo showing FDR swimming in Warm Springs, Georgia—the treatment center he had created for victims of infantile paralysis—the big-circulation tabloid called on readers to contribute funds to "build a pool for

Roosevelt" at his new home. Proclaimed the caption: "Franklin D. Roosevelt, who is leading the country out of depression, must have a pool for his health. There is none at the White House. Therefore, today *The News* undertakes to act as a medium for citizens of New York State to express affection for F. D. by giving him a pool."[32]

The paper made a strong case for what might otherwise have seemed an extravagance in a period of economic distress: "The water is his one form of healthful recreation. He's lost without it. It's the very essence of his existence. It is, in fact, in the long run, his life."[33] Worried that the appeal might persuade the public that their new leader was fragile, Louis Howe begged FDR to call a halt to it. But the family overruled him. The fundraising drive, boosted by small donations from "crippled children" and swelled by a nationally broadcast benefit featuring show business luminaries like Fred Astaire, Bette Davis, and Fanny Brice, raised nearly $22,000 (the equivalent of $552,000 in 2019 dollars). FDR got his pool without forfeiting an ounce of public confidence.[34]

But the alliance between the new president and the *Daily News* did not last forever. Although the paper would back Roosevelt for reelection in 1936 and again in 1940, the isolationist *News* turned against FDR in 1941 over the issue of prewar U.S. military aid to beleaguered Great Britain. The break should not really have surprised anyone who knew journalism history. *News* boss Joseph Medill Patterson traced his lineage to maternal grandfather Joseph Medill, the nineteenth-century owner of the *Chicago Tribune* and a founding supporter of the Republican Party. By the end of Roosevelt's first term, most of Patterson's pro-business family had united against the liberal administration: Patterson's cousin Colonel Robert R. McCormick, the archconservative *Chicago Tribune* publisher who had once attended Groton with FDR; and Eleanor Medill "Cissy" Patterson, who operated the *Washington Times-Herald*. The *Daily News* was the last holdout. Unfortunately for FDR, each paper became the most widely read in its home city.

FDR overcame their hostility not only through radio but through his breathtakingly ubiquitous presidential press conferences, conducting a remarkable 998 question-and-answer sessions during his twelve years in office. Whatever the pressures of domestic or global crises and wherever he happened to be—Washington, his family home in Hyde Park, his "Little White House" in Warm

Springs, and even aboard naval vessels on the high seas—Roosevelt made time to meet reporters, on average, twice a week for much of his long tenure. As he once quipped in justification of the self-imposed grind, "If ever something needed advertising publicity, it is Government."[35]

In a sense, publicity helped Roosevelt *become* the government, and no president ever took such delight in advertising himself. Drawing on his knowledge of both Theodore Roosevelt's and Woodrow Wilson's experiences with journalists, FDR conceived an entirely new form of press encounter. An FDR news conference would combine the businesslike routine of Wilson's formal Q&A sessions with reporters and the gregarious air of TR's free-form "barber's hours."

FDR savored his unscripted give-and-take with journalists, although he grew increasingly suspicious of the "press lords" they worked for and viewed newspapers overall as adversaries, not allies. Yet, as historian Arthur Schlesinger Jr. argued, "By the brilliant but simple act of making news and *being* news, Roosevelt outwitted the open hostility of the publishers and converted the press into one of the most effective channels of his public leadership."[36] That FDR managed to do so is all the more remarkable considering that nearly every answer he gave reporters over the years could not be quoted for publication without his permission.

Roosevelt's first presidential news conference set the tone for his New Deal in press relations.[37] At 10:00 A.M. on Wednesday, March 8, 1933—just four days into his term—White House ushers summoned correspondents to the cramped lobby outside the Oval Office, where they assembled in an "atmosphere heavy with smoke."[38] Ten minutes later a buzzer sounded from inside, indicating that the president was ready. When the door swung open, more than one hundred reporters surged into Roosevelt's sanctum. A participant confessed that the scramble seemed "more like the drive for unreserved bleacher seats at a World Series baseball game than a procession into the private office of the Nation's Chief Executive."[39]

The "tide" of writers squeezed into a semicircle surrounding FDR's big mahogany desk, miraculously failing to dislodge its clutter of "dolls, totems, and knick-knacks."[40] The correspondents stood, while Roosevelt sat in an upholstered armchair, his back to the windows, grandly flanked by American and presidential flags. "Cigarette holder in mouth at a jaunty angle," he fidgeted with his pince-nez spectacles, papers, and curios while waiting for all the reporters to file in.[41] (Later he began filling these awkward gaps with banter.) Journalists carried only pads and pencils; there would be no microphones at these early press conferences. The White House alone would make transcripts of the proceedings. An AP lensman took one staged photograph of the first session, but thereafter, cameras were prohibited, too.

Once the correspondents had at last assembled, an aide proclaimed, "All in!" and shut the door. Then, at Roosevelt's invitation, they filed past his desk one by one to shake hands. "Hello, I'm glad to see you," he greeted each. Astonished by the display of cordiality, one veteran reporter exclaimed, "I've never heard of anything like this."[42] Not until Roosevelt had welcomed every participant did he finally launch the event itself. "It is very good to see you all," he jovially began, "and my hope is that these conferences are going to be merely enlarged editions of the kind of very delightful family conferences I have been holding in Albany for the last four years."[43] Another communications revolution had begun.

"I am told that what I am about to do will become impossible," he added with a rare burst of self-doubt, "but I am going to try it. We are not going to have any more written questions and of course while I cannot answer seventy-five or a hundred questions because I simply haven't got the physical time, I see no reason why I should not talk to you ladies and gentlemen off the record just the way I have been doing in Albany and the way I used to do it in the Navy Department down here."

Before he could proceed, as if to underscore the "family" atmosphere he hoped to impose, his son Elliott "pushed his way into the room" to bid his father good-bye before departing on a trip. "Good luck to you, son," the president shouted back.[44] The humanizing distraction hearkened back to the days of Lincoln and TR, when presidential children roamed the White House at will and made superb copy for reporters. FDR's handsome grown sons exuded charisma of their own.

Methodically resuming his litany of stipulations, Roosevelt next cautioned writers to ask no speculative "'if' questions," warning, "I never answer them." As for those "which for various reasons I don't want to discuss or I am not ready to discuss or I don't know anything about," these would remain unanswered, too. Quotable quotes would come only "in writing" from mimeographed handouts distributed by the new White House press secretary, former UPI and AP correspondent Stephen T. Early.[45] (Early had amassed useful additional experience as an executive for Paramount Newsreels and, years before, as a World War I–era editor at the military newspaper *Stars and Stripes*. There he was fondly remembered by FDR as "the only man who could remain relatively sober in Paris."[46]) All other presidential comments would remain strictly off the record, that is, unless FDR made exceptions on the spur of the moment.*

FDR was not yet done listing his preconditions. He might also dispense "background information," he tantalizingly promised, which he defined as "material which can be used by all of you on your own authority and responsibility and just not be attributed to the White House, because I don't want to revive the Ananias Club"—his cousin Theodore's imagined purgatory for journalists who broke confidences. One final rule mandated that his replies be available "only to those who attend the conference."

"Now as to news," FDR at last declared to a round of laughter, "I don't think there is any." Thereupon he effortlessly fielded thirty-five questions. The "picture of ease and confidence," said one reporter on the scene, Roosevelt at one point casually "inserted a fresh cigarette in an ivory holder" as if he were discussing nothing more consequential than a rural pork barrel project.[47] Eventually, a voice called out, "Thank you, Mr. President," terminating the thirty-five-minute session at 10:45 A.M. to a spontaneous burst of applause from the ordinarily jaded press corps.[48]

The initial reviews proved ecstatic. One journalist who participated in the scrum judged it "the most amazing performance the White House has ever seen." Another reported, "The press barely restrained its whoopees. . . . [FDR] has definitely captivated an unusually cynical battalion of correspondents."[49] As the UPI's Raymond Clapper succinctly put it, "The correspondents saw him, and were conquered. He won them."[50]

Throughout the maiden press conference, Stephen Early hovered in the background while another newly named press aide, the gaunt Marvin "Mac" McIntyre, stood sentinel-like behind the president. McIntyre, also a former newsman, had worked on the censorious Creel Commission during World War I and, like Early, had known FDR for years.[51] Both men served initially as assistant secretaries to the president, officially reporting to the increasingly frail Louis Howe (who would die in 1935). "No President has ever had such a

---

* Later, the president violated his own strictures and began publishing edited transcripts of his favorite press conferences in volumes of his collected speeches and writings.

publicity-wise trio in his Secretariat," enthused veteran advertising executive William E. Berchtold.[52] Each of the three earned $10,000 per year.

The revamped press operation soon expanded well beyond this White House triumvirate. The new administration also dismissed career information officers at federal departments and agencies, replacing them with journalists better equipped to pitch stories to former colleagues (and more loyal to the president).[53] A cynical observer dubbed the new galaxy of PR professionals "Dr. Roosevelt's Propaganda Trust,"[54] while another complained that as a result of the government's recruitment efforts, "one great metropolitan newspaper has had its Washington bureau stripped twice of every man except the chief."[55] Admitting that much of the New Deal's "ballyhoo" emanated from this unsung PR corps, William Berchtold lauded it as "the largest and most efficient staff of publicity experts ever to grace the government's payroll."[56] Critics of the juggernaut warned that the "federal press agents" would cost taxpayers "millions."[57]

Although orchestrated publicity soon began flowing out of the agencies in a torrent, the emphasis at the White House remained fixed on Roosevelt's Panglossian notion of "family." As Eleanor's confidante, Marion Dickerman, described FDR's approach, "He had an easy, delightful give-and-take relationship with [reporters]—was always willing to discuss problems and incidents with them man to man, though without compromising his authority as President of the United States."[58] Seconding the appraisal, Raymond Clapper judged FDR's "good-humored and smiling spirit" as "the mark of a man at peace with himself and at ease in his job." Adding that he was "constantly amazed" at FDR's "knowledge of administrative detail," Clapper appreciated that he "never sent the reporters away empty-handed."[59]

Eclipsing another tradition, the president began socializing with journalists, too. He delighted in playing host to them at White House receptions, teas, and garden parties. A chosen few found themselves included in Sunday-night family suppers; others received invitations to state dinners. Eleanor welcomed correspondents to make use of the White House tennis courts and the newly installed pool. In the early days, FDR even joined them for occasional games of water polo, binding them ever closer and further blurring the lines long separating presidents from those who covered them.

Disabled or not, FDR proved remarkably peripatetic, and wherever he went, the press followed—at least the senior reporters and wire-service men. "He traveled incessantly, but took his local news with him,"[60] explained Charles Hurd, chief White House correspondent for the *New York Times* throughout

Roosevelt's first term and a rich source of anecdote and analysis about FDR's relationship with the press. Journalists who covered the president on these official trips grew into a particularly tight-knit band, flattered to be targets of FDR's cordial "ribbing."[61]

Roosevelt also became a master of what Hurd called "tenacious thoughtfulness."[62] When, for example, a presidential vacation to Florida threatened to delay one correspondent's long-planned honeymoon, FDR arranged to include the bride-to-be on the official manifest so the couple would not be separated while the reporter covered the trip. Learning that a bachelor journalist's mother had died, the president and his wife sent a condolence note, and Eleanor phoned to ask him to a White House meal.[63] And when the *New York Times*' Arthur Krock wrote disparagingly about FDR's foreign policy, he received an invitation to spend a weekend at Hyde Park, where the gregarious president inspired a remedial article by sharing his "great dream" for averting global war.[64]

Reporters particularly appreciated FDR's self-deprecating sense of humor. At one jolly Hyde Park press picnic, he took delight in reading aloud a recently published lampoon called *Frankie in Wonderland*, whose title character employs "rabbit tricks" to secure "forty-eight states to play with instead of one." Although the Lewis Carroll parody was meant to mock him, Roosevelt performed it with gusto. After the outing, a newly assigned reporter from an anti-Roosevelt paper sighed to Marion Dickerman, "What can you do with a man like that? You can't keep him down, that's sure."[65]

In a column titled "Why the Newspapermen Like Roosevelt," another Washington reporter offered a comprehensive explanation for FDR's popularity with the press. Unlike previous presidents, he "met the newspapermen on their own ground, while commanding the situation, sustaining the dignity of his office and functioning the processes of public opinion more effectively than any president in history."[66]

With rare exceptions, this meant that FDR's paralysis remained unmentioned. "The people of the United States find it hard," acknowledged one small-town paper in a rare but well-meaning exception, "to realize that their tornado of energy in the White House is a cripple."[67] In early June 1944, the White House press corps demonstrated its discreet respect by presenting FDR with $1,000 the reporters themselves had raised for polio research. Doubtless preoccupied with the imminent D-Day invasion, the president nonetheless managed to exclaim happily, "That's perfectly grand."[68]

True to his promise of regular access, Roosevelt invited reporters back to his office just two days after their initial give-and-take, apologizing for a twenty-minute delay by explaining that he "just got to chatting in the Cabinet." Came the first question: "Economics, Mr. President?" No, FDR casually explained, "I was just telling stories."[69] Devoting the entire session to the financial crisis he had inherited ("Oh, I am learning a lot about banking"), the president pledged to reignite public confidence by using "the language of the man on the street, of the average depositors, whereas these Treasury orders cannot be understood by the average person, including myself."[70] FDR continued to use colloquial American English at every press conference that followed.

The president did impose one final procedural demand on the correspondents. "I saw somebody edging toward the door in the middle of the talk" two days earlier, he sarcastically scolded. Henceforth, reporters would be required to remain inside the Oval Office once a press conference got underway. From then on, after aides sounded the "all in," the door would be locked. FDR wanted no one to gain an unfair advantage by sneaking out to contact his desk whenever a story broke. As a consequence, Charles Hurd observed that "if the news was 'hot,' there was a moment of bedlam [at the conclusion] while the news agency correspondents literally raced to their private telephones" to relay scoops.[71]

Asked late in this second session how he had enjoyed his "first week in the White House," FDR revealed, "Off the record, I haven't had enough sleep, otherwise fine." Laughter had barely subsided when AP bureau chief Francis Stephenson, himself exhausted by the president's schedule, blurted out, to another round of hilarity, "On the record, I haven't had enough, either."[72] The *New York Times* marveled at Roosevelt's "knack for making things sound personal and informal."[73]

For months to come, the president's thronged press conferences—now routinely scheduled for Tuesday afternoons and Friday mornings—abounded with cordial repartee and useful information.[74] Off the record the events remained, but the mere idea that they occurred so often resonated with both reporters and their readers. The new president came across as open, self-confident, and ultimately reassuring. Leo Rosten, a White House aide destined to become a best-selling humorist, described FDR's impact as nothing less than "galvanic." Just days after the president took office, Rosten asserted, "Roosevelt was lifted to the stature of savior by the public and a political wizard by the newspapermen."[75] *Providence Journal* correspondent Ashmun Brown offered a similar if more caustic appraisal: "If the New Deal was a success, we Washington correspondents were its parents. Day after day we informed the gullible public that FDR was by far the smartest politician who had ever occupied the White House. We even believed the myth ourselves."[76]

Relishing his role as fountain of behind-the-scenes information, FDR adroitly choreographed future press sessions, sometimes confiding advance word on new initiatives, at others deflecting inquiries he was not yet prepared to handle ("That is what they call premature," or "That is a secret.")[77] FDR might engage in a volley of give-and-take one day and on another launch a filibuster to demonstrate his grasp of complex issues while forestalling further inquiry. Reporters learned to follow his lead and steer coverage in directions he desired—if only because such deference generated reams of copy even if the president could not be quoted directly.

Of course, the "advantage," Raymond P. Brandt of the *St. Louis Post-Dispatch* came to realize, rested "always with the President." As Brandt pointed out: "While anyone can ask a question, there was and still is no way to get a satisfactory reply if the President wills otherwise. He can fail to hear the question; can give a facetious answer which usually calls forth thoughtless laughter from a small group of reporters who like to see a colleague ridiculed; he can say, 'there's no news on that subject'; he can merely smile and say nothing; or he can give a diplomatic answer." Remarkably, it was "one of the unwritten rules of the conference that once he has signified his intention of not answering a question, he must not be pressed on the same topic."[78]

To some reporters, the restraints soon became intolerable, particularly when Roosevelt began ignoring or scolding those who pressed him for follow-ups. FDR could be "utterly charming, disarming, and thoroughly likable," wire service reporter Merriman Smith conceded, but when riled "could be as rough and tough as a Third Avenue blackjack artist. It just depended on the question, who asked it and how Mr. Roosevelt felt when he got up that morning."[79] The love-hate relationship, however, veered mostly toward ardor. In 1935, a San Francisco press club named FDR "the best news source in America," predicting that "the nation's reporters will smile contentedly as long as F. R. sits on the throne dishing out 'hot copy.'"[80]

Indeed, smiles could often be seen at Oval Office press briefings, particularly when privileged senior correspondents took their reserved places in the front row and began chatting informally with the president while their younger colleagues scrambled for positions behind them. Queried during one such prelude on why he needed to charter a boat to fish for "hardheads"—a breed of catfish—FDR replied, "[T]he obvious answer is that there are so many softheads around here." Another lull inspired him to needle a correspondent about his drab new suit. Told it cost $15.75, Roosevelt quipped: "As much as that?"[81] Asked why he failed to sport a green necktie on St. Patrick's Day, FDR, a veteran of Irish American political rituals in New York, joked, "It wore out."[82] Beginning one 1935 press conference at 7:45 A.M., FDR drawled, "I am awfully sorry to get you up at this hour but it will give you a chance to play golf."[83] And when a journalist sought a comment on reports that Joseph P. Kennedy planned to write a book "on what is going to happen to children under Roosevelt," the president chuckled: "Very good, he has nine children and should qualify."[84] It is not difficult to comprehend, from the transcripts alone, how such engaging repartee endeared the president to his audience.

On several remarkable occasions that have escaped historical notice, FDR grew relaxed enough to joke with journalists even about his disability. Once he chided *Washington Times-Herald* correspondent Earl Godwin for taking too long to make his way inside the Oval Office. Came Godwin's unthinking reply: "You ought to join one of those rushes some time."[85] Roosevelt did not object; he had genuine reason to want the reporter he fondly called "the Earl of Godwin" to hasten to his usual front-row perch; Steve Early often planted questions with him to make sure administration priorities got mentioned.[86] When another journalist seemed too sluggish one afternoon in securing one of the chairs now set up along a side wall to accommodate older correspondents, an unselfconscious FDR joked, "About time. I know somebody else who has to sit down at press conferences."[87]

Until each interrogation commenced, FDR struck some observers as uncharacteristically tense. As journalists filed inside, he might "toy with his cigarette holder" or fiddle with his keepsakes. "Like most great actors," Charles Hurd speculated, "he always was palpably nervous and ill at ease just before each of his 'performances.'"[88] Yet once a session got underway, FDR became "thoroughly at ease: poised, confident, indicating his pleasure in the give and take."[89] One day Hurd saw the president clutching an antique gold saber as correspondents entered. "Are you going to cut off a few heads this morning?" Hurd inquired. "Charlie," replied Roosevelt, "you have to be good this morning. You watch your questions carefully." Later, when Hurd asked him, "Anything about the monetary situation?" FDR barked, "Give me that sword."[90]

Once formally launched, the sessions often proved equally jolly. Urged to comment on the 1897 Dingley Tariff, Roosevelt jested: "I never heard of it. I am too young."[91] When a journalist asked whether a controversial administration initiative might violate the Constitution, FDR exclaimed in mock horror, "Heavens above!"[92] Once, an objectionable question provoked FDR to complain, "off the record, that is crazy."[93] And when journalist Robert Post tried goading him into speculation about a third term just a few months after he had launched his second, FDR shouted: "Oh. My God! Go and sit in the corner over there and put on your dunce cap and stand with your back to the crowd."[94]

It was no wonder that Hurd called the conferences "the best show on earth."[95] Adding to the spectacle, FDR occasionally brought surprise guests to bear witness or participate. Eleanor joined the throngs from time to time, especially at Hyde Park, conspicuously occupying herself with her knitting. At one memorable 1941 session, White House visitor Winston Churchill joined FDR, the smoke from his trademark cigar intermingling with the plume from Roosevelt's omnipresent Camel. At one point, though he seldom took press questions at home, the British prime minister even stood on a chair to field a few inquiries from the American correspondents.[96]

At all these sessions, FDR shared inside information when he desired and condemned speculation if he preferred. "I have got a lot of news today," he might cheerfully open a conference; or he might irritably declare, "I really have no news today." At any given moment, he could cut short an awkward volley of queries by asserting, "That is all."[97] If he had not received a desired question, he might coax it by hinting, "If I were going to write a story, I would write it along the lines of . . ." In a similar manner, he might suggest, "I want to get something across, only don't put it that way"—or, more directly, "I would put it *this* way" (emphasis added). When he sensed reporters failed to grasp his hints, he might impatiently urge, "use your imagination."[98]

Like his cousin Theodore a deft floater of trial balloons, FDR often prefaced a newsworthy item by proclaiming, "Get out your pencils," or "I can give you a good tip on that if you don't say that I said it."[99] The *Atlanta Constitution* theorized in 1938 that "the friendliness of the conferences and the perpetuation of them are due in large measure to the fact that the President's confidence is never violated by accredited correspondents, even those who oppose him politically or represent newspapers opposed to him."[100] Leaks still found their way into the papers, but much as they infuriated FDR, White House speechwriter Samuel Rosenman suspected that Roosevelt himself "was often the one guilty of letting facts get out about which he had sworn others to secrecy."[101]

Charles Hurd cautioned that those who tried to outfox Roosevelt at press conferences did so at their peril, for "they were pitting inferior skills against a master of the art."[102] Even columnist Heywood Broun—who had once run for Congress in New York under the slogan "I'd rather be right than Roosevelt"—acknowledged that "Franklin Delano Roosevelt is the best newspaper man who has ever been President of the United States."[103]

By 1934 even the onetime chief of staff for Roosevelt's predecessor had joined the chorus of admirers attesting to FDR's public relations genius. While Hoover had fielded only written questions submitted in advance, "Roosevelt talks with amazing freedom," Theodore G. Joslin marveled. "There have been times when he has said little of consequence, but he has talked—and remember, that is the one thing the press wants the President to do."[104]

To be sure, Roosevelt's manipulative charm did not work on everyone. In 1935, the literary magazine *American Mercury* published a scathing assessment likening "pathetic" White House correspondents to "trained seals." Blasting Roosevelt's news conferences as "nothing but concentrated sales talks for the New Deal," critic Eugene A. Levy complained, "The reporters lean forward with popping eyes, gingerly scribbling each word of wisdom as it drops from the mouth of the potentate." Levy was not done. "For some inexplicable reason," he fumed, "as often as a statement emanates from the White House, no matter how asinine or palpably impossible, the correspondents flood the country with the glad tidings." As if in confirmation, the managing editor of the *New York Times* later estimated that by the end of Roosevelt's presidency, his paper alone had printed a staggering one million words about him.[105]

Such attacks did little to dent Roosevelt's popularity with working journalists. Even though most publishers opposed Roosevelt's reelection in 1936, the press corps continued to cover him straightforwardly, even sympathetically. Their bias might even provoke friendly sabotage. That year, one anti-Roosevelt paper ordered its White House photographer somehow to secure a shot of FDR being lifted helplessly about. "This editor thought he could use such a picture to discredit the President's capability as a person," Marion Dickerman believed. Fellow lensmen took to jostling him just as he focused his camera or knocking the instrument from his hands when he took aim. "Now, that was the kind of loyalty he had from the reporters," Dickerman commented. Just to make certain, the press office banned so-called "intimate" candid photos that caught the president "unaware."[106]

But the fact remained that the newspaper publishers lined up four-to-one against Roosevelt's 1936 reelection. "One would have thought," Roosevelt expert William vanden Heuvel told me, that "the enormous work of the New Deal would have permitted at least a passing salute. But it was the owners, not the journalists or subscribers, who represented the calcified resistance."[107]

FDR did attract his share of vitriol from the working press, especially from the new breed of bylined columnists. The anti–trade union writer Westbrook Pegler of the Scripps-Howard chain, for one, routinely castigated both FDR and his wife, whom he labeled "La Boca grande" (big mouth). *Baltimore Sun* columnist Frank A. Kent inhaled anti-FDR gossip at Alice Roosevelt Longworth's Washington cocktail parties and gleefully imparted it to his readers.

In rebuttal, foreign affairs specialist Dorothy Thompson (the wife of novelist Sinclair Lewis), whose column appeared in 170 newspapers, endorsed Roosevelt for a third term in 1940 by arguing that he was a bulwark against fascism. And Walter Winchell, the powerful syndicated Broadway columnist whose staccato voice could be heard on radio even more often than Roosevelt's, never concealed his admiration for the president. Like Thompson, Winchell (who was Jewish) believed that only FDR could save the world from Nazi tyranny. The widely respected veteran Raymond Clapper's "In Washington" column for the *Washington Post* generally backed the administration as well, no doubt motivated by his long friendship with Steve Early.[108] FDR battled for a fair shake from Drew Pearson's new syndicated column "Washington Merry-Go-Round," which occasionally assailed FDR from the left. Ever the cultivator, Roosevelt responded by inviting Pearson and his wife to White House dinners.[109]

Meanwhile, conservative press lords like the McCormicks and the Chandler family at the *Los Angeles Times* continued pummeling FDR on their editorial pages. Throughout World War II, the *Chicago Tribune* remained anti-labor, anti–New Deal, anti-Britain, anti-Russia, and anti-Roosevelt.[110] The indestructible William Randolph Hearst, a onetime booster who had slept in the Lincoln Bedroom early in the Roosevelt era, morphed into a fulminating enemy of the New Deal and ordered his vast newspaper chain to reflect his animus. At one point Hearst did put two of Roosevelt's children, Elliott and Anna, on his payroll, but as their brother James insisted, "[I]f he figured it would give him a grip on father, it didn't work."[111] A scornful Roosevelt took to labeling opposition publishers "The Tory Press" and once, at least according to Jimmy, snuck a look at Hearst's and Pegler's tax records in search of dirt.[112]

Some press attacks grew grotesque enough to be laughable: Roosevelt was a World War I draft dodger, a Communist, a closeted Jew, or a demented paranoiac, went a few of the slanders. Steve Early opted to ridicule rather than deny them in a deft 1939 *Saturday Evening Post* article called "Below the Belt." Early highlighted one series of incendiary stories that a pseudonymous columnist known as the "Squire of Krum Elbow" had published in an obscure upstate New York weekly called the *Highland Post*. The screeds accused FDR of "prenatal" sub-intelligence, and charged he had become the "smiling figurehead" for a cabal of Jews plotting to liquidate America. "The Squire" turned out to be the *Post*'s ultra-nationalist, anti-Semitic publisher (and FDR's fellow Hudson Valley resident) Howland Spencer, an extremist so provocative that he sold his estate to the African American religious leader Father Divine in order to irritate his neighbors.[113]

The *Saturday Evening Post* piece gave Early the useful additional opportunity to dismiss whispers about FDR's physical condition. One whopper, he reported, held that the president had been "found in a coma at his desk" and spirited from the White House for a recuperative trip on a "naval convoy which could not be penetrated" by reporters. Repeating such absurdities allowed the savvy press secretary to credibly maintain that the president's "marvelous health and splendid physical condition undoubtedly have proved a bitter disappointment to many who prattle about" his alleged infirmities.[114]

FDR's own favorite defensive weapon remained the press conference—which is why he held nearly a thousand of them during his twelve years in office. "If the newspapers report what I do and say," he maintained, "I am not concerned about the editorials and columnists." Yet he increasingly blamed beat reporters for their employers' hostility, and as Charles Hurd testified, when he did lose patience "he could be very angry indeed." Even Elliott Roosevelt had to admit, "At times, father did become bitter and vengeful."[115] When FDR's private secretary "Missy" LeHand and his advisor—and future Supreme Court appointee—Felix Frankfurter together begged him to cut down on his complaints for his own good, the president seized a pencil and drafted a memo: "I . . . do hereby solemnly agree to submit, in ample time for full discussion, to Marguerite LeHand and Felix Frankfurter any and all proposed attacks, direct or indirect, upon the press or parts thereof, under any form or pretext, so help me good [*sic*]." He defiantly signed the pledge, "Nerts—Franklin D. Roosevelt."[116]

Most reporters appreciated that FDR never hid his emotions behind a "poker face." His almost theatrical manner made him easy to read—and write about. As Hurd noted, "It was always essential to watch his expression to understand the real meaning of some of his replies. His mobile features expressed everything from deadly seriousness to irony to boredom to anger."[117]

Like Hurd, the *Washington Post*'s Hedley Donovan remained in the president's thrall no matter how often he lashed out at them. "Editorial writers might write harsh things about FDR," he observed, but a "large majority" of White House correspondents "were personally sympathetic to Roosevelt's policies, whatever their publishers may have thought, and few indeed were immune to his famous charm." Donovan, the future editor of *Time* magazine, admitted to feeling "greatly flattered one day, standing in my customary place at one end of the semicircle . . . to receive a large wink from the President as he delivered one transparent piece of humbug. FDR loved to make the reporter a fellow conspirator: you-know-and-I-know-you-know this is just a bit of flim flam."[118]

The tacit "conspiracy" that Donovan so casually recalled—in fact no less formidable than that which consigned Roosevelt's handicap to the shadows—kept the president content, the press sated, and the public reasonably well informed. It provided a platform to help FDR restore national confidence and may well have given him the sounding board to sell the most revolutionary social program the country had ever been asked to support: the New Deal itself.

— 9 —

FRANKLIN D. ROOSEVELT–II

Franklin Roosevelt did a spectacular job of battling for public opinion, in both the New Deal era and World War II, in broadcast and print media alike. But he could have done even more.

For all his availability and outreach, FDR long failed to utilize his twice-weekly press conferences to reach quite as many journalists—or readers—as he might have. For his first eleven years in office, even as FDR worked to woo African American voters to the Democrats from the party of Lincoln, his administration followed disgracefully hidebound traditions and barred reporters of color from the White House. Southern-born press secretary Stephen T. Early, a proud collateral descendant of Confederate general Jubal Early, offered the convenient excuse that only correspondents from daily newspapers could be accredited. But as Steve Early well knew, nearly all black-owned papers of the day appeared but once a week.[1]

More likely, in press relations just as in policy making, the administration feared alienating the white Southern Democrats, whose support it needed to achieve both electoral and legislative success. That meant going slowly on providing equal opportunity for African Americans. As a result, blacks found themselves not only disadvantaged in New Deal programs but excluded from White House press conferences. In fairness, journalists did little to integrate their own ranks, though some correspondents did sneak occasional tidbits to black reporters reduced to waiting for news outside the White House gates.[2]

Adding injury to insult, White House press secretary Early found himself involved in an embarrassing 1940 dustup with a black New York City policeman who claimed that the press secretary kneed him in the groin while trying to force his way into a Roosevelt campaign rally at Madison Square Garden. "He's lucky that's all he got," Early declared unapologetically, livid that the officer had failed to recognize him—and, perhaps more galling, that any black man had tried telling him what to do.[3] The ironic fact that an African American had imposed a barrier on Early instead of the other way around escaped notice. But Republicans (along with champion boxer Joe Louis) condemned Early over the fracas, which was widely reported in the black press. A political crisis was averted only when the aggrieved policeman revealed that he had "always voted for Roosevelt and intended to do so again."[4]

Not until February 1944—after many pleas for accreditation—did the White House Correspondents' Association finally recognize the *Atlanta Daily World*, the first African American daily newspaper of the twentieth century. As its initial Washington reporter, the paper hired Harry S. McAlpin, an aide to educator Mary McLeod Bethune, Director of Negro Affairs at Roosevelt's own National Youth Administration.[5] Perhaps to atone for past sins, Steve Early then labored to speed his credentialing. And when McAlpin at last gained admittance to his very first White House news conference—at Roosevelt's 934th such event—the president seemed transparently eager to take credit for the long-delayed breakthrough, welcoming the pioneering reporter as if he had been his greatest champion. Grasping his hand, FDR proclaimed, "I am glad to see you, McAlpin, and very happy to have you here."[6]

Yet no further steps to integrate the press corps came until May, when "the ban against Negro reporters was lifted for 24 hours" only to permit five black journalists to cover a White House visit by the president of Liberia.[7] Just two months after this latest minor milestone, African American correspondents were excluded from the "elaborate press box" set up for reporters at the Democratic National Convention that nominated FDR for a fourth term. The black press was compelled to cover Roosevelt's latest political coronation from a distant balcony.[8] Ultimately, FDR gets credit for taking small steps to extend opportunities to the black press. The pity is that the administration feared making genuine strides.

Women journalists faced only slightly less hostility. With a handful of exceptions—like May Craig, a julep-voiced, Southern-born correspondent for Maine's Gannett Papers whom FDR enjoyed teasing—few gained regular access to White House press conferences or secured the privilege of traveling with the president. Before one official trip, Steve Early flatly refused to make train reservations for female correspondents, arguing that he had no time to take calls "every fifteen minutes" from women invariably "changing [their] minds" about their plans.[9]

To narrow the journalistic gender gap, the First Lady launched a public relations revolution of her own. At the suggestion of AP reporter Lorena Hickok, a close friend, Eleanor Roosevelt became the first presidential spouse to host regular White House press conferences.[10] The inaugural session took place on March 6, 1933, two days *before* her husband's own. "Girl Reporters Get New Status in Washington," trumpeted one headline.[11] Eleanor's weekly sessions, which would total five hundred in all by the time she left the White House, offered access exclusively to female correspondents.[12]

Eleanor also sought to attack journalistic gender inequity at its roots by urging magazines and newspapers to hire more women. In addition she began writing articles for *McCall's* and *Ladies' Home Journal*, among other periodicals. Books followed, including *It's Up to the Women*, which cannily mixed child-rearing advice with subtle dogma on female empowerment. "Her typewriter has developed no inhibitions since its journey to the White House," huffed the *Chicago Tribune*.[13]

Undaunted, Eleanor broke yet another tradition and began broadcasting—for high pay, which she often donated to charity—on radio programs commercially sponsored by such manufacturers as Pond's cold cream, Sweetheart soaps, and the Simmons Beautyrest mattress. Her topic for the September 4, 1934, Simmons Program was "When Will a Woman Become President of the U.S.?" ("Someday," she ventured, "but I hope that it doesn't happen in the near future.")[14] Most notably, Eleanor launched a syndicated daily newspaper column called "My Day," an enormous popular success that by 1935 appeared in some 135 publications. (It would run continuously until 1962, the year of her death.)

No First Lady had ever attracted so much attention—or hostility. The virulent Westbrook Pegler declared her "impudent, presumptuous, and conspiratorial," snidely commenting "that her withdrawal from public life at this time would be a fine public service."[15] Yet a 1937 Gallup poll gave Eleanor a 67 percent approval rating—higher than the president's.[16]

Like many of his predecessors, FDR consumed newspapers voraciously—often dyspeptically—ranting privately about articles he had not sanctioned and editorials he felt he did not deserve. Each morning, apprehensive aides brought the

New York Times, *Washington Post*, and nearly a dozen other dailies to his bedside along with his breakfast tray. Press Secretary Early often accompanied the delivery, chiefly to absorb "The Boss's" inevitable gripes as he sped through each paper before tossing it dismissively onto the counterpane or floor.

Occasionally joining the ritual was economist Raymond Moley, a member of the White House "Brains Trust" who later turned against the New Deal. Testifying to FDR's "growing petulance about all criticism," Moley remembered that "when I came into his bedroom, he would comment angrily about the papers he had read over his breakfast. This paper had said 'something untrue'; that paper was being 'consistently unfair'; another paper was being run by a publisher who exploits his men."[17] Eventually, Moley noticed, the president began consoling himself that "[e]very time they made an attack upon him, he gained votes."[18]

FDR did not always confine his displeasure to his bedroom. At the end of one press conference during the fraught early days of World War II, he tauntingly presented a German Iron Cross to reporter John O'Donnell of the isolationist New York *Daily News*. Stunned fellow correspondents thought the president, long able "to absorb criticism and even to laugh at himself," had hit "below the belt"—the very phrase Steve Early had once used to deride press critics of FDR. The correspondents chalked up the O'Donnell episode to "war-frayed nerves." Then, in 1943, Drew Pearson criticized Roosevelt as insufficiently sympathetic to America's wartime Soviet allies, and FDR publicly labeled him a "chronic liar." Accusing the president of a "savage outburst of temper" meant to chill all criticism, the press rallied around the columnist.[19]

"We were antagonists," one correspondent summarized the evolving relationship between the press and FDR, "but we liked each other and we laughed and we had a perfect understanding of what each was trying to do."[20] In truth, the perfectionist president found far more fault with the journalists than vice versa. For example, while Roosevelt clearly benefited from personality-driven coverage, he even began chafing when journalists traveling with him filed frivolous reports "on whether I shake hands with Mr. X with my left hand, or looked away when Mr. Y greeted me, or spent forty seconds longer talking with Mr. Z than with his colleague. It would be a lot cheaper," he teased Steve Early, "if all your newspapers would hire Walter Winchell and save railroad fares."[21]

Not even the ever-resourceful FDR could sustain the buoyant atmosphere that prevailed at his early press conferences. The mood first darkened after the president encountered congressional and judicial resistance to the New Deal toward the end of his first term.

Roosevelt grew especially feisty when the Supreme Court invalidated the National Industrial Recovery Act. At a May 1935 press conference, he ridiculed the ruling by contending: "We have been relegated to the horse-and-buggy definition of interstate commerce."[22] Urged to put his colorful remark on the record, Roosevelt agreed—and the phrase entered the popular lexicon almost overnight, whether to his benefit or not remains a matter of historical dispute.

Similarly, when McCormick's ever-hostile *Chicago Tribune* warned that New Deal programs unchecked by the judicial branch would plunge America into Bolshevism, Roosevelt dismissed his fellow prep school alumnus: "Oh, tell Bertie he's seeing things under the bed."[23] For all his glibness, FDR proved incapable of convincing the press or public that his plan to pack the high court with friendlier judges was more than an act of petulance. The scheme went up in flames and the press assigned much of the fault to FDR, who in turn blamed the newspapers. At a special 1935 Q&A for faculty members from journalism schools, he let slip a "lack of confidence in the press" arising from its growing "tendency" to "color news stories" in order to placate publishers who were more concerned with profits than the public good. After rambling on about leaks and other perceived sins, FDR ended his diatribe by cautioning his visitors that his criticism must remain, as he put it, "just between us girls."[24] In the end, Roosevelt's strategy paid off. The reactionary court softened its anti–New Deal stance, the Social Security Act survived legal challenge, and Roosevelt, for losing a small battle with the press, won the war to save his legacy.

Off his peak press game or not, Roosevelt overwhelmed his 1936 election foe, Alfred M. Landon, winning forty-six of the forty-eight states to earn a second term. Steve Early flattered FDR that "newspapers, even the most unfriendly and hostile, believed in your reelection because they felt your popularity runs at flood tide and will continue to do so, despite anything the opposition can do."[25] He may have been right.

All the same, the president's news conferences never quite recaptured their original élan. Merriman Smith, who joined the White House press corps toward the end of FDR's second term, noted that Roosevelt now "debated with reporters," adding: "He insulted them, lectured them, and made them laugh. He called them liars and used the mighty weight of his high office against the press in pile-driving fashion."[26] Journalist Richard A. Stokes complained that the sessions had "degenerated into" something "less professional than social."[27]

Suddenly, reporters began finding Roosevelt's witticisms irritating, his "mugging" insincere, his habit of planting questions insulting, and his mere use of first names for reporters as "a form of psychological bribery."[28]

But the president could no more resist hosting his frequent press conferences than the reporters could hesitate in attending them. By then, the charged get-togethers had assumed almost legendary status in popular culture. Rodgers and Hart even included a spirited parody in their 1937 hit musical *I'd Rather Be Right*. For 290 performances, George M. Cohan sang and danced through a send-up called "Off the Record," portraying a strutting FDR reminding journalists: "Every word that I speak goes into the headlines; / When I speak all the papers hold their deadlines. / But I've found a way of dropping a hint, / Or a glint of the truth / That the boys cannot print . . . That's strictly off the record." The routine achieved such renown it was included in the 1942 Cohan biopic *Yankee Doodle Dandy*, with James Cagney reprising the routine in top hat, tails, and Rooseveltian pince-nez glasses.

Show business hoopla did little to ease growing tensions between the president and real-life journalists back at the White House. By 1937, FDR was accusing the press of "fostering a psychology of fear."[29] The following year, at a special news conference with the Society of Newspaper Editors, he aimed his wrath at his own guests, declaring, "I think [editors] have been more responsible for the inciting of fear in the community than any other factor." Pressed for specific examples, he exaggerated: "Well, I never expect an A.P. story to give my side in the lead. I have not for years." Growing angrier, he added, "the special bureau chiefs down here write what the owner of the newspaper tells them to write, and they leave out half of the truth. They give a one-sided picture to the American people. . . . I have got a letter here from an exceedingly good editor who was fired for writing a pro-Administration editorial—two." Still, he preened, "You never saw me walking up and down with a long face because of anything I ever read in any newspaper. . . . I have always managed to survive."[30]

More seriously, FDR also found himself periodically called on to defend the government against charges of outright manipulation. As early as summer 1934, Republican senator Thomas D. Schall of Minnesota warned that FDR planned to create "an un-American . . . National press service" to circumvent "the Associated Press, the Hearst News Services, and the United Press." Indignantly denying the "vituperative" charge, Roosevelt insisted that the administration contemplated no such "Government-controlled news agencies." But

Schall returned fire, blasting as "insincere" the president's attempt to present himself as a "champion of a free press" and accusing Roosevelt of attempting "to throttle the press and free speech." Reiterating his innocence, FDR snapped, "The incident is closed."[31]

Two years later, reporters learned that someone in the administration had indeed proposed creating just such a "Central Press Bureau." This time, Roosevelt merely shrugged off the report. "Off the record," he commented, "I never heard of it until I read it in the *Times*, and I don't want to hear any more about it." Unabashedly, FDR dubbed himself "Dean of the White House School of Journalism." When he followed up by suggesting, in 1944, that correspondents accompanying him from Warm Springs to Washington should clear their copy with him in advance, the AP reported that Roosevelt had "turned editor, too."[32]

Roosevelt often made news outside the cozy realm of the Oval Office. He delivered countless speeches in Washington and maintained a heavy travel schedule. The presidential trips and vacations—a mind-boggling fifty-two of them overseas from 1933 to 1945—usually attracted a retinue of reporters, leading FDR to half-seriously complain that they hovered "like vultures waiting for something to happen to me."[33] As always, photographers took no pictures as the president was lifted from automobiles, and journalists wrote no accounts of his efforts to cling tightly to rostrums or railings to avoid falling.

Longtime restrictions on spontaneous photography tightened even further after FDR's re-election, with surprisingly little resistance from the corps of professional photographers. Exceptions did occur. Once, after Steve Early banned all lensmen from a 1937 Democratic Party conference at Chesapeake Bay, both the AP and Acme News Photos surreptitiously purchased and published an amateur snapshot of the president taken by an unidentified congressman attending the retreat. An infuriated Early banned both agencies from the rest of the conference and threatened to bar them from Hyde Park as well. *Life* cameraman Myron Hoff Davis remembered, "Most newsmen made no attempt to take such pictures because (1) they supposed the Secret Service might revoke their White House Passes for doing so, (2) nothing could be gained by showing the extent of Roosevelt's infirmity." As a result, few Americans outside the government orbit ever knew the extent of FDR's disability.[34]

Always willing to socialize with journalists, FDR still turned up at many news organization banquets, where he genuinely enjoyed sitting through roasts and skits, especially when the barbs were aimed in his direction. On such occasions he also savored his opportunity for the final word, often responding in the same humorous style with which he had just been pilloried. Launching one such rejoinder at the 1934 Gridiron Club dinner, however, Roosevelt startled his audience by unleashing what sounded at first like a deadly serious attack on the press. "The evils that continue to beset American journalism," he lectured, must be blamed on the "stupidity, cowardice and Philistinism . . . [of] cheap, trashy, stupid and corrupt" writers reporting to editors who "could not pass an entrance examination for Harvard or Tuskegee, or even Yale." The press had grown accustomed to hearing the president's gripes, but not at this level of rancor. Not until the tirade had consumed a few more awkward minutes did the crowd finally begin to recognize the sentiments FDR was spouting: Baltimore newspaperman H. L. Mencken, who was in attendance that very night, had published them seven years earlier in one of his books on American journalism. The audience roared in approval, but Mencken, now a Roosevelt critic, did not find FDR's tongue-in-cheek rehash amusing. He vowed to his dinner companion, "I'll get the son-of-a-bitch; I'll dig skeletons out of his closet."[35]

Such threats rolled off Roosevelt's back. Attempting to get a rise out of him at a 1939 gathering, the Gridiron Club unveiled an eight-foot-high papier-mâché sculpture of FDR's face in the shape of a Sphinx, fashioned entirely from newspaper reports of his vexingly undeclared candidacy for a third term. The irreverent effigy was intended to tweak FDR for keeping reporters in the dark about his political future. Anything but offended, the president took the centerpiece home and installed it in his growing collection of souvenirs.[36]

Safely reelected by a ten-point margin later that year, FDR delivered his first formal speech for the annual White House Correspondents' Association dinner a few weeks after his third inauguration. With war now looming, the occasion called for genuine solemnity. But before launching into an address on American military preparedness, FDR reminded the gathering about the collegiality that he believed still anchored the relationship between the president and the press. His implication was clear: their partnership might soon become more important than ever in the looming fight to save democracy. "For eight years you and I have been helping each other," he acknowledged. Then he added that "in those lands where freedoms do not exist . . . it is a matter of constant amazement that press conferences such as ours can exist in any Nation in the World."[37]

Not surprisingly, World War II curtailed the free flow of news. But not even global conflict immediately altered FDR's routine or demeanor. He began his first news conferences after both Pearl Harbor and D-Day with off-the-record jocularity.

On December 9, 1941, the very day after FDR asked Congress to declare war on Japan, May Craig made her way into a presidential press conference sputtering about suddenly heightened White House security: "You've got a new system out there," she complained. ". . . It's going to take a long time to get in."

"What's that?" Roosevelt inquired to laughter. "What did you have to do? Have they frisked you?"

"Practically."

"Now, May, I don't think that's nice. I will have to hire female secret service agents around here to do the frisking."[38]

FDR welcomed reporters with similar panache on June 6, 1944, the day Operation Overlord successfully got underway in France, greeting reporters, "My Lord—all smiles." Replied one correspondent, "you don't look like you're so solemn yourself, Mr. President." Unable to suppress his relief that Allied forces had gained a toehold on the beaches of Normandy, Roosevelt allowed himself to admit, "No, I'm not solemn, I suppose."[39]

Like previous commanders in chief, however, the prospect of uninhibited press coverage in wartime became to FDR no laughing matter. Although he wisely rejected outright censorship, Roosevelt had already established an Office of Government Reports in 1939, and the following year, a White House Office of Facts and Figures, as well as a Division of Information within the federal Office of Emergency Management.[40] Like their World War I–era counterparts, these bureaus concentrated on supplying the country's rural newspapers and local government offices with positive news.[41] To his credit, FDR objected when the military suggested imposing tougher oversight. "Obviously," he replied, advocates for the crackdown knew nothing "about what the American public, let alone the American press, would say to a thing like this"—especially while America remained at peace.[42]

Two weeks after Pearl Harbor, however, FDR signed an emergency executive order creating an Office of Censorship after all and naming AP news editor Byron Price as its director. Under the motto "Least said, soonest mended" (soon supplanted by the popular credo "Loose lips sink ships"), the new bureau focused on blocking potentially injurious information at its source. Price (and FDR) hoped to avoid the reactive government overreach of the Civil War years, when the Lincoln administration shut down newspapers *after* they published objectionable material.[43] The onetime newsman vowed to interfere only with "information which the enemy would like to have," which included "defense matters, shipping data, weather conditions, and details of war production." As Price reassured the press, "Editorial opinions and criticisms never can be brought under government restraint, and ought not to be, so long as our present form of government endures."[44]

Responding to the call, radio networks voluntarily banned antiwar sentiments from the airwaves, spurred morale with patriotic programming, and restricted the flow of news emanating from combat zones. The industry even acquiesced to a temporary ban on quiz shows once experts warned that spies might infiltrate them to send coded messages to the enemy. Perhaps the Office of Censorship's greatest accomplishment was keeping the Manhattan Project a tightly guarded secret save for a lone *Cleveland Press* report that hinted that latter-day "Einsteins" were working on a powerful new bomb at Los Alamos. Inexplicably, the enemy never followed up on the potentially disastrous leak.

The expanding wartime oversight bureaucracy soon approached New Deal levels of overlapping complexity. In June 1942, FDR created yet another agency, the Office of War Information (OWI), consolidating prewar propaganda bureaus into a single operation that rivaled the old Creel Commission in power and scope. Naming CBS newsman Elmer Davis to run it, FDR ordered domestic and overseas OWI bureaus to "formulate and carry out, through the use of the press, radio, motion picture, and other facilities, information programs designed to facilitate the development of an informed and intelligent understanding, at home and abroad, of the status and progress of the war effort . . . and aims of the Government."[45] Under OWI prodding, Hollywood flooded American screens with anti-Axis movies and dispatched some of its greatest directors—John Ford, John Huston, Frank Capra, William Wyler, and George Stevens—to join the military and film the action for uplifting documentaries,[46] like Capra's astounding seven-part *Why We Fight* (1942–45), for which, ironically, he tried to re-create the hypnotic appeal of Leni Riefenstahl's notorious fascist propaganda film *Triumph of the Will*. To add to the confusion, publisher Henry Luce organized his own Commission on Freedom of the Press to study the proper role of the media in wartime, but named a college president, Robert Hutchins, as chair, and included no journalists on the panel at all. Its final report, delayed until after the war, endorsed Roosevelt's notion that in making journalistic choices, the press had an ethical responsibility to consider the social good.[47]

FDR made it clear he would tolerate no reports that jeopardized military operations. Information could continue to flow from press to public, he promised at the first news conference after Pearl Harbor, providing it was "accurate" and did "not give aid and comfort to the enemy." Added Roosevelt, "I should think that those two conditions ought to be put up in every office in Washington . . . that includes newspaper offices."[48] Pressed to be more precise about these vague instructions, FDR at least revealed who precisely would be judging what news could and could not be imparted: "The test is what the Commander in Chief of the Army and Navy thinks . . . would be harmful to the defense of the country to give out."[49]

Most veteran correspondents accepted the new restrictions but not the new atmosphere. When one *New York Times* reporter tried returning to an FDR press conference after a long leave, he found to his annoyance that he "had to have everything but a blood test" to gain readmission. Worse, he complained, the session itself lasted but ten minutes and elicited only softball inquiries. "We used to stand outside and load those questions like a Continental's musket," he reminisced somewhat hyperbolically, ". . . then march in and fire both barrels. But this was all politeness and punctilio and namby-pamby questions. Reporters . . . now seemed to figure: with all he has on his shoulders, should I really do this to him? The old rough-and-tumble give-and-take is another wartime casualty."[50]

War claimed another "victim" by virtually silencing isolationist right-wing newspapers, but FDR now found himself the occasional target of press disapproval from the left. In 1942, the liberal media strenuously objected to an unsavory, widely reported American "collaboration" with pro-fascist North Africans meant to pave the way for an Allied invasion (Operation Torch). FDR took a PR beating. Ironically, criticism also came from two new daily papers created specifically to offset conservative opposition to the administration. One was the feisty New York tabloid *PM*, for whose founding Roosevelt's aide Tommy Corcoran had helped secure investment money. Yet it morphed into a particular thorn in FDR's side. In a series of articles by its crusading Washington correspondent I. F. Stone, the paper lamented White House indifference to Jewish refugees. Then, along with another ostensibly sympathetic new paper, the *Chicago Sun*, designed as an alternative voice to the anti-FDR *Tribune*, the paper criticized Roosevelt for continuing to turn a blind eye to racial segregation. Jonathan

Daniels, an assistant to the president, confided that the White House had expected more loyalty: "This Negro business is only one aspect of the failure of *PM* and the *Chicago Sun* to give the administration the support they were designed to provide."[51] Whether coincidentally or not, the editor of *PM*, Ralph Ingersoll, soon found himself reclassified 1-A by a local draft board dominated by supporters of Father Coughlin's right-wing, isolationist magazine *Social Justice*.[52]

Finally, whether due to wartime obligations or growing impatience with the press, or both, FDR began curtailing his own press coverage. His news conference schedule dwindled from 374 during his second term to 279 in his third. The news sessions themselves produced fewer stories and more "no comments" than ever. In the name of wartime security, Roosevelt often slipped out of Washington to unknown locations for extensive, secret trips, out of the range of press scrutiny for the first time in years.

On one such jaunt, journeying by sea to Newfoundland in 1941 for the Atlantic Charter conference with Winston Churchill, he not only excluded journalists, he eluded them. British reporters accompanied Churchill to that shipboard summit, but FDR intentionally misled White House correspondents into believing he would be taking a vacation aboard the presidential yacht. "Even at my ripe old age," he guiltlessly confessed, "I feel a little thrill in making a get-away—especially from the American press." Indeed, Roosevelt's son Elliott, who was on the scene, remembered that FDR enjoyed "giving the press the slip, much as a twelve-year-old boy playing cops-and-robbers will enjoy shaking a playmate who is trying to 'shadow' him." The president was less amused, however, when the prime minister of England arrived "complete with press retinue not very well disguised as Ministry of Information officials." Elliott described it as the first, but not the last, time "that Churchill surprised father."[53]

Opportunities for press coverage widened only slightly at the Casablanca summit in 1943. Although he was not on hand to observe the conference personally, the recently discharged army veteran and future newscaster David Brinkley groused that correspondents there "were herded like farm animals into a theatrically staged event called a press conference but they were not allowed to ask questions. Military secrecy had to be kept, they were told."[54] Unrepentant, Roosevelt barred reporters altogether from a distinctly civilian international food conference soon thereafter at Hot Springs, Virginia. Raymond Clapper believed that FDR opted for "secrecy" there "because at Casablanca he found it so much more pleasant not to have newspaper reporters around." Seething over the new restrictions, Clapper scornfully added, "We newspaper workers . . . may not have the social graces that Groton and Harvard could have given us all had we been rich men's sons," but we "try as best we can to keep the American people informed about their government."[55]

FDR never restored full press access—or regained full press sympathy—again.

There was always radio—through which Roosevelt could entirely bypass the filter of journalistic oversight and speak directly to the public. FDR was no stranger to the medium. As New York governor, he had broadcast as early as 1929 reports on such topics as conservation, aid to disabled children, and the adoption of the state budget.[56] "If he could not control his publisher-critics," David Brinkley observed, "he could go around them." The airwaves gave FDR "a seamless pipeline running directly to the American people with nobody in between to turn the valves."[57]

No president ever used the airwaves so effectively. In the opinion of the *Times*' Arthur Krock, FDR became "the best showman the White House has lodged since modern science made possible such an effective dual performance."[58] By "dual performance," Krock meant to acknowledge FDR's concurrent mastery of press conferences and broadcast addresses alike. Instinctively, FDR approached these mediums from opposite extremes, inundating the newspapermen with opportunities while carefully limiting his appropriation of the airwaves.

His greatest impact unquestionably came from his Fireside Chats—nowhere near as ubiquitous as his twice-weekly press conferences but exponentially more influential. Altogether, FDR delivered just twenty-eight prime-time chats over the twelve years from 1933 to 1945, an average of only two or three annually. Yet, as contemporaries later testified, when they aired nationwide, time seemed to stand still. In 1932, the year of FDR's election, *New York Times* correspondent Anne O'Hare McCormick warned that the new medium of radio might exact an "almost anesthetic effect upon the mind."[59] If so, Roosevelt became its hypnotist in chief.

Technology and industry did their parts to make Roosevelt's domination possible. During the span of FDR's presidency, the percentage of American households with radios more than doubled, from a mere one-third in 1930 to 83 percent by 1940. This transformative period also brought audiences their first access to simultaneously broadcast nationwide programming, an impossibility until the Roosevelt era: the NBC radio network had launched in 1926, CBS in 1927, and ABC the year FDR took office, 1933.[60] The consolidations set the stage for FDR to conquer the medium, and he made the most of the opportunity. His talks may have been ingeniously crafted to speak to individuals, but they reached the entire country at once.

Decades later, those who had lived through the Roosevelt presidency imagined that he had been on the air almost continuously. To be sure, FDR could indeed be heard on radio often, since the networks aired many of his formal speeches, too. In 1936, he also began delivering State of the Union messages in the evening, and live on air—"another publicity stunt," according to the GOP. But nothing captivated audiences like the Fireside Chats—intimate conversations that made listeners almost believe their president had entered their own homes as a visitor. Interestingly, their evocative title was not Roosevelt's brainchild; it was coined by CBS's Washington station manager, Harry C. Butcher, after reading a press release announcing the initial broadcast. It was CBS newsman Robert Trout who became the first to use the phrase on air from the White House at the second of the chats.[61] The fortuitous branding enshrined the transmissions under a single, unifying label.

Back on March 12, 1933, Roosevelt had delivered his first Fireside Chat in an atmosphere of national trauma. Eight days earlier, he had assumed office with the nation's banks in catastrophic free-fall. FDR responded by ordering a four-day "bank holiday" to stanch further pressure from fearful depositors, then rammed reform legislation through Congress. But the crisis in confidence required more than regulation—or, he sensed, press conferences like the two expansive sessions he had already hosted by that date. FDR knew he must reassure the entire country. Electing to speak exclusively on the banking emergency, he established another enduring pattern: he would devote this and each of his subsequent chats to a single pressing theme.

At around 10:20 that historic night, aides wheeled the president into the Diplomatic Reception Room on the ground floor of the White House, the setting for most of these talks over the next twelve years. FDR carried his script in one hand and "the inevitable cigarette" in the other. The usually spacious twenty-nine-by-thirty-six-foot, oval-shaped chamber was filled to overflowing with temporary furniture, cables, and network personnel. Twenty or thirty family and staff members were already seated in "uncomfortable folding chairs" to observe the milestone broadcast. "There happened to be a real fireplace in the room," Sam Rosenman, one of these eyewitnesses, acknowledged, "but it was empty." The president was rolled to a "desk on which were bunched three or four microphones, a reading light, a pitcher of water, and glasses."[62] Minutes before entering the room, FDR had inserted an artificial tooth into his mouth. Without it, he had learned, radio picked up the fact that he whistled his *s*'s.

With ten minutes left to airtime, announcers for the three networks quietly began rehearsing their opening comments from individual cubicles that had been set up along the far walls of the room. "The President, once seated at his desk, exchanged greetings and pleasantries for a few moments with the guests and announcers. As the minute of ten-thirty approached, the atmosphere got more tense." At this and future broadcasts, he "would put out his cigarette, arrange his reading copy, and take a drink of water, as nervously as when he was about to address a visible audience. Then, on signal, complete silence, a nod from the chief radio engineer," and an announcement "stating tersely that the broadcast was coming live from" the White House from the president of the United States—"and finally, the clear resonant voice."[63]

"My friends," he began,

> I want to talk for a few minutes with the people of the United States about banking—to talk with the comparatively few who understand the mechanics of banking, but more particularly with the overwhelming majority of you who use banks for the making of deposits and the drawing of checks. I want to tell you about what has been done in the last few days, and why it was done, and what the next steps are going to be.[64]

The down-to-earth broadcast captivated the country. "The people listened," John Gunther reported, ". . . and felt that the man in the White House was their friend, as well as leader, who would save them from further catastrophe no matter what. Almost audible sighs of relief went up through the entire land." Gunther marveled at FDR's technique: "You could practically feel him physically in the room."[65] Echoed journalist Richard Strout: "[His] voice, calm, beautifully modulated, came right into the living room with you. You felt he was there talking to you, not to 50 million others, but to you personally."[66] Eventually, the bank crisis eased, and the stock market recorded major gains.

Time after time, this phenomenal connection recurred. Increasingly aware he was casting a powerful spell on his radio audiences, Roosevelt came to believe he had created the magic by using his own imagination. "[W]hile I sat in my study in the White House," he later reported on air, ". . . I had before my eyes the picture of all those Americans with whom I was talking. I saw the workmen in the mills, the mines, the factories; the girl behind the counter; the small shopkeeper; the farmer doing his spring plowing; the widows and the old men wondering about their life's savings." The point was, FDR could visualize his listeners as clearly as they could conjure up an image of their leader. Newsreel films of the Fireside Chats helped, but so did Roosevelt's intimate delivery. Usually speaking on Sunday nights (when the largest number of people would be home) between 9:00 and 11:00 P.M. eastern standard time, the president cornered huge swaths of the American radio audience—by one estimate, more than 80 percent on the eve of World War II. In 1934, an entertainment writer ranked Fireside Chats—along with Metropolitan Opera broadcasts and *Amos 'n' Andy*—as the "most popular programs" on the air.[67]

To FDR's opponents, they became too popular. During the 1936 election race, the Los Angeles station KFI announced it would no longer broadcast the president's Fireside Chats, calling them "nothing more than campaign speeches." If Roosevelt wanted to continue speaking on their stations, Earle C. Anthony's KFI and KCEA insisted, the Democratic organization would have to pay for airtime.[68] By popular demand, the ban was soon lifted.

Significantly, the broadcasts also helped neutralize the on-air vitriol from right-wing broadcast personalities like the anti-Semitic Father Charles Coughlin, whom FDR regarded as highly dangerous. Originally a Roosevelt supporter and New Deal advocate, the Detroit-based Coughlin had turned against the president in 1935 and continued his increasingly virulent broadcasts until forced off the air as a Nazi sympathizer in 1939. At one point his syndicated diatribes attracted forty million listeners.

Professional broadcasters like David Brinkley may have regarded FDR's efforts cynically, but Lorena Hickok, reporting from the South, where she had been dispatched by the Federal Emergency Relief Association (FERA) to assess the impact of its programs, marveled: "It's funny, but people down here all seem to think they know the President personally! It comes in part, I imagine, from their having heard him speak—so much more than any other President—over the radio, and in such friendly man-to-man fashion. They feel he is talking to each one of them, personally!"[69] As another FERA reporter, Martha Gellhorn, put it after canvassing folks in the same region, Roosevelt was "at once God and their intimate friend."[70]

Secretary of Labor Frances Perkins observed similarly hypnotic reactions whenever she, too, found herself in parlors where ordinary Americans heard the chats as they were broadcast. "I have seen men and women gathered around the radio, even those who didn't like him or who were opposed to him politically, listening with a pleasant, happy feeling of association of friendship," she testified. "The exchange between them and him through the medium of radio was very real. I have seen tears come to their eyes as he told them of some tragic episode" and "I have also seen them laugh."[71]

A listener who attested most vividly to FDR's spellbinding effect on air was the future Nobel Prize winner Saul Bellow. Then working in Chicago as part of the Works Progress Administration (WPA) writers' project, young Bellow found himself captivated by the mere sound of that "odd Eastern accent, which in anyone else would have irritated Midwesterners." He never forgot "walking eastward on the Chicago Midway on a summer evening" during the broadcast of one particularly entrancing Fireside Chat. Under the trees, "drivers had pulled over, parking bumper to bumper, and turned on their radios to hear Roosevelt. They had rolled down the windows and opened the car doors. Everywhere the same voice. . . . You could follow without missing a single word as you strolled by. You felt joined to these unknown drivers, men and women smoking their cigarettes in silence, not so much considering the president's words as affirming the rightness of his tone and taking assurance from it."[72] Bellow promenaded a full mile that night without once wandering out of earshot of Franklin D. Roosevelt.

Several of FDR's "intimate broadcasts" resonated as much for substance as style. One was the "Arsenal of Democracy" talk on December 29, 1940. It was "not a Fireside Chat on war," FDR cautioned at the outset, but "a talk on national security; because the nub of the whole purpose of your president is to keep you now, and your children later, and your grandchildren much later, out of a last-ditch war for the preservation of American independence and all of the things that American independence means to you and to me and to ours." Roosevelt ended the mesmerizing talk by declaring: "We must be the great Arsenal of democracy. For us this is an emergency as serious as war itself."[73] The calculated use of "we" and "you" personified a rhetorical style honed to bind the speaker to individual listeners. Historians credit the talk not only with winning popular support for the "Lend Lease" program in aid of Great Britain, but also for steeling Americans themselves for future battle. As a performance, it ranked as a masterpiece.

On February 23, 1942, with America now embroiled in that conflict, FDR asked listeners to follow along on their own household maps as he chatted frankly about recent military setbacks in the Pacific. "This war is a new kind of war," he preached:

> It is different from all other wars of the past, not only in its methods and weapons, but also in its geography. It is warfare in terms of every continent, every island, every sea, every air lane in the world. That is the reason why I have asked you to take out and spread before you a map of the whole earth, and to follow me in the references I shall make to the world-encircling battle lines of this war.

According to legend, advance word that the president planned asking listeners to follow along using their own visual aids had generated a nationwide run on maps and globes.[74]

On January 11, 1944, suffering from the flu and worn down by his recent voyage to Tehran to confer with Stalin and Churchill, FDR decided on doctor's orders to forgo his constitutionally obligated State of the Union address—at least as far as it, by recent tradition, required him to address Congress in person. Rather than make his way to Capitol Hill, FDR submitted his annual message in writing (nineteenth-century style) and then ingeniously adapted it into a Fireside Chat from the White House. For good measure, just as he had done from his New York City home the day after the 1932 election, he went on to offer highlights from the talk for the benefit of newsreel cameras. While opponents focused on his snub to senators and representatives, to those who tuned in to the live transmission or soon saw excerpts in their local movie theaters, the major takeaway was the president's landmark proposal for a "second Bill of Rights" to guarantee "economic security and independence" for all Americans "regardless of station or race or creed . . . to make this nation greater in a better world." The eight-point program aimed to guarantee the right to a job, a sufficient income, and access to markets for farmers; free trade unfettered by unfair competition; decent housing, adequate medical care, safeguards to protect older citizens, and good education for younger ones—a breathtaking agenda that would not be fully addressed for twenty years.[75]

A similar air of momentous solemnity characterized the chats Roosevelt began broadcasting to mark the turning points of the war. FDR may have greeted D-Day with an unrestrainable grin for the private benefit of White House reporters, but he eased into the story cautiously on the radio, broadcasting an invasion-eve chat in which he confirmed only the recent fall of Rome.

"The first of the Axis capitals is now in our hands," he exulted that night. "One up and two to go!" Although he ended the broadcast by asking God to "watch over . . . all of our gallant, fighting men," he offered no hint that Operation Overlord would commence only hours later.[76] The following evening, he returned to the airwaves, sheepishly admitting: "Last night, when I spoke *with you* [emphasis added] about the fall of Rome, I knew at that moment that troops of the United States and our allies were crossing the Channel in another and greater operation. It has come to pass with success this far. And so, in this poignant hour, I ask you to join with me in prayer." Even in announcing an invasion involving fifty-seven thousand Americans, FDR had made certain to speak reassuringly "with" and not "to" his listeners.

"Almighty God," he began the supplication he had worked so hard to compose, "Our sons, pride of our Nation, this day have set upon a mighty endeavor, a struggle to preserve our Republic, our religion, and our civilization, and set free a suffering humanity. Lead them straight and true; give strength to their arms, stoutness to their hearts, steadfastness in their faith. . . . Thy will be done, Almighty God."[77]

As Allied troops advanced overseas, the radio saturation continued at home. On June 12, barely a week after his most recent broadcast, FDR aired yet another chat, this time devoted almost perfunctorily to selling war bonds. It was as if the president sensed his voice alone could steady America's anxiety.

To Roosevelt's enemies, Fireside Chats posed serious political dangers, for they were all but unanswerable. "A fireside chat never filled an empty stomach," a Republican aspirant for the U.S. Senate from Illinois had tried sourly complaining before the war.[78] But the tide of public approbation for the great communicator—and his greatest communications innovation—swept such criticism away.

As spontaneous as Roosevelt sounded in his Fireside Chats, they were products of intense preparation. FDR required that the addresses be carefully scripted, and often revised them right up until airtime. For his debut talk, he had ordered up a script from Charles Michelson, a former journalist who had served as publicity director for the Democratic National Committee, specializing in bitter attacks on Herbert Hoover. But Roosevelt discarded Michelson's draft, then "lay on a couch, and dictated his own speech." Michelson remembered that as FDR stared at a wall, he conjured up images of a village mason "at work on a new building, a girl behind the counter and a farmer in his field," all of whom depended on their local banks.[79] Occasionally, Roosevelt improvised as he spoke on the radio. Presidential speechwriter Sam Rosenman recalled, "He loved to 'ad lib,'" and in many cases the "'Ad libbing' improved the prepared text."[80]

Rosenman, who came to share writing duty with Harry Hopkins and, later, prizewinning playwright Robert E. Sherwood, remembered Roosevelt dictating early drafts himself and mercilessly editing subsequent rewrites, insisting they be simple, direct, and frank. The language must be conversational, not oratorical; simple, not complex; and, above all, truthful. When one wartime pep talk "that had taken hours to write" was "ruthlessly discarded in a minute," Hopkins deduced that the boss found it too cheerful. "One thing the President does not want to do is to kid the American people into believing that this is anything but a tough son-of-a-bitch war against the toughest and cruelest bastards on earth."[81] As Rosenman came to understand, FDR believed that if Americans "were taken into the confidence of their government and received a full and truthful statement of what was happening, they would choose the right course."[82]

Roosevelt took every broadcast seriously. Eyewitnesses often noticed him sweating and trembling just before going on the air. Yet audiences detected neither his meticulous preparation nor his high anxiety. Frances Perkins, who often joined the circle of aides who watched him broadcast from the White House, noted that once he began speaking, he became "unconscious . . . of the twenty or thirty of us in that room" and focused "on the people listening at the other end. As he talked his head would nod and his hands would move in simple, comfortable gestures. His face would smile and light up as though he were actually sitting on the front porch or in the parlor" with his millions of listeners. "People felt this," she asserted, "and it bound them to him in affection."[83]

Roosevelt would deliver his twenty-eighth and, as it turned out, final Fireside Chat on January 6, 1945, calling again for an "American economic Bill of Rights" that guaranteed all citizens "the right to a decent home, to good education, to good medical care, to social security, [and] to reasonable farm income."

"Most important of all," he concluded that night's talk, "1945 can, and must, see the substantial beginning of the organization of world peace—for we all know what such an organization means in terms of security, and human rights and religious freedom. We Americans of today, together with our allies, are making history—and I hope it will be a better history than ever has been made before."[84]

A year earlier, FDR's health had begun a steep—and painfully visible—decline. According to reporter Merriman Smith, "He became listless and poor of voice . . . increasingly quarrelsome about petty things." Correspondents relegated to the rear of his office during press conferences "began to have difficulty in hearing" him.[85] At the very July 11, 1944, session at which he revealed his plans to run for a fourth term, observers noticed that his hands shook so much he could hardly light his cigarette.

Smith remembered that when the president ended that momentous announcement by joking to correspondents, "You've got your news, now get out," the newsmen commenced a wild "scrimmage" to get back to the press room to call in the scoop. Smith himself "drove, fullback style" toward the door, oblivious to his rivals. A Civil Aeronautics Board public relations man who had observed the event ended up trampled in the stampede. "Mr. Roosevelt was pop-eyed with amazement when the crowd cleared," Smith laughed. "Flat on the floor in front of the gadget-littered presidential desk was a figure looking for all the world like a corpse. Staff members quickly helped the public relations man to his feet."[86]

The big story the reporters missed—or ignored—that day was that the president seemed barely strong enough to get through his press conference, much less a presidential campaign. Visiting him for an exclusive interview, the *New York Times*' Turner Catledge was "shocked and horrified" by the president's emaciated appearance. Worse, FDR "would start talking about something, then in mid-sentence he would stop and his mouth would drop open and he'd sit in silence. I knew I was looking at a terribly sick man."[87]

Medical specialists who belatedly examined him at the insistence of his daughter Anna confirmed Catledge's diagnosis. They determined among themselves that Roosevelt suffered from stratospherically high blood pressure and congestive heart failure. Doctors pronounced his condition incurable, progressive, and fatal.[88] Official bulletins maintained he was merely fighting a stubborn flu.

The press never formally learned that Roosevelt was terminally ill but knew they were not being told the truth. Candid as they later became in their memoirs, they said nothing at the time to their newspaper readers. Just as reporters had once conspired to keep his disability out of print, now they refrained from elaborating on his undisguisable deterioration. Neither Catledge nor the White

House correspondents publicly questioned Roosevelt's physical capacity for office, even if most doubted he could survive a fourth term if elected.

While photographers still did not take spot pictures of the president in his wheelchair, even sanctioned shots could not camouflage his alarming weight loss or the dark circles now ringing his eyes. A picture taken in the observation car of his train as he broadcast his acceptance speech to the 1944 Democratic Convention—FDR was in San Diego en route to another physically draining military conference, this time in the Pacific—showed him looking dazed and slack-jawed.[89] Reportedly, when Steve Early saw the photo he ordered the cameraman who took it banished from the presidential entourage.

Still, with American troops now on a precarious march toward Berlin, even a reduced FDR seemed to some more indispensable than ever. Arthur Hays Sulzberger, the *New York Times* publisher who "disliked Mr. Roosevelt" and had endorsed his Republican opponent, Wendell Willkie, four years earlier, now switched sides again and backed the president for reelection.[90] The *Times* proved an exception: in all, only 230 newspapers endorsed Roosevelt in 1944, with 1,067 siding with Republican challenger, Thomas E. Dewey. The usual lopsided editorial opposition had little impact. Although voters gave FDR his narrowest victory yet, 53 percent of the popular vote, it was more than enough to give him 432 electoral votes to Dewey's 99. But Roosevelt's cadaverous pallor at a White House correspondents' dinner just a few months later so visibly shocked *Times* reporter Arthur Krock that FDR felt compelled to reassure the journalist as he departed the banquet: "Cheer up, Arthur. Things have seldom been as bad as you said they were."[91]

But they were. The strain of the February 1945 Yalta Conference, and the fourteen-thousand-mile round-trip journey it required, broke Roosevelt's health once and for all. En route home across the Atlantic aboard the USS *Quincy*, he spent most of his days resting below decks, venturing out only to attend movie screenings—or host an occasional press conference. On February 19, he summoned reporters to a surprisingly lucid oceangoing briefing. Fatigued or not, Roosevelt coherently recapped the Yalta summit and put in a word for the nascent United Nations.[92] But a few days later, in a nationally broadcast—and filmed—report to Congress, Roosevelt remained unapologetically seated, explaining publicly, for the first time, how difficult it had become to bear the extra weight of his ten-pound leg braces.

Back in the White House, he did resume his jocular ways at his very first press conference since the summit, commencing to tease May Craig as soon as the correspondents assembled. "It is a curious thing," he began in mock disappointment, "I didn't hear a thing from May the entire time I was away. She never wrote to me, or cabled me, or anything." To a round of laughter, Craig retorted, "I wrote you before you went, though." Answered FDR, "You mean you wrote me *up*—or down, in other words."[93] If the transcript can be believed, Roosevelt seemed his old self.

By early spring, however, his remaining energy fading, the president headed down to Warm Springs in one final effort to recapture his former vim. He was reported to be on a long vacation, out of the easy reach of reporters bivouacked eight miles away. On April 5, he unexpectedly staged his 998th press conference inside the "Little White House." Having met there earlier in the day with Philippine president Sergio Osmeña, Roosevelt wanted his distinguished visitor paraded before American journalists. FDR opened the 2:00 P.M. session by introducing his guest and instructing reporters, "I thought you could come up and write a story for release when we get back to Washington . . . in another week or ten days."[94]

Then the emaciated lion unleashed a captivating soliloquy on the war-ravaged Philippine islands, conceding at one point that the United States would now need to assume responsibility for policing the entire Pacific. Exhausted he may have been, but the president went on to field more than a dozen questions, at one point reenacting an entire conversation he had held with Joseph Stalin in Yalta. Osmeña got a word in only once.

"Mr. President," came one of the final questions for FDR, "do you think we will have a chance to talk with you again on other subjects before you go [back to Washington]?"

"I think you will see me several times before I go," came the optimistic reply. After all, he explained with one more joke, "Some of the boys cannot get their facts straight." His very last comment to the correspondents that afternoon was the long-familiar admonition: "By the way, this is all off the record."[95]

One week later, on April 12, FDR embarked on a therapeutic drive into the nearby Georgia hills. Returning to the Little White House, his car reduced speed as it approached a man on horseback. It was UPI correspondent Merriman Smith, out for a ride of his own. As the vehicle rolled closer, Smith later remembered, FDR "bowed majestically to me. The car was moving slowly as the President spoke. His voice was wonderful and resonant . . . like the Roosevelt of old. . . . Roosevelt hailed me with: 'Heigh-o Silver.' As far as I was concerned, those were his last words."[96]

To be sure, they were the last words FDR ever spoke to a journalist. A few hours later, the greatest public relations magician the White House had ever seen suffered a massive stroke and died.

At his passing—old well beyond his sixty-three years—Roosevelt earned accolades even from his most obdurate press adversaries, just as the relentlessly abused Lincoln had inspired reverential obituaries from opposition newspapers after his assassination. Well before his death, even the hostile *Chicago Tribune*—the paper that had once helped Lincoln devise public relations strategy—had acknowledged FDR as "one of the most skillful publicists America has ever known."[97]

The passage of time—and the introduction of advanced communication platforms of which Roosevelt never even dreamed—have not dimmed that appraisal. Looking back at his years of jousting with Roosevelt for quotable information, Merriman Smith credited him with a talent that transcended technology: he had been "a dramatic king."[98]

Roosevelt was not only an instinctive public relations wizard. He mastered powerful new media techniques and deployed them brilliantly to gain favor and undercut criticism, but never to divide and conquer the public—except to remind the powerful of their obligation to help the needy. Aside from legislative innovation and military might, press outreach became FDR's most potent weapon in fighting both the Great Depression and the Greatest War.

In pursuing monumental goals—resuscitating the economy and defeating the Axis—he could be ruthless and devious, self-righteous and demanding, intolerant and impatient, secretive and misleading. He charmed and befriended but also bullied and dissembled. He shared more information with journalists more often than any president ever had—or would again; but with equal panache, he withheld an enormous amount as well. For twelve years, he proved himself an ingenious, almost irresistible communicator. No one more adroitly corralled the press to advance public policy; and no press corps ever so willingly reported what a chief executive desired, or more graciously concealed what he wanted hidden.

Franklin D. Roosevelt, the chief executive who revolutionized presidential communications, would prove a very tough act to follow.

PART FOUR

“FAR GREATER PUBLIC INFORMATION”

10

JOHN F. KENNEDY

As early as 1939, midway through FDR's long tenure in the White House, Raymond P. Brandt, the Washington correspondent for the *St. Louis Post-Dispatch*, already believed it "hardly conceivable that the next President will be the virtuoso that President Roosevelt is in . . . furnishing the country with such a wealth of immediate news without injury to his administration."[1]

Brandt proved correct. Roosevelt's immediate successor, plainspoken Harry S. Truman, communicated with admirable forthrightness, but something magical had died with Roosevelt—and something intimidating as well. "Mr. Roosevelt was a far more imposing, fearful figure than Mr. Truman," the UPI's Merriman Smith explained, "and consequently it took more courage to bait him than it does to throw brickbats at the man from Missouri."[2] Many journalists wondered if Truman, reelected in his own right in 1948, was up to the job of managing the postwar economy at home or commanding both a Cold War with the Russians and a hot war in Korea.

"I only wish I could get the public to appreciate the Harry Truman I know," lamented his much-liked press secretary (and longtime friend) Charles G. Ross.[3] But the *Los Angeles Times* Washington bureau chief Robert S. Donovan ranked Truman as "awfully dull on the radio" and "very poor" on the infant medium of television.[4] One day, while preparing for a December 1950 TV interview, Ross keeled over sideways at his desk so suddenly that eyewitnesses at first thought he was playing a joke. The White House doctor pronounced him dead of a heart attack. That very night, Truman's daughter Margaret, a professional singer, was scheduled to give a recital at Washington's Constitution Hall. The president and his wife went ahead with their plans to attend but told Margaret nothing about Ross's death.

Washington Post music critic Paul Hume showed little sympathy when he panned Margaret's performance the next day. "Miss Truman cannot sing very well," he bluntly wrote. "She is flat a good deal of the time."[5] The review sent Truman over the edge. In a rage no doubt exacerbated by the traumatic events the day before, he dashed off a scathing handwritten rebuke that deserves to be ranked alongside Washington's Farewell Address and Lincoln's Greeley letter as the most extraordinary missives any president ever directed to a journalist before the Trump era.

Of course, Truman used saltier language. "I've just read your lousy review of Margaret's concert," Truman began. ". . . Some day I hope to meet you. When that happens you'll need a new nose, a lot of beefsteak for black eyes and perhaps a supporter below."[6] *Post* publisher Philip Graham declined to publish the screed, while Hume graciously exonerated its writer. "I can only say," the critic conceded, "that a man suffering the loss of a friend and carrying the burden of the present world crisis ought to be indulged in an occasional outburst of temper."[7] Word of the letter soon leaked out anyway and found its way onto the pages of the rival *Washington News*. It may have done more to bolster Truman's image than V-J Day.

Following Truman's retirement, Dwight D. Eisenhower, the first Republican president since Hoover, brought the respected James C. Haggerty to the White House as his chief spokesman and initiated the first on-the-record news conferences. But even with Haggerty's wise counsel, Ike managed to convey little of the forcefulness he had demonstrated as supreme commander of joint Allied forces in Europe during World War II. Arguably, his languor perfectly suited the comparatively bland 1950s. But Eisenhower put his disdain for self-promotion on view coast to coast when he held the first-ever live, televised presidential news conference on January 19, 1955, from the Indian Treaty Room in the Executive Office building. "Well, I see that we have a little experiment this morning," Ike dismissively began the proceedings. "I hope it doesn't prove to be a disturbing influence."[8]

Optimistically, Haggerty judged it "a good day!!!"[9] In truth, done in by the room's high ceilings and poor acoustics, the aging general came across as tired and timorous.[10] Unrelated technological innovations—the Russian Sputnik that beat America into space in 1958 and the sophisticated American U-2 spy plane downed by the Soviets in 1960, provoking a diplomatic crisis—seemed only to befuddle Eisenhower. Actor Robert Montgomery, fresh from hosting his own series on television, had joined the administration as TV advisor, but could do little to improve Eisenhower's ability on, or interest in, the medium. Neither Montgomery nor Haggerty could devise a winning strategy to respond to increasingly aggressive media inquiries about the American loss of face.[11]

Then came the energetic John Fitzgerald Kennedy and his savvy running mate and eventual successor, Lyndon Baines Johnson. The Roosevelt generation faded away and the torch passed to a new one that embraced modern media.

Although they never became warm friends, Kennedy and Johnson were in many ways made for each other—uneasy partners in a political marriage of convenience. What Senator Kennedy lacked in legislative achievement, Senator Johnson provided with his unrivaled record of productive arm-twisting. What Johnson lacked in urbanity, Kennedy supplied with abundant sex appeal and athletic grace. JFK could never have won the 1960 election without the garrulous Texan as his vice presidential running mate to reassure the balky white South. Needless to say, Johnson would not have succeeded to the presidency at Kennedy's death had the frustrated power broker not settled for the second spot on the Democratic ticket in 1960. A more dramatic contrast between running mates had not been so sharply evident since the sophisticated New Yorker Franklin Roosevelt first ran with Texan "Cactus" Jack Garner as his vice presidential nominee three decades earlier.

JFK brought not only movie star looks to the political table but also a substantial if slightly padded résumé. Like TR a genuine war hero and published writer, he was also, like FDR, the scion of multigenerational political royalty and, like both Roosevelts, a graduate of prestigious Harvard. Plus he was wealthier than either of them, younger than any presidential candidate of the twentieth century, and the first credible Catholic nominee since Al Smith lost to Herbert Hoover in 1928.[12] Kennedy could also boast of personal journalistic experience that provided him with valuable insight into the profession: in the summer of 1945, after returning from active naval duty in the Pacific, he had worked as a reporter for the Hearst-run International News Service, covering such milestones as the opening session of the United Nations in San Francisco, the shocking 1945 electoral defeat of Winston Churchill in Great Britain, and the Potsdam Conference in postwar Germany. Few knew that Kennedy had secured the job only because his father, the rich and powerful Joseph P. Kennedy, had importuned his friend William Randolph Hearst to hire him.[13]

A decade later, by then a U.S. senator from Massachusetts, JFK crowned his writing career by winning the Pulitzer Prize for Biography, even though *Profiles in Courage*, the 1956 book for which he notched the honor, turned out to have been largely written by an uncredited Senate staffer with help from an unnamed Georgetown University historian (Jules Davids).[14] Initially, the bestseller failed to make the final cut by the Pulitzer nominating committee, but the *New York Times*' Arthur Krock—by then an influential columnist—reportedly forwarded a strong recommendation to the full board, once again at the behest of JFK's father. Not surprisingly, Krock failed to mention this unorthodox behind-the-scenes effort in his memoirs. Instead he maintained that he had "certainly" observed JFK personally drafting *Profiles in Courage* while "on his back" recuperating from spinal surgery in 1955[15]—perhaps the first, but certainly not the last, time the press covered up for, instead of covering, John Kennedy.

In 1957, the year JFK received the Pulitzer, another noted columnist—Drew Pearson of the "Washington Merry-Go-Round"—appeared on ABC TV's live news show *The Mike Wallace Interview* and blurted out, "John F. Kennedy is the only man in history that I know who won a Pulitzer Prize for a book that was ghostwritten for him." Pearson then outed the senator's chief legislative aide, Ted Sorensen, as the unbilled author. "And he never acknowledged the fact?" asked an incredulous Wallace. To which Pearson replied—paraphrasing a withering comment first offered by Eleanor Roosevelt—"You know, there's a little wisecrack around the Senate about Jack . . . some of his colleagues say, 'Jack, I wish you had a little less profile and more courage.'"[16] Incensed, Kennedy's father threatened to sue the network for $50 million. Although Wallace refused to apologize, ABC meekly broadcast a retraction admitting that Pearson's charge was "unfounded and that the book in question was written by Senator Kennedy."[17]

Only in his own memoirs, published more than fifty years later in 2008, did Sorensen admit that in working with Kennedy on the book, he had, as he struggled to express it, "helped choose the words of many of its sentences." (He had insisted otherwise in a Kennedy biography published in 1965.) Now he volunteered, as if to justify his longtime silence on the question, that after *Profiles*' publication, JFK "unexpectedly and generously offered, and I happily accepted, a sum to be spread over several years, that I regarded as more than fair." Even so, he continued to argue that the book "was so deep a collaboration and I was so intimately involved at each stage that I know exactly where the credit ultimately lies—with JFK."[18]

Kennedy certainly retained that credit. None of the rumors about *Profiles in Courage* demonstrably hurt him in the 1950s or '60s, any more than the fact that the senators profiled in his book included such dubious choices as Edmund G. Ross, who cast the deciding vote in acquitting the racist Andrew Johnson at his 1868 impeachment trial; and Robert A. Taft, the conservative Ohio Republican who opposed the Nuremberg trials of captured Nazis. Journalist Krock later proudly took credit for recommending the anti-union Taft, boasting to Kennedy years afterward that it was "probably the best thing that I ever got you to do."[19]

The unique and, as it proved, unbeatable combination of attributes Kennedy brought to politics—good looks, discreet friends in the press, a dedicated staff prepared to say anything to protect him, and a fabulously wealthy and ruthlessly ambitious father—gave him both the tools to succeed and the audacity to tweak his own ascent. Rising to address the Gridiron Club in 1958, the year he successfully sought reelection to the Senate, he unleashed a routine as memorable as the "muckraker" attack that TR had launched at the same club half a century earlier. Pretending he had just received a telegram from his "generous daddy," he offered to read it aloud.

"Dear Jack," the imaginary wire began. "Don't buy a single vote more than is necessary—I'll be damned if I'm going to pay for a landslide."[20]

Drew Pearson may not have liked John Kennedy, but he did not believe his fellow Texan Lyndon Johnson had a prayer of overtaking him at the 1960 Democratic National Convention in Los Angeles. Still, Pearson resented the preballoting announcements, orchestrated by JFK and his brother Robert, at which delegation after delegation—in truth already locked into the Kennedy fold—proclaimed they had just decided to endorse him. "Johnson as president was later accused of managing the news," Pearson grumbled of the attempt to build momentum, "but there was no one more adept at managing the news than the two Kennedy brothers at that convention and sometimes later." In a drastic move, the columnist took out a full-page ad in the *Los Angeles Mirror* to denounce the Kennedy effort, as he put it, "to suppress the news."[21]

Pearson exaggerated on this occasion, but his would not be the last such charge leveled against JFK in the years to come. Like FDR before him, Kennedy worked not only to burnish his image but also to bury news he wished to conceal—including his extramarital affairs and his compromised health. To journalists, Kennedy's womanizing remained a taboo subject. And while the press did report on his almost quaint back problems, attributed to a wartime combat injury, it never learned of his dependence on both stimulants and sedatives or his struggle with Addison's disease, a rare adrenal insufficiency (first diagnosed in 1947) that required intravenous cortisone to control.

Again like Roosevelt, Kennedy found a means to sidestep the print press entirely and target American audiences through the newest of the new media: in his case, television. If FDR possessed the perfect voice for radio, JFK boasted the perfect appearance for TV—and his New England–accented tenor proved irresistible, too. Exuding "youth," "glamor," and "excitement," in the besotted assessment of CBS newsman Bob Schieffer, Kennedy "turned the black-and-white movie of American politics into blazing technicolor." In truth, actual color TV still remained an extreme rarity in American homes, but black-and-white screens proved adequate, as Schieffer recalled, to make Kennedy "our first television president."[22]

Before that, JFK became the initial television candidate. In fall 1960, he and his Republican opponent, Richard M. Nixon, agreed to face off in the first live television debates in history. Whether Nixon was unwise to accept the opportunity remains itself open to debate. Better known than Kennedy, the sitting vice president had little to gain and much to lose from one-on-one encounters. And as senator, Kennedy had already proved himself an "irresistibly kinetic" TV presence during the live telecasts of the McClellan Committee hearings on labor union corruption—"young, calm, and handsome beside his staid and wizened colleagues" in the words of historian Douglas Brinkley.[23] Yet like the nineteenth-century Illinois senator Stephen A. Douglas, who had reluctantly accepted Abraham Lincoln's debate challenge back in 1858 fearing it would look unmanly to turn him down, Nixon knew that rejecting debates with Kennedy could expose him to criticism for the rest of the campaign. In fact, the 1960 "challenge" came directly from the networks, an offer neither candidate could refuse.

On September 26, Kennedy and Nixon squared off for their initial debate at the studios of a CBS TV affiliate in Chicago. Few would remember what either nominee said that night. What stood out in high relief was how much Kennedy looked the part of a dynamic leader, and how much his opponent did not. Looking tanned and fit, JFK made Nixon appear haggard and weary by comparison. Genuinely weary he was: Nixon had recently spent time in the hospital recovering from a knee infection, shedding so much weight under a regimen of antibiotics that he had lost a shirt size—without bothering to buy new shirts. Worse, Nixon dressed for the event in a light-colored suit that blended into the pale backdrop, while Kennedy sported a dark outfit that contrasted vividly. Then, just before airtime, Nixon's persistent five o'clock shadow began visibly emerging. To conceal it, aides applied cheap Shavestick makeup that made him appear practically "clown white," in the words of a technician.[24] When Kennedy's own newly hired television advisor, William P. Wilson, a producer who had worked at this very studio, saw Nixon reluctantly submit to the touch-up, he raced to a nearby drugstore and returned with a compact of Max Factor Creme Puff for his client. "Do you know what you're doing?" asked a hesitant JFK. "Yes," Wilson assured him. "Okay," Kennedy answered, and Wilson lightly applied the powder that made the candidate look like he had just ventured inside from a game of touch football on a sunny afternoon. No one fathomed at the time that bronzed skin was a symptom of Addison's.

Once the broadcast began, Kennedy radiated cool confidence, Nixon, unease and exhaustion. Attempting to shed his image for aggressiveness, Nixon went out of his way to seek common ground with his opponent, saying at one point: "I subscribe completely to the spirit that Senator Kennedy has expressed tonight." As Ted Sorensen observed, "It sounded weak"—and worse, "Nixon looked weak."[25] Adding to the contrast, Nixon soon began to sweat under the hot television lights, beads of moisture forming on his upper lip. And while Kennedy kept his gaze fixed on the camera, establishing a connection with viewers at home, Nixon directed his comments to the panel of newsmen who questioned him. To those watching television, he seemed reluctant to make eye contact.

No postdebate polling statistics survive, but legend holds that those who heard the encounter on radio that evening believed Nixon had prevailed, while those who watched on television—an audience estimated at seventy million, more than three times the number of radio listeners—came away with the opposite impression. Long after the debate, its moderator, newsman Howard K. Smith, validated that theory by revealing: "I kept score. I gave Nixon eighteen-and-a-half points to Kennedy's eighteen. But I couldn't see them. They were ahead of me facing the camera. . . . So I was listening to it on radio, as it were. Later, when I went back and saw it replayed, I could see that Kennedy swept it. He was just so enchanting. His persona gave you confidence."[26]

Although Nixon corrected his cosmetic malfunctions in time for the next three telecasts, the initial impression that he (and Kennedy) made on September 26 proved indelible. "It is a devastating commentary on the nature of television as a political medium," Nixon later sourly observed, "that what hurt me the most in the first debate was not the substance of the encounter between Kennedy and me, but the disadvantageous contrast in our appearances. After the program ended," Nixon recalled with self-pity, "callers, including my mother, wanted to know if anything was wrong because I did not look well."[27]

On Election Day, Kennedy edged past Nixon by one of the narrowest margins in history—100,000 votes out of 68 million cast, less than two-tenths of one percent. Late returns from hotly disputed Illinois, site of the first debate, ended up tilting to the Democrats, guaranteeing JFK an electoral majority. No one on either side thought the television debates had been anything but decisive.

On January 20, 1961, Kennedy stood on the U.S. Capitol portico to deliver his nationally telecast inaugural address—one of the briefest and best in history. With breath escaping visibly from his mouth that freezing day, a bareheaded JFK challenged Americans: "Ask not what your country can do for you. Ask what you can do for your country." Pressed decades later to reveal who had written that memorable line—he or the new president—Ted Sorensen, who went on to serve as JFK's White House speechwriter, proved as reluctant to reply as he had long remained to admit primary authorship of *Profiles in Courage*. Sitting alongside this writer at an off-the-record roundtable on presidential oratory in early 2009, he shrugged to a group of journalists at the *New York Times*: "Ask not."[28]

In the thousand days of his presidency—a reign marked by such solid achievements as the establishment of the Peace Corps and the launch of America's race to the moon, not to mention victory in a nail-biting war of nerves with the Russians—Kennedy all but weaponized the medium that had helped elect him. Under Kennedy, presidential news conferences became not "experiments" but events. In a way, they came to overshadow his accomplishments. Not even FDR could have made (or would have wanted to make) such a claim.

Speaking for many print journalists, *Chicago Daily News* White House correspondent Peter Lisagor objected when he learned that intimate, informal Q&A sessions would now be replaced by live, televised events for hundreds of reporters in an arena-like setting.[29] Virtually echoing FDR, Kennedy privately remarked, "We should be able to go around the newspapers." Besides, he realized, "I don't know how we can justify keeping TV out if it wants in."[30]

When the new administration first announced its new approach, the *New York Times*' James B. Reston dismissed it as "the goofiest idea since the hula hoop." But Raymond P. Brandt, who had covered Washington since the days of the New Deal, reminded his fellow correspondents: "When Roosevelt ended written questions, there wasn't any trouble; when Eisenhower allowed direct quotation, there wasn't any trouble; when they admitted television cameras, there wasn't any trouble. The live conference is worth trying."[31]

Kennedy did more than try. He proceeded to field questions at sixty-four such events, averaging one for every two to three weeks of his tragically abbreviated presidency. And he sprinkled many of them with bracing examples of his sly wit. Although he fretted at one point that the sessions might descend into a "comedy hour," the surviving transcripts and videos show that they overwhelmingly dealt with serious domestic and foreign policy issues and elicited both challenging questions and complex answers.[32] Reporters eventually came to rely on the sessions to unearth genuine news, even if many television viewers tuned into the broadcasts to bear witness to Kennedy's radiant smile and regular flashes of humor. Like a skilled film actor emoting subtly for the big screen, JFK performed not alone for journalists but for home audiences. Subtle and restrained but exuding virile good looks and charm to spare, Kennedy became a genuine television star.

To stage-manage these groundbreaking events, Kennedy had turned to his debate advisor Bill Wilson, who immediately ruled out resuming press conferences in the Indian Treaty Room across the lawn from the White House. Even the mansion's own expansive East Room could not possibly contain the hundreds of domestic and foreign press demanding admission (418 would show up for the first conference). Seeking the ideal venue both to accommodate the journalists and provide a telegenic setting, Wilson settled on the plush auditorium at the nearby State Department. The space featured raked, theater-style seating for the press and an elevated stage for the president. Wilson suspended a blue curtain to serve as a warm backdrop and commissioned a made-to-order, two-tiered wooden lectern decorated with the eagle-festooned presidential seal. If the room was actually bigger than the press corps required, lighting could be manipulated to black out unoccupied seats. Besides, Wilson wanted space for a riser at the back of the house to accommodate a row of television and newsreel cameras.

All that was needed now was an innovative format to make the sessions reflect Kennedy's strengths. Wilson devised a clever way to heighten anticipation: the president would build suspense for his entrance by waiting in the wings while an announcer introduced the program to the home audience.[33] JFK also decided to begin most sessions with a detailed statement, not only to emphasize the news he wanted to convey to the press and public, but to demonstrate his overall grasp of both policy and management issues, essential for a new leader some critics had branded too young and inexperienced to be president. His style was so engaging that reports that seemed dour in print came off sounding cheerful on television.

The very first session got underway at 6:00 P.M. on January 25, 1961, just five days after his inauguration. Kennedy opened with updates on nuclear test ban negotiations and famine in the Congo. Then, dramatically, he announced the freeing of two downed Air Force pilots long imprisoned by the Soviets. The *New York Herald Tribune* had actually learned of their release earlier in the day. Using its influence with *Tribune* publisher John Hay Whitney, the administration had convinced the paper to hold the story until the president could break it at his news conference. As the episode demonstrated, the Kennedy White House would not refrain from managing—even hiding—news for the president's benefit.

The range of inquiries that followed at this first session gave Kennedy ample opportunity to present himself as lucidly well informed. Questions covered not only the pilots' imminent homecoming but relations with Cuba, trade agreements, the gold supply, military morale, New York Democratic politics, unemployment rates, national security, food aid for China, the space program, the federal budget, the electoral college system, and the use of executive privilege—all answered in complete sentences with appropriate gravity. Asked whether he was apprehensive about the "instantaneous broadcasts themselves"—since "an inadvertent statement is no longer correctible, as in the old days," and "could possibly cause some grave consequence"—Kennedy dismissed such concerns. Reserving the right to make future clarifications "in the interests of the country," he maintained that "this system has the advantage of providing more direct communication."[34] It also provided him with the fortnightly chance to act the part of a gladiator in full view of an average of eighteen million spectators.

In all, the young president handled thirty-seven separate press questions that first day, eclipsing FDR's record for an inaugural news conference and placing his grasp of complex matters on full display.[35] The only tense moment came when a correspondent wondered whether the president was in favor of "tightening" the flow of future news on sensitive subjects like national security. Here was a Pandora's box that Kennedy had cracked open in the first place by agreeing to take questions on camera. "I am anxious that we have a maximum flow of information," he calmly responded, ". . . but I think all of us here are aware that there are some matters which it would not be well to discuss at particular times. So we will just have to wait and try to work together and see if we can provide as much information as we can within the limits of national security." It was the right answer for the moment, but the thorny issue would crop up again within weeks.

Thirteen minutes into the otherwise solemn first session, another reporter asked Kennedy whether—consistent with his past vow to remain "in the thick of political battles"—he planned to intervene in a new effort by congressional progressives to expand membership on the all-powerful but reactionary House Rules Committee. Long dominated by senior Southerners, the panel was widely expected to bottle up the administration's civil rights initiatives. Eager to promote his agenda but reluctant to interfere with another branch of government, Kennedy launched into a windy, indirect response before finally reminding reporters, "I merely give my views as an interested citizen." The resulting ripple of laughter seemed to have taken Kennedy by surprise. Modern journalist Walter Shapiro has contended that "a puckish grin crosses Kennedy's face as he revels in his look-what-I-discovered-about-live-television moment."[36] In truth, the surviving video offers no such evidence; except for a hint of mischief behind the eyes, Kennedy's masklike expression remained unchanged, though the journalists' response undoubtedly demonstrated to him that a lighthearted moment could diffuse difficult questions in the future.

The nation's newspapers not only dutifully reported on the news Kennedy made that January evening but commented on his performance as if reviewing a show business opening. Although the BBC's voice in America, Alistair Cooke (long before his *Masterpiece Theatre* days), noted a "disturbing hint of Hollywood" in the proceedings, Kennedy's debut press conference largely drew raves. *New York Times* commentator Russell Baker hailed the birth of "a new star with tremendous national appeal and the skill of a national showman."[37] The *Chicago Daily News* likened Kennedy's achievement to "making love in Carnegie Hall."[38]

"Thus opened a new era of White House communications," declared the UPI's Merriman Smith. Not everyone celebrated (Smith included; he lamented the vanished "repartee" of the Roosevelt era). After observing a few more news conferences, Peter Lisagor called them "the nearest thing we have in this town to anarchy." *New York Herald Tribune* Washington correspondent Robert J. Donovan further complained that the loss of "intimacy" had "robbed the presidential press conference of much of its best flavor," while the paper's television critic John Crosby coarsely likened them to "a Chinese dinner," explaining, "You eat and eat of a dozen different dishes—but an hour later you find yourself hungry."[39] Kennedy managed to feed his audiences frequently enough to keep them sated. The *Los Angeles Times* probably came closest to understanding the enormous impact of Kennedy's press conferences by calling them "undisguised exercises of the Presidential power." As the Republican-leaning paper conceded: "Whatever the doubts his advisors and well-wishers—or even those who hoped he would come a cropper—had about the televised press conferences, they know now that television must have been invented for the use of this President."[40]

Ultimately, the news conferences grew best-known for the president's witticisms. At the second session, held just a week after the first, a correspondent asked Kennedy whether he planned to follow Dwight Eisenhower's example and self-identify as a moderate. "Well," came the droll reply, "I don't call myself anything but a Democrat who has been elected President of the United States." Laughter followed. Later that same afternoon, the most acclaimed debater since Lincoln was asked if he would commit now to another series of presidential face-offs in 1964. Kennedy provoked more laughter with the quick reply, "Oh, I would, yes."[41] This time the merriment was more robust, prodded by Kennedy's knowing smile. Informed at another session that Republicans had introduced a resolution declaring him a failure, Kennedy shot back, "I am sure it was passed unanimously."[42]

The mood did not remain consistently light. That first summer, JFK was compelled to confirm that Russia had again beaten America in the space race, sending a man into orbit around the earth for the first time. He handled the embarrassing question with aplomb. "Are you satisfied, from the evidence available to you, that they did do what they said they did?" demanded one reporter as if he could not believe the claim. Kennedy's one-word reply was a no-nonsense "yes."[43] Yet three months later, announcing America's modest effort to catch up by launching a chimpanzee into space, JFK could not resist humorously declaring of the primate astronaut: "He reports that everything is perfect and working well."[44] Kennedy's unwavering support for space exploration gained immeasurable traction when Walter Cronkite, the CBS news anchor during the JFK years, grew as passionate about the space race as the president.[45]

His confidence growing with each press conference, Kennedy responded fearlessly when challenged to address reports that the business community felt it had him just where it wanted him. "I can't believe," he slyly replied, "I'm where big business wants me." Back at the White House, Kennedy made it his habit to watch rebroadcasts of the conferences, often "chuckling appreciatively" at his best lines.[46]

Dubious at first about the new format, the press came to appreciate the opportunities for direct face time with the president, not to mention their own chances for exposure on national television. That first autumn, one correspondent even worried about a rumored reduction in frequency, asking JFK "if there was anything in particular you don't like about them, or anything we might do on our part to encourage you to meet with us more often?" The inquiry alone generated a laugh, but the president drew an even bigger one by replying, "Well, I like them . . . sort of." Then he ambiguously assured the 417 journalists packed into the auditorium for that session, "Let me just say that I am anxious to hold press conferences as often as I believe it to be in the public interest."[47]

Kennedy frequently faced questioners in an atmosphere of crisis. In April 1961 he ill-advisedly green-lit a CIA-backed invasion of Communist-controlled Cuba at the Bay of Pigs. Both the *Miami Herald* and *New York Times* unearthed news of the impending attack before it took place, but the administration successfully lobbied them to hold off publication in the name of national security.[48] The historian Arthur Schlesinger Jr.—then serving as a White House advisor—eventually revealed that the president had also persuaded the *New Republic* to kill an article on the CIA's plans to train Cuban exiles for the mission.[49] Secrecy did not prevent the actual operation from turning into a fiasco. Its failure produced a wave of finger-pointing at the State and Defense Departments along with a temporary clampdown on comments from the White House—followed unsurprisingly by resentment from the president and the press alike.

Going ahead with a previously scheduled news conference on April 21, the day after the Bay of Pigs mission imploded, Kennedy tried cautioning reporters that "no useful national purpose would be served by my going further into the Cuban question this morning." When NBC White House correspondent Sander Vanocur nevertheless persisted, Kennedy offered a memorable reply: "There's an old saying, that victory has 100 fathers and defeat is an orphan."[50] In the glare of TV lights, albeit only metaphorically, Kennedy had done something rare: accept responsibility. The noted scholar of rhetoric Thomas W. Benson pointed out that "most of the mainstream press appeared to rally to Kennedy's support" in response to his expressions of humility and contrition.[51] Only out of earshot of the press had he blamed scapegoats. Somehow forgetting that he had put a lid on advance news about the invasion, Kennedy even lashed out at *New York Times* editor Turner Catledge: "Maybe if you had printed more about the operation, you would have saved us from a colossal mistake."[52] As he grumbled to an aide, "Castro doesn't need agents over here. All he has to do is read our papers."[53]

Six days after his humbling news conference, Kennedy fulfilled a commitment to appear before the American Newspaper Publishers Association at the Waldorf-Astoria Hotel in New York City. Attired in white tie and tails, he entered the ballroom to a standing ovation from the 1,700-member audience. JFK's speech began in much the same confessional tone in which his press conference had left off. "This Administration intends to be candid about its errors," he proclaimed, "for as a wise man once said: 'An error does not become a mistake until you refuse to correct it.'" Besides, he added, "we expect you to point them out when we miss them." But the president also doubled down on the warning he had expressed at his very first news conference back in January, when he had predicted that, from time to time, the government might withhold news in the national interest. The "need for a far greater public information," he now elaborated, might indeed be outweighed by "the need for far greater official secrecy."[54]

He also told the group, comprised mostly of Republicans, that he had planned to name that evening's speech "'The President Versus the Press,'" but since "those are not my sentiments tonight," had decided to call the address "'The President *and* the Press'" (emphasis added). The softened title did little to warm the chilling message that came next. "I have no easy answer to the dilemma I have posed, and would not seek to impose it if I had one," he declared. "But I am asking the members of the newspaper profession and the industry in this country to reexamine their responsibilities, to consider the degree and the nature of the present danger, and to heed the duty of self-restraint which that danger imposes upon us all." Arthur Schlesinger believed Kennedy "went much too far" in his call for self-censorship that night, branding the speech a "misstep."[55]

The publishers and their leading Washington correspondents agreed. After all, the administration had not only withheld news about the Bay of Pigs operation but, as James Reston pointed out in the *New York Times*, had also exaggerated the size of the invading force when it was finally announced, then falsely described American participation merely as a supply operation once the invasion foundered. "Both times," charged Reston, "the press was debased for the government's purpose." The Castro regime and its Russian allies knew all along that Kennedy was dissembling, Reston added for good measure. The "American people were the only ones to be fooled." The influential columnist devised a new phrase to characterize the offense: "False News."[56]

Examining this controversy today—armed with all that we have experienced since 1961—it is clear that buying into Kennedy's justification for such press manipulation requires acceptance of his argument that America actually faced existential "peril" that year. As Kennedy had warned the publishers in full-throated Cold War language: "Our way of life is under attack. . . . If the press is awaiting the declaration of war before it imposes the self-discipline of combat conditions, then I can only say that no war ever posed a greater threat to our security." In retrospect, Kennedy obviously overstated the threat. But it is far easier for us to look back and condemn JFK's approach with the knowledge that the danger was exaggerated than it was at the time for Kennedy to look ahead and dismiss the threat entirely.

However serious the prevailing mood at most of his subsequent news conferences, Kennedy's rich sense of humor always lurked close to the surface, and often proved his salvation under tough questioning. Viewers waited expectantly for the inevitable bon mot as if they were baseball fans anticipating that a slugger might at any moment clout a home run. Kennedy watchers were seldom disappointed.

Occasionally, when the questioning grew dry and JFK sensed he might be losing his grip on the massive television audience, he would turn to the very same reporter FDR had enjoyed teasing at press sessions twenty years earlier. Seventy-two-year-old May Craig's inquiries were now "more likely to be puzzling than weighty," Ted Sorensen recalled.[57] Accordingly, Kennedy knew he would need only a brief riposte or a slight smile to provoke amusement.

One of their best-remembered exchanges came in early 1962, when Craig inexplicably pressed Kennedy about recently announced, but entirely local, plans to build a new stadium and freeway near the U.S. Capitol. Craig fretted that the scheme would cut visitors off from a park and a statue of Mary McLeod Bethune. "Could you inquire into that?" she beseeched JFK as he stared incredulously (to a smattering of preliminary laughter), "and see if the Freeway could be put a little farther beyond the park?" Kennedy merely replied: "Yes, I will." As the laughter built, he added, as if in appreciation: "Very gentle today, Miss [*sic*] Craig."[58]

Even if Craig's questions seldom advanced either her colleagues' agenda or the president's, the sight of the senior journalist in her trademark flowerpot-hat spouting whatever was on her mind—and of the bemused yet respectful glances Kennedy directed her way—produced a warm connection among television audiences no less effective than the sight of a cherished but eccentric guest returning to a TV talk show to chat with a sympathetic host.

Nobody's fool, Craig occasionally raised serious issues. She got painfully close to an unresolved one when she called on Kennedy to account for what he had done to live up to his party's 1960 platform pledge to secure equal pay for women. The president evoked a mild burst of laughter when he condescendingly replied, "Well, I'm sure we haven't done enough." Perhaps sensing he had been too glib, he added: "I must say I am a strong believer in equal pay for women, and I think we ought to do better than we've been doing, and I'm glad you reminded me of it, Mrs. Craig."[59] The amended response elicited a mixture of hilarity and applause, and apparently convinced the veteran journalist, reminiscing years later, that Kennedy "was always for women having a fair shake."[60] (Three weeks afterward, another journalist ventured to ask Kennedy if he and his wife would continue to attend functions at press clubs that refused to admit women. "The press should deal with that problem," he curtly responded.)[61]

Inevitably, questions also touched on the administration's thwarted efforts to advance civil rights. In 1962, as long-overdue legislation stalled in Congress, Craig rose to press Kennedy on a proposed compromise exception to new laws aimed at ending discrimination in small boardinghouses—an escape clause colloquially known as "Mrs. Murphy's Exemption." Inquired Craig: "Mr. President, do you think that Mrs. Murphy should have to take into her home a lodger whom she does not want, regardless of the reason, or would you accept a change in the civil rights bill to except small boardinghouses like Mrs. Murphy?" Replied Kennedy to laughter: "The question would be, it seems to me, Mrs. Craig, whether Mrs. Murphy had a substantial impact on interstate commerce."[62]

Kennedy may have come to regard May Craig with affection, but aides who worked in his press office remembered that he "always hated" the equally unpredictable but hard-edged, "klaxon-voiced" Texan Sarah McClendon. (President Eisenhower, whom she had once publicly urged to "leave off some of your golf and go out and visit some of the small cities," disliked her, too, and later taunted her: "Do you get fired every week?") The head of an eponymous, one-woman news agency, McClendon grew famous for shouting, "Mr. President, Mr. President" at news conferences until Kennedy allowed the onetime World War II WAC to pose an invariably disagreeable question.[63] The self-described "citizen journalist"[64] sounded more like Joseph McCarthy when, at a 1962 session, she demanded that Kennedy account for two State Department officials she branded "security risks." Rising to their defense, the president elegantly insisted they could carry on their work "without detriment to the interests of the United States, and I hope without detriment to their characters by your question." White House speechwriter Ted Sorensen was amazed that Kennedy continued to call on McClendon at nearly every conference. "I'd like to pass her by," JFK confessed, "but something always draws me to recognize her."[65] Perhaps he knew a usefully unsympathetic foil when he encountered one. For her part, McClendon resented that JFK had not paid her even more attention. "His pets," she bitterly complained in her memoirs, "mined Kennedy as if he were the mother lode."[66]

One of those "pets," if she can be believed, was Helen Thomas. The UPI correspondent was just starting her Washington career when Kennedy took office and had yet to earn her reputation for fierceness. In fact, Thomas had begun her coverage of the new First Family by staking out the hospital where John Kennedy Jr. was born a few weeks after the 1960 election. She called the assignment the "diaper detail." Later sent to cover the First Lady, she was shocked to learn that Jackie referred to the women on that beat as "the harpies." Belatedly promoted to cover the president, she found herself summoned to the Oval Office one day along with the rest of the press pool but was as surprised as the president that no other print reporter showed up. Accustomed to seeing the UPI correspondent in a crowd, Kennedy glanced her way and remarked, "Well, if it isn't Miss Thomas of the Universal Press."[67]

If JFK always appeared spontaneous at his public sessions with the press, it was in part the result of deep reading and intensive rehearsal. Actual news conference days began with an 8:45 White House breakfast briefing attended by a variety of administration officials, including Vice President Johnson, most armed with long lists of potential interrogatories. By the time the meetings began, Kennedy had already ingested their most recent reports and absorbed the front pages of the morning newspapers. Speechwriter Sorensen often proposed humorous lines, but JFK invariably judged them "too barbed." Besides, the president added, "It is dangerous to have them in the back of my head." Whenever State Department officials urged him to sidestep certain issues, Kennedy retorted, "If I followed your advice on every topic which you want me to avoid answering, I would stand up there with nothing to say."[68]

A final preparatory get-together took place at 3:00 P.M. in the president's second-floor bedroom to review "last-minute changes" while he dressed. Kennedy remarked that it was "like preparing for a final exam twice a month." As he hurried out for the quick ride to the State Department, JFK often worried aloud that "he felt doubtful and defenseless about the whole thing."[69] Invariably, he returned to the White House pleased with his latest outing.

As in FDR's case, JFK's news conferences became cultural touchstones in their own right. As such, they inspired gentle parody. In 1962, a previously obscure comedian named Vaughn Meader released a phenomenally successful record album titled *The First Family*, in which he delivered a spot-on presidential impersonation. Asked at a news conference whether the lampoon provided him "annoyment [*sic*] or enjoyment," Kennedy murmured, "Annoyment," before quickly adding: "No. I actually listened to Mr. Meader's record, but I thought it sounded more like [brother] Teddy than it did me, so *he's* annoyed."[70]

Reporters may have disliked being used—so it seemed to some of them—to feed such straight lines to the president at these events, but they could hardly stay away. At a certain point, some newspaper owners did commence muttering that their employees could easily glean the same amount of information by viewing the president's news conferences on TV. Kennedy assured the publishers that it remained "highly beneficial to have some 20,000,000 Americans regularly . . . observe, if I may say so, the incisive, the intelligent, and the courteous qualities displayed by your Washington correspondents."[71]

Managing the Kennedy press operation—from the 1960 campaign onward—was a rumpled, overweight, cigar-chewing onetime child piano prodigy, former journalist, and Capitol Hill flack named Pierre Salinger. Less experienced than his predecessor, Jim Haggerty, and granted less entrée to the inner circle than Truman's spokesman, Charlie Ross, Salinger nonetheless emerged as one of several administration figures to earn a degree of fame in his own right. He could often be observed by television viewers sitting on stage during presidential news conferences, or wearing Bermuda shorts when tagging along with his boss to

Kennedy family homes in Palm Beach, Florida, or Hyannis Port, Massachusetts. To the president's occasional annoyance, Salinger became a celebrity. The press liked Salinger because he always made himself available, but complained that he occasionally fed them misleading or inaccurate information—whether out of loyalty to the president or limited access to the facts, they could not ascertain.

Salinger endeared himself to the sixty principal White House correspondents by installing "a hot line, junior grade," so he could summon them for impromptu briefings whenever a major story broke.[72] He otherwise routinely briefed them two times a day. The press grew fond of the affable press secretary but continued to doubt whether he was privy to administration policy shifts.

Salinger assumed his post sensitive to the delicate balance between cooperation with the media and loyalty to the president, keenly aware that "the objectives of the two institutions collide." As Salinger recognized: "[T]he press, rooted in American history and a tradition of freedom, attempts to find and report every single piece of information. The government naturally wishes to present its programs and positions in the best possible light."[73] This ran somewhat counter to Kennedy's curt admonition: "Always remember that their interests and ours ultimately conflict."[74]

Soon enough, Salinger's nuanced view was put to the test—albeit on a minor matter. Briefing reporters in the early days of the administration, he let slip that freshly hired White House domestic staff had signed a pledge to write no books about the First Family. When Kennedy read the resulting news report, he "hit the roof." Demanding that Salinger report to the Oval Office for a dressing-down, JFK learned to his further irritation that his press secretary had gone out to lunch. He unleashed his fury on the nearest available aides. "Where does he get off volunteering this stuff?" Kennedy fumed. "Would Jim Haggerty have conducted a press conference this way?" Fortunately for Salinger, the president had "cooled down somewhat" by the time he returned to the White House, though he admitted it took JFK "several days to finally cool down completely."[75]

Salinger's miscue had exposed a serious bone of contention within the Kennedy household. For the most part, the president believed that public coverage of his beautiful family's private life would do him good, and wanted to encourage it. The First Lady, a onetime newspaperwoman herself, disagreed, above all insisting that their young children be shielded.[76] Salinger did a deft job balancing their conflicting priorities. On the one hand, he helped build Jackie's prestige by engineering the triumphant February 14, 1962, behind-the-scenes CBS television special *A Tour of the White House with Mrs. John F. Kennedy*. On the other, he conspired with the president to arrange photo shoots with the adorable Caroline and John-John while his wife was away.

When, for example, *Look* magazine proposed a photo spread that would showcase Kennedy's warm relationship with his little boy, Jackie told Salinger she was "dead set against it," regarding it as "an invasion of the family's privacy." As Salinger remembered, "The President smiled when I told him of her objections," then assured his press secretary: "We'll take another look at it the next time she leaves town." Two weeks later, Jackie departed for Italy, and sure enough, Salinger secured permission to summon writer Laura Bergquist and photographer Stanley Tretick to spend two hours in the Oval Office with JFK and John-John. When Mrs. Kennedy returned from abroad, Salinger dutifully reported what had transpired. She was "very upset," Salinger recalled. He tried soothing her, "Wait and see, you'll love the pictures." Replied Jackie icily, "You always say that." The result was "The President and His Son," a beguiling *Look* cover story boasting "marvelous pictures of JFK playing with John."[77] Sadly, the feature did not appear until December 3, 1963—two weeks after the president's death.

Notwithstanding JFK's fixation on television ("We couldn't survive without TV," he told Sorensen),[78] he kept a sharp eye on print publications, believing their impact was longer lasting than fleeting impressions on the tube. "JFK was a compulsive reader—and pilferer—of newspapers and magazines," Salinger testified. "When he came into my office and saw one he hadn't read on my desk, he would invariably walk out with it. No one on the staff was safe from his shoplifting." An accomplished speed-reader, Kennedy voraciously breezed through magazines like *Time*, *Newsweek*, *Life*, *Look*, *Harper's*, the *New Republic*, *Saturday Review*, and *U.S. News & World Report* (though Sorensen insisted that JFK shunned the last-named periodical because "it had little news and less to report").

Displaying an insatiable appetite for daily newspapers as well, he somehow found time to scan New York's *Times*, *Herald Tribune*, *Post*, and *Daily News*, along with three Washington papers, two from Chicago, plus the *Baltimore Sun*, *Atlanta Constitution*, *St. Louis Post-Dispatch*, and even the Sunday *London Times*.[79] To this list, Ted Sorensen added two Boston papers plus the *Philadelphia Inquirer*, the *Wall Street Journal*, and *Sports Illustrated*, although he admitted the president merely skimmed most of them.[80] Salinger believed the only thing that constrained Kennedy from reading every paper in the nation was what the California-born press secretary called JFK's East Coast "provincialism." Until the White House began subscribing to the *Los Angeles Times* midway through Kennedy's term, the president ignored the western dailies altogether.[81]

While he affirmed Roosevelt's judgment that newspapers were inherently adversarial, Kennedy kept in touch with many publishers, a task FDR had shunned. Like FDR, Kennedy also took pains to court star correspondents. He may have regarded newspapers as his "natural enemies," Sorensen observed, but he "regarded newsmen as his natural friends."[82] Wire service reporters like Merriman Smith of the UPI and Marvin Arrowsmith of the AP, whose stories appeared in hundreds of newspapers, got special access to the president, while syndicated columnists "Scotty" Reston, Rowland Evans, and the Alsop brothers (Stewart and Joseph) received advance notice of administration announcements as a courtesy. Veteran Washington correspondent Walter Lippmann earned flattering attention denied to him for years, including personal visits and requests for policy advice (seldom heeded). Star newscasters like CBS's Walter Cronkite secured invitations to film exclusive interviews.

Such gestures were no stretch for a president who had once, if briefly, served as a journalist himself. JFK also counted many reporters among his longtime friends and continued to socialize with them even when their competitors cried foul. "Kennedy liked newspapermen," Arthur Schlesinger attested, "they liked him; and he recognized that they provided him with a potent means of appealing to readers over the heads of publishers."[83] Or, as Sarah McClendon put it, "The public believed the press courted the Kennedys; it was actually the Kennedys who courted the press."[84] Pierre Salinger held a different view: "Kennedy was a guy who really enjoyed being with newspaper people."[85] Among the closest to him was the "imperious" and "scrupulously closeted" Joe Alsop, whose standing in Washington skyrocketed when the Kennedys stopped in at his town house after their 1961 inaugural ball. The friendship may have come with a global consequence: it was said that Alsop later urged the president to escalate U.S. involvement in Vietnam.

Then there was longtime pal Charles Bartlett of the *Chattanooga Times*, who had introduced Kennedy to his future wife and continued to join the president for dinners in the White House and vacations at Hyannis Port.[86] While Kennedy fed his old chum insights and scoops, Salinger observed that Bartlett's copy grew increasingly "dull" for fear of leaving readers the impression he was "trading in" on his close association with the president.[87] JFK also spent leisure time with Bill Lawrence of the *New York Times*, a frequent golfing partner. "I found with Kennedy," Lawrence frankly admitted, "that a round of golf could be much more fruitful in news terms than many formal presidential news conferences. John Kennedy thoroughly enjoyed 'leaking' a news story, and I was lucky enough to be the recipient." As a result, Lawrence later boasted without remorse, "I could and I did outreport and outwrite my rivals on story after story based on inside information."[88] *New York Post* Washington correspondent William V. Shannon came to the conclusion by 1962 that the president "devotes such a considerable portion of his attention to leaking news, planting reports, and playing off one reporter against another, that it sometimes seems his dream job is not being Chief Executive of the nation but Managing Editor of a hypothetical newspaper"[89]—much the same comment that had been made about previous presidents who had lavished attention on the press.

Add to this list longtime friend Ben Bradlee of *Newsweek*, and later the *Washington Post*, who insisted he never knew the details of the trysts Kennedy allegedly conducted, sometimes in the White House, with women ranging from Executive Wing interns to movie stars like Marilyn Monroe, Marlene Dietrich, and Angie Dickinson, not to mention Judith Campbell Exner, later (or simultaneously) involved in romances with both Frank Sinatra and Mafia don Sam Giancana. All Bradlee ever admitted to was the realization that Kennedy was "a fearful girler."[90] The one affair about which he did have personal knowledge—Kennedy's relationship with Bradlee's own sister-in-law, Mary Pinchot Meyer—he never discussed. As Bradlee told his biographer, "My rule used to be if private behavior didn't interfere with public business, then it stayed private."[91]

Kennedy might have enjoyed no well of residual goodwill from which to draw during the Bay of Pigs crisis had the public learned of his extramarital sexual adventures in and out of the White House. Fortunately for him, just as the press had shielded FDR for the innocent happenstance of his disability, it similarly chose to "protect" the public from news of JFK's guilty pleasures.

Historian Robert Dallek interviewed a number of 1960s-era journalists for his 2003 Kennedy biography, asking each, "Did you know that Kennedy was womanizing?" They said, "Yes, we always suspected." "Why didn't you write about it?" Dallek pressed them. "We didn't do it in the 1960s; you didn't intrude on the president's private life in that way. And so, it was hidden from the public."[92]

Veteran journalist Hedley Donovan was one of the observers who counted himself fully aware that "notwithstanding the storybook marriage" Kennedy presented to the public, he had "resumed the diversions of his bachelor days."

Later the editor of *Time* magazine, Donovan explained his own inattention by observing: "The press . . . was far more protective than now about the private lives of politicians." But Donovan admitted that a certain vicariousness among the predominately male press corps may have animated the conspiracy of silence. "After Kennedy entered the White House," he conceded, "the flagrant vulgarity and political recklessness of his philandering perhaps gave it an extra fillip."[93]

"A man as willfully self-indulgent as Kennedy in private life can carry over into public life a lordly assumption that what he wants he damned well should have," Donovan later admitted. He never quite passed judgment on either the president he had consciously or unconsciously shielded, or the journalists who had similarly hidden his indiscretions. "Perhaps," he rationalized, "a man can be dishonest and heartless in marriage and still be completely honest and compassionate in his public life."[94]

Like many of the journalists who covered the White House, Donovan maintained, "I knew much less of this then, even as an editor somewhat on the inside, than all of us have been able to read since." Fellow journalists "gossiped knowingly," Donovan admitted, "but few hints of his womanizing got into print."[95]

How much the other Washington correspondents knew about JFK's flings, when they knew it, and what they should have done with such information remains a matter of heated dispute six decades after the Kennedy presidency. Constrained by the prevailing culture of privacy but also vicariously awed by a boys' network admiration for the kind of prolific womanizing that was then referred to as "swordsmanship," they saw, heard, and reported no evil about the swashbuckler-in-chief.

Among the silent was the soon-to-become-legendary investigative journalist Seymour Hersh—who would achieve renown for exposing the My Lai massacre in Vietnam. Hersh began serving as an AP correspondent in Washington beginning in 1963. In a 1997 book titled *The Dark Side of Camelot*, he asserted that Kennedy's peccadillos left him continually teetering "just one news story away from cataclysmic political scandal."[96] Yet in 1963, like all his colleagues, Hersh turned a blind eye and wrote nothing.

JFK's reckless, catch-me-if-you-can sex life seemingly jeopardized both national security and his own presidency, but the priapic Kennedy knew the reigning journalistic culture still forbade scrutiny of a president's private life—even if this particular president took risks, as Garry Wills has observed, that "his father and brothers," all womanizers themselves, "thought foolish."[97] JFK got by with a great deal of help from his friends in the press. Dismissing them as "courtiers," Wills dubbed the group of enablers the "Honorary Kennedys."[98] Joseph Alsop put it more generously, conceding only that JFK "had in some sense a kind of court" of admirers that newspapermen like Alsop found hard to resist.[99]

Although he counted reporter-friends to spare, Kennedy regarded certain members of the press corps as irredeemable enemies (although they, too, kept his personal secrets). What he perceived to be their unfair reporting often sent him into expletive-laced tirades no less frightening than George Washington's or Teddy Roosevelt's legendary outbursts against journalists, and far more heated than FDR's comparatively benign grumbling over the morning papers in his bedroom. Like most of his predecessors, Kennedy had close to a zero tolerance for published criticism. "I am reading more and enjoying it less," he once complained to Sorensen, who credited him with "an inexhaustible capacity to take displeasure from what he read . . . and an equally inexhaustible capacity to keep on reading more than anyone else in Washington."[100] Joe Alsop found Kennedy both "sensitive" to and "scornful" of criticism.[101] Another reporter commented, "his skin is as thin as cigarette paper."[102]

Notwithstanding the longtime Kennedy family connection to Time-Life chairman Henry Luce, for example, the president came to scorn *Time* magazine as "highly readable but highly misleading." JFK so admired the company's presidential reporter Hugh Sidey that he convinced himself that Sidey's editors were mauling his copy to make the administration look bad. When *Time* began pounding Kennedy for failing to harness federal spending, the president got the postmaster general to find out how much Luce's magazines were costing taxpayers in postal subsidies. Presumably JFK relayed the staggering figure—$20 million—to the powerful publisher with whom he remained in frequent contact despite their disputes.[103]

Though a longtime reader of the pro-Republican *New York Herald Tribune*, a bastion of superb writing, Kennedy grew annoyed by what he regarded as its increasingly "smart-alecky style." His irritation came to a boil when the paper linked the new administration to a long-festering scandal involving Texas businessman Billie Sol Estes. In a pique, Kennedy ordered the White House to cancel its subscription (although Jackie took to smuggling its fashion page into her quarters). When news reports began suggesting that the president would read only stories that flattered him, he reversed himself and re-subscribed.

Meanwhile JFK continued grudgingly to peruse the *New York Times*, even though he griped to Ted Sorensen that its editorials were "90% unfavorable" against him personally despite the paper's enthusiasm for administration policies. "I'm convinced," he told his speechwriter, "that they keep in stock a canned editorial on our 'lack of leadership' and run it every few weeks with little change."[104] At one point, he ordered an FBI wiretap on the paper's chief military correspondent, Hanson Baldwin, over an alleged security breach. Then, when the paper's Saigon correspondent David Halberstam began questioning the legitimacy of South Vietnam's pro-U.S. Diem regime, Kennedy demanded that the *Times*' new publisher, Arthur Ochs "Punch" Sulzberger, reassign the "28-year-old kid" to a less sensitive outpost. Sulzberger refused.[105]

On his own initiative, Kennedy decided to host on-the-record White House lunches with leading newspaper publishers on a "state-by-state basis." As Salinger reported, "The publishers were generally pleased with the President's frankness and the honor of being invited to the White House." One grateful guest told Salinger upon his return home, "I will never be able to write another glib editorial attacking the President without thinking of that lunch and the great burdens on the American President."[106]

The events did not always inspire empathy. At one, E. M. "Ted" Dealey, publisher of the archconservative *Dallas Morning News*, hectored Kennedy, "[Y]ou and your administration are weak sisters. . . . We need a man on horseback to lead this nation, and many people in Texas and the Southwest think that you are riding Caroline's bicycle." When another attendee, the publisher of Dealey's rival paper, the afternoon *Dallas Times Herald*, wrote to Kennedy to apologize on behalf of his city, the president replied: "I'm sure the people of Dallas must be glad when afternoon comes." Recalling Kennedy's reaction to the Dealey outburst, Charlie Bartlett later confided, "I think he got a big kick out of it."[107] (Dealey would earn permanent notoriety by publishing a full-page anti-Kennedy ad in his paper on November 22, 1963—the day of JFK's assassination there.)

Both Pierre Salinger and John Kennedy faced the most serious challenge to their assiduously cultivated relationships with the press during the thirteen-day Cuban Missile Crisis that began in late October 1962.[108] U-2 aerial photographs had revealed the alarming presence of Soviet-built surface-to-surface missiles in Cuba, poised only ninety miles from U.S. territory. Now Russian ships believed to be transporting additional military supplies headed toward the Caribbean island. After UN Ambassador Adlai E. Stevenson dramatically reported the provocative buildup at a televised Security Council meeting on October 25, Kennedy imposed a naval "quarantine" and dared the Soviets to risk war by defying it. With U.S.–Soviet brinksmanship nearing a crescendo and the threat of nuclear annihilation looming credibly for the first time in world history, Kennedy addressed the nation on television. But then he restricted the usual flow of background information to the press from both the Pentagon and the State Department, not to mention the White House itself. Attempting to justify what amounted to a second quarantine—this one on news—he explained that he wanted government at this crucial moment to "speak with one voice."[109]

In fact, until publicly accusing the Russians at the United Nations, the administration had kept the press largely in the dark about the approaching showdown. When Kennedy cut short a campaign swing to head back to the White House to deal with the crisis—congressional elections were only a few weeks away—the press office put out word that he had merely come down with a head cold. After the full story of the Russian threat broke, correspondents thronged the White House press office demanding information, but generating few details. Even Kennedy's longtime friend Arthur Krock grew outraged over the news blackout, producing articles for both the *Times* and *Fortune* magazine that condemned administration attempts to referee coverage.[110] It was Krock who came up with the memorable phrase meant to rebuke the administration's efforts to control the message: "News Management."[111]

Adding fuel to the firestorm over the missile crisis, a Defense Department spokesman named Arthur Sylvester tried rationalizing the manipulation by telling the *Washington Star* that "in the kind of world we live in the generation of news by the government becomes one weapon in a strained situation. The results, in my opinion, justify the means." Pierre Salinger called it "the kind of statement which was to provide the flame to explode the powder keg of press resentment." Predictably, the *Star* itself soon editorialized that Sylvester had "let the ugly cat out of the bag," and chided the administration for "its efforts toward achieving managed control of the news. . . . The 'kind of world we live in' seems now to be a world in which the truth given the American people of what has happened is that part of the truth selected by officialdom to piece together a desirable image."[112] Helen Thomas of the UPI labeled the mess "the forerunner of the 'credibility gap' that precipatated the downfall of two of Kennedy's successors."[113]

Not entirely unsympathetic, at least in retrospect, Salinger called the episode "a symptom of a much greater problem which has never been seriously attacked in a mutual way by the American press and the U.S. government," namely "how a democracy . . . defends itself . . . against an enemy which can operate in secret."[114] Future administrations would have no more success in resolving that conundrum than Kennedy's. For certain, the episode permanently chilled Kennedy's generally warm relationship with the press. Thereafter, reporters remained on their guard about official updates—including the president's repeated assurances that he intended to send no American ground forces to Vietnam.

For his part, Kennedy never regretted his decision to block the flow of information in the fall of 1962. "It would have been a great mistake and possibly a disaster," he later defended himself to the National Association of Broadcasters, "if this news had been dribbled out when we were unsure of the extent of the Soviet build-up in Cuba, and when we were unsure of our response, and when we had not consulted any of our allies."[115]

To some, the episode only confirmed Kennedy's reputation for press manipulation. At a news conference in February 1963, the fearless May Craig raised the issue of "managed news" directly, asking Kennedy: "Would you give us your definition and tell us why you find it necessary to practice it?"

"You are charging us with something, uh, Miss Craig," Kennedy replied, "and then you are asking me to define what it is you are charging me with. . . . Let me just say we have had very limited success in managing the news, if that is what we have been trying to do. Perhaps you would tell us what you object to in our treatment of news?"

"Well, I don't believe in managed news at all. I thought we ought to get everything we want" [scattered laughter].

"Well, I think that you should, too, Miss Craig. I am for that" [a roar of laughter].[116]

But Kennedy remained dead serious in his efforts to massage the first draft of missile crisis history in his favor. When Charlie Bartlett earned an assignment from the *Saturday Evening Post* to produce an inside account of the events of October and November 1962, Kennedy took pains to tell his old friend he did not want it to appear that he was praising himself. But he agreed to cooperate when the journalist assured Kennedy in advance that he intended to portray "an effective operation." He thought it would be "a good magazine article because the President certainly looks good from everything I know." Bartlett did have one troubling question for Kennedy: Was it true, as he had heard, that Adlai

Stevenson had wanted to negotiate with, rather than face down, the Russians? "Are you going to put that in the article?" the president asked. "Yes," Bartlett replied. Kennedy not only raised no objections but, given the unusual opportunity to review and edit the article before Bartlett submitted it, left the revelation intact. He intended to emerge the sole hero of what some people were already calling the "Gettysburg of the Cold War."[117]

The Cuban Missile Crisis signaled a turning point not only in the Cold War but in the even longer history of tension between presidents and the press. As James T. Graham has noted, it marked the last time a president could mold (or kill) press stories by appealing to friendship and patriotism. And it also brought about "the final moments of an era of dominance for the print press that predated America's founding."[118] As early as 1961, Samuel Becker, a scholar of television and film, moreover attributed the "shift in the balance of power from the Congress to the President" to Kennedy's ability to speak "directly to each individual in the population."[119] After the Cuban Missile Crisis, during which Cronkite and the *Huntley-Brinkley Report* had provided blanket coverage of the nail-biting events, the medium that Kennedy dominated became the dominant medium in America. JFK was to enjoy its spotlight for only one more year.

The biggest impact Kennedy exerted on American television audiences came with his untimely murder. Nothing he had ever done in life earned the coverage lavished on him in death. On-air newsmen broke into regularly scheduled programming to report his assassination on November 22, 1963, and remained on the air almost without interruption to confirm his demise and report on the arrival of his body back in Washington and, over the next few days, his funeral and the capture and murder of his accused killer.

As the saying goes, seldom more accurately, Americans remained glued to their home screens that entire, surreal weekend: some to gape, others to worship at the altar of a burgeoning cult of personality, and a few to incubate ludicrous conspiracy theories. One and all eavesdropped on such unforgettable scenes as little John Kennedy Jr.'s heart-wrenching salute to his father's coffin.

Kennedy's canonization did not arise from television alone. Print journalists like Tom Wicker, a little-known *New York Times* Washington correspondent assigned to cover the president in Dallas, and Maurice Carroll, a *Daily News* political reporter ordered to hasten there after Kennedy's assassination, built their reputations by finding highly original ways to supplement the blanket television coverage with sparkling, behind-the-scenes features. New York columnist Jimmy Breslin added an unforgettable human touch to Kennedy's imposing state funeral by profiling the unassuming man who dug his grave.[120] But it was largely through television coverage that Kennedy escaped the bounds of ordinary scrutiny and assumed the status of myth.

Above all, JFK was a giant star of the small screen. However brief his tenure, his mastery of television—his discernible vitality and his extraordinary ease before the cameras—helped him become not only an immensely popular president in life (carrying an estimated 90 percent popularity rating into the 1964 campaign he would not get to wage) but an American icon in death. A 2007 Rasmussen poll found Kennedy to be one of only six presidents (the others being Washington, Lincoln, FDR, Jefferson, and TR) to be rated favorably by 80 percent of respondents. A 2011 Gallup poll ranked JFK fourth behind Reagan, Lincoln, and Clinton.[121] And that same year, a Vision Critical/Angus Reid survey ranked Kennedy first.

Professional historians are not far behind. A recent C-SPAN historian's survey of the first forty-three presidents ranked John F. Kennedy eighth best, arguably higher than his abbreviated tenure and scant legislative accomplishments might have earned absent his powerful impact on the eyes, minds, and hearts of surviving contemporaries who still remember his face and voice from TV.[122]

As do I. At age seventy, nearly sixty years after the fact, I can still vividly recall feigning a cold as an eleven-year-old so I could remain home from school on January 20, 1961, to watch the Kennedy inauguration, moment by moment, on a small black-and-white TV. Two and a half years later, my family and I huddled together, dazed but transfixed by the unfolding footage from Dallas, Washington, and Arlington, witnesses to a secular canonization by media. None of us who lived through any of it, even as pre-adolescents, will likely forget the powerful sights and sounds that brought America's young leader to his rest too violently and too soon.

The transcendent John F. Kennedy brought a New Frontier vigor to government by crossing a new frontier in presidential communications. As long as the medium of television dominated American politics and culture, no one seemed fresher, more vital, or more compelling. However melodramatic his Cold War rhetoric, however censorious his news management, however fruitless his efforts to advance civil rights or prevent American entanglement in Southeast Asia, and however irresponsible his sexual misconduct, he remains forever gilded on the highlight reels of a life and presidency cruelly interrupted.

— 11 —

LYNDON B. JOHNSON

The powerful "Washington Merry-Go-Round" columnist Drew Pearson once admitted that, at the beginning of their acquaintance, he had never imagined that Lyndon Johnson would ultimately become "one of the great leaders of the United States and the world."[1] So the veteran journalist took special pride in remembering that he had once contributed to the defeat of Johnson's 1948 Democratic primary opponent for the U.S. Senate in Texas, Coke R. Stevenson. A loss by Johnson that year might have ended his national political career before it began.

"I wanted to 'hep' Lyndon as he would say," Pearson remembered. So he exposed Stevenson as two-faced on labor issues, a report the columnist thought "maybe made the difference" in LBJ's slim 1948 victory. "Landslide Lyndon," as he was soon dubbed, won the race by just eighty-seven votes out of more than a million cast. Pearson recalled that a "very grateful" LBJ "was gracious enough to thank me for getting him elected," though the newspaperman added: "I'm sure he thanked a lot of other people."[2] Over the decades, LBJ would praise quite a few reporters—and direct rage at many others.

If Pearson imagined that Johnson's gratitude would blossom into lifelong indebtedness, he would discover otherwise. Learning some years later that Senator Joseph McCarthy planned to publicly denounce him as a Communist sympathizer, Pearson rushed to the office of by-then Majority Leader Johnson to ask for "a little help from you on the Senate floor." As Pearson reminded him, "Lyndon, you know that I'm not a Communist."

"Drew," Johnson changed the subject, "you've not been kind to me lately."

Stunned, Pearson returned to his own office and assembled a dossier proving that of the ninety recent items he had published about LBJ, eighty-five had been positive. He rushed the exculpatory data to Johnson. But "hep" would not be forthcoming. After McCarthy concluded his rant on the Senate floor, "Lyndon," the columnist acknowledged, "did not go to my defense." More than a decade later, pressed to consider whether the late president had required "a steady stream of praise . . . to maintain his good will," Pearson admitted, using the present tense as if Johnson were still alive and capable of again exacting revenge, that "he doesn't like to be criticized."[3]

Were it not for Vietnam, Pearson nonetheless insisted, history would have ranked LBJ as "one of our greatest Presidents," adding: "Roosevelt would have been proud of him." Asked whether Johnson's lifelong resistance to criticism hurt him, Pearson would say only: "He was a better talker than a listener. But then, after all, a newspaperman is there to listen and not to talk."[4]

Together and individually, John F. Kennedy and Lyndon B. Johnson dominated the media for most of the 1960s. Kennedy did so with a beguiling self-assurance that glittered on the increasingly dominant medium of television. Lacking Kennedy's élan, Johnson made his own mark by channeling a civil rights revolution into transformative new federal law but ultimately miring the country in an unwinnable war in Southeast Asia. Eventually launching a second front against the media, Johnson forfeited the goodwill he needed at home to sustain his military policy abroad.

Although Johnson had been included in cabinet meetings and briefings during Kennedy's White House tenure, JFK had made sure his press-savvy vice president was often occupied elsewhere, out of sight and, as much as possible, isolated from journalists. Kennedy named LBJ to chair various federal commissions and periodically sent him overseas as an envoy. Wondered the Copley News Service: "Why has Lyndon Johnson gone into eclipse?"[5] Privately, JFK explained, "I can't afford to have my Vice President, who knows every reporter in Washington, going around saying we're all screwed up, so we're going to keep him happy."[6]

The press, particularly the Eastern establishment media, never quite cottoned to the son of a Texas farmer, especially once he succeeded Kennedy in 1963. To them, he had committed an unpardonable sin: interrupting the reign of Camelot. Although Johnson "deported himself" flawlessly during the transition, in the view of NBC-TV news anchorman Chet Huntley, the "intellectuals . . . were so enamored of John Kennedy that they couldn't get over it when he was assassinated." As Texas-born newswoman Sarah McClendon sardonically observed: "How could someone from west of the Mississippi be as smart as someone from Boston?"[7]

Johnson branded the most resistant members of the press corps "the Georgetown Crowd," but much as he "loathed and detested them," he yearned for their approval. As LBJ crudely but plaintively asked *Time-Life* columnist Hugh Sidey, "How come when I say it, it comes out 'Horse Shit,' and when they say it, it comes out 'Chanel Number Five'?" Once-favored scribes soon found themselves excluded from White House functions. As Huntley recalled: "They resented it very bitterly. They began to attack Johnson very early, and I felt unfairly so."[8]

Boorish he may have been, but Lyndon Johnson was no rube. Polished, impeccably tailored, and relentlessly hardworking, he had used his leadership skills to bully a landmark 1957 civil rights bill through a U.S. Senate still dominated by Dixiecrats. No amateur when it came to the press, he had befriended innumerable journalists en route to national office and even counted himself—or at least his wife, Lady Bird—as a media mogul. Back in 1943, Mrs. Johnson had used an inheritance to purchase the small radio station KTBC in Austin, Texas. Like all such acquisitions, the deal required licensing approval by the Federal Communications Commission, so LBJ used his considerable influence to obtain it. Johnson biographers Robert A. Caro and Robert Dallek have surmised that then-congressman Johnson secured the license by pledging to back renewal of the soon-to-sunset FCC itself.[9] Later, LBJ helped convince CBS to embrace the station as a network affiliate, magnifying its value exponentially. Before long, the Johnsons added a TV station to their growing conglomerate. By 1960, the KTBC investment anchored a family financial empire worth millions.

Aside from wealth, LBJ had two other things in common with his lamented predecessor: bad health and a roving eye. Johnson had suffered a near-fatal heart attack in 1955 but had done little since to modify his hard-driving lifestyle, save for giving up cigarettes. A serial womanizer notwithstanding his cardiac problems, LBJ's infidelities ranged from tawdry flings to a longtime relationship about which his forbearing wife had full knowledge.[10] Just as the press had ruled Kennedy's private life off-limits—and Roosevelt's before him—they turned a blind eye to whatever they knew of Johnson's.

LBJ also shared with JFK a flair for generating publicity, even if he often sought it more clumsily. Aboard the very aircraft waiting to take him—together with Kennedy's remains—back to Washington from Dallas on November 22, 1963, Johnson delayed his swearing-in as president until the blood-splattered Jacqueline Kennedy was ready to emerge from her cabin and pose alongside him. Then LBJ was overheard barking, "We've got the press here, so we can go ahead."[11] The oath-taking recorded, the press disembarked with their film and the aircraft took off for the capital. For all his crass manipulation, the resulting photograph served to assure the nation that while Kennedy had died, the presidency lived.

When he first entered office, Johnson determined to outdo his predecessor with regard to press conferences, in quantity if not quality. In his first six months alone, he hosted twenty-six such sessions. "LBJ was a lot of things—mercurial and complex come to mind," UPI White House correspondent Helen Thomas later reminisced, "but he was accessible."[12] Contrary to logic, the press resented Johnson's early commitment to increased, if irregularly scheduled, press opportunities, criticizing the initiative as slapdash and inconsiderate; it gave them no time to prepare.

Unlike Kennedy's meticulously planned and professionally orchestrated news conferences, many of Johnson's early sessions were called on the spur of the moment, and staged wherever the president happened to be when the urge to share his views struck him. In a nod to his hero FDR, LBJ let nostalgia override practicality and hosted one such event inside the cramped Oval Office. Television reporters, not to mention their camera crews, found themselves outside, unable to fit inside, and vehemently expressed their displeasure. Johnson had FDR's "razzle-dazzle with the press," admitted J. Russell Wiggins, the managing editor of the *Washington Post*, but "arrived on the scene when the press was infinitely more sophisticated, cynical, and suspicious than it was in Roosevelt's day."[13] Defiantly, Johnson continued to host small-group press sessions in the office anyway. Kennedy's old newspaper pal Charlie Bartlett thought LBJ "made an enormous mistake" in "bringing the press in so much," believing such a practice "really doesn't pay off for a President. You've got to keep the press at a respectable distance."[14] Columnist Stewart Alsop agreed, huffing that Johnson seemed to be wasting an "extraordinary amount of time with the press."[15]

Meanwhile, LBJ and his staff scrambled to find alternate sites that might suit his style at more formal sessions. As Tom Wicker of the *New York Times* observed, Johnson was "perceptive" and "vain" enough to shun formats in which Kennedy had excelled.[16] Once, LBJ invited reporters to a news conference improbably situated in the White House family theater, a former cloakroom that the movie-loving FDR had converted into a screening room during World War II. Yet another Q&A took place during a picnic arranged for correspondents and their families on the White House grounds. And still another unusual opportunity was granted to select women correspondents amid a whirlwind tour LBJ personally led through the mansion's hitherto off-limits private quarters. Johnson even staged an impromptu news conference while loping around the White House lawn—seven laps in all—as reporters trailed him and fired questions whenever they could catch their breath. News may not have been generated that day, but LBJ left the impression that the journalists in his wake were eager to talk to him, a sharp contrast to Kennedy, who had seemed eager to engage journalists.

To one White House aide, LBJ's outdoor session amounted to "sheer madness—a press corps thirty to forty strong following him at a jog trot and elbowing each other for position where they could catch a few words." Still, Johnson remained "enormously reluctant" to schedule formal news conferences. "He preferred impromptu affairs—presumably because they did not afford reporters time to think up 'mean' questions."[17] The venerable columnist Walter Lippmann gave LBJ's unconventional approach his blessing: "I don't blame Johnson for not trying to do what Kennedy did with the press conference," he declared. "Kennedy was a virtuoso. It would be like asking Johnson to sing Tosca."[18]

Many of Johnson's press interactions took place on the road, and not only during official trips. He would spend nearly a quarter of his presidency at his sprawling ranch near Austin, requiring the press corps to follow him there and remain on call for his unpredictable announcements. Early in his term, Johnson hosted a Texas-style barbecue for two hundred correspondents, during which he simply ordered a rostrum hoisted onto an upended bale of hay so he could take questions on the spot. At the ranch, LBJ felt the most comfortable. Here he urged visiting reporters to mount up for horseback rides and join him for such activities as cookouts, visits to his idiosyncratic kinfolk, and boat rides on the nearby man-made lake he had once secured federal funding to dig. Press luminaries Tom Wicker, Douglas Kiker of the *Herald Tribune*, and Phil Potter of the *Baltimore Sun* enjoyed a post–New Year's fish fry on the ranch, after which they accompanied the president on one of his nightly calls to his aunt Aureole.[19] Reporters "who had scarcely known Johnson," columnists Evans and Novak observed, became "privileged listeners to confidential chats on the front porch of the ranch house, high-speed tours of the hill country, and hilarious parties aboard the President's motor launch."[20] If the press corps never became fully westernized, LBJ would make sure they at least looked the part: he bought the reporters Stetson hats.[21]

A week before Christmas 1963, barely a month after he took office, Johnson impulsively offered a gaggle of correspondents gathered at the ranch an unscheduled tour of his residence. Mrs. Johnson was putting the finishing touches on a dinner for relatives, so an irresistible force met an immovable object: Lady Bird did not want the journalists inside. The meal was cooked, the guests were hungry, and besides, she tried pointing out, "We're having a party for them [the press] in just a couple of days, and don't you think we could do it then?" Ignoring her, LBJ led the mortified throng on a room-by-room inspection as the other guests looked on, Merriman Smith of the UPI noted, wearing the "forlorn" expressions of "people . . . waiting for a behind-schedule bus." Finally, the party reached a closed door, which LBJ tried unsuccessfully to open. His knocking went unanswered, but the president would not give up. After calling out, "Lady Bird, let me in," he turned to the journalists and remarked, with no sign of embarrassment: "You know what? She's locked me out." Undeterred, he pounded again. Finally, Mrs. Johnson opened the door to what turned out to be the couple's bedroom. Reporters had no choice but to follow the president inside, where they encountered a disheveled bed that the "valiant" Mrs. Johnson had obviously tried hastily to cover. Then the president opened an interior door and proclaimed, "That's my bathroom!" Scattered there for all to see were an open toothpaste tube, discarded hair curlers, and wet towels. The awkward tour did little to endear the president to the press corps, but it did much to elevate their opinion of the First Lady.[22]

Back at the White House, the helter-skelter Q&A sessions resumed. Before his first year as president ended, Johnson also fielded press inquiries while visiting the World's Fair in New York and hosted a delegation of agricultural writers at the White House Cabinet Room. Columnist George Dixon joked that LBJ had "held press conferences almost everywhere except in Lincoln's bed and underwater."[23] During the 1964 presidential campaign, LBJ would even stage a small, unscheduled briefing aboard Air Force One—while disrobing until he was completely naked. On another flight, he demanded that reporters talk to a NATO official, then announced: "Now, you-all interview the hell out of him while I go take a leak."[24] Clearly he intended to separate himself from the Kennedy tradition of formality, if only to preempt unflattering comparisons.

Asked whether he worried he might become overexposed—not meant as a reference to his airborne display of nudity—Johnson replied that he only aimed "to please."[25] Yet by scheduling some sessions at the last minute, and at more modest-size venues, Johnson also reduced press participation (and scrutiny) more than 80 percent: only fifty or so correspondents now managed to squeeze into most LBJ news conferences, a far more manageable group than the hundreds who had thronged Kennedy's.

Eventually, LBJ did agree to host the press back at the State Department—but in its four-hundred-seat International Conference Room, not the cavernous auditorium where his predecessor had once held forth. For his own State Department debut, Johnson remained seated and spoke slowly and somberly. Just as he feared, the press noted the undisguisable contrast between the dour, basset-faced Johnson and the sparkling Kennedy—precisely why Johnson had avoided the site and format until then. Only later would LBJ launch a tradition of his own by using the East Room for his news conferences. But wherever he staged formal sessions, he seemed ill at ease. To Drew Pearson, Johnson was simply "not very good on these big televised press conferences, chiefly because he's not very photogenic and . . . studied it too carefully. He was too stilted. He was trying too hard."[26] Indeed, Johnson's cramming before formal press encounters rivaled Kennedy's for intensity, with all government hands on deck for exhaustive briefings. But much as he shared JFK's remarkable ability to retain detailed information, LBJ lacked his predecessor's uncanny knack for making well-rehearsed answers sound extemporaneous.

Johnson proved infinitely more effective in modest-size group sessions. The more select the guest list, the greater LBJ's impact; the smaller the room, the larger he loomed. Early in his term, for example, LBJ hosted a private White House lunch just for Luce empire journalists. There, he demonstrated what Time Inc. editor in chief Hedley Donovan called "appealing touches of humility." The man known as "Deadly Hedley" gushed, "If his purpose was to show us how fast and firmly he had taken hold of the President's business, he was entirely successful."[27] Soon the names of sympathetic correspondents began returning to invitation lists for White House receptions, at which Johnson made it a habit to lavish attention on them in front of their spouses. "He was a man who liked to entertain," testified one of his press aides. But "he would be outraged by any story he deemed to be hostile written by a reporter who had attended one of his soirees. He regarded such items as a breach of good manners."[28]

LBJ was especially masterful—and the most intimidating—one-on-one. In intimate situations the six-foot-three Johnson could deploy his already notorious "Treatment": looming close to a guest's face, throwing a big arm around his victim's shoulder, thumping his chest with the presidential index finger for emphasis, and offering ceaseless monologues and off-color jokes seemingly without pausing for breath. One of his targets, *Washington Star* columnist Mary McGrory, called it "a potent blend of badgering, cajolery, promises of favors, [and] implied threats" that left a visitor "absolutely helpless." Ben Bradlee cringed after one private meeting, "You really felt as if a St. Bernard had licked your face for an hour."[29] To future press secretary George E. Reedy, it was "like standing under Niagara Falls."[30]

Alternatively, Johnson was capable of remaining conspicuously still and staring wordlessly until a guest lost his appetite for confrontation. During LBJ's first weeks in the White House, Tom Wicker secured a coveted private meeting with the new president. The *Times* reporter found Johnson seated in the Oval Office, covered, save for his head, by a large sheet as he submitted to a haircut. It was Teddy Roosevelt's "barber's hour" all over again, except unlike TR, the usually voluble LBJ said nothing at all. He merely glared at Wicker, who remained frozen under the president's withering gaze. "I knew I was beaten," admitted the reporter, who finally "babbled" something about how glad he was that Johnson was now leading the nation. Hearing that praise, LBJ leapt from his chair, threw off the sheet, and launched into a one-sided conversation that lasted forty-five minutes.[31]

The objects of Johnson's overtures might be summoned to impromptu, off-the-record lunches in the family quarters or even granted face time in the presidential limousine. Once, he instructed two such startled passengers, Helen Thomas of the UPI and Peggy Stanton of ABC: "Wave to the crowds, as if you're Luci and Lynda"—LBJ's daughters.[32] On another occasion, Thomas scored a ride in the presidential helicopter, although Johnson spoiled the experience by handing her a comb after the windswept flight, telling her she looked "a mess."[33] Just as Kennedy had once passed inside information to journalist chums like Ben Bradlee, Bill Lawrence, Charlie Bartlett, and Rowland Evans, Johnson now sidled up to Drew Pearson, *Washington Post* publisher Katharine Graham (he called her "dearie"), magazine titan S. I. Newhouse, and *Philadelphia Inquirer* owner Walter Annenberg (whom LBJ believed "partial" to him).[34] Johnson conducted most of his overtures by telephone, recording the conversations and locking the tapes away for safekeeping.

Johnson undertook a particularly ardent effort to woo Walter Lippmann, at age seventy-four the dean of Washington opinion makers. Showing unusual deference, the president visited him at his home near the National Cathedral on December 1, 1963, barely a week after taking office. The Pulitzer Prize laureate found the president, clearly on his best behavior, to be "much less boisterous, more likeable than I'd known him before."[35] Lippmann's reaction should have surprised no one who could still recall the journalist's onetime infatuation with the first hyper-energized president he had covered: Theodore Roosevelt.

Flattering requests for advice and a shower of gifts followed the Lippmann house call, along with invitations to private meetings and White House social events. At one gathering, LBJ crowed to the other guests, "this man here is the greatest journalist in the world, and he's a friend of mine." Within the year, Lippmann would declare in his syndicated column, *Today and Tomorrow*, that "President Johnson is by instinct, temperament, conviction and experience, a man for this season." Astonished when Lippmann reiterated his admiration for LBJ at a high-toned London dinner party, his host, *Christian Science Monitor* correspondent John C. Harsh, countered, "Isn't he called 'Ol' Corn Pone?'" "Not by me" came Lippmann's emphatic reply.[36]

A month earlier, Lippmann had told a television interviewer: "Newspapermen cannot be the cronies of great men . . . much less a President."[37] But he came perilously close to violating his own standards in 1964, providing strong evidence of Lyndon Johnson's hypnotic powers during the early days of his presidency. In September, LBJ culminated his relentless courtship by awarding Lippmann the Presidential Medal of Freedom at the White House.

Soon Lippmann received an even greater compliment. Searching for a "New Deal"–like catchphrase to brand the administration's ambitious new agenda for social reform, someone on Johnson's staff exhumed Lippmann's 1937 book, *The Good Society*, and recommended adapting its title. It was said that the brilliant White House speechwriter Richard Goodwin suggested an editorial tweak to make the adjective stronger: they would call the program "The *Great* Society."[38]

Johnson unveiled his grand plan in a commencement address at the University of Michigan on May 22, 1964. "[I]n your time," he told the crowd of graduates, parents, and academics, "we have the opportunity to move not only toward the rich society and the powerful society, but upward to the Great Society." This meant, he vowed, a concerted effort to "shape the civilization that we want," one that included "an end to poverty and racial injustice."[39] The eighty thousand spectators repeatedly interrupted his speech with applause. Later that day, as Air Force One flew him back toward Washington, LBJ's mood escalated from "euphoric" to "manic" as he mulled over his triumph. After downing a celebratory cocktail, he headed to the press cabin at the rear of the aircraft, where he reiterated key phrases from the speech for reporters, adding "emphasis" to make sure, as he told his captive audience, that "you got this."[40]

One of his press secretaries later expressed regret that Johnson came to enjoy spending so much time with the airborne press pool in his section of the plane or theirs. Having witnessed a newsworthy event on the ground, the reporters usually wanted only to "rest." Unwilling to leave them to their own devices—or worse, interpretations—"the president became a bore," the aide admitted, "addicted to long, rambling conversations, some fueled by alcohol."[41] Even Helen Thomas, at first glad to be included when Johnson asked his aides to "bring the boys in here," wearied of the imposition. Pouring himself a highball, Johnson would "prop his feet up on the table" and "go on for hours," his voice often drowned out by the whine of the jet engines.[42] At some level, reporters came to understand, Johnson was essentially lonely.

The story of Lyndon Johnson's downhill relationship with the press after their post-assassination "honeymoon" might be subtitled "A Tale of Four Press Secretaries and One Chronically Dissatisfied Client." The four men were holdover Pierre Salinger, George Reedy, Bill D. Moyers, and George Christian. The last two, like Johnson, hailed from the Lone Star State.

When the presidency passed to Johnson in November 1963, one of his first acts was to persuade Salinger to remain in the job he had held under JFK. As LBJ flattered him, "I need you more than he ever did" (he would use a similar come-on to retain Ted Sorensen).[43] Johnson also summoned two Texas natives to White House service as advisors: the seasoned Houston public relations executive Jack Valenti and Moyers, the young deputy director of the Peace Corps who early in his career had worked at the Austin station owned by Lady Bird. Joining this group was Reedy, a onetime UPI correspondent who had served as an aide to Johnson beginning in his Senate days and doubtless had expected the top job when LBJ succeeded Kennedy. Johnson had instead opted to retain as much of the JFK team as he could, not only to emphasize continuity but to bend longtime Kennedy loyalists to his will.

For a brief time, the arrangement with Salinger flourished. Johnson granted him open-door access to the Oval Office, and once even accepted an invitation to his press secretary's home for dinner. As soon as the administration secured hotel space in Austin to accommodate journalists during LBJ's breaks at the "western White House," the president assigned Salinger a large suite and ordered it redecorated. "When a man works for me," LBJ told him, "he's a member of my family." The charm offensive reached its zenith when pianist Van Cliburn performed for Johnson inside a Texas high school gym; it was Salinger whom LBJ summoned to the stage to play an encore. Back in Washington, the press secretary joined the president twice a day in the White House pool. That meant seeing a great deal of LBJ, in every sense of the term, since Johnson, long infamous in Washington for conducting meetings while showering, shaving, or sitting on the toilet, remained shockingly uninhibited and often swam naked. It was another part of the Johnson "treatment": intimidation by exhibitionism.

"He gloried in exposing his body—which was not particularly handsome by normal aesthetic standards," Salinger's successor would distastefully recall.[44] Overweight and out of shape, Johnson remained eager to show himself off—especially the body part he had long referred to proudly as "Jumbo." Strolling once with Johnson at his ranch, journalist Sam Schaffer was startled to see him casually undo his fly and urinate in open view. On another occasion, the AP's James Marlow begged to speak to Johnson on the phone one night to answer some questions he needed resolved for his next column. To his surprise, LBJ summoned him to the White House. Ushered into the president's bedroom at 10:30 P.M., a startled Marlow found him "lying naked on a rubdown table getting his nightly massage." His replies in hand, Marlow tried to leave, but LBJ sprung from the table, still undressed, and bent down low to search for something on his closet floor, his "bare fundament . . . almost in the writer's face." Finally standing up, Johnson triumphantly handed Marlow a bound copy of his collected speeches as a gift.[45]

Johnson's propensity for exposing himself often placed Salinger in ludicrous situations. One afternoon, before commencing a scheduled White House lunch with Gardner "Mike" Cowles and four fellow staffers from *Look* magazine, LBJ on impulse beckoned Salinger and the visitors downstairs toward a locker room, barking: "Mike, your figure is as bad as mine. I'm not going to feed you until we have a swim." When Cowles hesitated, Johnson yelled out: "Mike! What's the matter with you? Are you afraid to see me nude? Come on in here and get undressed with me." The *Look* team, joined by Salinger, obligingly disrobed and plunged with LBJ into the historic pool, heated to boiling at ninety-two degrees. The six men found themselves wading self-consciously in the facility built for Roosevelt as LBJ did laps while continuing to talk without pause.

"Jumbo" evidently did not impress everyone. "Like most males of his age," Cowles recalled, "Lyndon was not a very prepossessing figure in the nude." But he was commanding. At one point that day he demanded that Salinger order the guests drinks. When the press secretary balked, "I don't know what they like," Johnson bellowed back: "They're damn Yankees. Just get them Scotch. I'll have a double bourbon." Several rounds, four hours, and one much-delayed meal later, the reporters finally staggered out of the White House, having been given new meaning to the term "*Look* magazine close-up."[46] Disproving George Dixon's observation, Johnson had indeed held a press conference underwater, leaving only Lincoln's bed as an unutilized forum. All Salinger would tactfully recall of such experiences was "I spent much more time with President Johnson at the White House than I had with JFK."[47]

In the end, time and access were not enough—"my fault," Salinger conceded, "not President Johnson's. I simply came to the realization that the memory of JFK was too overpowering, and that I wasn't functioning on all cylinders for LBJ." But Johnson had also become a tyrannical boss. He would "blow sky high" whenever a news story displeased him, which was most of the time, then demand that Salinger convey his displeasure and report back on how the wayward journalist took the reprimand. JFK had sent him on similar errands, Salinger admitted, but at least never required him to brief him on the results.[48] No matter how lavish or frequent Johnson's media coverage for his early achievements, it was never lavish or frequent enough to satisfy his omnivorous but fragile ego. As AP correspondent Douglas B. Cornell put it, Johnson became not only "sensitive to stories or events that reflect unfavorably on him," but "sensitive about being called sensitive."[49] As a result, historian Robert Dallek has noted, his aides "became the object of LBJ's fury for not getting the press more fully behind the Administration."[50] Each day, he scoured newspapers for evidence of his press officers' failures.

White House domestic policy advisor (and future secretary of health, education, and welfare) Joseph A. Califano Jr. wrote amusingly that Johnson "could never get enough of the news he so mistrusted."[51] Much as Kennedy had done, Johnson kept fully abreast of national reporting and opinion writing in the print press. His daily reading included the front-page stories and editorials in the *New York Times*, *Wall Street Journal*, *Baltimore Sun*, and *Christian Science Monitor.* Each night, he required that the early "bulldog" edition of the next morning's *Washington Post* be delivered to his bedside along with his briefing binders. A White House aide called LBJ "the best informed man in Washington."[52]

Simultaneously, Johnson directed obsessive attention to the electronic media and wire services. Fixated on radio, he instructed the Signal Corps to install sets throughout the White House, all connected to official channels. Once he ordered a bulk supply of Sony-brand pocket-size portables so his staff could monitor news reports with equal attention no matter where they happened to be.[53] Most of them ignored the directive, but Johnson himself could occasionally be observed strolling the White House grounds holding a tiny transistor radio tight to one of his enormous ears.

Equally fascinated by TV, Johnson "had three television sets in the office, three more in the green den next to it, and three each in his bedroom at the White House and ranch," attested Califano, who joined the White House staff in July 1965 and stayed to the bitter end. Johnson liked to begin each morning with the *Today* show. Then every evening, he tuned all three screens in his Oval Office console to the networks' 7:00 P.M. news shows, with the sound blaring only from his favorite, NBC. A remote control sat close at hand to activate either of the other channels if they showed LBJ's face. "He'd get annoyed whenever someone criticized him or didn't get the story right," Califano told me of LBJ's viewing habits. "If CBS didn't use the lead he wanted, he'd say, 'Call Cronkite.'"[54] The president ended each long workday in his bedroom, surrounded by briefing papers but glued to any late-night current-events programming he could find in the era before twenty-four-hour cable news.[55]

Johnson also checked the news at its source, before it could be analyzed—or, he feared, misinterpreted—by broadcasters or newspapers. As Califano recalled for me: "We had tickers in the office for the AP, UPI, all the wires, running all the time. He would jump up and look at them. And he would act on what he saw. When he read something on the wire he didn't like, he'd call me in and ask me to phone someone for a correction." Some of the wire stories evoked sympathy, Califano noted. "Once [in 1964], Henry Ford divorced his first wife [Anne], a very good Catholic. I was there when that came over the wire, and Johnson literally said, 'This has got to hurt her terribly,' and told someone to get her on the phone."[56]

In his own memoir, Califano wrote evocatively of the palpable hunger with which Johnson devoured the wire stories, "bending deep down into the machine, pulling at the rolls of paper, impatient for the next line of type."[57] When the president expressed annoyance that Califano did not have the AP and UPI wires running in his own office—"How the hell can you function without reading the tickers?" he complained—the feisty thirty-four-year-old replied: "I don't need them. I've got the best ticker reader in the world working for me in the Oval Office. He'll call immediately if there's anything I need to know."[58]

Johnson's expectations for unblemished coverage could obviously never be met, and journalists and press aides alike, especially those treated to food and drink one day, would taste "the famous LBJ wrath" the next if Johnson bristled at neglect or criticism. "The first six months in the White House he had the press eating out of his hand," George Reedy continued the metaphor. "But he kicked that away himself. He'd get mad at them for some reason."[59] Helen Thomas called it "the most extreme love-hate relationship I've ever seen in the White House."[60]

Even the bromance with Pierre Salinger ended in divorce. Once "absolutely convinced" that Salinger "had elected John F. Kennedy president of the United States," he soon "turned sour on Pierre," according to press secretary-in-waiting Reedy. The break came "not for any Salinger deficiency but simply because he was expecting results that no living human being could deliver, and when they were not forthcoming, he decided he was being treated with bad faith."[61]

In early 1964, after less than four months of service in the Johnson White House, Salinger found the perfect excuse to depart, informing LBJ he would resign to run for the U.S. Senate from his native California. Salinger went on to win the state's Democratic primary, then got what should have been a decisive boost with an appointment to temporarily fill that seat following the incumbent's death. It did not help. Unable to ride the crest of LBJ's huge California majority that autumn, Salinger lost ignominiously to Republican George Murphy, a onetime minor film star (and a harbinger of things to come). Salinger instead became a member of the press, serving for years as a television news commentator at home and abroad.[62] He remains the only presidential press secretary ever to serve as a senator.

His successor at the White House, the owlish, bespectacled Reedy, was far more accustomed to Johnson's controlling ways. When word arrived from LBJ that he was to replace Salinger, Reedy was in the hospital, trying to shed fifty pounds on a "starvation diet"—having been commanded to do so by the president.[63] For months, Johnson had dangled the top job before Reedy, providing that he first clean up his act. "You don't help yourself," he badgered him. "You come in in a damned old wrinkled suit . . . and a dirty shirt, and you come in with your tie screwed up. I want you to look real nice—get you a corset if you have to," adding what he doubtless believed the harshest criticism of all: "You look like a goddamned reporter."[64] Years earlier, Reedy had rebuffed a feeler to join the Kennedy White House, an act of fealty to LBJ that he later judged "one of the biggest mistakes of my life, as it would have increased my value in Johnson's eyes had he but known" of JFK's interest.[65]

Once appointed, Reedy not surprisingly found he had inherited a thankless task. Johnson, he claimed, "never understood the functioning of the press or its role. For him it was just a public relations outlet for whatever individual or group that was astute enough to manipulate the system." LBJ "had no subtlety whatever," "regarded newspapers and newscasts as partisan arenas," and maintained that "every news story (with the possible exception of the weather) was printed because it had been inspired by a public relations counsel."[66]

"Unfortunately," Reedy continued in a later assessment inflected by bitterness, "his concept of favorable was a story carrying flattering adjectives topped by a picture in which his hair was neatly combed, his suit was freshly pressed, and his left profile was prominent." (Johnson, who insisted on being photographed from his "good side," handed out autographed prints "like peanuts.") But as his blunt former spokesman complained, "He thought a good story was something that began, 'Lyndon Baines Johnson is a calm, collected statesman who is the finest representative of the American dream.'"[67]

"Anything that fell short of this ideal was 'unfavorable' and the writer marked down as an enemy," Reedy helplessly noted. And as Frank Cormier noted, LBJ never forgot "an article or broadcast that disturbed him. . . . [H]e had the memory of an elephant." Johnson "refused to regard the press as an organization having structure and machinery. He thought that a newspaper was something that appeared on the front doorstep every morning and a television newscast was something that happened when a switch was flicked. He was never clear on the process by which stories were written, edited, set up in type, printed, and eventually delivered to the consumer." Within Johnson's definition, conducting press relations meant "selling" journalists aggressively on administration priorities. The traditional facilitating of straightforward coverage came to be looked on as servile "bag carrying."[68]

Nonetheless, the press secretary always defended Johnson against suggestions that he could not match his predecessor's charismatic appeal, even in the all-important medium of television. "One of the more important lapses of the Washington press corps," he maintained long after he had broken with Johnson, "was the assertion that compared with John F. Kennedy he 'had no style.' I know of no better example of the ovine characteristics of capital journalists. However else Lyndon Johnson might be described, he had . . . style beside which Jack Kennedy, for all his attractive qualities, faded into the background.[69]

Still, Reedy's devotion never approached the levels the new president demanded—what LBJ colorfully described as the "kiss-my-ass-at-high-noon-in-Macy's-window loyalty" he required of all subordinates.[70] Inevitably, LBJ came to believe his new pressman was not doing enough to shield him from negative coverage. Johnson seethed, for example, when Reedy failed to divert media attention from a mortifying April 1964 spectacle of LBJ's own making: the now-infamous episode in which the president lifted up his beagle dogs by their ears "to make them bark." Johnson compounded the offense by adding, "It's good for them."[71] Photographs of the scene went viral before the term was coined, igniting a tornado of indignation from pet lovers. When Johnson learned that the AP's Doug Cornell had been the first to file an unflattering story about the incident, he snarled at Reedy: "I want to know what that son of a bitch looks like, and I want to give him the silent treatment for a while. . . . So he's got a great feeling for hurting a dog, huh?"[72] The ordinarily sympathetic *Christian Science Monitor* bureau chief Robert S. Allen, who tended to blame Johnson's "inadequate and incompetent" press secretaries for his friend's bad press, placed responsibility in this case squarely on LBJ for his "inexplicable faux pas." Even Allen characterized the act of "lifting that little dog up by his ears" as "grotesque."[73]

Notwithstanding his gaucheries, Johnson began the 1964 presidential campaign as the overwhelming favorite. Then he faced two potentially harmful scandals—one old, one new, but both fanned by the Republicans and the press.

The first centered on a resuscitated two-year-old charge that Bobby Baker—a wheeler-dealer who had once served Johnson on Capitol Hill as secretary to the majority leader—had swindled government contractors in a corrupt business venture. Johnson had not dealt directly with him since 1960, and Baker had resigned his Senate job in disgrace by 1963, but that did not stop the press from repeating Republican innuendos suggesting that Johnson surely had involvement in, or at least knowledge of, Baker's shenanigans. (Sarah McClendon eventually concluded that "Johnson knew plenty," and Baker himself later charged that Johnson had at the very least accepted an illegal kickback: a stereo set.)[74]

Evidence that LBJ struggled over how best to contain the fallout can be gleaned from his secret White House tapes. During a twenty-two-minute conference call with assorted advisors including Moyers, Valenti, Reedy, and the president's chief aide, Walter Jenkins, LBJ went back and forth with uncharacteristic indecisiveness about whether or not to rush out a detailed public denial. Finally he made the decision to stonewall reporters, quoting "the smartest man I've met in this White House," Ted Sorensen, who had supposedly told the president he "was a big, fat, cigar-puffing, potbellied numbskull" for trying to "get out here in front of the press." That's "all they want," Johnson seethed after the outburst. Obliging them was just "begging for trouble."[75]

Tainted but unbowed, Johnson survived the mess, but then a second scandal struck much closer to home, involving one of the confidants who had helped forge the Baker strategy: Walter Jenkins. On October 7—just twenty-seven days before the election—Washington police arrested the married Jenkins for soliciting sex from another man inside a YMCA washroom. For a full week, advisors like White House lawyer Abe Fortas pulled strings to stop the press from printing reports of Jenkins's arrest. But the rumors proved too persistent to quash.

On the 14th, after the *Washington Star* insisted on a comment from the White House, a "visibly weeping" George Reedy summoned the press corps to confirm the story and announce the well-liked Jenkins's resignation, along with his sham confinement to a hospital to rest his nerves.[76] In an era in which gay sex, especially the furtive kind, was viewed as both a security hazard and a moral abomination, not even a twenty-five-year professional connection to LBJ could shield Jenkins from exile. Although Lady Bird defied her husband's orders to say nothing about the matter—she issued her own brave statement of concern and support for the longtime family retainer—the administration otherwise circled the wagons and said no more.

Not even the Jenkins scandal could stem the Johnson momentum. On November 3, he amassed the most lopsided popular majority in electoral history: 61.1 percent, three-tenths of a percent more than the vote won in 1936 by FDR—the man he said was "like a daddy to me."[77] Experts interpreted the triumph as a ringing endorsement of LBJ's legislative accomplishments, not to mention the considerable public grace he had demonstrated after the Kennedy assassination. Surely his victory owed much to lingering public affection for the martyred JFK. But the victory also constituted a rejection of challenger Barry Goldwater, whom LBJ had successfully portrayed to the press and public as a warmongering extremist. On foreign policy, LBJ had offered voters the reassurance they wanted to hear—the same unsustainable vow that Roosevelt had pledged back in 1940: to keep Americans out of war.

Johnson reacted to the victory in perplexing ways. "He did not seem to believe entirely in the great mandate of 1964," Merriman Smith noted with surprise, "and continued to be super-sensitive about his press."[78] Agreed *Newsweek*'s Charles Roberts, LBJ remained "a frustrating paradox—the most accessible and yet the most thin-skinned of Presidents. He encourages contacts with [journalists], then reacts indignantly when their stories don't come out as pro-Johnson."[79]

An increasingly disenchanted George Reedy left an even more damning appraisal of Johnson's behavior in the period that followed his triumph at the polls: "His presidential style changed overnight, and it was not a good change." When Reedy suggested that the president hold a "long overdue news conference," an emboldened Johnson exploded: "I've been kissing asses all my life and I don't have to kiss them anymore. Tell those press bastards of yours that I'll see them when I want to and not before." Reedy prevented LBJ from canceling the press secretary's own daily White House briefings only by threatening to quit.[80]

Eliminating "ass kissing," Reedy chronicled, came to include, on Johnson's orders, barring selected reporters from Air Force One, keeping the presidential travel schedule secret as long as possible, and violating the so-called lid, a long-standing, informal agreement between the White House and the press corps that news would never be released during lunch hours and other predetermined breaks. "I am not sure whether he was being obtuse or taking a sadistic delight in tormenting the press," Reedy complained.[81] For correspondents seeking to maintain a cordial working relationship, the "only way to curry favor with him in this period was to damn the press" and "sympathize with him over his treatment by the others."[82]

The president's lifelong habit of trading favors for loyalty continued apace, but now the outreach seemed clumsier and more transparent. At one point, Johnson told Hedley Donovan, "If you ever get tired of what you're doing, I'd love to have you helping out around here." Perfectly happy at Time Inc., Donovan shrugged off the offer, assuming that an insincere Johnson "issued a fair number of those vague invitations that were in small danger of being accepted." (Donovan later did take a White House post—under Jimmy Carter.)[83]

The frustrating military stalemate in Southeast Asia, Reedy believed, coarsened Johnson's approach further. The casualty toll mounted, ground offensives stalled, draft quotas expanded, the antiwar movement grew, and still Johnson insisted publicly that America would prevail. Privately, his press secretary noted, his bravado often evaporated in the haze of alcohol. "With a few drinks under his belt," Reedy recalled, "he was ready to tell anyone within hearing range that the war would be his downfall." Reedy remembered "one bad night at Camp David when he entertained a small group of very eminent correspondents and really spilled his heart out to them. They all got so soused that night, however, that their memories of some startling revelations were lost in colossal hangovers.[84]

By resisting LBJ's ham-handed efforts to mete out rewards and punishment to journalists, Reedy's stock in the White House plummeted. By April 1965, LBJ was complaining in a secretly taped phone conversation with Abe Fortas, his Supreme Court nominee that year, that Reedy was "the *laziest*, no-good son-of-a-*bitch*!" He could no longer even depend on him, Johnson fumed, to ensure that teleprompters functioned properly at his press events.[85] When Reedy sheepishly told Johnson that the networks had balked at preempting regular programming to broadcast a presidential speech—his third in four days—Johnson exploded at him: "When a soap opera is more important, then I don't ever want to hear from you boys on televised news conferences or on equal time." He was not threatening them, Johnson quickly and unconvincingly clarified.[86]

Eventually LBJ marginalized Reedy entirely by excluding him from White House information sources. "He was afraid that whatever I knew," Reedy believed, "I might give to the press."[87] He tried assuring the president that he "had no problems at all that he wasn't creating for me," but Johnson continued to believe his press secretary was "pampering" hostile journalists, an unpardonable sin.[88] Reedy's professional nightmare ended only when he checked back into the hospital for foot surgery. Using his incapacity as a pretext, Johnson replaced him with Bill Moyers in early July 1965. Reedy had served a total of one year and 111 days. As columnist Robert Allen confirmed, Johnson "treated George atrociously, and George was at fault for allowing himself to be treated that way. He should have slammed him right back and told him to go to hell."[89] Reedy's subsequent recollections must be taken with a grain of salt. But similar horror stories from other staffers lend credibility to his baroque grievances.

For sure, the outgoing press secretary harbored no regrets about leaving. He had come to believe that a "man who is no longer dealing with reporters in a civilized way will soon find himself dealing with others along the same lines. That is what happened to Lyndon B. Johnson. His battle with the press became a large-scale battle with important segments of the public." In the tell-all memoir he published a few years later, Reedy went further. LBJ had exhibited "deplorable manners and barnyard speech. . . . He did disgusting things because he realized that other people had to pretend that they did not mind. It was his method of bending them to his designs." A "bully, sadist, lout, and egotist," he "seemed to take a special delight in humiliating those who had cast their lot with him," perhaps "the result of a form of self-loathing in which he concluded that there had to be something wrong with anyone who would associate with him." Reedy declared he was "glad to get him out of my life at last."[90]

For all this, Reedy's parole proved only temporary. His retributive memoir still only a dream, he would return to the White House as a special assistant for the final months of Johnson's presidency. As Sarah McClendon sneered, "once a Johnson employee, always a Johnson employee."[91] Later Reedy became dean of the Marquette University journalism school. He remained on reasonably friendly terms with LBJ until he published a 1970 book, *The Twilight of the Presidency.* Even though it served up no specific criticism of Johnson, merely warning future presidents against playing favorites among the press, a furious LBJ never again communicated with his onetime communications officer.[92]

Thirty-one-year-old Bill Moyers took over the toughest public relations job in America on July 8, 1965. He had already served for years as a White House counselor and had helped navigate Johnson through both the Baker and Jenkins imbroglios. He also knew what he was getting into as special assistant to the president ("You can call him press secretary though," LBJ hissed at reporters, "if it gives you any thrill."). "You aren't a man in your own right when you work for a President," Moyers told the *New York Times.* "To be the most effective you have to have an umbilical cord right to his character, nature and personality."[93]

Moyers carved out a unique and, as he later concluded, impractical portfolio: while serving as the president's spokesman, he also continued to function as a top policy advisor. That often meant emerging from top-level meetings and then advocating for some policies he had privately advised against. Moyers's successor would describe him as "a daring young quarterback who learned from his boss."[94] But the game took its toll; Moyers would remain in his post until only February 1, 1967, a tenure destined to exceed George Reedy's by ninety-seven days.

With or without Moyers's encouragement, Johnson soon began operating under the apparent belief, as columnist Arthur Krock wickedly put it in September, that there was no "such thing as Presidential overexposure." The man Krock called the "gifted press secretary" could do nothing to thwart the benign television appearances that began filling newscasts on an almost daily basis. Johnson seemed to be on-screen constantly, presiding over innocuous ceremonies, verbalizing "mimeographed handouts," or, as Krock twitted, reading "lengthy statistical statements at televised news conferences that limit the time for questioning by the reporters." In Krock's acerbic view, "So constant have been these electronic projections of the President to the people, that his footage on national news broadcasts may recently have been exceeded only by Huntley-Brinkley, Cronkite or Jennings."[95]

After 1965, Johnson's relationship with the press—indeed his presidency as a whole—spiraled downward, cleaving along fault lines separating domestic policy achievements from foreign policy failures. On one side stood the laudable triumphs of the Great Society, but on the other, the tragic morass of the Vietnam War.

Johnson had all but reshaped American life. In his first year in office alone, he had signed the historic Civil Rights Act and pushed through transformative legislation to fund urban mass transportation and food stamp programs. Then, bolstered by the veto-proof congressional majority swept into Washington astride his 1964 coattails, he added the Voting Rights Act, hiked federal aid to education, liberalized immigration, signed a fair housing act, launched the War on Poverty, passed Medicare and Medicaid, and created a cabinet-level Transportation Department. Later came the Freedom of Information Act, and even when his popularity was on the wane, a federal gun control law. In between landmark legislative triumphs, Johnson named Thurgood Marshall as the first African American on the Supreme Court. No president since Franklin Roosevelt had so utterly transformed society.

But overseas, thousands of young Americans continued to forfeit their lives in what television coverage escalated into the country's first "living room war." Protests, bombings, and body bags became regular features on the home-front evening news. The carnage horrified viewers and the stalemate frustrated LBJ. Never in history did such an acclaimed president fall so swiftly and so visibly.

Johnson's descent was abetted by an increasingly restive press corps. The administration could no longer secure its forbearance via social invitations and leaks. Bill Moyers preferred the professionalized atmosphere, stressing that "the press and the government are not allies. They are adversaries. . . . Reporters should do their best to find out what is going on, but they must also recognize that the President has . . . no obligation to spoonfeed them with a full disclosure of every facet of official thinking on every subject they see fit to probe."[96] Making clear to White House correspondents that as press secretary he was their intermediary, not their friend, the devoted but conscience-struck Moyers labored to keep both the journalists and Johnson content. To the *Times*, Moyers declared, "I work for him despite his faults and he lets me work for him despite my deficiencies."[97] But to his wife, he confided, "This is the beginning of the end because no man can serve two masters."[98]

Johnson's most hawkish press supporters suspected Moyers had gone soft on Vietnam. Robert S. Allen went so far as to charge that he "worked his way into Johnson's good graces" and "then maneuvered . . . always pushing Moyers and not the President."[99] But defending Johnson on the war was fast becoming a fool's errand. Moyers found himself struggling with his own moral values just as

Johnson determined both to escalate the war and limit his once almost-promiscuous accessibility to journalists. As events closed in around LBJ, Moyers told historian Robert Dallek, the president grew increasingly remote. "He would just go within himself, just disappear—morose, self-pitying, angry . . . a tormented man."[100]

Making matters more challenging, a new, damning catchphrase had taken firm hold in the American vernacular: the "credibility gap," a clever appropriation of the U.S.-Soviet "missile gap" of which John Kennedy had spoken during his 1960 campaign. Now the words defined the perceived chasm between what the administration told journalists and the facts they subsequently uncovered. Punctuated by antiwar demonstrations and urban riots, it signaled growing distrust for the entire government notwithstanding its accomplishments.[101] "When Lyndon Johnson lost his credibility on the war," the *Times*' White House correspondent Bill Lawrence believed, "he discovered he had lost his credibility on all issues, domestic as well as foreign. When you deceive the people on one thing, it does not take long for them to realize you would deceive them on all things. Johnson had proved again that old aphorism that you can't be only slightly pregnant."[102]

The credibility gap had first opened over a relatively innocuous issue: fiscal stewardship. Not long after warning that the 1964 federal budget might exceed $100 billion, LBJ dramatically submitted a figure lower than the one he had been predicting. Many correspondents concluded he had exaggerated the spending crisis in the first place so it would appear that he had resolved it in the end. Before long, journalists were taking few government announcements at face value. Suspicion infected even feature reporting. In one example, the press scoffed when the White House denied that reporters had caught Johnson, a beer on his car windshield, speeding near his ranch—noting that a press vehicle had accelerated to ninety miles per hour in pursuit. Even to his Texas-born admirer William S. White of the *New York Times*, the incident appeared "disorderly and somewhat shady." "But, Bill," Johnson protested over the report and its authors, "you don't understand. They were my guests."[103]

The gap widened into a canyon over conflicting reports from and about Vietnam. Joseph Califano remembered that an unreasonable Johnson "blamed much of his credibility problem on the Communists," the media, or both. "Angry about stories in the *New York Times*, he'd complain about how easily the Communists manipulated the paper." The president convinced himself that Communists exerted "heavy influence" at all the television networks save for ABC. To Califano, "LBJ became the most gullible victim of his own revisionist claims," for "he would quickly come to believe what he was saying even if it was clearly not true."[104] Caught in a vise, Johnson could not mellow his aggressive rhetoric on Vietnam without pro-war columnists like Joseph Alsop questioning his spine. Increasingly, LBJ preferred silence to correcting bad news. Moyers tried defending the president's—any president's—right to withhold things "simply not suited for telling on the time schedule an inquisitive press prefers."[105] By the summer of 1966, Moyers's private torment triggered a case of bleeding ulcers, sending him to the hospital.

For the most part, Johnson had begun confining his growing disdain for the press to his increasingly bizarre private telephone conversations. Even minor matters seized his attention. In a "gotcha" call to NBC anchorman John Chancellor in late March 1965, LBJ mocked the network's reliance on White House leaks to fuel speculation about administration appointments. "I like [correspondent] Ray Scherer," he began that diatribe, but when he says, "'Flash! I just want to tell you that the President has just named David Kennedy, Chicago banker, Secretary of the Treasury. . . . Now I'll be back in a moment with the news.' Then they come on and said, 'We want to sell you a little Crisco, right quick.' And they gave me a minute of Crisco. And he came back in and his face was red even without color television. He said, 'I hate to tell you, but it's just been announced that Mr. [Henry] Fowler is the one.'"[106]

That summer, to his greater horror, Johnson caught a CBS News report from Vietnam by Morley Safer, showing American soldiers placidly setting fire to the Vietnamese hamlet of Cam Ne as displaced villagers looked on in terror. The morning after the telecast, Frank Stanton, president of the network, picked up his phone to the roaring complaint: "Frank, are you trying to fuck me?" "Who is this?" Stanton inquired. Came the voice again, now unmistakable: "Frank, this is your president, and yesterday your boys shat on the American flag." As historian David Greenberg has recounted, LBJ soon ordered Safer investigated for suspected links to the Communists. The inquiry found only that the correspondent had been born in Canada. "Well," Johnson responded, "I knew he wasn't an American."[107]

Three years later, when North Korea precipitated a fresh international crisis by seizing the American spy ship USS *Pueblo*, another news broadcast reignited Johnson's fury against CBS. Correspondents Marvin and Bernard Kalb had reported South Korea's assurances that the *Pueblo*'s eighty-three-man crew would be released imminently. Johnson, who knew better, did not want to raise American hopes. "Your press is lying like drunken sailors every day," he lashed out to *Washington Star* White House correspondent Jack Horner, of all people. ". . . [H]ow can we . . . possibly win and survive as a nation and have to fight the press's lies. . . . [T]his son of a bitch Kalb . . . ought to be shot. I wish [Louisiana senator Russell] Long would just take a pistol and work on him . . . this little son of a bitch that never got in four miles of a front in his life is out here on CBS saying things."[108] This time at least, Johnson's rage was understandable, if misdirected. The eighty-two surviving crewmen would endure eleven months of psychological torture in confinement. By then Johnson had long reached the conclusion that all reporters were "just wicked men."[109]

Only occasionally did personal drama provide a welcome diversion, even if it produced unflattering media coverage. In October 1965, Moyers flooded White House correspondents with reassuring data (reinforced by gory medical images) after the president underwent a delicate gallbladder operation at Bethesda Naval Hospital. Moyers seemed to have the messaging under control until Johnson staged a press conference on the hospital lawn to personally demonstrate how well he was recuperating. "Apparently feeling words to be inadequate," reported Muriel Dobbin in the *Baltimore Sun*, "the President whipped up his blue knit sport shirt" and proudly displayed the twelve-inch surgical scar on his flabby stomach. Newspapers and magazines had a field day with this unexpected gift, and unflattering photographs of Johnson pointing to his swollen belly quickly popped up in newspapers and magazines. Among the many cartoonists inspired by the crude display, David Levine outdid them all with his classic caricature of a Pinocchio-nosed LBJ gesturing toward a scar that had assumed the shape of a map of Vietnam.[110]

Metaphorically speaking, the entire administration thereafter assumed the shape of Vietnam, including the press office. Whether on the brink of breaking with the president or not—he has never said—Moyers left the administration on February 1, 1967, to become publisher of the Long Island paper *Newsday*. "Lyndon Johnson was thirteen of the most interesting and difficult men I ever met," Moyers did admit nearly half a century later on the occasion of his eightieth birthday and retirement from an award-winning career on PBS. "He could be as couth as he was uncouth, as magnanimous as malicious, at times proud and sensitive, at times paranoid and darkly uneasy with himself. Freud would have had a field day with him." On Vietnam, Moyers conceded, LBJ was at his worst. But then he proudly added: "I was there during those years when he had resolved to finish what FDR started . . . when he seized unexpected moments and made the most of them by doing the right thing."[111]

Moyers's successor, George Christian, a thirty-eight-year-old, Austin-born former wire service reporter, leapt to Johnson's defense with gusto. The president is "a very candid man . . . rather open in his discussions with the press," he gushed to a television interviewer that summer. The credibility gap he dismissed as simply "the difference between what the president said and what some people wanted him to say." In Robert Allen's assessment, "Christian did a good job, but things were over the brink by then . . . everything was aggravated and exaggerated and intensified by the war. . . . I guess it was too late."[112] Christian's aggressive pushback did little to stanch Johnson's declining popularity, but it evidently pleased his boss. The last and longest-serving of LBJ's four press spokesmen would stay on in his job for the duration—notching nearly two years of service, a record in the Johnson White House.[113]

Initially a Vietnam hawk, Walter Lippmann turned against the war by late 1965, insisting of Johnson, "He misled me." The president never saw the pundit again. Like other journalists who had fallen under Johnson's thrall, the old crusader took the breakup like a spurned lover. As his biographer Ronald Steel put it, the relationship had begun, "like most seductions, with invitations and flattery, and it ended in recriminations and a feeling of betrayal." Predictably, Johnson felt no need to conceal his own disappointment. At one White House event, Idaho senator Frank Church, an early and outspoken opponent of the war, mentioned Lippmann's recent call for peace negotiations. Johnson snarled at him: "Frank, the next time you want a dam in Idaho, you just go to Walter Lippmann for it." Lippmann now rated Johnson "the most disagreeable individual ever to have occupied the White House."[114] His influence and access gutted, Lippmann soon abandoned his column and retired to Maine.

Katharine Graham, who had assumed the role of *Washington Post* publisher after her husband killed himself in 1963, found her early friendship with Johnson fading, too. "The war definitely got in the way of my friendly relationship with Lyndon Johnson," she later recalled, "but even before the war heated up, I seem to have been on his bad side. He had stopped calling me himself, and by 1966 our relations were definitely somewhat distant." The president tried explaining the rift by conveying the message that he no longer wanted insiders buzzing that his attention was meant to influence her (which surely it had been designed to do from the start). Graham did not buy it. "To Johnson," as she knew, "loyalty was everything—loyalty as he defined it." And now, she said, "Johnson saw me at times as masterminding the paper against his interests."[115]

With George Christian's encouragement, LBJ tried one more time to rally the American people. In November 1967, taking Christian's advice that an image transformation might help, Johnson shed his "pious, melancholy, and grandfatherly" tone and appeared at a White House news conference wearing a concealed microphone so he could roam the stage. "He waved his arms," reported the *New York Times*, "chopped the air, drew imaginary lines with his fingers, clutched his glasses, scowled, laughed and ran his voice through a range of sound from high-volume anger to quiet, self-deprecatory gentleness."[116] The president's friends hailed the performance as the return of "the real Johnson." But the real one had no greater power to persuade than the one he had replaced, and Johnson abandoned the new style after a single "performance."

The PR offensive took a new turn shortly before Christmas, when Johnson sat for a White House television interview with CBS (Dan Rather), NBC (Ray Scherer), and ABC (Frank McGee). All three networks broadcast a ninety-minute-long version simultaneously on December 19, attracting an audience of some fifty-one million—three million more than John Kennedy had lured for a similar conversation back in 1962, a statistic that no doubt gratified LBJ. But, a day after the telecast, Tom Wicker opined that while Johnson had argued his positions passionately on the telecast, he had "passed up the opportunity to display to equal advantage the warmer, more human and relaxed side of his nature." In a "contentious mood, yielding nothing to his critics, a little testy with reporters . . . this side of the President was buried in the constant hard-sell with which he presented his policies and attitudes."[117]

Making matters worse, *New York Times* television critic Jack Gould reported that same day that the broadcast had represented but a preapproved fraction of what the networks had recorded and that Johnson had ordered the taping stopped twice during the interview to request playbacks in order to "see how he was appearing on the screen."[118] The stories made LBJ appear more demanding and insecure than ever. Ten days later, Gould raised a more fundamental concern. The mere idea that the White House could demand "the right of reviewing a program before it goes on the air," he wrote, "seems a doubtful means of convincing the rest of the world that a free press in the United States is a fact and not a cliché."[119]

LBJ might have withstood both the criticism of his TV image and the defection of sages like Walter Lippmann. But he could not survive the steady loss of support from mainstream media. In 1967, *Life* magazine, long an enthusiastic cheerleader for the Great Society, broke with Johnson over Vietnam. Then in January, the Viet Cong and North Vietnamese launched the surprise Tet Offensive against one hundred targets in the South.[120] On February 27, CBS-TV aired a dramatic field report from the war zone featuring the revered Walter Cronkite, "the most trusted man in America." After putting American casualties on display for the cameras, Cronkite ended the now-famous telecast by offering an unsparing editorial comment: "[I]t is increasingly clear to this reporter that the only rational way out . . . will be to negotiate, not as victors, but as honorable people who lived up to their pledge to defend democracy, and did the best they could." According to legend, Johnson turned from his television set and lamented to staff aides: "If I have lost Cronkite I have lost middle America."[121]

Noting that Johnson "was never given to understatement," Hedley Donovan remembered the actual comment as "Cronkite and Hedley Donovan had cost him the war."[122] No doubt LBJ had by then given the Time Inc. executive so much grief over *Life* magazine's earlier defection that Donovan genuinely believed his version the more accurate. At a late March 1968 White House meeting, "Deadly Hedley" steeled his courage to ask LBJ whether he might now withdraw from the forthcoming presidential race, a possibility, LBJ later chortled in his own memoirs, that Tom Wicker thought as likely as seeing "[Secretary of State] Dean Rusk . . . turn dove" or "Dick Nixon . . . stop running."[123] On the 12th, antiwar Minnesota senator Eugene McCarthy, a long-shot challenger, had won 42 percent of the Democratic primary vote in New Hampshire, seven points fewer than the write-in total for LBJ (whose name did not appear on the ballot). The result had sent shock waves through the political and press establishments. LBJ refused to answer Donovan's yes-or-no question. Instead he responded, "[L]ike your magazines say, I feel sorry for myself, yes. I enjoy being a martyr, yes. But every so often I count my blessings."[124]

"I can prove that Ho-Chi-Minh is a son-of-a-bitch if you let me put it on the screen," a desperate LBJ had groused. "But television wants me to be the son-of-a-bitch."[125] On March 31, the "son of a bitch" went on national television and shocked the nation—and most of the press corps—by declaring that he would neither seek nor accept his party's nomination for another term. The bifurcated presidency of Lyndon Johnson was in a sense over. He would serve ten more months as a lame duck, the war still raging and his domestic achievements in danger of being minimized by contemporaries and overlooked by history.

The very day after withdrawing, Johnson, with the press corps in tow, dutifully boarded Air Force One for a long-scheduled trip to Chicago to address the National Association of Broadcasters. The president uncharacteristically kept to himself en route, but on the return flight, he walked back to the press cabin, where Max Frankel of the *Times*, Dan Rather of CBS, and Helen Thomas of the UPI, among others, were busily studying the transcript of his withdrawal statement of the previous night. "He saw me," Frankel told me, "grabbed my copy and autographed it cheerily at the top. Then, as he handed it back, he said: 'Well, Max, do you still believe in the First Amendment?'"[126]

"He talked, and he talked, and he talked," remembered Thomas of that visit, almost embarrassed to be observing him in "a frail moment." He spoke of the war and draft-card burners and national division—and the unavoidable fact that he had become "an object of contempt and controversy." Did he blame himself? "Yes, I feel I made several errors in the past," he admitted. But then the old defiance flared to life: "I came to the conclusion that if I signed the Lord's Prayer it would be objected to."[127]

The following month, a committee of the American Society of Newspaper Editors condemned the Johnson administration for long pursuing "a policy of obscurantism for its own sake." Asserting that "the credibility gap yawns wider" than ever, ASNE charged that much as previous governments had concealed "important information when it served their interests," with LBJ "official deceit is practiced both when there is reason for it and when there is not."[128]

In early June, LBJ's longtime political nemesis, Robert F. Kennedy, the putative heir to Camelot, lost his life to an assassin. After winning the California presidential primary, RFK had seemed destined to succeed Johnson—and his late brother—at the top of the Democratic ticket. Instead, the nod went to LBJ's vice president, Hubert H. Humphrey, who went on to lose an excruciatingly tight race to Kennedy's old foe Richard Nixon, 43.4 to 42.7 percent. Most of the remaining vote went to breakaway segregationist candidate George Wallace of Alabama, ending once and for all the era of the Solid Democratic South that LBJ had helped perpetuate for JFK and himself. Nixon had offered no proposals to extract America from the Vietnam quagmire, except to say he had "a secret plan" to end the fighting. Humphrey's defeat was widely interpreted as a rejection of Lyndon Johnson, but America's involvement in the war would continue for five more years.

Three weeks after Nixon's November victory, the national journalism society Sigma Delta Chi issued yet another report, this one declaring that Johnson would leave office with "the worst record for credibility of any President in history." He had not only "virtually abandoned the type of news conference which served the Washington press corps and the nation well from Franklin D. Roosevelt's time through the thousand days of John F. Kennedy"; LBJ had widened the credibility gap to "awesome proportions." He had even "interfered" with his own Freedom of Information law.[129] Outgoing press secretary George Christian tried for the last word when he appeared on *Meet the Press* on January 19, 1969, the penultimate day of Johnson's presidency. Neither he nor LBJ had ever knowingly lied to the press, he insisted to the last; they had merely withheld information. "In serving the people," he tried reminding viewers: "The Government has the right not to tell the full story."[130]

Left unspoken by both critics and defenders alike was a crucial fact that the watchdogs had—and indeed, history has—largely overlooked. Credibility gap or not, LBJ never allowed his military commanders to do what Lincoln had permitted General William T. Sherman and other Civil War officers to do: ban journalists from covering the battlefront, censor their reports, and shut down opposition newspapers if they embarrassed the administration. LBJ never jailed press critics, as Lincoln and Adams had; never sued newspapers for libel in the manner of TR; and never imposed limits on what news could be printed in wartime, as had FDR and Wilson. Ironically, his liberality in this regard may have hastened his undoing. The unvarnished reports and images from Vietnam that horrified Americans came back to haunt a president who had implicitly defended the right of the media to gather and publish them. Johnson still believed in the First Amendment, whatever the sarcastic comment he had shared on Air Force One with Max Frankel. Not all of Lyndon Johnson's successors would follow his self-defeating but admirable example.

Years later, near the end of his life—overweight, smoking cigarettes again, and wracked by angina pain—LBJ returned to Washington and appeared before the *Washington Post* editorial board to defend his entire career, legislative and executive, domestic and global. George Reedy, no longer "on speaking terms" with his old boss, nonetheless greeted with pleasure the news that the session had "ended with all the participants rising to their feet and cheering him wildly."[131]

Johnson was still capable of soaring moments. On December 12, 1972, he declared that his considerable civil rights accomplishments amounted to unfinished work, telling a symposium at the new LBJ Library in Austin: "I am confident we shall overcome."[132] As cameras captured the poignant moment, a visibly diminished LBJ popped a nitroglycerine tablet into his mouth. Yet he remained equally prone to jaw-dropping vulgarity. During a visit to Texas by UPI correspondent Bill Theis, Johnson reportedly complained that Richard Nixon's economic policies were "the worst thing that's happened to this country since pantyhose ruined finger-fucking."[133]

Unchanged and unchangeable to the end, Lyndon Johnson died of a coronary at the LBJ Ranch on January 22, 1973, two days after Nixon took the oath of office for the second time. LBJ was only sixty-four, having survived just a year longer than the man he had tried so hard to emulate, Franklin Roosevelt. During his own presidency, FDR had won victories against economic disparity at home, foreign enemies abroad, and, when required, against unsympathetic journalists in Washington. This trifecta Lyndon Johnson could not match.

LBJ's post-presidential press secretary, Tom Johnson, phoned the report of Johnson's sudden passing into CBS-TV while Walter Cronkite was still reporting live on the *Evening News*. In a final irony, the same journalist whose report from Vietnam had made Johnson a casualty of war five years earlier now broke the news of his death.

Bill Lawrence, by then the co-anchor of the rival *ABC Evening Report*, harbored no doubts about the cause of LBJ's political demise: "Vietnam killed Lyndon Johnson's Presidency as surely as a bullet struck down John F. Kennedy in Dallas.[134] But George Reedy always believed it "an oversimplification" to ascribe Johnson's downfall solely to the war. "Had it not been for Vietnam," he argued, "something else would have brought his career to an end. It was not the issue but his approach to the issue."[135]

Lyndon Johnson had spent most of his five and a half years in office revealing himself to be a "complex, coarse, courtly, cruel and compassionate" individual who "could preach honesty and practice deception," Helen Thomas testified; or, in Hedley Donovan's corroborative judgment, as a "mercurial, secretive, conniving, in some ways monstrous man" who "was also capable of deeply generous impulses and great visions for America."[136]

Donovan once speculated that if William Shakespeare had been able to study America's presidents for dramatic inspiration, "he might have found in Lyndon Johnson the richest theater. Or perhaps he would have been as powerfully attracted to the Presidency of Richard Nixon."[137]

— 12 —

RICHARD NIXON

On November 7, 1962, the day after suffering a decisive thrashing in a comeback bid for governor of California, Richard Nixon implied to a throng of a hundred journalists that his political career was over. The swan song was neither planned nor scripted: he had instructed his spokesman merely to read a routine concession statement on his behalf. But hearing the reporters clamoring, "Where's Nixon?" the defeated candidate changed his mind, entered the meeting room at the Beverly Hilton Hotel, and began unburdening himself. What followed may rank as the most famous press announcement in modern political history.

Nixon's attempted return to elected office had fallen far short. Final tabulations showed nearly three times more votes separating him from the Democratic candidate in his home state than had separated him from Kennedy two years earlier in all fifty.[1] Nixon left no doubt about whom he blamed for this latest humiliation. He directed his morning-after rant to "all the members of the press I know" who "are so delighted that I have lost."[2]

In a cramped space choked with cameras and microphones, Nixon began the postmortem by expressing high hopes for the future of the Republican Party and adding a rare if anodyne personal note: he planned "to go home . . . to get acquainted with my family again . . . to take a holiday." But he could not help unleashing a rambling barrage of criticism aimed at his longtime nemeses, the journalists he believed had plagued him unfairly for years. "I have no complaints about the press coverage," he insisted unconvincingly. But just once, he added, "I would appreciate if you would write what I say . . . in the lead—in the lead," and not give him "the shaft." Only one member of the entire press contingent, he groused, had reliably printed everything he'd said during the California campaign. All the others—and Nixon called out the offending papers by name—had failed to report his positions fully or accurately.[3]

He was on a roll now. Reaching the crescendo of what the *New York Times* called "a 15-minute monologue," his voice quavering, he insisted: "I believe a reporter has got a right to write it as he feels it. I believe if a reporter believes that one man ought to win rather than the other . . . he ought to say so. I will say to the reporter sometimes that I think, well, look, I wish you'd give my opponent the same going over that you gave me."[4] In a not-so-subtle swipe at President Kennedy, he added, "I have never canceled a subscription to a paper and also I never will" (a lie, according to *Washington Post* publisher Katharine Graham, who testified that Nixon had cut off his subscription to her paper years earlier).[5]

Then Nixon's eyelids fluttered in that characteristic blink that often made him look shifty, and he issued an immortal if premature farewell: "I leave you gentlemen now and you now write it. You will interpret it. That's your right. But as I leave you I want you to know—just think how much you're gonna be missing. You don't have Nixon to kick around anymore because, gentlemen, this is my last press conference."[6]

Ordinarily, it is dangerous for politicians to embolden journalists by ceding them the power to make or break careers. It is equally ill-advised to declare publicly that one is finished with politics (and the press) forever. Within days, as if to cement the morbid impression he had made, ABC News aired a report titled "The Political Obituary of Richard Nixon."[7] So not surprisingly, when Nixon returned to national politics six years later, the media did what it could to make his precipitate farewell return to haunt him. But while Nixon violated a basic rule of politics that day in Beverly Hills—never to say "never"—he survived and ultimately reemerged to enjoy the vindication he craved, even if it would prove temporary. In fact, Nixon's political resurgence in 1968 would be built on the very resentments he had bared in 1962: his belief that the liberal press was biased against him; that it improperly tainted news coverage with editorial opinion; and that the media itself constituted an Eastern elite devoted to stifling conservative voices to the detriment of ordinary Americans, particularly white ones.

Here was resentment that fueled resiliency. As the UPI's Helen Thomas put it, Nixon "lived by the credo: Never give up."[8] In 1968, in what must rank as the century's greatest political resurrection, Nixon rode his grievances all the way to the White House. Even safely ensconced there, he boasted to AP correspondent Saul Pett: "I believe in the battle, whether it's the battle of the campaign or the battle of this office, which is a continuous battle. It's always there, wherever you go. I, perhaps, carry it more than others because that's my way."[9] And the clash Nixon relished the most was his ongoing battle with the press. As for his perceived enemies, after decades spent amicably jousting with FDR, sparring with JFK on television, and alternating between flattery and fury from LBJ, the press encountered in Nixon the first American president to use press prejudice as a campaign theme and governing principle; the first to treat White House correspondents with undisguised and unrelenting hostility.

In doing it his way, the combative Richard Nixon ushered in a seismic—and, as it turned out, permanent—shift in the long-standing relationship between presidents and the press. Adversarial wariness gave way to open combat, inquiry to inquisition. What followed were not only the opening skirmishes of what we now often call the culture wars, but the earliest technological innovations and regulatory retreats that heralded the reduced power of the television networks Nixon so despised. For a while, vilifying the press worked wonders for Richard Nixon.

Perhaps we should not be surprised that Nixon had first revealed his uneasiness with the press while still a teenager. In a prize-winning speech he delivered as a sixteen-year-old student, he had only reluctantly acknowledged the guarantees of the First Amendment. "Yet the question arises," young Nixon asked, "how much ground do these privileges cover? There are some who use them as a cloak for covering libelous, indecent, and injurious statements against their fellow men. Should the morals of this nation be offended and polluted in the name of freedom of speech and freedom of the press?"[10] For the rest of his career, Nixon would grapple with that very question.

Fresh from service in the military, Nixon launched his political career with a 1946 challenge to a five-term, liberal Southern California congressman named Jerry Voorhis. Establishing a pattern that would characterize all his early races, Nixon disposed of the New Deal Democrat with red-baiting innuendo.[11] In Washington, freshman Nixon quickly built his reputation as an outspoken anti-Communist, attracting press attention—and criticism—through service on the House Un-American Activities Committee as it labored to root out alleged leftists.

In his most celebrated and controversial undertaking in the House—a case that metastasized into a lifelong obsession—Nixon focused his wrath on a State Department official named Alger Hiss after a HUAC witness named him as a Soviet espionage agent. When an indignant Hiss appeared before the panel to endure a withering examination by Nixon, the *Washington Post* likened the accused man to "an innocent pedestrian, splattered with mud by a passing vehicle."[12] Hiss openly expressed contempt for Nixon during his congressional testimony, and Nixon returned the scorn in full—and for life. Later judged guilty of perjury, Hiss served several years in prison but would maintain his innocence until his death in 1996. While most politicians would have savored the vindication that came with Hiss's conviction, the *Washington Post*'s criticism of Nixon's Javert-like pursuit so infuriated him that he carried a grudge against the paper for the rest of his career.

Sixty-five years later, most historians now regard Hiss as guilty, based on long-hidden Cold War documents and fresh interviews made public in the late 1980s. More recent scholarship, however, has held that this so-called evidence may have been fabricated and that those who surfaced to testify to Hiss's guilt lack credibility.[13] As for Nixon, all he chose to remember was that in retaliation for what he considered God's work, he was "subjected to an utterly unprincipled and vicious smear campaign" by the liberal media.[14] Historian Evan Thomas has pointed out that press reports on Nixon's pursuit of Alger Hiss actually played out in the congressman's favor.[15] Yet Nixon chose to obsess about his critics, nursing his anger for decades. As he would remind journalists in 1962 during his "farewell" press conference in California, "For 16 years, ever since the Hiss case, you've had a lot of fun," taking "every opportunity to attack me."[16]

With his anti-Communist reputation established, and the McCarthy witch hunt providing an increasingly comfortable environment for Cold War zealotry, Congressman Nixon decided to run for the U.S. Senate in 1950. His Democratic opponent was a show-business luminary, Congresswoman Helen Gahagan Douglas, a former actress married to one of the film industry's leading liberals, Melvyn Douglas.[17] In Hollywood terms, the Nixon-Douglas campaign proved noir-ish, replete with dark accusations of Communist sympathies on both sides. An element of farce crept into the race as well when Nixon charged, and the press reported, that Douglas had accepted a $100 campaign contribution from Eleanor Roosevelt—a gesture, Nixon argued, that made a prima facie case for Douglas's leftism. The check turned out to be a donation from Eleanor *Alexander* Roosevelt, widow of World War II hero Theodore Roosevelt Jr., a Medal of Honor recipient, not to mention a Republican. *Los Angeles News* publisher Manchester Boddy (who had fought for the Senate seat himself, thus becoming another early Nixon press enemy) provided additional fodder by labeling Nixon "Tricky Dick" and nicknaming Douglas "the Pink Lady."[18] The Douglas sobriquet proved the greater liability once the Korean War broke out in June. Nixon swept to victory by 600,000 votes.

Two years later, when Dwight D. Eisenhower won the Republican presidential nomination, Nixon emerged as the ideal running mate: a young (only thirty-nine) and aggressive counterpoint to the avuncular sixty-one-year-old former general. Midway through the 1952 campaign, however, Nixon's murky finances nearly cost him his place on the slate. On September 14, in a story headlined "Secret Rich Men's Trust Fund Keeps Nixon in Style Far Beyond His Salary," the pro-Democratic *New York Post* charged that the vice presidential nominee had taken money from Republican donors to build a secret bank account meant to augment his meager congressional salary. Nixon ridiculed its author, the tabloid's West Coast political reporter, Leo Katcher, as "a Hollywood movie writer" who specialized in "gossip."[19] But Katcher's report stung; it documented a stash of donor money that Nixon had tapped over the years to reimburse himself for so-called political expenses that included Christmas cards.[20] Within days, columnist Drew Pearson inquired into the matter, prompting Nixon campaign advisor William P. Rogers (his future secretary of state) to fire off a warning that if Pearson went with the story, "Nixon would have no recourse but to retaliate by discrediting Drew as a Communist operative."[21]

Even without additional exposure in Pearson's "Washington Merry-Go-Round" column, the Katcher report alone was enough to prompt editorials from newspapers like the *Washington Post* and, more troublingly, the pro-GOP *New York Herald Tribune*, demanding that Nixon step aside. "If the most influential Republican paper in the East, if not the country . . . was calling for my resignation from the ticket," the beleaguered candidate admitted, "the fat was in the fire."[22] Nixon's advisors warned him that the only way to save himself was by responding directly to voters via television, a novel tactic at the time, not to mention an expensive one. To buy airtime on NBC preempting the *Milton Berle*

Show, the Republican National Committee would spend five times more than the value of Nixon's entire $15,000 slush fund.

On September 23, 1952, sitting behind a desk on the stage of the deserted El Capitan Theatre on Hollywood Boulevard, a visibly perspiring Nixon made the case that he was simply a family man of modest means trying to make ends meet. His wife owned nothing fancier than a "Republican cloth coat," he declared that night (adding that she "looked good" in anything). And he had taken but one gift during his entire career in public service: a cocker spaniel named Checkers. Clearly trying to evoke FDR—who, eight years earlier to the very day, had eviscerated Republicans for trying to make a campaign liability of his Scotch terrier Fala—Nixon vowed he would never give up the family dog that his young daughters now cherished. The audience for the address that became known as the Checkers speech—estimated as high as sixty million—would be rivaled in size that season only by the masses who tuned into CBS a few months later for the *I Love Lucy* episode devoted to the birth of her baby.

How the political correspondents rated Nixon's performance proved irrelevant. Wanting no reports of his pre-event jitters, and no distractions during the telecast itself, Nixon's staff barred reporters from observing the proceedings in the flesh. Instead, they watched the address on TV monitors set up in a room adjacent to the set.[23] And on television, in the parlance of show business, it "played." While the *St. Louis Post-Dispatch* dismissed the spectacle as "a carefully contrived soap opera," most editorials lauded Nixon's speech, with the old Hearst paper, the *New York Journal American*, calling it "simply magnificent."[24] Vindicated by a performance that seems mawkish by today's standards, Nixon remained the GOP candidate for vice president and returned to form with a series of red-baiting attacks on Democratic standard-bearer Adlai Stevenson.

Republicans triumphed in November. Perhaps most important for Nixon—and for history—he had shown he could marginalize hostile print journalism by communicating through other means. Yet he was never one to look on the bright side. When he ran into Leo Katcher's brother, also a reporter, Nixon asked him to deliver a message to the man who had helped break the slush-fund story: tell Leo, Nixon urged, that he was a "son of a bitch."[25] Actually, Nixon should have thanked him for the opportunity he had generated. "From then on," said the advisor who had arranged the Checkers speech, Edward A. "Ted" Rogers, Nixon "didn't give a damn about the regular press. He saw what television can do and he was . . . spellbound." Print journalists? Rogers summarized Nixon's new attitude in two words: "Fuck them."[26]

The vice presidency did little to soften the battle-scarred Nixon. At one point he praised America's new chief diplomat, John Foster Dulles, by declaring it "wonderful to have a Secretary of State who isn't taken in by the Communists." When the *Washington Post* objected to the implied smear on Dulles's predecessor, Nixon placed a personal call to the paper to terminate both his home and office deliveries—the cancellation he later failed to recall at Beverly Hills. "What do you think he'll do in the morning," the circulation manager asked the publisher, "when he discovers there's no alternative?"[27]

By 1960, eight years after his boffo Checkers speech, Nixon's proven mastery of the medium should have given him a distinct advantage over—or at least put him on an equal footing with—his telegenic opponent in the first presidential debate. Instead, as documented in Chapter 10, Nixon's stiff outing proved, in the words of ABC-TV political correspondent Bill Lawrence, a "spectacular fiasco." Lawrence was not particularly surprised, noting that the Republican candidate seemed "distant and reserved with most reporters covering his campaign."[28] Ben Bradlee, obviously predisposed to his friend Kennedy, was "struck" by Nixon's "inability ever to be natural, or comfortable in his own skin." His 1960 effort seemed "joyless, strangely dull, almost hostile."[29] The campaign's response to the press was "Stuff the bastards." As one Nixon aide told journalist Theodore H. White, "They're all against Dick anyway."[30]

If so, much of the animosity was personal rather than political, even if Nixon always preferred to believe that journalists objected to his views, not his manner. "Teddy" White later remembered that whenever the charming JFK strolled through his campaign plane and invited a reporter to join him for a nightcap, "even though you've spent eighteen hours with him that day, you're eager to talk about the day's events. But when Nixon walked through the plane, every reporter was looking fixedly out the window."[31]

For all his missteps and contempt, Nixon came within a whisker of winning the presidency in 1960. (And contrary to his belief that the press remained stacked against him, he actually earned an overwhelming majority of the nation's newspaper endorsements—the same level of editorial support Herbert Hoover had won—in losing the election—in 1932.) Then came the humiliating loss in California; the bitter, premature farewell to the press; a long political hibernation; and finally, Lyndon Johnson's 1968 withdrawal. A resurgent "New

Nixon" then reentered the arena—but, like the old Nixon, fully expecting to be kicked around by press once again.

This time out, abetted by savvy public relations advisors like speechwriters William Safire and Pat Buchanan, along with press secretary Herbert G. Klein, a former San Diego newspaper editor, Nixon made a virtue of his unpopularity with journalists. At the same time, he kept reporters at a safe and relatively harmless distance.

To help him get the most out of television, Nixon added experts like Frank Shakespeare of CBS and a young producer named Roger Ailes, whom the candidate had met the previous year when he appeared on *The Mike Douglas Show*, a genial staple of daytime television. Traditional press activities fell by the wayside. When the *New York Times* invited Nixon to its long-obligatory pre-election editorial board interview, he declined; he did not care to be interrogated with a view toward an endorsement he knew he would not receive. The young *Philadelphia Inquirer* columnist Joe McGinnis, who infiltrated the 1968 Nixon campaign and eavesdropped on a number of media strategy sessions, came away convinced of the team's determination to circumvent traditional press scrutiny and focus on advertising, well-staged campaign rallies, and orchestrated photo opportunities. McGinnis called his memoir of the experience *The Selling of the President*.[32]

Oddly, Nixon had by then convinced himself that his 1962 humiliation had "served a purpose." McGinnis notwithstanding, the nominee wanted to believe (at least at the outset) that his stormy history had softened his image. "The press," he mused, now operated from "a guilt complex about their inaccuracy . . . they've been generally accurate, and far more respectful." Journalists still opposed his views, Nixon acknowledged, but "I like to take them on in a give-and-take. I used to be too serious about it. Now I treat it like a game."[33] And reporters now liked *him*, Nixon hallucinated, because he gave them "a lot of news." Newspaperman Timothy Crouse, who also covered the '68 race, saw matters otherwise: "His basic campaign strategy (which was to keep himself isolated from reporters) and his basic attitude (which was that reporters were scum) hadn't changed. But he had smartened up and learned one crucial lesson—to 'give correspondents a lot of news,' in the form of handouts and a few discreet one-to-one interviews."[34] And since the Vietnam War continued to consume human lives and provoke national anguish, the "news" included vague allusions to a secret peace plan for which Nixon offered no details—because none existed.

After a campaign unblemished by misstatements or scandals—the most controversial thing he did in 1968 was appear for five seconds on the comedy series *Laugh-In* to ask, "Sock it to *me*?"—Nixon prevailed by a margin nearly as thin as Kennedy's had been in defeating him eight years earlier: a mere 500,000 votes out of 63 million cast. He even survived a last-minute "October surprise" designed to tilt the race to Democratic opponent Hubert Humphrey: a Lyndon Johnson–ordered pause in the bombing of North Vietnam meant to trigger peace negotiations. Only later did it come to light that Nixon likely worked behind the scenes to sabotage the peace initiative. LBJ's gesture might have been cynical and desperate, but Nixon's attempt to undermine the cease-fire proposal may well have been treasonous.[35]

Once in office, Nixon ushered in major changes in White House press operations. Uncomfortable with the close proximity of the longtime press room—he did not want reporters observing who came in and out of the Oval Office—he ordered FDR's indoor swimming pool covered over to create a larger space to house the press on the mansion's lower level. Roomier it may have been, complete with soundproof booths from which to conduct broadcasts, but the new press headquarters was also well removed from the vantage point journalists had enjoyed since the days of Teddy Roosevelt. The Nixon administration equipped the expanded space with a theater-style TV set—from which the president's press secretary would conduct briefings and the president himself could make special announcements. To the press, it was a banishment softened by an upgrade.

Nixon also created a new job for longtime loyalist Herb Klein, making him the first-ever communications director for the entire executive branch. Klein's assignment was to reach out beyond the jaded White House press corps to influence broadcast and print media nationwide, including network moguls and newspaper publishers. His real goal, Klein later said, was "destroying any image that 'Tricky Dick' was in the White House." To do so, Klein had one suggestion for Nixon: "appear more on television."[36] That simple advice would reinvent the traditions of White House communications. Ironically, Nixon recognized the power of the medium even if he could never quite master it.

To carry out the day-to-day functions of press secretary, Nixon named the relatively raw, twenty-nine-year-old Ron Ziegler, who had first developed his communications skills as a tour guide aboard the Disneyland "Jungle

Cruise"—a résumé credit his critics would never let him forget. Ziegler's indoctrination proved a trial by fire. Correspondents quickly concluded that he not only lacked credibility but enjoyed limited access to Nixon. As *Newsweek* later commented, Ziegler became "the press agent for an Administration that sorely mistrusted the press. His two-a-day briefings were a game of fox and hounds, the secretary leading the newsmen through a labyrinth of skewed syntax and sleight-of-hand evasions—and occasionally his own ignorance of what was happening." Before long the press secretary earned a derisive nickname from correspondents—"Zigzag"—while his "stumble-tongued answers" became known as "Ziegles."[37]

Cosseted by a longer-than-usual press honeymoon, Nixon governed both pragmatically and creatively. He surprised longtime critics by enforcing civil rights laws, supporting cost-of-living adjustments for social security beneficiaries, and signing bills that established federal agencies to protect the environment and safeguard occupational health and safety. He named Warren Burger as chief justice of the Supreme Court, and Harry Blackmun, Lewis Powell, and William Rehnquist as associate justices. But bad press still plagued him. Before falling back on Powell, Nixon stoked partisan and regional divisions by nominating two Southern judges who had left a trail of segregationist sentiment: Clement F. Haynsworth and G. Harrold Carswell. After contentious, widely publicized hearings, the Senate rejected both. Then, nine months before the 1972 election, the old anti-Communist startled the world by undertaking his historic journey to the People's Republic of China—accompanied by a huge press contingent—one of the signal diplomatic breakthroughs of the century, and a television triumph to boot.

As Nixon, once relegated to the role of attack dog, morphed into a statesman, he found an ideal partner to assume the bad-cop role he had once played for Eisenhower. Nixon's dark side would be given voice by his own surprise choice for vice president, the previously obscure Maryland governor Spiro Agnew. By impulse and record, Agnew had counted himself a liberal. But he embraced the assignment the White House gave him after the campaign. He would serve as principal spokesman for the aggrieved "Silent Majority"—the coded phrase Nixon himself would invent to describe voiceless white Americans supposedly marginalized by the expanding circle of opportunity championed by Democrats.

At first, Agnew proved only a gaffe machine. On a plane returning him from a 1968 campaign stop in Nevada, he noticed *Baltimore Sun* reporter Gene Oishi dozing in his seat. Remarked Agnew, "What's the matter with the fat Jap—too much Las Vegas?" Asked by an African American *New York Times* reporter if he planned to visit depressed urban neighborhoods, Agnew dismissively responded, "If you've seen one slum, you've seen them all."[38] Democrats unleashed a torrent of criticism focused on the dangers of Agnew in high office, but Nixon, seeing parallels to his own political experience, came to his defense, arguing that the media was treating his running mate unfairly. Both Nixon and Agnew, even Herb Klein would admit, tended unwisely "to coil back, to pull away in a sea of bitterness rather than to make an effort to correct the problem realistically."[39] As if repeating Nixonian history, Agnew even withstood a financial inquiry by the *New York Times*.[40] (Not for another four years would press revelations of impropriety resurface and force Agnew's resignation.)

Within a year of assuming office, Agnew took on a specific task: leading an offensive designed to undermine the credibility of the media itself. Four months after the inauguration, the administration armed the new vice president with a bombastic new vocabulary to pursue attacks on intellectuals, bleeding hearts, antiwar activists, and other real and imagined villains—but especially the supposedly liberal-dominated print press and broadcasters. Television news had been devoting far too much coverage to antiwar demonstrations, the administration reckoned, and far too much airtime to second-guessing the president's words and deeds. Although he endorsed the plan to send Agnew into battle mode, Nixon himself stayed above the fray. So when five hundred thousand protestors thronged the Washington Mall to demand an immediate end to the fighting that still raged in Vietnam, the president invited the press into the Oval Office to bear witness to his casual indifference. "I'm going to watch football this afternoon," he declared, a line the *Washington Post* likened to Marie Antoinette's immortally dismissive "Let them eat cake."[41]

On November 13, 1969, the vice president launched his well-planned assault with a speech in Des Moines that attracted an almost masochistic level of attention from the very targets of his criticism. The fiery White House speechwriter Pat Buchanan, an ultraconservative former journalist and future presidential contender, had crafted Agnew's astringent remarks as a response to "instant" TV news criticism of Nixon's Silent Majority appeal ten days earlier. (Such glib on-air commentary seemed a new and dangerous phenomenon to the Nixon camp at the time; talking heads routinely deconstructing every remark a president utters would not become staples of television news for decades.) Buchanan had advised White House chief of staff H. R. Haldeman, "This is the time really to take on the networks directly." Buchanan's memo came back with Haldeman's comment: "P[resident] has seen, go ahead."[42]

To ensure maximum attention for the Agnew response, the White House press office issued an advance blurb promising he would challenge the "dozen anchormen, commentators, and executive producers" who "decide what forty or fifty million Americans will learn of the day's events."[43] The networks responded by covering the Agnew appearance live, the first time in memory that television had broadcast an address by a sitting vice president. (Nixon had been only a vice presidential candidate when he delivered the Checkers speech—and the RNC had been compelled to pay for his airtime.)

Agnew lived up to the hype. After charging in Des Moines that Nixon's "words and policies" had been "subjected to instant analysis and querulous criticism . . . by a small brand of network commentators" whose "minds were made up in advance," the vice president hinted at retribution: "I am asking whether a form of censorship already exists when the news that forty million Americans receive each night is determined by a handful of men . . . and filtered through a handful of commentators who admit their own set of biases. . . . It is time that the networks were made more responsive to the views of the nation and more responsible to the people they serve." Precisely how the networks were to be brought to heel, and who should define and enforce their conformity—all this was left unsaid.[44]

However vague, Agnew's brute warning put the networks on notice: thenceforth they would be closely scrutinized, which the industry took to mean that their broadcast licenses might be revoked when they came up for renewal. After a flurry of predictable objections—the networks at first accused Agnew of trying to intimidate them, which was clearly the case—media criticism of the administration indeed softened, and coverage of the antiwar movement temporarily ebbed. "Overnight," observed newsman Bill Lawrence, "Agnew became a national hero to some, and a national bum to others." More important, his "threat—clearly backed up by the President . . . had the effect of intimidating some broadcasters into soft-pedaling sharp news commentary and hard-hitting reporting lest at some future date renewal problems would be created for valuable licenses."[45]

Just a week after his Des Moines blast, in another Buchanan-crafted speech, Agnew resumed his administration-sanctioned war on the media with an attack on the print press. This time the remarks came in Mobile, Alabama, the epicenter of Nixon's new "Southern Strategy": the cynical plan to use the Democrats' civil rights and voting rights reforms as a wedge to tilt the once solidly Democratic white South permanently to the Republicans.

The vice president focused part of his Mobile speech on the Washington Post Company—which also owned *Newsweek* magazine and assorted broadcasting assets—describing it as "an example of a trend toward monopolization." He was not recommending its "dismemberment," he clarified, as if issuing a pardon—though the mere mention of the word was clearly meant to intimidate Katharine Graham. Rather, he meant simply to warn the company's consumers "that these four powerful voices hearken to the same master"—or in this case, mistress. As Graham remembered: "There is no doubt that he worried all of us—perhaps more than he should have—by striking a popular chord in a vulnerable area."[46] Then Agnew looked northward to add stiltedly but threateningly that the day when "the gentlemen of the *New York Times* enjoyed a form of diplomatic immunity from criticism of what they said is over."[47]

In a memo to the president after the speech, a jubilant Pat Buchanan saluted Agnew as "the Robespierre of the Great Silent Majority." It was evidently lost on the speechwriter that Maximilian Robespierre's radical overreach during the French Revolution had once subjected the pro-France American president Thomas Jefferson to intense press criticism. Then there was the fact that the Reign of Terror, which Robespierre helped incite, had culminated with his own execution. However dubious the accolade, an enthusiastic Nixon scrawled on Buchanan's "Robespierre" memorandum: "Right!"[48]

Feeling encouraged, the ghostwriter ran amok. The more the media covered Agnew's invective, the more hyperbolic—and flamboyantly alliterative—it became. In 1970, Agnew assailed "pusillanimous pussyfooting liberals," and in his most purple explosion, assailed "the nattering nabobs of negativism" who had "formed their own 4-H Club—the 'Hopeless, Hysterical, Hypochondriacs of History.'"[49] This time the diatribe was not aimed specifically at the media but against liberals and peace advocates in general. But, as William Safire told journalism scholar Norman P. Lewis years later, "it's tough to go up against a myth—especially since Agnew came to believe it, too."[50] By then the press had begun referring to the vice president as "Nixon's Nixon." From a media perspective, the designation was not meant as a compliment.

Now the president's communications operation became a White House divided against itself. On the one side, at least by Herb Klein's account, stood Klein and the professional public relations men who wanted to focus on Nixon's unifying accomplishments. They resisted proposals that "amateurs" plant positive stories that "glorified" Nixon or, worse, produce documentaries that told "the Administration side of what was happening in Vietnam and Cambodia." (Klein insisted the public would regard such initiatives as bald "propaganda.")[51] On the other side sat the adrenalized speechwriting team, putting angry words flogging the networks into the mouth of a malleable surrogate intoxicated by his newfound prominence. Firmly in the take-no-prisoners camp was young staffer Roger Ailes, hired as Nixon's television advisor to make him more likeable on the small screen. Ailes later said that the attack-dog methods he learned in the Nixon White House inspired his blueprint for operating Fox News as its founding CEO.

Further pushback to the strategy of network-bashing came from the White House Office of Telecommunications Policy. A young staffer at the OTP, future founder and CEO of C-SPAN, Brian Lamb, remembers that the group believed that the administration should instead have worked harder to create alternatives to the big-three broadcasting giants by encouraging communication satellites and working for deregulation. Ultimately, the OTP vision prevailed—but not because the Nixon administration anticipated the forthcoming seismic shift that ultimately brought America cable television.

"Ron Ziegler and Herb Klein preferred currying favor with local broadcasters across the country because they believed their owners were sympathetic Republicans and because the White House just hated the networks," Lamb told me. "On the other side was Clay T. Whitehead, who ran our office—a 'Brainiac' Ph.D. out of MIT who wanted to change the structure of communications rather than the substance of it. Klein wanted to use the Fairness Doctrine as a lever against the networks; Whitehead said, just get rid of it; it's holding back the possibility of deregulating all the voices. Nixon understood this once it got to his desk. It was just hard getting to his desk."[52]

As these revolutionary ideas percolated, Agnew's rants continued. Technically speaking, the president himself never uttered the divisive phrases Agnew mouthed during his oratorical road show. But in a sense, Nixon bears historical responsibility for every word. His speechwriters crafted them. His administration sanctioned their delivery, urged the media to cover Agnew's appearances, and savored the results. Even while insisting that Nixon "can't read speeches in advance," communications director Klein admitted at the time to the *Washington Post* that "the President tells them which way to go."[53] And the direction in which he sent his speechwriters—and Spiro Agnew—set the rancorous tone that would permeate his entire presidency. As Pat Buchanan himself might have expressed it, Nixon became the villainous ventriloquist of venom.

In March 1970, believing themselves to be winning the public relations battle, Nixon and Agnew felt confident enough to make a joint appearance at the annual Gridiron Club press dinner, a highlight of the Washington social calendar, which presidents had been attending, with misgivings, for fifty years. Both Theodore and Franklin Roosevelt had made unforgettable presentations there in the past, and now it was Nixon's turn. Taking the stage to perform a comedy routine with music, the usually dour Nixon gamely found humor in his Southern Strategy. The rare display of self-deprecation, never the president's forte, got underway with the two leaders sitting down together at a piano—an instrument Nixon played with some proficiency.

In their act, Nixon proposes they demonstrate multi-partisanship by playing theme songs associated with previous presidents. The gimmick is that every time Nixon begins hammering out a tune—be it Truman's favorite, "Missouri Waltz," or LBJ's "The Eyes of Texas"—Agnew interrupts by tinkling a few notes of "Dixie." Finally, Nixon introduces a tune everyone can embrace: "God Bless America." The climax inspired the entire, well-liquored crowd of journalists to struggle to their feet and sing along.[54]

Yet Nixon's capacity to enjoy his small success remained limited, his anger at the press undimmed. Even at his public relations zenith—the trip to China two years later—Nixon's hatred of the media flared up. At a reception in Beijing's Great Hall of the People, Chinese premier Zhou Enlai courteously asked the American reporters if they were having a good time. Helen Thomas remembers hearing Nixon whisper audibly, "More than they deserve."[55]

As for Agnew, he later pleaded no contest to a charge of failing to report income to the IRS, quit the vice presidency, and paid a six-figure fine. Although the administration leaked word of Agnew's impending resignation to hasten it, publicly Nixon would accept the departure with reluctance. If any doubts remained about his enthusiasm for Agnew's oratory while in office, Nixon made sure to lavish the disgraced politician with praise and gratitude for his efforts: "As Vice President, you have addressed the great issues of our times with courage and candor."[56]

His suspicion of the newspapers notwithstanding, Nixon had remained a dutiful reader of the big dailies. Each morning, he received the *New York Times* and

Washington Post, and each night aides left the *Washington Star* at his bedside. But not even a workaholic like Nixon could keep up with the papers as Kennedy once had, especially once the administration went into crisis mode. So, each day at 7:00 A.M., Pat Buchanan began preparing a "daily press briefing" that summarized the most recent media and wire reports on the Nixon administration in a thick booklet. In some instances, especially Mondays, when it included distillations from the weekly magazines, it ran to fifty pages.[57] By spring 1972, the news had grown so bleak in so many publications—and the stories themselves so explosive and so complex—that no summary could contain them.

Earlier, for example, the *New York Times* had broken the news, gleaned from unnamed sources, that for more than a year the administration had conducted secret bombing raids against North Vietnamese troops in Cambodia—a major, covert expansion of the war. On April 30, 1970, Nixon confirmed the report—having devoted months to bugging the phones of reporters in an effort to identify the source of the leak. Then on May 4, amid growing unrest on the nation's college campuses, state troopers in Ohio shot and killed four young antiwar demonstrators, injuring another nine in what became known as the Kent State massacre. The horrifying photograph of one teenage girl, arms outstretched and mouth agape in terror as she kneels over the body of a dead protestor, filled the nation's newspapers. Nixon, too, felt the anguish. But as journalism professor Louis W. Liebovich accurately described its impact, taken together with "Nixon's Vietnam policy decisions," the "tragic confrontation in Ohio, and the force of seven years of pent-up public frustration, unraveled the carefully cultivated Nixon image."[58]

Not long thereafter, a member of Nixon's staff directed a particularly delusional public relations summary to Herb Klein. Klein had no doubt that the "lengthy third-person assessment" represented "the President's perception of his own image."[59] Its source, he said, was "obvious": Nixon himself. Reflecting Nixon's belief that he now had "no friends in the press," the "PR POINTS TO BE MADE" memo failed to attribute his image problems to their true source. The recently revealed "Cambodian venture," for example, was "a devastating indication of the lack of credibility" not of the administration but "of the national media," especially *Time*, *Newsweek*, the *New York Times*, *Washington Post*, "and the three networks." When Nixon first entered office, the memo exaggerated, "there was a credibility gap as far as the presidency was concerned. Now, ironically, there is a credibility gap as far as the press is concerned." In this self-congratulatory yet distant manner the anonymous writer continued:[60]

This is not something new. RN is the first President in this century who came into the Presidency with the opposition of all these major communication powers. Since he has been in office, with only very few exceptions, he has been heavily opposed—not just editorially by these publications and networks—but primarily by the slant of the news coverage due to the attitude of reporters.

The fact that he now survives this with 55-60% approval by the people indicates not so much something about RN as it does something about the news media. . . .

In other words this is a time for soul-searching on the part of the press as to whether it is they who are out of tune with the people rather than the President.

The President has taken all this with good grace. He has never during his period of office, called a publisher, commentator, editor, etc., for purposes of criticizing them. . . .

Some of his critics complain that he doesn't have enough press conferences, but when he has one and does well, they complain because they weren't able to knock him out of the box—in other words, he can't win. . . .

The key to all this, of course, is that RN, very consciously, has taken an entirely different tact [sic] from LBJ's and a different tact than was urged upon him by some of his friends. Instead of trying to win the press, to cater to them, to have backgrounders with them, RN has ignored them and talked directly to the country by TV whenever possible. . . . With the exception of TR, Wilson, and Hoover, RN is probably the only President in this century who still sits down from time to time and completely writes a major speech himself. This makes it possible for him to use the television medium much more effectively than anyone had before him. . . . He has used the press and not let the press use him. He has particularly not allowed the press, whenever he could avoid it, to filter his ideas to the public. This is a remarkable achievement.

On Memorial Day 1970, a date most Americans devoted to honoring those who had died in war, Richard Nixon decided to build on his "remarkable achievement" by reigniting his lifelong war against the press. That day, he issued "very strict instructions" to all his aides: "[N]o one from the White House staff under any circumstances is to answer any call or see anybody from *The New York Times*.

With regard to *The Washington Post*, [Ron] Ziegler under no circumstances is to see anybody from *The Washington Post* and no one on the White House staff is to see anybody from *The Washington Post* or return any calls from them."[61] He even banned the *Post* from his daughter Tricia's June 1971 White House wedding. But even Nixon could not ignore the powerful dailies for long.

Within months, he found himself doing direct battle with these very newspapers in a spectacular struggle over leaked Defense Department documents that came to be called the Pentagon Papers.[62] A rigorously documented, forty-seven-volume chronicle of America's twenty-two-year-long involvement in Vietnam, it had been assembled in the late 1960s by order of then-secretary Robert S. McNamara. In the understatement of his career, McNamara characterized the result as "encyclopedic." In fact it was explosive.[63] Filled with evidence of unreported military escalation and unacknowledged presidential dissembling, the report was meant for internal use only, or, as has been speculated since, as a briefing for Robert Kennedy had he lived to run against Nixon in 1968. Eventually, one of the outside experts preparing the document grew so dismayed by its revelations about longtime U.S. missteps and secrecy that he determined to leak it. After secretly making photocopies, Daniel Ellsberg of the Center for International Studies at MIT tried sharing the results with both the Nixon administration and antiwar senators J. William Fulbright and George S. McGovern. He got no takers.

Then Ellsberg offered the material to onetime war correspondent Neil Sheehan of the *New York Times*, who instantly recognized its enormous news value. The newspaper's legal advisors, however, cautioned against publication of the government-owned report. *Times* publisher "Punch" Sulzberger told me years later that his decision to overrule the attorneys marked his "proudest—and scariest—moment at the paper."[64] It was also his bravest. The blockbuster excerpts that began appearing serially on June 13, 1971, showed how each presidential administration since Truman's—including those of Eisenhower, Kennedy, and Johnson—had successively escalated the American commitment in Vietnam from advisory status to all-out war. The documents were particularly harsh on Johnson, revealing that he had expanded U.S. involvement a full year before announcing the buildup to the public.

For a while, ruefully acknowledging the *Times* exclusive, the *Washington Post* relegated itself to summarizing its rival's scoops with full credit. Then, responding to a Nixon administration request to restrain the New York paper, a federal court issued an injunction enjoining the *Times* from further publication. While the *Times* prepared an appeal, Ellsberg leaked another trove of photocopied pages to *Post* national editor Ben Bagdikian. After several rounds of frenzied discussions between publisher Katharine Graham, managing editor Ben Bradlee, and the newspaper's own lawyers—while reporters struggled to make coherent sense out of the four thousand pages of material—the Washington daily began on June 18 to pick up where the New York paper had left off.[65]

The Nixon administration took its case for suppression all the way to the Supreme Court. Its zealousness remains something of a mystery, since the Pentagon Papers offered no criticism of Nixon, only of his predecessors. He might more profitably have used their appearance to defend the military stalemate he had inherited when he assumed office. For once, he may well have been thinking about the office of the presidency and not himself. "How the hell can a president . . . do anything?" he wondered. "How can they make a contingency plan if it's going to be taken out of a trunk and be given to a goddam newspaper?"[66]

Yet in private conversations with his staff, he seemed to take the matter more personally. "Goddamn *Post*," he cursed at a July 2 Oval Office meeting, "saying that 'Well, that's the price of the First Amendment.'" Publisher Katharine Graham's son (the paper's future publisher), he bellowed, was a "little shitass," and the administration's critics "all draft dodgers." Then he pivoted, acknowledging with a non sequitur: "The press must think of it in terms of circulation. We understand that they have to print everything. I have to look at it in terms of the life of American men and their glory." Ricocheting yet again from his sense of obligation to his feelings of persecution, he proclaimed *Times* reporter Sheehan "guilty as hell," admitting: "But you prosecute a newspaper man, you're in a difficult position." Nixon concluded his diatribe by comparing Daniel Ellsworth unfavorably even to his lifelong bête noire Alger Hiss: "I got to say for Hiss, he never ratted on anybody else. Never."[67]

Along with a fellow source, Ellsberg—the man Nixon now took to calling "the Jew"—now faced a treason charge under Woodrow Wilson's old 1917 Espionage Act (a case later dropped when the courts learned that the administration tried to steal incriminating documents from Ellsberg's psychiatrist).[68] But first, on June 30, in deciding perhaps the most consequential freedom of the press case in American legal history—following the most intrusive attempt at government censorship since the Civil War—the high court ruled 6–3 against the government. The *Times* and *Post* could resume publication of the Pentagon

Papers without further interference or legal exposure. Writing for the majority, eighty-five-year-old Associate Justice Hugo L. Black (destined to die a few months later) offered this opinion:

> In the First Amendment the Founding Fathers gave the free press the protection it must have to fulfill its essential role in our democracy. The press was to serve the governed, not the governors. . . . The press was protected so it could bare the secrets of the government and inform the people. Only a free and unrestrained press can effectively expose deception in government. And paramount among the responsibilities of a free press is the duty to prevent any part of the government from deceiving the people and sending them off to distant lands to die of foreign fevers and foreign shot and shell.[69]

With the case settled in the newspapers' favor, Nixon weighed retaliating against the *Washington Post* anyway. He yearned at least to "screw around" with its parent company's television license. Relishing the thought of blackballing its next renewal application, Nixon told his special counsel Charles Colson (later to be imprisoned), "I hope to God it comes up this year."[70]

In Nixon's distorted view, the press assumed increasing responsibility for the Vietnam quagmire itself. "In the short run," he (presumably) joked on Washington's birthday, 1971, "it would be so much easier . . . to kill all the reporters and carry on the war." Five days later, Nixon used an Oval Office meeting whose attendees included the chairman of the Joint Chiefs of Staff to suggest that, for PR purposes, the time had come to publicize newsworthy battlefield victories, even tiny ones ("Take a stinking hill"). The alternative was to offer the press no news at all ("I do it all the time"). "The press is your enemy. Enemies. Understand that?" he lectured his visitor. ". . . Now never . . . give them a drink, you know, treat them nice. You just love it, you're trying to be helpful. But don't help the bastards. Ever. Because they're trying to stick the knife right in our groin."[71]

As late as 1973, Nixon was still cursing Ellsberg as a "sonofabitching thief" whom the press had "made a national hero" to the extent that "the *New York Times* gets a Pulitzer Prize for stealing documents. . . . What in the name of God have we come to?"[72] (The Pentagon Papers would not be fully declassified until 2011.)

Privately—but in front of others—Nixon harbored few doubts as to why so much of the print and broadcast media remained, in his warped view, arrayed against him, especially those print and electronic moguls clustered on both coasts. Their hostility reflected the same "problem" that distorted Hollywood entertainment, he believed: "Eleven out of twelve writers are Jewish." In a secretly taped conversation on February 1, 1972, Nixon shamelessly expounded on his prejudice in an Oval Office conversation with, of all people, religious leader Billy Graham—conducted, to add to the irony, immediately following a White House prayer breakfast:

> Now, *Life* [magazine] is totally dominated by the Jews. *Newsweek* is totally, is owned by Jews, and dominated by them, their editorials. The New York Times, the Washington Post, are totally Jewish. The ownership of the Los Angeles Times is now totally Jewish. Poor [publisher] Owen Chandler, who sits on the top of the heap. The . . . three networks . . . they have front men—they have Howard K. Smith, or [David] Brinkley or a [Walter] Cronkite [who] may not be of that persuasion—but the writers though, ninety-five percent are Jewish. Now, what does this mean? Does this mean that all the Jews are bad? No. It does mean that most Jews are left-wing. . . . They're way out. They're radical. They're for peace at any price, except where the support of Israel is concerned.[73]

At the end of the rant, Rev. Graham can be heard opining that "this ugly stranglehold has got to be broken or this country is going to go down the drain." "Do you believe that?" asks Nixon, sounding hopeful. "Yes, sir," Graham replies. "Boy!" Nixon responds. "I can never say it though, but I believe—," prompting America's most prominent minister to interrupt and suggest: "But if you've been elected a second time, you might be able to do something." (Graham later denied the audible evidence and claimed he had not endorsed the president's anti-Semitic tropes).

After China, and despite the Pentagon Papers humiliation, most observers considered Nixon's 1972 reelection likely. The belief grew into certainty once Democrats tacked left and nominated liberal antiwar senator George S. McGovern to oppose him. McGovern's slim chance for success evaporated altogether when his running mate, Thomas Eagleton, stepped off the ticket after the press reported he had once undergone electroshock therapy to treat clinical depression. Nixon took no chances, approving several illegal initiatives to stifle critics. Early in the year, for example, the White House sought "evidence" it could use against "Washington Merry-Go-Round" columnist Jack Anderson "*before* his next attack." Among the tactics considered were lacing his car's steering wheel with LSD, poisoning his medications, or passing the word that Anderson might be a homosexual.[74]

Nixon's campaign appearances that year, such as they were, amounted to well-oiled productions featuring music, rallies, canned speeches, and limited press access to the candidate. "Gonzo" journalist Hunter S. Thompson, national affairs editor of *Rolling Stone*, was one of several counterculture reporters who experienced difficulty merely obtaining the credentials needed to cover these events. Even then, he and the rest of the "press mob" seldom got closer to Nixon than did the supporters gathered on airport tarmacs to greet his plane. At one event, Thompson and his colleagues were reduced to observing a campaign speech from a crowded hallway, peering into the main room to catch occasional glimpses of the president. "Jesus," Thompson exclaimed to Bob Greene of the *Chicago Sun-Times*, "is it *always* like this?" "Hell," replied Greene, "this is *accessible*! We can actually see him."[75]

Thompson concluded that the president had regarded all journalists as "biased bastards" since his 1962 loss in California. "He rarely holds press conferences," Thompson noted of the 1972 Nixon, "and his personal relationship with the working press is almost nonexistent. In the White House or on the road, he 'communicates' . . . through his mouthpiece, press secretary Ron Ziegler, an arrogant thirty-three-year-old punk . . . who treats the White House press corps like a gang of troublesome winos who will only be tolerated as long as they keep out of the boss's hair."[76] Nixon sometimes treated Ziegler as roughly as he did the reporters. On one occasion he was seen physically shoving his spokesman toward a lineup of journalists as if to remind him they were his responsibility, not the president's.

Graduating inexplicably from the press plane to a seat on Air Force One, the caustic Thompson was startled to find that even this rarefied proximity did not increase access to its passenger in chief. Unlike LBJ, Nixon never strolled into the press area for chats or invited reporters forward to his cabin for a meal or drink. When such access had been proffered in 1960, the press had shunned it; typically, now that it was denied, the journalists resented Nixon even more. "We never leave the compartment; just sit in there and play cards," a veteran UPI pool reporter advised Thompson. "They could all be running around naked up in front, for all we know." The real "tragedy," of 1972, Thompson lamented, was that McGovern proved "so goddamn maddeningly inept."[77] But nearly half a century later, that assessment seems harsh. The truth is that once Eagleton quit the Democratic ticket, McGovern never had a fighting chance in the general election.

Another renegade journalist, Timothy Crouse, judged "Nixon's 1972 non-campaign" a "triumph of public relations," explaining: "Agnew was calm and conciliatory. The President was Presidential. Peace was at hand." But more crucially, "The Press had become too weak, frightened, and demoralized to try to dent the Administration's handsome veneer."[78] (Crouse and other reporters had no way of knowing at the time what extra lengths the Nixon campaign had taken to crush the opposition.) On Election Day, Nixon notched a historic victory, winning everywhere but Massachusetts and the District of Columbia, and outpolling his opponent by eighteen million votes. Decades later, with earnest sincerity, McGovern told my wife and me, at a dinner with writer Kurt Vonnegut, activist Gloria Steinem, and Vonnegut's wife, photographer Jill Krementz: "If only I'd had a few days more, I would have caught up with him."[79]

McGovern's delusions were exceeded only by Nixon's insecurities. At the beginning of a campaign he probably could have won without even campaigning, the Committee to Re-elect the President (or as some referred to the group, CREEP) ushered in the age of "Dirty Tricks" to ensure, but forever taint, Nixon's triumph. On June 17, 1972, at around 2:30 A.M., five intruders wearing rubber surgical gloves forced their way into the Democratic National Committee headquarters on the sixth floor of a fancy Washington apartment-hotel-office complex near the newly opened Kennedy Center: a building called the Watergate. CREEP's objective was to photograph documents and install eavesdropping devices—more accurately, it would later be revealed, to repair faulty bugging equipment installed three weeks earlier.[80] But the gang that couldn't wiretap straight was caught in the act. A grand jury indicted them—along with two White House functionaries, G. Gordon Liddy and H. Howard Hunt—on September 15, but with no discernible damage to the ongoing Nixon campaign.

And with no immediate outpouring of coverage, much less indignation, Nixon eagerly embraced his chief aide Bob Haldeman's early assessment: "I felt sure that it was just a public relations problem that only needed a public relations solution."[81] In his first press briefing after the news broke, Ron Ziegler memorably minimized the crime as "a third rate burglary," presciently conceding, "Certain elements may try to stretch this beyond what it is."[82]

The "elements" who did the most to put the event under a sustained and increasingly revealing microscope were two young reporters at the *Washington Post*: a twenty-nine-year-old, Illinois-born recent hire named Bob Woodward and a twenty-eight-year-old college dropout from Washington, Carl Bernstein.[83] But the *Post* owed its original knowledge of the story to an early tip about the break-in from a lawyer who represented both the DNC and the paper: the same Joe Califano who had once worked in the Johnson White House.[84] For months thereafter, Woodward and Bernstein investigated every aspect of the break-in, slowly but inescapably linking it to a web of clandestine operations by the Nixon campaign designed to infiltrate and damage the opposition. Congresswoman Elizabeth Holtzman, soon to gain fame for her work on the House Judiciary Committee, told me she believed "the reporting by Woodward and Bernstein" proved "vital to the public demand for House action."[85] The term "Watergate"—coined originally because the five clumsy spooks had been caught in the Watergate building in June—expanded in meaning to embrace all aspects of CREEP's, and the government's, sordid activities to interfere with the elections and conceal their activities from legal authorities.

Encouraged in their investigation by *Post* managing editor Ben Bradlee, Woodward and Bernstein's first exposé, published at the end of September, revealed the existence of a secret campaign fund that outdid in subterfuge anything Nixon had established twenty years earlier in California. Republican operatives had created the stash specifically to bankroll spying on Democrats, and, as Woodward and Bernstein reported, it was overseen in part by Attorney General John Mitchell. Given a chance by Bernstein to respond on the phone, Mitchell let out what sounded like a "primal scream" and threatened: "Katie Graham's gonna get her tit caught in a big fat wringer if that's published. Good Christ! That's the most sickening thing I ever heard." Graham recalled that she did not know what offended her more: the vulgarity of Mitchell's warning or the fact that he called her "Katie" when all her friends knew her as "Kay." Bradlee approved a sanitized version of the quote in the paper—Mrs. Graham "was gonna get caught in a big fat wringer"—but the authentic words quickly made the rounds in Washington.[86]

Evidence never surfaced to suggest that Nixon knew of in advance, much less approved, the June 1972 DNC caper. What became increasingly clear was that as soon as it was brought to his attention, he authorized a cover-up. On August 29, Nixon insisted otherwise at an outdoor press conference at his "western White House" in San Clemente, California, the first of many press sessions that would focus on Watergate. No special prosecutor was needed to look into the matter, Nixon argued that day, because White House counsel John W. Dean III had completed his own inquiry. "I can say categorically," Nixon asserted, "that his investigation indicates that no one on the White House staff, no one in this administration, presently employed, was involved in this very bizarre incident."[87]

Meanwhile the administration doubled down on its criticism of the *Post*'s managing editor. In a speech to New England newspaper editors, Charles Colson, head of the White House Office of Special Liaison, labeled Ben Bradlee "the self-appointed leader of"—and here he appropriated a quote from Theodore H. White—"that tiny little fringe of arrogant elitists who infect the healthy mainstream of American journalism with their own peculiar view of the world." Unmoved, Bradlee maintained of Watergate, "you would have to be Richard Nixon himself to say this was not a story."[88]

Not until April 30, 1973, did Nixon go on national TV, not to take blame for the affair but to accept responsibility, as he put it, for "people whose zeal exceeded their judgment."[89] His belated and half-hearted explanation did not work. House and Senate committees opened impeachment inquiries the following year. Woodward and Bernstein's remarkable run of scoops transfixed not only the readers of the *Washington Post* but the rest of the media, which reprised their stories and profiled the authors, transforming the duo into celebrities. Using remarkable, ongoing access to a man Woodward blandly described at first only as "a source in the Executive Branch," the team gained extraordinary insight into the White House cover-up. It was *Post* managing editor Howard Simons who seized inspiration from a recent porn film and its star, Linda Lovelace, to name the source "Deep Throat." (Not until 2005 did Deep Throat reveal himself to be FBI associate director Mark Felt.)[90]

Back at the White House, in the glare of his twice-daily press briefings, Ron Ziegler began unraveling under relentless questioning from the press corps. Increasingly "militant," blaming his inquisitors and not his boss, Ziegler maintained he was more shocked by the inquiries than by the deeds that required explanation. "People are preoccupied with the answers to the questions," he protested, "and I think they should look to the questions asked as well."[91] Pressed about why his responses sounded less and less believable, Ziegler squirmed:

"Credibility is a matter of the attitudes of those who are listening. I have done the best I could with the information available and the facts as I know them."[92]

When the *New York Times* asked Herb Klein that same month if Nixon should quit, Klein insisted that the president had adamantly replied: "I wouldn't give a damn if they proved red-handed that I was in the Watergate, you know, and wearing a red beard, collecting the evidence. Hell . . . the President of the United States isn't going to resign . . . over this chicken shit stuff."[93]

Not long thereafter, Klein, who by then had left the administration to take a job with Metromedia in New York, turned down a plea to return to the White House to manage emergency Watergate public relations strategy. Arguing that the offer "came two years too late," when the "presidency was already gone," the former communications director later implied that Nixon might have weathered the crisis had he better understood how his predecessors had handled journalists. Nixon admired Kennedy's "dramatic way with words," Klein pointed out, "but he never understood the Kennedy relationship with the press. I have no doubt but that when he was confronted with some of the crucial decisions as to Watergate and the cover-up . . . he was influenced by thinking that both Kennedy and Johnson had wended their way through troublesome personal spots by just hanging tough."[94] Clearly, Nixon forgot that JFK had survived the 1961 Bay of Pigs fiasco by taking full responsibility at the outset.

Nixon's secret "Enemies List," exposed amid the avalanche of Watergate revelations in June 1973, cemented the administration's reputation for harboring resentment and plotting vengeance. The McCarthy-era blacklist was long dead and discredited, so when Nixon's roster of targets was revealed to the public, it transformed a number of its previously anonymous designees into heroes. More accurately the sum of several lists compiled by various administration staffers, it overflowed with both liberal activists and supposedly biased journalists. In addition to members of Congress (Bella Abzug), celebrities (Barbra Streisand), labor leaders (Lane Kirkland of the AFL-CIO), civil rights activists (Ralph Abernathy), and men who had been prominent in the Kennedy and Johnson administrations (Ted Sorensen and Jack Valenti respectively), the roster came to encompass more than sixty media people from magazines, television, and newspapers. The watch list featured three entire news organizations: the *Washington Post*, *New York Times*, and *St. Louis Post-Dispatch*.

Individuals condemned to Nixon's dishonor roll included syndicated columnists Joseph Kraft, Carl Rowan, Garry Wills, Frank Mankiewicz, Clayton Fritchey, Rowland Evans and Robert Novak, Mary McGrory, Jack Anderson, and even Jim Bishop (who would later write the bestseller *The Day Christ Died*). Then there were reporters James Reston and Tom Wicker of the *New York Times*; Max Lerner, James Wechsler, Pete Hamill, and Harriet Van Horne of the *New York Post*; and White House correspondents James Deakin of the *Post-Dispatch* and Peter Lisagor of the *Chicago Daily News*. From the broadcast world, Eric Sevareid, Harry Reasoner, Marvin Kalb, and Daniel Schorr of CBS all made the lists, as did Lem Tucker and Sander Vanocur of NBC, along with their boss, network CEO Julian Goodman.[95] Schorr, who read twenty of the names aloud, including his own, on-air one night, recalled decades later at age ninety-two: "It was such a distinguished list. My lecture fees went up."[96] Schorr did not know it at the time, but he also became the subject of an FBI investigation on orders from the White House.[97]

The day the list became public, the pugnacious ABC correspondent Sam Donaldson, whom Ronald Reagan later called "the Ayatollah of the press corps," ran into *Washington Star* columnist Mary McGrory on Capitol Hill. Showing her the newly released list that featured her name, he teased her: "It says here that you write daily 'hate Nixon' articles." In what Donaldson called the "ever-so-sweet manner" that masked "the instinct of a barracuda," McGrory replied: "That's not true. I only write three days a week."[98]

Heading into the summer of 1973, Nixon still clung to the belief, no matter what the press wrote, that he retained a strong residue of support from his base. And he maintained his view that the crisis of confidence he had inspired had more to do with political differences than with any underlying crime. Using "crap," he warned his newly named chief of staff, General Alexander Haig, the liberal media intended to "destroy the president because they realize that that will destroy the Republican Party." He still had the opportunity and obligation, he said, "to go forth" and build on "the greatest foreign policy this country has ever had," adding: "That is what the goddamn *New York Times* and the *Washington Post* ought to be writing. . . . Well, they never will, but it doesn't make any difference because they are not with the country and the country isn't with them."[99]

By July the reality finally began to sink in. "They've killed me," Nixon said of the media on the 12th, after reading another daily press summary bulging with fresh revelations about the scandal. "The only time the press corps will ever be happy is when they write my obituary." That same night, a spiraling case of viral pneumonia forced Nixon into the hospital. "I told Ziegler to make the announcement," the president told his personal secretary, Rose Mary Woods, "because I said it's the only time in his career he will hear the press corps clap."[100]

To the UPI's unsympathetic Helen Thomas, Nixon's cascading unpopularity with the press was no one's fault but his own. During his presidency, she complained, secrecy in the White House had mushroomed from "endemic" to "epidemic." Her catalog of Nixonian abuses included "the secret bombing of Cambodia to stonewalling about Watergate, from the creation of the 'plumbers' unit [a clandestine White House investigations group] to the 'enemies list,' to Kissinger turning over to the FBI a list of his top aides whom he suspected of leaking information." As for his strategy for convincing reporters of his innocence, Thomas added, Nixon "always had two battle plans, and had a bad habit of choosing the wrong one. Either that, or he had one of the most off-kilter moral compasses that ever guided the Oval Office."[101]

One afternoon, with Nixon's presidency nearing free fall, Thomas unexpectedly bumped into the president as he slouched toward his tiny hideaway retreat in the Executive Office Building, the century-old structure where Dwight Eisenhower had once met the press in calmer days. "Good evening, Mr. President," she greeted him, "and good luck." Nixon seized her hand and said, "I know we don't have the same religion. But will you say a prayer for me?" Thomas remembered being asked the following year, just before the president resigned "in disgrace": "When did you first know Nixon was lying?" Replied the unsentimental veteran, "In nineteen forty-six."[102] On July 31, Congressman Robert Drinan—a Catholic priest—formally introduced a House resolution to consider Nixon's impeachment.

That October, as congressional hearings dominated the television news, Nixon unleashed a new constitutional crisis by firing Archibald Cox, a special prosecutor he had installed to investigate the Watergate affair, but whose independence threatened the president. The decapitation in turn triggered the resignations of Attorney General Elliot Richardson and Deputy Attorney General William Ruckelshaus. In his memoirs, Nixon focused on the press response, noting that the "television networks broke into their regular programming with breathless, almost hysterical bulletins." Later he seemed surprised that the networks ran nineteen different attacks and only five defenses. "Some called it the 'Night of the Long Knives,'" Nixon complained, "in a tasteless and inflammatory comparison with Hitler's murderous purge of his opposition in 1934. Within twenty-four hours the television and press had labeled the events with the prejudicial shorthand of a 'Saturday Night Massacre.'" He seemed comforted only when the *Washington Star* editorialized, "The jackboots that some observers seem to hear . . . are largely in their own minds."[103]

On October 26, Nixon allowed his growing resentments against the media go on full national display at a televised news conference from the White House. "I have never heard or seen such outrageous, vicious, distorted reporting in twenty-seven years of public life," he berated the press corps. Asked whether the country could endure the continuing crisis, Nixon again blamed news coverage: "When people are pounded night after night with that kind of frantic, hysterical reporting, it naturally shakes their confidence." The unmistakable implication that TV had been particularly irresponsible prompted CBS News correspondent Robert Pierpoint to rise and ask, "What is it about the television coverage . . . that has so aroused your anger?" Nixon made no further effort to mask his contempt. "Don't get the impression that you arouse my anger," he sneered at Pierpoint. "You see, one can only be angry with those he respects." Rookie NBC News correspondent Tom Brokaw knew exactly what he had just witnessed: "the latest in the long-running Nixon knife fight with the American press."[104]

Continuing to insist that Nixon's troubles owed more to "questions" than "answers," Ziegler maintained as late as January 1974 that he had "not lost faith in the nation's press" even though it continued to put the administration "in the position of proving the negative." Watergate was indeed a tragedy, he conceded, but so was the way the press had covered it. "And if we allow a President to be destroyed as a result of excesses in this system, then we have a real problem in our society."[105] In May, one of Nixon's last press defenders, the long-closeted columnist Joseph Alsop—who once believed Lyndon Johnson had ordered his phone tapped—finally abandoned the president. In a note to publisher Kay Graham saluting the *Washington Post*'s brave Watergate coverage, he graciously conceded: "You're dead right and I was nearly dead wrong . . . for giving our miserable President the benefit of the doubt."[106] Even Ziegler ended up publicly apologizing to the *Post* along with its star reporters Woodward and Bernstein.

"I can understand why Richard Nixon believes that he received harsher treatment from the press than any president before him," the feisty Sarah McClendon later explained. "This is partly because reporters are so much better at their jobs . . . and even seem to have more nerve than in the old days. Once these young reporters saw how thinly covered up Nixon and Company's misdeeds really were, they tore into the Watergate story and never let go."

"Nixon," she continued, ". . . tried to make the American public believe that reporters were out to get him and that he was the underdog. Many people believed him, too; even after the [secret White House] tapes were discovered, the press was still being blamed for running Nixon out of office." To his final day in the White House, she believed, Nixon "whipped up so much public opinion against the press that I would not have been surprised to have seen a reporter tarred and feathered by Nixon supporters."[107]

On March 19, 1974, a desperate Nixon headed to Houston to hold a televised news conference before the National Association of Broadcasters—the same group, coincidence or not, that Lyndon Johnson had addressed the day after announcing his decision not to seek reelection five years earlier. Nixon, asked by a reporter there whether he yet hoped to mend his frayed relations with journalists, sneered, "The president should treat the press just as fairly as the press treats him." Toward the end of the event, Nixon called upon a famously aggressive television correspondent.

"Dan Rather of CBS News," the questioner began for the benefit of the few who did not recognize him—unleashing a wave of applause mixed with boos. Seeing an opportunity to taunt a longtime enemy, Nixon asked him (off camera, unfortunately): "Are you running for something?" As Rather remembered what happened next: "If I'd been allowed half a day, or even half a minute, to think, my response *might* have been different. But in those sandspecks of time I only had long enough to think, well, you don't want to stand here simply mute. And so I said, '*No, sir, Mr. President, are you?*'"[108] In the days to come, most journalists criticized Rather for competing with the president for the spotlight. But if Nixon won that battle, he was destined soon to abandon the war. The Houston appearance would be his final press conference.

For a time longer, Nixon tried to hold off the inevitable—defying a subpoena to produce the secret audio tapes he had long kept running in the Oval Office, yet, astonishingly, had never destroyed. A stack of edited transcripts failed to satisfy Congress, although Theodore H. White—once quoted by the administration in its war against the media elite—found them sufficient to reveal "a profanity of such commonness as to make the imaginative level of Lyndon Johnson's obscenities seem artful by comparison."[109] Newspapers that had long backed Nixon, including the staunchly Republican *Chicago Tribune*, now demanded his resignation.

In a unanimous 9–0 decision, the Supreme Court quickly ordered that the original tapes be sent to Capitol Hill. The infamous "smoking gun" contained within them revealed that Nixon indeed had tried to obstruct the investigation of Watergate and conceal its ripple effect of associated criminal acts. As the front-page headline of the *Washington Post* blared: "President Admits Withholding Data: Tapes Show He Approved Cover-up."[110]

Two days later, on August 8, barely a week after a faithful supporter, Rabbi Baruch Korff of Massachusetts, begged the president to defy "the jackals in the media," Nixon decided to resign as president of the United States.[111] "One thing, Ron old boy," he said to Ziegler as he headed toward the White House residence to work on a farewell address, "at least we won't have to have any more press conferences and we won't even have to tell them that, either."[112] Nixon had said much the same thing in Beverly Hills twelve years earlier, but this time there was no possibility of another Lazarus-like comeback.

After one more televised speech to the nation, tearfully delivered the next day to the echo of audible sobbing from staff members gathered in the East Room, came a final photo opportunity. At Ron Ziegler's urging, Nixon would not slink out of the White House in shame. Instead, he ascended the steps of the presidential helicopter one last time as it waited for him on the lawn, turned to face the cameras, and defiantly raised both arms and waved his trademark "V" for "victory" sign. Nixon's last advice to his supporters had been, "Always remember, others may hate you—but those who hate you don't win unless you hate them, and then you die yourself."[113] By being hated and hating venomously in return, Nixon had ignored his own wisdom and died many deaths.

As *New Yorker* editor David Remnick put it, Richard Nixon departed Washington "believing that the imperial presidency had been disastrously hobbled by a now imperial press."[114] Indeed, having done all in his power to avoid or suppress media scrutiny, Nixon instead emboldened it. But while Nixon left the press far more aggressive, he left the nation far more cynical. Presidential secrecy, private and public alike, would be respected no more. Benefits of the doubt would cease to exist. In one sense, Nixon contributed to the public good by liberating the press at last from its almost Victorian restraints, thus assuring the public more scrutiny and imposing greater transparency on the operations of its government. But Nixon also eroded the respect with which Americans long held the presidency and its occupants. Journalists after Nixon made "gotcha" their credo. And presidents ever since have reaped the whirlwind.

In 1977, three years after Nixon's fall and subsequent pardon, the British-born television host David Frost paid the ex-president $600,000—the equivalent of $2.9 million in 2019—plus a percentage of future profits to sit for a series of special on-camera interviews. These were the probing Q&A sessions that later inspired the play and movie *Frost/Nixon*.

The actual programs proved far less dramatic than the subsequent adaptations for theater and film. Nixon never dropped his guard for Frost, and never fully yielded to the host's request that, once and for all, he accept both responsibility and guilt for the pain the Watergate scandal had caused his administration, his country, and himself.

Only after hours of grilling did Nixon finally admit, "I brought myself down." Even then, his remorse proved fleeting. He could not quite allow himself to absorb sole blame for his disgrace. Always, always there was the press.

"I gave them a sword and they stuck it in," he volunteered. "And they twisted it with relish."[115]

PART FIVE

"TRUTH IS THE GLUE"

Left: A 1793 Edward Savage engraving of George Washington: first in war, first in peace, and the first president obsessed with, and criticized by, the press. *(Library of Congress)* Right: Philip Freneau (1752–1832), founding editor of Philadelphia's *National Gazette*, a journal underwritten by Thomas Jefferson specifically to heap rebuke on the Washington administration. *(New York Public Library)*

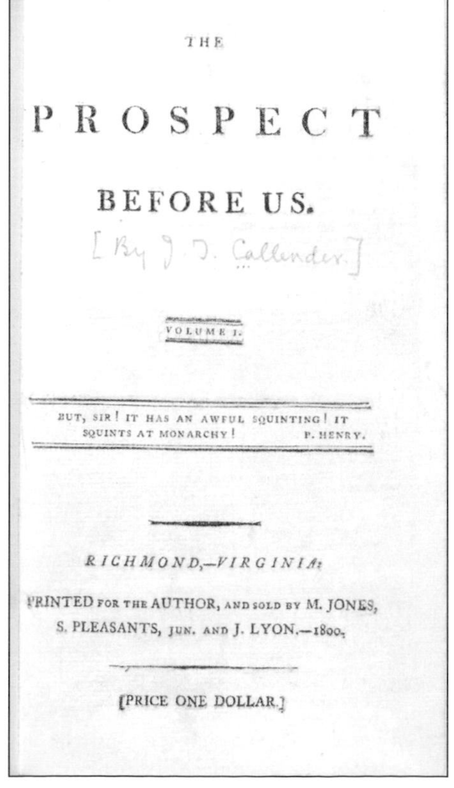

THE

PROSPECT

BEFORE US.

[By J. T. Callender.]

VOLUME I.

BUT, SIR! IT HAS AN AWFUL SQUINTING! IT SQUINTS AT MONARCHY! P. HENRY.

RICHMOND,—VIRGINIA:

PRINTED FOR THE AUTHOR, AND SOLD BY M. JONES, S. PLEASANTS, JUN. AND J. LYON.—1800.

[PRICE ONE DOLLAR.]

Above: John Adams signed and enforced the 1798 Sedition Act, making it a federal crime for the press to criticize the president. Right: With Jefferson's encouragement, James T. Callender (1758–1803) wrote this anti-Federalist pamphlet in 1800. Prosecuted, fined, and jailed, he was later pardoned by Jefferson, but Callender turned on him and broke the story of Jefferson's sexual liaison with the enslaved Sally Hemings. *(Library of Congress)*

Left: Thomas Jefferson helped conceive and nurture the partisan press but ended his long life believing advertising was "the only truths to be relied on in a newspaper." *(Library of Congress)* Right: One of Jefferson's key press supporters, William Duane (1760–1835), editor of the *Philadelphia Aurora*, was twice arrested under the Sedition Act. *(National Portrait Gallery, Smithsonian Institution; gift of Mr. and Mrs. Paul Mellon)*

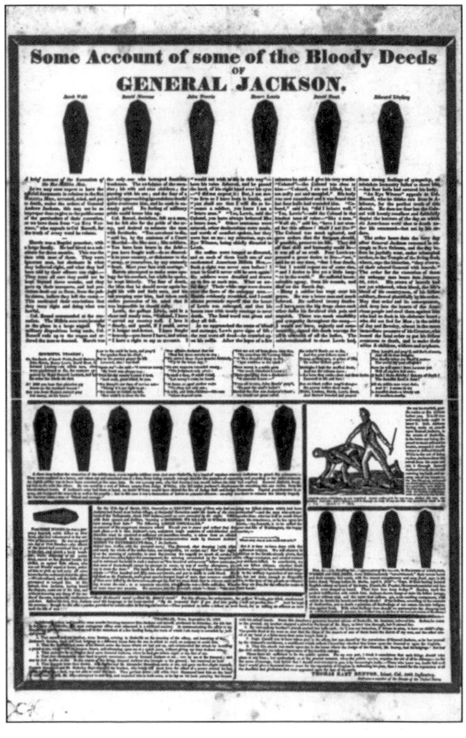
Some Account of some of the Bloody Deeds OF GENERAL JACKSON.

Two hostile views of Andrew Jackson: *King Andrew the First* (left), depicting him as a despot trampling on the Constitution; and *The Bloody Deeds of Andrew Jackson* (right), a "coffin handbill," produced by anti-Jackson newspaper editor Jacob Binns to accuse the former general of habitual violence. *(Library of Congress)*

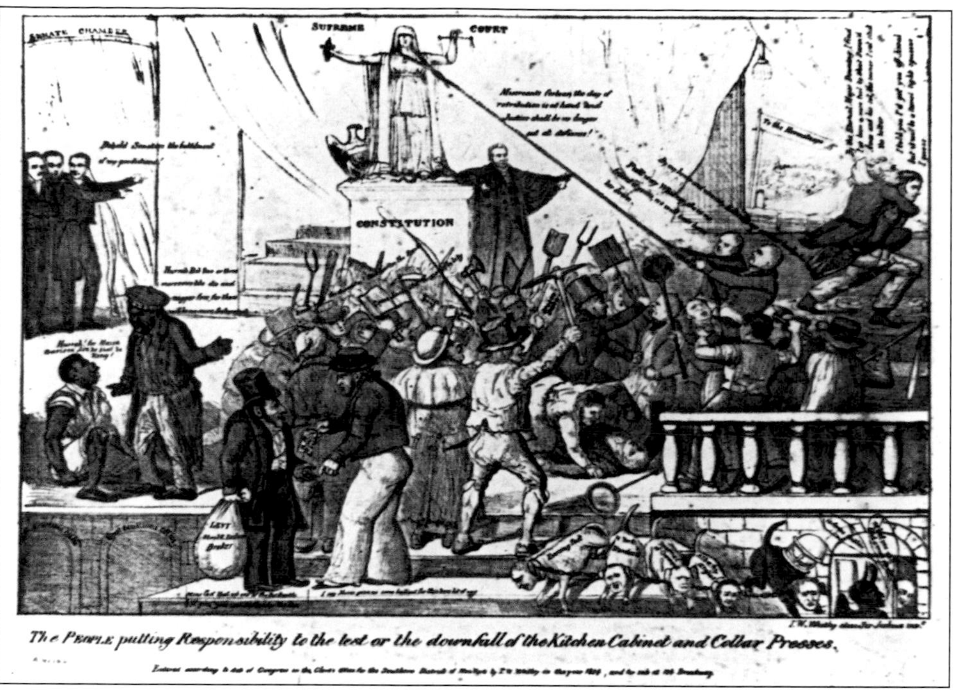

This 1834 lithograph, *Downfall of the Kitchen Cabinet and Collar Presses*, laments Jackson's hostility to the national bank. The artist aimed particular scorn at newspapers loyal to the president: the *Albany Argus* and New York's *Evening Post*, *Standard*, and *Journal of Commerce*, and the *Washington Globe* (a cur balancing a globe on its back), whose editors are depicted in the foreground as chained dogs. *(Library of Congress)*

Jackson's press supporters. Left: Amos Kendall (1789–1869) edited the *Argus of Western America*. Relocating to Washington, he became a member of the "Kitchen Cabinet" and Jackson's postmaster general. *(National Archives)* Right: Jackson favorite Francis Preston Blair, Sr. (1791–1876), who ran the *Washington Globe*, official organ of the administration, from 1830 to 1845. *(Courtesy Blair House, U.S. Department of State)*

Right: A casual Gerald R. Ford takes a question from redoubtable UPI correspondent Helen Thomas, who covered the White House from the Kennedy administration through the first years of Barack Obama's presidency. *(Library of Congress)* Below: Jimmy Carter chats with CBS anchorman Walter Cronkite before the two begin a March 5, 1977, radio call-in show from the Oval Office. *(AP photo by Charles Tasnadi)*

The infamous, hazy photo showing Carter seizing a paddle to repel a "killer rabbit" swimming toward his canoe on a Georgia lake on April 20, 1979. The incident provoked an embarrassing sensation. *(Jimmy Carter Presidential Library and Museum, Atlanta)*

Above: Ronald Reagan confers with media advisors Larry Speakes (right) and David Gergen (center, in white shirt) in the Oval Office, April 24, 1982. Left: Reagan preferred photo ops to press conferences. Here he welcomes his council on physical fitness to the East Room on February 2, 1982, by demonstrating his prowess with weights. Below: President Reagan broadcasts a radio address to the nation, February 26, 1983. Aides began using a larger, more visible "ON THE AIR" sign after Reagan spoke about bombing Russia into what he thought was a dead microphone in August 1984. *(Ronald Reagan Presidential Library & Museum, Simi Valley, CA)*

Presidential candidate Bill Clinton and his wife Hillary sit for an interview with CBS reporter Steve Kroft that aired on *60 Minutes* on January 26, 1992. The broadcast helped rescue Clinton's campaign following charges of his marital infidelity. During the taping, Clinton also rescued Hillary—from a falling klieg light. *(Photo by CBS via Getty Images)*

Surrounded by reporters, President Clinton delivers his weekly radio address on August 7, 1993. His early relations with the press strained, he fell back on many Reagan-era PR innovations, including radio talks like this one. *(William J. Clinton Presidential Library and Museum, Little Rock)*

Two of George W. Bush's best-known photo opportunities—one triumphant, the other premature. Above: Bullhorn in hand, "W" encourages rescue and cleanup workers in the rubble of the World Trade Center on September 14, 2001. *(George W. Bush Presidential Library and Museum, Dallas)* Left: Bush addresses crew aboard the aircraft carrier USS *Abraham Lincoln* on May 1, 2003, standing in front of a sign declaring "MISSION ACCOMPLISHED" before the Iraq War in fact ended. *(AP photo by Scott Applewhite)*

A master of the press conference, Barack Obama held eleven such sessions in his first year in office, but the number dwindled as he pioneered outreach via social media. Meanwhile the forty-fourth president approved wiretaps on journalists suspected of leaking secret information. *(White House photo by Lawrence Jackson)*

Donald Trump campaign rallies like this one, many of which featured fierce criticism of the press, drew large crowds and attracted live television coverage during the 2016 presidential campaign. This event took place two weeks before Election Day. *(Photo by Michael Candelori)*

As president, Trump shunned formal news conferences but held frequent, often combative, scrums with correspondents on the White House lawn before boarding his helicopter. *(White House photograph)*

— 13 —

GERALD FORD AND JIMMY CARTER

The most effective presidential communicators—leaders who conquered new technologies or successfully dominated prevailing ones—invariably left the most indelible marks on history, for better or for worse.

Those who best navigated the evolving media landscape included the Founders, Jackson, Lincoln, both Roosevelts, Kennedy, Johnson, and Nixon. After Nixon, presidents faced a new reality that would have daunted any of their predecessors: an intense level of often combative scrutiny unseen since the days leading up to the Civil War. Once, sectionalism and partisanship had propelled coverage. Now press attention was driven by an intense skepticism fueled by a new expectation that only relentless press oversight could keep leaders honest and the republic safe. For most of the four decades to come, until social media offered leaders an altogether new means of bypassing press oversight and speaking directly to the public, the emboldened media by and large held the upper hand. Only occasionally did the power of the press yield to the force of personality.

The next eight occupants of the White House dealt with the post-Nixon environment in different ways, most of them cognizant of the new expectations for transparency. Nearly all fell into inevitable conflict with the institution long expected—and now freshly empowered—to question their motives, policies, and, increasingly, their moral standing.

GERALD R. FORD

Genial Jerry Ford, never elected to an office higher than congressman from Grand Rapids, assumed the presidency burdened with an inescapable handicap: he had been anointed by a disgraced predecessor. Handpicked by Nixon to succeed Spiro Agnew as vice president under the new Twenty-Fifth Amendment and quickly confirmed by his old congressional colleagues, Ford became president just eight months later, when Nixon resigned. Unelected or not, Ford went on to enjoy a charmed press honeymoon—and one that lasted "longer than most," Helen Thomas sarcastically attested: all of a month.[1]

On August 9, 1974, the day Nixon left office, Ford took the oath in the East Room and addressed the American people on television. Wisely, the new president identified his chief mission as healing the wounds opened by Watergate. "My fellow Americans, our long national nightmare is over," he declared in his first and, as it turned out, only quotable speech. Before uttering that memorable line, this fundamentally decent man came as close as he could to acknowledging the deception that had brought Nixon down: "I believe that truth is the glue that holds government together, not only our government, but civilization itself. . . . In all my public and private acts as your President, I expect to follow my instincts of openness and candor with full confidence that honesty is always the best policy in the end."[2] By and large he did so.

Ford earned early goodwill by shunning some of the trappings long associated with the presidency. The press reported admiringly that he worked in his shirtsleeves and still preferred toasting his own English muffins for breakfast. He did himself further good by naming one of the most popular journalists in town as his press secretary. Jerald terHorst, who had long covered the White House for the *Detroit News*, took over the job amid high expectations for the restoration of both access and honesty. TerHorst saw his principal job as helping Ford "make a sharp break between himself and Richard Nixon . . . to create a new climate."[3] Ford assured terHorst, somewhat more ambiguously, that he was "very interested in keeping a friendly press corps," or at least "appearing to be accommodating to what he felt were legitimate things."[4]

Within weeks, the new president proved far too accommodating to suit his spokesman. In the first week of September, Ford pardoned Richard Nixon unconditionally, and both the honeymoon and terHorst's brief tenure came to a crashing end. The press secretary promptly handed in his resignation, explaining: "I do not know how I could credibly defend that action in the absence of a like decision to grant absolute pardon to the young men who evaded Vietnam military service as a matter of conscience," not to mention the Nixon underlings already doing prison time for their misdeeds. As terHorst told Ford: "Try as I can, it is impossible to conclude that the former President is more deserving of mercy than persons of lesser station in life whose offenses have had far less effect on our national well-being."[5]

TerHorst's real gripe may have been that Ford had failed to confide the pardon decision to him in advance, and worse, that senior White House staff had led him to believe the new president was instead leaning toward allowing the legal process against Nixon to unfold unimpeded. That assumption may have emboldened terHorst, in turn, to inadvertently misinform journalists, a cardinal sin as far as the former reporter was concerned. Ford tried hard to get his fellow Michigander to reconsider. "Jerry, I regret this," he wrote terHorst. "I think you've made a mistake. I respect your views, and I'm sorry if there was a misunderstanding. As to the pardon, it was a decision I felt I had to make. I've made it and I'm going to stick with it. I hope that you will reconsider and change your mind."[6] TerHorst stuck by his own decision as well.

Facing an avalanche of criticism, Ford maintained his characteristic good cheer. A few days later, he fulfilled a September 18 commitment to speak at the National Press Club, where he evidenced no loss of optimism. "Anybody in public life is well aware of how important the judgments of the press are," he declared that night. "I'm firmly convinced that if the good Lord had made the world today, he would have spent six days creating the heavens and earth and all the living creatures upon it. But on the seventh day, he would not have rested. He would have had to justify it to Helen Thomas." In turn, the UPI veteran found Ford "cordial and frank," even after learning that the new president had described her reporting style as "a fine blend of journalism and acupuncture."[7]

As Jerry terHorst's successor, Ford named NBC News correspondent Ron Nessen, the first press secretary to come from the world of television news. "I'm a Ron, but not a Ziegler," Nessen reintroduced himself to the press corps, vowing, "I will never knowingly lie." Soon he was accusing reporters of "cynicism and mistrust," and reacting to negative media reports on Ford as if they were "some kind of personal attack on him." Still grousing about terHorst's sudden departure, reporters began whispering among themselves: "Two Rons don't make a right."[8]

Nessen went on to oversee Ford's central role in one of the most inspiring, sustained photo opportunities ever: the 1976 bicentennial of American independence. Ford scored other PR successes as well: a multinational peace accord at Helsinki and the long-awaited, if chaotic, withdrawal of American troops from Vietnam. Ford also tried uniting long-estranged factions at home by later issuing conditional amnesty for Vietnam draft evaders. Meanwhile, his exceptionally popular wife, Betty, shared with the American people her courageous battles against breast cancer and alcohol dependence. In going public with her ailments, the First Lady ended long-standing taboos against public discussion of both types of health challenges. (Mrs. Ford later established a Palm Springs, California, addiction clinic bearing her name that became synonymous with the treatment of substance abuse.)

Her husband proved far less successful in sustaining public sympathy. In one of the administration's early PR missteps, Ford signaled his concern over runaway consumer prices with a marketing campaign called "Whip Inflation Now"—and for emphasis began sporting a WIN lapel button at public appearances. The hollow sloganeering reassured no one and made Ford appear slightly ridiculous. America's withdrawal from Vietnam may have occasioned a collective sigh of relief, but the endlessly re-televised scenes of panicked, pro-U.S. Vietnamese fleeing from Saigon pierced America's longtime reputation for loyalty to allies.

And then came Ford's literal fall from grace—or in his case, falls. Inexplicably, this physically fit president—who had once played football for the University of Michigan—began earning a reputation as a lummox. Ford commenced tripping and stumbling in public, highlighted by a June 1974 slip down the rain-soaked stairway leading from Air Force One to an airport tarmac in Austria. "There was no way," he admitted, "the press was not going to run that picture."[9] Not long thereafter, Ford stumbled again heading *up* the same staircase in Michigan. Although an accomplished skier, Ford also managed to tumble on the slopes at Vail, with TV newsmen recording the "wipeout." Once, he nearly suffered decapitation there when a passing ski lift struck him in the head. Long a decent golfer, Ford now began hooking and slicing errant shots into crowds of spectators as if he were aiming at them. In June 1974, he conked a teenager on the head so seriously in Minneapolis that medics rushed the victim to an emergency room. All these mishaps played out as cameras rolled and reporters took notes.[10]

Ford's reputation for epic clumsiness grew so pervasive that the new NBC satire series *Saturday Night Live*, launched in October 1975, cast one of its principal stars to portray the accident-prone Ford on a regular basis. Week after week, a stone-faced Chevy Chase lurched toward the stage floor, or down staircases, in wildly exaggerated pratfalls seemingly triggered by nothing but his character's tangled feet and impaired balance. To demonstrate its sportsmanlike acceptance of the joke, the White House allowed Ron Nessen to serve as guest host on *SNL*, the first—and thus far, the last—time a presidential press secretary appeared on the now-long-running show. Ford himself popped up on tape to introduce the April 17, 1976, episode by intoning the now-familiar catchphrase: "Live from New York, it's *Saturday Night*!"

Whether Ford's good-natured acceptance of his new image as "Klutz in Chief" humanized him or reduced his stature beyond repair remains open to debate.[11] "At the time," Ford later rationalized the situation, "the media and general public still resented any hint of 'imperial' trappings in connection with the presidency." Ford wanted to believe that the "portrayal of me as an oafish ex-jock made for good copy," which might ultimately enhance his reputation. As he put it: "It wouldn't surprise me if there was a measurable correlation between humor in an administration and the popularity of that administration's policies." Besides, he continued to maintain: "I believe it is always better to err on the side of more exposure and access rather than less."[12]

The jovial laughter never quite compensated for the ill will Ford had engendered when he made the difficult decision to pardon Nixon. Moreover, as historian Kathryn Cramer Brownell astutely noted on the fortieth anniversary of Ford's historic *SNL* appearance, his efforts to "humanize" his presidency by volunteering himself as the butt of ridicule made him "more relatable" at the cost of making future presidents less accessible to the professional press. Having "struggled to navigate a shifting media landscape," Brownell argued, Ford "reluctantly turned to entertainment television as a last resort."[13]

Indeed, presidents after Ford turned increasingly to entertainment venues rather than appearing before large crowds or exposing themselves to regular scrutiny by journalists. Of course, this latest transformation was not attributable only to Ford's sense of fun and emotional security but to the increased cultural dominance of television itself. Brownell made a valid point about the growing trend toward hiding in plain sight on TV; but compared with all that followed in Ford's wake—presidential appearances on late-night and afternoon talk shows, not to mention the subsequent rise of both a former movie actor and a reality-TV star to the presidency itself—Ford's brief, isolated guest shot on *Saturday Night Live* today seems quaintly inconsequential.

Besides, Ford had more than earned comic relief on his own terms. Not everything about his accidental, and accident-prone, presidency ranked as amusing—including the life-threatening struggles of his wife. Within a span of only seventeen days in September 1975, two different women, Manson "family" admirer Lynette "Squeaky" Fromme and Sarah Jane Moore, a volunteer for a charity called People in Need, each attempted unsuccessfully to assassinate the president. Fromme, whose handgun misfired, would serve thirty-four years in prison, and Moore, who got off several shots at Ford but missed, thirty-two. It is no wonder Ford submitted himself to softer coverage when possible. When the White House pool reopened after a renovation, Ford staged the ultimate he-man photo op, christening the space by gracefully diving in (unlike LBJ, wearing bathing trunks), swimming a few laps, and emerging without a single pratfall. "It was . . . silly," Ford admitted, "and I knew it. . . . Still, there was a good reason to go along with it. As in so many other instances, in allowing the coverage, we created a bond between the people in front of and the people behind the camera. Somewhere down the line, you figure, those photographers will have the option of whether or not to take a less than flattering picture of you. . . . I would like to believe (though I can't prove it) that if they don't regard you as a pretentious president in a pretentious White House, they might choose to give you a break."[14]

Like Lyndon Johnson before him, Ford ultimately decided to run for president in his own right. But in his 1976 race against born-again reformer Jimmy Carter, he found it difficult to escape the stigma of the Nixon pardon or his own growing reputation for epic obtuseness. During an October 6 televised campaign debate against Carter, Ford replied to a question by *New York Times* associate editor Max Frankel by denying the obvious reality of Soviet influence in Eastern Europe. "I don't believe that the Rumanians consider themselves dominated by the Soviet Union," Ford maintained. "I don't believe that the Poles consider themselves dominated by the Soviet Union. Each of those countries is independent, autonomous. . . . And the United States does not concede that those countries are under the domination of the Soviet Union."[15]

"I immediately recognized Ford's reply as a terribly mangled version of the rehearsed reply he must have been given by [former Secretary of State Henry] Kissinger," Frankel told me forty-three years after the event. True to *New York Times* tradition—"we do not play 'gotcha,'" Frankel emphasized—he lobbed Ford a soft follow-up to give him "a chance to explain." To his "amazement," the president "dug in deeper in his clumsy way." Offered a chance at rebuttal, Carter pounced: "I would like to see Mr. Ford convince the Polish-Americans and the

Czech-Americans and the Hungarian-Americans in this country that those countries don't live under the domination and supervision of the Soviet Union behind the Iron Curtain." The Ford White House did not generate a clarification until the next day. As Frankel put it: "Too late."[16] In Helen Thomas's understated view, Ford's gaffe caused his campaign "a bad setback."[17]

By the end of the race, however, Ford nearly made up the thirty-point gap by which polls showed him trailing Carter at the outset. The Republican's late surge owed much to the fact that reports of sexual indiscretion still scandalized voters more than flagrant ignorance on foreign policy—even when the indiscretion turned out to be a product of the imagination. Thus the morally pure Georgia Sunday-school teacher suffered almost fatal political damage when a *Playboy* interview released in October revealed that he had "looked on a lot of women with lust" and "committed adultery in my heart many times."[18] If nothing else, the resulting brouhaha served as a caution that politicians exposed themselves not only to great opportunity but also grave danger by expressing themselves to nontraditional media.

In the end, Ford fell short on November 2 by 3 percent, 1.6 million votes out of 80 million cast. Evidently voters agreed in the end with correspondent Sarah McClendon's description of Ford as "a nice, clean-cut, friendly man—the perfect next-door neighbor—but not the leader our country needed."[19] Of more lasting significance, as the *New York Times* commented editorially, "the legitimate boundaries of [politicians'] private lives and intimate feelings" had now been permanently breached.[20]

In the end, Ford may not have dazzled the journalists who covered him, but as Howard K. Smith would later put it, he did provide the nation precisely "what was so badly needed at that moment": an awakening from a national nightmare.[21] Jimmy Carter would graciously acknowledge this at his swearing-in, commencing his inaugural address with a unifying gesture of his own: "For myself and for our nation," he said on January 20, 1977, "I want to thank my predecessor for all he has done to heal our land."[22]

JIMMY CARTER

James Earl Carter Jr. did not much like the press, and the feeling was largely mutual. Running against Gerald Ford in 1976, Carter found the alleged disparity in coverage between the incumbent and the challenger—himself—"absolutely shocking." He would not risk further alienation by suggesting outright that the press treated him unfairly, but he came close. Seeing "President Ford impervious to . . . cross-examination and scrutiny and intense personal criticism," he complained, "made me look very bad in contrast to him on the evening news."[23]

The notorious *Playboy* interview, best remembered for Carter's confessions about mental lust, contained a quickly forgotten observation about journalism that deserves the attention it has seldom received. It revealed Carter's disdain for the press before he even entered the White House. "[T]he national news media have absolutely . . . zero interest in any issues unless it's a matter of making a mistake," he commented. "What they're looking for is a 47 second argument between me and another candidate or something like that."[24] One of Carter's great failures was his stubborn reluctance to share with the press an issues-driven vision beyond his promise to bring honesty to government. But he was absolutely right that reporters long seemed to be lying in wait for his improbable, dark-horse candidacy to implode—or doing what they could to light the fuse.

Carter's subsequent press honeymoon nonetheless endured a bit longer than had Ford's. Just eight weeks after his inauguration, the new president sat down with Walter Cronkite for an unusual, Oval Office CBS radio call-in show, fielding forty-two unfiltered calls from twenty-six states. Cronkite later commented favorably, "No matter how far out the question, he had in his head a textbook of information about it." But the show earned no accolades from among Cronkite's jealous colleagues. One of them, Sander Vanocur, went so far as to charge in the *Washington Post* that the CBS anchor had played an obsequious "Mr. Interlocutor to President Carter's Mr. Bones."[25]

"When Carter was elected president," his "outspoken" press admirer Sarah McClendon insisted, "he started working like a prairie fire." Describing the new president's early press relations as "excellent," McClendon noted appreciatively that, unlike his immediate predecessors, Carter liberated White House staff to respond to press inquiries without preclearance and did "a great job" providing "well rounded and specific" answers at his own press conferences.[26] Such praise from the crusty journalist might have been written off as enthusiasm for a fellow Southerner, but she had shown little affection for Lyndon Johnson, like McClendon a Texan. "I want to be close to you," Carter told reporters after he took office.[27] Most wanted to believe him.

Thirty-five-year-old Jody Powell, a longtime, vital part of Carter's support staff from Georgia, became White House press secretary, and for a time boasted a level of presidential access unseen since the days of Jim Hagerty under Eisenhower. One day, the dogged Sam Donaldson of ABC-TV News walked into the press secretary's office to ask what the president intended to do on a particular issue. "I don't know," Powell admitted frankly. "Just a minute, I'll ask him." Powell rose, strolled toward the nearby Oval Office, and, after just a few minutes, returned and gave Donaldson the information he had requested. "Now, that's service," the usually pugnacious broadcaster commented. *Newsweek* Washington correspondent Thomas DeFrank called Powell "the most promising presidential spokesman in years," likening him to a "Southern breeze" that swept away "the bitterness and distrust in the Ziegler-Nessen press operations."[28]

Popular as he was at first with the press corps, when Powell's own grace period inevitably ended, no one doubted where his principal loyalty lay. When the *New York Times* quoted unnamed Carter aides as worrying that the president was becoming a "recluse," a rampaging Powell, determined to plug leaks, subjected a number of White House staffers to an investigation.[29] In his formal relations with the press—standing at the press room rostrum to field questions at the mini-press conferences known as daily briefings—Carter's spokesman "could dodge and weave with the best of them," Donaldson recalled. On one occasion, a reporter asked Powell if Carter had spent a recent meeting with a Southern senator brokering judicial appointments in the old-school manner. No, Powell insisted, the subject had never come up during their get-together. Then Powell posed a question to the inquisitive reporter: what was the senator's own recollection? It turned out the senator denied that any meeting had taken place, so the press secretary did a brazen pirouette. "That," said Powell without embarrassment, "was, upon reflection, the president's recollection also."[30]

For Powell, as even the persistent Donaldson acknowledged, there was "no requirement that a press secretary volunteer information out of the blue." As the veteran TV journalist put it: "Ask Powell . . . or any other press secretary the question 'What's new today?' and he is under no obligation to tell you, even though there may be fifty things new. Ask him a specific question about a specific subject, and the transaction gets more complicated."[31] NBC-TV White House correspondent Judy Woodruff complained in 1979, "As a reporter I never feel that we are being told enough about what the President is doing."[32] Years later, Powell frankly admitted that the Carter team had cut back on press conferences because "they weren't helping us." For his own part, Carter later insisted he "looked forward to press conferences," yearned to do more, and blamed their reduction on "Jody's natural inclination . . . to procrastinate."[33]

Donaldson and Powell engaged in a number of "knock-down drag-out fights" during the Carter years. Once, the broadcaster confessed, he provoked an infuriated Powell into hurling a glass of wine at him aboard Air Force One. Donaldson, who believed that what happened on the president's plane should stay on the plane, recalled only that he was "glad" that Powell "didn't have a full bottle handy."[34] Powell told Donaldson, "You know, it's not the fact that you trash us so much that I mind. What I mind is you seem to get such a kick out of it."[35]

Aside from its efforts to manage the press, the Carter communications operation (soon overseen by yet another Georgian, Gerald Rafshoon) worked to build on the president's fresh, folksy appeal. On February 2, 1977, just two weeks after his inauguration, Carter delivered an FDR-style televised fireside chat on the energy crisis. When the event began, viewers saw Carter sitting before a lit fireplace in his West Wing study dressed in an unbuttoned cardigan sweater. While his attire was clearly intended to hint that Americans ought to be turning down their thermostats, lighting their own hearths, and wearing additional layers of clothing, the overall effect made the president look more like Mister Rogers than Mr. Roosevelt.[36] A 2009 blog issued by the usually benign *Encyclopedia Britannica* not only called the speech an example of "How Carter Lectured, Not Led," but ranked it number eight among the all-time, top ten mistakes ever made by U.S. presidents—even though public opinion polls initially ranked the stunt a success.[37]

Soon, the down-home Carter made even the unprepossessing Ford look like a potentate. Acting as he had campaigned—as a virtuous "outsider"—the new president proceeded to do away with the traditional playing of "Hail to the Chief," carried his own suitcase in public, sold off the presidential yacht, and banned hard liquor from White House receptions. Not all his press observers expressed approval. "He wanted to deimperialize the presidency," Helen Thomas acknowledged, but "in doing so stripped the office of some of the qualities that give it that sense of awe so many of us are still moved by." To Thomas, Carter remained uncertain, "a man in search of an image."[38]

Washington's leading hostess, publisher Katharine Graham, tried to break the ice by inviting Jody Powell and chief of staff Hamilton Jordan to a reception honoring the American Society of Newspaper Editors. Jordan sent his regrets, but Powell, who should have seized the opportunity, never even responded, and when Graham called his office to tell him how helpful (to him) she thought his appearance might be, the press secretary refused to take her call—and never returned it. Years later, when Jordan finally joined one of Graham's celebrated dinners, she raised a glass to him with the amusing toast, "Hamilton, welcome to the establishment." Jordan responded by conceding that had he joined earlier, "Jimmy Carter might still be in the White House." A gracious Graham remembered: "I don't know that that's true but I do believe that the Carter administration missed some good opportunities."[39] From his perspective, a resentful Carter reckoned that after but nine months in office, his entire Georgia staff "delegation" had been "seriously roughed up by the news media," Graham's empire included. Within three years, he would conclude: "At one time or another everyone who is close to me has been worked over by the press in an extremely frivolous way."[40] But the president would not play the Washington insiders' game: taking negative stories on the chin and waiting until the proverbial next time.

The more embittered side of Carter's nature became evident when he was under pressure. His toothy smile failed to conceal a glum and occasionally hostile approach. When Judy Woodruff asked him to justify federal rules that made it difficult for poor women to afford abortions, Carter coldly replied, "There are many things in life that are not fair, that wealthy people can afford and poor people can't." On another occasion, after concluding a televised address on diplomatic relations with China, Carter griped into what he believed to be a dead microphone, "That sound you hear is the applause of a grateful nation."[41] Under Carter, the line between sanctimony and cynicism blurred.

The foreign policy highlight of Carter's presidency was unquestionably the September 1978 peace pact hammered out at Camp David during thirteen days of American-brokered negotiations between Menachem Begin of Israel and Anwar el-Sadat of Egypt. The accord earned the two Middle Eastern leaders the Nobel Peace Prize and won significant acclaim for Carter's patient diplomacy. Few members of the public knew that Carter had kept American reporters far from the actual talks or that, as Helen Thomas sourly noted that "the Israeli press were getting better and more accurate information than [Jody] Powell was passing on to us"—no one, that is, except correspondents like Thomas famous for their long memories and longer knives.[42]

Carter, whose failures came to outpace his triumphs, soon gave press critics ample fodder for filleting. An assortment of financial scandals—involving his budget director Bert Lance, his troublesome brother Billy (who got cozy with the Libyans), and the alleged mismanagement of his family peanut business in

Georgia—amounted to little of legal consequence but did injury to the president's squeaky-clean image.[43] The *Atlanta Constitution* said of Billy Carter, "If he's not working for the Republican Party, he should be."[44] The worsening economy proved more threatening than the president's alcohol-impaired sibling. As the energy crisis worsened, lines grew longer at the nation's fuel pumps. As interest rates soared, home buyers found it increasingly difficult to afford mortgages. Unable to improve either situation, the president took the heat.

The year after the Camp David deal, a seemingly trivial event unleashed the most lethal of all public relations consequences on Carter: mockery. On April 20, 1979, during an otherwise uneventful Georgia vacation, he took a canoe onto a tranquil pond near his Plains hometown to do some solitary fishing. His idyll ended when a so-called swamp rabbit being pursued by hounds on shore "jumped in the water," Carter recalled, "and swam toward my boat," hissing and baring its teeth. In response, the president did no more than shoo the creature away by using his paddle to splash it with water. The rabbit never posed a real danger—its species are herbivores—and apparently the president had difficulty back in Washington merely convincing his staff that the bizarre incident had actually occurred. To prove a point he would have been wiser to drop, he actually ordered the White House photographer who had been shadowing him that day to process what turned out to be an inconclusive snapshot. All it showed was a creature paddling through the water and Carter, his back to the camera, raising his oar as if to defend himself.

The evidence was enough to make a believer of Jody Powell, who concluded that the tale revealed the president as a man of courage. So he leaked it to Associated Press reporter Brooks Jackson "over tea," he later claimed, but according to Carter, "in a bar after a lot of drinking had gone on."[45] Jackson's wire story, issued four months after the actual incident, and only then because there was so little else to write about at the end of summer, landed on the front page of the *Washington Post* under the headline "Bunny Goes Bugs: Rabbit Attacks the President." The report, also published in the *New York Times*, described the animal as a "killer rabbit" and quoted unnamed "White House staff members" who boasted that "the President beat back the animal with a canoe paddle."[46] Carter "was not injured," the story made clear.

Prolonged nationwide media ridicule followed in print and on air, in both words and pictures. Columnist Robert Novak claimed the incident had provoked the invasion of Afghanistan. Mary McGrory joked that the president's use of a paddle was "a clear example of excessive force." And the *New Republic* hinted that Carter's attempt to pummel the rabbit was "an indication of what he would do to Israel if he was elected to a second term." To Jody Powell, it was all "a nightmare." He even faced a Freedom of Information suit to compel release of the White House photo showing Carter brandishing his paddle.[47]

From the time of Andrew Jackson onward, newspaper cartoons had illustrated, prolonged, and often magnified presidential vulnerabilities. Caricature was an old-fashioned genre, to be sure, but it had long been capable of doing significant damage: lampooning Jackson as a violent brawler, Lincoln as a satanic despot, TR as a bully, Wilson as a foggy professor, and LBJ as a boor displaying a surgical scar resembling an outline map of Vietnam. Now the *Washington Post* capped the Carter feeding frenzy with a devastating takeoff on the iconic movie poster for the 1975 film *Jaws*, which portrayed a shark rising menacingly toward the water's surface. The 1979 parody replaced the sea monster with a rabbit and bore the title *Paws*.

Unfathomably deaf to the cascading injury to his reputation, Carter continued to provide new ammunition to the press critics he now blamed for misinterpreting his adventure. At a White House Labor Day picnic, he told a group of union leaders: "I believe in killer rabbits—and killer reporters. But a killer rabbit has never come after me and a killer reporter has." This comment ended up in the *Washington Post*, too, giving the swamp bunny story new life. The bizarre episode would remain a permanent staple of Carter biography throughout his long life.[48] His pollster and counselor Pat Caddell had always advised his boss that style mattered more than substance, and in the case of the killer rabbit versus the president, he proved right. To his credit, Jody Powell took full "blame for the consequences" and admitted that he bore "the burden of guilt and self-recrimination" for years. Yet in his 1984 memoir, he could not restrain himself from adding his opinion that by the time of the swamp rabbit encounter, "if the President had been set upon by a pack of wild dogs, a good portion of the press would have sided with the dogs and declared that he had provoked the attack."[49]

Between the actual incident and its later revelation, Carter ponderously called a multiday "domestic summit" at Camp David to explore—with an eye toward curing—what Caddell had termed the "national malaise."[50] Those long lines at filling stations had driven the president's approval ratings down to record lows. Counterintuitively, Carter canceled a planned energy speech to focus on what Caddell convinced him was a much larger concern: an overall coast-to-coast crisis in confidence. One wag told Howard K. Smith that America had found itself "between a marshmallow and a hard place."[51] But Caddell convinced the president to seize on the stagnant mood to produce a modern "ask what you can do for your country" rallying cry.

On July 15, after days of consultation with an assortment of voices at Camp David (including, curiously, Haynes Johnson, a reporter for a paper the administration disliked: the *Washington Post*), Carter came down from the mountain and delivered a televised address from the Oval Office. The speech called for renewed commitment to the American can-do spirit. Not once did the president use the word "malaise"—by which, to Carter's detriment, the speech nevertheless became instantly and perennially known.

Initial polls showed a dramatic spike in Carter's approval. But then the president followed up by demanding the resignations of all his cabinet members, then accepting only five and expressing confidence in the others. The move, meant to demonstrate the president's control over the government, instead flattened Carter's approval bump, erasing the public relations advantage he had produced with his address. As an incredulous *Time* magazine reporter put it, "The President basked in the applause for a day and then . . . set in motion his astounding purge, undoing much of the good he had done himself." An administration source told the *New York Times* that the unforced error represented Carter's "Armageddon."[52] The setback may also have hastened the rise of the conservative movement, emboldened by liberal government's evident inability to come to grips with economic and confidence crises alike. Once again, Carter and the country fell into the doldrums. And the worst was yet to come.

In November 1979, with just a year remaining before the next presidential election, a gang of radical Iranian students seized American hostages in Tehran, beginning an ordeal destined to last an agonizing 444 days. Amid the turmoil, Iran's pro-American shah fled his country, abandoning control to religious extremists. Iran soon released several of the captives—a woman, two African Americans, and a hostage who fell ill—but dragged several others before TV cameras to denounce the United States in an obviously staged and deeply humiliating press conference. At first, the kidnapping united Americans in anger. But as the situation dragged on without resolution into 1980, the stalemate aroused growing frustration. Surely, critics complained, the most powerful nation in the world should be able to recover the hostages by negotiation or, if required, other means. Then on April 24, 1980, eight American military helicopters dramatically landed in Iran on a bold mission to liberate the prisoners by force. There, most of the choppers became disabled while another crashed, killing several crew members. The military aborted what seemed like a Keystone Kop rescue attempt, and the standoff went on.

Once again, the Carter administration faced criticism for timidity and ineffectuality. Already battered by a challenge from a fellow Democrat, Senator Ted Kennedy, Carter barely secured renomination that summer, and endured further humiliation when Kennedy refused to shake his hand at the televised national convention. Awaiting the president was a formidable Republican challenger: Ronald Reagan.

At their presidential debate on October 28, Reagan effortlessly deflected Carter's barrage of charges with a casual, now-famous rebuff: "There you go again." The former California governor capped his relaxed performance by facing the cameras and asking viewers: "Are you better off than you were four years ago?" Carter did score points on specifics, but then diminished himself by solemnly reporting, in response to a question from moderator Howard K. Smith, that his thirteen-year-old daughter, Amy, believed that "the control of nuclear arms" (which Carter pronounced "*nook*-you-lar") was "the most important issue" of the campaign.[53] That November, Carter became the first elected president to lose reelection since Hoover had fallen to Roosevelt half a century earlier. Reagan clobbered Carter by ten points—more than 8 million popular votes—and swept the electoral college by a lopsided count of 489–49.[54]

Carter had unseated Gerald Ford in 1976 by promising to cleanse the federal government. Arguing that liberal Washington spending had done little to solve new problems since, Reagan defeated Carter four years later by vowing to reduce it vastly in size and scope. Whether the result represented a rejection of Carter, an embrace of the telegenic Reagan, the first skirmish of the culture wars (Reagan had won the endorsement of Jerry Falwell's Moral Majority), or a genuine conservative revolution, no one could yet be sure. While Carter used his final months in office to negotiate the return of American hostages from Iran, the always lucky Reagan earned the public relations credit for their freedom when Tehran thrust a final thumb in Carter's eye and released the captives during the new president's inauguration.

One journalist who had anticipated a Reagan landslide, *Time* magazine correspondent Laurence I. Barrett, always believed that "if Carter had somehow managed to spring the hostages in Iran before election day . . . he would have been reelected. The real question about the '80 election, I think, is when did it become clear that Reagan was plausible?"[55] In fact, public acceptance came much sooner than Carter's supposedly poll-sensitive staff believed. *Harper's* magazine may have mocked Reagan as "The Candidate from Disneyland"; the respected journalist Elizabeth Drew may have wondered, "What is he doing with these public relations people as key advisors?" But such warnings failed to alarm voters.[56] Democrats and journalists alike may have begun the race convinced that a second-rate movie star could never unseat a seasoned politician. But when the credits rolled, it was Reagan in the lead.

Jody Powell left the White House convinced that "the relationship between press and President" remained "basically flawed." The problems were not "primarily the product of malice or bias on the part of reporters, although there is some of that," he argued, "nor are they chiefly caused by dishonesty and deceit in the White House, although that also crops up now and then" (in his memoir, Powell solemnly argued for the "right to lie"). To Powell, the perpetual standoff was attributable not to conflict but to a similarity. Both institutions, he argued, remained slaves to "artificial deadlines." Each made decisions "based upon . . . sometimes woefully inadequate information." And presidents and the press, Powell argued, were "influenced by forces which neither is willing to fully acknowledge: money and profit in the case of the fourth estate, politics in the case of the White House."[57]

Powell had a solution in mind, but predictably aimed it only at journalists. What the media needed, he suggested, was a more adversarial relationship not with the presidents they covered but among themselves: the correspondents who battled each other for scoops. Powell could not have known it yet, but that is exactly what would soon transpire with the advent of cable television and deregulated radio.[58] Jimmy Carter's press secretary, who died in 2009, would at least live to see his ideas flower. Whether or not the innovations succeeded in improving press coverage of the White House remains open to debate.

Two years after he lost his bid for a second term, Carter had become somewhat more wistful about his stormy days with the press. "There was a strong adversarial relationship that's probably inherent," he conceded, "which, if I were God, I don't think I would want to change particularly, but which was unpleasant. I think since Kennedy, there probably hasn't been any President who's had a good relationship with the press. I mean a constructive relationship with the press. I think this includes Johnson . . . Nixon, and even Ford," Carter noted of his former opponent, "who was stigmatized by the press as a fumbling incompetent, whereas he's probably the best athlete that ever lived in the White House and think he was in the top third of his law class at Yale [in fact he was in the top 25 percent]. . . . I think it was an attitude of the press, maybe in the wake of Watergate . . . and because I was an alien in Washington it was inevitable."[59]

But Carter still believed the media had helped propel his downfall. "[T]he greatest disappointments of mine in Washington," he asserted, "were lethargy, inertia of the Congress, and irresponsibility of the press." Above all, the ex-president still resented the accusations of financial impropriety the media had repeated about his family: "[N]ever did a reporter come to me and say, 'Mr. President, is this true? Did you cheat or use this money illegally?' There was nobody on the *Washington Post* or *New York Times* who tried to investigate the allegations and discern if they were true . . . no element in the press inclined to prove the facts."

The breakdown in relations between the president and the press Carter called "a very serious problem." But "how to address it," he admitted, "I do not know."

Reporters did not know it at the time, but Ronald Reagan's supremely confident 1980 debate performance against Jimmy Carter owed at least something to an unfair and, at the time, undisclosed advantage: his staff had gained advance knowledge of Carter's strategy for the confrontation. As *Time* magazine's Laurence Barrett ultimately revealed two years later, a Reagan mole in the Carter White House had spirited a copy of the president's briefing book to the Republicans before the televised event.

As it turned out, every issue Carter raised in the debate, save for his daughter's passion for nuclear disarmament, had been detailed in the purloined material. Reagan entered the arena that night extremely well prepared.[60] Barrett had first tried reporting the dirty trick in 1980, but his *Time* editors had cut the mention from his final article. Only when Barrett's 1982 Reagan biography appeared did the story finally come to light.

At first, its belated revelation aroused no more than a smattering of local press coverage; only later did journalists label the incident "Debategate" and begin digging into the source of the theft. Blame fell on an assortment of alleged culprits, including Reagan's White House chief of staff James Baker and his CIA director William Casey, who soon engaged in a public battle of denial and accusation, essentially blaming each other. Suspicion also dogged a prominent member of the press: the influential conservative *Washington Post* columnist George Will.[61] By 1983, *Newsweek* further reported that the pro-Reagan White

House source had also stolen "a trove of briefing papers, policy memos, and government reports," adding to speculation that "the Carter White House had been leaking like a sieve."[62]

More than twenty years afterward, Carter himself revived the still-unsolved mystery, accusing Will anew of accepting delivery of the briefing material. While the journalist unapologetically admitted that he had enjoyed access to it, he went on the attack, condemning the former president as a "recidivist fibber" and, in a withering letter to Carter, added of the book itself: "My cursory glance at it convinced me that it was a crashing bore and next to useless—for you, or for anyone else." Carter ultimately walked back his accusation, telling the *Washington Post*: "I never thought Mr. Will took my book" or "that the outcome of the debate was damaging to my campaign."[63] In that last assertion he was certainly wrong. Reagan may have been heading toward victory by the time of the 1980 debate, but the encounter with the well-prepared Reagan sealed Carter's doom and may have turned a relatively close election into a wipeout.

Only later did George Will further reveal that he had personally helped coach Reagan during his 1980 debate prep, and had indeed been armed with the "excruciatingly boring" book that had been pilfered from the Carter camp. The columnist likened his participation in the coaching session merely to that of "a sportswriter . . . being invited into the locker room." But his colleagues would not buy the explanation, hinting at a conflict of interest: Washington-based columnists Jack Germond and Jules Witcover condemned Will for blatantly—and covertly—violating journalistic ethics. The irrepressible New Yorker Jimmy Breslin had another word for it: Will had become "a shill."[64]

The mystery of Debategate has never been solved. Nor has the matter of whether Reagan's advisors made the candidate aware at the time that they had obtained stolen information. At the very least, his team, George Will included, knew precisely how to rehearse Reagan for that decisive encounter. Of far more consequence, as historian Douglas Brinkley later discovered, Republicans fearful of an October surprise from Carter had done far worse: they had likely approached Palestinian leader Yasser Arafat that fall with an offer of future arms sales providing he could persuade his Iranian allies to keep American hostages imprisoned until after the election. American voters learned nothing of this matter either.

It would not be the last time Reagan's telegenic affability proved more crucial to his political success than his administration's controversial policies and bare-knuckle tactics.[65]

14

RONALD REAGAN AND GEORGE H. W. BUSH

Where's the rest of me?" Ronald Reagan asked in the title to his prepresidential autobiography—borrowing the most famous line of dialogue he had ever uttered in motion pictures.[1] The memoir appeared in 1965, a year before the onetime actor ran for the first of his two terms as governor of California. But the words on the dust jacket were no doubt meant to suggest an even grander political future—an unlikely second career yet unfinished.

For the dozens of journalists who went on to cover Reagan in Sacramento and, later, in Washington, the phrase would also come to summarize the nagging riddle they never got close enough to the man to solve: Was the Ronald Reagan who dominated television news for the next two decades authentic or contrived? Was what we saw all there was—or was something withheld, or simply lacking? Where, reporters long wondered but never quite discovered, was the rest of him?

Ronald Reagan proved a transformational communicator without really trying—or at least, without giving the appearance of trying. Seeming indifference may have been his one personal flaw. Or was it his greatest asset?

A onetime radio sports announcer, the Illinois-born Reagan had gone on to achieve celebrity without true stardom in a Hollywood career spanning sixty-nine films over twenty-five years.[2] Beginning as a juvenile lead and supporting player, he had peaked with a fine performance as an amputee in 1940's *King's Row* (from which came "Where's the rest of me?"). But after the war, Reagan fell into routine, increasingly embarrassing parts: a psychologist babysitting a chimp in 1951's *Bedtime for Bonzo* and a dour submarine commander in 1957's *Hellcats of the Navy*—which at least gave him the chance to play opposite his adoring second wife and future White House costar, the actress then known as Nancy Davis.

Slipping further, Reagan made his last film appearance fourth-billed as a gangster in *The Killers*, a 1964 film noir loosely based on a Hemingway story that required him (to his eternal regret) to slap costar Angie Dickinson hard in the face.[3] The scene is particularly jarring today because the character who does the slapping is not the callow Reagan who rode alongside Errol Flynn in *Santa Fe Trail* but a fifty-three-year-old who looks remarkably like the gentle individual who ran for the White House sixteen years later. The uncharacteristic burst of anger could only have been more discordant had Reagan mauled his beloved Nancy.

From 1964 on, the onetime Screen Actors Guild president focused his principal attention on politics.[4] In the preceding years, he had unapologetically morphed from "a near-hopeless hemophiliac liberal" who "bled for causes," as he put it, into a firmly conservative Republican proud that his heart bled no longer.[5] Journalists never accused Reagan of "flip-flopping"—a term introduced decades later—and the veteran performer was glib enough to make a humorous virtue of his philosophical transformation. Professionally, in a remarkably brief span of time, he went from host of television's *GE Theater* and *Death Valley Days* to governor of California (1967–75) to president of the United States—the oldest man elected to the office since William Henry Harrison, who had died within a month of his inauguration 140 years earlier.

The "Great Communicator," as he came to be known, found himself in precisely the right place at exactly the right time to ride the crest of a media revolution—and cultural counterrevolution—in which a show business background not only failed to disqualify candidates for high office but actually helped them. As "hugely successful" in politics "as he had been a loser in pictures," declared the acerbic and perceptive film historian David Thomson, Reagan the president proceeded to "amass more camera time than anyone else in the Actors' Guild" while "America made a gentle transition—from nation to show—that disturbed no one's fun."[6]

The media transfiguration that accompanied Reagan's rise included the growth of C-SPAN, the cable news network founded by Brian Lamb in 1979 and destined soon to reach twenty million policy wonks, including, to the surprise of many who thought he had no interest in minutiae, Reagan himself. With the District of Columbia not yet wired for cable, C-SPAN found its way onto White House television sets when a George Mason University–based broadcaster aimed a microwave-dish transmitter at downtown Washington. Long before Donald Trump began his workdays by watching, and reacting to, morning news and talk shows on the Fox network, Reagan retreated periodically to the White House residence to watch C-SPAN. Those vying for the president's attention soon caught on to his viewing habits. As the "Funding Father of the Conservative Movement," Richard Viguerie, described matters, legislators who encountered difficulty gaining direct access to the president found that the best way to get his attention on policy initiatives was to appear on C-SPAN's gavel-to-gavel coverage of congressional debates, which he was likely to watch.[7]

In time, Reagan's alleged C-SPAN fandom grew into something more complex and less casual. Georgia congressman (and future House Speaker) Newt Gingrich remembered "routinely" visiting Reagan speechwriter Terry Dolan in the White House "to discuss strategies and language" for future policy proposals. Gingrich would then "take the ideas back to the Hill and we would originate 'special orders' and 'one minutes' around them." The tradition of "special orders" entitled any congressman to speak from the floor (and in front of the cameras feeding the proceedings to C-SPAN) following adjournment on official legislative business. "One minute" speeches of some three hundred words each—perfect for listeners with limited attention spans—could precede calls to order each morning. In both formats, members of Congress seized valuable television time to air their opinions.

As Gingrich described for me what happened next: Reagan would subsequently "make speeches on the topics" Republicans addressed each morning and evening. "We would then put Reagan's speeches in the Congressional Record." And then "we would do special orders talking about his speeches to give them additional impact"—generating three bites of the same publicity apple for each initiative. Whether or not Reagan personally viewed the televised special orders and one-minute orations from Capitol Hill cannot be determined with certainty. But Gingrich does remember one "vivid moment" that occurred after "I did a special order defending Nancy when she was under attack for using an astrologer. The next day I got a call from the president thanking me for standing up for his wife."[8]

Brian Lamb vividly remembers the day in February 1983 that Reagan attended—and C-SPAN telecast—a young people's press conference with the president live from the Executive Office Building. Reagan had wanted for months to revive this format, which had served him well in California, and Lamb had helped enlist the Close Up Foundation, specialists in organizing student tours of the capital, to bring a group of teenagers before the president. After the main event ended, Lamb hosted the kids for a post-press-conference phone-in Q&A, also carried live on the network. At one point he noticed on his prompter that an incoming call was waiting from Washington, D.C. Advised from off camera to put it through quickly—the network customarily gave preference to out-of-towners paying long-distance rates to hold on until they got their turn on-air—Lamb, the youngsters, and the C-SPAN audience heard a woman saying, "Will you hold on one moment please for the President?" Lamb maintained a tight smile on-air, but as he remembers, "I felt like I swallowed the coal mine and the canary and everything."[9]

A few seconds later the gentle, unmistakable voice sounded forth: "I just came up to the study here, turned on the set and there you were," Reagan began, validating the habitual C-SPAN surfing others had described. The president then launched into a long, detailed explanation of his position on the Exclusionary Rule barring tainted evidence from courtrooms. He had answered a question on the issue during the earlier press conference, but now wanted to expand and clarify. Yes, he wanted to preserve the rights of the accused, but he was also concerned about giving a free pass to criminals who were "as guilty as sin." Reagan sidetracked to instruct the class on the meaning of case law—precedents established by bench opinions rather than statute and regulation—and even alluded to the dangers of premarital sex. "Big time," one of the dazzled students can be heard commenting.

The growth of the low-key, nonpartisan C-SPAN was accompanied by the debut of rowdy television talk shows like *The McLaughlin Group* (1982), a kind of WrestleMania mosh pit for Washington journalists on which "TV talk became theater," political operative Richard Viguerie chortled, "and the decibel level went through the roof."[10] Just behind it came the explosion in cable news—and the all-news formats at CNN, MSNBC, and later, Fox, featuring disputatious talking heads regurgitating the day's stories. Journalists did not win starring roles on such shows by pulling their punches as they did in print. Fred Barnes, one of the longest-serving McLaughlin panelists, declared the new motto of Washington reporters to be "If you don't have anything nice to say, let's hear it."[11]

Reagan's own laid-back persona—whether reflective of self-assurance or bewilderment, no one ever really knew—was kept aloft by a brilliant White House communications team that focused on flag-bedecked photo opportunities and benign television appearances while limiting serious one-on-one and group encounters with journalists. Astute White House communications advisor David Gergen believed the passive-aggressive media strategy perfectly suited both Reagan and the institution of the presidency. No president, Gergen maintained, should "be out on the line every day, particularly on bad news. Eisenhower was the last President . . . to ride above the storm. They kept him out of harm's way. My theory on that is that you only have one four-star general in battle, but you've got a lot of lieutenants who can give blood. And if the going is getting hot and heavy, it is far better to have your lieutenants take the wounds than the general. Because once that happens to your President, it is very difficult to recover from it. One of the most destructive aspects of the Carter administration was that they continually let him go out there and be the point man, on everything! A lot of our strategy had to do with *not* having the President out answering questions every day."[12] In their version of the Hippocratic Oath for doctors, Reagan's communications team dedicated itself to doing no harm.

Together with White House deputy chief of staff Michael K. Deaver and Reagan's other public relations counselors, Gergen elevated Reagan's ceremonial appearances into an impeccably stage-managed art form. Reagan was often seen but seldom heard—except at well-choreographed public events where he hit his mark as effortlessly as he had on movie sets and dependably emphasized only what his staff called "the line of the day," deflecting any and all inquiries that compromised "the lead." At meticulously staged speaking engagements, he read flawlessly from a teleprompter or index cards.

It was not as if the president became invisible; indeed, he appeared almost constantly, but only in orchestrated settings and situations where the old actor could pose smilingly or deliver scripted lines without challenge. Deaver called it "manipulation by inundation."[13] Castigating the strategy as an exploitation of television's "insatiable appetite for visuals," Washington-based investigative reporter Mark Hertsgaard observed: "The networks wanted visuals of the President? Fine. But they would be visuals carefully designed to promote the Reagan agenda." With only a slight tweak on the outright media hostility that prevailed in the Nixon era, "the Reagan apparatus projected its messages to the American public not only by going over the top of the press but also by going right through it."[14] The administration embraced the age-old theory that any news was good news, especially if they had stage-managed it and illustrated it with visuals of the president. After airing a report criticizing the Reagan team's image-building efforts, CBS correspondent Leslie Stahl unexpectedly received a call from the White House thanking her for telecasting "four minutes of great photographs of Ronald Reagan."[15]

In another creative innovation, Reagan began broadcasting weekly Saturday-morning radio addresses, a practice that would endure for more than thirty years, giving presidents routine dominance of weekend news coverage when the rest of official Washington was taking a break. Not surprisingly, the veteran sportscaster commanded the medium with all the magical skill he had once brought to vividly re-creating baseball games from mere wire reports. Reagan did misstep once while warming up for one such Saturday broadcast from his vacation home in Santa Barbara on August 11, 1984. Unaware that he was speaking into an open microphone, Reagan tested his voice level by intoning: "My fellow Americans, I am pleased to announce that I have just signed legislation which outlaws Russia forever. The bombing begins in five minutes."[16] The flippant remarks were never carried over the airwaves, but reporters tuning in to the official feed from various outposts overheard them. Ignoring administration pleas to keep the comments off the record, the press widely reported them. The official Soviet news agency Tass condemned the comments as "simple-minded" and "irresponsible," but the White House never acknowledged, much less apologized for, the embarrassing lapse in judgment. It was just Reagan being Reagan.[17] Not only did the president dismiss the flap; on yet another occasion he reacted to the seizure of American hostages on a TWA airliner by remarking into another presumably cold mic: "After seeing *Rambo* last night [the Sylvester Stallone film series about a one-man vengeance machine], I know what to do the next time this happens." The White House finally ordered a big ON THE AIR warning sign to display in the studio for the president's benefit whenever the microphones were hot.[18]

The Reagan team cannily revived another PR initiative that dated back to the Kennedy and Nixon years: making the president available to groups of small-town editors and correspondents who invariably enjoyed the thrill of visiting the White House and reflected their awe in their reports back to the heartland. The events seldom stimulated headlines, but the idea was to generate warm feature stories, long-term gratitude—and, of course, pictures. Some years later, Reagan began hosting off-the-record cocktail hours for small groups of journalists. For the first time in memory, however, some correspondents refused to join in the social gatherings, arguing that they should be able to report what transpired. Reagan enjoyed cordial personal relationships with a handful of journalists—columnists George Will, Hugh Sidey, and James J. Kilpatrick, a onetime segregationist whose column "A Conservative View" appeared in more than 150 papers. For a time, Mrs. Reagan befriended NBC's Chris Wallace, presumably out of affection for his father, the legendary Mike Wallace; but she cut him off after he broadcast several negative stories about her husband.[19] Reagan, who had few close friends, made no special effort to widen his circle of journalistic intimates.

With the emphasis on marketing over press relations, Reagan's affable press secretary James Brady initially found himself out of the White House loop. David Gergen, who believed in theory that "the press secretary ought to have unquestioned access," later confessed that counselor Edwin Meese overruled him, insisting that "you tell the press secretary after the fact." Rumors flew that the First Lady thought the portly, balding Brady too unattractive to shine on televised daily press briefings ("I think he's divine," she insisted). Brady, armed with a self-deprecating sense of humor, gamely determined to "do his best" in the absence of face time with his boss while simultaneously battling for the right to attend important meetings, Moyers-like, at which policy decisions were made.[20] When doors finally began opening to him, Brady found he was neglecting his press-handling obligations. "I couldn't get the job of press secretary done," he joked, "because I was so busy having access."[21] Helen Thomas observed, "There was affection for Jim Brady I've never seen for a press secretary, ever."[22]

Brady may have represented a throwback to the back-slapping days of Pierre Salinger and George Reedy. But beneath the genial facade, the rest of the White House treated journalists according to the more contentious assumptions articulated by the president's strategist (and onetime gubernatorial press secretary) Lyn Nofziger. "The press does not allow it to be fun," he reminded White House colleagues. "They have become personally nasty, personally vindictive"[23]—and therefore, perennially under suspicion of antipathy to the Reagan Revolution. Brady's successor would describe the relationship bluntly as "Us Against Them" and likened the confrontation to a battle between "a handful of relatively underpaid but dedicated public servants" and the "Rich and Famous and Powerful" among the press corps.[24] After 1981, Michael Deaver even forbade reporters from pestering the president with queries while his picture was being taken. Frustrated, journalists took to shouting long-unanswered questions from behind rope lines as Reagan walked to or from his helicopter.

The president typically fended them off by cupping his ear with his hand or pointing to his wristwatch. The elaborate, silent-film-style pantomime meant to signal that he was too deaf to hear or too rushed to venture closer.

"Through all of this," remembered Helen Thomas, "we reporters marveled—and chafed—at the state-of-the-art management and manipulation of the news that the Reagan staffers brought with them." Mike Deaver, she recalled with some bitterness, "would decide what was the 'story of the day' or the 'picture of the day' and we were at his mercy." With an "audacity and arrogance" that was "something to behold," Reagan's "troika"—Deaver, James Baker, and Edwin Meese—"scripted their boss every day, every inch of the way. I always thought Reagan was more than adept at handling himself in any situation, including dealing with us, but we hardly ever got the chance to find out."[25] Thomas may have been right. A March 1981 television interview with Walter Cronkite (on the occasion of the anchorman's retirement from the *CBS Evening News*) showed Reagan fully at ease, effectively parrying with the veteran journalist on U.S. relations with Russia. Even if the interview amounted to foreign-policy-by-television, the broadcast not only showed the president in command of the facts but may well have shown the Soviets a path for improved dialogue.[26]

An argument can be offered that the once-vigilant press corps, now blocked from close scrutiny and perhaps exhausted after helping to unseat three consecutive presidents, relaxed their guard under Reagan and neglected to peer closely at an emperor who may not have been wearing clothes. Journalist Mark Hertsgaard embraced that theory, declaring that—with the exception of Sam Donaldson and columnist Richard Cohen (who attributed Reagan's success to a new "standard of just bare mediocrity")—the new "palace court press" was guilty of a "witless complicity in selling" Reagan's policies to the public.[27] If that is so, then the political opposition proved equally complacent and complicit. Reaganomics, which strove to undo government programs and regulations, effectively rolling back the New Deal and Great Society, attracted sufficient Democratic support in Congress to win more than one for "the Gipper"—including tax reductions and cutbacks to the social safety net.[28]

An equally strong case can be made that Ronald Reagan simply proved an irresistibly effective unifier whose messages of patriotism, resistance to Soviet authoritarianism, and an end to government interference in individuals' lives genuinely resonated with the public, politicians from both parties, and an overmatched press corps.[29] In other words, Reagan may have skirted close scrutiny, but perhaps deserved the free ride he built through geniality. "I would agree that Reagan has gotten the breaks in terms of press coverage," admitted *Newsweek* editor Maynard Parker at the time, "for the reason that most reporters covering him genuinely like the man and find it difficult to be as tough as they might like."[30]

Certainly Reagan's public brush with death made him almost impervious to press criticism. On March 30, 1981, just two months after the inauguration, a would-be-assassin named John W. Hinckley Jr. fired a barrage of bullets at the president as he left the Washington Hilton hotel and strolled toward his limousine on the street.[31] In the process, Hinckley—who fantasized that his attack would impress the object of his erotic obsessions, actress Jodie Foster—inflicted a crippling injury on Jim Brady. Reagan, sped to a nearby hospital, went into shock and nearly bled to death before doctors rushed him into life-saving emergency surgery.

The public soon learned, via the press, that Reagan had not only walked into the hospital on his own power (no stretcher had been available) but had uttered such witticisms as "Honey, I forgot to duck" (to wife Nancy) and, to his surgeons, "I hope you are all Republicans."[32] In the recovery room, his mouth covered by an oxygen mask, he had scribbled on a pad: "All in all, I would rather be in Philadelphia."[33] It hardly mattered that Reagan, ever the actor at his best reciting other people's lines, had cribbed the "duck" comment from boxer Jack Dempsey (uttered after a rare knockout) and the "Philadelphia" remark from comedian W. C. Fields (his supposed self-authored epitaph). Reagan's courage and memory for one-liners seemed undiminished.

Those brave wisecracks earned wide circulation, along with reports that Reagan had required little pain medication in the hospital and began recovering with miraculous speed. Such tales masked the truth about his considerable suffering, a touch-and-go postoperative infection, and a chaotic White House response to managing the government during the emergency.[34] Reagan did rebound quickly for a man his age, and, just a month after the shooting, journeyed to Capitol Hill to bask in a hero's welcome and deliver a rousing nationally televised address to Congress. The appearance gave his stalled, controversial economic agenda the personal boost it needed to pass. As David Gergen frankly told a journalist years later, the assassination attempt gave the administration "a second honeymoon."[35] Reagan's close call may not have increased his popularity, but it helped sustain it. Communications experts refer to such effects as "rallies." Typically, even in extreme situations, they prove short-lived. Within three months, Reagan's approval levels were back where they had been before

Hinckley fired his gun—but it was a level that most presidents would be grateful to achieve at the end of their first year in office.[36]

James Brady remained official press secretary but, paralyzed by the Hinckley shooting, never returned to his job. Lyn Nofziger handled briefings during Reagan's stay at the hospital, and Deaver provided "lighter touches" that demonstrated the president's bravery, resilience, and good cheer. Later, Deaver granted the AP and UPI the first post-recovery interviews with the president, at which Reagan memorably told Helen Thomas that "he felt the 'hand of God' was on his shoulder" that day "and that his mission in life was still to be accomplished." His list of priorities would still not include gun control, he stated for the record.[37]

Wheelchair-bound, Brady made an emotional return visit to the White House that November for the dedication of the newly renovated White House press headquarters, soon to be named in his honor. "As happy as we are about the reopening of the press room today," Reagan forced himself to say on that occasion, "we are even happier, more elated by the presence of a man . . . whose courage has been an inspiration to all of us." After Helen Thomas shouted out, "We miss you, Jim," Reagan kept the humor flowing. "You know, of course, that the floor of this press room is built over the old swimming pool," he remarked, "but it isn't true that that the floor has been hinged and will spring like a trap any time you ask the wrong question." Contradicted Brady on cue: "Yes, it is!"[38]

Brady was succeeded (in practice if not in title) by Larry Speakes, a onetime Mississippi newspaper editor and Senate public affairs specialist who boasted the perfect surname for a press spokesman. The following year, Speakes earned permanent notoriety when he responded to the first question ever posed at a White House briefing on the subject of gay men's health. "Larry," came the interrogatory from Globe Syndicate radio correspondent Les Kinsolving, "does the President have any reaction to the announcement by the Centers for Disease Control in Atlanta that A-I-D-S [spelling out the still-unfamiliar term letter by letter] is now an epidemic in over 600 cases? . . . It's known as the gay plague." To this, Speakes glibly replied, "I don't have it. Do you?"

In truth, the press corps proved no more enlightened on the HIV/AIDS crisis than the White House. One journalist counted thirteen separate occasions on which correspondents laughed aloud at questions about the worsening epidemic. Once, Speakes teased that Kinsolving maintained "an abiding interest in the disease" because he was "a fairy." As it happened, the Baltimore-based radio personality, a former Episcopal priest, had long derided gay rights organizations as "the sodomy lobby."[39] Speakes tried to keep Kinsolving at arm's length—and certainly out of camera range—by warning Reagan not to call on him at press conferences. Equipped with a strapped-on tape recorder that made him look like an organ grinder, Kinsolving overcame the ban by barking out questions even when the president called on others. At one point, an exasperated Reagan shot back: "My finger must be crooked—every time I point at somebody, Lester Kinsolving starts asking a question."[40] Fortunately, one of the most improbable of those questions had started the desperately needed national conversation on AIDS.

As for Speakes, he would later reveal that he periodically invented quotes and attributed them to Reagan. That ex post facto admission unleashed a belated firestorm and cost him a $400,000-a-year, post–White House sinecure as press spokesman for Merrill Lynch.[41]

Unlike his predecessors, Reagan seldom kept up with the newspapers. He "glances" at the papers that arrived in his office each morning—the *New York Times*, *Washington Post*, *Los Angeles Times*, *USA Today*, and the relatively new and decidedly conservative *Washington Times*—Speakes noted during his White House tenure. When Reagan did open a paper, Speakes revealed without embarassment, his "habit is to read the comics first." Speakes found it surprising only that the onetime sportscaster did not routinely check the box scores.[42]

However limited his reading, Reagan, like other presidents before him, complained from the outset that he was "up to his 'keister' in leaks and wanted them stopped."[43] In a November 5, 1981, diary entry, Reagan plaintively noted: "A very secret paper somehow made its way to the N. Y. Times. We have to find a way to end this endless and dangerous leaking."[44] By mid-January 1982, the president complained at a press conference that leaks had "reached a new high." While "the Sporting News does not keep administration-by-administration statistics," Brookings Institution senior fellow Stephen Hess commented that Reagan's "claim was probably correct." But Hess argued that the proliferation of off-the-record tips was a direct result of the high number of ideologues—so-called Reaganuts—that Reagan had attracted to Washington, who now wanted to advance their agendas by whatever means at their disposal, high-level leaking included.

The *Wall Street Journal* advanced a different view, blaming the outbreak of loose lips on Reagan's hands-off management style: "If every policy is constantly up for a committee decision," it warned in an editorial, "you are constantly inviting contending parties to fight it out through leaks in the press."[45] Whatever the reasons for the unauthorized stories, Reagan eventually invited the FBI to investigate his own staff—reportedly subjecting all of them to lie detector tests to determine who was siphoning inside stories to the media. Even that crackdown failed to plug the leaks. Convinced his private comments were no longer secure, Reagan took to glancing at the Oval Office chandelier during meetings and joshing, as if a microphone were hidden there, "Get that, *Washington Post*, and be sure you get it right!"[46]

On a more serious level, Reagan authorized unprecedented crackdowns to limit the free flow of information. In late August 1983, the administration issued a "contract" which all high-level government officials would be obliged to sign, requiring them to obtain advance approval for anything they wrote about their work in newspapers or books—for the rest of their lives. The American Society of Newspaper Editors branded the proposal "peacetime censorship of a scope unparalleled in this country since the adoption of the Bill of Rights in 1791." Commenting that the Reagan White House seemed hostile to "the concept that the public has a serious and continuing interest in being informed," First Amendment lawyer Floyd Abrams labeled the "exuberant effort" a far greater risk to the nation than the threat posed by an occasional leak. "In less stable times," he warned of the idea of a clampdown, it would "too easily be used to suppress information essential to the self-government of the country."[47]

From time to time, even Reagan felt compelled to hold the occasional press conference. He proved neither illuminating nor particularly adept at the time-honored format, although he seemed occasionally to enjoy the give-and-take with journalists, especially in his early years as president. Attempting to explain why both Richard Nixon and Ronald Reagan had averaged so few press conferences, William Safire offered, "Reagan because he hated the preparation, Nixon because he hated the press."[48] Reagan still managed a total of forty-six televised press conferences in his eight years in office, an average of less than six annually, but almost all of them in prime time. The overwhelming majority of sessions took place in the White House, save for the first three, staged in the Old Executive Office Building, and one each during later presidential trips to Portugal, Japan, Chicago, Italy, the USSR, and Canada.[49] More often than not, Reagan shone under the bright lights.

Reagan biographer H. W. Brands has observed of these performances: "If his mastery of policy minutiae was less than Jimmy Carter's, his camera presence was far greater. And he understood that presence mattered more to television viewers."[50] From time to time, a detailed question on an unanticipated topic might elicit a helpless, deer-in-the-headlights expression and an addled response replete with factual errors. Following any such occurrence, Reagan's staff "Spin Patrol" went into overdrive, descending on reporters to "correct" mistakes before they could be published. Robert Sims, an assistant to Larry Speakes, quickly gained a reputation as the supreme administration spinmeister. Whenever the press readied to report a presidential gaffe, as Sam Donaldson recalled, "Sims would come back to try to explain, argue, wheedle, and jolly us into softening the edges of the presidential goof, all in the name of fairness and good sportsmanship."[51] Reagan's second White House chief of staff, Donald Regan, acknowledged, "Some of us are like a shovel brigade following a parade down main street cleaning up."[52]

Reagan's doddering unfamiliarity with details bothered neither him nor his admirers. Mimics from Rich Little to Johnny Carson evoked affectionate laughter by impersonating the president's trademark, head-shaking opening word—"Well"—a verbal placeholder that came to symbolize the president's modesty, not his confusion. Regardless of what he said, Reagan's erect posture, self-effacing humor, and consummate grace seemed to give Americans confidence. After four years of scolding from Carter, the public obviously approved of the morale-building figurehead who delegated the real work of government to his staff. It was "morning in America."

New York governor Mario M. Cuomo, a Democrat who firmly believed that Reagan's policies dangerously widened the gap between rich and poor, confided to friends that even his elderly, Italian-born mother grew enamored of the president. Particularly pleased by Reagan's demonization of "welfare queens," Immaculata Cuomo told her son that she had come to agree with Reagan that too many people received welfare. "But, mom," the governor reminded her, "when you and Pop came here, *you* were on relief." "That was relief," she insisted in her thickly accented English, "not welfare." Besides, Mrs. Cuomo declared of Reagan, "God must love him." When her son asked how she could know that, she replied, "Look at his hair!"[53]

With his dark-hued pompadour still unflecked by gray, the seventy-three-year-old Reagan, the oldest candidate yet to run for president, sought a second term in 1984. And his relations with the press immediately became an issue—at least for the press. "Every President has sought to limit what reporters call access," an exasperated Steven R. Weisman wrote in the *New York Times Maga-*

zine with three weeks to go before Election Day. But "even Presidents who have disliked and distrusted the press have met with reporters on a fairly regular basis and given spirited, detailed answers to their questions. Mr. Reagan has been an exception. During his Administration, he has tended to operate in a kind of cocoon, sheltered from the press." Weisman enumerated Reagan's elusiveness: he refused to answer questions that went beyond "the line of the day"; often staged news events at picturesque sites to deflect close scrutiny on specific issues; cut down on press conferences (to twenty-six at that point from Carter's fifty-nine); and in those sessions "proved to be a master of evasion—he joked, he changed the subject, he even filibustered" to limit the number of questions. Reagan's evident "success" with the strategy, Weisman warned, "could blunt one of the traditional checks and balances that have given flexibility and strength to the American political system." But Weisman conceded the administration was unlikely to alter its successful formula of "controlled access." As a blunt sign on Larry Speakes's desk made clear to the press corps: "You don't tell us how to stage the news and we don't tell you how to cover it."[54]

The 1984 campaign inspired yet another breakout debate moment. Two weeks after appearing desultory at his first encounter with his fifty-six-year-old Democratic challenger, Walter Mondale, Reagan faced a tough but unsurprising question from *Baltimore Sun* diplomatic correspondent Henry Trewhitt: Considering his advanced age, were there "any doubts" in his mind that he could summon the energy to confront a future international crisis? Reagan had a glib reply at the ready: "I will not make age an issue in this campaign. I am not going to exploit, for political purposes, my opponent's youth and inexperience." Even Mondale joined in the laughter that greeted the perfectly timed remark.[55] In November, Reagan carried forty-nine states, defeating Mondale by 17 million popular votes and amassing 525 electoral votes to his opponent's 13.

The Reagan presidency was certainly not without its low points. It had begun with Reagan insisting that trees caused more pollution than cars (for joking about that comment later, Jim Brady was banished for a time from Air Force One).[56] Helen Thomas remembered that "Mr. Nice Guy" also maintained that "the homeless sleep on grates 'because they want to,'" and that the administration counted ketchup "a vegetable for school lunch programs." Still, she reported, "his engaging style" and "charm" soothed and pleased the public no matter what the president said by accident or his staff did intentionally. Merely bemused by reports of his own laziness, Reagan enjoyed telling people that he was "burning the midday oil." At one point he good-naturedly emblazoned his cabinet room chair with a sign reading "Ronald Reagan slept here."[57]

Scandals, Debategate included, never gained much traction in the press or with the public in the Reagan era. Early in his presidency, the press learned that a Japanese magazine had offered First Lady Nancy Reagan a $1,000 cash gift—apparently a long-standing custom in that country—in return for an interview. National security advisor Richard Allen intercepted the check to avoid a conflict, but instead of returning it, nonchalantly placed it in a safe near his desk—where it was discovered months later when he switched offices. As Reagan optimistically noted in his diary: "I don't think it amounts to much."[58] But the episode assumed a life of its own when David Gergen told the press the president knew nothing about it—when in fact Reagan had learned about the diverted payment two months earlier. As *Time* magazine's Larry Barrett put it, "The Allen affair could have been a brief shower of bad publicity, but it turned into a rainy season lasting until the new year."[59]

In March 1982, Reagan accused television networks of creating such a "constant downbeat" of bad news in reporting the country's economic woes that the coverage threatened to "contribute psychologically" to the problem. Going further, he suggested to the *Daily Oklahoman* that TV news had become "more concerned with entertainment than they are with delivering news."[60] It was a familiar refrain, sung by several of his predecessors (not to mention Spiro Agnew), but Reagan added a unique if somewhat muddled spin for emphasis: "Is it news that some fellow out in South Succotash someplace has just been laid off, that he should be interviewed nationwide, or someone's complaint that the budget cuts are going to hurt their present program?"[61] No one quite knew what the president was getting at, but, propelled into damage control, David Gergen felt it necessary to assure reporters that no "campaign" was underway to vilify the press.

Taking no chances, the White House acted decisively to limit the damage, a rare occurrence for an administration that generally offered a "no comment" to embarrassing questions in order to prevent negative stories from taking on extra oxygen. The same day as the *Times* reported his "Succotash" comment, Reagan got ahead of the story by offering a rare presidential apology in the form of a well-rehearsed "ad-lib" during a speech to the friendly National Association of Manufacturers. "You know," he began, "some people think there's a storm brewing between me and the news industry. That simply isn't true. My feelings about the media haven't changed a bit"—a line that triggered laughter. "No, no, no," he said, "I have always been and always will be in complete agreement with Thomas Jefferson on this subject." Then he paraphrased Jefferson's famous line about preferring newspapers without government to a government without newspapers, adding: "Of course, he also said, 'Perhaps the editor might divide his paper into four chapters, heading the first 'truths'; second, 'probabilities'; third, 'possibilities'; fourth, 'lies.'" Not surprisingly, Reagan had said it better than Jefferson had—certainly more succinctly. As another round of laughter subsided, he added, "I always agree with Jefferson."[62]

The one-upmanship flawlessly delivered, Reagan continued: "Presidents, even Thomas Jefferson, have their moods just like everyone else, including members of the press. Some of the things we say and do regarding each other may cause a little momentary frustration or misunderstanding, but that's all it is. So I hope I didn't touch a nerve with any of the press a few days ago, because I think that most of the time the overwhelming majority of them do a fine job, and as a former reporter, columnist and commentator myself, I know just how tough their job can be. Now, back to our regularly scheduled program."[63]

Reagan's simple-sounding statement put a quick end to the "Succotash" flap. Behind the seemingly ordinary phrases, however, resided an ingenious, subtly diversionary set of messages meant to raise generic doubts about press fairness. At first blush, the remarks revealed Reagan to be contrite—but not too much so; after all, as he reminded his listeners, all presidents get angry, even Thomas Jefferson, not a bad predecessor with whom to be compared. More important, Reagan seemed to be saying, let's remember (even though it was off the point), that reporters get mad, too—in other words, they often say terrible things. So keep in mind (without specifically restating it) the thoughts I first conveyed the other day (and don't really mean to retract): press negativity can indeed be harmful. Finally, I'm not hostile to the press—they're just doing their job, and it's a difficult one (translation: they can sometimes botch it up). And in case anyone has forgotten, I know this profession inside out because I once practiced it myself.

Just what Reagan meant by claiming he had once been a reporter, columnist, and commentator remains unclear. At most he had broadcast football and baseball games and generated radio spots for General Electric. Presidential fact-checking was not yet standard practice, and image still counted more than fact.

So Reagan reclaimed the high ground simply by identifying himself with past presidents and current journalists, and leaving it to others to continue debating whether or not Reaganomics was causing people in South Succotash to lose their jobs. It was a small matter, but a powerful reminder of Reagan's effectiveness, given the right script, and the right setting, to prove his abilities as communicator in chief. As always, he was at his best reciting what David Gergen called "parables"—even if some were exaggerated or even invented.[64]

Reagan forfeited a measure of that abundant goodwill in 1985, when, during a state visit to Germany, he agreed to join Chancellor Helmut Schmidt in laying a wreath at a military cemetery that housed the remains of some fifty veterans of the Hitler SS. Amid the understandable firestorm of criticism, David Gergen's replacement as White House communications director, Pat Buchanan, reportedly advised Reagan to stick to his planned itinerary so as not to offend his German host. The visit to Bitburg Cemetery proceeded, and when the president added a visit to the Bergen-Belsen death camp, Buchanan reportedly scrawled on a notepad that Reagan was "succumbing to the pressure of the Jews." Whether the complaint represented the advisor's own reaction—Buchanan later became a Holocaust denier—or merely took note of someone else's opinion has never been ascertained.[65] Whatever the case, Buchanan brought a new, hard-edged aggressiveness to a job David Gergen had once handled with equanimity.[66]

Things took another dark turn after a 1986 U.S. bombing raid on the Libyan capital of Tripoli in retaliation for a deadly terrorist attack at a Berlin discothèque. After the punishing raid, the administration leaked a false report to the *Wall Street Journal* and other papers hinting at an imminent second strike. Former newsman Bernard Kalb, who had left television to become assistant secretary of state for public affairs, quit his post in protest over what he labeled a White House "disinformation program."[67]

By far the biggest disgrace of the Reagan era was the Iran-Contra affair, which came to light in late 1986. After imposing a trade embargo on Iran and urging America's allies to do likewise with terrorist nations, Reagan authorized the secret sale of arms to Iran for that rogue state's use in its war against Iraq. The administration crafted the deal to secure the freedom of seven American hostages being held by pro-Iranian Hezbollah forces in Lebanon. Under the convoluted plan, some of the profits from the arms sale were then secretly diverted to anti-Sandinista "contras" fighting in distant Nicaragua. The affair exploded in the press after a Lebanese weekly broke the story (possibly after an American leak) in November.

Reagan at first denied knowledge of, much less involvement in, the deal. Moreover, he confessed to *Time* magazine, "What is driving me up the wall is that this wasn't a failure until the press got a tip from that rag in Beirut and began to play it up." Now the besieged president warned that lives were being endangered by "wildly speculative and false stories about arms for hostages and alleged ransom payments."[68] A November 25 press conference failed to convince journalists or the public that the deal had not violated the law. The scandal ultimately triggered investigations by both Congress and a special prosecutor, and resulted in fourteen indictments against administration officials, including national security advisor Robert McFarlane, Colonel Oliver North, and Secretary of Defense Caspar Weinberger, who would be pardoned before his trial by Reagan's White House successor, George Bush.

Though wounded, Reagan himself once again skirted blame, coasting on the near-universal belief that he had no knowledge of (and thus, no responsibility for) what his own administration was doing. One veteran journalist blamed a gullible, jaded public for developing no appetite for pursuing the president. "The press did investigate Iran-Contra to a fare-thee-well," Ben Bradlee insisted, ". . . and still never managed to engage the nation's attention or conscience." Reagan's poll numbers did plummet, but he was no Nixon: victimhood was never his chosen role.[69] At a tense, perhaps make-or-break news conference for which he was exhaustively briefed at both the White House and Camp David, Reagan "stood tall and gave not an inch," in the admiring words of his third press secretary, Marlin Fitzwater, who took over from Speakes on February 1, 1987. "The reporters' dreams would not be fulfilled that night." To the new spokesman's astonishment, Reagan had prepared himself by writing out a detailed explanation of Iran-Contra in longhand and committed it flawlessly to memory. He was "an actor," Fitzwater told himself, and "followed the scripts. . . . If he read a fact from a source he respected, it stayed with him."[70]

The press corps echoed Fitzwater's assessment, but with resentment undisguised. "He was number one tonight," Sam Donaldson declared of Reagan, adding snarkily, "Hollywood came right through." Although "heavily perspiring," Dan Rather observed, Reagan "seemed to be in charge and in command." Chris Wallace of NBC concurred, declaring Reagan's "performance first rate." Once again, style triumphed over substance. And in the case of Iran-Contra, the press shared the blame even as Reagan seized the credit: journalists had foolhardily anticipated a major stumble, and in merely exceeding low expectations, the beleaguered president emerged triumphant.[71] Reagan reclaimed his starring role as "the Prospero of American memories," in *Time*'s descriptive appraisal, "a magician who carries a bright, ideal America like a holograph on his mind and projects its image in the air."[72]

"The public's throat was never seized by Iran-Contra as it had been by Watergate," admitted Ben Bradlee. "Ronald Reagan was popular; there was no one to impeach him on the Hill. He was near the end of his term."[73] Chris Wallace spoke for most White House correspondents when he later concurred: "I guess I didn't have a good enough imagination to envision Ronald Reagan selling arms to [the Ayatollah] Khomeini."[74] Even so, special prosecutor Lawrence E. Walsh ultimately concluded that "President Reagan created the conditions which made possible the crimes committed by others." According to some sources, Walsh decided against pursuing an indictment against Reagan himself only because the president left the White House in fading health.[75]

To a remarkable degree, Reagan never stopped enjoying the benefit of the doubt. When the October 1986 Reykjavík summit conference unexpectedly came closer than expected to achieving a major breakthrough in missile reduction, White House spokesmen hastily briefed the press on the unanticipated progress. Then, when the Reagan–Gorbachev meeting broke down over Russian resistance to America's Strategic Defense Initiative—the "Star Wars" shield—the press was told that no one had expected a deal in the first place. Finally, the administration changed its story one more time, telling reporters "that great progress had been achieved" after all—that the "ball had been moved to the one-yard line."[76] Just the sight of Reagan back on the world stage was enough to drive up his poll numbers.

In this case, the final official line proved prophetic: in December 1987, the United States and USSR signed the Intermediate-Range Nuclear Forces Treaty. A few months earlier, as television cameras rolled, Reagan had reached his apogee. Standing at the Brandenburg Gate near the concrete barrier that had separated East and West Berlin since 1961, he said, "Mr. Gorbachev, tear down this wall." His powerful message easily drowned out the voices of the fifty thousand German demonstrators who had protested his visit when it began. Although the Berlin Wall did not come down until 1989, when George Bush resided in the White House, history gave Reagan much of the credit not only for opening the city but also for removing the entire Iron Curtain.

Nearly as popular when he departed as he had been when he entered the White House, the ever-placid Reagan exited with his dignity and reputation intact—something that could not be said for most of his recent predecessors.

"What I'd really like to do," Reagan once said, "is go down in history as the President who made Americans believe in themselves again."[77] His controversial policies notwithstanding, Reagan will likely go down in history for precisely that achievement. Whether it was the triumph of personality and public relations over politics and principle will continue to be debated by scholars—and, of course, by the television talking heads who first began proliferating at the end of his reign. But the Great Communicator more than earned his title.

Forty years after his first election, admirers still regard Reagan both as the savior who generated the patriotic renewal America so desperately craved and the father of his country's conservative revolution. To his detractors, he remains a bewildered actor who played the part of president with the same limited proficiency that had made him a star of B-pictures but no more than the leading man's sidekick in feature films. Studio boss Jack Warner, Reagan's longtime employer, had once been so shocked by his contract player's political ambitions that he reportedly quipped: "No, Jimmy Stewart for President. Ronald Reagan for his best friend."[78] Yet few presidents ever played the part better than the Gipper—a prince of underplayers as subtly adept at close-ups as he was graceful in long shots. "Above all," Larry Speakes said without apology, "Reagan was an actor, and if being an actor made him a better communicator, so be it."[79] Reagan did not disagree. "There have been times in this office," Reagan conceded in a remarkably frank exchange with ABC's David Brinkley shortly before his tenure ended, "when I've wondered how you could do the job if you hadn't been an actor."[80]

Time magazine's Larry Barrett, granted unprecedented access to Reagan in order to write a book, conceded that the president's "temperament seemed to resemble Coolidge's and his intellect, Harding's." Indeed, Barrett acknowledged, "Reagan came to the White House with important flaws in terms of personal capacity" that made him a "mediocre administrator, ever vulnerable to errors born of indifference or incomprehension." But in his ability to rise to the occasion at moments that counted, Barrett maintained, Reagan could "demonstrate will and vigor that evoked memories of the two Roosevelts."[81]

In that judgment, no less experienced an observer than Hedley Donovan concurred. The veteran correspondent, who had covered nine administrations over the course of forty years on the White House beat, always believed that an effective president must above all "be a communicator." In that crucial role, Donovan maintained, Reagan was quite simply "the best since FDR."[82]

Reagan's media advisor David Gergen thought he understood why. Through experience and instinct, the Great Communicator "knew that his audiences were more interested in hearing about themselves than about him."[83]

GEORGE H. W. BUSH

Seldom has a single magazine piece defined a presidential candidate more indelibly—or more destructively—than the October 1987 *Newsweek* cover story on George Bush: "Fighting the 'Wimp Factor.'"[84] It was not the article that did the damage but the headline.

"The profile of Bush had been fair and complete," publisher Katharine Graham always insisted. But she admitted that "the effect of the word 'wimp' crying out from the cover on newsstands everywhere was hard to overcome." Bush—who had earned the Distinguished Flying Cross and three air medals as a World War II fighter pilot—understandably regarded the article as a personal insult. His staff cut off all communications with *Newsweek* until a summit could be arranged at the vice president's Washington residence. Graham herself received an invitation, along with *Newsweek* editors Richard Mills "Rick" Smith and Evan Thomas.

Graham remembered that an understandably angry Bush raged at that frosty meeting that "the whole story had been wildly distorted by playing up the word on the cover, for which he accurately blamed the editors. His family, whom he'd asked to cooperate on the story, was naturally upset and angry and had advised him that further cooperation with the magazine, in any but a technically correct manner, would only prove the point: that he was indeed a wimp."[85]

The situation only got worse. What had begun as an isolated criticism of Bush's WASP comity quickly widened: unlike Reagan, the rumors began flying, Bush bent with the political wind; he had no real principles of his own; he was certainly not an authentic conservative. The prevailing joke, Howard K. Smith remembered, was that "what made the gangster John Gotti different from Bush was that the former had one conviction."[86] Indeed, Bush himself had told *Time* back in 1984, "I'm a conservative, but I'm not a nut about it."[87] Marlin Fitzwater, who served as press secretary to both Reagan and Bush, was powerless to change the perception that Bush lacked substance. He believed both the leaders he served to be "men of vision who look to the future," but explained that "one looks through the gauzy lens of his dreams, the other through the viewfinder of a telescope. Unfortunately," Fitzwater acknowledged, "the Bush vision was seldom recognized."[88]

The following summer, Bush struck back against the "wimp" image by channeling Clint Eastwood (as filtered by speechwriter Peggy Noonan) to assure fellow Republicans at the 1988 convention that nominated him for president: "Read my lips: no new taxes."[89] This televised pledge he ultimately broke, reinforcing the "wimp" stereotype he had struggled so hard to overcome. Howard K. Smith believed Bush had only himself to blame for placing himself in such a "ridiculous straitjacket."[90] *Time* magazine would later include the ill-considered promise in its all-time list of "Top 10 Unfortunate Political One-Liners."[91]

As a presidential candidate, Bush tried to walk the finest of lines, promising continuity but freshness: he would maintain Reagan's conservative policies, he vowed that campaign year, but try to make America "kindler" and "gentler" as well. He hoped to shine "a thousand points of light" on America's downtrodden, but only to spur volunteerism, not increase federal funding for the poor. He had attended Andover and Yale, but now considered himself a Texan. A onetime college baseball player, he loved horseshoes, of all sports, but loathed broccoli. To some, Bush was not so much a contradiction as a caricature. But he seemed incapable of malevolence or deception, his background as CIA director notwithstanding. When he insisted he was "out of the loop" on Iran-Contra, people believed him.

Then, toward the end of the 1988 campaign, a Los Angeles weekly revived longtime Washington rumors of Bush's alleged extramarital affairs. The whispers never quite made their way to mainstream media and stimulated no genuine investigation, and when the young Democratic campaign operative Donna Brazile demanded that Bush tell America who "will share that bed with him in the White House," Brazile was compelled to resign.[92] The story resurfaced in 1992, when the *New York Post* ran its own speculative story in the midst of ongoing reports of extramarital affairs by Bush's presidential challenger, Bill Clinton.

At a press briefing called to discuss Yitzhak Rabin's election as leader of Israel, Martha Tillotson of CNN bluntly asked the president if he had been engaged in a sexual affair. "No," Bush shot back. "It's a lie." As Marlin Fitzwater remembered, "The Bush family attitude toward the media hardened that day to granite, and I didn't blame them. . . . At that moment, I hated the press corps."

To the press secretary, the "ugly moment" was "unfair;" the press "couldn't wait to embarrass the President." And he blamed Clinton aide James Carville for sending "fax after fax" to journalists to keep the story alive.[93] Fitzwater's fury was understandable, but decades later, a biography of Barbara Bush suggested that she had long known of her husband's ongoing affair with a staff member, a dalliance that reportedly almost drove her to suicide.[94]

But in the fall of 1988, a televised debate comment may once again have turned the campaign tide toward Bush: in this case, a chillingly unemotional response by Democratic nominee Michael Dukakis to CNN newsman Bernard Shaw's provocative opening question on October 13: "If Kitty Dukakis were raped and murdered, would you favor an irrevocable death penalty for the killer?" Refusing to take the bait and show his human side, the Massachusetts governor replied, "No, I don't, Bernard," and lapsed into a statistics-driven argument that capital punishment did not deter violent crime.[95]

Shaw, who would later ask Al Gore how he might react if he or his children came down with AIDS, always defended his "gotcha" approach. "I'm from the Chicago school of journalism," he explained. "I believe in asking tough questions." He had come up with this particular one at 2:00 A.M. the night before he took the moderator's chair. "Did he really say that?" the press room erupted when Shaw opened the broadcast with it. Dukakis later tried explaining that he had been under the weather with a fever that night, but his excuses came too late. *Politico* understandably highlighted his "Kitty Dukakis" moment among its list of "questions that kill candidates' careers."[96] After a bruising campaign in which Bush played good cop to his own hard-hitting and, some charged, race-baiting television advertising campaign managed by attack dogs Roger Ailes and Lee Atwater, the vice president defeated Dukakis by 54 to 46 percent, with 426 electoral votes to his opponent's 111.

To his detriment, Bush's studied new muscularity soon inspired *Saturday Night Live* to assign a gifted new cast member, Dana Carvey, to create another unforgettable presidential impersonation. Carvey's amiable Bush performances outdid Chevy Chase's earlier portrayals of Gerald Ford because Carvey uncannily mimicked Bush's voice and gestures. Yet this same, supposedly insincere conservative ended up appointing Clarence Thomas to the Supreme Court and standing by his beleaguered choice when Anita Hill testified before the Senate Judiciary Committee that he had subjected her to sexual harassment. The nationally televised hearings marked the first time—but not the last—that a woman's testimony on such matters was dismissed.

Bush, the man so well informed that he needed no briefings, conducted some two hundred press conferences over the next four years—five times more than Reagan had hosted and in half the time.

Like most incoming presidents, Bush sought to distance himself from his predecessor—in style if not in substance. Bush eschewed Reagan-type image management but, as some of Reagan's old advisors believed, sacrificed clarity in the process. Acknowledging that Bush "has shied away from what he has called 'the vision thing,'" David Gergen noted only six weeks into Bush's presidency that he had given the impression that he merely stood ready to "manage problems as they came his way." The onetime communications director said that "surely the country needs more. . . . For the moment, it [the White House] is being nibbled and nicked to death by small stories because the administration is generating so few big stories to dominate the news."[97]

Bush engendered criticism—and on one occasion, alarm and pity—in coverage of his relationships with foreign leaders. When he decided against expressing indignation over Chinese crackdowns at Tiananmen Square, Lesley Stahl of CBS reported that he seemed "distracted and disinterested." Bush "was furious with the press," Fitzwater reported, "but he didn't want to do anything publicly" to correct the record, in the belief that quiet diplomacy could achieve more than public anger. On a trip to Japan in 1992, suffering from an intestinal flu at the end of a twelve-day trip to the Western Pacific, Bush insisted on attending a banquet with Prime Minister Kiichi Miyazawa and ended up vomiting, fainting on the Japanese leader, and sliding onto the floor in full view of NHK television and an enormous contingent of international press. The "goddam film," Fitzwater cursed the endlessly rebroadcast visual record. Asked if he had viewed it, an ashen but spirited Bush told a press conference the next day, "I'm not sure I want to."[98]

Yet Bush achieved unheard-of public approval numbers—as high as 90 percent—after waging the brief, successful, and almost bloodless 1991 Gulf War against Saddam Hussein's forces in Kuwait. One reason the war attracted so much support was that the administration imposed so much control over battlefield coverage. "By keeping television crews away from the fighting and releasing its own visually hypnotic films of high-technology bombing raids," observed political scientist John Anthony Maltese, "the Pentagon sanitized the war."[99] Unable to sustain the goodwill in the midst of economic challenges at home, Bush found himself running for a second term against an appealing Southern governor, Bill Clinton, and an upstart millionaire independent, H. Ross Perot. Better-known prospective Democratic challengers like Mario

Cuomo had declined to make the race, perhaps convinced that Bush's postwar popularity gave them little chance of success. But Clinton pushed hard against the incumbent's seeming cluelessness about economic hardships facing ordinary Americans.

In February 1992, Bush unwittingly validated that cliché during a visit to a grocers' convention in Orlando. There, the *New York Times* reported, he paused to inspect an ultramodern cash-register bar-code system. The new technology, he gushed, "amazed" him.[100] What had begun as a cheerful photo op turned into a public relations debacle that suggested Bush had no comprehension of Americans' everyday experiences. It brought new life to the line Texas governor Ann Richards had delivered at the 1988 Democratic National Convention—that "George Bush was born with a silver foot in his mouth."[101] It hardly mattered—as the AP pointed out the week after Bush's Orlando visit—that in fact he had been shown a brand-new iteration of a bar-code cash scanner capable of reassembling torn labels to accurately register prices. Neither the AP nor CBS broadcaster Charles Osgood succeeded in getting the "bum rap" reversed.[102]

Bush nonetheless benefited enormously from what political operative Richard Viguerie called "The Talk Radio Revolution." With the long-standing FCC Fairness Doctrine relegated to the regulatory dustbin in 1987, broadcasters became free to drop equal-time requirements among political candidates and fill the airwaves with hyperpartisan talk-show hosts. Viguerie had a valid point: the old-time doctrine had "made second-class citizens of broadcasters compared to their printing cousins when it came to the free speech protections of the Constitution and the Bill of Rights." Bush submitted to more than eighty radio interviews in his first two years. But in 1992, Bill Clinton, as *Talkers Magazine* editor Michael Harrison put it, "played talk radio like a piano."[103] Meanwhile, as Helen Thomas noted, Bush's campaign became "a disorganized mess."[104] Clinton won only 43 percent of the popular vote but amassed pluralities in thirty-two states, plus the District of Columbia, to amass 370 votes in the electoral college to Bush's 168. Bush's 37 percent popular vote was among the lowest totals for an incumbent since William Howard Taft had fallen to Woodrow Wilson eighty years earlier.

If he blamed the press, Bush never let on. In one of his last acts, he granted mock "amnesty to Helen Thomas and all the rest of you guys" in the White House correspondents corp.[105] George Bush was never as amusing as he thought he was—he just lacked the Reagan touch or the Clinton poise—but he was a class act.

Relations with Katharine Graham's media empire had warmed long before that point, but Bush never entirely escaped *Newsweek*'s assault on his machismo. Ironically, he later chose a subsequent *Newsweek* editor in chief, Jon Meacham, to write his official biography, published in 2015.[106] And he cast his net wide in his search of the historical validation he believed he deserved. In 2004, I sat in a private dining room at his Houston country club with the ex-president and Mrs. Bush and a small party of guests that included Time-Life presidential columnist emeritus Hugh Sidey. At a convivial supper ostensibly devoted to discussing Abraham Lincoln's presidency, the conversation turned inevitably to Bush's—with most guests agreeing it had been underrated, or at least unappreciated. Sidey led the cheers.[107]

In a final bow to Bush's rapprochement with the media that had injured him, the president delivered the eulogy at Sidey's memorial service in 2005, and Meacham delivered a eulogy at Bush's Washington funeral thirteen years later.

15

BILL CLINTON

"If there's one thing we've learned about Bill Clinton," journalist Chris Bury intoned on ABC's *Nightline* two weeks before the forty-second president's final day in office, ". . . it's just as he gets through with one scrape, another one's right around the corner."[1] Bury neglected to mention that it was the press that kept the spotlight relentlessly aimed at Clinton's "scrapes," from his days as governor of Arkansas to his 1992 presidential campaign, on through his two terms in the White House. Churned by the conservative media, and perhaps bending over backward to appear fair, the mainstream press often paid too little attention to the major policy issues dividing conservatives and liberals in the 1990s and gave too little credit to Clinton's often successful efforts to navigate common ground.

The media—increasingly endowed with all-new, all-day, high-speed platforms—instead filled space and time with titillating speculation about scandals and conspiracies, never quite forgiving itself, or its favorite target, for withstanding the constant criticism. If Bill Clinton deserved shame for hedonistic behavior, a number of journalists deserved blame for giving every indication they took it personally when he failed to succumb to their often cannibalistic feeding frenzies.

That the public maintained the capacity to separate their president's private failures from his public successes demonstrated either an increasing sophistication among the electorate or the diminished power of what was once called "yellow journalism"—and perhaps both. Bill Clinton and the media devoted too much time to diversionary side issues when each might have more usefully focused on what truly counted, including the evolution of—and the opportunity to harness—the most potentially powerful communications tool yet: the Internet. But the media that Hillary Clinton would later link to a "vast right-wing conspiracy" often preferred to demonize her husband rather than cover him straightforwardly.[2] And the competitive new twenty-four-hour news cycle demanded constant grist for its mill, the simpler and more sensational the better.

In this roiling environment, the media perpetuated nearly every alleged misstep and obfuscation by the man an Arkansas editor had first memorably dubbed "Slick Willie" back in 1980.[3] Where Clinton was concerned, private matters that would have slipped under the radar in the days of JFK (perhaps accompanied by a collective wink) routinely made it to the airwaves and into print. Clinton's rise coincided with a post-Watergate climate in which latter-day Woodwards and Bernsteins dreamed of setting the World Wide Web ablaze with scoops that generated front-page print pickup, major book deals, and movie portrayals by the likes of Robert Redford and Dustin Hoffman. The combination of post-Watergate cynicism and careerist ambition combined to trap Clinton in a whirlpool of seemingly perpetual press (and political) investigation. Yet somehow, the most closely scrutinized president in history survived negative multimedia inquiries that would have torpedoed others.

William Jefferson Clinton was either the media's greatest twentieth-century creation or its most egregiously hounded victim. Some thirty years before announcing his candidacy for president, the teenage Clinton had met—and been photographed with—President Kennedy in the White House Rose Garden. The UPI's indefatigable Helen Thomas had not only stood nearby during young Bill's brush with history; she claimed decades later that she could be glimpsed off to the side in one of the alternate versions of the now-famous picture, "looking skeptical as usual. . . . Little did I know at the time that there was a future president in the wide-eyed group in the presence of Kennedy, who, of course, urged them all to think about a career in public service."[4] Ambitious ever after, Clinton never stopped thinking about tomorrow—the name of the song that later became his campaign theme. And it seemed as if Helen Thomas never stopped covering the White House; Clinton would be the eighth president to fall under her gaze. But he was the first to be hounded by a long, well-organized, and politically motivated effort to discredit him in the press: the so-called

"Arkansas Project," channeled through *American Spectato*r magazine and funded by Clinton hater Richard Mellon Scaife, the ultra-conservative heir to one of America's wealthiest families.[5]

An obscure Arkansas governor given little chance at first of winning the 1992 Democratic presidential nomination, Clinton soared to prominence in a weak field, only to "hemorrhage" in the public opinion polls following reports of extramarital adventures.[6] He defiantly labeled himself "the comeback kid" after rebounding to a second-place finish in that year's New Hampshire primary. Earlier politicians had misbehaved, but Clinton was the first to do so under the microscope of twenty-four-hour news coverage and fed by relentless and well-organized enemies. Yet "There was not really a barrier between him and the press" during the early race for the Democratic nod, his future press secretary Richard L. "Jake" Siewert testified. Reporters like Joe Klein of *New York* magazine and Ron Brownstein of the *Los Angeles Times* traveled with the campaign and spent hours in "relaxed and informal" conversation with the dark-horse candidate.[7]

Clinton learned the hard way that camaraderie with reporters would not exclude him from surveillance over what he naively believed should remain private and off-limits. Traditionally, campaign-embedded journalists tended to go easy on their subjects; after all, if the presidential candidate they covered triumphed, their employers were likely to assign them to the most prestigious beat in journalism: the White House. The widespread coverage of Clinton's earliest scandal at least proved that most reporters could rise above that obvious conflict of interest. Looked at another way, the smell of blood in the water—namely Clinton's—proved more alluring to journalists in 1992 than the prospect of future employment in Washington.

The turbulence began in January of that year, not long before Democratic voters were scheduled to head to the polls in New Hampshire. An Arkansas singer named Gennifer Flowers came forward to claim she had engaged in a twelve-year sexual affair with the married governor. The campaign teetered on the brink of collapse until the 26th, when Hillary Clinton came roaring to her husband's defense in a dramatic interview on the top-rated CBS news magazine *60 Minutes*. Her appearance represented the third and final phase of what aides described as the classic "Clinton crisis playbook": first parse each negative story, then attack the accusers, and finally bring in the cavalry—namely Hillary.[8]

"You know, I'm not sitting here, some little woman standing by my man like Tammy Wynette," a "cool and unruffled" Mrs. Clinton declared that night from

Boston (in a pronounced Southern drawl) with Bill at her side. "I'm sitting here because I love him, and I respect him, and I honor what he's been through and what we've been through together. And you know, if that's not good enough for people, then heck—don't vote for him."[9] We do not know whether anyone on set took it as divine intervention when a burning-hot television light came loose during the taping and toppled down toward Hillary—who was yanked to safety at the last second by her husband. It was not the kind of peril the Clintons expected to face that day.

During the taping, Clinton acknowledged "causing pain in my marriage" through "wrongdoing," but hit the Flowers allegations as "false" and, in response to reporter Steve Kroft's intensely personal questioning, denied that his marriage was a mere "arrangement" ("I wanted to slug him," Clinton remembered).[10] For this, his most consequential media appearance to date, he added an ingenious syllogism. "I can remember a time when a divorced person couldn't run for president," he said, "and that time, thank goodness, has passed. . . . Are we going to take the reverse position now that if people have problems in their marriage and there are things in their past which they don't want to discuss which are painful to them, that they can't run?"[11]

Not surprisingly, the highly rated *60 Minutes* installment attracted even more viewers than usual, nearly forty million that night, in part because of the publicity storm enveloping Clinton but also because the broadcast followed the most popular television event of the year on the same network: the Super Bowl.[12] Few people knew it at the time, but the Clintons had originally planned to submit to the grilling on CNN, cannily moving it to CBS only "at the last minute, augmenting the audience tenfold." In retaliation, Clinton came to believe, the jilted cable network "pushed scandal after scandal" in the coming years to "get even."[13]

The CBS appearance very likely saved Bill Clinton's candidacy as much as it may have later come back to haunt his wife's when it was exhumed in order to damage Hillary's own presidential hopes a quarter century later.[14] It also placed an "enormous barrier" between Clinton and the media.[15] When Steve Kroft concluded the 1992 interview by asking the candidate if he thought his appearance had helped put his self-generated problems behind him, Clinton offered an answer that indicated whom he really blamed for the Flowers mess. "That's up to the American people," he replied, "and to some extent up to the press. This will test the character of the press. It is not only my character that is being tested."[16]

Clinton's relationship with zealous journalists thereafter worsened, but few politicians save for Kennedy and Reagan proved so successful at bypassing them and connecting directly with audiences via television. Whether maintaining his innocence, staying on message by advocating economic reform, smiling uncannily through frowns, or biting his lower lip, Elvis-like, for sympathy-inducing close-ups, candidate Clinton proved too fascinating—and too resilient—for the pack journalistss to dislodge, however hard they tried. The media piled on with reports that Clinton's youthful transgressions had included dodging the military draft (and burning his draft card, a fabrication) and, in his student days, smoking marijuana. Clinton adamantly denied the first charge but admitted the second—albeit with an implausible caveat: he had smoked but not inhaled.

In a book written the year before Clinton ran for the White House, political scientist Larry Sabato had presciently warned of a future marked by "junkyard dog journalism on the prowl," predicting dire consequences for both the political system and the press if journalists did not develop more discernment and restraint.[17] By 1992, others disagreed. Denying that the campaign had descended into an anti-Clinton feeding frenzy, a *New York Times* op-ed columnist argued instead that the "press has heroically tried to save him." Ellen Landowsky maintained: "The press is enamored of Mr. Clinton. This is the real secret love affair of the 1992 campaign."[18]

The gifted "natural" dipped in the polls after the draft-evasion charge but rebounded with no lasting damage. Here was a baby boomer who seemed to resonate with a generation of media-savvy voters who had dealt with Vietnam and drugs in ways they perhaps wanted to obscure, too, but at least understood. As Republican media guru David Gergen put it, "I didn't know any saints from the sixties generation, and I was not one myself."[19] Marveling at Clinton's ability to "turn the tables on the press"—to "come back repeatedly from the precipice"—his staff took to calling him "Secretariat" after the Triple Crown–winning thoroughbred, perhaps an unfortunate comparison considering that the famous horse had been put out to stud and later euthanized. "The remarkable thing about Bill Clinton is how good he is at pulling himself out of the tailspins," agreed Gergen. But as he added: "The other remarkable thing about Bill Clinton is how he gets himself into trouble so he goes into tailspins. That's what's so hard to reconcile."[20]

Some of Clinton's Teflon-like immunity that year must be credited to innovative young media consultant Mandy Grunwald, daughter of onetime *Time* magazine editor Henry Grunwald. She counseled Clinton to look beyond mainstream journalism—obsessed as it remained with his alleged peccadilloes—and seize on invitations to appear on soft-news or outright entertainment shows. Clinton could soon be found chatting on air with sympathetic hosts Phil Donahue and Larry King, donning sunglasses to play a "Heartbreak Hotel" saxophone solo on *The Arsenio Hall Show*, and getting personal on Gen X–friendly MTV. He liked Elvis Presley and El Greco, he endearingly told the young MTV studio audience, adding, for what it was worth, that he believed Anita Hill's claims of sexual harassment against Clarence Thomas.[21] On such appearances, a "magnetic" Clinton deftly mixed personal anecdote with issue-driven advocacy, a combination that clicked with younger audiences even if, as advisor Sidney Blumenthal noticed, the guest spots "offended Washington pundits who felt he had violated norms of propriety." As Blumenthal put it, Clinton created "a crossover appeal that the traditionally minded warned was the devil's sign."[22]

By summer, *Evening Shade* television producer Linda Bloodworth-Thomason's beautifully made documentary short, *The Man from Hope*, had enthralled the Democratic convention crowd along with millions of viewers watching at home. It featured a double entendre destined to emerge as a political catchphrase: Clinton saying of his Arkansas birthplace, "I still believe in a place called Hope."[23] Thomason later dubbed herself, with some hyperbole, "the woman who introduced Bill Clinton to America in the now famous biopic."[24] In truth, by convention time, thanks to the media circus that had surrounded him for months, the public needed no introduction to the man from Hope.

Generating feel-good news was only one of the campaign's specialties. At the other extreme, the Clinton team organized a twenty-four-hour war room to provide what the candidate called "focused and fast" replies before political attacks could gain unanswered traction on cable news. Kennedyesque young George Stephanopoulos, who, along with flint-eyed "Ragin' Cajun" James Carville, ran the media team, described their strategy as quickly flooding the media with "talk, talk, and more talk" whenever the candidate faced criticism.[25] Carville hung a sign on the war room wall bluntly reminding staffers: "Speed Kills . . . Bush." Additional posters instructed the squad to stay focused on key issues:

Change vs. More of the Same
The Economy, Stupid
Don't Forget Health Care

"It's all routine stuff now," Clinton recalled of the rapid-response operation, "but then it was new."[26] Indeed, it was so new that the operation would inspire another documentary film, *The War Room*, the following year.

Outgunned, the press corps temporarily eased up on Clinton, but only to pursue his Republican opponent's running mate, Dan Quayle. The conservative vice president had launched a quixotic moral crusade against a popular television character, TV newswoman Murphy Brown, and implicitly its liberal star, the popular Candice Bergen. Quayle maintained that the show had done injury to family values by depicting Murphy as a shamelessly happy, single expectant mother. Surely his outrage was meant to remind voters that Bill Clinton was unrepentantly promiscuous, too, but Quayle overreached: Murphy won the battle for public sympathy, and Bush and Quayle lost the election to Clinton and Al Gore. In a three-way contest that included independent Ross Perot (who drew equally from both major-party candidates, exit polls showed), Clinton beat Bush in thirty-two of the fifty states plus the District of Columbia.

According to reporters as well as his own staffers, Clinton failed to use the ensuing transition to prepare himself adequately for the scrutiny he would face when he entered the White House. Outgoing Bush press secretary Marlin Fitzwater offered to show the Clinton communications team the ropes, but was told "we'd rather make our own mistakes." And they did, Helen Thomas remembered, "in spades."[27] To staff the White House press office, Clinton chose trusted but inexperienced campaign aides over seasoned Washington professionals.

The press assessment of the new president's first hundred days, Clinton himself conceded, was "mixed."[28] In truth, it was worse. Clinton protested that he "never really had a 'honeymoon' in the press"—the usual grace period granted incoming White House occupants—and was compelled to focus on "sensational leaks rather than substantive politics."[29] Even the cantankerous Sam Donaldson, newly reassigned to the White House, admitted that "Bill Clinton never had a honeymoon."[30] While Helen Thomas, too, agreed that "the usual honeymoon with the press never materialized," she put the blame squarely "on the White House staff's attitude."[31] The administration had started things off with a provocation, sealing off the passageway that had long led from the ground-floor press room to the press secretary's office.[32] The Clinton people simply did not want journalists wandering in and out of the Executive Wing without appointments, but the administration paid dearly for the insult. "I've been here since Kennedy," Thomas fumed to George Stephanopoulos, the newly installed communications director, "and those steps have never been blocked to us, and the press secretary's office has never been off limits. Ever."[33] She declared the locked door "an act of war."[34]

"Early on, there were some problems we made worse," a frank Bill Clinton told me, "like stopping the press from roaming the West Wing halls and popping in on people with open doors." As he explained that decision: "It's tight in there. People need open doors. But we could have handled it better. I don't think it would have changed the fundamental thread of the [later] Whitewater stories. The major papers were too wedded to a false storyline and loath to abandon it."[35]

Clinton fared no better with the media when, responding to pressure from General Colin Powell and Georgia Senator Sam Nunn, chairman of the Armed Services Committee, he directed his early attention to a campaign pledge to grant gays the right to serve openly in the military. Politically, Clinton took a typically centrist approach, proposing a "Don't Ask, Don't Tell" policy and making clear he unrealistically (and unfairly) expected "a very high standard of conduct" from gay soldiers.[36] He ended up taking heat from both the right and the left, not to mention journalists. As Clinton told author Taylor Branch, he regretted that the initiative "enshrined the double standard he sought to remove."[37] Yet he attributed the resulting bad press not to misplaced priorities but to administration sources who shared the proposal with the media too soon.

Clinton also endured bad press on high-level appointments. Committed to naming a woman as attorney general, he reeled as his first two choices, Zoë Baird and Kimba Wood, withdrew after the media revealed they had failed to pay taxes for their children's caregivers. "Nannygate" ended only when Clinton settled on Harvard-trained Janet Reno. "Public service was her life," Clinton rejoiced—perhaps a coded way of reminding the press that the unmarried Reno had neither children nor nannies.[38]

The administration took still more heat when federal forces raided an enclave held by a reclusive sect whose Messianic leader, David Koresh, was suspected of stockpiling weapons. The April 19 FBI assault on the Branch Davidians' heavily enforced stronghold near Waco, Texas, culminated in a huge conflagration. Some seventy-five people, including children, perished at the fiery scene. Libertarian commentators accused the FBI of aggressive overreach and even mainstream media suggested "government missteps."[39] When word later got out that two months after Waco, Clinton had held Air Force One on the ground at LAX so he could get a $200 haircut, the press reported the false charge that he had delayed hundreds of passengers as planes idled on nearby runways.[40] Clinton's poll numbers plummeted, and he blamed the press.

His early PR catastrophes failed to motivate a stubborn Clinton to deal more directly—or more affably—with the press. *Newsweek* columnist Jonathan Alter was astonished that Clinton did not prove "more skillful in making the jump from Little Rock" to the Washington vulture culture, which required him not only to behave prudently but to present himself at the salons dominated by the likes of media power couple Sally Quinn and Ben Bradlee. But Quinn had greeted Clinton's inaugural with a provocative *Post* column headlined "Welcome to Washington, but Play by Our Rules," warning the new team in town to keep in mind that "When the Clinton administration is gone and forgotten, the Congress, the media and the establishment will remain."[41] Clinton would not be intimidated—especially after his earliest overtures were rebuffed.

"I went over there," the president maintained of his futile attempts to woo veteran reporters, "I kissed their fat asses, and what do I get from it?"[42] Clinton "never got to the stage where he despised the press corps as an undifferentiated whole," an aide insisted, and he remained open to exclusive interviews with Washington heavyweights like Mary McGrory of the *Star* and E. J. Dionne of the *Post*. But Clinton's chronic tardiness, among other incurable traits, irked reporters eager to interpret his inability to hew to a schedule as an overall lack of discipline. Even so, one of his spokesmen believed "the level of candor" between the administration and those who covered it actually became "too high," as a result of which the press "saw a lot more of the sausage-making than you would in a Bush White House."[43]

Clinton argued that he became a victim of the "trivialization of press culture." As far as he was concerned, the media had replaced "classic," fact-based reporting with "spin" meant "to pamper consumers rather than inform citizens"—to provide "entertainment and subjective gamesmanship."[44] Defiantly, he turned to some of the alternative media arenas that Reagan had made his own. Over the next eight years, for example, Clinton would deliver 455 weekly radio addresses. He used his downtime—even while flying aboard Air Force One—for interviews with local radio stations. Innovatively, Clinton also began holding televised town hall meetings, charming crowds as effortlessly as he had stirred enthusiasm along campaign rope lines. And he focused unprecedented attention on the black press, particularly the Trotter Group, an association of African American journalists who "were in and out of the White House" frequently "over the years."[45]

Clinton "never shied away from answering questions," acknowledged CBS Radio's White House correspondent Mark Knoller, one of the reporters assigned to follow Clinton wherever he went, even if it meant piling into a van at the crack of dawn to cover the president's morning runs along the Washington Mall. Ronald Reagan may once have feigned hearing loss to avoid the reporters at his heels, but as Knoller recalled of Clinton: "Every time he would run by us on a jog, we'd shout a question, and in huffs and puffs, he'd give us a one- or two- or three-word answer."[46] Less appreciative of such opportunities, seventy-three-year-old Helen Thomas, who often joined the press motorcade pursuing Clinton on the jogging path, sardonically noted, "He could run but he couldn't hide."[47]

In another apparent bow to the Reagan playbook, Clinton agreed to place himself on the firing line before a roomful of what he assumed would be adoring kids. But the White House unwisely ceded control of the first such event to ABC News, which chose the young participants, making sure they represented aggrieved constituencies and could articulate their families' problems. The give-and-take turned into "an absolute nightmare," a press aide recalled. ". . . They'd bring in a cattle rancher's kid whose father was worried about losing their farm because of Clinton's new grazing rights" policy, or another "who lived underneath an electromagnetic field and was worried about some obscure energy regulation and how it was going to turn their house unlivable."[48]

"Because it was kids," the frustrated staffer added, Clinton "wouldn't concentrate" on preparation "until the last second." Worse, the events were scheduled on Saturday mornings, when the president "wants to play golf, wants to do the radio address and leave. . . . So he hates being there." According to the aide, "in a press conference, you can talk over the heads of the press corps directly to the American people when you get a snotty question. Or you can turn the people against the press by talking past them and making them look small. Can't do that with kids, right? They already look small." The staffer's advice, learned too late to benefit his boss, was to "never put the President with children, especially when the media is hand-picking the kids."[49]

Frustrated by these early missteps, Clinton tried another effort to widen outreach: he went after the young-adult sector within the Democratic base by sitting for a *Rolling Stone* interview conducted in the White House by founding publisher Jann Wenner and former *Washington Post* correspondent William Greider. It did not go well, either. Recalling the experience of defending himself to the hip liberal magazine as "traumatic," Clinton at one point wagged his finger at Greider and berated him as "a faulty citizen." Then he lectured the reporter: "You don't mobilize or persuade, because you only worry about being doctrinaire and proud, you are betraying your own principles with self-righteousness." The president all but boasted, "I did everything but fart in his face."[50]

The resulting story, which appeared on newsstands in November 1993, came across as if Clinton had done precisely that. The article made him seem like a defensive leader under siege, unsparing in his self-pitying criticism of his critics. Clinton excoriated journalists' "compulsion to make instantaneous judgments and make big things little and little things big." He denied he disliked the press, but grumbled anew: "Used to be a president got a honeymoon." As they were packing up to leave the White House, the *Rolling Stone* duo asked Clinton one final, provocative question: Had he not gone back on his original commitment to change Washington? At this, the president "turned and glared," his "face reddened, and his voice rose to a furious pitch," Wenner and Greider reported, "as he delivered a scalding rebuke, an angry, emotional encounter, the kind of which few have ever witnessed: 'But that is the press' fault, too, damn it. I have fought more damn battles here for more things than any president has in 20 years, with the possible exception of Reagan's first budget, and not gotten one damn bit of credit from the knee-jerk liberal press, and I am sick and tired of it, and you can put that in the damn article.'"[51] They did so; and to Clinton's further detriment, his exit-line outburst inspired coverage not just in the niche-market *Rolling Stone* but in daily newspapers that picked up the story and reran it across the country.[52] Usually the target of conservative media, Clinton had now been ambushed from the left.

Dee Dee Myers, the first woman ever to serve as a presidential press secretary, proved powerless to stop the bleeding. Less than two weeks after the inauguration, the *Boston Globe* was already reporting, "Clinton appears to have lost control of the political agenda."[53] Things went downhill from there. Myers found herself relegated to desk duty—and not even at the desk long assigned to press secretaries. "Her job was doubly difficult," David Gergen opined, not only because she lacked Washington experience but "because a male-dominated staff left her out of the loop too often and Hillary, worried about her ability, was frequently on the warpath against her."[54] George Stephanopoulos, the "boy wonder" communications director, assumed responsibility for most daily press briefings—often with less-than-impressive results. *New York Times* reporter Thomas Friedman admitted after watching him falter one day: "I just wanted to get a hook, and pull George Stephanopoulos off stage and say, 'George, go back, get your ducks in order, and then come out here, because this is too serious.'"[55]

The Clinton team "did a lot of little things to alienate" the White House correspondents, future spokesman Jake Siewert admitted: not just by closing off the press room door but by "going to the regional press" and staging town meetings and satellite interviews. The press "really disliked George . . . had no time for him at all," Siewert added, yet the administration made it "impossible" for the "extremely smart" Myers "to succeed." By sending others out to brief the press on the most critical issues, Siewert believed, Clinton signaled he "had trust in people other than Dee Dee. . . . She didn't have quite the authority you needed to do . . . a brutal job."[56] As a result, Myers's status fell among journalists "more obsessed with . . . who's up and who's down than they are with policy."[57]

As a remedy, Clinton rather gullibly agreed to grant special access to two tough veteran journalists, Elizabeth Drew and Bob Woodward, both of whom planned books on the administration's early efforts. Although Clinton convinced himself that his cooperation would soften their judgment, both authors produced "devastating indictments" of his first hundred days, depicting "a White House in disarray, a president leading by the seat of his pants, and an administration apparently in over its head." Clinton, who was said to lose his temper several times a day over minor matters, "went up in smoke when he read the results, as he should have."[58]

After only four months, heads rolled. Clinton transferred Stephanopoulos to an undefined "senior advisor" position, invited Reagan media advisor David Gergen back to the White House as a "counselor" (outraging liberals), and named White House deputy chief of staff Mark Gearan as the new communications director. (The post would be subsequently held, under various titles, by Don Baer, Ann Lewis, and Loretta Ucelli, with input from such seasoned media hands as Sidney Blumenthal, a veteran political reporter who had worked most recently for the *New Yorker.*) The "Communications Director is supposed to be [doing] long-term planning," Siewert said, "which we always used to joke at the White House meant tomorrow as opposed to today. . . . [We] needed a lot more discipline around the calendar and the schedule and the agenda, and we didn't have it."[59] According to one jaded observer, White House communications office duties soon boiled down to three priorities: planning events, promoting policy, and confronting scandals.[60]

Gergen at least succeeded in reopening the sealed-off door to the press room. Seeking to heal festering wounds, he boldly asked Hillary Clinton why she hated the press so much. "I don't really," she insisted. "They've been tough on us from the start, but we need to repair relations." She even agreed to belatedly begin courting Bradlee and Quinn. "We know we should do that," the first lady told Gergen. "We've been thinking about some dinners this summer at the White House."[61] The parties went off as scheduled, many journalists attended, and both Clintons "agreed to talk with reporters more often. . . . The war against the press was moving toward a truce." Yet Gergen ultimately concluded, "I am afraid the Clintons carried too large a chip on their shoulders toward the press and would have had a far more productive relationship if they had been more open and respectful of reporters." Gergen came to admire their ongoing rapid-response operation but not their "pattern of spinning stories beyond their legitimate bounds."[62]

Myers escaped the purge only temporarily, remaining press secretary even after unexpectedly discovering a premature report about her own departure in the September 22, 1994, *Washington Post*.[63] Two months later, State Department spokesman Mike McCurry—an original aspirant for the top job—replaced her and, according to Gergen, proved so successful he "earned a spot in the hall of fame for press secretaries."[64] Myers had an ironic last laugh fifteen years later with a bestselling memoir, *Why Women Should Rule the World*. To observers at the time, however, even with a woman putatively ruling the press office, McCurry inherited a media operation that was, in Jake Siewert's words, "a shambles."[65]

Whatever the early turmoil in messaging, Clinton went on to notch notable domestic and diplomatic accomplishments, although some of his home-front achievements, widely applauded at the time, have come under fire from twenty-first-century progressives. The successes included a national service program, welfare reform, the North American Free Trade Agreement, and a balanced budget (achieved in part through a tax increase on the wealthy). An anti-crime bill helped reduce violent offenses but disproportionately impacted people of color and may have contributed to what later became known as mass incarceration (though the law also funded education grants for prisoners). Under Clinton, crime declined and the economy rebounded.

On the global stage, Clinton brought together bitter antagonists Yitzhak Rabin and Yasser Arafat in September 1993 to sign the Oslo Accords—and all but shoved the leaders together for a historic press photograph showing them shaking hands for the first time. Clinton also moved courageously to stop ethnic cleansing in the former Yugoslavia, and his administration brokered an end to the violent, long-intractable "Troubles" in Northern Ireland. The most Clinton will say is that "press coverage was mixed." As he told me, "On foreign policy and major domestic events, most coverage was fair and felt positive." But the former president remains "surprised" at "how reluctant the press was to recognize the fact that the one-vote passage of my economic plan and my other economic initiatives led to the fairest income distribution in the last fifty years."[66]

In November 1993, Clinton signed the "Brady Bill" limiting handgun sales—named for the Reagan press secretary so grievously injured by an assassin's bullet twelve years earlier—though its background-check provision would later be voided by the Supreme Court. While opposition from the National Rifle Association proved insufficient to stop that bill, a mammoth advertising pushback by medical and pharmaceutical lobbies helped doom Hillary's effort to push universal health care. In the end, the Clintons—who had made such a powerful impression as a couple on *60 Minutes*—saw their signature health initiative fall victim to a fictional husband and wife named "Harry and Louise" who emoted anxiety about the proposal in a series of effective, if cynical, television commercials. Operating under standard procedure—meaning that no attack went unanswered—the president was soon publicly dismissing "Thelma and Louise, whoever it is."[67] His derisive comments only guaranteed the spots additional television exposure on the news.

Increasingly, Clinton faced not only policy pushback but also what Helen Thomas described as a "visceral and vitriolic" hatred from enemies. "Not even Nixon," she conceded, "generated that kind of hostility at his worst times."[68] Neither she nor the president could explain it. But one source was certainly the right, emboldened and empowered after Republicans took control of the House of Representatives in the off-year elections of 1994.

"We constantly struggled to get out competing messages," former House Speaker Newt Gingrich told me of his often stormy relationship with Clinton, disagreement with whom once led to a government shutdown. "He had a very likeable personality, enormous energy, and personal exuberance. He once told me he was like the blow-up clown with sand in the bottom that you had as a kid. You could knock him down but he would come back up. He had learned early on in Arkansas to do whatever it took to survive."[69]

With regularity, press coverage veered from legislative and diplomatic triumphs to alleged ethical violations. "The reporters would just stampede and print anything," Clinton seethed at the time.[70] Even before he and his wife entered the White House, the Clintons had faced accusations that they had participated in a shady Arkansas real estate deal known as Whitewater. The controversy followed them to Washington and reignited when they refused to turn over documents to investigators. Wrongdoing was never proved—in fact, neither was ever charged with a misdeed. But the charges alone opened perilous floodgates, provoking the appointment of a special investigator who would later widen his scope to hound the president on unrelated charges: Ken Starr. For the next five years, Starr would function as both detective and grand inquisitor—for Clinton, a nightmarish combination of Javert and Torquemada who passed judgment before he made inquiries, and in the process leaked compulsively to the press.

Another brouhaha erupted in May 1993 when the Clintons decided to reorganize the White House travel office amid reports of gross and possibly illegal mismanagement. But its staff had long served correspondents by arranging charter flights for presidential trips, and the press corps resented the unexpected dismissal of longtime friends. Not surprisingly, critics denounced the move to hire new staff as cronyism and dubbed the affair "Travelgate." The overdue housecleaning triggered another dead-end inquiry that nonetheless remained officially unresolved for five years, ultimately to be dropped without fanfare. Columnist Lars-Erik Nelson likened the Clintons' ordeals to a "Stalinist-era trial," noting ruefully that "the President and First Lady have been publicly charged and secretly found innocent."[71] Agreeing that both the *New York Times* and *Washington Post* had devoted far too much coverage to nonstories, Clinton vented: "I think these papers have corrupted themselves over Whitewater."[72]

Without reducing its attention on earlier red herrings, the press moved on to allegations that the president and First Lady routinely offered overnight lodging in the sacred Lincoln Bedroom in exchange for campaign contributions. Denying the charge, Clinton groused that the story had "legs without a brain."[73] Yet for some reason he later brought it back to the forefront himself. At the 1997 White House Correspondents' Association dinner, held in the recently opened Newseum on Pennsylvania Avenue, he would note that the new tourist attraction boasted a special wing "dedicated to historic scoops." Turning to one of the association's longest-serving members, he joked, "For example, did you know that Helen Thomas broke the story about the Lincoln Bedroom—while Lincoln was sleeping in it?"[74]

Years later, guiding my wife and me on a private tour of this historic chamber—where Abraham Lincoln had once signed the Emancipation Proclamation and fumed about his own press coverage—Clinton focused on telling us with pride that he had installed a small trove of old books of the type Lincoln himself had read as a young man. Upset to see one of the brittle volumes sitting upside down, he took it from its place, turned it right side up, and carefully replaced it. (Years later, Hillary would reveal that her husband was a chronic reorganizer of books and bookshelves.)[75] Then, glancing at a Mary Lincoln portrait hanging on the wall, Clinton wistfully commented about that maligned First Lady—in a way, the Hillary of the 1860s—"You know, she got a raw deal."

Perhaps the most personally devastating of the crises the Clintons faced during their first year in the White House occurred in July 1993, when their longtime family friend (and Hillary's former Arkansas law partner) deputy White House counsel Vincent Foster, unable to overcome crippling depression, shot himself to death in a Virginia park. His suicide prompted conspiracy fantasists to advance the libel that the president and his wife had ordered him murdered because he knew too much about their legal and personal travails. Conservative shock jocks and columnists speculated wildly that the White House had not only ordered a cover-up but perhaps even moved and rearranged Foster's corpse to make the shooting look self-inflicted. A shredded suicide note discovered in Foster's briefcase pointed to factors truly fueling his despondency, including what he viewed as unfair press scrutiny: "WSJ [Wall Street Journal] editors," Foster had written, "lie without consequence"—a lament likely inspired by recent editorials raising questions about his administration role.

"I heard a lot of the right-wing talk show people . . . and the sleazy stuff they said" about the Foster suicide, Clinton later agonized. "They didn't give a rip that he had killed himself or that his family was miserable. . . . It was just another weapon to slug us with, to dehumanize us with."[76] Even "respectable newspapers like the *Washington Post*," the president chafed, reported "ghoulish theories."[77] Clinton privately maintained that for all its famous probity, the *Journal* had "hounded Vince Foster to death with malice."[78] As he further reflected to me in late 2019: "The Whitewater coverage was flawed from the beginning, fueled by false information, fed by a source reporters found reliable years earlier. The press would turn it down, but wouldn't let the storyline go, even when the Resolution Trust Corporation's official report said neither of us had done anything wrong, and [that] Hillary's billing records were consistent with her sworn testimony."[79]

Despite the swirl of false leads and leaks, Clinton tried keeping himself in view of the public and press, fighting back with indignation and, when required, humor. On April 12, 1994, he gave a hilarious speech at the Radio and

Television Correspondents' Dinner, poking fun at everything from the Whitewater imbroglio to his image as the "Man from Hope" famous for the empathic assurance "I feel your pain." Clinton proudly remembered that he "got off some good lines" that night, among them: "I really am delighted to be here. If you believe that I've got some land in northwest Arkansas I'd like to sell you. Some say my relations with the press have been marked by self-pity. I like to think of it as the outer limits of my empathy. I feel my pain . . . and I still believe in a place called Help."[80] The very next day, Clinton returned to MTV, where he endured a tasteless "boxers or briefs" inquiry without evident embarrassment ("usually briefs").[81]

Two months later, Clinton resumed his criticism of the media. In a freewheeling radio interview, he lashed out at two conservative critics, radio host Rush Limbaugh and televangelist Jerry Falwell, for offering "a constant unremitting drumbeat of negativism." But Clinton berated the entire press corps for focusing on scandal-mongering. "The American people keep being told that things are bad and politicians are corrupt and the system's broken," he railed. "It's not true."[82] At the time, the press had found a new "scandal" to overreport: a rumor that White House staff members had stolen towels from aircraft carrier staterooms during a recent presidential trip to Europe. There were "lots of other people on that boat," Clinton argued back, including "the press." Rush Limbaugh reacted by declaring, "The gauntlet has been thrown."[83] In the years to come, he would hurl vile personal insults at the Clintons' daughter, Chelsea, and as First Lady Hillary Clinton took on unprecedented official responsibilities, Limbaugh castigated women's rights advocates as "feminazis."

The 1994 appointment of Mike McCurry as Dee Dee Meyer's successor at least helped stabilize day-to-day White House press operations. The new press secretary "created an atmosphere of friendliness—after we were spat upon and treated as the enemy," Helen Thomas cheered through clenched teeth. McCurry charmed the press corps with laid-back humor. Asked once if he would ever lie for the president, he replied, "No, but I'd tell the truth slowly."[84] McCurry ably assumed responsibility for daily "gaggles"—informal morning meetings at which the press secretary outlined the president's news-making schedule for the day. He also took the podium for televised daily briefings—events that a future press secretary called an "artificial environment" designed merely to provide correspondents with "footage of them whacking around a White House official."[85]

Clinton eventually rebounded with the press and public, though it took a national catastrophe to pave his own path to PR redemption: the April 19, 1995, truck bombing of a federal office building in Oklahoma City, which killed 168 people, including 19 children. The act of domestic terrorism had been carried out by an anti-government Gulf War veteran and militia movement enthusiast named Timothy McVeigh to mark the second anniversary of the Waco raid. Clinton denounced the "attack on innocent children and defenseless citizens" and declared in an address to the nation that night, "We will not tolerate it, and I will not allow the people of this country to be intimidated by evil cowards."[86] The president's soaring eulogy at a nationally televised memorial service in Oklahoma City, and his slow walk up the aisle to personally soothe mourners, firmly established him as the nation's consoler in chief.

Recalling Clinton's "unique ability to communicate" directly with the people—on a level that helped him withstand negative press coverage—Sidney Blumenthal attributed the president's "highly personal" gifts to his upbringing. "They were based on the experiences of his birth (his father dying before he was born)," Blumenthal suggested, "his childhood (raised early by his poor grandparents in rural Arkansas), and boyhood (his mother's remarriage, domestic violence, Clinton's intervention), his close relationship with his flamboyant, emotionally warm and empathetic mother, and the high natural intelligence that he persistently trained through great education (Georgetown, a Rhodes Scholar at Oxford, and Yale Law). No modern president combined Clinton's charismatic bond and his mastery of public policy."[87]

Again, however, the Comeback Kid's comeback proved fleeting. The following January, Random House published a sensational, anonymously written roman á clef titled *Primary Colors: A Novel of Politics*. It was the thinly disguised account of a well-oiled presidential campaign suddenly upended by the misdeeds of a randy candidate (Southern governor "Jack Stanton"), then saved from ruin by his ruthlessly tough wife, "Susan." "Who Is Anonymous," wondered the trade journal *Booklist*, "and why is he saying such terrible things about Bill Clinton?"[88] For months, as the book maintained its place on bestseller lists, journalists openly conjectured about the book's authorship, calculating that it could have been written only by someone who had enjoyed full access to Clinton's 1992 inner circle. Much speculation focused on Joe Klein, but the columnist repeatedly disavowed authorship. Only when the *Washington Post* reported in July that it had conducted a handwriting analysis of a draft manuscript of the novel did Klein at last confess that he had written *Primary Colors*.[89]

In the end, neither the book nor the fact that it had been created by a genuine journalistic insider—not even its disturbing reminder of the darkest days of Clinton's rocky 1992 campaign—made much of an impact on the 1996 race. That November, Clinton handily defeated Republican challenger Bob Dole (and Ross Perot, again) to win a second White House term. Clinton outpolled Dole by nearly eight million votes. When the movie version of *Primary Colors* opened two years later, Clinton felt secure enough to invite the man who had portrayed Stanton, John Travolta, to visit the White House. It is said that Travolta declined.

Helen Thomas once remarked of Bill Clinton: "There was just one test he failed: the test of self-discipline." In at least one instance, she proved correct. On January 21, 1998—just one year after his re-inauguration—the *Washington Post* published a bombshell story, first broken by the bottom-feeding *Drudge Report* four days earlier: Clinton had pursued a sexual liaison with the young White House intern Monica Lewinsky. Amid the ensuing uproar, columnist George Will declared Clinton's presidency "deader really than Woodrow Wilson's was after he had a stroke."[90] Facing a "feeding frenzy," Mike McCurry admitted that "in the first couple of days there was a sense that Clinton was going down."[91] The president broke his silence on the 26th—on live TV from the White House, Hillary once again at his side—by denying that he had ever had "sexual relations with that woman, Miss Lewinsky."[92]

The very day the *Post* legitimized the *Drudge* story, the president also went ahead with a previously arranged pre–State of the Union interview with Jim Lehrer for the *PBS NewsHour.* To no one's surprise, the veteran anchorman launched the broadcast by asking the president about the Lewinsky revelations. Clinton insisted, "There is no improper relationship," an emphasis on the present tense that McCurry and other staff members noticed with concern. "On the first day that it broke," Sam Donaldson said of the story, "I realized he was lying."[93] According to political scientist Richard Pious, an "eclectic Clinton" borrowed from both the "Nixon and Reagan tactics" of denial and obfuscation, "but also improvised his own" by insisting on a "zone of privacy."[94]

But in raw terms, the president fibbed to Jim Lehrer. In his own 2004 memoir, Clinton admitted, "[M]y answer was misleading and I was ashamed of telling Lehrer that." Whatever his "terrible mistake," however, he determined he would not be hounded from office. "Since 1991," he said, the sense of perceived injustice still in evidence, "I had been called a liar about everything under the sun, when in fact I had been honest in my public life and financial affairs, as all the investigations would show. Now I was misleading everyone about my personal failings."[95] Clinton once told me he regarded these battles as "the small struggles which consume the political class"—but few others. In this analysis he proved correct: the "small struggles" would never fatally rile Americans outside the Beltway or media aristocracy, at least not to the point of invalidating the recent presidential election.[96] As polls would show, most of those repelled by Clinton's private behavior nonetheless wanted him to remain in office.

If the universally respected Jim Lehrer believed that Clinton defrauded him that January 1998 night on PBS, he never said so. In fact, he remembers Clinton with genuine respect, believing he was endowed with "TV communication skills that were extraordinary, and definitely unique among the other presidents I covered"—skills that particularly shone in the interview format.

"Not even Ronald Reagan's or Barack Obama's, in my opinion," he told me, "could match Clinton's. The key to it was his seemingly innate ability to adapt to the tone and voice as well as the intellect of anyone who joined him before a public microphone and/or camera. He never appeared to speak down, over, or up. There he was, eye-to-eye, mind-to-mind, fact-to-fact while he listened or talked directly to and fully engaged with whomever was there across the table, studio, or room. He made journalists like me feel worthy—and special. And I never felt it was an act or a technique he trained for on his way to political glory-dom. That was just the way he was. Bill Clinton was born to glow in a spotlight that required company for it to shine its very brightest."[97]

The third of Clinton's four White House press secretaries—the man who inherited "Monicagate" from Mike McCurry—was New York–born former NBC News producer Joe Lockhart, who had served as the 1996 campaign spokesman. After an Oval Office job interview at which the beleaguered president did all the talking, admonishing Lockhart to bypass the "elite press" and "talk to the real people out in the states," the thirty-nine-year-old took over from Mike McCurry on August 4, 1998.[98] At that time, the White House staff still did not know that the president had lied about Monica Lewinsky. After Lockhart held his initial Q&A session with the press corps, Helen Thomas approached him to inquire: "So how'd you like your first briefing?" "I loved it, Helen," Lockhart replied, "it was great." Thomas shot back, "They all say that at the beginning. It's going to be an albatross. Trust me."[99]

Once again, Thomas proved right, for the scandal that had been simmering for six grueling months—as other women came forward to say Clinton had romanced or groped them—was about to explode epically. Just two weeks later, Clinton testified under oath before a grand jury at the White House and finally admitted to "inappropriate intimate contact" with Lewinsky. On September 11, Ken Starr released the infamous videotaped deposition at which the president, denying he had perjured himself earlier, insisted, "It depends on what the meaning of the word 'is' is."[100] Journalist Jacob Weisberg prophesied that the answer "was destined for inclusion in *Bartlett's*," asserting that "Clinton is to hairsplitting legalisms what Yogi Berra is to tautological absurdities."[101] In the end, some viewers judged Starr's gross questions about specific sex acts as more outrageous than Clinton's terse, agonized answers. But the president had no choice but to deliver a second television address to apologize for his earlier falsehoods and admit: "Indeed, I did have a relationship with Miss Lewinsky that was not appropriate. In fact, it was wrong. It constituted a critical lapse in judgment and a personal failure on my part for which I am solely and completely responsible."[102] Flushed and tight-jawed, he seemed both remorseful and indignant. His attitude suggested he still believed the matter should have remained private.

The president and Mrs. Clinton tried to endure the resulting media frenzy with dignity, but the press pursued them, parsing and psychoanalyzing their every move. Photographers captured their strained body language as they departed the White House for a long-planned family vacation, their daughter walking referee-like between them, and the president clinging to his pet dog's leash as if it were a lifeline. Pictures later captured husband and wife embracing (in bathing suits) on the beach (a shot that unrelenting critics labeled a setup meant to promote their alleged reconciliation). The press would not let up on Lewinsky, either. When she appeared at a federal courthouse to provide her own testimony, the grounds outside overflowed with so many satellite trucks and reporters that a wag dubbed the stakeout "Monica Beach."[103]

At daily briefings for the rest of the year—which proved as unpleasant as Helen Thomas had predicted—Lockhart fended off most questions about the scandal by referring journalists to the White House legal team. The administration had "made the decision," he explained, "that we were not going to litigate this on television."[104] A press spokesman could not risk advancing explanations that could later come back to haunt Clinton in court, especially after more women came forward to charge Clinton with past sexual harassment. Finally, some four months after Lockhart became press secretary, the Republican-controlled House Judiciary Committee recommended that Clinton be impeached on charges of perjury and obstruction of justice.[105] The crisis understandably spawned mixed metaphors. "This was a tidal wave going over us," Lockhart recalled. "You talk about fires. Every 15 minutes there was a new one."[106]

Just a few days after the committee vote, Bill Clinton ordered four days of high-intensity, widely televised precision airstrikes against Iraq over its failure to heed UN orders to disarm. Operation Desert Fox spawned charges of a White House conspiracy to invent a military crisis to divert public attention from the president's legal and political troubles—the kind of cynical made-to-order conflict that had been depicted in the 1997 black comedy *Wag the Dog*.[107] (Ironically, Republicans had led the calls for aggressive action against Iraqi dictator Saddam Hussein.) Lockhart, who conceded that the "wag the dog" charges proved "a nuisance," would admit later to stealing after-hours time aboard Air Force One to stealthily watch the movie, laughing so hard he woke nearby journalists from their sleep. "This is my last trip," Lockhart fretted to himself, certain the president was about to stride to the back of the plane to fire him.[108] Just one day after the bombing campaign ended, the full House voted along party lines to impeach—making Clinton the first elected president in history to face a Senate trial. Yet within days, the *Washington Post* reported that his popularity numbers had soared upward by 10 points.[109]

In March, the president summoned the courage to undertake the traditional annual appearance at the Gridiron Club, telling its members to "please withhold the subpoenas until all the jokes have been told." Otherwise, a reportedly "traumatized" Clinton "avoided the press when he could, allowing only still photographers into the Oval Office and answering questions only at news conferences with heads of state." It took months for him to dive "back into high-profile events around the White House."[110] Joe Lockhart believed that Clinton managed to endure by remaining "detached" from the media storm. "There's all this political scandal," Lockhart marveled, "and he'll come in in the morning and say, 'I feel great today.' And you think, *you obviously haven't read the paper this morning.*"[111] Through it all, the communications staff remained notably loyal. As Jake Siewert marveled, "No one ever walked out the door and said, 'I quit because of this.'"[112]

Precisely how Clinton managed to weather humiliating media exposure (as well as congressional rebuke)—not only retaining office but actually increasing his poll ratings—remains one of the abiding mysteries of presidential and press history. Analysts have attributed his endurance to such factors as America's distaste for prosecutorial overreach, its increasingly tolerant moral climate, its disgust with the press hysteria the Lewinsky story unleashed, and its strong desire to keep Clinton at the helm of a prospering economy. Always controversial, Clinton evoked a more emotional response than ever from both enemies and admirers. Ann Devroy of the *Washington Post* confessed that every time she wrote about him, her voice mail overflowed with complaints from detractors or supporters who disagreed with her conclusions. "Either way, callers were usually emotional and vulgar."[113]

Many Americans saw through the legislative sanctimony as well, particularly after one of the Clinton critics so eager to cast the first stone, incoming House Speaker Bob Livingston, confessed inside the chamber on live TV that he, too, had strayed from his marriage—and then dramatically resigned and marched off the House floor. *Hustler* publisher Larry Flynt, eager to root out what he viewed as "hypocrisy," took full credit. He had placed a brazen *Washington Post* ad offering a million dollars to "anyone who could prove that they had had an illicit affair with a senator or congressman." Among the many women who stepped forward to claim the bounty, one claimed a relationship with the new speaker, and Livingston got word he was about to be "Flynted." Although Flynt claims he later learned that Clinton was grateful and hoped one day to thank him personally, the president and the pornographer did not meet until 2006, when the two encountered each other at a Las Vegas fundraiser. "He walked directly to me," Flynt boasted, "stuck out his hand . . . and said, 'I just want you to know you're my hero.'"[114]

One factor often overlooked regarding Clinton's resilience under fire was the diminished capacity of both the mainstream media and its embryonic new offshoots on cable, talk radio, and the Internet to stir and sustain outrage. Having earlier made life a misery for Ronald Reagan—but without doing him fatal harm—the traditional press had lost some of its Watergate-era power to persuade, much less topple. Once print and broadcast began relying on fringe media as a news source, mainstream journalism could no longer count on readers and viewers to heed its moralizing and clamor for punishment, especially if it did not fit the so-called crime.

Not only had the news cycle "become continuous," David Gergen noted, but journalists had grown "more cynical and judgmental than those covering the White House" a generation earlier.[115] Sidney Blumenthal contended that Americans also saw through Ken Starr's efforts to "mislead the press corps as well as put the nation through a politically motivated trauma." He notes that "Starr's favorite designated leaker was one of the authors of the deliberately pornographic Starr Report, Brett Kavanaugh," adding that their work "stoked the fires of the right wing media."[116] And conservative media was growing in influence and reach. Back in October 1996, Australian media tycoon Rupert Murdoch had expanded his American empire (which already included the right-leaning *New York Post*) by founding the Fox News network. Murdoch named the conservative political veteran Roger Ailes to run the new operation. Although it took to the airwaves under the slogan "Fair and balanced," Fox and its prime-time stars—notably Bill O'Reilly—went after Clinton ferociously. (Years later, both O'Reilly and Ailes would be forced to quit Fox under a cloud of sexual harassment complaints.)

Both Fox and CNN flooded the airwaves with commentators who alternatively lobbed accusations and justifications that invariably muddied the waters or hardened party-line opinions. Liberal public intellectual Todd Gitlin labeled the new press corps "barking heads" for whom the "thrill of a breaking story" propelled a "dynamic that keeps . . . the 24-hour news channels, along with the tabloids, scraping the bottoms of all accessible barrels."[117] Of this new media environment, Joe Lockhart concluded, "There were some people I trusted" and "some people I didn't"—specifically, those whose "mission was not even-handed journalism." Lockhart referred scornfully to the "small but growing—and it's grown expansively—conservative right-wing media I did not trust at all."[118] Readers and viewers understandably lost faith in party-line opinion with which they did not already agree. The result—a general breakdown of public confidence in the press—felt more profound and permanent than any temporary reduction of respect for the presidency.

Then there was the potent information source still in its infancy: the unfiltered news one could only access on a computer. During this transformative period, even with Matt Drudge breaking stories online, the Clinton White House remained unaware of the growing power (and danger) of Internet communications. Jake Siewert credited two unsung administration staffers, Jock Gill and Thomas Kalil, as the first "to understand the power of the Internet as a communications device."[119] Gill "had the Internet, whatever it was, on his computer.

At the time it was, what's the Internet?" Kalil "got someone to donate a bunch of monitors." The press office installed the screens in the upper reaches of the Old Executive Office Building, and Kalil "would try to drag people up there and show them what it was capable of." Up to then, "everyone else in America" was still getting their news "in chunks, morning, middle of the day, night, more or less. All of a sudden," Siewert discovered, ". . . everyone is seeing all the garbage floating around in Washington."[120] It was a less-than-brave new world that the Clinton staff discovered a bit too late, and answered with far too little.

From whatever media platform reports of his demise emanated, the Clinton deathwatch proved, like Mark Twain's, exaggerated. Nothing could bring him down, although the press corps never abandoned the quest. Journalist-turned-novelist Joe Klein perhaps revealed his own "primary colors" when he went on CNBC to try rationalizing his profession's unrelenting obsession with the president's foibles. "The things that we are most upset with Bill Clinton about," Klein told host Tim Russert, "are the things that I think we're most upset with ourselves about. . . . One, he put marketing over substance, which is something that we in the media are very, very conscious of . . . number two, the sexual revolution. . . . Most of us who have lived through the last 30 years, including a lot of the people who are writing these pompous editorials, have done things that we are not proud of, and by casting out Bill Clinton, maybe we can cast out some of our own demons. But the third thing . . . the most profound . . . is there's a sense in Bill Clinton's generation, our generation, that we skated, that we cut corners, that we got off easy, and man, if there was ever a guy who skated and cut corners and fudged and got off easy, it was Bill Clinton."[121] In other words, Klein seemed to be suggesting, Clinton deserved to pay for the indiscretions of an entire generation, journalists included.

Feminist icon Gloria Steinem strongly disagreed—identifying with Hillary Clinton's fears of a right-wing coup. Media and congressional persecution of Clinton, she argued in a 1998 *New York Times* op-ed, represented "another case of the double standard"—as well as an organized threat by conservatives to destroy a womanizing president sympathetic to the women's movement. His extramarital affairs may have made him a "candidate for sex addiction therapy," she said. "But feminists will still have been right to resist pressure by the right wing and the news media to call for his resignation or impeachment. . . . If President Clinton were as vital to preserving freedom of speech as he is to preserving reproductive freedom," Steinem asked, "would journalists be condemned as 'inconsistent' for refusing to suggest he resign? Forget it."[122]

In fact, as Steinem likely knew, through adversity and under unprecedented scrutiny, Clinton nevertheless maintained a strong commitment to the ideal of a free and independent press—which he made manifest in at least two undervalued cases. He indeed proved "vital to preserving freedom of speech."

At first Clinton had alarmed First Amendment purists by flirting with "decency" legislation designed to restrict sexually explicit content on the Internet; Floyd Abrams accused his administration of doing "more than any other since Richard Nixon's to control television content" and confessed he expected more from a "former war protester" and "constitutional law teacher."[123] Clinton redeemed himself in 1999 by vetoing a proposed National Security Bill, though it must have offered the most investigated president in history the sweet temptation to inhibit future press access to government officials. "We meet enough obstacles that are meant to keep our wrongs secret," applauded one watchdog. "Let's not add another one to the list."[124]

It was not the last time Clinton put his influence behind the cause of journalistic independence. Sidney Blumenthal recalled that, preceding a South American trip, Clinton confronted the fact that press autonomy had dwindled on that continent. The climate was especially chilling in the host country, Argentina, which at the time, Blumenthal said, was "killing journalists." Most presidents avoided discussing human rights violations on foreign trips—it was considered impolite. But as Blumenthal attested: "President Clinton never confused the friction he had with the press corps at home—especially during the unpleasant days—with the principle of upholding freedom of the press everywhere. He was determined to do that with foreign leaders who were suppressing freedom of the press in their own countries."[125] Clinton ultimately pushed for appointment of a special rapporteur within the Organization of American States to monitor and report on press freedom in the region.

Near the end of his two terms in office, following his Senate acquittal and the subsequent 2000 race that saw his vice president, Al Gore, lose a disputed election to George W. Bush, Clinton sat down for an exit interview with PBS anchor Jim Lehrer, their first one-on-one conversation for television since the session that had taken place the day the press broke the Lewinsky story. Lehrer asked Clinton to comment on a recent *New York Times* editorial lamenting that he had "missed the greatness that once seemed within his grasp."

Clinton began his response with a rote, achievement-by-achievement accounting of his eight years in the White House (omitting one of the most significant: that he had cheated the press out of its lust for his destruction). Implying that he knew he was departing without the media's affection, but convinced that journalists reported only the first draft of the American story, Clinton knowingly added, "I had read enough history to know that it is constantly being rewritten."[126] Seventeen years later, ninety-one "presidential historians and professional observers of the presidency" ranked Clinton fifteenth among the first forty-three American presidents in a C-SPAN survey. He surely would have settled for that middle-to-high rating when he left office. "Bill Clinton," biographer David Maraniss explained on the network, would always be "a great story."[127]

Did Clinton sabotage his chance to enter the echelon of great and near-great presidents? Sam Donaldson thought so, arguing that the "man side of him" too often gave way to "the child side of him, and you want to gently shake him by the neck and say, 'Get out of the sandbox.'"[128] Others argued that whatever his flaws and demons, Clinton brought the office the greatest gifts among recent presidents—politically, intellectually, and as a beguiling communicator. In the face of intransigent opposition from a Republican-controlled Congress and a record-high level of antagonism from the media, he kept hope alive for the American social contract, repaired a frayed economy, improved race relations at home, and stood for peace and human rights abroad. Yet he never escaped scrutiny over real and imagined misconduct. Even after he departed, the press reported that his outgoing staff had pilfered White House property and vandalized office computers by childishly prying loose *W* keys from computers to protest the arrival of George W. Bush. "And the press wolfed them down," Clinton remembered ruefully of those rumors.[129] Only later did the incoming administration reveal that such stories had no basis in fact.

As judgment passes from journalism to history, Clinton himself has remained mostly silent about the way the press treated him in the 1990s—until responding to questions for this book. But in the 2018 thriller *The President Is Missing* that he coauthored with novelist James Patterson, he allowed their fictional "President Duncan" to express what most real-life presidents have been reluctant to put into words themselves. And Duncan—perhaps a stand-in for Clinton himself—places much of the blame for national cynicism on the nation's press.

"We're using modern technology to revert to primitive kinds of human relations," the Duncan character warns. "The media knows what sells—conflict and division. It's also quick and easy. All too often anger works better than answers; resentment better than reason; emotion trumps evidence. A sanctimonious, sneering one-liner, no matter how bogus, is seen as straight talk, while a calm, well-argued response is seen as canned and phony. . . .

"We can't survive without a free press, dedicated to preserving that fine line and secure enough to follow the facts where they lead," the fictional president declares. "But the current environment imposes serious pressures on our journalists, at least those who cover politics, to do just the reverse. Everybody knows it's wrong, but the immediate rewards are so great that we stagger on, just assuming that our Constitution, our public institutions, and the rule of law can endure each new assault without doing permanent damage to our freedoms and way of life."[130]

Was Clinton justifiably aggrieved or irrationally self-pitying? Speaking for himself, Clinton told me more than eighteen years after the end of his second term: "I was fortunate to be covered by some fine reporters, and to be both praised and criticized by many fine, intellectually able, and honest columnists."[131] Time may have healed his earlier indignation. By contrast in 2007, a few years before her own departure from the White House, eighty-seven-year-old Helen Thomas appeared on *Meet the Press* for a wide-ranging interview on all the presidents she had covered during her astonishingly long career. Inevitably, the conversation turned to Bill Clinton. "My impression," she said, oblivious to her own complicity, "is that this man . . . did not know one second—and I won't even say a minute—in the White House when he was not being investigated by the right-wing. . . . I don't know how he stood it."

Yet Thomas did not think either prosecutors or prosecutorial journalists deserved full blame for the many years of dysfunction and diversion. It was "incredible," she maintained of Clinton—as if his earlier reluctance to woo the press sealed his doom—"that he didn't realize that you don't play into their hands."[132] For journalists then and since, Bill Clinton remains the president reporters most loved to hate, or most hated to love.

16

GEORGE W. BUSH

Toward the end of the bitter 2000 election contest to succeed him in the White House, Bill Clinton assailed media coverage of the presidential campaign as "a bunch of bull." Holding forth at a Democratic fundraiser in Houston, he unleashed one more salvo against the journalists he felt had plagued him during his own eight years in office. Now, he warned, they threatened to trivialize the race to choose his successor, turning a genuine philosophical battle into a contest about personality. "I do not think America is very well served by all this rigmarole trying to confuse people into thinking that if you can just find which one has the worst quirks, you'll know to vote for the other," Clinton complained. "That's a bunch of hooey."[1]

Perhaps he was thinking back to an opinion piece the previous June by *New York Times* star columnist Maureen Dowd, in which she likened Clinton's vice president (and political heir), Al Gore, to the Tin Man in *The Wizard of Oz*—"immobile, rusting, decent, badly in need of that oil can"—and compared Republican aspirant George W. Bush to "the Scarecrow: charming, limber, cocky, fidgety, seeking to stuff his head with a few more weighty thoughts."[2] Clinton may rightly have objected to such coverage as "hooey," but later that same year, Dowd won the Pulitzer Prize. What now counted as meaningful political journalism bore little resemblance to the work produced by the muckrakers or Woodward and Bernstein.

To be fair, the 2000 presidential candidates—Al Gore and George W. Bush—boasted quirks galore, not to mention flaws. The press regarded Gore as self-aggrandizing—he had once fantastically taken credit for the Internet, a claim journalists seldom let him forget—while Bush preferred not to talk about his early days, when alcohol had reportedly gotten the better of him.

It was hard to know whether Election Day 2000 validated or disproved Bill Clinton's fears about the tenor of the campaign. Whether reacting to quirks, a significant rightward turn on issues, or what was often called "Clinton fatigue," voters gave Gore only a 500,000-vote popular majority—not enough of a cushion, it turned out, to win him the presidential election. Once the Supreme Court halted a recount in disputed Florida, Republican candidate Bush prevailed by a single vote in the electoral college. The interrupted re-tally in Florida ended in a near dead heat—with Bush leading by just five hundred votes out of nearly six million cast, but countless ballots still unexamined. (An independent commission later determined that Bush would have prevailed in Florida—by three times that margin—had the high court allowed the recount to proceed.)

NBC News star Tim Russert had spent so much election night airtime charting different electoral-vote scenarios on a piece of white oak-tag that the poster board later entered the Smithsonian Institution as a national icon. But Bush entered the White House under a cloud, judged by half the electorate as an illegitimate president crowned by a 5–4 high court ruling, which associate justice Sandra Day O'Connor, who voted with the majority, later came to regret.[3] Bush brought a rare combination of diffidence and swagger to the office—a brew of Texas-bred machismo, Yale- and Harvard-trained self-confidence, the knowledge that he had turned too often to drink yet had overcome his dependence, and the humbling experiences he had absorbed as the son of a former president who had lost a bid for a second term.

Election controversies notwithstanding, Bush enjoyed a surprisingly placid honeymoon with both the public and the media—even though, with his election validated only in mid-December, he had been given less time than any president in history to prepare for governing. Of course, the press had already exposed his shortcomings, focusing early and often on Bush's ear-bending campaign-season malaprops. Bush would never "hold our allies hostile," he had said at one point; on another, he pledged he would work to "put food on your family." Elaborating on economic priorities at a debate, Bush declared, "We ought to make the pie higher." Explained campaign press secretary Mindy Tucker, who might have offered a better defense of her boss, "His brain works faster than his mouth."[4]

Bush proved no more facile of tongue in his early years as president, especially with the spotlight aimed on every public appearance. "You teach a child to read, and he or her will be able to pass a literacy test," he declared in defense of his education initiatives. "Too many OB-GYNs aren't able to practice their love with women all across the country," he explained of his health care priorities in Missouri. And in Nashville, he ruminated about his own learning curve: "There's an old saying in Tennessee—I know it's in Texas, probably in Tennessee—that says, 'Fool me once, shame on—shame on you. Fool me—you can't get fooled again.'" Appearing on National Public Radio, he decried Washington cynicism. "I am surprised, frankly, at the amount of distrust that exists in this town," Bush told listeners. "And I'm sorry it's the case, and I'll work hard to try to elevate it."[5]

Bush proved far more agile in charming individual journalists, a tactic that worked to extend his grace period further. One of his quaint obsessions was assigning nicknames to members of the press corps, then remembering and using them endearingly. Thus two particularly tall correspondents, Bill Sammon of the *Washington Times* and David Gregory of NBC News became, respectively, "Super Stretch" and "Little Stretch." CNN's Candy Crowley was "Dulce," a synonym for "sweet." *New York Times* reporter Frank Bruni was inexplicably assigned a derogatory name for Hispanic Americans, "Panchito," and the fearsome Maureen Dowd was dubbed "The Cobra." None of these designations surprised observers who knew that the president referred to House Republican leader John Boehner as "Boner" and nicknamed his political advisor Karl Rove "Turd Blossom." Yet Bush biographer Jean Edward Smith perceived an almost diabolical effort at mind control behind the seemingly innocent rechristenings: "The recipient of the nickname felt flattered," Smith insisted, and thereby "Bush established his authority."[6]

During unscripted moments, Bush proved far less jovial in his choice of sobriquets. At a 2000 Labor Day rally in Naperville, Illinois, candidate Bush spotted a frequent press critic among the gaggle of reporters covering the event. "There's Adam Clymer," he muttered to his running mate, Dick Cheney, "a major-league asshole from the *New York Times*." Cheney could only agree: "Oh, yeah, he is, big time." Bush's vulgarity was caught on a hot microphone and widely rebroadcast. A campaign spokesman tried justifying the epithet by explaining that the candidate had been upset by Clymer's "very unfair" coverage. For his part, the veteran reporter seemed to enjoy the sudden notoriety. "You know," he all but boasted, "if they all love you, you might as well just be driving a Good Humor truck."[7]

As his first White House press secretary, Bush named Ari Fleischer, the fifty-year-old veteran congressional and Senate press aide who had worked in the George H. W. Bush presidential campaign back in 1992 before serving as spokesman for "W's" race in 2000. Longtime Bush II aide Karen Hughes became communications director, while Karl Rove operated from the West Wing as senior advisor and chief political counselor, a job that involved message control and crisis management. Like Bush a Lincoln admirer, Rove kept a collection of Civil War–era engravings in his office. Together, this skilled group worked to put Bush in full view of television cameras for ceremonial occasions while keeping his actual encounters with journalists well structured and, even then, to a minimum.

Otherwise, aides restricted the president's press availabilities to no more than "two or three questions a day, two or three times a week," admitted Fleischer, who added: "While Bush wasn't a fan of formal news conferences and rarely held any, he was regularly available to answer inquiries from the hot news of the day." Bush established a new tradition by appearing unannounced for informal Q&A sessions during the press secretary's daily televised briefings (at least during the early years of his presidency). He also ushered in the practice of allowing reporters to ask questions in the Oval Office during the photo opportunities that preceded or followed his meetings with visiting world leaders. In all the venues, a thoroughly prepped Bush remained tightly disciplined. He knew what he wanted to say, and seldom veered "off message." By this, Fleischer meant that Bush "would often repeat the same statement to the press, no matter how many different ways they asked their questions." Always "looking for the next big story," Fleischer recalled with evident satisfaction, reporters found the consistency "frustrating."[8]

Fleischer and his colleagues functioned from the start as if they faced antipathy from a "liberal" media. "Like every other institution," he maintained, "the Washington and political press corps operate with a good number of biases and predilections. They include, but are not limited to, a near-universal shared sense that liberal political positions on social issues like gun control, homosexuality, abortion and religion are the default, while more conservative positions are 'conservative' positions. . . . Reporters dismiss the notion that they're largely liberal, or they say it doesn't matter, it's not reflected in their writings. I beg to differ."[9]

On a purely social level, ever above the fray, Bush continued reaching out amicably even to those who did not share his political beliefs—including me, a onetime press secretary in liberal Democratic campaigns in New York. In mid-July 2001, a few months after the president served as the commencement speaker at my daughter's graduation from Yale, I accepted an invitation to join a small, handpicked crowd assembled on the White House lawn to greet Bush as his helicopter, Marine One, brought him back from a sojourn at Camp David. (I learned later that crowds were routinely gathered for such arrivals so photographers and TV cameras could record images of adoring admirers welcoming the president home from even the briefest trips.) A few minutes later, after he had quickly changed into casual clothes, we met to chat one-on-one inside the mansion on a range of subjects, including baseball; he was about to host a T-ball game for physically challenged youngsters on a diamond he'd ordered built on the grounds.

At one point he surprised me by asking, "What books have you read lately?"—which I admit was the last subject I expected to be raised by a leader whose alleged lack of interest in reading had become something of a national joke. "*John Adams*," I answered, referring to the then-recently published biography by David McCullough. "I read that, too," the president quickly replied. "I liked it, though I think McCullough was soft on Adams on midnight judges and the Alien and Sedition Act."

"I've never put the publisher of the *New York Times* in jail," Bush added with a smile. Then he winked and added, "much as I'd like to." In my arrogance, I could not decide what was more surprising: the idea that Bush had tackled an eight-hundred-page doorstopper of a book or that he had recognized the over-the-top abuses that a White House predecessor had committed against the press.*

Just two months later, 9/11 ushered in the worst of times for America and, in a sense, the best of times for George W. Bush. The terrorist attacks against the United States deflected increasingly critical press attention on controversial domestic issues like the limitations Bush imposed on government-funded

* Full and grateful disclosure: President Bush later invited actor Sam Waterston and me to perform our program *Lincoln Seen and Heard* at the White House on February 11, 2005, and honored me with the National Humanities Medal in 2008.

stem-cell research and the establishment of a White House Office of Faith-Based and Community Initiatives. Progressives regarded the latter as an attempt to circumvent the constitutionally guaranteed separation of church and state. After September 11, 2001, the country, and the press, focused primarily on terrorism.

Caught somewhat flat-footed when the attacks occurred—a subsequent investigation chided federal agencies for failing to anticipate the aggression—the president himself was in Sarasota, Florida, on September 11. When a hijacked airliner struck the first World Trade Center tower, an unsuspecting Bush was being filmed reading a children's book aloud to an elementary school class. After another plane hit the second tower, White House Chief of Staff Andrew Card approached Bush and whispered the horrific news into his ear: the first crash had been no accident; America was under attack. Bush remained in his seat—seemingly frozen in immobility, his critics later said; but to his defenders, admirably unwilling to alarm the children by racing from the scene—captured for TV news and posterity reading *My Pet Goat* for another seven minutes.

Ari Fleischer's first instinct was to maneuver himself in front of Bush and hold up a handwritten sign that warned, "Don't say anything yet." Heeding the advice to remain mum, the president and the press corps then returned to Air Force One and commenced flying around the country until Washington (near which the Pentagon had also come under attack) had been judged secure. Along the circuitous way home, administration and military officials displaced and stranded journalists at several intermediary stops—to their loudly expressed chagrin. Only five of the original thirteen pool reporters who had accompanied the president to Florida returned with him to the capital. To keep the president's location secret, officials forbade the remaining correspondents from using their cell phones along the way.[10] Once back in the capital, Bush took firm charge. And over the next few months, he morphed into a combination consoler and angel of vengeance.

Perhaps his finest moment—as a leader and communicator—came on September 14, when he visited Ground Zero in Manhattan. There, he climbed onto a pile of rubble to address the emergency crews working on clearing debris and searching for signs of life in the ruins of the World Trade Center. With television cameras rolling, Bush shouted encouraging words into a bullhorn, but not loudly enough to reach all the nearby workers. One of them shouted back that he couldn't hear, to which Bush offered the memorable reply: "I can hear you.

The rest of the world hears you and the people . . . who knocked these buildings down will hear all of us soon." The crowd erupted into the chant "USA, USA, USA."[11] Seven weeks later, as a huge national television audience again tuned in, Bush appeared unannounced to throw out the ceremonial first pitch at a delayed World Series game at Yankee Stadium. Bush, a onetime baseball executive, had rehearsed for the big moment by hurling practice pitches to his press secretary on the White House lawn. Now, as if a higher power were guiding his hand, he tossed a perfect strike as more than fifty thousand spectators again greeted him with a loud chorus of "USA!"

The president scheduled his first post-9/11 press conference a month after the terrorist attacks, practicing for the pressure-packed event at a succession of half-hour sessions at which he effortlessly fielded sample questions from Karen Hughes, her deputy Dan Bartlett (who had managed the Rapid Response team for the 2000 campaign), Ari Fleischer, Andy Card, and National Security Advisor Condoleezza Rice. Fleischer believed Bush did "great" in the actual press conference, and Bush "felt good too, as he reclined in his chair" after the ordeal and "lit a cigar."[12] The president was riding high.

Bush avenged 9/11 with Operation Enduring Freedom, a retributive military campaign against chief perpetrator Osama bin Laden plus the "terrorist camps of Al Qaeda and the military installations of the Taliban regime in Afghanistan." From the start, the president warned of a long war against what he described as an "axis of evil," and he proved right. The administration began planning the operation in the summer of 2002 but delayed action until after Labor Day. As Andy Card callously admitted, "From a marketing point of view, you don't introduce new products in August."[13] A year after the 9/11 attacks, Bush asked Congress to authorize an expansion of what he called a "crusade"—an unwise if unwitting offense to Muslims all over the world who still regarded Medieval Christian Crusades as a barbaric attempt to destroy their religion.[14] Bush now proposed military action to depose Iraqi dictator Saddam Hussein, who, Bush warned, was hoarding weapons of mass destruction.

A few days later, Bush argued his case for a broader war before the UN Security Council, and in March 2003, backed by a 77–23 authorization by the U.S. Senate and support from a coalition of global allies, launched the war against Iraq with a televised "shock and awe" bombing attack on Baghdad. Pleased with what he, too, saw on TV, an overconfident Bush told the Sunday interview show *Face the Nation* that the war might require "weeks, rather than months."[15] But after the shock and awe wore off, the war proved more challenging than Bush had imagined—and less popular. Within a matter of weeks, the president felt compelled to dismiss growing media doubts about the military effort. "I'm not paying attention to the press," he assured a visiting delegation of veterans. ". . . We don't adjust the plan based on editorials."[16]

Just two months afterward, Bush was indeed ready to claim victory. On May 1, 2003, he dramatically landed in a sleek Viking fighter jet on the flight deck of the mammoth aircraft carrier USS *Abraham Lincoln* as it steamed in the Pacific. Bush emerged from his warplane, Ari Fleischer remembered with admiration, "looking perfectly comfortable and dashing in his flight suit." The president "*wanted* to land like a fighter pilot," his press secretary later admitted, "having been one himself in the [National] Guard." Under a giant banner hanging from the flight tower proclaiming "MISSION ACCOMPLISHED," Bush greeted hundreds of enthusiastic sailors. A few hours later, the commander in chief delivered a rousing deckside speech claiming success in the first phase of the Iraq War. But the "MISSION ACCOMPLISHED" banner loomed so large and so declaratively that it all but obscured Bush's carefully calibrated message, which in fact emphasized, "Our mission continues."[17] An administration that had used background graphics to their advantage almost as cannily as had Ronald Reagan's team would soon find itself hoisted on its own visual petard.

The dazzling spectacle had been made to order for television news. Political opponents feared it would be put to later use in campaign commercials, prompting Democrats to howl in outrage. Their complaints grew in number and volume when journalists came to regret their own wide-eyed original reports. As Chris Matthews had rhapsodized on MSNBC, for example, "I think we like having a hero as our president."[18] Later inquiry revealed that Bush might less grandiosely (and more securely) have landed on the *Abraham Lincoln* via helicopter, for the carrier was close enough to San Diego at the time to facilitate easy chopper access. "Helicoptergate" grew in intensity when it became evident, more consequentially, that the Iraq mission had not yet been accomplished after all. Although major operations had ended, insurgents soon reignited the fighting. Fleischer maintained in his memoir, "Many in the White House press corps wondered why it had taken the President so long to declare victory."[19] But the riskiest photo opportunity of Bush's presidency turned out to have been a colossal overreach that came too soon, not too late. U.S. forces did not capture Saddam Hussein until December, and even then sporadic violence continued flaring. (Following a trial, Saddam died on the gallows three years later.)

Bush would always strongly defend the aircraft carrier stunt, insisting: "I was there to thank the troops. My statement was a clear statement basically recognizing that this phase of the war for Iraq was over and there was a lot of dangerous work" left to do. Asked if the "MISSION ACCOMPLISHED" banner had left a misleading impression, Bush replied only that it had not been created or displayed by his own staff.[20]

In July 2003—the same month the CIA admitted that Saddam Hussein had not attempted to purchase enriched uranium to build WMDs, the very rationale for the Iraq War—the administration found itself embroiled in a scandal over retaliatory leaks. In an apparent effort to punish an administration official who had cast doubt on the WMD argument, Karl Rove and I. Lewis "Scooter" Libby, Vice President Dick Cheney's chief of staff, allegedly revealed the identity of a covert CIA operative named Valerie Plame, exposing her to potential danger. Her husband, diplomat Joseph C. Wilson IV, had openly questioned administration claims that Saddam Hussein had sought enriched uranium from Africa to fuel nuclear weapons.[21]

The Plame leak—along with the accusations against her husband—were picked up first by longtime Washington columnist Robert Novak, who outed the CIA agent in his syndicated "Washington Merry-Go-Round" column on July 14, provoking an immediate sensation.[22] Parenthetically, the Novak report may have represented the last gasp of what writer Thomas Mallon called the now "radically . . . contracted" power once wielded by "individual Washington correspondents."[23] Attention turned quickly to the source of the revelation, with some speculating that Ari Fleischer had passed the information on, placing the secret agent's life in peril.[24] "If there is a leak out of my administration," Bush assured the press corps, "I want to know who it is. And if the person violated the law, the person will be taken care of."[25] But "Plamegate," as the scandal was invariably (but only temporarily) named, did considerable damage to the entire Bush administration, not only calling into question its argument for committing troops to Iraq but also raising doubts about its willingness to protect U.S. operatives on their missions overseas. After a subsequent investigation and indictment, Cheney aide Scooter Libby was convicted of both perjury and obstruction of justice. A disillusioned Bush rejected his vice president's entreaties for a presidential pardon, which came only when Donald Trump reviewed the case years later.

Robert Novak altered his recollections of the Plame leak several times over the ensuing years, always insisting that his "role and role of the Bush White

House have been distorted." But he never revealed his confidential source or sources. "If I did," he tried explaining in October 2003, "I would be finished in journalism."[26] He lived another six years without shedding further light on how he had secured the information that, as Valerie Plame later told the *New York Times*, "wrecked her espionage career and nearly took down" her marriage.[27] Both Plame and her husband went on to write books about their experiences, and her memoir inspired a film adaptation, *Fair Game*, in which she was portrayed by Naomi Watts. (The couple ultimately did divorce in 2017, and Bill Plame died two years later.)[28] Another journalist peripherally embroiled in the affair did not fare quite so well. *New York Times* reporter Judith Miller, whose articles had frequently confirmed that Iraq possessed WMDs, also wrote extensively on the Plame leak. Unlike Novak—who, some speculated, cooperated secretly with a grand jury to avoid prosecution—Miller refused to reveal her own sources and subsequently served prison time for contempt and lost her job at the paper. Out of her ordeal came a book of her own.[29]

Fleischer departed the White House in July 2003, exhausted after some two and a half years as press secretary, and at Karen Hughes's suggestion, Bush named Fleischer's deputy, Scott McClellan, as his new press secretary. McClellan served even longer, but he left the job feeling far more disillusioned than his predecessor. In an explosive 2008 memoir, McClellan charged that "the presidency of George W. Bush wandered and remained . . . far off course by excessively embracing the permanent campaign and its tactics." By "permanent campaign," McClellan used "a shorthand term" for "the way political leaders today work 365 days a year, year in and year out, to shape and manipulate sources of public approval as the primary means for governing." In other words, McClellan alleged, the Bush White House became "*primarily* focused" on "using such tools as the news media, political blogs, popular web sites, paid advertising, talk radio, local organizations, and propaganda disseminated by interest groups to shape narratives" to the administration's "advantage." To this already toxic brew of manipulative churning, McClellan confronted another political ingredient that dated back to the Nixon era: a "perpetual scandal culture . . . born in the permanent campaign."[30]

Although McClellan took up his post just a few weeks after Valerie Plame's identity had been leaked, he totally exonerated Bush from the subsequent scandal. The president, he insisted, floated "above the fray, uninvolved in the aggressive, under-the-radar counterpunching of his advisers," explaining: "He purposely chose to know little if anything about the tactics they employed" to combat the media.[31] But McClellan did not overlook the ironic fact that the Valerie Plame "bombshell" had been revealed "not by members of 'the liberal press,' but by a noted conservative reporter, pundit, and commentator, the feisty, beetle-browed Robert Novak."[32]

Bush sought reelection in 2004 against Massachusetts liberal and decorated Vietnam veteran John Kerry. Bush's victory did not come without press controversies. During the race, CBS newsman Dan Rather aired a report questioning the legitimacy of Bush's own Vietnam-era service in the National Guard—using what Ari Fleischer angrily branded as "forged documents" to validate the charges that the president had been a shirker. (At the same time, veterans opposing Kerry were engaged in "Swift Boating" the Democrat—spreading the false charge that he had exaggerated his war record.)[33] "Only after pressure mounted," Fleischer recalled, "did CBS admit they were duped and hadn't performed proper due diligence before putting the inflammatory story on the air." To the Bush White House, the incident provided further evidence that reporters "made things up—facts, events, and quotes—reported them as gospel, and later, much later, got fired once they were caught."[34] That suspicion inflected the team's attitude toward the press for the rest of the campaign, and through its next four years in the White House. Rather lost his job over the report but swore to its accuracy for years. The episode later inspired a 2015 movie, *Truth*, in which the anchorman is portrayed by the man who had once played Bob Woodward: Robert Redford.[35] More so even than Reagan, George W. Bush otherwise maintained affable-enough relationships with journalists while his aides worked under the belief that the press constituted a dangerous, shamelessly partisan enemy class.

Vindicated, Bush began his second term continuing and defending American wars against terror while promoting tax cuts, the privatization of social security, and other conservative priorities. He also made a sincere effort to pass bipartisan immigration reform, which failed twice to gain approval from a sharply divided House of Representatives.

Within a year, however, public opinion turned against both Bush and the war. The media "counterinsurgency" began with pushback from a familiar and seasoned press veteran. Helen Thomas had quit United Press International in 2000 after a media conglomerate controlled by Rev. Sun Myung Moon's Unification Church acquired the fading wire service. Within weeks, Thomas reestablished herself as a White House–based columnist for the Hearst chain, still entitled by seniority to occupy the front-row center seat for every presidential news conference with the right to ask the lead question and end each session with the familiar "Thank you, Mr. President."

That privilege did not last long. For one thing, the Lebanese American veteran began to use her questions to challenge long-standing American policy on Israel. In March 2002, she asked Ari Fleischer to justify American arms shipments to the Jewish state. The following month she asked the press secretary if the president believed "that the Palestinians have a right to resist thirty-five years of brutal military occupation and suppression." As Fleischer understood it, "Helen wasn't really a reporter any longer. She was a columnist . . . freeing her up to give her opinion and not have to act like a neutral reporter who simply asked tough questions. . . . As long as I was the press secretary, she was going to keep [her front-row seat] and be welcome in it."[36]

Once Fleischer left his perch, however, so did Thomas—and not voluntarily. In January 2003 she was overheard telling a fan at a Society of Professional Journalists banquet, "I'm covering the worst president in American history." The admirer turned out to be a writer for the *Daily Breeze*, and he quickly published her comment. At the next presidential press conference she attended, the White House ignored her attempts to ask her customary question. For the first time in forty years, Thomas was silenced. Although she apologized to Bush in writing, the press office temporarily moved her to a back-row seat. Thomas rationalized that the reassignment seemed appropriate since she no longer worked for a wire service. Eventually, she regained both her premier chair and the right to pose questions, but forfeited the privilege of terminating each session with the traditional "thank you." As Thomas understood, "They don't like me." Her questions were "too mean."[37]

A few years later, the indestructible veteran exacted her revenge. At a press conference on March 21, 2006, Thomas as usual led off the interrogation, but this time with the most provocative question with which she had launched a news session since the Nixon era. An unapologetic opponent of the Iraq War who believed Pentagon reporters had been too gullible in accepting the administration's explanations for the conflict, she now directed her doubts to the commander in chief.[38] "I'd like to ask you, Mr. President," she began, "your decision to invade Iraq has caused the death of thousands of Americans and Iraqis, wounds of Americans and Iraqis for a lifetime. Every reason given, publicly at least, has turned out not to be true. My question is, why did you really want to go to war?"

Startled, Bush tried citing 9/11. The Iraqis had not attacked on 9/11, Thomas shot back. "They did," Bush insisted, "the Taliban provided safe haven for al Qaeda." The veteran reporter would not let the president get away with that misstatement, either. "I'm talking about Iraq," she countered. Correcting himself to acknowledge that the Taliban had indeed operated out of Afghanistan, Bush insisted that Iraq had posed a dangerous threat of its own. He rambled on that the UN had not achieved a diplomatic solution, yet he took credit for making sure "that Saddam Hussein heard the message of the world."[39] It was not Bush's finest moment before the press. His approval ratings plummeted, and he never again crossed above the dismal 40 percent mark. Scott McClellan would serve nearly three years, the longest tenure of any of Bush's White House spokesmen, but left with a sour taste. (He would endorse Barack Obama in 2008.)

Bush's public relations nadir came in the wake of an act of God: Hurricane Katrina, which struck New Orleans on August 29, 2005. More than 1,800 people died in the storm that breached the city's levees. Whole sections of the city vanished underwater, while other areas succumbed to looting. The federal government took much of the heat for the natural disaster by appearing to respond lethargically while Bush himself continued a working vacation at his Texas ranch. In the wake of Katrina, the administration committed a perfect storm of PR blunders.

"The president understood his role as comforter in chief in such situations," Scott McClellan asserted, "and he performed it remarkably well"—in most circumstances. "The standard practice of the Bush White House," McClellan knew, "was not to have the president rush to the scene of a natural disaster." Bush preferred to let emergency workers perform their tasks unimpeded, and he remained disinclined to seek a publicity advantage from other people's suffering. As McClellan rationalized, Bush had avoided New York's Ground Zero for three days before his acclaimed bullhorn-message visit on September 14, 2001. But *Newsweek* reported that Bush had neither read newspaper reports nor viewed television coverage of the Katrina disaster, watching video of the hurricane for the first time only when he belatedly headed to New Orleans to inspect the damage.[40]

Until then, the Bush team had stubbornly maintained the president's previously announced schedule without alteration. The day after Katrina made landfall, Bush flew to an event in San Diego to mark the anniversary of V-J Day and the end of World War II. His only deviation from the pre-Katrina game plan was to begin his prepared remarks with a dutiful comment on hard-hit New Orleans and its residents. Then disaster of the man-made kind struck Bush, out of the public's sight—but not that of the press. Backstage after the ceremony, country music star Mark Wills, who had entertained at the V-J event, presented Bush with a guitar emblazoned with the presidential seal. With a grin, Bush took the instrument and began strumming chords. Unbeknownst to the president, ABC News Pentagon correspondent Martha Raddatz was standing just a few feet away armed with a small camera, and of course took a picture of Bush playing Nero-like with his new toy. Within hours, McClellan painfully remembered, her snapshot "hit the AP wire, juxtaposed with one showing a stranded family in coastal Mississippi being rescued from the rooftop of their SUV, and others showing New Orleanians clinging to the rooftops of their submerged homes. This was exactly what I feared: the image of a seemingly carefree President Bush pursuing his original schedule and disregarding the plight of Katrina's victims—the dead, the homeless, the lost. Was it fair? You decide."[41]

Further Katrina-related publicity nightmares lay ahead. McClellan had strongly objected to Karl Rove's suggestion that, en route back to Washington, Air Force One should descend low enough over New Orleans for Bush to inspect Katrina damage from the air. McClellan warned, "He'll look out of touch and detached. If he goes, he needs to be on the ground visiting with those affected and seeing the damage up close."[42] The flyover took place anyway, with the plane dipping down to an altitude of 2,500 feet as Bush sat by a side window to peer down at the devastation while photographers inside the cabin snapped pictures.

According to Wayne Slater and James Moore, biographers of Karl Rove: "It was among the most damaging photos of [Bush's] presidency. The president appeared detached and powerless, unable even to comprehend how he might use the government to help his own people."[43] Finally hitting the ground to visit the disaster area on September 2, Bush compounded his clumsy errors by praising Federal Emergency Management Agency director Michael D. Brown with the unforgettable words, "Brownie, you're doing a heck of a job."[44] Soon thereafter, Bush fired the FEMA chief and finally admitted that "Katrina exposed serious problems in our response capability at all levels of government."[45] By then it was too late for public relations redemption. Even the president's mother had contributed to the growing sense that the entire Bush family was indifferent to the suffering. When the government shipped homeless hurricane victims to Houston's Astrodome for emergency shelter, Barbara Bush commented on radio that the lodging was "working very well" for the "underprivileged" who had lived in substandard housing in New Orleans.[46]

Bush never regained his popularity—which had topped 90 percent approval in the weeks after 9/11—yet never seemed as perpetually embroiled in career-threatening controversy as had his White House predecessor. Regardless of who served as press secretary, the administration managed to maintain an aura of calm, even if the prevailing mood occasionally suggested complacency and indecisiveness. The press remained outside looking in, granted few opportunities to penetrate the bubble. Media resentment fell on the press secretaries, not the president, who continued uncannily to remain above the fray.

"In many ways, the lesson of the Bush administration," said Bill Clinton's last press secretary, Jake Siewert, "is that *we* [emphasis added] were much too nice to the press. I think there was a tendency in the [Clinton] Press Office, particularly, specifically, to blame things on the President . . . rather than take the hit for themselves. I think what Ari and his staff did very effectively . . . they just took the hit themselves so the President was the good guy. The animosity of the reporters was all directed at Ari and his team and not at the President."[47]

"The current White House is adept at so many things," Siewert continued of the Bush team, adding one major reservation: "They don't seem quite as nimble. They like to develop their long-range plan and stick with it, and I think they were hurt in the Katrina aftermath by the fact that it didn't fit anyplace. There was nobody who had the job of saying, 'Hey, everybody else is talking about this and we're not.'"[48] This unyielding dynamic might have altered under Bush's third spokesman, the popular TV journalist Tony Snow. But Snow suffered a recurrence of colon cancer early in his tenure and served less than a year before taking medical leave. He died in 2008.

"The president wants to have a good relationship with the press," Bush's fourth and final press secretary, Dana Perino, told political spokesman-turned-historian Woody Klein in 2007. "I have been trained to get the media a correct answer as quickly as possible with as much detail as possible. . . . When I am asked a question that I know the answer to but the president does not want the information released, I say 'That's not something I can get into right now.'" Bush, she noted admiringly, did not "have a vindictive bone in his body. . . . He lets criticism roll off his back."[49]

Perino was serving as press secretary during the outgoing president's final trip to Iraq, where she witnessed one more notable example of Bush's remarkable sangfroid. At a press conference in Baghdad on December 14, 2008, a journalist from the newspaper *Al-Baghdadia* hurled two shoes in Bush's direction, shouting: "Dog. . . . This is from the widows, the orphans and those who were killed in Iraq." Ever athletic, Bush deftly dodged and ducked, avoiding both pieces of footwear as they flew toward him. In the melee that followed when security men descended on the assailant, a microphone stand fell over and injured Perino in the eye. Unfazed, Bush resumed his press conference by remarking, "All I can report is it is a size 10."[50] Still, the incident—even if it took place in a volatile war zone—ranked as the first and, so far, only time a reporter ever physically attacked an American president during a press conference.

Back home, it was Helen Thomas who threw the shoes—even if they were only symbolic. Increasingly outspoken on the issue of Palestinian rights in her new role as a columnist, she had outraged press secretary Tony Snow in 2006 by charging, "We have gone for collective punishment against all of Lebanon and Palestine." Snow had replied sharply, "Thank you for the Hezbollah view."[51] The following November 30, Thomas asked Snow's successor why the public should "depend" on General David Petraeus to decide on a lingering American troop presence in Iraq. As Dana Perino attempted to answer by calling the general "the one who is making sure that the situation is moving," Thomas interrupted with, "You mean how many more people we kill?" Perino, who had been born twelve years after Thomas began covering the White House, decided it was time to talk back to the older woman. "Helen," she lectured her publicly, "I find it really unfortunate that you use your front row position, bestowed upon you by your colleagues, to make such statements. This is . . . an honor and a privilege to be in the briefing room, and to suggest that we, the United States, are killing innocent people is just absurd and very offensive." As usual, Thomas had the final word. When Perino volunteered that America had "expressed regret" for the loss of innocent lives in Iraq, Thomas said, "Oh, regret. It doesn't bring back a life."[52] Notwithstanding her fraught experiences on the job, Perino later wrote a cheerful book called *And the Good News Is: Lessons and Advice from the Bright Side.*

Bush left office after spending a year confronting the worst economic crisis of the new century, a collapse that came dangerously close to escalating into a full-blown depression. Many economists blamed laissez-faire Republican economic policies and deregulated banks gone amok with risky lending. To his credit, Bush helped avert a catastrophe by doing what fellow Republican Herbert Hoover had failed to do in 1929: using the federal government to fight back.

In December 2008, Bush authorized a bailout of General Motors and Chrysler to save both giant companies—and their tens of thousands of employees—from bankruptcy. When Bush left office in January 2009, the fate of the economy remained unknown, the causes for its downturn still a muddle. Credit for the emergency rescue generally went to Treasury Secretary Henry Paulson, Federal Reserve Chairman Ben Bernanke, and New York Fed President Timothy Geithner. But the press may have granted Bush insufficient credit for responding to the crisis with an elasticity shown by no Republican president since Teddy Roosevelt. In a 2018 analysis, the *Wall Street Journal* belatedly reminded readers, "Mr. Bush's unsung role merits greater appreciation today."[53]

Just before the 2008 presidential election, the *New York Times* asked a number of current and recent White House staff veterans, along with longtime observers, to contribute to an op-ed titled "What I Will Miss About President Bush." *Slate* editor Jacob Weisberg replied whimsically: "Mr. Bush's battle with English has enriched our political language. It is no longer possible to say a person or a factor has been underestimated. Thanks to him, that word is now misunderestimated. In trade negotiations, tariffs and barriers have become bariffs and terriers. Kosovo is the land of the Kosovians, Greece the ancient homeland of the Grecians. . . . When words won't do what he wants, he tries to wrestle them into submission. . . . In the face of defeat, Mr. Bush remains unbowed by grammar. You've got to admire that, kind of."

But according to *GQ* correspondent Robert Draper, who had gone on to write a biography of the forty-third president, there was more to the Bush legacy than miscommunication. "His sense of loyalty blinded him to the shortcomings of several senior aides," he said, "—among them Scott McClellan, who rewarded Mr. Bush's generosity with a lacerating tell-all book. He [Bush] kept the press away from his two daughters, when their charm could have been deployed to buoy up his sagging numbers. When the vault of the 43rd presidency is sealed, it will include, among many things, evidence of President Bush's virtue."

But it was Bush's first press secretary who tried to make a virtue of what many considered Bush's worst fault: the tendency to oversimplify and moralize. "Mr. Bush saw the presidency as a place to call the American people to big challenges—in morally clear terms," Ari Fleischer tried explaining. "As his spokesman, I knew that many people would be uncomfortable with how easily he made such moral judgments. I also knew that many Americans welcomed his tough, direct and unambiguous moral clarity. . . . I hope his successors recognize the strength that moral clarity can provide." But Bush's second and longest-serving White House spokesman, Scott McClellan, hoped that "the next president will share his passion for human dignity—and also find ways to express it with greater wisdom and judgment."[54]

Whether or not the press "misunderestimated" George W. Bush remains to be decided by researchers and historians. But that analysis may prove difficult to undertake because of a dearth of available sources. One of the persistent criticisms of the Bush White House was described by the *New York Times* as "its penchant for secrecy," a resistance to scrutiny affirmed by historian Alan Brinkley—the son of TV news icon David. The younger Brinkley charged that the Bush administration consistently endeavored "to release nothing" to the public or press, not because it was worried that its trove of documents contained embarrassing secrets, but because of "what's in there that they don't know about." As Ari Fleisher told the *Times* in response: "The bottom line remains the president is dedicated to an open government, a responsive government, while he fully exercises the authority of the executive branch."[55]

The *New York Times* report argued that this was not really the case. And in doing so, the paper of record provided a reminder that the press, not the president, usually gets the last word, even if it represents only the initial draft of what later becomes history. Sometimes the press gets the last laugh as well. The damaging 2003 *Times* exposé on government secrecy carried the byline of the very reporter George W. Bush had once called "a major-league asshole": Adam Clymer.

17

BARACK OBAMA

Barack Obama made history—not only as America's first African American president but as its first social media president as well. Whether his extraordinary success on new, high-tech communications platforms should be attributed to instinct, opportunity, or a combination of talent and circumstance, Obama mastered a system of rapid messaging that greatly expanded the president's direct access to the people but further distanced the professional press from the president.

Obama enjoyed the benefits of wide exposure to the American public, but he paid a price for reaching over the heads of professional journalists. Back in the 1960s, Lyndon Johnson had been observed at the White House clutching transistor radios and monitoring wire service tickers, and was judged remarkably modern for utilizing such devices to keep current with the news. Half a century later, Obama turned for information to the BlackBerry and, later, the iPhone. But unlike LBJ, he and his administration used these and equally advanced tools not just to receive information but to deploy it.

By relying less than any of his predecessors had on traditional journalism to convey news, Obama accomplished what all the truly revolutionary presidential communicators had done from Jefferson to Lincoln to Kennedy: he expanded and personalized his messaging by using the most modern available technologies to reach the widest possible audiences. Not since JFK turned to television did a president so successfully harness a new technology to communicate directly to the American people.

Even so, the traditional press still held considerable power during the

Obama years, and inevitably came to resent the new president's communications independence. Obama never let journalists forget that they needed him more than he needed them; and the press never forgave him for the same reason.

Not that Obama shied away entirely from conventional media encounters. When necessary, he showed himself to be a virtuoso of the press conference as well—impeccably prepared, resourceful, amusing, able to usefully consume time by filibustering his responses, and when appropriate, for all his famous "coolness," showing genuine passion. And no one, not even Bill Clinton, demonstrated more empathic oratorical skills when salving national wounds in times of trauma and mass mourning. Obama proved himself an extraordinary healer-communicator after the massacre of children at the Sandy Hook elementary school, the sniper-attack murder of policemen in Dallas, and the racially motivated slaughter at Charleston's Emanuel African Methodist Episcopal Church—where the president broke into a spontaneous chorus of "Amazing Grace" as millions watched on live television.

Like Clinton, but more so, Obama took his case not only to news programs but to entertainment TV venues as well. But increasingly, Obama preferred to generate news on his own Internet platforms: Facebook, Flickr, Snapchat, Instagram, YouTube, Myspace, Tumblr, and even iTunes, as well as through the content supplied for the millions of followers who enrolled to receive updates from the official White House website. By 2015, he added Twitter to his arsenal, announcing in his initial post: "Hello, Twitter! It's Barack. Really! Six years in, they're finally giving me my own account." Introducing himself as a "Dad, husband, 44th President of the United States," and a devoted fan of various Chicago sports teams, the tweeter in chief with the handle @POTUS instantly attracted hundreds of thousands of followers. A White House social media strategist called the account "a new way for President Obama to engage directly with the American people, with tweets coming exclusively from him."[1]

But in a regrettably old-fashioned sign of the times, his inaugural post quickly drew scores of racist rants, with one post reading, "Get back in your cage monkey," and another showing an image of Obama's head in a noose, accompanied by the message: "we need 'ROPE FOR CHANGE.'" Press secretary Josh Earnest insisted that "the president's new Twitter handle is one that can be used to important effect," while Obama advisor Dan Pfeiffer, who had urged the president to make use of social media, maintained: "We know these sentiments exist, we know those comments are on Twitter or other social media platforms, but you'd be missing a terrific chance to engage with a lot of really good nontrolls if you stayed off them because of the tiny fraction of people who are doing it." Ultimately the Secret Service felt compelled to establish an "Internet Threat Desk" to monitor the uglier online insults.[2]

By the end of his presidency, by one count, Obama had posted thousands of tweets and attracted more than 104 million followers—more than anyone in the country at the time, even runner-up singing sensation Katy Perry.[3] Inevitably, Obama's social media posts reduced mainstream journalists to playing catch-up. The administration began making its major announcements online, with journalists receiving news at the same time it reached audiences who had once depended on the press alone to dispense such information.

Rapidly changing communications technology made Obama's innovative methods possible. Yet for all his efforts to expand outreach, Obama conversely did more than most of his predecessors to restrict access, and not only because in a high-tech age a president no longer needed to rely exclusively on a friendly press. Although he entered office vowing an unprecedented level of transparency, Obama proceeded to place obstacles on the free flow of information—a crackdown his administration justified in the name of national security in a still-dangerous world. As a result, Obama may deserve a place alongside John Adams, Abraham Lincoln (his political hero), and Woodrow Wilson as the most aggressive presidents in blocking press scrutiny and making professional life difficult for his critics. His efforts ranged from the overt (investigating journalists his administration regarded as security risks) to subtle (blackballing unfriendly media outlets).

Obama's most combative effort to hamstring press coverage came at the beginning of his presidency, in 2009, when he launched a blanket public relations blitz to win public support for his major domestic initiative, and in the end, signature accomplishment: health care reform. On September 20, he made his arguments on five different Sunday talk shows—that is, those that aired on CBS, ABC, NBC, CNN, and Univision. Conspicuously, he shunned *Fox News Sunday.* The snub was clearly meant as an act of revenge. Two weeks earlier, the president had addressed a joint session of Congress on the health care issue, and Fox, sister network of cable television's most conservative all-news outlet, had alone declined to broadcast the speech live. Instead, the network had aired the latest episode of its entertainment series *So You Think You Can Dance.*

Asked to provide an official explanation for the president's reluctance to take his case to the vast *Fox News Sunday* audience, deputy White House press secretary Josh Earnest lived up to his given name by taunting, "We figured Fox would rather show *So You Think You Can Dance* than broadcast an honest discussion about health insurance reform." In a more sober and revealing vein, administration communications director Anita Dunn declared of Fox News: "We're not going to legitimize them as a news organization. . . . We're going to treat them the way we would treat an opponent. As they are undertaking a war against Barack Obama and the White House, we don't need to pretend that this is the way that legitimate news organizations behave." Fox News anchor Chris Wallace replied, "They are the biggest bunch of crybabies I have dealt with in my 30 years in Washington."[4]

In a follow-up campaign to further promote its health care proposals, the administration next organized a series of televised town hall meetings featuring congressmen and senators taking questions from ordinary citizens. Obama himself appeared at one. When the mainstream press began reporting that some of the sessions had been marked by anger, anxiety, and confusion, Obama blamed the media, not the message. "TV loves a ruckus," he seethed. "What you haven't seen on TV and what makes me proud are the many constructive meetings going on all over the country."[5] He may have been right, but the White House neglected to reach out to all the press to make the argument in the traditional manner. The ostracism of Fox News continued. That same year, the administration ordered the Treasury Department's special master for compensation—"Pay Czar" Kenneth Feinberg—to decline an invitation to appear on Fox News to discuss efforts to prevent runaway compensation for executives whose companies took federal assistance from the Troubled Assets Relief Program (TARP). Feinberg hit all the major news networks but one.

In 2012, the administration yet again excluded Fox News from official briefings, this time a series of White House and CIA backgrounders on the September terrorist attack against the U.S. consulate at Benghazi, which had resulted in the death of U.S. ambassador to Libya J. Christopher Stevens. That particular decision may have helped provoke years of Benghazi investigations by pro–Fox News Republicans, particularly into Secretary of State Hillary Clinton's alleged failure to guarantee security for U.S. diplomatic outposts abroad. Ostracizing Fox News came to trigger not only media resentment but political retribution.

In his antipathy toward Fox News, Obama certainly demonstrated a keen understanding of the rapidly evolving—some would say deteriorating—broadcast news culture. To Obama, Fox personified an existential shift: the gaping partisan divide now inflecting much of cable news, with Fox News tilting hard to the right and CNN and MSNBC to the left. As Obama sensed, here was media history repeating itself, with the increasing dominance of politicized news resurrecting the long-discarded traditions of the party-aligned print press of earlier days. Nearly a century and a half earlier, an admittedly pro-Republican journalist had likened party-affiliated newspapers to "'hand organs,' for the simple reason that hand-organs can only grind out those particular tunes which the machines are manufactured to play."[6] Newspapers then not only covered politics but participated—as advisors, official printers, and organizers. In the modern world of cable news, the unmistakable synergy between politics and networks became more philosophical than organizational; but because of cable's vast reach and twenty-four-hour reporting cycle, the "hand organs" grew louder, more dissonant, more influential, and certainly more immediate.

Liberals decried Fox News, but conservative observers countered that the new generation of MSNBC and CNN anchors had come to include such unapologetically progressive stars as Chris Matthews, a former staff aide to onetime Democratic House Speaker "Tip" O'Neill and Chris Cuomo, son of one Democratic New York governor and brother of another. Obama's Fox News critics may not have spent time of their own in government or politics, but they came to reflect, even inspire, conservative political dogma, especially the marquee stars Bill O'Reilly and Sean Hannity. O'Reilly, the onetime host of the innocuous series *Inside Edition*, appeared now on *The O'Reilly Factor*, offering a "no spin zone" in which the host in fact spun the news blatantly and shouted down guests who disagreed with him. Hannity, a radio broadcaster, rose to TV fame as the right-leaning voice on a conceptually balanced give-and-take show called *Hannity & Colmes*. Liberal Alan Colmes's departure during the first year of the Obama presidency opened the way for Hannity to reestablish the nightly program as an exclusively conservative soapbox. Both O'Reilly and Hannity attracted huge followings.

Conservative talk radio host Mark R. Levin nonetheless insisted that the Obama-era media remained strongly biased toward liberals, pointing now to an array of print journalists who had floated between media jobs and employment at the White House. These included *Time* magazine editor Richard Stengel, who became an undersecretary of state for public diplomacy and public affairs in the early Obama years, one of twenty-four journalists hired by the administration, according to *The Atlantic*.[7] Yet Levin conveniently ignored the fact that presidents had been appointing friendly journalists to government posts since the Founding Era. In the weeks leading up to Abraham Lincoln's 1861 inauguration, one of *New York Tribune* editor Horace Greeley's rivals chortled that Lincoln had plucked so many new diplomatic appointees from the ranks of the pro-Republican daily that "it became the talk in newspaper circles that the *Tribune* would be depleted of its writers in consequence of the necessity of the new administration for suitable men to send abroad as ministers, *chargé d'affaires*, and consuls."[8] By 2009, media patronage and media partisanship alike approached pre–Civil War levels.

Obama actually underestimated this resurgence when he told *Rolling Stone* in October 2010 that the new wave of journalistic bias seemed the most blatant since the Hearst chain had directed its hostility toward early twentieth-century progressives. He might as convincingly have compared increasingly politicized television coverage to the Federalist-Democratic newspaper feuding of the Revolutionary period, or the splenetic Democratic-Republican antagonisms that marked press coverage before the Civil War. During those fraught periods, factual reporting had vanished altogether. Democratic and Republican coverage of the same events had borne scant resemblance to each other. Now, while most newspaper reporting aspired to objectivity, the same could seldom be said of conflicting accounts airing on liberal and conservative cable networks. Responding with a laugh to the question "What do you think of Fox News?" the president told *Rolling Stone*:

> Look, as president, I swore to uphold the Constitution, and part of that Constitution is a free press. We've got a tradition in this country of a free press that oftentimes is opinionated. The golden age of an objective press was a pretty narrow span of time in our history. Before that, you had folks like [William Randolph] Hearst who used their newspapers very intentionally to promote their viewpoints. I think Fox is part of that tradition—it is part of the tradition that has a very clear, undeniable point of view. It's a point of view that I disagree with. It's a point of view that I think is ultimately destructive for the long-time growth of a country that has a vibrant middle class and is competitive in the world. But as an economic enterprise, it's been wildly successful. And I suspect that if you ask Mr. [Rupert] Murdoch what his number-one concern is, it's that Fox is very successful.[9]

"Few presidential candidates ever enjoyed better news coverage than Barack Obama in 2008," veteran Bloomberg News columnist Al Hunt remembered of the freshman Illinois senator's White House runs against Democratic primary opponent Hillary Clinton and Republican nominee John McCain.[10] During the campaign, media observer Ken Auletta agreed: "Obama was the object of near veneration, possessed of a persona and a campaign that were irresistibly compelling to all but his rivals and the right-wing press." As evidence, Auletta offered the persuasive fact that *Time* put Obama on the magazine's cover six times in just eleven months.[11]

In fact, the press had taken notice of—and heaped praise on—Obama from the time he first claimed the national spotlight as a riveting, nationally televised keynote speaker at the 2004 Democratic National Convention. There, Obama arguably made an even greater impression than Roosevelt had notched with his comeback convention speech eighty years earlier. "A superstar is born," raved Clarence Page in the *Chicago Tribune* after the 2004 keynote. "It is difficult for many of us to contain our enthusiasm for Barack Obama." Page all but predicted that Obama would seek the presidency himself in 2012. He was off by four years; Obama did not feel the need to wait.[12]

As Obama weighed a 2008 bid, the press encouraged him lavishly. Lynn Sweet of his hometown *Chicago Sun-Times*—the reporter who, colleague Glenn Thrush believed, held Obama "most accountable"—noted that the senator now occupied "a pedestal." Writing in *Newsweek*, Ellis Cose called him "a political phenomenon unlike any previously seen," a reaction echoed in a *Time* cover story by the longtime cynic Joe Klein, who called Obama "the equivalent of a rainbow—a sudden preternatural event inspiring awe and ecstasy." Obama improved his image—as if further embellishment were needed—with an electric guest appearance on *Oprah*, followed by equally impressive turns on the *Today* show, *Meet the Press*, and *All Things Considered*, ostensibly to promote his well-timed new book, *The Audacity of Hope*. By the time his book tour reached Philadelphia, press coverage had approached the rhapsodic. To the *Inquirer*, Senator Obama seemed "as handsome as John F. Kennedy and as charismatic as Bill Clinton."[13]

No candidate ever launched a presidential campaign with a more scenic and symbolic announcement event. On February 10, 2007, two days before Abraham Lincoln's 198th birthday, Obama appeared outside the Old State Capitol in Springfield, the historic building where Lincoln had delivered his "House Divided" speech in 1858 to begin a candidacy of his own for the U.S. Senate. Unlike Lincoln—who had warned the country could not endure "half *slave* and half *free*"—Obama had quoted the preamble to the Constitution to promise "a more perfect union."[14] Still, Obama did not retreat from emphasizing his natural connection to the man who had issued the Emancipation Proclamation; it was as if Lincoln himself had planted the seeds that had blossomed into the historic announcement by the first African American male to seek a major-party presidential nomination. "And that is why," Obama declared that frigid day in Springfield, and to the audience watching on live TV, "in the shadow of the Old State Capitol where Lincoln once called on a house divided to stand together, where common hopes and common dreams still live, I stand before you to announce my candidacy for President of the United States of America."[15]

Obama's storied run did not lack for moments of peril. A *Rolling Stone* story published just before his announcement ceremony revealed that his longtime Chicago pastor, Rev. Jeremiah Wright, had once delivered an incendiary sermon from the pulpit. Obama, who had asked Wright to deliver the invocation at his Springfield launch, rescinded the invitation at the last minute, fearful that a public appearance by the minister might steal the headline from his own big moment. Media interest in Wright faded, but only temporarily. In March of the following year, a few days after Hillary Clinton bested Obama in the Ohio and Texas primaries, ABC broke the news that the minister had also delivered a fiery sermon interpreting the 9/11 attacks as God's retribution for U.S. "state terrorism against the Palestinians and black South Africans" and for its World War II bombings of Hiroshima and Nagasaki. "America's chickens!" he had railed. "Are coming home! To roost!"—echoing, perhaps intentionally, the controversial statement Malcolm X had made about the death of John F. Kennedy in 1963. Worse for Obama, this particular rant had been captured on video, along with a 2003 sermon, "Confusing God and Government," in which Wright had declared: "Not God bless America. God damn America."[16] Whether or not Barack and Michelle Obama had occupied a pew for either harangue became irrelevant as the inflammatory clips aired repeatedly on television, generating an uproar that threatened to sink the campaign. Fox News began calling Wright "Obama's Minister of Hate."[17]

After trying without success to ignore the firestorm, Obama attempted a bold recovery in a forum few politicians ever mastered as brilliantly: the televised speech. Appearing at the National Constitution Center in Philadelphia ten days after the Wright controversy erupted, Obama delivered a measured but eloquent oration titled "A More Perfect Union." Reintroducing himself as "the son of a black man from Kenya and a white woman from Kansas," Obama confided that during his youth, his beloved white grandmother had occasionally used racially insensitive language that had made him cringe. He would renounce neither Wright nor his grandmother now, he said, straining logic but evoking sympathy; each had been too important in making him the man he had become. Obama did repudiate the minister's toxic sermons, while clarifying that Wright had served only as his spiritual—but not his political—mentor. As Obama declared, "I can no more disown him than I can disown the black community."[18] TV cameras occasionally cut to show audience members weeping.

Reaction to the address predictably split along partisan lines, with conservative talking heads continuing to rail against both Obama and his pastor. But in an editorial called "Mr. Obama's Profile in Courage," the *New York Times* spoke for many progressive opinion makers in declaring that the candidate had "not only cleared the air over a particular controversy—he raised the discussion to a higher plane."[19] Hailing it as the "best speech ever given on race in this country," MSNBC's Chris Matthews urged that Obama's text become required reading for students from first grade to college—as "an American tract." The speech never achieved that status, but ABC's George Stephanopoulos, a veteran of Clinton-brand political turmoil and redemption, immediately recognized that it "held his campaign together."[20] For a time, Fox News tried keeping the Wright matter before its viewers, but the public lost interest. The "More Perfect Union" speech not only ended the uproar but reinvigorated the campaign. "We were triumphant," Obama's savvy media guru David Axelrod allowed himself to rejoice, "and riding a media wave."[21]

In an especially nuanced analysis of the episode, Georgetown University sociology professor Michael Eric Dyson—an African American intellectual who also serves as a commentator on cable news—emphasized an aspect of the story that the white liberal media missed. "The conflict between Wright and Obama," he pointed out, represented "a showdown of two archetypes in black America: the prophet and the politician." Citing Frederick Douglass, Martin Luther King Jr., and Jesse Jackson, Dyson argued that prophets had hitherto prevailed in influence without achieving electoral success. "Barack Obama's rise may not be the first instance of the prophetic taking a backseat to the political," Dyson asserted, "but it is surely the most visible example in black history"—made possible, he pointed out, because so many people of color already regarded his candidacy as "divinely inspired."[22]

For the most part, after the Wright furor dissipated, Obama haters were left to rally around the borderline racism that continued to be aired on talk radio. Rush Limbaugh, who by now attracted some thirteen million viewers each week, took to calling the mixed-race candidate a "halfrican American" or portraying him as an African of Arab descent who hated the United States—smears that the most extreme conservative media would deploy for years.[23] Fox News hiked the volume and vitriol of its own Obama bashing as the viability of his candidacy increased. The network repeated unsubstantiated charges that Obama had been born outside the United States and somehow forged his Hawaiian birth certificate—making him ineligible for the presidency. Bill O'Reilly later claimed to have investigated and dismissed the accusation—going so far as to say so on air to a New York developer and reality-TV star who continued insisting otherwise: Donald Trump. "I told Donald to his face on national TV that the conspiracy was total BS," O'Reilly said in an effort to exonerate himself—but not until 2019, years after the story had gained traction on his network.[24]

Bombarded by the constant repetition of the lie, a "birther" movement took hold in the American imagination, at least that part of it that identified as Republican. In a phenomenon that reporter-turned-historian Jonathan Alter would call "Obama Derangement Syndrome," a third of Republicans concluded within two years of Obama's inauguration that he had indeed been born outside the country, while 25 percent came to believe that he practiced the Muslim religion—even though Obama had come under earlier scrutiny over his membership in Jeremiah Wright's Trinity United Church of Christ.[25]

The Obama campaign might at this point have turned for support to inherently sympathetic media voices already besotted with the Democratic candidate—or those professionally offended by the tactics of Fox News and the radio shock jocks. Instead, fueled by the conviction that it had discovered a better way to inform the public, the Obama team limited access by traditional media across the spectrum. Avoiding the press became standard operating procedure, especially after the *Huffington Post* and others reported that Obama had been secretly recorded remarking at a private fundraiser that some voters "cling to guns or religion or antipathy to people who aren't like them." Unsurprisingly, the complaint earned endless repetition on the news shows. Obama himself conceded that his words had been "ill-chosen."[26]

Aware that the new media environment blurred the lines between private and public, indeed between journalism and eavesdropping, the campaign "began exploring ways to re-exert control," staffer Reid Cherlin recalled. The revised strategy called for "ignoring the media altogether." As Cherlin put it, "Campaign manager David Plouffe and other senior advisors made a virtue, even a show, of shrugging off press criticism. Instead they amped up efforts to put the campaign's unfiltered message directly in voters' inboxes, social-media feeds, and television sets."[27] The strategy came with risks: it meant Obama would focus on preaching to the choir—his Internet followers—aiming to maximize turnout, not broaden support. Michael Eric Dyson argued that the "fractured media landscape" had left Obama no alternative. "We are reduced to forging workable rather than wide consensus," Dyson maintained, ". . . and short-term alliances with potentially increased numbers of allies." The Obama campaign recognized the new reality earlier than most, Dyson argued, "when he transformed the American political campaign with his unprecedented success in fund-raising and message-sharing on the Internet."[28]

The media was not about to cede its longtime power without a fight. During the summer of 2008, believing Obama would likely win the White House, Rupert Murdoch, chairman of the News Corporation, which owns Fox News, initiated a face-to-face meeting with the Democratic candidate in an effort to restore civility, if not to make outright peace. After enjoying eight years of goodwill from, and direct access to, the Bush White House, Murdoch did not want his network left on the outside looking in during a potential Obama presidency. Obama was less than eager to take the meeting but finally agreed to see Murdoch at a neutral venue: New York's Waldorf-Astoria Hotel. Reportedly their chat got off to a cordial enough start—until combative Fox News chairman Roger Ailes entered the room to join the discussion. From that point, the conversation deteriorated. Obama, who not unreasonably viewed Ailes as an outright enemy, voiced his displeasure that Fox had repeatedly libeled him as a "terrorist." As far as Obama was concerned, Ailes bore direct responsibility for tolerating, if not encouraging, the calumny. Ailes denied that such a charge had been allowed on air, but Obama insisted that "Sean Hannity does it every night." Backed into a corner, Ailes tried explaining that shows like Hannity's were supposed to dispense opinions, not news.[29]

The one and only Obama-Fox summit ended without rapprochement, although in the weeks to come Obama did submit to an interview with Chris Wallace and taped a four-segment appearance on *The O'Reilly Factor.* Calling the O'Reilly face-off "a wonk vs. wacko match," *New York Times* media reporter Alessandra Stanley described the tone as "civil, but thankfully not too civil," explaining: "Mr. O'Reilly, as is his wont, spoke brusquely, interrupted, argued and didn't let his guest off the hook," while the candidate "remained pleasant, respectful and good-humored."[30] While the relationship soured further from that point on, once he handily defeated John McCain in the election the new president did magnanimously keep Ailes and his Fox colleagues on the coveted White House Christmas party A-list. Pausing on the receiving line at one such reception to pose for a photograph with Ailes, the president even flattered his fiercest critic by declaring, as Ailes's wife looked on, "I just saw on the cover of a magazine that you're the most powerful man in the news." Obama had circumspectly omitted the fact that the magazine passing judgment was *Newsmax*, a conservative monthly founded by another of the president's unrelenting media foes, Christopher Ruddy.[31]

The Obama White House did not exude Christmas spirit every day. Further escalating its war with Fox News in late 2010—ostensibly over recent leaks of classified information—the administration went after one of the network's on-air correspondents, James Rosen. The FBI regarded Rosen as "an aider [and] abettor" who had received secret government data and published sensitive information about a possible nuclear buildup by North Korea. Citing the seldom-enforced Espionage Act of 1917, the Justice Department named Rosen an unindicted "criminal co-conspirator" and seized phone records from his office, home, and cell phone lines—along with those of his parents. The surveillance included tracing Rosen's emails in order to document his visits to the State Department, where he had allegedly received leaked information from a contractor named Stephen Jin-Woo Kim, who had later been indicted on espionage charges.[32] Appearing on the morning show *Fox & Friends*, conservative commentator Andrew Napolitano decried the crackdown: "This is the first time that the federal government has moved to this level of taking ordinary, reasonable, traditional, lawful reporter skills and claiming they constitute criminal behavior." Placing equal blame on Obama's press secretary, host Brian Kilmeade added: "I don't know how Jay Carney sleeps at night, because he came from the reporting world."[33] (Carney had replaced Robert Gibbs as presidential spokesman in 2011 and would be succeeded three years later by Josh Earnest.)

Washington Post correspondent (and Harvard-trained lawyer) Ruth Marcus called the administration's war on Fox News "dumb on multiple levels." While she understood the argument that Fox News practiced "opinion journalism masquerading as news," Marcus maintained that the White House went "overboard in its decision to treat Fox as an outright enemy." It made the administration look "weak," "childish," and "Nixonian," even "Agnew-esque." As Marcus argued, "There's only one thing dumber than picking a fight with people who buy ink by the barrel—picking a fight with people who don't even have to buy ink"—meaning television networks. Marcus cited an earlier interview in which the president had more confidently said: "I don't always get my most favorable coverage on Fox, but I think that's part of how democracy is supposed to work. You know, we're not supposed to all be in lock step here."[34]

Even the reliably pro-Obama *New York Times* protested the crackdown. "With the decision to label a Fox News television reporter as a possible 'co-conspirator' in a criminal investigation of a news leak," the paper editorialized, "the Obama administration has moved beyond protecting government secrets to threatening fundamental freedoms of the press to gather news."[35] *Times* reporter Charlie Savage came up with a phrase to describe the administration's blanket insistence that national security supersede freedom of the press: "Acting Like Bush."[36]

Another journalist subjected to what *Washington Post* media reporter Erik Wemple called "the Obama administration scorched-earth stance on leaks" was *New York Times* reporter James Risen (not to be confused with James Rosen), who also ran afoul of the 1917 Espionage Act.[37] In pursuing Risen under a law enacted to catch spies, not "to go after government officials who talked to journalists," the latest target argued that the government again overreached on wiretaps. Later the Justice Department ordered Risen to testify in the trial of onetime CIA official Jeffrey Sterling, an alleged source accused of feeding the reporter classified data about a Clinton-era plan to sabotage Iranian nuclear facilities. Risen and his *Times* colleague Eric Lichtblau refused to appear, a jury convicted Sterling anyway, and the administration took no further action against the journalists. "The government only relented," Risen later speculated, "because they feared the negative publicity that would come from sending a *New York Times* reporter to jail."[38]

Rather than plugging the leak culture, the Risen affair may well have stiffened journalists' resolve to probe the administration even more aggressively. When the U.S. Court of Appeals ruled that reporters like Risen enjoyed no inherent First Amendment right to protect the confidentiality of their sources in national security cases, watchdog groups sounded the alarm. The cofounder of the Freedom of the Press Foundation, lawyer-turned-journalist Trevor Timm, warned that the ruling had "eviscerated" privileges long granted to journalists in pursuit of news.[39]

"I am a strong believer in the First Amendment and the need for journalists to pursue every lead and every angle," Obama insisted in a rare interview. "I think that when you hear stories about us cracking down on whistle-blowers or whatnot, we're talking about a really small sample. Some of them are serious, where you had purposeful leaks of information that could harm or threaten operations or individuals who were in the field involved with really sensitive national security issues." Consciously or not, here Obama channeled FDR, who decades earlier had expressed his frustrations about the mainstream media to a group of journalism students. In this case, Obama had defended himself to the student newspaper at Rutgers.[40]

As it turned out, the hair-trigger technology that made it possible for Obama to reach millions of followers on social media also enabled tech-savvy critics of censorship and surveillance to retaliate by engineering massive data dumps. In 2010, Julian Assange, a former journalist and founder of WikiLeaks, an online clearinghouse specifically created to host leaked documents, began periodically posting large troves of top-secret material. The posts came in blatant defiance of the Obama administration's increasingly strict enforcement of statutes like the Terrorist Surveillance Act of 2006, the Protect America Act of 2007, and the thirty-year-old Foreign Intelligence Surveillance Act (FISA), which had been updated in 2008. As far as the administration was concerned, these measures provided legal justification for warrantless domestic wiretapping, even against journalists, in the name of national security.[41]

In defiance, WikiLeaks made public such top-secret files as the "Iraq War Logs," a collection of nearly four hundred thousand documents related to the protracted American military presence there. It was one of the biggest single leaks of classified data since the Pentagon Papers. Admirers hailed Assange as a free-speech hero while critics blasted him as a traitor. Bill Keller reported in the *New York Times* that "reporters came to think of Assange as smart and well educated, extremely adept technologically but arrogant, thin-skinned, conspiratorial and oddly credulous . . . openly contemptuous of the American government and certain that he was a hunted man."[42]

Assange's source for the most sensational trove of material turned out to be a "disillusioned" army private named Bradley Manning, who was arrested and placed in solitary confinement for stealing and sharing the data. The saga grew even more complex when Manning transitioned from male to female and became Chelsea Manning but remained inside a succession of military prisons before receiving a formal sentence of thirty-five years. In a humane gesture, Obama commuted the sentence, but Manning ended up confined in an Alexandria, Virginia, jailhouse after refusing to testify against Assange. Facing charges of his own under several statutes, the WikiLeaks founder sought asylum in various overseas embassies before British authorities extradited and imprisoned him. Assange could yet face prosecution in the United States, although press freedom purists here continue to argue in his defense that he is a legitimate journalist who deserves exoneration.[43]

In 2013, a disgruntled former National Security Agency contractor named Edward Snowden set off another firestorm by summoning two journalists and a filmmaker to his Hong Kong hotel room and giving them a top-secret archive containing thousands of documents about global surveillance that he had lifted from the NSA. Snowden, too, became a fugitive from justice, stranded in Moscow, unwilling to set foot back in the United States and face arrest for infractions ranging from theft to treason. Like Assange, Snowden has attracted a considerable number of sympathizers. His supporters still maintain that he is a legitimate whistle-blower with every right to share alleged proof of government overreach with the public and the press. Readers of the *Guardian*—to whose reporters Snowden had initially leaked the documents in Hong Kong—even elected Snowden their 2013 "Person of the Year."[44]

The domestic media never quite lionized Assange, but it did eventually turn against Obama on the issues of oversight and censorship. Former *Washington Post* executive editor Leonard Downie Jr. called "the administration's war on leaks and other efforts to control information . . . the most aggressive I've seen since the Nixon administration, when I was one of the editors involved in the *Washington Post*'s investigation of Watergate."[45] Two years later, James Risen labeled the Obama team "the greatest enemy of press freedom in a generation."[46] By then the administration had not only struck at Rosen and Risen, but seized two months' worth of work and personal phone calls flowing to and from at least twenty Associated Press editors and reporters.[47] In an understatement, the *New York Times* described the AP surveillance as "a fishing expedition" and credited Edward Snowden for exposing "how much data American intelligence agencies were collecting and hoarding."[48]

Ironically, as he sought reelection in 2012, a leak helped tilt another bitter presidential race in Obama's favor. Perhaps no one should have been surprised when an unauthorized amateur video made at a Mitt Romney fundraiser that year helped sink the Utah Republican's challenge to Obama's reelection. In an echo of the flippant Obama comments that had injured, but not destroyed, his 2008 campaign, Romney was heard—and reheard—glibly telling a room of supporters: "There are 47% of the people who will vote for the president no matter what. All right, there are 47% who are dependent upon government, who believe they are victims, who believe the government has a responsibility to care for them, who believe that they are entitled to health care, to food, to you-name-it."[49] Though presumably meant to warn potential donors that he faced tough odds that year, Romney's tone-deaf insensitivity made even his damaging four-year-old op-ed piece "Let Detroit Go Bankrupt" seem enlightened by comparison.[50]

Leakers, scoop-seeking print reporters, and Fox News were not the only journalists exiled to Obama-era purgatory in an attempt to control all messaging. So was the scrupulously nonpartisan Brian Lamb of C-SPAN, who had conducted six separate interviews with George W. Bush and, all told, interrogated seven different presidents on camera during and after their terms. In total, Lamb enjoyed but one brief on-air encounter with Barack Obama, and it came late. Limited by mutual agreement to "soft questions," the session did not take place until August 2010, eighteen months after the inauguration.

Knowing he had only ten minutes to conduct the entire interview, Lamb ordered up a shoulder camera to eliminate setup time, then entered the Oval Office and began benignly by asking the president why he had not refurnished the room—as had all recent incoming presidents. "Given that we are in the midst of some very difficult economic times," Obama replied, ". . . we decided to hold off last year in terms of making changes."[51] But before the interview could be aired, Lamb got a call from the Obama press office to alert him that the administration was about to announce just such a redecoration, not only of the Oval Office but the entire White House. In short, Lamb's long-sought session had become outdated before it could be telecast. It was a minor matter, but the kind of experience journalists remember.

"We were stunned," Lamb recalls. "President Obama obviously knew. He had even decided on the words that would be embroidered on the new rug." Lamb informed the press office that he would run the interview that very night, whomever it might embarrass. The White House retaliated in kind. "They cut us off for the rest of his term," Lamb remembers. "We had no more interviews and they even cut the number of C-SPAN people at the Christmas party. We never got another peep out of them."[52] Interestingly, Lamb had spent some of his precious on-camera time with Obama exploring the president's disdain for the opinion-laden "twenty-four-hour news cycle" on commercial news networks—from which C-SPAN provided an antidote, or at least an occasional respite. C-SPAN sought no vengeance of its own. Although there would be no further one-on-one opportunities, the cable network continued to cover the president wherever and whenever he delivered speeches. Today, counting telecasts from the 2008 campaign and the post-presidential years, the C-SPAN online archive boasts more than three thousand telecasts featuring Barack Obama.[53]

C-SPAN and Fox News were not alone in feeling the sting of Obama's cold shoulder. The new president also grew increasingly reluctant to engage the resident White House press corps on a routine basis. As Jonathan Alter remembered, the president "didn't cater to White House reporters other than to occasionally bring them cupcakes on their birthdays." In his first term, Obama held only thirty-six press conferences, an average of one every month and a half, fewer than had Reagan, George H. W. Bush, or Bill Clinton, and a far cry from FDR's two-per-week regimen in the 1930s and '40s. (Obama conducted a total of eleven in his initial year, compared to a dozen by Clinton.)[54] He did introduce one controversial but sugar-coated innovation: reporters would be called upon by pre-arrangement, rather than by raising hands and shouting for attention—but as a concession, they would be recognized by name. Though he lacked Washington experience, David Axelrod, the aide who had helped Obama get to the White House in the first place, now served as senior advisor, rigorously maintaining campaign-style focus: media initiatives were carefully researched, scientifically tested, and introduced on social media platforms that the White House controlled.

Defying long-standing norms, the Obama White House took pride not only in making news but producing it. Journalists Mike Allen and Jim VandeHei credited the Obama White House with pioneering and perfecting the art of "government creation of content—photos of the president, videos of White House officials, blog posts written by Obama aides—which can then be instantly released to the masses through social media." As a result, complained Chris Shlemon, a Washington-based producer for a British news channel, "When you call the White House press office to ask a question or seek information, they refer us to the White House websites. We have to use White House website content, White House videos of the president's interviews with local television stations and White House photographs of the president."[55]

Historian David Greenberg called the operation "the latest embodiment of the new, faster-paced Beltway media" but did not mean the description as a compliment. He believed the administration had turned to self-generating, nontraditional media when the "adulatory coverage" of the 2008 campaign quickly yielded after the inauguration "to the old adversarial dynamic."[56] The

Obama White House hired dozens of new federal employees just to staff online PR platforms, among them the first presidential "new media director." To place these innovations in historical context, Obama thus achieved what previous presidents Woodrow Wilson and Franklin Roosevelt had only threatened (to the horror of the press corps): he established a government news service.

Obama remained unwelcoming to TV news. "This breathless, moment by moment, eternal cycle of cable news—that's what he doesn't like," noted *Washington Post* White House correspondent David Nakamura. "It's superficial . . . about the 'gotcha.' That probably gets on his nerves." At an August 1, 2014, news conference, Obama complained that he had not been asked serious questions that might allow him to emphasize economic recovery and what he called "the power of persistence." Such journalistic indifference, he bristled—ignoring the fact that he had done little to endear himself to the press corps—would never have occurred at "a press conference like this" during his first term. When reporters insisted on asking about Ebola and the CIA anyway, Obama dismissively remarked, "You're not that pent up. I've been giving you questions lately."[57] Clearly, the relationship had gone from bad to worse. FDR and JFK had similarly emphasized new media—respectively, radio and television—but they had also prudently maintained connections to the working press. Obama gravitated toward an "out with the old, in with the new" approach, and the media resented him for it.

Former campaign staffer Reid Cherlin was not surprised that the president's relationship with the press had descended so low. "Obama, during his two campaigns for the presidency, had made a point of going over the heads of the media (denigrated as 'the filter') and communicating directly with voters," he admitted. "With Obama in office, reporters have complained that the approach has sometimes bordered on pathology." CNN White House correspondent Jake Tapper agreed. "At the White House," he said, "you're cordoned off like veal."[58]

As the nonprofit, nonpartisan Committee to Protect Journalists (CPJ) noted, while the "Obama administration used social media, videos, and its own sophisticated websites to provide the public with . . . large amounts of favorable information and images generated by his administration," it systematically withheld "the information most needed by the press and public to hold the administration accountable for its policies and actions." Indeed, Obama gave more interviews than his predecessors Clinton and Bush, but many of them took place on entertainment venues like the late-night talk shows hosted by Jay

Leno and David Letterman. In such settings, Obama routinely received rousing standing ovations and fielded mostly softball questions.

Meanwhile, editors griped that the administration routinely excluded press photographers from major events and banned journalists from traveling on First Lady Michelle Obama's aircraft even when the White House described her overseas trips as policy-oriented. Once, in what White House reporter Julie Mason described as "a bleak episode of unintended irony," President Obama received an award for transparency—but excluded the press from the Oval Office bestowal ceremony.[59]

To the Committee to Protect Journalists, Obama's anti-press record ranked as unsurpassed. "In the Obama administration's Washington," the CPJ complained in a fall 2013 report, "government officials are increasingly afraid to talk to the press. Those suspected of discussing with reporters anything that the government has classified as secret are subject to investigation, including lie-detector tests and scrutiny of their telephone and email records." Eight Americans, the report pointed out—six government employees and two contractors (including Edward Snowden)—had thus far been subjected to "felony criminal prosecutions since 2009 under the Espionage Act . . . compared with a total of three such prosecutions in all previous U.S. administrations." That number later rose to nine.

CPJ included this comment from *New York Times* national security correspondent Scott Shane: "I think we have a real problem. Most people are deterred by those leaks prosecutions. They're scared to death. . . . If we consider aggressive press coverage of government activities [as] being at the core of American democracy, this tips the balance heavily in favor of the government." Shane's *Times* colleague and longtime Washington correspondent David E. Sanger succinctly concurred: "This is the most closed, control-freak administration I've ever covered."[60]

In 2010, Obama did sign the Daniel Pearl Freedom of the Press Act, named for the *Wall Street Journal* correspondent brutally murdered in Pakistan in 2002. The law "puts us clearly on the side of journalistic freedom," the president declared at the bill-signing ceremony.[61] Critics pointed out that Obama was promoting a standard of press freedom overseas that he would not tolerate at home. Three years later, Obama tried to rectify matters by proposing a federal shield law to protect journalists and their sources in the United States. Again the effort was greeted with cynicism. Margaret Talbot of the *New Yorker* sardonically commented that the new law "would protect reporters from the sort of thing the Justice Department has done to the A.P." Talbot reminded readers of a further inconsistency: Obama had refused to support a stronger version of the legislation back in 2009. Its original Senate cosponsor, Chuck Schumer of New York, had called Obama's earlier opposition "an unexpected and significant setback." Without the president's support, the original bill had failed. (As a senator, Obama had voted for an even earlier shield law.)[62]

Industry frustration toward Obama was not isolated. ABC News correspondent Ann Compton, who had been patrolling the White House beat since the days of Gerald Ford, called Obama "the least transparent of the seven presidents I've covered in terms of how he does his daily business." Compton elaborated: "There is no access to the daily business in the Oval Office, who the president meets with, who he gets advice from. In the past, we would often be called into the Roosevelt Room at the beginning of meetings to hear the president's opening remarks and see who's in the meeting, and then we could talk to some of them outside on the driveway afterward. This president has wiped all that coverage off the map."[63] No less critically, *Politico* described Obama in 2013 as "a master at limiting, shaping, and manipulating media coverage." Earlier administrations had tried similar tactics, admitted *Politico*'s Jack Shafer three years later. "What distinguishes the Obama administration's propaganda machine from previous efforts," he argued, "is its cold, casual style." According to Shafer, one prominent White House advisor habitually dismissed all querulous reporters as "the Blob," and used supportive ones as "force multipliers . . . to disseminate" positive news.[64]

The one unflappable, battle-scarred watchdog who might have held Obama's feet to the fire on transparency abruptly vanished from the scene just when it surely seemed to some that she might endure forever: Helen Thomas. On February 9, 2009, Obama had recognized Thomas at his very first news conference. "All right, Helen," the president said in calling on her toward the end of the session. "This is my inaugural moment here. I'm excited."[65] Within months, however, Thomas joined her colleagues denouncing the new administration's efforts to control the flow of information and limit access by journalists. That July, Obama press secretary Robert Gibbs deflected a question by NBC News White House correspondent Chip Reid by suggesting he submit it on Twitter or Facebook for a response the following day. While Reid reacted with laughter,

Thomas was not amused. "I'm amazed at you people who call for openness and transparency," she declared. Accusing the administration of "controlling the press," she enumerated such grievances as making "formal engagements . . . prepackaged." When Gibbs asked her if she had submitted a question of her own, Thomas shot back: "I don't have to e-mail it—I can tell you right now!" The tense exchange went on for some four minutes.[66]

As she approached age ninety, Thomas persevered, even though colleagues now had to help her up and down the stairway leading from White House press headquarters to press conferences in the East Room. Thomas managed to get through one such session on May 27, 2010, then made her way outside to the North Lawn. There she encountered a rabbi who had been visiting the White House with his son for an event marking Jewish Heritage Month. "Any advice for these young people over here?" the rabbi called out to the instantly recognizable reporter. Thomas paused to offer them encouragement. Then the rabbi asked her if she had any comments on Israel, explaining, "We're asking everybody today." Thomas did not mince words. "Israel should get out of Palestine," she replied, pointedly adding: "Remember, these people are occupied, and it's their land. It's not Germany and it's not Poland." Where could Israeli Jews go? the rabbi persisted. "They could go home," Thomas answered. "Where is their home?" the rabbi challenged her. "Poland, Germany . . . America, and everywhere else. Why push people out of there who have lived there for centuries?" After the rabbi posted the exchange on his website, the dialogue went viral on YouTube. For once, Thomas herself became the story. Within days, after fifty years on the White House beat, she resigned from the Hearst organization.[67]

Thomas died three years later in 2013, just weeks shy of her ninety-third birthday. At her passing, Obama issued a generous statement of condolence: "Helen was a true pioneer, opening doors and breaking down barriers for generations of women in journalism. . . . She never failed to keep presidents—myself included—on their toes. What made Helen the 'Dean of the White House Press Corps' was not just the length of her tenure, but her fierce belief that our democracy works best when we ask tough questions and hold our leaders to account."[68] Additional tributes came from the presidential press secretaries with whom she had so often battled. Acknowledging that no one had done "more for the role of women in journalism," Reagan spokesman Marlin Fitzwater remembered admiringly, "She was just always at the door saying, 'I have a right to be here.'" Clinton press secretary Mike McCurry added, "She has single-handedly gotten under the skin of every president since JFK."

Indeed, Thomas loved to recall that a Washington cabbie had once recognized her and inquired: "Aren't you the woman the presidents love to hate?"[69] Asked by the *New York Times* a few years earlier to "define the difference between a probing question and a rude one," Thomas had answered: "I don't think there are any rude questions."[70] For more than half a century, from Kennedy to Obama, Helen Thomas had asked hundreds of tough, even rude questions—forfeiting her record-long career only when she gave one ill-advised answer.

Ultimately, watchdog groups charged that the Obama administration amassed the worst record in history on Freedom of Information Act requests, too. In the administration's final year in the White House, according to the AP, it spent $36.2 million in legal fees just to defend its reluctance to release documents. In its first year, the administration had refused 65 percent of FOIA requests. By its final two, the proportion of inquiries generating redacted files or "nothing" at all had risen to 77 percent.

In its own defense, the White House argued that it had simply been overwhelmed: by 2016 it had been compelled to assign a staggering 4,263 employees in nearly a hundred federal agencies to handle the record 788,769 FOIA requests submitted that year alone. But the fact remained that even when it caught up to these inquiries, the government granted access to only a quarter of them.[71] The *New York Times* reported that "agencies are talking the talk, but few are yet walking the walk."[72] Coincidentally or not, that story was filed by one of the journalists exposed to surveillance: James Risen's colleague Eric Lichtblau.

In fairness, Obama seldom got the acknowledgment his spokesmen believed he deserved for the efforts he did make to widen transparency. From the outset, he committed the administration to preserve his records on accessible, downloadable digital archives and created the new job of White House director of product management in the Office of Digital Strategy (naming a former Facebook specialist to the post). But instead of celebrating, some critics unreasonably complained that Obama had permitted communications technology to run rampant; one even held him partly accountable for the social upheavals supposedly caused by new technology. Media scholar Ian Bogost, chair of media studies at the Georgia Institute of Technology, charged of Obama that "the digital tools he quietly celebrated have also hollowed out American life. Surveillance capitalism has made data extraction, aggregation, resale, and speculation the hidden engine of wealth and progress." Perhaps, Bogost speculated, "what America needed from 2009 to 2017 wasn't a cool dad to tweet and stream alongside its citizens. Maybe it needed a guardian to watch and safeguard it against its own worst habits."[73]

As for his widely reported hostility toward the rigorous but increasingly minimalized White House press corps, Obama made light of it during a March 9, 2013, speech at the Gridiron Club dinner. "Now, since I don't often speak to a room full of journalists," he began, to laughter, "I thought I should address a few concerns tonight. Some of you have said that I'm ignoring the Washington press corps—that we're too controlling," he declared. "Well, you know what? You were right. I was wrong, and I want to apologize in a video you can watch exclusively at whitehouse.gov." He jokingly promised he would at last take one question from the press. And then he posed it to himself: "'Mr. President, will you be taking any questions tonight?' I'm happy to answer that. No . . . I will not."[74]

Obama reflected a far grimmer mood the following April toward the end of a long trip to Japan, South Korea, Malaysia, and the Philippines, after two *New York Times* reporters declared the tour a debacle while it was still in progress. En route home, Obama made his way to the press cabin in the rear of Air Force One for the now-customary off-the-record debrief. Livid, he accused journalists by name of "scoring" foreign policy "like a campaign debate" and insisted his overall diplomatic goal was simply "Don't do stupid shit." The private remark quickly landed in the *Huffington Post* under the headline "Obama Criticized News Coverage During Off-the-Record Meeting with Reporters." When administration sources subsequently leaked the "stupid shit" mantra, it appeared in the *New York Times*, *Los Angeles Times*, and *Chicago Tribune*, too. Not surprisingly, columnists piled on, castigating Obama as a whiner.[75]

In the parting shot of his explosive 2013 CPJ report, Leonard Downie Jr., by then a journalism professor at Arizona State University's Walter Cronkite School, had written this: "President Obama is faced with many challenges during his remaining years in office, the outcome of which will shape his legacy. Among them is fulfilling his very first promise—to make his administration the most transparent in American history amid national security concerns, economic uncertainty, political polarization, and rapid technological change. Whether he succeeds could have lasting impact on U.S. government accountability and on the standing of America as an international example of press freedom."[76] If Downie's view is correct, then Obama's failure to meet his own original standards helped set the harsh tone made harsher by the president who succeeded him.

In truth, the defamatory journalism that greeted Obama's ascent and only intensified during his time in office may well have justified his increasing reluctance to engage the traditional media. Jonathan Alter and others have attributed the outbreak of press hostility to the reemergence of what historian Richard Hofstadter had once called "the paranoid style in American politics."[77] In the eyes of the extreme right-wing press—and despite his success in reversing economic collapse, passing health care reform, and eliminating 9/11 mastermind Osama bin Laden—Obama unjustifiably remained an alien threat to the republic. Oprah Winfrey may have dubbed him "The One," but to his enemies he was still "The Other."

Perhaps Obama might have done more to woo that portion of the press corps inclined from the first to report on him positively. But he and his opaque, somewhat remote White House proved unwilling or unable to do so, and thereby turned a powerful group of potentially faithful allies against him when he needed all the support he could get. Few American presidents ever entered office battered by so much media hostility on one hand and blessed with so much media sympathy on the other—and managed to leave office with almost no real friends in the press. Yet in a 2017 C-SPAN survey of America's presidents, historians ranked Obama twelfth among forty-four—an unusually high rating for a recent leader.[78]

On Super Bowl Sunday, February 2, 2014, Obama agreed to his third on-air interview with Bill O'Reilly. The "purveyor of anti-Obama sentiment was given 10 minutes to question the man he decries to millions nightly," an incredulous Dana Milbank reported in the *Washington Post*, describing the session as "a milepost on the conservative movement's road to Obama hysteria." O'Reilly "interrupted the president 42 times" as he grilled him on his purported lapses of judgment on health care, security failures at Benghazi, and alleged weaponizing of the IRS. At one point, prevented from answering under a barrage of interruptions, Obama was reduced to saying, "I'm trying to explain . . . if you want to listen."[79] O'Reilly failed to hector the president out of his legendary composure that night—but the rancorous spectacle might have convinced the president and his advisors that the administration had been wise all along to minimize such encounters while maximizing their own news platforms.

As Obama departed office he told the press corps: "America needs you and our democracy needs you. Having you in this building had made this place work better. It keeps us honest, it makes us work harder."[80] But noting that Obama had prosecuted so many cases against whistle-blowers—three times the number pursued by all his predecessors combined—James Risen commented, "If Donald Trump decides as president to throw a whistle-blower in jail for trying to talk to a reporter, or gets the FBI to spy on a journalist, he will have one man to thank for bequeathing him such executive power: Barack Obama."[81]

Two years after leaving the White House, Obama addressed students at the University of Illinois at Urbana-Champaign, urging them to vote Democratic in the upcoming 2018 midterm elections. Toward the end of his speech he turned his attention to the attacks on the press that had been unleashed by his successor, Donald Trump. "It shouldn't be Democratic or Republican to say that we don't threaten the freedom of the press because they say things or publish stories we don't like," he said. "I complained plenty about Fox News—but you never heard me threaten to shut them down, or call them enemies of the people."[82]

Barack Obama may not have called hostile journalists "enemies of the people." But those whom his administration tried to isolate or prosecute might argue that some of his actions spoke louder than his successor's words.

— 18 —

DONALD TRUMP

In the fall of 2005, a full decade before Donald Trump began running for president, *New York Times* reporter Timothy L. O'Brien published a book called *TrumpNation: The Art of Being the Donald.* In reviewing it, *USA Today* hailed the work for cutting through the hype "to separate Trump the reality from Trump the reality show."[1]

Not surprisingly, Donald Trump disagreed with that assessment. And Trump relished nothing more than doing battle with journalists who diverged from his own rendition of the Trump life story—especially when his rebuttals stimulated further media attention.

What particularly irked Trump about *TrumpNation*, he admitted, was that it "purposely and knowingly" underestimated his wealth at $250 million, a fraction of the fortune he claimed he had amassed. Trump himself had already saturated the book market with bestselling titles like *The Art of the Deal*, *Surviving at the Top*, and *Think Like a Billionaire*. Now *TrumpNation* threatened to undermine his swaggering brand. At his prodding, *Forbes* magazine recalculated his net worth "conservatively" at $2.7 billion.[2]

"I don't like him," Trump said of O'Brien in his own subsequent book, aptly called *Never Give Up*, "This guy was despicable. . . . writing for attention and money."[3] Trump, who thus implied that he himself never wrote books in anticipation of such rewards, urged his admirers to consult another recent biography whose contents—and surely its title—more accurately reflected his credo: *No Such Thing as Over-exposure* by Robert Slater.[4]

Trump did more than complain about *TrumpNation*. He also hit its author with a $5 billion lawsuit for libel and defamation. Trump believed that, however costly, the legal challenge would serve as a warning to all journalists: they would "pay a big price" for venturing beyond the boundaries that encapsulated his official biography—for being, to use a phrase he later adopted to castigate critics, "nasty." Trump rationalized his insistence on enjoying the final word: "Many people would say, why bother? I say, why give up? I do not back down. I don't need the money from winning the case—I need to set the record straight and maybe make it harder for other disreputable writers to knock people for the fun and profit of it." Two separate courts later dismissed the lawsuit, yet Trump proudly chronicled the litigation in *Never Give Up*, devoting an entire chapter to regurgitating O'Brien's transgressions and his own scorched-earth response. He titled the section "When You're Attacked, Bite Back."

In the years since, critics have often reproached Donald Trump as wildly unpredictable. Yet as the O'Brien saga suggests, he has in fact demonstrated a remarkable consistency. "When You're Attacked, Bite Back" would long remain his public relations mantra. Whether feuding with local journalists, championing discredited causes, improbably seeking national office, or unconventionally conducting his presidency, he has operated by his own golden rule: quash the message and squash the messenger.

Powerful personality aside, what has set Trump apart has been his ability to counterattack with increasingly sophisticated tools. At first content merely to stage photo opportunities and work the phones to promote himself, he later so cunningly weaponized high-speed media technologies that, love him or loathe him, the forty-fifth president became one of the most effective communicators in White House history. Separating fact from fiction never preoccupied him. He dedicated himself to deploying and repeating the strongest possible message in the shortest possible time. No one ever nursed a grudge as long or fought back as hard, as often—and with such vast reach and breathtaking immediacy—as Donald Trump.

It is hard to pinpoint the precise moment at which the younger Trump became as adept at wrangling the cynical New York media as he proved early in his career at navigating the New York real estate market. The son of a successful, outer-borough realtor, Trump achieved fortune and fame in Manhattan with high-profile development projects like the old Commodore Hotel near Grand Central Terminal, which he gutted and reimagined into a glitzy Hyatt. Then came the historic Plaza Hotel opposite Central Park, which he acquired, preserved, and restored; and the crown jewel of his portfolio, Trump Tower on Fifth Avenue, where he took up residence in a gilded triplex penthouse modeled after the Palace of Versailles. None of these megaprojects got planned or built without stirring media controversy.

Trump blunted criticism by reviving a long-stalled New York civic project. In 1986, he took over the rehabilitation of the deteriorating Wollman Skating Rink in Central Park and completed the work in a matter of months. A grateful Mayor Ed Koch gave Trump major press exposure at the ceremony marking the laying of the first concrete. "Think of it," Trump remarked after posing for photographers that day, coming close to claiming he was by nature camera-shy. "A couple of guys in pinstripe suits shoveling wet concrete. But I like to be accommodating. As long as they want to shoot, I'll shovel."[5] Proving he was hungrier for publicity than he had admitted, Trump scheduled additional media opportunities to mark subsequent construction milestones—including the installation of the first ice—populating each event with marquee skaters like Peggy Fleming. City officials simply stopped attending. To his credit, Trump succeeded in transforming an endangered landmark he had labeled "one of the great losers" into a genuine "winner," generously donating all future revenues to the city. As *Forbes* grudgingly admitted of Trump: "Even if he is the bacteria necessary to make yogurt, he is very effective bacteria."[6]

The Wollman Rink project transformed Trump into a municipal celebrity. But good local press was not enough. Trump craved great national press, and often. As he unselfconsciously quoted an anonymous journalist's diagnosis, "Publicity is Trump's cocaine."[7] Traditional news cycles seldom constrained him, as he would later demonstrate as dawn-to-dark tweeter in chief. He courted reporters by day and badgered editors far into the night. The bigger his latest project, the more grandiose his marketing initiatives, and the smaller his tolerance for criticism. And so followed well-promoted investments in Atlantic City casinos, complete with a widely publicized feud with TV icon (and hotelier) Merv Griffin that usefully landed Trump on *60 Minutes*. Then came the sponsorship of televised beauty pageants and the ballyhooed acquisition of a private plane and opulent yacht, the latter, Trump reminded the press, larger than the craft owned by media titan Malcolm Forbes.

Trump did more than gaudily stamp his name on each of his tangible assets; he also sought coverage meant to build his reputation as a business "player" and, between marriages, an irresistible playboy. He set a new bar for audacity, irrepressibly promoting hyperbole as fact. In New York, they call such bravado *chutzpah*—Yiddish for "brazen nerve." And though an anomaly in Big Apple real estate circles—a blond-haired Christian in a largely Jewish industry—Trump boasted *chutzpah* to spare. Above all, he steadfastly refused to confess weakness even when financial setbacks forced him to sell his hotels, plane, and boat and sent him spiraling toward bankruptcy. Merely escaping ruin, he defiantly argued, burnished his image. His method of operation was evident even then: bombast, behind-the-scenes manipulation, and Barnum-like hyperbole.

Trump not only refused to confess, much less correct, errors; when caught, he pounded back mercilessly against detractors. On one occasion, he ridiculed an "ordinary"-looking *Time* reporter because she had "sauntered" into his office "like Marilyn Monroe . . . seething with hostility" (a mixed simile, to be sure). A *Forbes* journalist who dared downgrade his net worth was judged "mediocre." A "vicious" *Village Voice* profile by Wayne Barrett mattered little because the paper "was not exactly overloaded with Pulitzer Prize winners." And syndicated gossip columnist Liz Smith, who sided with Trump's first wife, Ivana, in their 1991 divorce, could not be trusted because she "used to kiss my ass so much that it was downright embarrassing."[8] Trump still welcomed requests for press access, but never sat back quietly if the results displeased him. "I know that the real danger in criticizing the media is that they will have the last word about everything I'm ever involved in, personally and professionally," he acknowledged in 1990. ". . . Frankly, I don't care."[9]

Willing to take unorthodox risks in pursuit of self-aggrandizement, Trump even took to phoning journalists using a badly disguised voice to pretend to be his own publicist. Adopting unimaginative aliases like "John Miller" or "John Barron," he began touting his real estate triumphs and romantic conquests in the third person. Several reporters recognized Trump's distinctive manner of speech. ("Many, many people try to imitate me," he tried arguing without quite denying the charge.) One journalist found it "creepy" to hear "Miller" or "Barron" boast of Trump: "Actresses just call to see if they can go out with him and things." Even the *New York Times* fell victim to the charade, quoting the fictitious "John Barron" defending Trump's refusal to preserve the decorative relief sculptures at the Bonwit Teller department store, the retail landmark he razed to make way for Trump Tower. The Metropolitan Museum of Art had asked him to rescue and donate the art deco friezes, and Trump had initially agreed. But when he learned the effort would delay demolition, he reneged and ordered the sculptural elements jackhammered into dust.[10] The *New York Times* observed, "obviously big buildings do not make big human beings." Trump admitted of the fallout: "It's not the sort of publicity you like to get." But those who criticized his change of heart, he added, "were phonies and hypocrites."[11]

Trump and his imaginary publicist grew particularly incensed in 1990 when Liz Smith's flagship paper, the New York *Daily News*, began giving Ivana sympathetic coverage during the couple's breakup. According to Jill Brooke, then a reporter at the rival *New York Post*, Trump phoned her paper late one night to deride *News* editors as "fucking bitches" and suggest that the *Post* initiate an old-fashioned tabloid war by publicizing his newfound prowess as single man about town. Brooke recalled that Trump himself supplied the idea for a subsequent, notorious *Post* headline that allegedly quoted his new fiancée, entertainer Marla Maples: "Marla brags to her pals about Donald: 'Best Sex I've Ever Had.'" As Brooke put it, "Shameless and wily, he instinctively knew even then how to steer the media conversation."[12] The Donald-Ivana divorce earned tabloid headlines for eleven consecutive days. But the story of Trump's masquerade as his own PR man attracted no real scrutiny until the year he ran for president, at which time he shrugged it off without harm.

Meanwhile, Trump became a ubiquitous presence in other media. He popped up regularly on radio and television talk shows and, over the years, appeared in cameo roles in thirteen movies, usually playing himself. For fourteen seasons, he also hosted a highly popular reality-TV series, *The Apprentice*, growing notorious for pointing to weak contestants and barking what became his catchphrase: "You're fired." *The Apprentice* franchise eventually spun off a dating show called *Donald J. Trump Presents the Ultimate Merger*, starring a onetime *Apprentice* contestant named Omarosa Manigault-Stallworth (later Newman). Omarosa would go on to serve briefly as a White House aide, then abruptly quit, claiming she possessed an audiotape of Trump using the *n*-word. She would later write a tell-all book detailing alleged Trump administration dysfunction.[13]

Guided by lessons he had absorbed from his mentor, the controversial (and ultimately disbarred) attorney and fixer Roy Cohn, Trump meanwhile continued to pursue a take-no-prisoners approach to media critics. Trump's zero-tolerance policy resurfaced in 2005, just as the *TrumpNation* book aroused his ire. That same year he struck back against a set of *New Yorker* profiles assembled into book form by staff writer Mark Singer. The collection included a less-than-flattering eight-year-old story quoting an anonymous source saying of Trump: "Deep down, he wants to be Madonna."[14]

Trump retaliated only after the *New York Times* published a warm notice for the book. Even when struck with a feather, Trump responded with an Uzi. In an indignant letter to the *Book Review*, he lashed out at Singer ("not born with great writing ability"), book critic MacGregor ("writes poorly"), and Tina Brown, the editor who had assigned the original profile ("dragging the *New Yorker* to a new low"). Trump knew great writing when he encountered it, he unconvincingly added: "I've read John Updike, I've read Orhan Pamuk, I've read Philip Roth." And, as he pointed out: "I've been a bestselling author for close to twenty years," noting that the *Times* had acknowledged "that I had produced 'a steady stream of classics' that together ranked as an 'astonishing achievement.'" That Trump had written them with an even steadier stream of credited, uncredited, and occasionally disillusioned coauthors remained unmentioned.

One of those ghostwriters, Tony Schwartz, who penned Trump's 1987 bestseller, *The Art of the Deal*, later countered: "I seriously doubt that Trump has ever read a book straight through in his adult life." The man who by then had earned the title of Trump's "Dr. Frankenstein" added, "I put lipstick on a pig."[15] In 2019, Schwartz claimed that throughout their collaboration, Trump "lied as a matter of course, without apparent guilt."[16] By then, Trump had long grown accustomed to having the last word. In 2005, dismissing "losers" like Mark Singer and Jeff MacGregor, he had snarled, "they just don't have what it takes."[17]

Singer actually found Trump's over-the-top attacks amusing. When the kerfuffle propelled his book to number 375 on the Amazon bestseller list, a rarefied height for his work, he provocatively sent Trump a check for $37.82 as "a small token of my enormous gratitude" for the extra royalties his diatribe had generated. No fan of irony, Trump returned the letter, marked up with large capital letters: "Mark, you are a total loser! And your book (and writings) sucks [*sic*]." According to Singer, Trump also cashed the $37.82 check.[18]

On the darker side, whether to promote, provoke, or simply attract attention, the prepresidential Trump also embraced inflammatory causes and absurd conspiracy theories. One was the inherently racist "birther" movement. But Trump's most notorious such undertaking dated all the way back to 1989, when New York City police arrested more than a dozen African American teenagers after a female jogger was raped and severely beaten in Central Park. Under intense questioning without benefit of counsel, five young black men admitted to the crime. Though they later recanted their confessions, a jury convicted them and a judge sentenced them to lengthy prison terms. Unsatisfied with this result, Trump took out full-page ads in city newspapers demanding that the young men face even harsher punishment. His headline blared, "Bring Back the Death Penalty." Appearing on *Larry King Live*, Trump added, "Maybe hate is what we need if we're gonna get something done."[19]

Twelve years later, an entirely different man serving time for an unrelated murder would admit to sole responsibility for the attack, a confession police validated through DNA testing. Exonerated and freed, the "Central Park Five" went on to win a $41 million wrongful arrest lawsuit against the city and inspired a Ken Burns documentary. Trump never voiced remorse for his suggestion that the ultimate, irreversible penalty be exacted against the improperly interrogated and unfairly incarcerated teenagers.

Already ambitious for public office, but well aware that his "marital problems and business reverses have dragged me through the newspapers," Trump worried (for the first and only time) that his public and private escapades might render him forever unelectable. Thereafter, he flirted with several political races, but ultimately declined to run in any. His explanation was that "Americans have become so accustomed to professional politicians that when they are faced with a strong personality—a man or woman of action—they are afraid, or at least wary."[20] For once, Trump underestimated himself.

According to *New York Times* political reporter Michael Barbaro, Trump had grown by the dawn of the new millennium into "a serial exploiter of old-line media."[21] Of far more consequence, Trump soon discovered a fresh and more effective communications outlet—one that no longer required him to cajole (and inevitably be disappointed or infuriated by) jaded professional reporters.

The turning point came in 2009, when his staff asked him to authorize the creation of @realDonaldTrump, an account to be situated on a three-year-old microblogging site called Twitter. Initially, the aides conceived the effort chiefly to promote the boss's books and business enterprises to a younger demographic. At the time, Trump did not even have a computer in his office and still relied on assistants to print out his emails. "I like the sound of that," he nonetheless reacted to the Twitter suggestion. "Let's do it." His first recorded tweet, on May 4 of that year, probably composed by a staffer, was the benign alert: "Be sure to tune in and watch Donald Trump on Late Night with David Letterman as he presents the Top Ten List tonight."[22] It was not quite a harbinger of tweetstorms to come, but it signaled a true milestone.

Soon enough, Trump learned to use the new tool himself, becoming, in

Barbaro's telling, "a virtuoso of the tweet." Trump's detractors at first sneered that the medium—which initially limited postings to just 140 characters of type—suited Trump because he lacked the attention span to devote further energy to reading or writing. Such wags vastly undervalued both Trump's instinctive feel for communications and the new platform's enormous potential. At the same time that Barack Obama began using the high-tech medium to spotlight policy initiatives, Donald Trump commenced deploying Twitter to promote his television series, flog his hotels and residential properties, and, most of all, tout himself. It was the perfect merger of technology and personality, medium and messenger. Trump and Twitter were made for each other.

The same could not be said about Trump and Obama. But on April 30, 2011, the two found themselves in the same Washington hotel ballroom at the White House Correspondents' Association dinner. The encounter would provoke another tipping point. The annual event, as the *Washington Post*'s Roxanne Roberts reported, had by then "devolved from a little-known media evening into a black-tie mash-up of the Super Bowl and the Oscars." Here was the kind of live television spectacle that Donald Trump ordinarily loved, but not so much when he was relegated to sitting mutely in the audience enduring the slings and arrows of Barack Obama's monologue.

The president was in fine form that night. "No one is happier, no one is prouder to put this birth certificate matter to rest than Donald," he joked. "That's because he can finally get back to focusing on the issues that matter, like: 'Did we fake the moon landing? What really happened in Roswell? And where are Biggie and Tupac?'" As the rest of the audience roared, cameras caught the target of the barbs scowling. According to the *New York Times*, "That evening's public abasement, rather than sending Mr. Trump away, accelerated his ferocious efforts to gain stature within the political world." Writing in the *New Yorker*, Adam Gopnik further speculated that the public humiliation persuaded Trump to "pursue the Presidency after all, no matter how nihilistically or absurdly," just to "redeem himself."[23] Such observations perhaps exaggerated the fissures that Obama opened in the Trump ego that night. Trump later insisted he'd had a "fantastic" time at the roast. Yet he would never attend a White House Correspondents' Association gala again. By then, his Twitter feed was attracting far more viewers than the correspondents' affair anyway.

A *New York Times* assessment of Trump's prepresidential Twitter proficiency estimated that as of 2015 he had already dispatched some twenty-eight thousand messages, averaging twelve a day, while amassing more than four million followers and gaining further traction through his fans' eagerness to repost his messages on their own social media accounts. By then, Trump was regularly dispensing barbs not only about political issues but about the physical appearance of women who dared question him. Bette Midler, Arianna Huffington, and Rosie O'Donnell were among those who became recurring targets, often derided as unattractive harridans. Occasionally, his crueler online comments produced sad consequences. When the reclusive Hollywood legend Kim Novak ventured a comeback appearance at the 2014 Oscars, Trump tweeted to his followers, "Kim should sue her plastic surgeon." Reportedly, the fragile Novak retreated again from the Hollywood scene in despair.[24]

The unrepentant master of the Twitter putdown went into overdrive once he entered the race for president in 2015, lacing his posts with unforgettably derisive nicknames for his rivals. His roster of targets expanded to include Republican primary opponents Jeb ("no energy") Bush, "Lyin' Ted" Cruz, "Little Marco" Rubio, and eventually the Democratic rival he traduced as "Crooked Hillary." Although he never assembled a traditional campaign organization, Trump's social media mastery, repeatedly augmented in the echo chamber of high-voltage rallies and Fox News—not to mention rogue online trolls and bots from both domestic and foreign sources—proved more than enough to compensate for the lack of political infrastructure.

Often, the unacknowledged collaboration between Trump and conservative media went beyond the republication and exaltation of his Twitter posts. Liberals tended to describe the relationship with a word Trump and the press would later thrust into the national vocabulary: "collusion." Trump's tweets did not only garner attention from the conservative press; in turn, some of the most outlandish stories advanced on the most extreme platforms ended up recirculated by @realDonaldTrump. In one example, Trump repeated a scurrilous charge from the supermarket tabloid *National Enquirer* (published by his friend and supporter, American Media Inc. chairman David Pecker) suggesting that Ted Cruz's father had conspired in the 1963 assassination of John F. Kennedy. By then, Trump's exaggerations on Twitter had ceased to arouse furor; their very frequency gave them currency among his supporters while numbing outrage among his critics.

Pecker media cheered Trump early—with the *National Enquirer* endorsing him for the White House in a front-page March 16 editorial, "Trump Must be

Prez."[25] Even more usefully, the company also helped silence his accusers, buying and then burying accusations from women who periodically came forward to charge Trump with past sexual misconduct. Working in tandem with the candidate's attorney, Michael Cohen (who later pled guilty to eight felony charges, including campaign finance violations, for paying off one such accuser), Pecker financed legally binding nondisclosure agreements to keep more than one allegation under wraps.[26]

In 2019, investigative reporter Ronan Farrow elaborated further on how (and why) American Media purchased, then quashed reports of Trump's peccadilloes. On one occasion, Farrow alleged, AMI had paid Trump's New York doorman $30,000 to confirm an unverifiable rumor that the future president had fathered an illegitimate child by his housekeeper. Then the media company not only withheld the story's publication but also used its suppression to gain favors from the White House. Farrow went so far as to allege that Pecker's "steadily accumulating blackmail power over Trump" gave the publisher access, directly through the Oval Office, to "potential sources of funding for AMI." Farrow was so taken with the term for the complicated scheme that he adapted it as the title of his 2019 bestselling book: *Catch and Kill.*[27]

Shielded from damage and buttressed by conspiracy theorists, candidate Trump also revived the discredited birther-movement attacks on President Obama. Five years earlier, Trump had gone on Fox News to charge without proof that Obama had spent "millions of dollars in legal fees trying to get away from the issue." Even the Rupert Murdoch–owned *New York Post* had lamented Trump's "weird embrace of birthers." Now Trump told Laura Ingraham's radio audience that Obama continued to conceal his birth certificate because he supposedly knew it listed his religion as Muslim. According to *Morning Joe* cohost Mika Brzezinski, Trump confided of his shameful effort after another such interview (once the cameras were off), "I know it's bad but it works."[28] Not until seven weeks before Election Day did Trump finally concede Obama's valid citizenship. Accepting no blame for the foray, Trump maintained that "2008" had started the birther controversy, but "I finished it."[29]

Candidate Trump further rallied his base by warning online and in person of the alleged dangers posed by Muslim immigration—and by Muslims already living in America. At a November 2015 campaign rally in Birmingham, he claimed that "thousands upon thousands of people" had been observed cheering from a Muslim neighborhood in New Jersey after the twin towers fell on 9/11. When fact-checkers challenged Trump's recollection, the campaign referred to a September 18, 2001, *Washington Post* article noting that "law enforcement authorities detained and questioned a number of people who were allegedly seen celebrating the attacks." The *Post* report had not specified the number of suspects interrogated—a journalistic oversight. But the article's coauthor, Serge F. Kovaleski, now working for the *New York Times*, cautioned, "I certainly do not remember anyone saying that thousands or even hundreds of people were celebrating."[30] Asked on ABC News to justify his exaggeration, Trump insisted to George Stephanopoulos: "It was on television. I saw it."[31]

At a subsequent rally in Myrtle Beach, South Carolina, Trump provoked derisive laughter by mocking Kovaleski with a cruel imitation of the disabled journalist's awkward arm gestures—the result of the congenital joint disease arthrogryposis. "You've got to see this guy," Trump smirkingly told the crowd, coiling his wrists and flapping his arms for effect. Yet he later insisted to NBC News, "If Mr. Kovaleski is handicapped, I would not know because I do not know what he looks like." He reiterated to the *Times*, "Despite having one of the all-time great memories, I certainly do not remember him." How he had summoned the familiarity to so precisely ape Kovaleski's rare disability remained unexplained.[32]

Trump's insensitivity toward one of their own aroused waves of criticism from Kovaleski's press colleagues.[33] For days, sensing blood, news programs re-aired Trump's derisive mimicry. Hillary Clinton even adapted the clip into a negative campaign commercial. But widespread public outrage never materialized. Trump's swagger had by then convinced so many media consumers that he was the tough leader they needed to "make America great again" that no bluster, however distasteful, could pierce his armor.

Whether Trump was deploying tweets or generating free airtime for his rallies, no one else had ever used the media to dispatch so many opponents so effectively. But the most significant and permanent victim of Trump bashing was the press itself. Trump persuaded nearly half the voting population in 2016 that the mainstream media could not be trusted and that therefore criticism of him must raise doubts—even when he erred egregiously or crossed the line of civil discourse. His relentless debunking of the press made him all but impervious to its rebuke, even when evidence of a flagrant outrage or exaggeration could be viewed unalloyed on TV and the Internet. Making America great again required making the media irrelevant for the first time.

Trump's campaign against the press really took flight when he first faced charges that Russians were generating "fake news" against Hillary Clinton for his benefit. Trump simply co-opted the phrase (he later claimed he had invented it) and redirected it against the media.[34] What constituted one of his most cynical initiatives also turned out to be one of his most effective. In adopting the "fake news" expression as his own, Trump adroitly deflected attention from the toxic subject of Russian election interference and in the bargain further eroded American faith in the ability—even the right—of the press to pursue meaningful inquiry. Meanwhile, conservative and liberal media alike repeatedly broadcast each tirade—granting Trump some two billion dollars in free airtime even before the Republican National Convention nominated him—perhaps willing to absorb the relentless criticism in return for the high ratings (and increased advertising revenues) that wall-to-wall Trump coverage generated.[35]

As the presidential race progressed, outspoken women—not just Clinton—served anew as foils for Trumpian disdain. During the first Republican primary debate, Fox News reporter Megyn Kelly pressed Trump for referring to unfriendly females as "fat pigs, dogs, slobs, and disgusting animals." Taking a swipe at one celebrity with whom he had long feuded, Trump shot back, "Only Rosie O'Donnell." Then he added, to cheers from his followers, "I think the big problem this country has is being politically correct." Soon thereafter, he implied on CNN that Kelly's hostility had been magnified by her menstrual cycle: "You could see there was blood coming out of her eyes, blood coming out of her—wherever." Trump paid no political price for his vulgarity. In fact, he boycotted the next Fox-sponsored debate without consequence when the network refused to remove Kelly as the moderator, dismissing her on Twitter as a "lightweight" and retweeting several posts characterizing her as a "bimbo."[36]

Kelly tried reminding viewers that Trump "doesn't get to control the media," but soon discovered otherwise, at least as far as her Murdoch-owned home network was concerned. Fox News viewers turned decidedly against her, and eventually so did management. Two weeks before Trump's inauguration, she would abandon her show *The Kelly File* and step away from her $15 million–per–year Fox contract (although she later signed an even more lucrative deal with NBC).[37] Conservative talk-radio host Hugh Hewitt—who like Kelly served as a GOP debate moderator—may have been the first journalist to understand Trump's increasingly mesmeric power. Trump had once derided him as "a very low ratings radio talk show host . . . a third-rate 'gotcha' guy."[38] But Hewitt sensed early on that of the seventeen aspirants for the 2016 Republican nomination, only "one of them was an honest-to-goodness television star, who knew how to turn the primary into a reality TV show."[39] In that milieu, Trump reigned supreme.

At a nationally broadcast rally in Sioux City, Iowa, in January 2016, Trump infamously boasted, "I could stand in the middle of Fifth Avenue and shoot somebody, and I wouldn't lose voters." He may have been right. The previous month, speaking in Grand Rapids, Michigan, he had made a joke of Russian leader Vladimir Putin's habit of eliminating unfriendly journalists. "I would never kill them. I would never do that," Trump declared in a sardonic tone. Then he added: "Uh, let's see, uh?"[40] CNN reporter Jim Acosta reported several ugly confrontations with Trump's fans at the candidate's public events. At one Minnesota campaign rally, a Trump supporter was spotted in the crowd wearing a T-shirt emblazoned with the words: "Rope. Tree. Journalist. Some Assembly Required."[41]

By this time, no one could outperform Trump on TV or social media. It took an archaic news medium to nearly derail the Trump bandwagon: the old-fashioned audiotape. Eleven years earlier, during a bus ride with TV host Billy Bush, Trump had been recorded boasting of an inability to keep his hands off women, even strangers. "You know," Trump had bragged while en route to an appearance on the NBC show *Access Hollywood*, "I'm automatically attracted to beautiful—I just start kissing them. It's like a magnet. Just kiss. I don't even wait. And when you're a star, they let you do it. You can do anything. Grab 'em by the pussy. You can do anything." The *Washington Post* revealed the existence of the tape on October 16. Tim Alberta, chief political correspondent for *Politico*, called it an "October surprise for the ages."[42]

The *Access Hollywood* audio earned endless replay on the networks. "This doesn't sound like me," Trump at first protested. "Well, that's me," he later conceded, dismissing his remarks as "locker room banter, a private conversation that took place many years ago." Then he gratuitously added, "Bill Clinton has said far worse to me on the golf course—not even close." With his campaign in free fall, Trump ultimately provided something he almost never offered: regrets: "I apologize if anyone was offended." Republican leaders weighed dumping him.

But barely an hour after the tapes became public, in what must rank as either an overt attempt to limit their damage or else a miraculous coincidence, WikiLeaks flooded social media with two thousand emails it had lifted—via Russian hackers, some intelligence officials believed—off the personal account of Clinton campaign manager John Podesta. It turned out to be but the first round in a cache of fifty thousand hacked messages that WikiLeaks began systematically dumping online.[43] As a result, just as Trump was teetering on the precipice of political oblivion, many Americans turned their attention from the *Access Hollywood* mess to focus instead on Hillary Clinton and what seemed to some—without justification—a revival of her previous, widely covered problems with her private email server.[44]

Having escaped a near-death campaign experience, Trump resumed feeding his "Make America Great Again" base with red meat. Jim Acosta, the son of Cuban immigrants, worried that in calling for a ban on Muslim immigration, construction of a southern border wall to be paid for by Mexico, and closer scrutiny of press coverage, Trump stirred genuine outrage against "the 'three M's': Muslims, Mexicans, and the media." The press got the worst of it. Acosta repeatedly heard the candidate label journalists "disgusting, dishonest, scum, thieves, crooks, liars, and so on," admitting in an understatement: "Trump simply could not stand us."[45] At one event, Trump did single out a journalist for praise. Matthew Boyle, the candidate declared, was a "very good reporter."[46] Boyle served as Washington political editor for far-right Breitbart News.

MSNBC political analyst Joy-Ann Reid saw danger signs merely in Trump's overt appeal to white males. "Trump's campaign," she wrote, "amplified by Russian bots and the American far right media machine, tapped into the fear among some white Americans that they have lost their place atop America's cultural firmament. Trump vowed to give it back to them, to wind back the clock, to hurt the 'right people,' and rebalance the scales."[47] Equally dismayed, *New York Times* media critic James Rutenberg wondered: "If you're a working journalist and you believe that Donald J. Trump is a demagogue playing to the nation's worst racist and nationalistic tendencies . . . how the heck are you supposed to cover him?" In the view of many conservative journalists, such confessions only validated Trump's argument that the liberal media was biased against him. One pundit believes that the *New York Time*s portrayed Trump from the start as "a liar, a racist and a traitor," and thereafter trashed all "standards of fairness" and morphed into "the media wing of the resistance movement."[48]

With faith in mainstream media in decline, eroded largely by Trump's onslaught of criticism, the resistance proved inadequate to stay Trump's momentum. He marched toward November on a tsunami of televised speeches and daily tweets. "We've never seen this before in politics," marveled Mike Berland, a veteran of Hillary Clinton's campaign. "This is not just a rally that happens once in a while. This is a continuous Trump rally that happens on Twitter at all hours. He fills the Twitter stadium every day."[49] CNN's Jake Tapper would call Trump's Twitter feed "the window into his soul."[50] But just enough Americans liked the view.

On Election Day, Clinton won nearly three million more popular votes than Trump, but by small margins lost swing states Michigan, Pennsylvania, and Wisconsin, tipping the electoral majority to Trump, 306–222.[51] A few months later, bruised by criticism that she had come up short in Wisconsin by failing to campaign there late in the race, Mrs. Clinton told me she still believed that a rash of online mischief—aimed at suppressing Democratic turnout and driving undecideds to Trump at the last moment under the pollsters' radar—had helped cost her that key state.[52] Who can say that in an era in which social media so often trumped both traditional coverage and retail politics—pun intended—Secretary Clinton was wrong in her conclusion?

Stephen K. Bannon, the former Breitbart News CEO who had served as Trump's chief campaign strategist, offered a different explanation. "We got elected on Drain the Swamp, Lock Her Up, Build a Wall," Bannon said. "This was pure anger. Anger and fear is what gets people to the polls. The Democrats don't matter. The real opposition is the media. And the way to deal with them is to flood the zone with shit." As Trump himself taunted reporters a few months later, "I certainly didn't win by people listening to you people."[53] The 2016 Trump campaign, Jim Acosta maintained, "was an attempt to tell the public that up was down, that black was white, that real was fake. And it was all happening in front of our eyes."[54] Here was climate change that Trump not only believed in but championed. And the climate changed little after Election Day.

On January 21, 2017, his first full day as president, Donald Trump paid a visit to CIA headquarters in Langley, Virginia, the media in tow. There, he was expected to reassure agency professionals that despite his campaign-season attacks on the so-called deep state, not to mention his recent characterization of CIA officials as "Nazis," he indeed valued the American intelligence community. But once he started speaking, Trump almost immediately veered off script to denounce the press. "I have a running war with the media," he volunteered. "They are among the most dishonest human beings on earth."[55] It was the press, he charged—notwithstanding his own recent CIA critique—that had fabricated his "feud with the intelligence community."[56]

In fact, what had most likely provoked Trump's sour mood that day were reports that his inaugural day crowd the previous morning had fallen short of his predecessor's. The story infuriated Trump. "We caught them in a beauty," he insisted during his Langley visit, "and I think they're going to pay a big price."[57]

Aerial photographs only validated the unwinnable comparison to Obama's immense 2009 inaugural throng, but his successor was never one to let evidence get in the way of fixation. So Trump ordered his newly minted press secretary Sean Spicer to respond to the media's alleged efforts "to belittle and disparage the incoming administration from the get-go." Spicer, who had hoped to devote his initial day on the job focusing on "the president's policy agenda," instead issued a statement insisting, "This was the largest audience to ever witness an inauguration—period—both in person and around the globe"—perhaps adding that final caveat in an attempt to factor in worldwide TV ratings to support the president's claims to crowd-size superiority. Appearing in the White House press room for his first daily briefing, Spicer not only accused the press of "deliberately false reporting." He ominously added: "There's been a lot of talk in the media about the responsibility to hold Donald Trump accountable. And I'm here to tell you that it goes two ways. We're going to hold the press accountable as well." Freshly assigned CNN White House correspondent Jim Acosta called it "the stuff of despots and dictators."[58]

The attempted clarification backfired. "Fact-checkers said my pants were on fire," Spicer admitted, "fashion critics mocked my light gray pinstripe suit for the way it rode up my neck, and my first appearance before the media in the Press Briefing Room set an unfortunate precedent of a belligerent press confronted with an equally belligerent press secretary." In return for falling on his sword, poor Spicer even earned a thumbs-down from his exacting boss: Trump, he recalled, "wasn't happy at all with the way I performed."[59] Adding insult to injury, actress Melissa McCarthy then introduced a robotic Spicer parody on *Saturday Night Live*. Temporary relief came only when the program crossed a line by tastelessly ridiculing the president's young son, Barron, inciting Trump to lash out (understandably, if inaccurately), "It's a failing show. It's not funny. . . . It's a disgrace." As for actor Alec Baldwin's uncanny and hilarious on-air impersonation of the president, Trump labeled it "a disaster," adding, "He's terrible on the show."[60] Trump's tolerance for ribbing had not expanded in the six years since the 2011 White House Correspondents' Association dinner.

Although he had already forfeited his credibility, Spicer actually took a second stab at vouching for Trump's allegedly record-breaking inaugural crowd, reappearing the day after he had botched the original message to clarify that the throng on the ground had indisputably ranked as the largest in history—even though it had not. "That's my Sean," Trump greeted him this time. "Good job. Right way to do it." *Washington Post* columnist Richard Cohen taunted that "Spicer's account made no mention of a doggie biscuit."[61]

On day three of the Trump administration, the White House dispatched presidential counselor Kellyanne Conway to the Sunday talk-show circuit to perpetuate the inaugural-crowd fantasy. On *Meet the Press*, host Chuck Todd asked her to explain why the president had compelled Spicer to "utter a falsehood" in his very first act as press secretary. "*You're* saying it's a falsehood," Conway shot back (emphasis added). Spicer, she contended—coining yet another Trump-era turn of phrase—had simply provided "alternative facts."[62] Another uproar ensued. Before long, Conway had begun her own war with the press, filibustering on some interview shows, assailing the hosts of others, and eventually wearing out her welcome on several. To add to the chaos, Conway's own husband commenced a years-long Twitter assault on Trump, suggesting several times that the president had lost his reason.[63] In 2018, Michael Conway would lament that Trump was "seeking, and to a startling degree succeeding, in discrediting the entire media profession." He warned that Trump's public crusade against journalism was "more pernicious and damaging" even than Richard Nixon's private media war nearly half a century earlier.[64]

Still, when the time approached for the first White House Correspondents' Association dinner of the Trump era, it surprised many Washington old-timers that the new president decided not to deliver the traditional keynote roast. Not since Ronald Reagan skipped a dinner—only after being shot—had any recent president shunned the traditional event. One of Trump's spokespeople later justified his boycott, "If a Girl Scout egged your house, would you buy cookies from her?"[65] (In 2018, Trump would even stage a political rally in Michigan on the same night as the Washington banquet, tweeting a boast that his own event had been "a big success" and the correspondents' dinner "a very big, boring bust.")[66] As Sean Spicer put it: "To attend that dinner would be to submit to an evening-long public immolation, not really Trump's style. . . . He saw no benefit in spending a night pretending everything was okay with a press that was at war with him."[67]

The war only intensified. On February 17, Trump memorably tweeted to his vast following—which had now ballooned to twenty-five million—that the "fake news media" was "not my enemy, it is the enemy of the American people." Chuck Todd angrily responded on his own social media platform: "I'm sorry, delegitimizing the press is unAmerican."[68] Trump only increased his multi-pronged effort to reduce American confidence in mainstream journalism. The campaign took three distinct forms: intimidation (ostracizing select reporters), fabrication (spewing exaggerations and outright falsehoods), and demonization (arousing suspicion and resentment that called the media itself into question).

Not that the press let Trump's prevarications go unnoticed. During the first year of his presidency, journalists called him to account often, albeit politely, at first referring to Trump's exaggerations only as "erroneous claims." But even in cataloging his questionable statements under the benign headline "Fact-Checking President Trump," the *New York Times* reported in April that he had uttered misleading statements at least once a day for the first forty days of his presidency. By June, the paper published an updated appraisal more belligerently titled "Trump's Lies."[69] The *Times* confronted Trump for, among other fabrications, suggesting that Hillary Clinton's 2016 popular vote plurality had been produced by people "who are dead, who are illegals . . . millions of votes, in my opinion"; for likening immigrants to "professional anarchists, thugs and paid protestors"; for charging that outgoing president Obama had wiretapped Trump Tower during the 2016 campaign ("This is McCarthyism!"); for claiming he'd never suggested he would "repeal and replace Obamacare" (though he had said precisely so countless times and would soon back just such an effort); for boasting, "I don't think anybody has done what we did over the first 100 days" (ignoring the accomplishments of the initial three months of FDR's New Deal); and for suggesting that "the murder rate in our country is the highest it's been in 47 years" (in fact it was dramatically lower than it had been in the 1990s).[70]

Soon the *Guardian* took to commenting on "the 'exhausting' work" its researchers faced merely tracking "Trump's barrage of lies."[71] And the *Washington Post* launched a "Democracy Dies in the Darkness" website to chronicle "President Trump's proclivity for spouting exaggerated numbers, unwarranted boasts and outright falsehoods." By mid-August 2019 the *Post* would charge that Trump had made "12,019 false or misleading claims over his initial 928 days" in office. The paper further revealed that a public opinion survey showed that only three in ten Americans believed Trump's "most-common false statements," although slightly more than four in ten continued to support him—the same bedrock 40-plus percent that he had won on Election Day 2016.[72] In apparent retaliation for the unflattering scorecard, Trump began threatening the *Post*'s parent company, Amazon (then fighting a legal battle to maintain its tax status). And he questioned the paper's longtime right to discounted postal rates (an issue George Washington had addressed in a more generous vein two centuries earlier). "The Amazon Washington Post has gone crazy against me ever since they lost the Internet Tax Case in the U.S. Supreme Court two months ago," Trump tweeted. "Next up is the U.S. Post Office, which they use, at a fraction of real cost, as their 'delivery boy' for a BIG percentage of their packages." Added the president in a second tweet minutes after the first: "In my opinion the Washington Post is nothing more than an expensive (the paper loses a fortune) lobbyist for Amazon."[73]

In an atmosphere poisoned by mutual suspicion, Trump also shunned formal press conferences, holding but one in his entire first year in office (compared with seven by Obama, four by George W. Bush, eleven by Clinton, and twenty-seven by George H. W. Bush).[74] In their place, Trump generated Twitter storms targeted to please supporters and provoke opponents. Visual amplification came at the scrums Trump conducted with print and broadcast reporters on the White House lawn before boarding his helicopter. Strutting up and down the rope line to respond to questions and follow-ups, he drummed home talking points and occasionally berated reporters he did not admire. Critics chafed, but his public loved the show; novelist Gary Shteyngart called it "Must See TV."[75]

The political campaign was over, but the Trump rallies continued. At one February 2017 event in Melbourne, Florida, the president showcased his growing ability to defy press scrutiny—this time over the charge that he had made inappropriate comments to a Russian diplomat during a White House visit. "The dishonest media which has published one false story after another with no sources, even though they pretend to have them," he countered, "they make them up in many cases, they just don't want to report the truth. . . . They have their own agenda. And their agenda is not your agenda." Trump drew distinct historical parallels in his victimhood. "Thomas Jefferson, Andrew Jackson, and Abraham Lincoln and many of our greatest presidents fought with the media and called them out often times on their lies," he pointed out, oversimplifying the comparison but coming close enough to the truth. "I will never, ever, let them get away with it."[76]

Increasingly focused on retaliation, the president spent more time vilifying the press than generating coverage for early political successes like getting Congress to pass tax cuts. Trump may have found it especially difficult to convey a positive message because his press operation—like the rest of his administration—suffered from record-high turnover. Early in his tenure, angered by a steady trickle of leaks from the White House, Trump summoned

Sean Spicer and his then-deputy, Sarah Huckabee Sanders, to the Oval Office. Spicer found the president seated at a table inside the adjacent dining room, his eyes glued to a television screen tuned to cable news. Said Trump: "Sean, we're getting killed in the media. No matter what we do we're getting killed. I know it's not your fault. I know you guys are trying. I think we need to change some things. We need to get some new people in here. We need to get Anthony in here."[77]

By "Anthony," an incredulous Spicer realized, the president meant Anthony Scaramucci, a tough-talking, sharply dressed onetime delivery boy for the Long Island daily *Newsday* who had evolved into a successful entrepreneur and, in 2016, from a Jeb Bush supporter to a Trump champion. Now Trump believed he "might have a magic touch with the media" and invited Scaramucci to become the new White House communications director (even though Mike Dubke already held the job). "Though he bestowed me with that official title," Scaramucci remembered, "job one, the president told me, was to find and fire the leakers."[78] The media, Trump bemoaned to "The Mooch," "used to love me." Scaramucci convinced himself that Trump yearned for not only their attention but also their affection. "We gotta have an armistice with the media," Scaramucci proposed. "You might not like them, they might not like you, but we have to stop battling each other." Press criticism was unavoidable. "You have to let it roll off of you. Like water off a duck's ass." Trump agreed to try. "Okay," he said. "Let's fix this."[79]

The very next morning, a humiliated Spicer submitted his resignation, effective in July.[80] He may have acted prematurely. The Scaramucci "era" lasted all of ten days. Early in his absurdly brief tenure, Scaramucci, who came to his job with no media experience, made the colossal mistake of confiding to the *New Yorker*'s Washington correspondent, Ryan Lizza, that he planned "to fire the entire comms staff and start over"—a "stupid remark," Scaramucci later conceded, particularly since it meant putting "thirty-five people out of work." What made the comments even stupider was that Scaramucci had neglected to take them off the record. For good measure, he'd added a vulgarity about one of his nemeses, White House advisor Steve Bannon. Suspecting that Bannon—who had opposed his hiring—was one of the principal sources of leaks (along with chief of staff Reince Priebus), Scaramucci accused Bannon of the anatomically challenging act of "sucking his own cock."[81] Of course, Lizza published everything that Scaramucci blabbed. "Adios Moochacho!" ran one headline announcing the communication director's hasty exit.[82] If it provided Scaramucci any consolation, Trump's new chief of staff, John J. Kelly, ousted Bannon as well. Sarah Sanders took over as press secretary and began her own stormy relationship with the White House media. And Trump floated the censorious idea of "limiting press briefings to once a week" and requiring correspondents to submit their questions to Sanders in advance—and in writing.[83]

By then, it mattered little who formally ran White House "comms." Trump needed no help to maintain his extraordinary dominance of the media. A Harvard Kennedy School study found that during his first hundred days in office, Trump was the principal subject of broadcast news stories an astonishing 41 percent of the time—"three times the amount of coverage received" by his predecessors at the outset of their terms. In releasing the study, the Shorenstein Center on Media, Politics and Public Policy chided the press for failing "to give Trump credit when his actions warrant it," but criticized the administration for emphasizing personality over policy. The experts urged the press corps to "spend less time peering at the White House" and called on Trump to devote less energy lashing out at the press. Not surprisingly, neither the president nor the media heeded the advice.[84]

As president, Donald Trump increasingly made media-bashing a staple not only of his messaging but also of his policy. It would be hard to argue that he did not intend to permanently fracture American confidence in the press—at least that sector of the bifurcated partisan media that often found fault with him.

Above all there were the tweets. In his first year in office, Trump tweeted an average of seven times a day, not only breaking genuine news but also routinely castigating the "Fake News Media" over its negative coverage.[85] His audience grew exponentially. By mid-June 2017, Trump's principal Twitter account boasted a staggering 32.4 million followers, and his corollary @POTUS account 18.8 million more. By then Trump had also attracted 1.7 million Facebook friends, 4.3 million followers on YouTube, and another 7 million on Instagram—some 64 million followers in total. "Not too shabby," acknowledged his frequent punching bag, CNN.[86] Yet CNN and the other cable networks continued almost ritualistically to promote Trump's online presence. Even though he devoted his platforms in large part to assailing "Lamestream Media," the aggrieved print and broadcast press as often amplified Trump's scornful online content as it contradicted it. Presidential Twitter posts not only filled cyberspace; they generated constant repetition on mainstream media.

Each day, Trump's tweets reached millions of his followers online and tens of millions more on television. In previous decades, the wire services and *New York Times* had set the table for coverage in the national broadcast media: what they published each morning dictated what other outlets reported throughout the day. Now "those tweets quickly turned into headlines," MSNBC's Joy-Ann Reid complained, "to the horror of media watchdogs who view it as a way of co-opting and manipulating the legitimate press into transmitting Trumpian propaganda."[87] Like all the true pioneers of presidential communications—Lincoln with his telegraphed messages and public letters, Franklin Roosevelt through radio chats, Kennedy on televised news conferences, and Obama as an Internet trailblazer—Trump dominated a revolutionary new medium. Uniquely, he compelled the old media to bear witness.

So skillfully did Trump command messaging that he easily withstood public relations calamities that might have crippled earlier administrations. In August 2017, an alt-right, neo-Nazi rally in Charlottesville, Virginia—ostensibly called to protest the removal of a statue of Robert E. Lee—grew violent. Trump held a news conference at his New Jersey golf club to "condemn in the strongest possible terms this egregious display of hatred, bigotry, and violence"—but then ad-libbed, "on many sides." As *Politico*'s Jim Alberta saw matters, Trump had drawn "a moral equivalence between the white supremacists marching in Charlottesville and the counterprotesters opposed to their ideology." Faced with condemnation from within his own party, Trump promptly scheduled a second press conference back at the White House, this time castigating only "the KKK, neo-Nazis, and other hate groups." But the very next day he told a gaggle of reporters at Trump Tower that there were indeed "very fine people on both sides" of the Charlottesville unrest.[88]

Standing near Trump's side in full view of the television cameras that day in New York, his Jewish economic advisor, Gary Cohn, visibly winced. A few days later, he prepared his resignation and told the *Financial Times* that the president "can and must do better" to "heal the deep division that exists within our communities."[89] Cohn decided to stay on but exited six months later. Trump blamed the press for obsessing about Charlottesville, defended Confederate monuments as indelible relics of history, and warned that further questions could lead to the invalidation of slave-holding founders like George Washington and Thomas Jefferson.

Just as the Charlottesville news began dying down in late 2017, word came that Attorney General Jeff Sessions would name former FBI director Robert

Mueller as a special prosecutor to investigate lingering charges of Russian election interference and possible Trump campaign collusion. The move reignited Trump's belief that the press and Deep State were collaborating in a "witch hunt" designed to undo the results of the 2016 race. He took to Twitter to mock the investigation as well as his own attorney general for recusing himself from the process. As always, Trump reserved his angriest rebukes for the media.

As campaigning got underway for the 2018 midterm elections, Trump increasingly bypassed the established press corps and took the Republican case directly to social media and to his boisterous trademark rallies. His anger at the media was reaching a fever pitch. In Wilkes Barre, Pennsylvania, that August, Trump asked, "What ever happened to fair press? What ever happened to honest reporting?" The media, he insisted, "can make anything bad because they are the fake, fake, disgusting news."[90] Most of all, Trump lashed out at the notion that he had won in 2016 only because of Russian interference. That such interference had actually been attempted was by then recognized across party lines. Yet at the July 2018 Helsinki summit meeting with world leaders, Trump refused to endorse reports issued with "high confidence" by American intelligence officials that Russia had at least tried to impact the 2016 campaign—and planned to try again in 2018. Trump reacted as if acknowledgment would tarnish his victory—even if denial meant exposing future campaigns to repeat mischief. At a joint press conference in Helsinki with Russian leader Vladimir Putin, Trump issued what one network called "a stunning rebuke of the US intelligence community" by declaring, "I have great confidence in my intelligence people, but I will tell you that President Putin was extremely strong and powerful in his denial today."[91] Then he tweeted: "The summit with Russia was a great success, except with the real enemy of the people, the Fake News Media."[92]

Although threats against liberal commentators spiked in the wake of Trump's fusillades, the president did nothing to defuse the hostility he had helped foment. However, when an armed intruder nursing an unrelated grudge against a neighborhood paper killed five people in a mass shooting at the Annapolis, Maryland, *Capital Gazette* in June 2018, Trump did appropriately comment: "Journalists, like all Americans, should be free from the fear of being violently attacked while doing their job."[93] Yet he had recently retweeted a cartoon showing a locomotive labeled "TRUMP" barreling into a CNN reporter. "Nothing can stop the Trump Train!!" he had added for emphasis.[94] CNN's New York offices were repeatedly evacuated in response to bomb threats. (In

February 2019, authorities would arrest Coast Guard officer and self-declared white nationalist Christopher Paul Hasson for plotting a mass shooting of politicians and on-air personalities from MSNBC and CNN.)[95]

New York Times editorials and opinion columns continued to lead the chorus of Trump critics, but in late July 2018 the president sat down for what he called "a very good and interesting" private White House meeting with the paper's recently elevated publisher A. G. Sulzberger. Afterward, Trump dispelled any notion of a pending truce by unleashing what the *Washington Post* called "a Twitter tirade" from his Bedminster, New Jersey, golf estate the following Sunday. In one post, Trump tweeted: "Spent much time talking about the vast amounts of Fake News being put out by the media & how that Fake News has morphed into phrase, 'Enemy of the People.' Sad," he concluded, as if he had not promoted the phrase himself.[96] In subsequent blasts, Trump added: "When the media—driven insane by their Trump Derangement Syndrome—reveals internal deliberations of our government, it truly puts the lives of many, not just journalists, at risk! Very unpatriotic!" Running out of space, he continued in yet another tweet: "I will not allow our great country to be sold out by anti-Trump haters in the dying newspaper industry."[97] Young Sulzberger had apparently "warned" Trump that his "inflammatory language" about journalists was "contributing to a rise in threats against journalists and will lead to violence."[98] A few days later, Sarah Huckabee Sanders blamed the media for continuing "to ratchet up the verbal assaults against the president."[99]

In August, the *Boston Globe* called on newspapers around the country to push back against Trump's "blitzkrieg" of criticism by reaffirming the rights and obligations of a free press. More than three hundred papers, large and small, responded with editorials. "The biggest injustice of Trump's smear of the press presumes that a Trump supporter cannot and will not think critically and fairly about their news," declared the *Brattleboro Commons*. "The president's supporters deserve to be held to a higher standard." Argued the *San Jose Mercury News and East Bay Times*: "Journalists are trying to do a job. We're not trying to tear down our nation. We're trying to strengthen it." The *Globe* itself warned that the principles that had "protected journalists at home and served as a model for free nations abroad" were now under siege. "And it sends an alarming signal to despots from Ankara to Moscow, Beijing to Baghdad, that journalists can be treated as a domestic enemy."[100]

Trump responded to the outpouring with a tweet asserting that "the Globe is in COLLUSION with other papers on free press. PROVE IT!"[101] At a subsequent meeting with reporters, he again branded the well-choreographed editorial campaign as "collusion," characterizing participants as the "opposition party," and addressing them directly with what sounded like a veiled threat: "If you'd like, you can stay [in America]. If you'd like, you can leave. Freedom of the press."[102] Later he added the tweet: "I just cannot state strongly enough how totally dishonest much of the Media is. Truth doesn't matter to them, they only have their hatred & agenda."[103]

As Election Day neared, Trump risked further media rebuke when he failed to condemn Saudi Arabia after *Washington Post* columnist Jamal Khashoggi entered that nation's Istanbul consulate on October 2, 2018, never to exit alive. Trump appeared satisfied with the Saudi royal family's explanation that Khashoggi had either died accidentally during a vigorous interrogation or been murdered by renegade operatives. Karen Attiah, Khashoggi's *Post* editor, expressed horror when the White House repeated the additional Saudi charge that the slain journalist had been "an 'enemy of the state,'" implying that he deserved his brutal fate. "It was infuriating and frankly quite scary to see the blatant carrying of the Saudi line," Attiah said. "I realized, wow, okay: if something like this can happen to Jamal, somebody who's arguably one of Saudi Arabia's most famous journalists . . . if he could be eliminated in this way and have the president look the other way, what chance do the rest of us stand if we happen to fall prey to Saudi Arabia or some other so-called ally?"[104]

Not long after the Khashoggi murder, Trump appeared to hint that he condoned violence against overinquisitive journalists at home. A Republican running for Congress in Montana had recently responded to a disobliging question from a *Guardian* reporter by knocking him to the ground. Now, headlining yet another campaign rally, Trump said of candidate Greg Gianforte (who had pleaded guilty to assault but received a suspended sentence), "Any guy that can do a body slam, he's my kind of—he's my guy." In that assessment, Trump aligned himself with Rush Limbaugh, who had called Gianforte "manly and studly."[105]

Yet Trump continued to insist on Twitter: "A very big part of the anger we see today in our society is caused by the purposely false and inaccurate reporting of the Mainstream Media that I refer to as Fake News. It has gotten so bad and hateful that it is beyond description. Mainstream Media must clean up its act, FAST!"[106] Although his daughter and advisor Ivanka announced that she disagreed with her father's contention that the press had become "the enemy of the people," the president thereafter took the stage at a campaign rally in Wilkes-Barre, Pennsylvania, and spent ten minutes restating all his grievances:

the media had delayed 2016 election returns from Pennsylvania so the Keystone State could not claim "credit" for electing him; failed to lavish him with sufficient kudos for negotiating a temporary halt in North Korean nuclear testing; and misreported his Helsinki meeting with Vladimir Putin. "They can make anything bad because they are the fake, fake disgusting news," Trump concluded.[107] At another late-summer campaign rally, he cautioned his followers: "Don't believe the crap you see from these people, the fake news. Just remember: What you're seeing . . . is not what's happening."[108]

Reiterating the phrase he had borrowed—one hopes unknowingly—from historic villains like Goebbels and Stalin, Trump tweeted at the end of October: "There is great anger in our Country caused in part by inaccurate, and even fraudulent, reporting of the news. The Fake News Media, the true Enemy of the People, must stop the open & obvious hostility & report the news accurately & fairly. That will do much to put out the flame of Anger and Outrage and we will then be able to bring all sides together in Peace and Harmony. Fake News Must End."[109]

Perhaps it was no coincidence that around the same time, a suspicious package arrived at CNN's New York studio, causing a panic. Network chief Jeff Zucker asserted, "The President, and especially the White House Press Secretary, should understand their words matter." In response, Sarah Sanders called it "absolutely disgraceful" that CNN had placed "responsibility of this despicable act on the president and on me personally." Yet earlier in the week, Trump had told a crowd in Wisconsin, "The media also has a responsibility to set a civil tone and to stop the endless hostility and constant negative—and oftentimes, false—attacks and stories."[110]

Highlighting a climactic Republican campaign rally in Missouri on election eve, twenty-first-century history was made—and nineteenth-century history revived—when Fox News hosts Sean Hannity and Jeanine Pirro actually took the stage at Trump's invitation. Not since New York editors Horace Greeley and Henry Raymond had hit the campaign trail for Abraham Lincoln in 1860 had working journalists so conspicuously campaigned for a political party. Hannity lost no time in assailing his press colleagues from the rostrum. Taking note of the reporters covering the event, the cable superstar reminded the audience, "all those people in the back are fake news." The crowd responded with loud boos. Then the president summoned Pirro to join the celebration, telling the crowd, she "treats us very, very well." Pirro responded by telling the throng, "If you like the America that he is making now, you've got to make sure you get out there tomorrow." The progressive watchdog group Media Matters labeled the mere appearance of journalists at a political event "dangerous for democracy and a threat to a free press."[111] Fox News issued only an indirect rebuke of its top-rated stars, saying it did not "condone any talent participating in campaign contests."[112]

The 2018 election proved a disappointment to Trump and the Republicans: Democrats took back the House of Representatives. Left unresolved was the hostility raging between much of the press and most of the administration. The liberal media showed no indication it would soften its tough coverage—accusing Trump of, among other misdeeds, mistreating immigrant children in refugee camps while directing official visitors, lobbyists, and meetings to his golf courses and resorts, sometimes at government expense. The president showed no interest in muffling his anti-press rhetoric, though experts at the United Nations had warned that his ongoing criticism of the American media might encourage violence against reporters worldwide. Trump, the UN specialists on freedom of expression pointed out, had "failed to show even once that specific reporting has been driven by any untoward motivations."[113] Insisting that freedom of the press came with the "responsibility to report the news . . . accurately," Trump countered that since "90 percent of media coverage of my Administration is negative, despite the tremendously positive results we're achieving, it's no surprise that confidence in the media is at an all-time low."

Many public opinion surveys confirmed his assessment. As early as October 2016, despite warnings about looming Russian tampering with the upcoming American election, a *USA Today*/Suffolk University poll concluded that only 20 percent identified "foreign interests such as Russian hackers" as the biggest threat to the "integrity" of the vote; more than 45 percent instead named "the media."[114] That particular statistic suggests that candidate Trump had cleverly tapped into, rather than created, mass distrust of the press. By the following April, three months into the Trump presidency, a Gallup poll found that 62 percent of American adults, and 77 percent of Republicans, believed "the media has a favorite [political party]," up 10 to 20 percent in recent years. As the Gallup headline made clear: "Americans' Trust in Mass Media Sinks to New Low."[115] Asked during the 2018 congressional campaign whether Trump should shut down CNN, the *Washington Post*, and the *New York Times*, an alarming 23 percent of Republicans responded yes.[116] An NBC/*Wall Street Journal* survey revealed that half of all Americans thought that press coverage of collusion charges was "overdramatized," while only 34 percent viewed it as "responsible and proper."[117] And in April 2018, a Monmouth University poll found that nearly half of all Americans believed that the major media "occasionally" published fake news, while almost a third thought the media did so "regularly." That result represented a 12 percent higher loss of confidence than was reported the previous year, but not surprisingly coincided with studies that showed Americans losing faith in democracy itself.[118]

The year 2019 brought no respite from the media wars. Facing the prospect of investigations by a House of Representatives now under Democratic control, Trump and his admirers lashed out more virulently than ever. On February 12—Lincoln's birthday—a spectator at a Trump event in El Paso, Texas—wearing a red "Make America Great Again" cap—shoved a BBC cameraman "very hard" before being escorted out, spewing curses, by security. Eleanor Montague, a BBC Washington news editor, tweeted that the El Paso audience had been "whipped into a frenzy against the media by Trump and other speakers all night."[119]

Amid plummeting public trust, it was no wonder that outspoken critics began facing ostracism without provoking much outrage. A frustrated Trump had earlier complained of the press, "They're kicking the crap out of me." Attorney John Dowd had advised: "I'd pull all their credentials. I'd throw them the fuck out of here. I don't think they have any right to come into the White House and behave the way they do." Trump agreed, adding, "But I always get overruled. . . . I want to pull everyone's credentials."[120] Eventually, the president began doing just that. "These people shouting questions are the worst," Trump complained at one point to an aide. "Why do we have them in here?" In July 2018, the White House barred CNN correspondent Kaitlan Collins from a media event in the Rose Garden. The administration objected, she was told, to a question she had asked the president earlier in the day. "President Trump is the most accessible president in modern history," Sarah Huckabee Sanders insisted in defending the move. That same month, Jim Acosta tried to pose a question to the president during a joint news conference in London with British prime minister Theresa May. "I don't take questions from CNN," Trump replied. "CNN is fake news." Declaring, "Let's go to a real network," Trump then called on John Roberts of Fox.[121]

In November, the administration took what the *Times* called "the exceedingly rare step" of withdrawing Acosta's White House press pass. Two days earlier, at a news conference called in the wake of Republican election defeats, the president had switched gears to label Central American migration to the United States "an invasion." Aggressively questioned by Acosta, Trump at first shot back, "Honestly, I think you should let me run the country—you run CNN." When Acosta refused to surrender the microphone to the next questioner, Trump called him a "rude, terrible person" and added, "You shouldn't be working for CNN." The next day, press secretary Sanders charged that in staving off the female intern who had tried to reclaim the mic, Acosta had put "his hands on a young woman." When CNN dismissed that charge and branded the ouster both an act of "retaliation" and "a threat to our democracy," Sanders doubled down: "The fact that CNN is proud of the way their employee behaved is not only disgusting, it is an example of their outrageous disregard for everyone, including young women, who work in this administration."[122] En route to Paris, Trump warned he might expand the ban to other reporters, arguing: "You have to treat the White House with respect. You have to treat the presidency with respect."[123] Once home, he hinted that the government might even create its own media network. "Something has to be done," he tweeted, "including the possibility of the United States starting our own Worldwide Network to show the World the way we really are. GREAT!"[124]

Acosta's colleagues meanwhile rushed to his defense. Jeff Mason of Reuters, who was seated next to the CNN correspondent at the heated press conference, repudiated the charge that Acosta had manhandled the young intern.[125] Both the ACLU and the White House Correspondents' Association protested the banishment. And Elisabeth Bumiller, the *New York Times*' Washington bureau chief, issued a reminder that the "president should not pick and choose who covers him." Yet Acosta remained in journalistic purgatory, his press pass invalid, until a court ruled that his credentials must be restored. Even when he regained access, Acosta received online threats, including "images of a decapitated goat and its severed head."[126]

The CNN star was not the only reporter to feel Trump's wrath. The president also lashed out at frequent critic April Ryan, an African American White House correspondent for the American Urban Radio Networks and a news analyst for CNN. Ryan had asked back in April if Trump would consider resigning in the wake of the Mueller Report. (She told CNN that she thereafter received death threats.)[127] Branding her a "loser" who "doesn't know what she's doing," Trump complained: "She gets publicity, and then she gets a pay raise or a contract with, I think, CNN. But she's very nasty. She shouldn't be."[128]

The White House also imposed a technical rule to strip credentials from additional reporters: those who did not spend half their work time at the mansion. Among those ousted was Dana Milbank of the *Washington Post*, who had covered presidents for twenty-one years.[129] Ted Boutrous, attorney for *Playboy* White House correspondent Brian Karem, whose access was later terminated as well, called the bans "powerful evidence . . . that this White House is wielding the hard pass credentialing process as a weapon to punish and chill reporters who publish stories the President doesn't like. It's totally brazen and shows a total disrespect for basic First Amendment principles."[130]

In a sense, the remaining press corps lost access as well, and not just because presidential press conferences had become such rarities. In early 2019, Sarah Sanders grew so weary of her contentious daily briefings with journalists that she suspended the traditional sessions altogether. By the time she resigned in June, she had held no briefings for ninety-four days. Her hibernation had been prolonged after the Mueller Report revealed that she had twice lied to reporters about Trump's 2017 dismissal of FBI director James Comey. Although she tried attributing her misstatements to the "heat of the moment," April Ryan had called for her ouster, and *Washington Post* columnist Margaret Sullivan had condemned Sanders for doing her job "disrespectfully, and apparently without shame." An equally unsympathetic Lawrence O'Donnell reminded his MSNBC audience: "She lied about her lie to people who knew she was lying."[131] On the day Sanders announced her departure, President Trump bestowed a public kiss on his outgoing spokeswoman and declared her a "warrior."[132]

To be sure, plenty of opinion makers sympathized with Sanders's ordeal in facing down a hostile press corps and enduring cruel taunts at the White House Correspondents' dinner and on *Saturday Night Live* about her body weight and makeup preferences.[133] Some moreover agreed with Trump's overall pushback against partisan journalists and journalism. One consistent Trump defender was Michael Goodwin, an award-winning political columnist for the *New York Post*. Beginning with the 2016 campaign, Goodwin maintained, Trump had been "slandered like no other candidate in memory." Goodwin blamed the *Washington Post* and *New York Times* "for causing the breakdown," asserting, "They set the tone, and most of the media followed like lemmings."[134]

Now Goodwin decried what he perceived as a snowballing bias against the president. "I think if you read the *Times* any day from the front page to last—the sports, the cultural pages, the television coverage—it's all anti-Trump, and it's right in the headlines," he elaborated on Fox News in the summer of 2019. "It's not subtle."[135] Yet according to Bob Woodward, who chronicled the first two years of the Trump administration in a series of books, the president may have "attacked the mainstream media with relish, especially the *Times*—but despite the full-takedown language, he considered the *Times* the paper of record and largely believed its stories."[136] Indeed, as president-elect, Trump had visited the paper for a Q&A, Kellyanne Conway at his side, and the following April had granted a White House interview to *Times* correspondents Maggie Haberman and Glenn Thrush, though the president devoted parts of each session to criticizing the paper.[137] As the relationship between the paper and the president deteriorated, Trump continued to play the roles of critic and suitor simultaneously. In early February 2019, he granted a long Oval Office interview to publisher Sulzberger and correspondents Haberman and Peter Baker. Describing himself as a "victim" of "unfair" coverage, he told them: "I do notice that people are declaring more and more fake news, where they go, 'Fake News!' I even see it in other countries. I don't necessarily attribute that to me." Informed by his visitors that foreign despots were increasingly echoing that phrase to justify their own press crackdowns, Trump said, "I don't like that." But he added: "I do think it's very bad for a country when the news is not accurately portrayed. I really do. And I do believe I'm a victim of that, honestly. . . . I would love if I was just covered fairly. . . . The New York Times treats me terribly."[138]

The February sit-down did not bridge the chasm. After the *Times* published an article a few weeks later suggesting Trump had tried to obstruct justice in the investigation of his sullied lawyer Michael Cohen, Trump issued one of his most denunciatory tweets yet: "The New York Times reporting is false. They are TRUE ENEMY OF THE PEOPLE."[139] Bristling at the outburst, *Times* publisher Sulzberger warned: "The phrase 'enemy of the people' is not just false, it's dangerous. As I have repeatedly told President Trump face-to-face, there are mounting signs that this incendiary rhetoric is encouraging threats and violence against journalists at home and abroad."[140] The rejoinder failed to inhibit Trump. On June 15, he tweeted: "Do you believe that the Failing New York Times just did a story stating that the United States is substantially increasing Cyber Attacks on Russia. This is a virtual act of Treason by a once great paper so desperate for a story, any story, even if bad for our Country."[141]

Sean Spicer, who had abandoned his White House job but not his loyalty to Trump, believed press coverage had become not only partisan, but trivialized. "Today's media is obsessed with palace intrigue instead of issues of substance, prioritizing the number of clicks, viewers, and subscriptions," Spicer said, ". . . And journalists, rather than critique and improve each other's reporting, are captives of a pack mentality—driven largely by the shrinking economics of the news business." Yet even Spicer decried his former boss's chief means of communication. "Twitter is not glue," he emphasized. "It's solvent. It is breaking us down and breaking us apart. And yes, I see the irony of Donald Trump's former press secretary making this observation."[142] Twitter's creators could not have disagreed more strenuously. In May 2019, cofounder Ev Williams hailed Trump's use of social media as "genius" and called him "a master of the platform."[143] Two months later, it was learned that Trump had retweeted online comments from sixteen subsequently suspended accounts, including one that accused Bill and Hillary Clinton of the "torture and sacrifice of children."[144] By then the number of Trump's followers had passed the sixty million mark.

Even if they did not endorse the president's Twitter profligacy, other observers concurred with the notion that the mainstream media had demonstrated a liberal bias in Trump coverage. Andrew H. Malcolm, a onetime press aide in the George W. Bush administration, observed that "much of today's political journalism has fallen into advocacy, intentionally inflammatory, using or omitting selective details, quotes, and background to make a case against President Donald Trump." He titled his opinion piece "Media's Anti-Trump Addiction Amps Up the Outrage and Fuels the Public's Suspicions."[145]

Reporter Howard Kurtz, who migrated from CNN to Fox to launch a show called *Media Buzz*, wrote that "melodramatic coverage of Trump's troubles was blotting out his efforts to change the country." For this he blamed the press as well as the president, arguing: "To be sure, Trump has at times made mistakes, stretched or obscured the truth, and gone too far in attacking journalists and painting them as enemies of the country. And while the media still play a vital role in separating fact from fiction, the president's criticisms—and their own blinders and blunders—have cast that role in doubt. . . . Donald Trump will not be president forever, but the media's reputation, badly scarred during these polarizing years, might never recover."[146]

Conservative talk radio host Mark Levin added: "So many of the media allegations against President Trump and his administration are overwrought and, in many respects, utterly dishonest. To read their daily blitzkrieg of outrages . . . you would think that the president has corruptly used the instrumentalities of his office and executive authority in ways unimagined by past presidents and administrations. But in truth, he has done no such thing."[147]

Levin had a valid point. John Adams had signed a sedition law to muzzle journalists and ordered the prosecution of those who defied it. Abraham Lincoln had shut down newspapers and jailed Democratic editors for urging young men not to enlist in the Union Army. Teddy Roosevelt had sent his Justice

Department after Joseph Pulitzer. Both Woodrow Wilson and Franklin D. Roosevelt had imposed wartime press censorship. And the Nixon administration had filed a lawsuit to silence the *New York Times* and *Washington Post*. Judging by those standards, Donald Trump's bark far exceeded his bite.

Yet to First Amendment lawyer Floyd Abrams, who had raised warning flags against previous presidents of both parties for trying to muzzle the media, Trump's verbal assaults were sufficiently chilling to elicit concern. "Never has any U.S. president been so hostile to the press," he told me, "spoken of it in such a repeatedly defamatory and accusatory manner, and sought as a matter of policy—of design—to persuade the public (or even his 40 percent of the public) to disbelieve it and to reject its factual revelations as false. This is new in our history."

"No other president," Abrams added, "has ever pointed to the press at his rallies, denounced those journalists who attended, and encouraged his supporters to scream obscenities at them. No other president has . . . said anything like this: it is 'frankly disgusting the way the press is able to write whatever they want to write' and that 'the people should look into that.' The 'that' in that sentence is, of course, nothing less than the First Amendment itself."[148]

Through all his battles with the press, Trump remained an ardent fan of top-rated Fox News, whose most widely watched hosts, Sean Hannity, Tucker Carlson, Jeanine Pirro, and Laura Ingraham, regularly heaped praise on him and shut down dissenting views by their guests. An early riser, Trump became a faithful viewer of the network's morning show *Fox & Friends*, and every so often rewarded its equally loyal anchors with spontaneous on-air phone calls that thickened the atmosphere of mutual congratulation. His official daily schedule began at 11:00 A.M. with his daily national security briefing, but media observer Matt Gertz scoffed that "the real briefing is on 'Fox & Friends.'" Gertz reported that from August 2018 to early 2019, Trump tweeted more than two hundred items he had heard on Fox News.[149]

Trump also stayed up late, watching pro-administration conversations on Fox, as well as the more critical chatter on CNN and MSNBC, to which he often responded with Twitter blasts. By day, he habitually wandered between the Oval Office and the nearby dining room, where another seventy-inch TV screen remained switched on, always tuned to Fox News. When crises unfolded, Trump typically viewed Fox News live and recorded the liberal networks so he could screen them later.[150] Aides took to defining the growing gaps in his official schedule—left free so he could binge-watch television—with the euphemism "executive time." According to one White House source, Trump directed some 60 percent of his attention immediately after the 2018 midterms—some 297 hours—so engaged. Not even Lyndon Johnson had focused so relentlessly on how television portrayed a presidency. Trump's press secretary tried explaining that Trump boasted a "different leadership style than his predecessors and the results speak for themselves." He was "the most productive president in modern history."[151]

Since his most ill-considered tweets "were often triggered by the president's obsessive TV watching," some staff members cautiously "looked for ways to shut off the television," reported Bob Woodward. "But television was Trump's default activity. Sunday nights were often the worst. Trump would come back to the White House from the weekend at one of his golf resorts just in time to watch political talk on his enemy networks, MSNBC and CNN." The president kept "a giant TV going much of the time, alone in the bedroom with the clicker, the TiVo, and his Twitter account" locked and loaded for instant commentary. Reince Priebus referred to the president's bedroom as "'the devil's workshop' and the early mornings and carefree Sunday nights 'the witching hour.'"[152] Out of such immersion might come a tweet referring to himself as a "very stable genius," or a thirteen-message storm on a single morning in July 2019 (in which he misspelled "Barrack" Obama). The *Daily News* attributed such outbursts to "itchy finger" syndrome.[153]

Many such tweets emerged in direct response to reports on Fox. In July 2019, after the House Oversight Committee subpoenaed documents from Ivanka Trump and her husband, White House advisor Jared Kushner, Trump went on a Twitter rant against the committee's chairman, veteran Maryland congressman Elijah Cummings, deriding his predominantly African American Baltimore district as "a disgusting, rat and rodent infested mess" in which "no human being would want to live." As always oblivious to irony, the president branded Cummings, by then in declining health, as "a brutal bully."[154] Commentators on Fox News were left uncomfortably to report the president's overheated attack against a revered legislator who counted friends on both sides of the political aisle. Cummings died in October at age sixty-eight.

In the constant affirmation from Fox, conservatives saw a corrective to "fake news," while the liberal media feared a new kind of collusion. Columnist Paul Krugman declared of Trump in 2019: "He has de facto state media in the form of Fox News and the rest of the Murdoch Empire."[155] Media writer Erik Wemple went further, charging Sean Hannity with pursuing "a Trumpian strategy for breaking the news: Flood airwaves with so much ethical depravity that people stop caring or they chalk it up to the routine activities of an opinion host."[156]

But as impeachment fever grew toward the end of 2019, cracks opened in Trump's long-secure media firewall. Several Fox hosts openly criticized the president over the now-infamous quid pro quo call to Ukrainian president Volodymyr Zelensky in which Trump insinuated that American aid would be withheld until Ukraine agreed to investigate potential 2020 rival Joe Biden. Among the critics was veteran Fox News political reporter Ed Henry, whose on-air comments provoked Trump to retweet more than twenty posts accusing the broadcaster of spreading "fake news." Conservative media criticism increased when Trump abruptly pulled U.S. forces from northern Syria, exposing pro-American Kurds to a potential massacre by the long-hostile Turkish military.

After twenty-two years at the network, chief Fox News anchor Shepard Smith, widely considered a straight shooter, abruptly resigned on October 10. Suspiciously, Smith's departure followed by only a few days a meeting between Trump's attorney general, William Barr, and Fox News founder Rupert Murdoch. The network downplayed the coincidence, but the president, who had begun lamenting that Fox had become "much different than it used to be in the good old days," had earlier castigated Smith by name, suggesting he would be a better fit at CNN. "God help the journalists at Fox," commented Carl Cameron, an on-air reporter who had departed two years earlier and emerged as a critic of his onetime employer.[157] In November 2019, Smith resurfaced to donate $500,000 to the Committee to Protect Journalists, commenting: "Intimidation and vilification of the press is now a global phenomenon. We don't have to look far for evidence of that."[158]

Smith's exit did not completely calm Trump, who had taken to tweet-bashing the entire network as "HOPELESS AND CLUELESS," complaining, "@Fox News doesn't deliver for US anymore." Trump also phoned Fox News CEO Suzanne Scott and "let loose" with a barrage of grievances, making it clear he expected more support and less censure. When network star Chris Wallace raised new concerns in December, Trump excoriated him as "nasty" and a Republican official branded Fox impeachment coverage as "bullshit." Admitted a network insider of Trump: "He's clearly worried we're really going to cover this fairly, and he's starting to freak." Anthony Scaramucci resurfaced to liken the

Fox defections to the watershed moment a legendary CBS broadcaster had dared criticize the Vietnam War in the 1960s. To Scaramucci, now a Trump basher who regularly vented against his former boss on CNN, history was repeating itself. "Fox News is Trump's Walter Cronkite," Scaramucci told the *New York Times*. "Once he loses the majority of them, it's over. He knows it, which is why he is bashing and intimidating them."[159] But Trump did not lose them. By the time Congress began seriously weighing impeachment, Fox by and large resumed its characteristic defense of the president.

Throughout 2019, even rapid-fire communications technology could barely keep pace with Donald Trump's escalating vitriol against the press. In January, he charged on Twitter that the "Fake Media" had "become crazed lunatics who have given up on the TRUTH!"[160] In February, he condemned a television parody with: "Nothing funny about tired Saturday Night Live on Fake News NBC! Question is, how do the Networks get away with these total Republican hit jobs without retribution?"[161] In April, Trump urged *New York Times* writers "to get down on their knees & beg forgiveness—they are truly the Enemy of the People!"[162] Even pro-Trump columnist Rich Lowry, noting that Trump had instructed aides to "think of each presidential day as a TV show," soon wondered, "Can Americans bear for the show to go on?"[163]

In June, after Trump labeled the *Times* guilty of "a virtual act of treason" for printing a story on American plans to target the Russian power grid, A. G. Sulzberger took the unprecedented step of responding with an opinion piece in the rival *Wall Street Journal*. "There is no more serious a charge a commander in chief can make against an independent news organization," Sulzberger lamented, "which presents a troubling question: What would it look like for Mr. Trump to escalate his attacks on the press further? Having already reached for the most incendiary language available, what is left but putting his threats into action?"[164]

Although Trump did not do so, the relationship between the president and the press sunk to a new low. In August, the *Times* reported that a "loose network of conservative operatives allied with the White House" planned a campaign to "discredit" critical news organizations "by publicizing damaging information about journalists."[165] The following month, as scrutiny of the president's threat to Ukraine increased, Trump called the White House press corps "crooked as hell."[166]

That same month, Trump tweeted from the Biarritz G7 summit: "The question I was asked most by fellow World Leaders, who think the USA is doing so well and is stronger than ever before, happens to be: 'Mr. President, why does the American media hate your Country so much? Why are they rooting for it to fail?'"[167]

On September 7, Trump tweeted that Philip Rucker and Ashley R. Parker of the *Washington Post*, "two nasty lightweight reporters, shouldn't even be allowed on the grounds of the White House because their reporting is so DISGUSTING & FAKE."[168]

Later that month, Trump summoned the press corps to the Oval Office to display a hand-altered chart suggesting, in defiance of National Weather Service forecasts, that Hurricane Dorian might soon strike Alabama. Greeted with ridicule, Trump blamed the press for questioning his Sharpie-imposed meteorological prediction. "The Fake News Media," he tweeted, "went crazy, hoping against hope that I made a mistake (which I didn't). . . . Four days of corrupt reporting still without an apology."[169] Trump never retracted his inaccurate forecast, and never issued an apology of his own for, if nothing else, unnecessarily alarming Alabama.

Then in October he interrupted a press conference with the visiting president of Finland to declare, "Much of the media in this country is not just fake, it's corrupt." He was reportedly annoyed that the *Washington Post* had revealed his alleged interest in building a moat along the nation's southern border and filling it with alligators and snakes to deter refugees.[170]

Did Trump's increasingly melodramatic scorn for journalists embolden his most extreme followers? That same October, a crowd attending a pro-Trump conference at the president's Doral resort in Miami screened a violent cartoon video depicting an animated "Trump" figure conducting gory attacks against his political opponents inside a "Church of Fake News." The cartoon character could be seen drawing a gun and mowing down such foes as Black Lives Matter, Hillary Clinton, Rosie O'Donnell, and Bernie Sanders. At one point in the video, as "parishioners" like PBS, NPR, NBC, *Politico*, and the *Washington Post* looked on, the character drives a stake into the head of a figure labeled "CNN."[171] The film debuted just days after Trump had railed against "an unholy alliance of Democrat politicians, deep-state bureaucrats and the fake news."[172] Intense press attention only increased the video's circulation. Within days, 200,000 viewers had watched it on YouTube.[173]

And then, on a late October Saturday night, Trump teased by tweet about a "really big" but unspecified announcement soon to come. It turned out to be news of the daring American military raid that resulted in the death of ISIS leader Abu Bakr al-Baghdadi in Syria. The next morning, Trump held a rare live-TV White House press conference to offer details of the operation, one of which he apparently invented: that al-Baghdadi had fled "whimpering and crying and screaming all the way" before detonating a suicide bomb that killed him along with his children. Military officials could not verify, much less explain, the assertion. By this point, the *Washington Post* tabulation of Trump's fabrications and exaggerations had crossed the thirteen thousand mark.[174]

And then Trump appeared on Sean Hannity's prime-time Fox News show to reveal his plan to cancel government subscriptions to the *New York Times* and *Washington Post*. "Look, they give Pulitzer Prizes to people that got it wrong, okay?" Trump told Hannity, "We don't even want them in the White House anymore. We're going to probably terminate that and the *Washington Post*—they're fake." More than half a century earlier, Kennedy's petulant decision to cancel his *New York Herald-Tribune* deliveries had spurred an uproar. Accused of being thin-skinned, JFK reversed his decision. A century before that, Lincoln had ceased reading the once-loyal *Chicago Tribune* after the paper questioned his decision to impose a military draft. The paper's editors had responded by threatening, "If he does not want it—declines to read it—we will discontinue sending it." Fearful of public outcry, Lincoln's chief of staff encouraged the editors to keep shipping the paper but admonished them for "condemning" Lincoln "in the bitterness of ill-temper."[175] In 2019, Trump's foot-stamping hardly caused a ripple. New White House press secretary Stephanie Grisham suggested the cancellations were meant as a "cost saving" move.[176]

And then Grisham suggested that Trump's former chief of staff, John Kelly, had resigned because he was "unequipped to handle the genius of our great president."[177]

And then the *New York Times* published a special ten-page section crammed with presidential tweets, featuring such stories as "How Trump Used Social Media to Transform the Government" and "The Grim Undertow in His Feed: Conspiracies, Racists and Spies." The section was titled "The Twitter Presidency."[178]

And then Trump visited an Apple computer factory in Austin, Texas, where he took credit for inspiring its opening even though the facility had been in operation for six years. Before anyone could question the president, he castigated "the fake press." In December, the *Washington Post* reported that Trump's "false or misleading statements" now exceeded 15,000.[179]

And then liberal and conservative commentators ramped up their alternative versions of the impeachment hearings—with MSNBC'S Rachel Maddow, for example, arguing on air one November night that Trump had been "caught doing something illegal," while from Fox News headquarters, just one Manhattan block away, Sean Hannity condemned the "radical, extreme, socialist Democrats and their top allies known as the media mob." The *New York Times* headlined its report of the wildly disparate coverage: "In the Fractured Lens of Cable News, Two Impeachments for Two Nations."[180] As CNN analyst John Avlon warned, "America is self-segregating itself into separate political realities and partisan media is largely to blame." Avlon blamed "bots and trolls who hijack civic debate with disinformation," as well as a fragmented media "where most folks pursued a narrow but intense niche audience and kept them . . . addicted to anger and anxiety." Nor did Avlon spare Trump, calling him "a creature of partisan media . . . amplifying conspiracy theories from the Oval Office while denouncing uncomfortable facts . . . canceling regular press conferences and hiring more than a dozen Fox News personalities as White House staffers."[181]

A report by the *Columbia Journalism Review* similarly warned of a "distinct and insulated media ecosystem" amplified by "social media as a backbone," in which, as *New York Times* critic Michiko Kakutani put it, "the shared worldview" of a platform's own cadre of followers "shielded them from journalism that challenged" their preconceived opinions. To survive, concluded the *CJR* study, traditional media needed to "reorient," not only by "developing better viral content and clickbait to compete in the social media environment, but by recognizing that it is operating in a propaganda and disinformation environment" for which there seems to be no immediate cure.[182]

And then Trump remarked, at the traditional White House ceremony to pardon a symbolic Thanksgiving turkey, "I expect this pardon will be very popular with the media. After all, turkeys are closely related to vultures."[183]

And then, after former New York mayor and Bloomberg News founder Michael Bloomberg entered the crowded Democratic field for president, the Trump reelection campaign announced that it would no longer issue press credentials to Bloomberg News.[184]

And then, a few days later, Trump headed home from a NATO meeting in

London—at which allied leaders had publicly and privately insulted him—tweeting: "The Fake News Media is doing everything possible to belittle my VERY successful trip to London for NATO."[185]

And then . . .

"Journalists should not have a dog in the political fight," Bob Woodward declared at the White House Correspondents' dinner back in April 2017, "except to find that best obtainable version of the truth. . . . Whatever the climate, whether the media is revered or reviled, we should and must persist, and, I believe, we will."[186]

A year later, newly elected Utah senator Mitt Romney penned an op-ed column for *USA Today*—the same daily that had reviewed the book *TrumpNation* thirteen years earlier. Trump's GOP enemy argued that America should be "indebted" to "the free press for truths it has uncovered, for truths it has disseminated, and for falsehoods it has repudiated." Taking note of President Trump's latest indignant tweets, he added: "Surely every president has endured stories that he knew were inaccurate and has chafed at one or more news publications. . . . But no American president has ever before vilified the American press or one of its professional outlets as an 'enemy of the people.'"

In Romney's view, the media remains "essential to our Republic, to our freedom, to the cause of freedom abroad, and to our national security. It is very much our friend."[187]

Where the press was concerned, as the 2020 election season approached, Donald Trump had good reason to feel friendless outside the ecosystem of Fox News, Breitbart, and conservative radio. Yet in an era of factionalized ideologies and fragmented media analyses, he remains to admirers far more credible than the press establishment he so often associated with the swamp he swore to drain. To his foes, Trump is the greatest threat to a free press since the founding era.

In reporting "Trump's War on Journalism" as early as 2017, the *Los Angeles Times* posited that "Trump's strategy is pretty clear. . . . By undermining trust in news organizations and delegitimizing journalism and muddling the facts so that Americans no longer know who to believe, he can deny and distract and help push his administration's far-fetched storyline." But as the editorial acknowledged, "it's an effective strategy."[188] By the end of 2019, fewer people trusted the press than ever; more liberals remained tuned exclusively to liberal media, and more conservatives to conservative platforms.[189]

When it comes to communications, Trump has proven himself a transformative genius, even if he is not always the "very stable" one he has often claimed to be. He has shattered norms and remade presidential messaging in his own style and image. Trump can hardly be called the first president to detest and lambast the press. But he is surely the first to create, if not state-run media, then a one-person alternative. And he has done so with an iPhone.

As Howard Kurz said, Trump will not be president forever. Whoever succeeds him will face an emboldened if diminished press corps eager to reassert the balance of power that has always swung—depending on the audacity of journalists and the popularity of presidents—between relentless inquiry and headstrong defiance. As we have seen, that delicate but enduring balance can easily be upended by a puerile press, runaway technology, and unfettered demagoguery. But only temporarily, if the past is any guide.

The press has faced, and survived, far greater presidential hostility in the past: sedition laws, outright censorship, and even shutdowns and arrests. Whether Trump permanently fractures the working relationship, merely recalibrates it, or yields to a White House successor who simply returns it to its former status, no one can yet know.

Which unconstrained institution meanwhile poses the greater danger to the body politic—a hyper-partisan media flailing to retain readers and viewers, or a presidency with direct access to tens of millions of cult-like admirers—remains a matter of dispute. In an age in which traditional news sources are consulted less and doubted more, the final answer may ultimately come not from the press but through the social media platforms Donald Trump has so relentlessly dominated.

At last count, with 68 million followers, Trump ranks an impressive eleventh in global popularity, well ahead of media sources like CNN Breaking News (56 million) and the *New York Times* (45 million). Yet Trump still languishes behind Ellen DeGeneres, Lady Gaga, Justin Bieber, Katy Perry, and soccer heartthrob Cristiano Ronaldo, among others. As of December 15, 2019, the most popular "handle" in the entire Twitter world still belonged to the man who launched presidential tweeting in the first place. Whether or not it galls Trump (and surely it does), @BarackObama now reaches an astounding 111 million followers.[190] But Trump outpaces one and all in loquacity. In September 2019 alone he averaged sixteen posts a day (totaling 797 for the month). On a single day in mid-December 2019, he unleashed 115 Twitter posts. And by the end of the calendar year, he had dispatched a mind-boggling 7,500 tweets. CNN called it "Trump unleashed."

But was he ever less so? At his very first White House press conference in February 2017, a reporter had asked Trump why he believed he needed not only to create such frequent alternative messaging but to assail established media as "fake news." As the questioner attempted to remind him, "you're undermining confidence in our news media."[191]

"Look," Trump replied, "I want to see an honest press . . . it's so important to the public to get an honest press. The . . . public doesn't believe you anymore. Now, maybe I had something to do with that. I don't know. . . . I would be your biggest fan if you treated me right."[192]

In fact, the greatest threat to the traditional equilibrium that usually exists between the press and our presidents comes from neither the rogue belligerence of an independent media nor the jarring bellicosity of a headstrong president. It comes with the loss of a universal acceptance of objective truth. As the *Times*' Charles M. Blow, a persistent Trump critic, has wondered: "How is a democracy supposed to survive when this many people deny a basic common set of facts?"[193]

In a famous warning attributed to both the late senator Daniel Patrick Moynihan and onetime CIA director James R. Schlesinger—the former a Democrat, the latter a Republican—"everyone is entitled to his own opinion, but not his own facts." The Trump era may usher in a permanent upheaval in which Americans never again agree on basic information or trust in traditional sources of news. Or, as *New York Post* columnist Rich Lowry suggested, the Trump presidency may only be a show—a show on which the curtain must one day fall.

Taking a page from John Adams, Donald Trump began his 2020 reelection campaign by filing lawsuits for libel and defamation against the *New York Times*, *Washington Post*, and CNN.

ACKNOWLEDGMENTS

The author of a book ranging over so many periods of our history—some of them admittedly outside his zone of comfort and lifelong study—inevitably (if he is wise) turns to accomplished friends and colleagues for advice and counsel. I am enormously grateful to those who gave of their time and expertise in response: historians, public figures, and journalists who helped guide me from the Civil War all the way back to the founding, and all the way forward to the modern era. I hope I have justified their encouragement and reflected their good advice.

Sincere thanks go especially to: Jonathan Alter, for his input on Jimmy Carter; John Avlon and Ron Chernow for their essential guidance on George Washington; Sidney Blumenthal for his first-hand insights into the Clinton years; Douglas Brinkley for sage advice on my chapters about the Kennedy and Johnson administrations; Brian P. Lamb, the founding chairman of C-SPAN, for reading the Nixon and Reagan sections and sharing his own recollections of their respective White House press operations; Patricia O'Toole for reviewing, analyzing, and improving my chapter on Woodrow Wilson; Annette Gordon-Reed for providing a key reading of my Jefferson chapter; Geoffrey C. Ward for offering crucial advice and catching more than a few errors in my Theodore Roosevelt and Franklin D. Roosevelt sections; Jonathan W. White, who shared some of his research into the origins of American libel law; and Sean Wilentz for reading and most usefully (and forcefully) commenting on my chapters on JFK, LBJ, Bill Clinton, and Barack Obama. While each of these friends has helped to improve this book, any factual and interpretive errors that remain are mine alone.

I am also most grateful to those who granted interviews to share their lived experiences: Former Speaker of the House Newt Gingrich discussed the Clinton years with his usual insight and wit. First Amendment defender Floyd Abrams inspired me with his published writing, his preparatory notes for a speech, and his personal insights about the Trump era. Joseph Califano Jr. shared vivid recollections of the Johnson White House, while former ambassador William vanden Heuvel spoke of his early interactions with the Roosevelt family and then reviewed my FDR chapters with a keen eye for nuance. And former congresswoman Liz Holtzman generously discussed press coverage of the Watergate hearings in which she played such a memorable role. Journalists have weighed in at my request, too: Sid Blumenthal, who spoke openly and knowledgably about his time as a Clinton White House advisor; the PBS icon Jim Lehrer, who shared his own memories of the Clinton years; and legendary *New York Times* executive editor Max Frankel, who had amazing stories to tell about Lyndon Johnson. Years before this book was even an idea, I enjoyed unforgettable discussions with Ted Sorensen about John Kennedy, with Bill Moyers about the relationship between presidents and the press, and with former president George W. Bush about previous chief executives and their interactions with journalists.

Most of all, I am indebted to President Bill Clinton for so generously and thoughtfully responding to questions about his own relationship with the press during his eight years in office—and to members of the Clinton team Angel Urena and Tina Flournoy.

At my new publisher, E. P. Dutton, I have very much enjoyed working with my editor, Brent Howard, whose guiding hand, enthusiasm, patience, and good company have been much appreciated and, hopefully, have contributed to a better book. I want also to thank Dutton's president Ivan Held, publisher Christine Ball, editor in chief John Parsley, assistant editor Cassidy Sachs, production editor Andrea St. Aubin, and senior publicist Sarah Thegeby. My indefatigable agent, Geri Thoma, has been advocating for my books for more than twenty-five years, and has never failed to offer the best advice on what project to undertake next—and for whom.

Thanks go also to my research assistant, Avi Mowshowitz, who so patiently gathered and copied material for me from many sources; to my former assistant, reliable scourer of the Internet, and informal travel agent, Kraig Smith; and to my terrific office staff at my home base, Hunter College's Roosevelt House Public Policy Institute: historian/archivist Deborah Gardner (for sharing her expertise on FDR and Eleanor) and my assistants AmyRose Aleonar Yee and Jacki Mariana Summerfield, for their invaluable help every day of the year.

My inexhaustible and inspiring boss, Hunter College president Jennifer J. Raab, has been a constant source of encouragement—and moreover granted me some critical time away from the office to finish this project. I am much indebted to her for her support. President Raab also invited me to preview several of the book's themes before audiences of Hunter alumni, whose response and input helped provide valuable guidance in finalizing the manuscript.

On the home front, my amazing wife, Edith, once again proved an invaluable and beloved partner, whether traveling with me to Washington to do research, keeping me reasonably healthy, or patiently reading the manuscript as it emerged, president by president, from the computer. Thanks for their constant understanding and support go, too, to my brilliant daughters Remy and Meg, their wonderful respective spouses Adam Kirsch and Rhiana Swartz, and the two lights of my life: my grandsons, twelve-year-old Charles Ezra Kirsch (who read several chapters in advance, too) and Leo Rhys Holzer-Swartz, born June 2019, who, judging by his early fascination with picture books, will probably be reading full paragraphs by the time this volume comes out. My love goes to all of them.

Rye, New York
December 1, 2019

BIBLIOGRAPHY

Presidential Papers, Memoirs, and Autobiographies

The Writings of George Washington from the Original Manuscript Sources, 1745–1799. Edited by John C. Fitzpatrick. 39 vols. Washington, D.C.: U.S. Government Printing Office, 1931–1944.

Alexander Hamilton: Writings. Edited by Joanne B. Freeman. New York: Library of America, 2001.

Letters of Mrs. Adams, the Wife of John Adams. Edited by Charles Francis Adams. 2 vols. Boston: Charles C. Little & James Brown, 1840.

Letters of John Adams Addressed to His Wife. Edited by Charles Francis Adams. 2 vols. Boston: Charles C. Little & James Brown, 1841.

The Works of John Adams, Second President of the United States, with a Life of the Author, Notes and Illustrations. Edited by Charles Francis Adams. 10 vols. Boston: Little, Brown, 1851–54.

The Works of Thomas Jefferson. Edited by Paul Leicester Ford. 12 vols. New York: G. P. Putnam's Sons, 1897.

The Writings of Thomas Jefferson: Memorial Edition. Edited by Andrew A. Lipscomb and Albert Ellery Bergh. 20 vols. Washington, DC: Thomas Jefferson Memorial Association, 1903–04.

Memoirs of John Quincy Adams, Comprising Portions of His Diary from 1785 to 1848. Edited by Charles Francis Adams. 12 vols. Philadelphia: J. B. Lippincott, 1875–77.

The Papers of Andrew Jackson. Edited by Daniel Feller et al. 10 vols. to date. Knoxville: University of Tennessee Press, 1980–2016.

The Collected Works of Abraham Lincoln. Edited by Roy P. Basler et al. 8 vols. New Brunswick, NJ: Rutgers University Press, 1953–55.

Papers of Abraham Lincoln (a.k.a. Robert Todd Lincoln Papers), Manuscript Division, Library of Congress.

The Papers of Ulysses S. Grant. Edited by John Y. Simon, John F. Marszalek et al. 32 vols. 1962–2012.

Addresses and Presidential Messages of Theodore Roosevelt, 1902–1904. New York: G. P. Putnam's Sons, 1904.

The Works of Theodore Roosevelt. Edited by Hermann Hagedorn. 20 vols. New York: Charles Scribner's Sons, 1923–26.

Letters of Theodore Roosevelt. Edited by Elting Elmore Morison and John Morton Blum. 8 vols. Cambridge, MA: Harvard University Press, 1951–54.

Papers of Woodrow Wilson. Edited by Arthur S. Link. 69 vols. Princeton, NJ: Princeton University Press, 1966–94.

The Public Papers and Addresses of Franklin D. Roosevelt. Edited by Samuel Rosenman. 13 vols. New York: Random House, Macmillan, and Harper & Bros., 1938–50.

F.D.R., His Personal Letters, 1928–1945. Edited by Elliott Roosevelt and Joseph Lash. 2 vols. New York: Duell, Sloan & Pearce, 1950.

Press Conferences of President Franklin D. Roosevelt, 1933–45. Franklin D. Roosevelt Presidential Library and Museum. www.fdrlibrary.marist.edu/archives/collections/franklin/?p=collections/findingaid&id=508.

FDR's Fireside Chats. Edited by Russell D. Buhite and David W. Levy. Norman: University of Oklahoma Press, 1992.

Franklin D. Roosevelt Day by Day: A Project of the Lorenz Center. Franklin D. Roosevelt Presidential Library. www.fdrlibrary.marist.edu/daybyday.

John F. Kennedy: Press Conferences. John F. Kennedy Presidential Library. http://www.jfklibrary.org/archives/other-resources/john-f-kennedy-press-conferences.

The Presidential Recordings: John F. Kennedy—The Great Crises. Edited by Timothy Naftali, Philip D. Zelikow, and Ernest W. May (July 30, 1961–August 1962; September–October 21, 1962). 2 vols. New York: W. W. Norton, 2001.

Listening In: The Secret White House Recordings of John F. Kennedy. Edited by Ted Widmer. New York: Hyperion, 2012.

Johnson, Lyndon Baines. *The Vantage Point: Perspectives of the Presidency, 1963–1969.* New York: Holt, Rinehart and Winston, 1971.

Reaching for Glory: Lyndon Johnson's Secret White House Tapes, 1964–65. Edited by Michael Beschloss. New York: Touchstone, 2001.

The Presidential Recordings: Lyndon B. Johnson. Edited by Kent B. Germany, Robert David Johnson, David Shreve, and Max Holland. 6 vols. New York: W. W. Norton, 2005–7.

Nixon, Richard. *My Six Crises.* New York: Doubleday, 1962.

———. *RN: The Memoirs of Richard Nixon.* 2 vols. New York: Warner Books, 1978.

Abuse of Power: The New Nixon Tapes. Edited by Stanley I. Cutler. New York: Free Press, 1971.

The Nixon Tapes. Edited by Douglas Brinkley and Luke A. Nichter. 2 vols. Boston: Houghton Mifflin Harcourt, 2014.

Public Papers of the Presidents [Reagan–Obama], National Archives. https://www.archives.gov/federal-register/publications/presidential-papers.html.

Ford, Gerald, R. *A Time to Heal: The Autobiography of Gerald R. Ford.* New York: Harper & Row, 1979.

———. *Humor and the Presidency.* New York: Arbor House, 1987.

Carter, Jimmy. *Keeping Faith: Memoirs of the President.* New York: Bantam Books, 1982.

———. *White House Diary.* New York: Farrar, Straus and Giroux, 2010.

Reagan, Ronald, and Richard G. Hubler. *Where's the Rest of Me? The Ronald Reagan Story.* New York: Duell, Sloan and Pearce, 1965.

Reagan, Ronald, with Robert Lindsey. *Ronald Reagan: An American Life.* New York: Simon & Schuster, 2001.

———. *A Life in Letters.* New York: Free Press, 2003.

———. *The Reagan Diaries.* Edited by Douglas Brinkley. New York: HarperCollins, 2007.

Clinton, Bill. *My Life.* New York: Alfred A. Knopf, 2004.

Obama, Barack. *Dreams from My Father: A Story of Race and Inheritance.* New York: Broadway Books, 2004.

———. *The Audacity of Hope: Thoughts on Reclaiming the American Dream.* New York: Crown, 2006.

Bush, George W. *Decision Points.* New York: Crown, 2010.

Trump, Donald J., and Tony Schwartz. *Trump: The Art of the Deal.* New York: Random House, 1987.

Trump, Donald J., with Charles Leerhsen. *Trump: Surviving at the Top.* New York: Random House, 1990.

Trump, Donald J., with Kate Bohner. *Trump: The Art of the Comeback.* New York: Times Books, 1997.

Trump, Donald J., and Bill Zanker. *Think Big.* New York: HarperBusiness, 2007.

Trump, Donald J., with Meredith McIver. *Trump: Never Give Up: How I Turned My Biggest Challenges into Success.* Hoboken, NJ: John Wiley & Sons, 2008.

Trump, Donald J. *Crippled America: How to Make America Great Again.* New York: Threshold Editions, 2015.

Books

Abramson, Jill. *Merchants of Truth: The Business of News and the Fight for the Facts.* New York: Simon & Schuster, 2019.

Acosta, Jim. *The Enemy of the People: A Dangerous Time to Tell the Truth in America.* New York: Harper, 2019.

Agnew, Spiro. *Go Quietly . . . or Else: His Own Story of the Events Leading Up to His Resignation.* New York: William Morrow, 1980.

Alter, Jonathan. *The Defining Moment: FDR's Hundred Days and the Triumph of Hope.* New York: Simon & Schuster, 2006.

———. *The Center Holds: Obama and His Enemies.* New York: Simon & Schuster, 2013.

Anderson, Jack, with James Boyd. *Confessions of a Muckraker.* New York: Random House, 1979.

Anderson, Terry. *Bush's Wars.* New York: Oxford University Press, 2011.

Avlon, John. *Washington's Farewell: The Founding Father's Warning to Future Generations.* New York: Simon & Schuster, 2017.

Axelrad, Jacob. *Philip Freneau, Champion of Democracy.* Austin: University of Texas Press, 1967.

Axelrod, Alan. *Selling the Great War: The Making of American Propaganda.* New York: Palgrave Macmillan, 2009.

Axelrod, David. *Believer: My Forty Years in Politics.* New York: Penguin, 2015.

Baker, Bobby, and Larry L. King. *Wheeling and Dealing: Confessions of a Capitol Hill Operator.* New York: W. W. Norton, 1978.

Baker, Ray Stannard. *American Chronicle: The Autobiography of Ray Stannard Baker.* New York: Scribner's, 1945.

Balin, Peter, and Paul Shaw. *Blackletter: Type and National Identity.* Princeton, NJ: Princeton University Press, 1998.

Banner, James M., ed. *Presidential Misconduct: From George Washington to Today.* New York: New Press, 2019.

Barrett, Laurence L. *Gambling with History: Reagan in the White House.* New York: Doubleday, 1983.

Barry, David S. *Forty Years in Washington.* Boston: Little, Brown, 1924.

Beasley, Maurine H. *Eleanor Roosevelt and the Media: A Public Quest for Self-Fulfillment.* Urbana: University of Illinois Press, 1987.

Becker, Stephen. *Marshall Field III: A Biography.* New York: Simon & Schuster, 1964.

Belko, W. Stephen. *The Invincible Duff Green: Whig of the West.* Columbia: University of Missouri Press, 2006.

Bemis, Samuel Flagg. *John Quincy Adams and the Foundations of American Foreign Policy.* Baton Rouge: Louisiana State University Press, 2013.

Bennett, James Gordon. *Memoirs of James Gordon Bennett and His Times by a Journalist.* New York: Stringer & Townsend, 1855.

Bennett, James O'Donnell. *Joseph Medill: A Brief Biography and an Appreciation.* Chicago: Chicago Tribune, 1947.

Benson, Thomas. *Writing JFK: Presidential Rhetoric and the Press in the Bay of Pigs Crisis.* College Station: Texas A&M University Press, 2004.

Berg, A. Scott. *Wilson.* New York: G. P. Putnam's Sons, 2013.

Berger, Meyer. *The Story of the "New York Times," 1851–1951.* New York: Simon & Schuster, 1951.

Bernays, Edward. *Propaganda*. Orig. pub. 1928; Brooklyn: Ig Publishing, 2005.

———. *Crystallizing Public Opinion*. Orig. pub. Boni & Liveright, 1923; New York: Ig Publishing, 2011.

Berry, Joseph P., ed. *John F. Kennedy and the Media: The First Television President*. Lanham, MD: University Press of America, 1987.

Beschloss, Michael. *Reaching for Glory: Lyndon Johnson's Secret White House Tapes, 1964–1965*. New York: Simon & Schuster, 2001.

———. *Presidential Courage: Brave Leaders and How They Changed America*. New York: Simon & Schuster, 2007.

———. *Presidents of War: The Epic Story from 1807 to Modern Times*. New York: Crown, 2018.

Bleyer, Willard Grosvenor. *Main Currents in the History of American Journalism*. Boston: Houghton Mifflin, 1927.

Blondheim, Menahem. *News over the Wires: The Telegraph and the Flow of Public Information in America, 1844–1897*. Cambridge, MA: Harvard University Press, 1994.

Blumenthal, Sidney. *The Permanent Campaign: Inside the World of Political Operatives*. Boston: Beacon Press, 1980.

———. *The Clinton Wars*. New York: Farrar Straus & Giroux, 2003.

Borchard, Gregory A. *A Narrative History of the American Press*. New York: Routledge, 2019.

Bowers, Claude G. *The Party Battles of the Jackson Period*. Boston: Houghton Mifflin, 1922.

Bradlee, Benjamin. *Conversations with Kennedy*. New York: Bantam Books: 1975.

———. *A Good Life: Newspapering and Other Adventures*. New York: Simon & Schuster, 1995.

Branch, Taylor. *The Clinton Tapes: Wrestling History with the President*. New York: Simon & Schuster, 2009.

Brands, H. W. *Reagan: The Life*. New York: Doubleday, 2015.

Brinkley, David. *Washington Goes to War*. New York: Ballantine Books, 1988.

Brinkley, Douglas. *Cronkite*. New York: HarperCollins, 2012.

———. *Rightful Heritage: Franklin D. Roosevelt and the Land of America*. New York: Harper, 2016.

———. *American Moonshot: John F. Kennedy and the Great Space Race*. New York: Harper, 2018.

Brody, Richard A. *Assessing the President: The Media, Elite Opinion, and Public Support*. Stanford, CA: Stanford University Press, 1991.

Brokaw, Tom. *The Fall of Richard Nixon: A Reporter Remembers Watergate*. New York: Random House, 2019.

Brown, Walt. *John Adams and the American Press: Politics and Journalism at the Birth of the Republic*. Jefferson, NC: McFarland, 1995.

Brownell, Kathryn Cramer. *Showbiz Politics: Hollywood in American Political Life*. Chapel Hill: University of North Carolina Press, 2014.

Bruni, Frank. *Ambling into History: The Unlikely Odyssey of George W. Bush*. New York: HarperCollins, 2002.

Buchanan, Pat. *Nixon's White House Wars: The Battles That Made and Broke a President and Divided America Forever*. New York: Crown, 2017.

Bulla, David. *Journalism in the Civil War*. New York: Peter Lang, 2010.

Burlingame, Michael, ed. *Lincoln's Journalist: John Hay's Anonymous Writings for the Press, 1860–1864*. Carbondale: Southern Illinois University Press, 1998.

———., ed. *Dispatches from Lincoln's White House: The Anonymous Civil War Journalism of Presidential Secretary William O. Stoddard*. Lincoln: University of Nebraska Press, 2002.

Califano, Joseph A., Jr. *The Triumph and Tragedy of Lyndon Johnson: The White House Years; a Personal Memoir by President Johnson's Top Domestic Advisor*. New York: Touchstone, 1991.

———. *Our Damaged Democracy: We the People Must Act*. New York: Touchstone, 2018.

Campbell, W. Joseph. *Yellow Journalism: Puncturing the Myths, Defining the Legacies*. Orig. pub. 2001; Westport, CT: Praeger, 2003.

Cannon, James. *My Time and Chance: Gerald Ford's Appointment with History.* Ann Arbor: University of Michigan Press, 1973.

Cannon, Lou. *Reagan.* New York: G. P. Putnam's Sons, 1982.

———. *President Reagan: The Role of a Lifetime.* New York: Simon & Schuster, 1991.

Carew, Michael G. *The Power to Persuade: FDR, the Newsmagazines, and Going to War, 1939–1941.* Lanham: University Press of America, 2005.

Caro, Robert A. *The Years of Lyndon Johnson, Vol. 1: The Path to Power.* New York: Alfred A. Knopf, 1982.

———. *The Years of Lyndon Johnson, Vol. 2: Means of Ascent.* New York: Alfred A. Knopf, 1990.

———. *The Years of Lyndon Johnson, Vol. 3: Master of the Senate.* New York: Alfred A. Knopf, 2002.

———. *The Years of Lyndon Johnson, Vol. 4: The Passage of Power.* New York: Alfred A. Knopf, 2012.

———. *Working: Researching, Interviewing, Writing.* New York: Alfred A. Knopf, 2019.

Carpenter, Francis B. *Six Months at the White House with Abraham Lincoln: The Story of a Picture.* New York: Hurd & Houghton, 1866.

Catledge, Turner. *My Life and "The Times."* New York: Harper & Row, 1971.

Cheathem, Mark R. *Andrew Jackson, Southerner.* Baton Rouge: Louisiana State University Press, 2013.

Chernow, Ron. *Alexander Hamilton.* New York: Penguin Press, 2004.

———. *George Washington: A Life.* New York: Penguin Press, 2010.

Clinton, Hillary Rodham. *What Happened?* New York: Simon & Schuster, 2017.

Cole, Donald B. *A Jackson Man: Amos Kendall and the Rise of American Democracy.* Baton Rouge: Louisiana State University Press, 2004.

Conason, Joe. *Big Lies: The Right-Wing Propaganda Machine and How It Distorts the Truth.* New York: Thomas Dunne Books, 2003.

Conason, Joe, and Gene Lyons. *The Hunting of the President: The Ten-Year Campaign to Destroy Bill and Hillary Clinton.* New York: Thomas Dunne Books, 2000.

Cook, Blanche Wiesen. *Eleanor Roosevelt.* 3 vols. New York: Penguin, 1993, 2000, 2016.

Christian, George. *The President Steps Down: A Personal Memoir of the Tragedy of Power.* New York: Macmillan, 1970.

———., ed. *The World of Texas Politics.* Austin: Lyndon B. Johnson Library, 1989.

Cormier, Frank. *LBJ the Way He Was: A Personal Memoir of the Man and His Presidency.* New York: Doubleday, 1977.

Cortissoz, Royal. *The Life of Whitelaw Reid.* 2 vols. New York: Charles Scribner's Sons, 1921.

Cowan, Geoffrey. *Let the People Rule: Theodore Roosevelt and the Birth of the Presidential Primary.* New York: W. W. Norton, 2016.

Coyne, James R., Jr. *The Impudent Snobs: Agnew vs. the Intellectual Establishment.* New Rochelle, NY: Arlington House, 1972.

Creel, George. *How We Advertised America: The First Telling of the Amazing Story of the Committee on Public Information That Carried the Gospel of Americanism to Every Corner of the Globe.* New York: Harper's, 1920.

Creelman, James. *On the Great Highway: The Wanderings and Adventures of a Special Correspondent.* Boston: Lothrop, 1901.

Cronkite, Walter. *A Reporter's Life.* New York: Random House, 1996.

Crouse, Timothy. *The Boys on the Bus.* Orig. pub. 1972; New York: Random House, 2003.

Crouthamel, James L. *Bennett's "New York Herald" and the Rise of the Popular Press.* Syracuse, NY: Syracuse University Press, 1989.

Crowley, Monica. *Nixon in Winter.* New York: Random House, 1998.

Dallek, Robert. *Flawed Giant: Lyndon Johnson and His Times, 1961–1973.* New York: Oxford University Press, 1998.

———. *An Unfinished Life: John F. Kennedy, 1917–1963.* Boston: Little, Brown, 2003.

———. *Lyndon B. Johnson: Portrait of a President.* New York: Oxford University Press, 2004.
———. *Camelot's Court: Inside the Kennedy White House.* New York: HarperCollins, 2013.
Daniels, Jonathan. *White House Witness, 1942–1845: An Intimate Diary of the Years with F.D.R.* Garden City, NY: Doubleday, 1975.
Daniels, Josephus. *The Wilson Era.* 2 vols. Chapel Hill: University of North Carolina Press, 1944–1946.
Davis, Deborah. *Guest of Honor: Booker T. Washington, Theodore Roosevelt, and the White House Dinner That Shocked a Nation.* New York: Simon & Schuster, 2012.
Davis, Kenneth. *Invincible Summer: An Intimate Portrait of the Roosevelts Based on the Recollections of Marion Dickerman.* New York: Atheneum, 1974.
Davis, Oscar King. *Released for Publication: Some Inside Political History of Theodore Roosevelt and His Times, 1898–1918.* Boston: Houghton Mifflin, 1925.
De Borchgrave, Alexandra Villard, and John Cullen. *Villard: The Life and Times of an American Titan.* New York: Doubleday, 2001.
De Brosse, Jim. *See No Evil: The JFK Assassination and the U.S. Media.* Walterville, OR: Trine Day, 2018.
Denton, Robert E., Jr., and Rachel L. Holloway, eds. *The Clinton Presidency: Images, Issues, and Communication Strategies.* Westport, CT: Praeger, 1996.
Derby, J. C. *Fifty Years Among Authors, Books, and Publishers.* New York: G. C. Carleton, 1884.
Dickenson, Mollie. *Thumbs Up: The Life and Courageous Comeback of White House Press Secretary Jim Brady.* New York: William Morrow, 1987.
Donaldson, Gary A. *The First Modern Campaign: Kennedy, Nixon, and the Campaign of 1960.* Lanham, MD: Rowman & Littlefield, 2007.
Donaldson, Sam. *Hold On, Mr. President.* Orig. pub. 1987. New York: Ballantine, 1988.
Donovan, Hedley. *Roosevelt to Reagan: A Reporter's Encounters with Nine Presidents.* New York: Harper & Row, 1985.
Donovan, Robert S. *Conflict and Crisis: The Presidency of Harry S Truman, 1945–1948.* New York: W. W. Norton, 1977.
———. *Tumultuous Years: The Presidency of Harry S Truman, 1949–1953.* New York: W. W. Norton, 1982.
Douglas, George H. *The Golden Age of the Newspaper.* Westport, CT: Greenwood Press, 1999.
Draper, Robert. *Dead Certain: The Presidency of George W. Bush.* New York: Free Press, 2007.
Drew, Elizabeth. *Washington Journal: Reporting Watergate and Richard Nixon's Downfall.* New York: Overlook Duckworth, 2014.
Durey, Michael. *"With the Hammer of Truth": James Thomas Callender and America's Early National Heroes.* Charlottesville: University Press of Virginia, 1990.
Dyson, Michael Eric. *The Black Presidency: Barack Obama and the Politics of Race in America.* Boston: Houghton Mifflin, 2016.
Ehrlichman, John. *Witness to Power: The Nixon Years.* New York: Simon & Schuster, 1982.
Eizenstat, Stuart E. *President Carter: The White House Years.* New York: St. Martin's Press, 2018.
Ellis, Sylvia. *Freedom's Pragmatist: Lyndon Johnson and Civil Rights.* Tallahassee: University Press of Florida, 2013.
Ellsworth, Daniel. *Secrets: A Memoir of Vietnam and the Pentagon Papers.* New York: Viking, 2002.
Emery, Michael, Edwin Emery, and Nancy L. Roberts. *The Press and America: An Interpretive History of the Mass Media.* 9th ed. Boston: Allyn & Bacon, 2000.
Essary, J. Frederick. *Covering Washington: Government Reflected to the Public in the Press, 1822–1926.* Boston: Houghton Mifflin, 1927.
Evans, Rowland, and Robert Novak. *Lyndon B. Johnson: The Exercise of Power.* New York: New American Library, 1966.
———. *Nixon in the White House: The Frustration of Power.* New York: Random House, 1971.

Farrell, John A. *Richard Nixon: The Life*. New York: Doubleday, 2017.

Feldstein, Mark. *Poisoning the Press: Richard Nixon, Jack Anderson, and the Rise of Washington's Scandal Culture*. New York: Farrar, Straus and Giroux, 2010.

Fenster, Julie M. *FDR's Shadow: Louis Howe, the Force That Shaped Franklin and Eleanor Roosevelt*. New York: St. Martin's Griffin, 2009.

Fermer, Douglas. *James Gordon Bennett and the "New York Herald": A Study of Editorial Opinion in the Civil War Era, 1854–1867*. Royal Historical Society Studies in History 46. New York: St. Martin's Press, 1986.

Fitzwater, Marlin. *Call the Briefing! Reagan and Bush, Sam and Helen: A Decade with Presidents and the Press*. New York: Times Books, 1995.

Fleischer, Ari. *Taking Heat: The President, the Press, and My Years in the White House*. New York: William Morrow, 2005.

Frum, David. *Trumpocracy: The Corruption of the American Republic*. New York: Harper, 2018.

Gallagher, Hugh Gregory. *FDR's Splendid Deception: The Moving Story of Roosevelt's Massive Disability—and the Intense Efforts to Conceal It from the Public*. 3rd ed. St. Petersburg, FL: Vandamere Press, 1999.

Garrow, David J. *Rising Star: The Making of Barack Obama*. New York: William Morrow, 2017.

Gergen, David. *Eyewitness to Power: The Essence of Leadership, Nixon to Clinton*. New York: Simon & Schuster, 2000.

Germond, Jack. *Mad as Hell: Revolt at the Ballot Box, 1992*. New York: Warner Books, 1993.

Goeglein, Timothy S. *The Man in the Middle: An Inside Account of Faith and Politics in the George W. Bush Era*. Nashville: B&H Publishing Group, 2011.

Goldman, Eric. *The Tragedy of Lyndon Johnson*. New York: Alfred A. Knopf, 1969.

Goodwin, Doris Kearns. *Lyndon Johnson and the American Dream*. New York: Harper & Row, 1976.

———. *No Ordinary Time: Franklin and Eleanor Roosevelt—the Home Front in World War II*. New York: Simon & Schuster, 1994.

———. *The Bully Pulpit: Theodore Roosevelt, William Howard Taft, and the Golden Age of Journalism*. New York: Simon & Schuster, 2013.

———. *Leadership in Perilous Times*. New York: Simon & Schuster, 2018.

Goodwin, Richard. *Remembering America: A Voice from the Sixties*. Boston: Little, Brown, 1988.

Graham, Katharine. *Personal History*. New York: Alfred A. Knopf, 1997.

Graham, Otis L., Jr., and Meghan Robinson Wander. *Franklin D. Roosevelt: His Life and Times—an Encyclopedic View*. Boston: G. K. Hall, 1985.

Graham, Tim. *Pattern of Deception: The Media's Role in the Clinton Presidency*. Alexandria, VA: Media Research Center, 1996.

Greeley, Horace. *Recollections of a Busy Life*. New York: J. B. Ford, 1868.

Greenberg, David. *Republic of Spin: An Inside History of the American Presidency*. New York: W. W. Norton, 2016.

Greene, John Robert. *The Presidency of George Bush*. Lawrence: University Press of Kansas, 2000.

Greene, Laurence. *America Goes to Press: Headlines of the Past—the History of the United States as Reported in the Newspapers of the Day from the Boston Tea Party to the World War*. Garden City, NY: Doubleday, 1938.

Grondahl, Paul. *I Rose like a Rocket: The Political Education of Theodore Roosevelt*. Lincoln: University of Nebraska Press, 2004.

Grossman, Michael Baruch, and Martha Joynt Kumar. *Portraying the President: The White House and the News Media*. Baltimore: Johns Hopkins University Press, 1981.

Gunther, John. *Roosevelt in Retrospect: A Profile in History*. New York: Harper & Bros., 1950.

Haggerty, James C. *The Diaries of James C. Haggerty: Eisenhower in Mid-Course, 1954–1955*. Edited by Robert H. Ferrell. Bloomington: Indiana University Press, 1983.

Halberstam, David. *The Powers That Be*. New York: Alfred A. Knopf, 1979.

Haldeman, H. R., with Joseph DiMona. *The Ends of Power.* New York: Times Books, 1978.

Haldeman, H. R. *The Haldeman Diaries: Inside the Nixon White House.* New York: G. P. Putnam's Sons, 1994.

Halperin, Terri Diane. *The Alien and Sedition Acts of 1798: Testing the Constitution.* Baltimore: Johns Hopkins University Press, 2016.

Hamilton, James A. *Reminiscences of James A. Hamilton; or, Men and Events at Home and Abroad, During Three Quarters of a Century.* New York: Charles Scribner's Sons, 1869.

Harper, Robert S. *Lincoln and the Press.* New York: McGraw-Hill, 1951.

Hartmann, Robert T. *Palace Politics: An Inside Account of the Ford Years.* New York: McGraw-Hill, 1980.

Harvey, George Brinton McClellan. *Women, Etc.: Some Leaders from an Editor's Diary.* New York: Harper & Bros., 1908.

Hayden, Joseph. *Covering Clinton: The President and the Press.* Westport, CT: Praeger, 2002.

Hemingway, Mollie Ziegler. *Trump vs. the Media.* New York: Encounter Broadsides, 2017.

Hersh, Seymour M. *The Dark Side of Camelot.* Boston: Little, Brown, 1997.

Hertsgaard, Mark. *On Bended Knee: The Press and the Reagan Presidency.* New York: Farrar, Straus and Giroux, 1988.

Hess, Stephen. *The Government/Press Connection: Press Officers and Their Offices.* Washington, DC: Brookings Institution, 1984.

Himmelman, Jeff. *Yours in Truth: A Personal Portrait of Ben Bradlee.* New York: Random House, 2012.

Holden, Charles J., Zach Messitte, and Jerald Podair. *Republican Populist: Spiro Agnew and the Origins of Donald Trump's America.* Charlottesville: University Press of Virginia, 2019.

Hoopes, Roy. *Ralph Ingersoll: A Biography.* New York: Atheneum, 1985.

Hudson, Frederic. *Journalism in the United States from 1690 to 1872.* New York: Harper & Bros., 1873.

Hughes, Karen. *Ten Minutes from Normal.* New York: Viking, 2004.

Huntzicker, William E. *The Popular Press, 1833–1865.* Westport, CT: Greenwood Press, 1999.

Hurd, Charles. *When the New Deal Was Young and Gay: F.D.R. and His Circle.* New York: Hawthorn Books, 1965.

Ingersoll, L. D. *The Life of Horace Greeley, Founder of the "New York Tribune," with Extended Notices of Many of His Contemporary Statesmen and Journalists.* New York: Union Publishing, 1873.

Irwin, Will. *Propaganda and the News: Or What Makes You Think So?* New York: Whittlesey House, 1936.

Isikoff, Michael. *Uncovering Clinton: A Reporter's Story.* New York: Three Rivers Press, 1999.

Jamieson, Kathleen Hall, and Paul Waldman. *The Press Effect: Politicians, Journalists, and the Stories That Shape the Political World.* New York: Oxford University Press, 2003.

Johnson, Haynes. *Sleepwalking Through History: America in the Reagan Years.* New York: W. W. Norton, 1991.

Jordan, David M. *FDR, Dewey, and the Election of 1944.* Bloomington: Indiana University Press, 2011.

Jordan, Hamilton. *Crisis: The Last Year of the Carter Presidency.* New York: G. P. Putnam's Sons, 1982.

Kalb, Marvin. *One Scandalous Story: Clinton, Lewinsky, and Thirteen Days That Tarnished American Journalism.* New York: Free Press, 2001.

Kern, Montague, Patricia W. Levering, and Ralph B. Levering. *The Kennedy Crises: The Press, the Presidency, and Foreign Policy.* Chapel Hill: University of North Carolina Press, 1983.

Kerney, James. *The Political Education of Woodrow Wilson.* New York: Century, 1926.

Klein, Herbert G. *Making It Perfectly Clear: An Inside Account of Nixon's Love-Hate Relationship with the Media.* New York: Doubleday, 1980.

Klein, Woody. *All the Presidents' Spokesmen: Spinning the News—White House Press Secretaries from Franklin D. Roosevelt to George W. Bush.* Westport, CT: Praeger, 2008.

Klement, Frank. *The Limits of Dissent.* Orig. pub. 1970; New York: Fordham University Press, 1998.

Klotter, James C. *Henry Clay: The Man Who Would Be President.* New York: Oxford University Press, 2018.

Knudson, Jerry W. *Jefferson and the Press: Crucible of Liberty.* Columbia: University of South Carolina Press, 2006.

Kohlsaat, H. H. *From McKinley to Harding: Personal Recollections of Our Presidents.* New York: Scribner's, 1923.

Krock, Arthur. *Memoirs: Sixty Years on the Firing Line.* New York: Funk & Wagnalls, 1968.

Kumar, Martha Joynt. *Managing the President's Message: The White House Communications Operation.* Baltimore: Johns Hopkins University Press, 2007.

Kurtz, Howard. *Hot Air: All Talk, All the Time.* New York: Times Books, 1996.

———. *Spin Cycle: Inside the Clinton Propaganda Machine.* New York: Free Press, 1998.

———. *Media Madness: Donald Trump, the Press, and the War over the Truth.* New York: Regenery, 2018.

Kutler, Stanley I. *Abuse of Power: The New Nixon Tapes.* New York: Free Press, 1997.

Lamb, Brian, and Susan Swain, eds. *The Presidents: Noted Historians Rank America's Best—and Worst—Chief Executives.* New York: PublicAffairs, 2019.

Lawrence, Bill. *Six Presidents, Too Many Wars.* New York: Saturday Review Press, 1972.

Leary, John J., Jr. *Talks with T. R.: From the Diaries of John J. Leary, Jr.* Boston: Houghton Mifflin, 1920.

Leary, Lewis. *That Rascal Freneau: A Study in Literary Failure.* New York: Octagon, 1971.

Lelyveld, Joseph. *His Final Battle: The Last Months of Franklin Roosevelt.* New York: Alfred A. Knopf, 2016.

Leuchtenburg, William E. *Franklin D. Roosevelt and the New Deal, 1932–1940.* New York: Harper & Row, 1963.

———. *The American President: From Teddy Roosevelt to Bill Clinton.* New York: Oxford University Press, 2015.

Levin, Linda Lotridge. *The Making of FDR: The Story of Stephen T. Early, America's First Modern Press Secretary.* Orig. pub. 1963. Amherst, NY: Prometheus Books, 2008.

Levin, Mark R. *Unfreedom of the Press.* New York: Threshold Editions, 2019.

Levy, Leonard W., *Freedom of Speech and Press in Early American History: Legacy of Suppression.* Orig. pub. 1960; New York: Harper Torchbooks, 1963.

———. *Jefferson and Civil Liberties: The Darker Side.* Orig. pub. 1963; Chicago: Ivan R. Dee, 1963.

———., ed. *Freedom of the Press from Zenger to Jefferson: Early American Libertarian Theories.* 2 vols. Indianapolis: Bobbs-Merrill, 1966.

———. *Emergence of a Free Press.* New York: Oxford University Press, 1985.

Levy, Leonard, and Harold W. Nelson. *Freedom of the Press: From Hamilton to the Warren Court.* 2 vols. Indianapolis: Bobbs-Merrill, 1967.

Lewandowski, Corey R., and David N. Bossie. *Trump's Enemies: How the Deep State Is Undermining the Presidency.* New York: Center Street, 2018.

Liebovich, Louis V. *The Press and the Modern Presidency: Myths and Mindsets from Kennedy to Clinton.* Westport, CT: Praeger, 1998.

———. *Richard Nixon, Watergate, and the Press: A Historical Perspective.* Westport, CT: Praeger, 2003.

Link, Arthur S. *Wilson: The Road to the White House.* Orig. pub. 1947; Princeton, NJ: Princeton University Press, 1965.

Lipman, Theo, Jr. *The Squire of Warm Springs: FDR in Georgia, 1914–1945.* Chicago: Playboy Press, 1977.

Lippmann, Walter. *Liberty and the News.* Orig. pub. 1920; Princeton, NJ: Princeton University Press, 2008.

Lomazow, Steven, and Eric Fettmann, *FDR's Deadly Secret.* New York: Public Affairs, 2009.

Louchheim, Katie, ed. *The Making of the New Deal: The Insiders Speak Out.* Cambridge, MA: Harvard University Press, 1983.

Loughran, Trish. *The Republic in Print: Print Culture in the Age of U.S. Nation Building, 1770–1870.* New York: Columbia University Press, 2007.

Lowitt, Richard, and Maurine Beasley, eds. *One Third of a Nation: Lorena Hickok Reports on the Great Depression.* Urbana: University of Illinois Press, 1983.

Lowry, Edward George. *Washington Close-ups: Intimate Views of Some Public Figures.* Boston: Houghton Mifflin, 1921.

Lukas, J. Anthony. *Nightmare: The Underside of the Nixon Years.* New York: Viking, 1976.

Lull, James, and Stephen Hinerman, eds. *Media Scandals: Morality and Desire in the Popular Culture Marketplace.* New York: Columbia University Press, 1997.

Maltese, John Anthony. *Spin Control: The White House Office of Communications and the Management of Presidential News.* Chapel Hill: University of North Carolina Press, 1992.

Manber, Jeffrey, and Neil Dahlstrom. *Lincoln's Wrath: Fierce Mobs, Brilliant Scoundrels and a President's Mission to Destroy the Press.* Naperville, IL: Sourcebooks, 2005.

Mapes, Mary. *Truth and Duty: The Press, the President, and the Privilege of Power.* New York: St. Martin's Press, 2005.

Maraniss, David. *First in His Class: A Biography of Bill Clinton.* New York: Simon & Schuster, 1995.

Marcosson, Isaac F. *Adventures in Interviewing.* New York: Dodd, Mead, 1919.

Marszalek, John F. *The Petticoat Affair: Manners, Mutiny, and Sex in Andrew Jackson's White House.* New York: Free Press, 1997.

Mattson, Kevin. *"What the Heck Are You Up To, Mr. President?": Jimmy Carter, America's "Malaise," and the Speech That Should Have Changed the Country.* New York: Bloomsbury, 2009.

McAdoo, Eleanor Wilson. *The Woodrow Wilsons.* New York: Macmillan, 1937.

McClellan, Scott. *What Happened: Inside the Bush White House and Washington's Culture of Deception.* New York: PublicAffairs, 2008.

McClendon, Sarah. *My Eight Presidents.* New York: Wyden Books, 1978.

McGinnis, Joe. *The Selling of the President 1968.* New York: Trident/Simon & Schuster, 1969.

Meacham, Jon. *Destiny and Power: The American Odyssey of George Herbert Walker Bush.* New York: Random House, 2015.

Meacham, Jon, with Timothy Naftali, Peter Baker, and Jeffrey A. Engel, *Impeachment: An American History.* New York: Modern Library, 2018.

Miller, John C. *Crisis in Freedom: The Alien and Sedition Acts.* Boston: Little, Brown, 1952.

Miller, Judith. *The Story: A Reporter's Journey.* New York: Simon & Schuster, 2015.

Miller, Merle. *Lyndon: An Oral History.* New York: G. P. Putnam's Sons, 1980.

Mills, Walter. *Road to War: America 1914–1917.* Boston: Houghton Mifflin, 1935.

Mitgang, Herbert, ed. *Lincoln as They Saw Him.* New York: Rinehart, 1956.

Mock, James R., and Cedric Larson. *Words That Won the War: The Story of the Committee on Public Information, 1917–1919.* Princeton, NJ: Princeton University Press, 1939.

Moley, Raymond. *27 Masters of Politics in a Personal Perspective.* New York: Funk & Wagnalls, 1949.

———. *The First New Deal.* New York: Harcourt, 1966.

Moley, Raymond, with Elliot A. Rosen. *After Seven Years.* New York: Harper & Bros., 1939.

Morris, Edmund. *The Rise of Theodore Roosevelt.* New York: Coward, McCann & Geoghegan, 1979.

———. *Theodore Rex.* New York: Random House, 2001.

———. *Colonel Roosevelt.* New York: Random House, 2010.

Morris, James McGrath. *Pulitzer: A Life in Politics, Print, and Power.* New York: Harper, 2010.

Mott, Frank Luther. *A History of American Magazines*. Vol. 2, *1850–1865*. Orig. pub. 1938; Cambridge: Harvard University Press, 1957.

Moyers, Bill. *Moyers on America: A Journalist and His Times*. New York: New Press, 2004.

Murphy, Paul L. *World War I and the Origins of Civil Liberties in the United States*. New York: W. W. Norton, 1979.

Myers, Dee Dee. *Why Women Should Rule the World*. New York: Harper, 2008.

Neely, Mark E., Jr. *The Fate of Liberty: Abraham Lincoln and Civil Liberties*. New York: Oxford University Press, 1991.

Nelson, W. Dale. *Who Speaks for the President? The White House Press Secretary from Cleveland to Clinton*. Syracuse, NY: Syracuse University Press, 1998.

Nessen, Ron. *It Sure Looks Different from the Inside*. Chicago: Playboy Press, 1978.

New York Times. *The Pentagon Papers: The Secret History of the Vietnam War*. New York: Quadrangle, 1971.

Newman, Omarosa Manigault. *Unhinged: An Insider's Account of the Trump White House*. New York: Gallery Books, 2018.

Noonan, Peggy. *What I Saw at the Revolution: A Political Life in the Reagan Era*. New York: Random House, 1990.

O'Reilly, Bill. *The United States of Trump: How the President Really Sees America*. New York: Henry Holt, 2019.

O'Toole, Patricia. *The Moralist: Woodrow Wilson and the World He Made*. New York: Simon & Schuster, 2018.

Oudes, Bruce, ed. *Richard Nixon's Secret Files*. New York: Harper & Row, 1988.

Oulahan, Richard. *The Man Who . . . The Story of the 1932 Democratic National Convention*. New York: Dial Press, 1972.

Paine, Charles. *The Resistant Writer: Rhetoric as Immunity, 1850 to the Present*. Albany: State University of New York Press, 1999.

Parmet, Herbert. *Jack: The Struggles of John F. Kennedy*. New York: Dial Press, 1980.

Parton, James. *The Life of Horace Greeley, Editor of "The New York Tribune" from His Birth to the Present Time*. Boston: James R. Osgood, 1889.

Pasley, Louis W. *"The Tyranny of Printers": Newspaper Politics in the Early American Republic*. Charlottesville: University Press of Virginia, 2001.

Paine, Charles. *The Resistant Writer: Rhetoric as Immunity, 1850 to the Present*. Albany: State University of New York Press, 1999.

Payne, George Henry. *History of Journalism in the United States*. New York: D. Appleton, 1920.

Peck, Harry Thurston. *Twenty Years of the Republic, 1885–1905*. New York: Dodd, Mead, 1906.

Perino, Dana. *And the Good News Is . . . Lessons and Advice from the Bright Side*. New York: Twelve, 2015.

Perlstein, Rick. *The Invisible Bridge: The Fall of Nixon and the Rise of Reagan*. New York: Simon & Schuster, 2014.

Peterson, Merrill D. *The President and the Biographer: Woodrow Wilson and Ray Stannard Baker*. Charlottesville: University Press of Virginia, 2007.

Pitney, John J., Jr. *After Reagan: Bush, Dukakis, and the 1988 Elections*. Lawrence: University Press of Kansas, 2019.

Plame, Valerie. *Fair Game: My Life as a Spy, My Betrayal by the White House*. New York: Simon & Schuster, 2007.

Pollard, James E. *The President and the Press*. New York: Macmillan, 1947.

———. *The Presidents and the Press: Truman to Johnson*. Washington: Public Affairs, 1964.

Poniewozik, James. *Audience of One: Donald Trump, Television, and the Fracturing of America*. New York: Liveright, 2019.

Ponsonby, Arthur (Baron of Shulbrede). *Falsehood in War-Time: Containing an Assortment of Lies Circulated Throughout the Nations During the Great War*. New York: E. P. Dutton, 1928.

Poore, Ben Perley. *Perley's Reminiscences of Sixty Years in the National Metropolis Illustrating the Wit, Humor, Genius, Eccentricities, Jealousies, Ambitions and Intrigues of the Brilliant Statesmen, Ladies, Officers, Diplomats, Lobbyists and other noted Celebrities of the World that gather at the Centre of the Nation Describing imposing Inauguration Ceremonies, Gala Day Festivities, Army Reviews, &c., &c., &c.* 2 vol. Philadelphia: Hubbard Bros., 1886.

Porter, William E. *Assault on the Media: The Nixon Years.* Ann Arbor: University of Michigan Press, 1977.

Powell, Jody. *The Other Side of the Story.* New York: William Morrow, 1984.

Purvis, Hoyt, ed. *The President and the Press.* Austin, TX: Lyndon B. Johnson School of Public Affairs, 1976.

Rather, Dan. *The Camera Never Blinks: Adventures of a TV Journalist.* New York: William Morrow, 1977.

Ratner, Lorman A., and Dwight L. Teeter Jr. *Fanatics and Fire-Eaters: Newspapers and the Coming of the Civil War.* Urbana: University of Illinois Press, 2003.

Rawls, Walton. *Wake Up, America! World War I and the American Poster.* New York: Abbeville Press, 1988.

Reedy, George E. *The Twilight of the Presidency.* Orig. pub. 1970; New York: New American Library, 1971.

———. *Lyndon B. Johnson: A Memoir.* New York: Andrews & McMeel, 1982.

Reeves, Richard. *President Kennedy: Profile of Power.* New York: Simon & Schuster, 1993.

———. *President Nixon: Alone in the White House.* New York: Simon & Schuster, 2001.

Regan, Donald. *For the Record: From Wall Street to Washington.* New York: Harcourt Brace Jovanovich, 1988.

Reid, Joy-Ann. *The Man Who Sold America: Trump and the Unraveling of the American Story.* New York: William Morrow, 2019.

Remini, Robert V. *Andrew Jackson and the Course of American Freedom, 1822–1832.* New York: Harper & Row, 1981.

———. *The Life of Andrew Jackson.* New York: Harper & Row, 1988.

Remnick, David. *The Bridge: The Life and Rise of Barack Obama.* New York: Alfred A. Knopf, 2010.

Reynolds, Donald E. *Editors Make War: Southern Newspapers in the Secession Crisis.* Carbondale: Southern Illinois University Press, 2006.

Riley, Russell L. *Inside the Clinton White House: An Oral History.* New York: Oxford University Press, 2016.

Roosevelt, Eleanor. *This I Remember.* New York: Harper & Bros., 1946.

———. *The Autobiography of Eleanor Roosevelt.* New York: Harper & Bros., 1958.

———. *Eleanor Roosevelt's My Day: Her Acclaimed Columns*, 3 vols. New York: Pharos, 1989–91.

Roosevelt, Elliott. *As He Saw It.* New York: Duell, Sloan and Pearce, 1946.

———, and James Brough. *The Roosevelts of Hyde Park: An Untold Story.* New York: G. P. Putnam's Sons, 1973.

———. *The Roosevelts of the White House: A Rendezvous with Destiny.* New York: G. P. Putnam's Sons, 1975.

Roosevelt, James, with Bill Libby. *My Parents: A Differing View.* Chicago, Playboy Press, 1976.

Roosevelt, James, and Sidney Shalett. *Affectionately, F.D.R.: A Son's Story of a Lonely Man.* New York, Avon, 1959.

Rosenfeld, Richard N. *American Aurora: A Democratic-Republican Returns; the Suppressed History of Our Nation's Beginnings and the Heroic Newspaper That Tried to Report It.* New York: St. Martin's Press, 1997.

Rosenman, Samuel I. *Working with Roosevelt.* New York: Harper & Bros., 1952.

Rosenstiel, Tom. *Strange Bedfellows: How Television and the Presidential Candidates Changed American Politics, 1992.* New York: Hyperion, 1993.

Ross, Stewart Halsey. *Propaganda for War: How the United States Was Conditioned to Fight the Great War of 1914–1918.* Joshua Tree, CA: Progressive Press, 2009.

Rove, Karl. *Courage and Consequence: My Life as a Conservative in the Fight.* New York: Threshold, 2010.

Rozell, Mark J. *The Press and the Carter Presidency.* Boulder, CO: Westview Press, 1989.

Rubin, Richard L. *Press, Party and the Presidency.* New York: W. W. Norton, 1981.

Rumsfeld, Donald. *When the Center Held: Gerald Ford and the Rescue of the American Presidency.* New York: Free Press, 2018.

Sabato, Larry J. *Feeding Frenzy: How Attack Journalism Has Transformed American Politics.* New York: Free Press, 1991.

Sachsman, David B., S. Kittrell Rushing, and Roy Morris Jr. *Words at War: The Civil War and American Journalism.* West Lafayette, IN: Purdue University Press, 2008.

Safire, William. *Before the Fall: An Inside View of the Pre-Watergate White House.* New York: Da Capo Press, 1975.

Salinger, Pierre. *With Kennedy.* New York: Doubleday, 1966.

Salkin, Allen, and Aaron Short. *The Method to the Madness: Donald Trump's Ascent as Told by Those Who Were Hired, Fired, Inspired—and Inaugurated.* New York: All Points Books, 2019.

Savage, Charlie. *Power Wars: Inside Obama's Post-9/11 Presidency.* Boston: Little, Brown, 2015.

Scaramucci, Anthony. *Trump: The Blue-Collar President.* New York: Center Street, 2018.

Schlesinger, Arthur M., Jr. *The Age of Jackson.* Boston: Little, Brown, 1945.

———. *A Thousand Days: John F. Kennedy in the White House.* Boston: Houghton Mifflin, 1965.

Schouler, James. *History of the United States of America, Under the Constitution.* 7 vols. New York: Dodd, Mead, 1880–1917.

Schram, Martin. *Running for President 1976: The Carter Campaign.* New York: Stein and Day, 1977.

———. *The Great American Video Game: Presidential Politics in the Television Age.* New York: William Morrow, 1987.

Schreiber, G. R. *The Bobby Baker Affair: How to Make Millions in Washington.* New York: Henry Regenery, 1964.

Singer, Mark. *Character Studies: Encounters with the Curiously Obsessed.* New York: Houghton Mifflin Harcourt, 2005.

———. *Trump and Me.* New York: Tim Duggan Books, 2016.

Small, Melvin. *The Presidency of Richard Nixon.* Lawrence: University Press of Kansas, 1999.

Smith, A. Merriman. *Thank You, Mr. President: A White House Notebook.* New York: Harper & Bros., 1946.

———. *Merriman Smith's Book of Presidents: A White House Memoir.* Edited by Timothy G. Smith. New York: W. W. Norton, 1972.

Smith, Culver H. *The Press, Politics, and Patronage: The American Government's Use of Newspapers, 1789–1875.* Athens: University of Georgia Press, 1977.

Smith, Howard K. *Events Leading Up to My Death: The Life of a Twentieth-Century Reporter.* New York: St. Martin's Press, 1996.

Smith, James Morton. *Freedom's Fetters: The Alien and Sedition Laws and American Civil Liberties.* Ithaca, NY: Cornell University Press, 1956.

Smith, Jean Edward. *FDR.* New York: Random House, 2007.

———. *Bush.* New York: Simon & Schuster, 2016.

Smith, Jeffrey A. *War and Press Freedom: The Problem of Prerogative Power.* New York: Oxford University Press, 1999.

Smith, Stephen Drury. *The First Lady of Radio: Eleanor Roosevelt's Historic Broadcasts.* New York: New Press, 2014.

Sorensen, Ted. *Kennedy.* New York: Harper & Row, 1965.

——. *Counselor: A Life at the Edge of History.* New York: Harper, 2008.

Speakes, Larry, with Robert Pack. *Speaking Out: The Reagan Presidency from Inside the White House.* New York: Charles Scribner's Sons, 1988.

Spear, Joseph C. *Presidents and the Press: The Nixon Legacy.* Cambridge: MIT Press, 1984.

Spencer, David R. *The Yellow Journalism: The Press and America's Emergence as a World Power.* Evanston, IL: Northwestern University Press, 2007.

Spicer, Sean. *The Briefing: Politics, the Press, and the President.* Washington, DC: Regenery, 2018.

Spragens, William C. *The Presidency and the Mass Media.* Washington, DC: University Press of America, 1979.

Spragens, William C., with Carole Ann Terwoord. *From Spokesman to Press Secretary: White House Media Operations.* Washington, DC: University Press of America, 1980.

Sprague, Dean. *Freedom Under Lincoln: Federal Power and Personal Liberty Under the Strain of Civil War.* Boston: Houghton Mifflin, 1965.

Starr, Paul. *The Creation of the Media: Political Origins of Modern Communications.* New York: Basic Books, 2004.

Startt, James D. *Woodrow Wilson and the Press: Prelude to the Presidency.* New York: Palgrave Macmillan, 2004.

Steel, Ronald. *Walter Lippmann and the American Century.* New York: W. W. Norton, 2004.

Steele, Richard W. *Propaganda in an Open Society: The Roosevelt Administration and the Media, 1933–1941.* New York: Praeger, 1985.

Steffens, Lincoln. *The Autobiography of Lincoln Steffens.* New York: Harcourt, Brace, 1931.

Stein, M. L. *When Presidents Meet the Press.* New York: Julian Messner, 1969.

Stephanopoulos, George. *All Too Human: A Political Education.* Boston: Little, Brown, 1999.

Stewart, Donald H. *The Opposition Press of the Federalist Period.* Albany: State University of New York Press, 1969.

Stewart, James B. *Blood Sport: The President and His Adversaries.* New York: Simon & Schuster, 1996.

Stiles, Lela. *The Man Behind Roosevelt: The Story of Louis McHenry Howe.* Cleveland: World Publishing, 1954.

Stone, Geoffrey R. *Perilous Times: Free Speech in Wartime from the Alien and Sedition Act of 1798 to the War on Terrorism.* New York: W. W. Norton, 2004.

——. *War and Liberty: An American Dilemma, 1790 to the Present.* New York: W. W. Norton, 2007.

Stone, I. F. *The War Years, 1939–1945.* Boston: Little, Brown, 1990.

Stuart, James D. *Woodrow Wilson and the Press: Prelude to the Presidency.* New York: Palgrave Macmillan, 2004.

Symonds, Craig L. *World War II at Sea: A Global History.* New York: Oxford University Press, 2018.

Tagg, James. *Benjamin Franklin Bache and the "Philadelphia Aurora."* Philadelphia: University of Pennsylvania Press, 1991.

Takiff, Michael. *A Complicated Man: The Life of Bill Clinton as Told by Those Who Know Him.* New Haven, CT: Yale University Press, 2010.

Tebbel, John. *An American Dynasty: The Story of the McCormicks, Medills and Pattersons.* New York: Doubleday, 1947.

Tebbel, John, and Sarah Miles Watts. *The Press and the Presidency: From George Washington to Ronald Reagan.* New York: Oxford University Press, 1985.

TerHorst, Jerald. *Gerald Ford and the Future of the Presidency.* New York: Third Press, 1974.

Thomas, Evan. *Being Nixon: A Man Divided.* New York: Random House, 2015.

Thomas, Helen. *Dateline White House: A Warm and Revealing Account of American Presidents and Their Families, from the Kennedys to the Fords.* New York: Macmillan, 1975.

———. *Front Row at the White House: My Life and Times.* New York: Scribner, 1999.
———. *Thanks for the Memories, Mr. President.* New York: Scribner, 2002.
———. *Watchdogs of Democracy? The Waning Washington Press Corps and How It Failed the Public.* New York: Scribner, 2006.
Thompson, Charles Willis. *Presidents I've Known and Two Near Presidents.* Indianapolis: Bobbs-Merrill, 1929.
Thompson, Hunter S. *Fear and Loathing on the Campaign Trail '72.* New York: Simon & Schuster, 1973.
Thompson, Kenneth W., ed. *Ten Presidents and the Press.* Latham, MD: University Press of America, 1983.
———. *Three Press Secretaries on the Presidency and the Press—Jody Powell, George Reedy, Jerry terHorst.* Latham, MD: University Press of America, 1983.
———. *The Johnson Presidency: Twenty Intimate Perspectives of Lyndon B. Johnson.* Lanham, MD: University Press of America, 1986.
———. *The Bush Presidency, Part Two: Ten Intimate Perspectives of George Bush.* Portraits of American Presidents 11. Latham, MD: University Press of America, 1998.
Toobin, Jeffrey. *Too Close to Call: The Thirty-Six-Day Battle to Decide the 2000 Election.* New York: Random House, 2001.
Troy, Gil. *See How They Ran: The Changing Role of the American Campaign.* New York: Free Press, 1991.
Tugwell, R.W. *The Brains Trust.* New York: Viking, 1968.
Tumulty, Joseph P. *Woodrow Wilson as I Know Him.* New York: Doubleday, Page, 1921.
Turner, Justin G., and Linda Levitt Turner, eds. *Mary Todd Lincoln: Her Life and Letters.* New York: Alfred A. Knopf, 1972.
Turrell, David J. *Government by Political Spin.* Lafayette, LA: Huntington House, 2000.
Tye, Larry. *The Father of Spin: Edward L. Bernays and the Birth of Public Relations.* New York: Crown, 1998.
Valenti, Jack. *A Very Human President.* New York: Pocket Books, 1977.
Viguerie, Richard A., and David Franke. *America's Right Turn: How Conservatives Used New and Alternative Media to Take Power.* Chicago: Bonus Books, 2004.
Villard, Henry. *Memoirs of Henry Villard.* 2 vols. Boston: Houghton Mifflin, 1904.
Villard, Oswald Garrison. *Fighting Years: Memoirs of a Liberal Editor.* New York: Harcourt, Brace, 1939.
Ward, Geoffrey C. *A First-Class Temperament: The Emergence of Franklin Roosevelt, 1905–1928.* New York: Harper & Row, 1989.
———. *Closest Companion: The Unknown Story of the Intimate Friendship Between Franklin Roosevelt and Margaret Suckley.* New York: Houghton Mifflin Harcourt, 1995.
Ward, Geoffrey C., and Ken Burns. *The Roosevelts: An Intimate History.* New York: Alfred A. Knopf, 2014.
Warshauer, Matthew. *Andrew Jackson and the Politics of Martial Law: Nationalism, Civil Liberties, and Partisanship.* Knoxville: University of Tennessee Press, 2006.
Washington, Booker T. *Up from Slavery: An Autobiography.* New York: Doubleday, Page, 1901.
Weisberg, Jacob. *The Ultimate George W. Bushisms: Bush at War with the English Language.* New York: Fireside, 2007.
———. *The Bush Tragedy.* New York: Random House, 2008.
Weisberger, Bernard A. *Reporters for the Union.* Boston: Little, Brown, 1953.
Weiss, Nancy J. *Farewell the Party of Lincoln: Black Politics in the Age of FDR.* Princeton, NJ: Princeton University Press, 1983.
Werth, Barry. *31 Days: Gerald Ford, the Nixon Pardon, and a Government in Crisis.* New York: Anchor, 2007.
White, Graham J. *FDR and the Press.* Chicago: University of Chicago Press, 1979.

White, Theodore H. *The Making of the President—1960.* New York: Atheneum, 1961.
———. *The Making of the President—1964.* New York: Atheneum, 1965.
———. *The Making of the President—1968.* New York: Atheneum, 1969.
———. *The Making of the President—1972.* New York: Atheneum, 1973.
———. *Breach of Faith: The Fall of Richard Nixon.* New York: Atheneum, 1975.
White, William Allen. *Woodrow Wilson: The Man, His Times and His Task.* Boston: Houghton Mifflin, 1925.
———. *Masks in a Pageant.* New York: Macmillan, 1928.
———. *The Autobiography of William Allen White.* New York: Macmillan, 1946.
Wickham, Dewayne. *Bill Clinton and Black America.* New York: One World, 2002.
Wilentz, Sean. *The Rise of American Democracy: Jefferson to Lincoln.* New York: W. W. Norton, 2005.
———. *The Age of Reagan: A History, 1974–2008.* New York: HarperCollins, 2008.
Wills, Garry. *Nixon Agonistes.* Boston: Houghton Mifflin, 1970.
———. *The Kennedy Imprisonment: A Meditation on Power.* Boston: Little, Brown, 1981.
Wilmer, Lambert A. *Our Press Gang; or, A Complete Exposition on the Corruption and Crimes of the American Newspapers.* Philadelphia: J. T. Lloyd, 1859.
Wilson, Edith Bolling. *My Memoir.* Indianapolis: Bobbs-Merrill, 1937.
Wilson, Joseph. *The Politics of Truth: A Diplomat's Memoir—Inside the Lies That Led to War and Betrayed My Wife's CIA Identity.* New York: Carol & Graf, 2004.
Winfield, Betty Houchin. *FDR and the News Media.* Orig. pub. 1990; New York: Columbia University Press, 1994.
Wingate, Charles F. *Views and Interviews on Journalism.* New York: F. B. Patterson, 1875.
Wise, David. *The Politics of Lying: Government Deception, Secrecy, and Power.* New York: Random House, 1973.
Wise, Henry A. *Seven Decades of the Union.* Philadelphia: J. B. Lippincott, 1872.
Witcover, Jules. *White Knight: The Rise of Spiro Agnew.* New York: Random House, 1972.
———. *Very Strange Bedfellows: The Short and Unhappy Marriage of Richard Nixon and Spiro Agnew.* New York: PublicAffairs, 2007.
Wolff, Michael. *Fire and Fury: Inside the Trump White House.* New York: Henry Holt, 2018.
———. *Siege: Trump Under Fire.* New York: Henry Holt, 2019.
Wolfskill, George, and John A. Hudson. *All but the People: FDR and His Critics, 1933–39.* New York: Macmillan, 1969.
Wood, Gordon S. *Friends Divided: John Adams and Thomas Jefferson.* New York: Penguin Press, 2017.
Woodward, Bob. *The Agenda: Inside the Clinton White House.* New York: Simon & Schuster, 1994.
———. *Shadow: Five Presidents and the Legacy of Watergate.* New York: Simon & Schuster, 1999.
———. *Bush at War.* New York: Simon & Schuster, 2002.
———. *Plan of Attack: The Definitive Account of the Decision to Invade Iraq.* New York: Simon & Schuster, 2004.
———. *State of Denial: Bush at War, Part 3.* New York: Simon & Schuster, 2007.
———. *Fear: Trump in the White House.* New York: Simon & Schuster, 2018.
Woodward, Bob, and Carl Bernstein. *All the President's Men.* New York: Simon & Schuster, 1974.
———. *The Final Days.* New York: Simon & Schuster, 1976.
———. *The Secret Man: The Story of Watergate's Deep Throat.* New York: Simon & Schuster, 2005.
Woolner, David B. *The Last 100 Days: FDR at War and at Peace.* New York: Basic Books, 2017.
Wyatt, Clarence. *Paper Soldiers: The American Press and the Vietnam War.* New York: W. W. Norton, 1993.
Yellin, Eric. *Racism in the Nation's Service: Government Workers and the Color Line in Woodrow Wilson's America.* Chapel Hill: University of North Carolina Press, 2013.
Zeitz, Joshua. *Building the Great Society: Inside Lyndon Johnson's White House.* New York: Viking, 2018.

Chapters in Books and Selected Journal and Magazine Articles

Abrams, Floyd. "The New Effort to Control Information." *New York Times Magazine*, September 25, 1983, 22–28, 72–73.

———. "Clinton Versus the First Amendment." *New York Times Magazine*, March 30, 1997, 42–44.

Ames, William E., and S. Dean Olson. "Washington's Political Press and the Election of 1824." *Journalism Quarterly* 40 (Summer 1963): 343–50.

Anderson, Patrick. "No. 2 Texan in the White House." *New York Times*, April 3, 1966.

Anderson, Paul Y. "Hoover and the Press." *The Nation*, October 14, 1931, 382–84.

Auletta, Ken. "Non-Stop News: With Cable, the Web, and Tweets, Can the President—or the Press—Still Control the Story?" *New Yorker*, January 25, 2010, 38–47.

Bain, George. "How Negro Editors Viewed the New Deal." *Journalism Quarterly* 44 (Autumn 1967): 552–54.

Barclay, Thomas S. "The Bureau of Publicity of the Democratic National Committee, 1930–32." *American Political Science Review* 27 (February 1933): 63–65.

Becker, Samuel L. "Presidential Power: The Influence of Broadcasting." *Quarterly Journal of Speech* 47 (February 1961): 10–18.

Benjamin, S.G.W. "Notable Editors Between 1776 and 1800." *Magazine of American History* 17 (February 1887): 97–127.

Benson, Krystina. "The Committee on Public Information: A Transmedia War Propaganda Campaign." *Journal of Cultural Science* 5 (2012): 62–86.

Berchtold, William E. "Press Agents of the New Deal." *New Outlook*, July 26, 1934, 23–30, 61.

Berns, Walter. "Freedom of the Press and the Alien and Sedition Laws: A Reappraisal." *Supreme Court Review* 1970 (1970): 109–59.

Blumenthal, Sidney. "Marketing the President." *New York Times Magazine*, September 13, 1981, 43, 110, 112, 116, 118.

Blyer, Willard Grosvenor. "Freedom of the Press and the New Deal." *Journalism Quarterly* 11 (March 1934): 22–35.

Boeckel, Richard. "The Man With the Best Story Wins." *The Independent* 102 (May 1920): 244–45.

Bogen, David S. "The Origins of Freedom of Speech and Press." *Maryland Law Review* 42 (1983): 429–65.

Bonafede, Dom. "The Selling of the Executive Branch—Public Information or Promotion?" *National Journal* 27 (June 1981): 1153–57.

Braden, Waldo W., and Ernest Brandenburg. "Roosevelt's Fireside Chats." *Speech Monographs*, November 1955: 290–307.

Brandt, Raymond P. "The President's Press Conference." *Sunday Graphic* 28 (July 1939): 446–57.

Brinkley, David. "An Age Less Than Golden: Roosevelt vs. the Wartime Press." *Washington Journalism Review* 10 (June 1988): 30–44.

Brody, Richard A., and Catherine R. Shapiro. "Policy Failure and Public Support: The Iran-Contra Affair and Public Assessments of President Reagan." *Political Behavior* 11 (December 1989): 353–69.

Brown, Ashmun. "The Roosevelt Myth." *American Mercury* 37 (April 1936): 390–94.

Carcasson, Martin. "Herbert Hoover and the presidential campaign of 1932: The failure of Apologia." *Presidential Studies Quarterly* 28 (Spring 1998): 349–65.

Carroll, Gordon. "Dr. Roosevelt's Propaganda Trust." *American Mercury* 52 (September 1937): 1–31.

Carroll, Thomas F. "Freedom of Speech and of the Press During the Civil War." *Virginia Law Review* 9 (May 1923): 516–61.

Cherlin, Reid. "The Presidency and the Press: The White House Distrusts the Media, Reporters Feel Persecuted—a Former Obama Spokesman on the History of the Toxic Relationship."

Rolling Stone, August 4, 2014. https://www.rollingstone.com/politics/politics-news/the-presidency-and-the-press-74832/.

Clapper, Raymond. "Why Reporters Like Roosevelt." *Review of Reviews and World's Work* 89 (June 1934): 14–17.

Clark, Delbert. "The President's Listening-in Machine: What the People Think About Him Is Conveyed to His Ear by an Efficient Organization." *New York Times*, September 1, 1935.

Clement, Edward H. "19th-Century Boston Journalism," Parts 1–11. *New England Magazine* 35 (November 1906): 277–81; (December 1906): 415–21; (January 1907): 523–28; (February 1907): 707–13; *New England Magazine* 36 (February 1907): 41–49; (April 1907): 170–76; (May 1907): 321–30; (June 1907) 462–67; (July 1907): 558–64; (August 1907): 729–35; *New England Magazine* 37 (September 1907): 92–98.

Crouthamel, James L. "The Newspaper Revolution in New York, 1830–1860. *New York History* 45 (1964): 91–113.

Culbert, David. "Johnson and the Media." In *The Johnson Years—Volume I*, edited by Robert A. Divine. Lawrence: University Press of Kansas, 1987.

Curry, Roy Watson. "The Newspaper Presses and the Civil War." *West Virginia Magazine of History* 6: 225–64.

Daly, Christopher B. "How Woodrow Wilson's Propaganda Machine Changed American Journalism." Smithsonian.com, April 18, 2017. https://www.smithsonianmag.com/history/how-woodrow-wilsons-propaganda-machine-changed-american-journalism-180963082/.

Davenport, Walter. "The President and the Press." *Collier's Magazine*, January 27, 1945, 11–14, 47; February 3, 1945: 16–17, 45.

Downie, Leonard, Jr., with Sara Rafsky. *The Obama Administration and the Press: Leak Investigations, and Surveillance in Post-9/11 America*. Report of the Committee to Protect Journalists, October 13, 2013. https://cpj.org/reports/2013/10/obama-and-the-press-us-leaks-surveillance-post-911.php.

Early, Stephen T. "Below the Belt." *Saturday Evening Post*, June 10, 1939, 7, 111–13.

Ewing, Gretchen Garst. "Duff Green, John C. Calhoun, and the Election of 1828." *South Carolina Historical Magazine* 79 (April 1978): 126–37.

Fay, Bernard, "Benjamin Franklin Bache, a Democratic Leader of the Eighteenth Century." *Proceedings of the American Antiquarian Society* 40 (1930): 277–304.

Ford, Worthington Chauncey. "Jefferson and the Newspapers." *Records of the Columbia Historical Society Review* 8 (1905): 78–111.

Gitlin, Todd. "The Clinton-Lewinsky Obsession: How the Press Made a Scandal of Itself." *Washington Monthly* 30 (December 1998). http://www. washingtonmonthly.com/features/1998/9812.gitlin.obsession.html.

Glassock, J. Walter. "Did the 'Dishonest Media' Really Take On Lincoln, Jefferson, and Jackson?" *Christian Science Monitor*, February 20, 2017.

Goldman, Peter. "Inside Nixon's White House." *Newsweek*, January 21, 1974, 21–23.

Graham, James T. "Kennedy, Cuba, and the Press." *Journalism Quarterly* 24 (1998): 60–72.

Grantham, Dewey W. "Dinner at the White House: Theodore Roosevelt, Booker T. Washington, and the South." *Tennessee Historical Quarterly* 17 (June 1958): 112–30.

Grossman, Michael Baruch, and Martha Joynt Kumar. "The White House and the News Media: The Phases of Their Relationship." *Political Science Quarterly* 94 (Spring 1979): 37–53.

Haight, Timothy R., and Richard A. Brody. "The Mass Media and Presidential Popularity: Presidential Broadcasting and News in the Nixon Administration." *Communication Research* 4 (January 1977): 41–60.

Hale, Matthew Rainbow. "On Their Tiptoes: Political Time and Newspapers During the Advent of the Radicalized French Revolution Circa 1792–1793." *Journal of the Early Republic* 29 (Summer 2009): 191–218.

Harris, Richard. "The Presidency and the Press." *New Yorker*, October 1, 1973.

Hawthorne, Nathaniel [A Peaceable Man]. "Chiefly About War Matters." *Atlantic Monthly* 10 (July 1862): 43–61.

Herring, E. Pendleton. "Official Publicity Under the New Deal." *Annals of the American Academy of Political and Social Science* 179 (May 1935): 167–75.

Heyse, Amy L., and Katie L. Gibson. "John F. Kennedy, 'The Presidency and the Press' . . . American Newspaper Publishers Association." *Voices of Democracy* 9 (2014): 23–40.

Hong, Sounman, and Daniel Nadler. "Which Candidates Do the Public Discuss Online in an Election Campaign?" *Government Information Quarterly* 29 (October 2012): 455–461.

Hong, Sounman and Sun Hyoung Kim, "Political Polarization on Twitter: Implications for the Use of Social Media on Digital Governments. *Government Inforrmation Quarterly* 33 (October 2016): 777–82.

Irwin, Will. "The American Newspaper: A Study of Journalism in Relation to the Public." *Collier's* 46–47. Part 1, "The Power of the Press" (January 21, 1911): 15–18; Part 2, "The Dim Beginnings" (February 4, 1911): 14–17; Part 3, "The Fourth Current" (February 18, 1911): 14–19; Part 4, "The Spread and Decline of Yellow Journalism" (March 4, 1911): 18–20, 36; Part 5, "What Is News?" (March 18, 1911): 16–18; Part 6, "The Editor and the News" (April 1, 1911): 18–21; Part 7, "The Reporter and the News" (April 22, 1911): 21–22, 35–36; Part 8, "'All the News That's Fit to Print'" (May 6, 1911): 17–19, 30; Part 9, "The Advertising Influence" (May 20, 1911): 15–16; 23–25; Part 10, "The Unhealthy Alliance" (June 8, 1911): 17–19, 28–29, 31–34; Part 11, "Our Kind of People" (June 17, 1911): 17–18; Part 12, "The Foe from Within" (July 1, 1911): 17–18, 30; Part 13, "The New Era" (July 8, 1911): 15–16, 25; Part 14, "The Press of Two Cities" (July 22, 1911): 15, 25, 26; Part 15, "The Voice of a Generation" (July 27, 1911): 15–16, 23, 25.

Jacobs, James A. "The President, the Press, and Proximity: The Creation of the White House Press Center." *White House History* 37 (Spring 2015): 4–23.

Johnson, Thomas J., Wayne Wanta, John T. Byrd, and Cindy Lee. "Exploring FDR's Relationship with the Press: A Historical Agenda-Setting Study." *Political Communications* 12 (1995): 157–72.

Joslin, Theodore G. "President Meets the Press: White House More Important News Center Today Than Ever Before—Vital News Comes from Conferences." *Washington Sunday Star*, March 4, 1934.

Juergens, George. "Theodore Roosevelt and the Press." *Daedalus* 111 (Fall 1982): 113–33.

Keller, Bill. "Dealing with Assange and the WikiLeaks Secrets." *New York Times Magazine*, January 26, 2011. https://www.nytimes.com/2011/01/30/magazine/30Wikileaks-t.html.

Kelly, Eugene A. "Distorting the News." *American Mercury* 34 (March 1935): 307–18.

Kielbowicz, Richard B. "Speeding the News by Postal Express, 1825–1861: The Public Policy of Privileges for the Press." *Social Science Journal* 22 (January 1975): 49–63.

Kirscheim, Dick. "In Reagan's White House, It's Gergen Who's Taken Charge of Communications." *National Journal* (July 25, 1981): 1329–31.

———. "For Reagan Communication Team It's Strictly One Week at a Time." *National Journal* (March 8, 1986): 594–95.

Kumar, Martha Joynt. "The Contemporary Presidency: Energy or Chaos? Turnover at the Top of President Trump's White House." *Presidential Studies Quarterly* 49 (March 2019): 219–36.

Lepore, Jill. "Party Time: Swear Tactics, Skullduggery, and the Debut of American Democracy." *New Yorker*, September 17, 2007.

Levy, Leonard W. "Liberty and the First Amendment, 1790–1800." *American Historical Review* 68 (October 1962): 22–37.

Lewis, Norman P. "The Myth of Spiro Agnew's 'Nattering Nabobs of Negativism.'" *American Journalism* 27 (Winter 2010): 89–115.

Lienesch, Michael. "Thomas Jefferson and the Democratic Experience: The Origins of the Partisan Press, Popular Political Publishers, and Public Opinion," 316–39. In *Jeffersonian Legacies*, edited by Peter S. Onuf. Charlottesville: University Press of Virginia, 1993.

Longaker, Richard. "Was Jackson's Kitchen Cabinet a Cabinet?" *Mississippi Valley Historical Review* 44 (June 1957): 94–108.

Lord, Donald C. "JFK and Civil Rights." *Presidential Studies Quarterly* 8 (Spring 1978): 151–63.

Maurer, Paul J. "Media Feeding Frenzies: Press Behavior During Two Clinton Scandals." *Presidential Studies Quarterly* 29 (March 1999): 65–79.

Mayer, Jane. "The Making of the Fox News White House: Fox News Has Always Been Partisan. But Has It Become Propaganda?" *New Yorker*, March 11, 2009. https://www.newyorker.com/magazine/2019/03/11/the-making-of-the-fox-news-white-house.

———. "Hard News: The State of Journalism." *New Yorker* (January 28, 2019): 18–24.

Mellett, Lowell. "Government Propaganda." *Atlantic Monthly* 168 (September 1941): 311–13.

Milligan, Susan. "The President and the Press." *Columbia Journalism Review*, March–April 2015. https://www.cjr.org/analysis/the-president-and-the-press.php.

Pasley, Jeffrey L. "The Two National 'Gazettes': Newspapers and the Embodiment of American Political Parties." *Early American Literature* 35 (2000): 51–86.

Patterson, Thomas E. "News Coverage of Donald Trump's First 100 Days." Report by Harvard Kennedy School, Shorenstein Center on Media, Politics, and Public Policy, May 18, 2017. https://shorensteincenter.org/news-coverage-donald-trumps-first-100-days.

Pious, Richard M. "The Paradox of Clinton Winning and the Presidency Losing." *Political Science Quarterly* 114 (Winter 1999–2000): 569–93.

Ponder, Stephen. "The President Makes News: William McKinley and the First Presidential Press Corps, 1897–1901." *Presidential Studies Quarterly* 24 (Fall 1994): 823–36.

Poore, Ben: Perley. "Washington News." *Harper's New Monthly Magazine* 26 (January 1874): 361–67.

Pressman, Matthew. "Ambivalent Accomplices: How the Press Handled FDR's Disability and How FDR Handled the Press." *Journal of the Historical Society* 13 (September 2013): 325–59.

Price, Byron. "Government Censorship in War-Time." *American Political Science Review* 36 (October 1942): 837–49.

Reedy, George E. "The President and the Press: Struggle for Dominance." *Annals of the American Academy of Political and Social Science* 427 (September 1976): 65–72.

Robinson, Elwyn Burns. "The *Press*: President Lincoln's Philadelphia Organ." *Pennsylvania Magazine of History and Biography* 65 (April 1941): 157–70.

Roosevelt, Theodore. "Latitude and Longitude Among Reformers." *Century Magazine* 40 (June 1900): 211–16.

———. "The Men with the Muck-Rake." *Putnam's New Monthly Magazine* 1 (October 1906): 42–47.

Rosenberg, Norman L. "The Law of Libel and Freedom of the Press in Nineteenth Century America: An Interpretation." *American Journal of Legal History* 17 (October 1973): 336–52.

Rosten, Leo C. "President Roosevelt and the Washington Correspondents." *Public Opinion Quarterly* 1 (January 1937): 36–52.

Shanks, William Franklin Gore. "How We Get Our News." *Harper's New Monthly Magazine* 34 (January 1867): 511–22.

Sharp, Harry, Jr. "Live from Washington: The Telecasting of President Kennedy's News Conferences." *Journal of Broadcasting* 13 (Winter 1968–69): 23–32.

Simon, Joel. "Barack Obama's Press Freedom Legacy." *Columbia Journalism Review*, April 3, 2015. https://www.cjr.org/criticism/barack_obamas_press_freedom_legacy.php.

Singer, Mark. "Trump Solo." *New Yorker*, May 12, 1987. https://www.newyorker.com/magazine/1997/05/19/trump-solo.

Smalley. George W. "Chapters in Journalism." *Harper's New Monthly Magazine* 89 (August 1894): 426–435.

———. "Notes on Journalism." *Harper's New Monthly Magazine* 97 (July 1898): 213–23.

Smelser, Howard. "George Washington and the Alien and Sedition Acts." *American Historical Review* 49 (January 1954): 322–34.

Smith, Hedrick. "Viewpoint: When the President Meets the Press." *Atlantic Monthly* 226 (August 1970): 65–67.

Smith, James Morton. "The Sedition Law, Free Speech, and the American Political Process." *William and Mary Quarterly* 9 (October 1952): 497–511.

———. "Sedition in the Old Dominion: James T. Callender and *The Prospect Before Us*." *Journal of Southern History* 20 (May 1954): 157–82.

Spragens, William C. "The Myth of Johnson's 'Credibility Gap.'" *Presidential Studies Quarterly* 4 (Fall 1980): 629–35.

Steele, Richard W. "The Great Debate: Roosevelt, the Media, and the Coming of War, 1940–1941." *Journal of American History* 71 (June 1984): 69–92.

———. "News of the 'Good War': World War II News Management." *Journalism Quarterly* 62 (Winter 1985): 707–16.

Stone, Geoffrey R. "On Secrecy and Transparency: Thoughts for Congress and a New Administration." Paper for the American Constitution Society for Law and Policy, June 2008.

Swinton, John. "The New York Daily Papers and Their Editors." *Independent* 52 (January 18, 1900), part 1, 168–70; (January 25, 1900), part 2, 237–40.

Trewitt, Henry L. "Meet the Press: What Does the President's Spokesman Think of the Press and Its Reporting on an Administration in Crisis?" *Newsweek*, January 21, 1974, 23.

———., et al. "Inside Nixon's White House: Stepping Up the Pressure." *Newsweek*, January 21, 1974, 19–30.

Turner, Kathryn. "Republican Policy and the Judiciary Act of 1801," *William and Mary Quarterly* 22 (January 1965): 3–32.

Vaughn, Stephen. "First Amendment Liberties and the Committee on Public Information." *American Journal of Legal History* 23 (April 1979): 95–119.

Villard, Oswald Garrison. "A Question of Preparedness." *New York Evening Post*, October 23, 29, 30; November 3, 6, 10, 13, 17, 1915.

———. "Woodrow Wilson and the Negro," *The Crisis* 45 (December 1938): 384–85.

Watson, Mary Ann. "How Kennedy Invented Political Television: The 35th President's Introduction of the Televised Press Conference and His Use of the Medium During the Cuban Missile Crisis Shifted Power Closer to the White House." *Television Quarterly* 26 (1991): 61–71.

Waxman, Olivia B., and Merrill Fabry. "From an Anonymous Tip to an Impeachment: A Timeline of Key Moments in the Clinton-Lewinsky Scandal." *Time*, May 4, 2018. https://time.com/5120561/bill-clinton-monica-lewinsky-timeline/.

Weisenburger, Francis P. "Charles Hammond: The First Great Journalist of the Old Northwest." *Ohio Archaeological and Historical Quarterly* 43 (October 1934): 338–427.

Weisman, Steven R. "The President and the Press," *New York Times Magazine* (October 14, 1984): 34–37, 71–74, 80–82.

Wilentz, Sean. "Race Man." *New Republic*, February 27, 2008. https://newrepublic.com/article/62357/race-man.

Dissertations

Davies, David R. "An Industry in Transition: Major Trends in American Daily Newspapers, 1945–1965." Ph.D. dissertation, University of Alabama, 1997.

Collman, Megan H. "From Party to Publicity: The Traditional Role of Three Publicity Experts on the Road to Modern Campaigning." Master's thesis, Louisiana State University, 2018. https://digitalcommons,lsu.edu/gradschool_theses/4623.

Erikson, Erik McKinley. "The Establishment and Rise of the Washington Globe, a Phase of Jacksonian Politics." Master's thesis, State University of Iowa, 1921. https://doi.org/10.17077/etd.35kl1pj2.

Haight, Timothy. "The Mass Media and Presidential Popularity." Ph.D. dissertation, Department of Communications, Stanford University, 1978.

Mannerberg, Lauren. "The Presidency and the Press: An Analysis of the Fundamental Rule of Traditional Press for the American Democracy." Thesis for SUNY Albany Political Science Honors College, May 2017.

Moore, William McKinley. "FDR's Image: A Study in Pictorial Symbols." Ph.D. dissertation, University of Wisconsin, 1946.

Schoenherr, Steven E. "Selling the New Deal: Stephen T. Early's Role as Press Secretary to Franklin D. Roosevelt." Ph.D. dissertation, University of Delaware, 1976.

NOTES

Introduction

1. Thomas Jefferson, notes on cabinet meeting, August 2, 1793, Andrew A. Lipscomb and Albert Ellery Bergh, eds., *The Writings of Thomas Jefferson: Memorial Edition*, 20 vols. (Washington, DC: Thomas Jefferson Memorial Association, 1903–4), 1:254.
2. George Henry Payne, *History of Journalism in the United States* (New York: D. Appleton, 1920), 19–21.
3. Great Law of Pennsylvania (1682), www.phmc.state.pa.us/portal/communities/documents/1681-1776/great-law.html.
4. Roger Sherman quoted in Akhil Reed Amar, *The Bill of Rights* (New Haven, CT: Yale University Press, 1998), 36.
5. Phillips made the statement in January 1852.
6. Kennedy challenged incumbent president Jimmy Carter for the 1980 Democratic nomination. This author worked on press efforts for Kennedy's New York campaign that year. Kennedy won the statewide primary.
7. Governor Cuomo flirted with a race for the 1992 Democratic presidential nomination but famously left an airplane sitting idly on the runway at Albany airport on the deadline day for filing for the New Hampshire primary. The governor never told me or, as far as I know, his other senior staff, that he indeed ever really considered the possibility.

Chapter One: George Washington

1. Communication to Congress, May 5, 1777, in John C. Fitzpatrick, ed., *The Writings of George Washington from the Original Manuscript Sources, 1745–1799*, 39 vols. (Washington, DC: U.S. Government Printing Office, 1931–44), 8:16–18 (hereinafter referred to as *Writings of Washington*).
2. George Washington to Matthew Cauley, June 25, 1788, *Writings of Washington*, 30:7–8. See also Ron Chernow, *George Washington: A Life* (New York: Penguin, 2010), 685.
3. Paul Leicester Ford, ed., *The True George Washington* (Philadelphia: J. B. Lippincott, 1896), 206.
4. Washington to Matthew Carey, quoted in James E. Pollard, *The Presidents and the Press* (New York: Macmillan, 1947), 9.
5. For a good analysis, see Geoffrey R. Stone, *Perilous Times: Free Speech in Wartime from the Alien and Sedition Act of 1798 to the War on Terrorism* (New York: W. W. Norton, 2004), 26.
6. Washington to David Stuart, March 28, 1790, *Writings of Washington*, 31:28.

7. Gordon S. Wood, *Revolutionary Characters: What Made the Founders Different?* (New York: Penguin, 2006), 260.
8. Gordon S. Wood, *The Idea of America: Reflections on the Birth of the United States* (New York: Penguin Books, 2011), 281.
9. *Gazette of the United States*, March 1790, quoted in George Henry Payne, *History of Journalism in the United States* (New York: D. Appleton, 1920), 159–60.
10. Lewis Leary, *That Rascal Freneau: A Study in Literary Failure* (New York: Octagon Books, 1971), 213. As an additional subvention, Fenno may also have served on the government payroll as a clerk. At the outset, Jefferson, too, made certain Fenno enjoyed patronage in the form of State Department printing orders.
11. William Grosvenor Bleyer, *Main Currents in the History of Journalism* (Boston: Houghton Mifflin, 1927), 108. In desperate need of $2,000, Fenno sought half from Hamilton and the rest from local investors, but also tried to raise money in small increments from loyal subscribers—an early example of GoFundMe crowdsourcing.
12. Jefferson to James Madison, July 21, 1791, Michael Lienesch, "Thomas Jefferson and the American Democratic Experience: The Origins of the Partisan Press, Popular Political Parties, and Public Opinion," in *Jeffersonian Legacies,* ed. Peter S. Onuf (Charlottesville: University of Virginia Press, 1993), 321.
13. S. G. W. Benjamin, "Some Notable Editors Between 1776 and 1800: Influence of the Early American Press," *Magazine of American History* 17 (February 1887): 125–27.
14. As students, the two had cofounded the American Whig-Cliosophic Society at the college. See Alexander Leitch, *A Princeton Companion* (Princeton, NJ: Princeton University Press, 1978).
15. Madison quoted in Leary, *That Rascal Freneau*, 188.
16. Quoted in Ron Chernow, *Alexander Hamilton* (New York: Penguin Press, 2004), 403.
17. Boston *Independent Chronicle*, September 6, 1792, in David Stewart, *The Opposition Press of the Federal Period* (Albany: State University of New York Press, 1969), 9.
18. Quoted in Pollard, *Presidents and the Press*, 12.
19. Payne, *History of Journalism*, 161.
20. Chernow, *George Washington*, 671.
21. Jefferson to Thomas Mann Randolph Jr., April 19, 1792, Founders Online, http://founders.archives.gov/documents/Jefferson/01-23-02-0389.
22. George Washington to Gouverneur Morris, October 20, 1792, *Writings of Washington*, 32:189.
23. John Adams to Abigail Adams, January 24, January 31, 1793, in *Letters of John Adams, Addressed to His Wife*, ed. Charles Francis Adams, 2 vols. (Boston: Charles H. Little and James Brown, 1841), 2:121, 123.
24. Thomas Jefferson to James Madison, June 9, 1893, in *The Writings of Thomas Jefferson*, ed. Paul Leicester Ford, 10 vols. (New York: G. P. Putnam's Sons, 1894), 6:293.
25. Diary entry (the "Anas"), August 2, 1793, *Writings of Thomas Jefferson,* 1:254.
26. Diary entry, May 23, 1793, ibid., 1:231.
27. Stephen Decatur Jr., *The Private Affairs of George Washington: From the Records and Accounts of Tobias Lear, Esquire, His Secretary* (Boston: Houghton Mifflin, 1933), 302.
28. Jacob Axelrad, *Philip Freneau: Champion of Democracy* (Austin: University of Texas Press, 1967), 260–62; Martin S. Pernick, "Politics, Parties, and Pestilence: Epidemic, Yellow Fever, and the Rise of the First Party System," *William and Mary Quarterly* 29 (October 1972): 579–80.
29. *Philadelphia Aurora*, November 8, 1794, in James Tagg, *Benjamin Franklin Bache and the Philadelphia Aurora* (Philadelphia: University of Pennsylvania Press, 1991), 104.
30. Bernard Fay, "Benjamin Franklin Bache, a Democratic Leader in the Eighteenth Century," *Proceedings of the American Antiquarian Society* 40 (1930): 284.

31. Jefferson's diary entry, February 26, 1793, quoted in Fay, "Benjamin Franklin Bache," 290n2.
32. John Adams to Abigail Adams, January 2, 1794, in Adams, *Letters of John Adams, Addressed to His Wife*, 2:134.
33. See Joseph Ellis, *His Excellency, George Washington* (New York: Alfred A. Knopf, 2004), 225. At most, Washington merely inspired the troops in northwestern Pennsylvania, and did no actual fighting. As for similar incidents in presidential history, James Madison would come dangerously close to British forces during the War of 1812. Abraham Lincoln would lead an assault on Norfolk, Virginia, in May 1862 (although the Confederate position was abandoned before Union troops arrived) and come under Confederate fire two years later at Fort Stevens, near Washington. Otherwise, "military" presidents from Andrew Jackson to Zachary Taylor to Ulysses S. Grant to Dwight D. Eisenhower would all notch their martial experiences before their White House years. Theodore Roosevelt, who also gained military glory before he took office, did prove another exception in that he volunteered for World War I service years after his presidency, a request President Woodrow Wilson denied.
34. Quoted in Pollard, *Presidents and the Press*, 19.
35. Washington to Jefferson, October 16, 1794, *Writings of Washington*, 34:2–3.
36. Wendy C. Wick, *George Washington, an American Icon: The Eighteenth-Century Graphic Portraits* (Washington, DC: Smithsonian Institution, 1982), 130–31. This particular Cornelius Tiebout print did not appear until 1798 but was preceded by many pictorial tributes to the first president, as this definitive study shows.
37. Pollard, *Presidents and the Press*, 16.
38. Although it was whispered that Jefferson himself had leaked the treaty to Bache (a rumor Jefferson denied), it appears the source was Senator Stevens Thomson Mason of Virginia. Stewart, *Opposition Press*, 198.
39. Tagg, *Benjamin Franklin Bache*, 261; Henry Cabot Lodge, *George Washington*, 2 vols. (Boston: Houghton Mifflin, 1889), 2:240; *Philadelphia Aurora*, September 23, 1795, quoted in Stewart, *Opposition Press*, 212.
40. For other anti-Washington criticism, see Walt Brown, *John Adams and the American Press: Politics and Journalism at the Birth of the Republic* (Jefferson, NC: McFarland, 1995), 55.
41. Philadelphia *Aurora General Advertiser*, October 29, 1795.
42. *Philadelphia Aurora*, December 29, 1795.
43. Benjamin Rush to John Adams, June 4, 1812, in John A. Schultz and Douglas Adair, eds., *The Spur of Fame: Dialogues of John Adams and Benjamin Rush, 1805–1815* (San Marino, CA: Henry Huntington Library, 1966), 223.
44. Quoted in Ford, *The True George Washington*, 264.
45. George Washington to Timothy Pickering, July 18, 1796, in *Writings of Washington*, 35:143–45.
46. Ibid.
47. Quoted in Pollard, *Presidents and the Press*, 14.
48. Washington to Oliver Wolcott Jr., July 6, 1796, *Writings of Washington*, 35:126.
49. Washington to Jefferson, July 6, 1796, *Writings of Washington*, 36:120.
50. Washington to Alexander Hamilton, July 6, 1796, ibid., 126; Pollard, *Presidents and the Press*, 16.
51. Washington to Henry Knox, April 4, 1796; Washington to Alexander Hamilton, June 26, 1796, *Writings of Washington*, 35:13, 103.
52. Benjamin Rush to John Adams, June 4, 1812, Schultz and Douglas, *Spur of Fame*, 223.
53. John Adams to Abigail Adams, March 26, 1796, in Adams, *Letters from John Adams, Addressed to His Wife*, 2:214–16.
54. Chernow, *George Washington*, 752. Biographer Chernow made this the title of one of the final chapters of his masterful biography.
55. Washington had first contemplated retiring, and begun work on an earlier farewell, four years before. In its final form, the Farewell Address proved so timeless that, some four score

years later, in the midst of a civil war, Abraham Lincoln ordered the "immortal" message to be read aloud on the floor of Congress on Washington's 130th birthday. It has been intoned there ever since. See Abraham Lincoln, Washington's Birthday Proclamation, February 19, 1862, in Roy P. Basler, ed., *The Collected Works of Abraham Lincoln*, 8 vols. (New Brunswick, NJ: Rutgers University Press, 1953–55), 5:136.

56. Washington had contemplated retirement after a single term but was persuaded to seek reelection in 1792; he again won unanimously.
57. Washington to Alexander Hamilton (with a draft of his Farewell Address), May 15, 1796, *Writings of Washington*, 35:59.
58. John Avlon, *Washington's Farewell: The Founding Father's Warning to Future Generations* (New York: Simon & Schuster, 2017), 82. Avlon's vivid account includes a report on the controversy over the first rereading of the address before Congress on February 22, 1862.
59. Ibid., 234–36.
60. Washington's Farewell Address, Avalon Project, https://avalon.law.yale.edu/18th_century/washing.asp.
61. Washington to Alexander Hamilton, August 10, 1796, *Writings of Washington*, 35:178.
62. The *Daily Advertiser* had been the first to publish the Declaration of Independence twenty years earlier. See Washington to Alexander Hamilton, August 25, 1796, ibid., 192; John Fanning Watson, *Annals of Philadelphia and Pennsylvania, in the Olden Time*, 2 vols. (Carlisle, PA: Applewood Books, 1830), 2:397.
63. Alfred McClung Lee, "Dunlap and Claypoole: Printers and News-Merchants of the Revolution," *Journalism Quarterly* 11 (June 1934): 160–78.
64. See, for example, William Cobbett, *Porcupine's political censor, for November 1796: Containing observations on the insolent and seditious notes, communicated to the people of the United States by the late French Minister Adet* (Philadelphia: William Cobbett, 1796). Cobbett (1763–1835) later gained infamy after libeling Dr. Benjamin Rush for maltreating yellow fever sufferers. After an $8,000 fine was levied, the journalist-pamphleteer known as "Peter Porcupine" headed back to England and launched a royalist newspaper there.
65. Washington to David Stuart, January 7, 1797, *Writings of Washington*, 35:358.
66. Ibid., 358, n.93.
67. John Adams to Abigail Adams, December 4, 1796, in Adams, *Letters of John Adams, Addressed to His Wife*, 2:231; Washington to David Stuart, January 8, 1797, *Writings of Washington*, 35:358–59.
68. *Porcupine's Gazette*, quoted in Tagg, *Benjamin Franklin Bache*, iv.
69. Washington to David Stuart, January 18, 1797, *Writings of Washington*, 35:360.
70. *Philadelphia Aurora*, December 23, 1796; Bleyer, *Main Currents in the History of Journalism*, 116.
71. Washington to David Stuart, January 8, 1797, *Writings of Washington*, 35:359.
72. Washington to Benjamin Walker, January 12, 1797, ibid., 35:364.
73. Ibid.
74. Washington to Jeremiah Wadsworth, March 6, 1797, ibid., 35:420–21.
75. Washington to William Gordon, October 15, 1797; Washington to Timothy Pickering, March 3, 1797, ibid., 36:50; 35:416–18.
76. Washington to Gordon, October 15, 1797, ibid., 36:50.
77. *Philadelphia Aurora*, March 6, 1797; Pollard, *Presidents and the Press*, 26.
78. Richard N. Rosenfeld, *American Aurora: A Democratic-Republican Returns; the Suppressed History of Our Nation's Beginnings and the Heroic Newspaper That Tried to Report It* (New York: St. Martin's Press, 1997), 31, 35.
79. Thomas Scharf and Thompson Westcott, *History of Philadelphia, 1609–1884*, 3 vols. (Philadelphia: L. H. Everts, 1884), 1:495.

80. James Tagg, *Benjamin Franklin Bache*, 160.
81. John Marshall, *The Life of George Washington*, 5 vols. (Philadelphia: G. P. Wayne, 1804–7), cited in Richard Harris, "The Presidency and the Press," *New Yorker*, October 1, 1973, https://www.newyorker.com/magazine/1973/10/01/the-presidency-and-the-press.
82. For guidance on these conclusions, I am grateful to the brilliantly worded advice of Ron Chernow.
83. Washington to William Gordon, October 15, 1797, *Writings of Washington*, 36:50.
84. Ibid.; Pollard, *Presidents and the Press*, 23–24.
85. Washington to Henry Lee, July 21, 1793, *Writings of Washington*, 33:22–24.

Chapter Two: John Adams

1. Jefferson to Edward Rutledge, December 27, 1796, in *The Works of Thomas Jefferson*, 12 vols., ed. Paul Leicester Ford (New York: G. P. Putnam's, 1904), 8:257 (hereinafter cited as *Works of Jefferson*).
2. Quoted in James E. Pollard, *Presidents and the Press* (New York: Macmillan, 1947), 37.
3. Adams to John Luzak, December 13, 1781, in *The Works of John Adams, Second President of the United States with a Life of the Author, Notes and Illustrations*, 10 vols., ed. Charles Francis Adams (Boston: Charles C. Little and James Brown, 1851–54), 7:490 (hereinafter cited as *Works of John Adams*). At the time, Dutchman Luzak was the editor of the Leyden *Gazette* and one of the most prominent journalists in the world.
4. Adams to George Washington, May 17, 1789, *Works of John Adams*, 8:491.
5. Walt Brown, *John Adams and the American Press: Politics and Journalism at the Birth of the Republic* (Jefferson, NC: McFarland, 1995), 73. Brown's remains the best study of Adams's evolving relationship with the newspapers, particularly during the winter–spring 1797 honeymoon period.
6. *Philadelphia Aurora*, February 22, 1797.
7. Adams's inaugural address is online at avalon.law.yale.edu/18th_century/adams.asp. For Bache's reaction, see *Philadelphia Aurora*, March 11, 1797.
8. John Adams to Abigail Adams, March 17, 1797, in *Letters of John Adams, Addressed to His Wife*, 2 vols., ed. Charles Francis Adams (Boston: Charles C. Little and James Brown, 1841), 2:252.
9. Abigail Adams to her sister, June 3, 1797, in *New Letters of Abigail Adams, 1788–1801*, ed. Stewart Mitchell (Boston: Houghton Mifflin, 1947), 94.
10. Michael Durey, *"With the Hammer of Truth": James Thomson Callender and America's Early National Heroes* (Charlottesville: University Press of Virginia, 1990), 96.
11. *New Hampshire Gazette*, February 15, 1794, quoted (with data on Atlantic crossings) in Matthew Rainbow Hale, "On Their Tiptoes: Political Time and Newspapers During the Advent of the Radicalized French Revolution, Circa 1792–1793," *Journal of the Early Republic* 29 (Summer 2009): 199–200.
12. *Philadelphia Aurora* editorials in mid-May and early June 1797 in Brown, *John Adams and the American Press*, 90.
13. Ibid., 91.
14. *Philadelphia Aurora*, April 2, 1798.
15. The French diplomats who conveyed Talleyrand's demands were named Hottinguer (X), Bellamy (Y), and Hauteval (Z). See Thomas Ray, "'Not One Cent for Tribute': The Public Addresses and American Popular Reaction to the XYZ Affair, 1798–1799," *Journal of the Early Republic* 3 (Winter 1983): 389–90.
16. Marshall Smelser, "George Washington and the Alien and Sedition Acts," *American Historical Review* 59 (January 1954): 329.

17. Abigail Adams to Mary Smith Cranch, April 28, 1798, in *New Letters of Abigail Adams*, 167.
18. George Washington to Thomas Pickering, February 6, 1798, in *Writings of Washington*, 36:156. As usual, Washington did not make these comments public.
19. Geoffrey R. Stone, *Perilous Times: Free Speech in Wartime from the Sedition Act of 1798 to the War on Terrorism* (New York: W. W. Norton, 2004), 17.
20. Merrill D. Peterson, *Thomas Jefferson and the New Nation*, 2 vols., orig. pub. 1970 (Newtown, CT: American Political Biography Press, 2001), 2:606.
21. *Philadelphia Aurora*, quoted in Terri Diane Halperin, *The Alien and Sedition Acts of 1798: Testing the Constitution* (Baltimore: Johns Hopkins University Press, 2016), 97.
22. James Morton Smith, "The Sedition Law, Free Speech, and the American Political Process," *William and Mary Quarterly* 9 (October 1952): 498.
23. Washington to James McHenry, July 4, 1798, in *Writings of Washington*, 36:306. See also Smelser, "George Washington and the Alien and Sedition Acts," 331–32.
24. Washington to William Vans Murray, December 26, 1798, in *Writings of Washington*, 37:72.
25. Jefferson to James Madison, June 7, 1798, Founders Online, https://founders.archives.gov/documents/Jefferson/01-30-02-0284.
26. Jefferson to Elbridge Gerry, January 26, 1799, in *The Writings of Thomas Jefferson*, Memorial Edition, ed. Andrew A. Lipscomb and Albert Ellery Bergh, 20 vols. (Washington, DC: Thomas Jefferson Memorial Association, 1903–4), 10:78 (hereinafter cited as *Jefferson Memorial Edition*).
27. Walter Berns, "Freedom of the Press and the Alien and Sedition Laws: A Reappraisal," *Supreme Court Review* 1970 (1970): 122.
28. Leonard W. Levy, "Liberty and the First Amendment: 1790–1800," *American Historical Review* 68 (October 1962): 32–36. Levy notes that the language of the First Amendment was less definitive than that adopted earlier by Virginia, which forbade *any* branch of government (not just the legislative) from impinging on absolute press freedom.
29. Ibid., 198–99.
30. Reprinted in the Boston *Columbian Centinel*, May 26, 1798, and in Brown, *John Adams and the American Press*, 101.
31. Akhil Reed Amar, *America's Constitution: A Biography* (New York: Random House, 2005), 216. As Amar puts it, the law gave "inferior federal courts the last judicial word."
32. Quoted in Pollard, *Presidents and the Press*, 42.
33. Smith, "The Sedition Law," 503.
34. Bruce A. Ragsdale, *The Sedition Act Trials* (Washington, DC: Federal Judicial Center and Federal Judicial History Office, 2005), 12–13.
35. Abigail Adams to Mary Smith Cranch, April 21, 1798, in *New Letters of Abigail Adams*, 159.
36. Abigail Adams to Mary Smith Cranch, December 12, 1797, April 21, April 26, May 10, June 15, 1798, ibid., 116, 159, 165, 193.
37. *Philadelphia Aurora*, June 27, 1798.
38. James Tagg, *Benjamin Franklin Bache and the "Philadelphia Aurora"* (Philadelphia: University of Pennsylvania Press, 1991), 396.
39. *Porcupine's Gazette*, July 22, 1799, in Richard N. Rosenfeld, *American Aurora: The Suppressed History of Our Nation's Beginnings and the Heroic Newspaper That Tried to Report It* (New York: St. Martin's Press, 1997), 663.
40. Stone, *Perilous Times*, 65.
41. Thomas Pickering to Adams, July 24, 1799, in *Works of John Adams*, 9:3.
42. Adams to Thomas Pickering, August 1, 1799, ibid., 5.
43. Washington to Secretary of War James McHenry, August 11, 1799, *Writings of Washington*, 38:328.
44. *Philadelphia Aurora*, March 29, 1800, in John C. Miller, *Crisis in Freedom: The Alien and Sedition Acts* (Boston: Little, Brown, 1952), 19.

45. Peterson suggests that the number of sedition charges was closer to twenty-five. See Peterson, *Thomas Jefferson and the New Nation*, 1:605.
46. Mrs. Greenleaf's journeyman printer was convicted and jailed.
47. Miller, *Crisis in Freedom*, 229.
48. Adams to members of his cabinet, April 23, 1800, *Works of John Adams*, 9:50–51.
49. James Morton Smith, *Freedom's Fetters: The Alien and Sedition Laws and American Civil Liberties* (Ithaca, NY: Cornell University Press, 1956), 340; Peterson, *Jefferson and the New Nation*, 2:637–38.
50. Adams to Jonathan Trumbull, September 10, 1800, *Works of John Adams*, 9:83.
51. New York State's presidential electors were chosen by the state legislature in 1800. Burr's campaigning, and Hamilton's newspaper attacks on Adams, probably swayed enough popular votes to secure a Republican legislative majority and thus guarantee that the Jefferson-Burr ticket won the Empire State's electors.
52. It was originally understood that Jefferson and Burr were Republican candidates for president and vice president, respectively, but when each man earned 73 electoral votes, Burr ignored the arrangement and sought the higher office.
53. Jefferson to John Taylor, June 1, 1798, Ford, *Works of Thomas Jefferson*, 8:432.
54. *Philadelphia Aurora*, February 20, 1801.
55. Adams to Benjamin Stoddert, March 31, 1801, *Works of John Adams*, 9:582–83.
56. Adams to Thomas Jefferson, June 30, 1813, ibid., 10:48–49.
57. Adams to James Lloyd, February 11, 1815, ibid., 116–17.
58. Halperin, *Alien and Sedition Acts*, 61–62.

Chapter Three: Thomas Jefferson

1. Jefferson to Thomas Cooper, November 29, 1802, Andrew A. Lipscomb and Albert Ellery Bergh, eds., *The Writings of Thomas Jefferson: Memorial Edition*, 20 vols. (Washington, DC: Thomas Jefferson Memorial Association, 1903–04, 10:341.
2. *Richmond Examiner*, February 11, 1800.
3. Michael Durey, *"With the Hammer of Truth": James Thomson Callender and America's Early National Heroes* (Charlottesville: University Press of Virginia, 1990), 27, 29–30, 53, 56, 61.
4. James T. Callender, *The Prospect Before Us* (Richmond, VA: M. Jones, S. Pleasants, jun. and J. Lyon, 1800), 30, 124. See also, James Morton Smith, "Sedition in the Old Dominion: James T. Callender and *The Prospect Before Us*," *Journal of Southern History* 54 (May 1954): 157–82.
5. Terri Diane Halperin, *The Alien and Sedition Acts of 1798: Testing the Constitution* (Baltimore: Johns Hopkins University Press, 2016), 88, 90.
6. Jefferson to James Monroe, May 26, May 29, 1801, Paul Leicester Ford, ed., *The Works of Thomas Jefferson*, 12 vols. (New York: G. P. Putnam's Sons, 1897), 9:260, 263; "that Callender . . . substantially defended," quoted in James Simon, *Thomas Jefferson, John Marshall, and the Epic Struggle to Create a United States* (New York: Simon & Schuster, 2001), 113.
7. Jefferson to Monroe, May 29, 1801, *Works of Jefferson*, 9:263.
8. Callender to Jefferson, April 12, 1801, in Durey, *"With the Hammer of Truth,"* 144.
9. Jefferson to James Monroe, May 29, 1801, *Works of Jefferson*, 9:265.
10. *Richmond Recorder*, September 1, 1802; Durey, *"With the Hammer of Truth,"* 158.
11. See Fawn M. Brodie, *Thomas Jefferson: An Intimate History* (New York: W. W. Norton, 1974); Annette Gordon Reed, *The Hemingses of Monticello: An American Family* (New York: W. W. Norton, 2008).
12. Quoted in S. E. Forman, *The Life and Writings of Thomas Jefferson, Including All of His Important Utterances on Public Questions . . .* (Indianapolis: Bobbs-Merrill, 1900), 143.
13. Abigail Adams to Thomas Jefferson, July 1, 1804, Founders Online, http://founders.archives.gov/documents/Adams/99-03-02-1285; also quoted in Lynne Withey, *Dearest Friend: A Life*

of Abigail Adams (New York: Touchstone, 2001), 273. Abigail complained to Jefferson, "One of the first acts of your administration was to liberate a wretch."

14. Jefferson to Abigail Adams, July 22, 1804, Founders Online, http://founders.archives.gov/documents/Jefferson/99-01-02-0125.
15. Leonard Levy, *Jefferson and Civil Liberties: The Darker Side* (Chicago: Ivan R. Dee, 1989), 59.
16. Quoted in Thomas Fleming, "Verdicts of History IV: 'A Scandalous, Malicious, and Seditious Libel,'" *American Heritage* 19 (December 1967), https://www.americanheritage.com/verdicts-history-iv-scandalous-malicious-and-seditious-libel.
17. Jefferson to Abigail Adams, September 11, 1804, https://founders.archives.gov/documents/Jefferson/99-01-02-0348.
18. Chauncey Worthington Ford, "Jefferson and the Newspapers," *Columbia Historical Society Review (*1905): 82.
19. Jefferson to Edward Carrington, January 16, 1787, Founders Online, https://founders.archives.gov/documents/Jefferson/01-11-02-0047.
20. Jefferson's "Anas," quoted in James E. Pollard, *The Presidents and the Press* (New York: Macmillan, 1947), 56.
21. Jefferson to James Currie, January 28, 1786, Monticello Online, www.tjrs.monticello.org.
22. Specifically, Adams had criticized the Federalist-dominated Massachusetts legislature for refusing to endorse the resolves. See Geoffrey R. Stone, *Perilous Times: Free Speech in Wartime from the Alien and Sedition Act of 1798 to the War on Terrorism* (New York: W. W. Norton, 2004), 68.
23. Culver H. Smith, *The Press, Politics, and Patronage: The American Government's Use of Newspapers, 1789–1875* (Athens: University of Georgia Press, 1977), 38, 281n11.
24. Hunt Gaillard, *The First Forty Years of Washington Society, Portrayed by the Family Letters of Mrs. Samuel Harrison Smith (Margaret Bayard) from the Collection of Her Grandson, J. Henley Smith* (New York: Charles Scribner's Sons, 1906), 7–8.
25. Baron Wilhelm von Humboldt of Prussia, quoted in Pollard, *Presidents and the Press*, 72.
26. Quoted in Willard Grosvenor Bleyer, *Main Currents in the History of American Journalism* (Boston: Houghton Mifflin, 1927), 133.
27. Quoted in Alfred Owen Aldridge, *Man of Reason: The Life of Thomas Paine* (Philadelphia: J. P. Lippincott, 1959), 269.
28. Jefferson to Thomas Paine, March 18, 1801, *Works of Jefferson*, 9:213.
29. *Gazette of the United States*, July 21, 1801, in Jerry W. Knudson, *Jefferson and the Press: Crucible of Liberty* (Columbia: University of South Carolina Press, 2006), 71.
30. Boston *New England Palladium*, quoted in W. E. Woodward, *Tom Paine: America's Godfather, 1737–1809* (New York: E. P. Dutton, 1945), 309.
31. Jefferson to Peregrine Fitzhugh, February 23, 1798, *Works of Jefferson*, 8:376.
32. Jefferson to Elbridge Gerry, March 29, 1801, Library of Congress, http://www.loc.gov/resource/mtj1.023_0465_0467.
33. Pollard, *Presidents and the Press*, 83.
34. For an excellent study, see Kathryn Turner, "Republican Policy and the Judiciary Act of 1801," *William and Mary Quarterly* 22 (January 1965): 3–32.
35. *Gazette of the United States*, November 19, 1801, in Knudson, *Jefferson and the Press*, 129–30.
36. Merrill D. Peterson, *Thomas Jefferson and the New Nation*, 2 vols., orig. pub. 1970 (Newtown, CT: American Political Biography Press, 2001), 2:695. The controversy ended only with the Supreme Court's 1803 *Marbury v. Madison* decision, which reaffirmed the independence and status of the judicial branch.
37. Boston *Columbian Centinel*, July 13, 1803; *Boston Independent Chronicle*, July 14, 1803, quoted in Knudson, *Jefferson and the Press*, 96–97.
38. *New York Evening Post*, July 5, 1803, ibid., 88.
39. Jefferson to Marc-Auguste Pictet, February 5, 1803, *Jefferson Memorial Edition*, 10:356–57.

40. Knudson, *Jefferson and the Press*, 111. The front-page black borders appeared continuously from July 13 to July 21, 1804.
41. *Boston Independent Chronicle*, July 24, 1804, ibid., 119.
42. *Boston Independent Chronicle*, July 26, 1804, ibid., 125.
43. Ibid.
44. Jefferson, second inaugural address, Avalon Project, https://avalon.law.yale.edu/19th_century/jefinau2.asp.
45. *National Intelligencer*, December 23, 1807; *New York Evening Post*, February 2, 1808, quoted in Knudsen, *Jefferson and the Press*, 145, 164.
46. Jefferson to John Norvell, June 11, 1807, Papers of Thomas Jefferson online, Library of Congress, https://www.loc.gov/resource/mtj1.038_0592_0594/?st=gallery.
47. Ibid.
48. William Waller Hening, *The New Virginia Justice, Comprising the Office and Authority of a Justice of the Peace in the Commonwealth of Virginia Together with a Variety of Useful Precedents* . . . (Richmond: Johnson & Warner, 1810), 253.
49. Jefferson to John Adams, January 21, 1812, Founders Online, https://founders.archives.gov/documents/Jefferson/03-04-02-0334.
50. Jefferson to Nathaniel Macon, January 12, 1819, quoted in Harold Holzer, *Lincoln and the Power of the Press: The War for Public Opinion* (New York: Simon & Schuster, 2014), xvii.
51. Jefferson to Walter Jones, January 2, 1820, Founders Online, https://founders.archives.gov/documents/Jefferson/03-07-02-0052; to Richard Rush, October 20, 1820, in J. G. de Roulhac Hamilton, *The Best Letters of Thomas Jefferson* (Whitefish, MT: Kessenger Legacy Reprints, 2010) 242–44.
52. Quoted in Pollard, *Presidents and the Press*, 119.
53. Jefferson to Roger C. Weightman, June 24, 1826, Library of Congress, https://www.loc.gov/item/mtjbib024904/.
54. Jefferson to Lafayette, November 4, 1823, quoted in Margaret A. Blanchard, *History of the Mass Media in the United States* (Chicago: Fitzroy Dearborn, 1998), 284.
55. Jefferson to Charles Yancey, January 6, 1816, Founders Online, https://founders.archives.gov/documents/Jefferson/03-09-02-0209.

Chapter Four: Andrew Jackson

1. *New York Evening Post*, February 7, 1815; "The Hero of New-Orleans. From the Enquirer," reprinted in the *Poughkeepsie* (NY) *Journal*, February 15, 1815.
2. Adams was chief negotiator in a delegation that also included James Bayard, Henry Clay, Albert Gallatin, and Jonathan Russell.
3. Quoted in Matthew Warshauer, *Andrew Jackson and the Politics of Martial Law: Nationalism, Civil Liberties, and Partisanship* (Knoxville: University of Tennessee Press, 2006), 62.
4. Louis Louaillier, "A Citizen of Louisiana of French Origin," *Louisiana Courier*, March 3, 1815, ibid., 35. For Warshauer's account of *U.S. vs. Jackson*, see 35–39.
5. Only when Congress reviewed the case in 1844 did the government reimburse Jackson. In 1863, Abraham Lincoln cited the Louaillier episode to assure critics that his own habeas corpus suspensions would be similarly impermanent. See Lincoln to Erastus Corning and others, June 12, 1863, in Roy P. Basler, ed., *The Collected Works of Abraham Lincoln*, 8 vols. (New Brunswick, NJ: Rutgers University Press, 1953–55), 6:268.
6. See, for example, *Burlington* (VT) *Weekly Free Press*, August 29, 1828.
7. Quoted in Samuel Flagg Bemis, *John Quincy Adams and the Foundations of American Foreign Policy* (New York: Alfred A. Knopf, 1949), 253.

8. Mark R. Cheathem, *Andrew Jackson, Southerner* (Baton Rouge: Louisiana State University Press, 2013), 39–41. The dispute with Jackson's dueling opponent, Charles Dickinson, may have involved more than the unauthorized forfeiture of a horse race; Cheathem suggests that Dickinson may also have insulted Mrs. Jackson.
9. Quoted in James C. Klotter, *Henry Clay: The Man Who Would Be President* (New York: Oxford University Press, 2018), 102.
10. Diary entry, November 28, 1832, in *Memoirs of John Quincy Adams, Comprising Portions of His Diary from 1795 to 1848*, 12 vols., ed. Charles Francis Adams (Philadelphia: J. B. Lippincott, 1875–77), 6:98, 5:469 (hereinafter cited as *JQA Memoirs*).
11. *Washington Gazette*, March 20, 1822, quoted in William E. Ames and S. Dean Olson, "Washington's Political Press and the Election of 1824," *Journalism Quarterly* 40 (Summer 1963): 350.
12. Diary entry, November 7, 1822, *JQA Memoirs*, 6:94. Force later served as mayor of Washington, D.C.
13. Diary entry, December 19, 1826, *JQA Memoirs*, 7:189.
14. Diary entry, April 29, 1828, *JQA Memoirs*, 7:507.
15. Ibid.
16. Diary entry, April 19, 1828, *JQA Memoirs*, 7:514.
17. Diary entry, December 6, 1827, *JQA Memoirs*, 7:370.
18. Cheathem, *Andrew Jackson, Southerner*, 108. The conflicts of interest went beyond the two men's affiliation with the *Gazette*: at the time, Green also served as official U.S. Senate printer, with Jarvis on the payroll as his associate.
19. W. Stephen Belko, *The Invincible Duff Green: Whig of the West* (Columbia: University of Missouri Press, 2006), 127.
20. Quoted in James E. Pollard, *The Presidents and the Press* (New York: Macmillan, 1947), 152.
21. *Albany Spirit of the Times*, August 23, 1828.
22. These "coffin handbills," proliferated during the campaign, are widely considered the most famous political prints of the 1820s. See Bernard Reilly, *American Political Prints, 1766–1876: A Catalog of the Collections in the Library of Congress* (Boston: G. K. Hall, 1991), 32–33.
23. *Burlington Sentinel and Democrat*, March 14, 1828.
24. Quoted in Pollard, *Presidents and the Press*, 148.
25. Jackson to Duff Green, August 10, 1827, Harold D. Moser, Daniel Feller, et al, eds., *The Papers of Andrew Jackson*, 10 vols. to date (Knoxville: University of Tennessee Press, 1980–2016), 6:375.
26. Diary entry, May 31, 1828, *JQA Memoirs*, 7:536.
27. Green to Jackson, July 8, 1827, in Pollard, *Presidents and the Press*, 150.
28. Robert V. Remini, *The Life of Andrew Jackson* (New York: Harper & Row, 1988), 165.
29. *Nashville Republican*, reprinted by the *United States Telegraph*, January 13, 1829, in Belko, *Invincible Duff Green*, 167.
30. Quoted in Pollard, *Presidents and the Press*, 152.
31. *Argus of Western America* (Kentucky), March 18, 1829, in Remini, *Andrew Jackson*, 181.
32. The quote has been attributed to veteran Supreme Court justice Joseph Story, who promptly resigned and left Washington to teach at Harvard.
33. Josephine Seaton, *William Winston Seaton of the "National Intelligencer": A Biographical Sketch. With Passing Notices of His Associates and Friends* (Boston: James R. Osgood, 1871), 210.
34. The statistics appeared in the *National Journal*, quoted in John Tebbel and Sarah Miles Watts, *The Press and the Presidency from George Washington to Ronald Reagan* (New York: Oxford University Press, 1985), 85.
35. Diary entry, April 16, 1829, *JQA Memoirs*, 8:138.
36. Quoted in Pollard, *Presidents and the Press*, 161.

37. *National Journal*, August 19, 1829; Jackson to John Randolph, November 11, 1831, in Pollard, *Presidents and the Press*, 161, 163.
38. Diary entry, June 6, 1828, *JQA Memoirs*, 8:28. Reportedly, Kendall "warmed to the cause" in return for $1,500 to repay creditors; see Donald B. Cole, *Amos Kendall and the Rise of American Democracy* (Baton Rouge: Louisiana State University Press, 2004), 95–96.
39. Harriet Martineau, *Retrospect of Western Travel*, 3 vols. (London: Saunders & Otley, 1838), 1:258.
40. Richard P. Longaker, "Was Jackson's Kitchen Cabinet a Cabinet?," *Mississippi Valley Historical Review* 44 (June 1957): 100.
41. Henry A. Wise, *Seven Decades of the Union* (Philadelphia: J. B. Lippincott, 1872), 117.
42. Quoted in George H. Douglas, *The Golden Age of the Newspaper* (Westport, CT: Greenwood Press, 1999), 18.
43. Diary entry, March 4, 1840, *JQA Memoirs*, 10:366.
44. "Statement by Duff Green," in Frederic Hudson, *Journalism in the United States from 1860 to 1872* (New York: Harper & Bros., 1873), 237.
45. Duff Green to William Snowden, November 16, 1827, in Gretchen Garst Ewing, "Duff Green, John C. Calhoun, and the Election of 1828," *South Carolina Historical Magazine* 79 (April 1978): 126. The original is in the Duff Green letter books in the Manuscript Division, Library of Congress.
46. Jackson to William Berkeley Lewis, June 26, 1830, *Papers of Andrew Jackson*, 8:396.
47. Cole, *Amos Kendall*, 145; Culver H. Smith, *The Press, Politics, and Patronage: The American Government's Use of Newspapers, 1789–1875* (Athens: University of Georgia Press, 1977), 123.
48. James Schouler, *History of the United States of America, Under the Constitution*, 7 vols. (New York: Dodd, Mead, 1880–1917), 3:502.
49. Benjamin Perley Poore, *Perley's Reminiscences of Sixty Years in the National Metropolis . . .*, 2 vols. (Philadelphia: Hubbard Bros., 1886), 1:191.
50. Hudson, *History of Journalism*, 238.
51. Jackson to Charles Jones Love, March 7, 1831, *Papers of Andrew Jackson*, 6:121.
52. Claude G. Bowers, *The Party Battles of the Jackson Period* (Boston: Houghton Mifflin, 1922), 166.
53. *Washington Globe*, January 22, 1831.
54. *National Intelligencer*, January 27, 1831.
55. The best study is John F. Marszalek, *The Petticoat Affair: Manners, Mutiny, and Sex in Andrew Jackson's White House* (Baton Rouge: Louisiana State University Press, 2000).
56. Tebbel and Watts, *Press and the Presidency*, 75.
57. *Philadelphia National Gazette*, May 16, September 26, 1832.
58. Ibid., May 8, 1832.
59. *Alexandria* (VA) *Gazette* editorial, reprinted in the *Philadelphia National Gazette*, October 16, 1832.
60. Kendall to an unknown correspondent, July 25, 1832, in Remini, *Andrew Jackson*, 233. Kendall's papers are in the New York Historical Society.
61. Remini, *Andrew Jackson*, 233–34.
62. *Washington Intelligencer*, August 7, 1832; *Philadelphia National Gazette*, May 8, 1832.
63. Belko, *Invincible Duff Green*, 232.
64. Ibid., 1.
65. Diary entry, December 24, 1832, *JQA Memoirs*, 8:510–11.
66. For Jackson's Proclamation on Nullification, December 10, 1832, with all drafts including Kendall's, see *Papers of Andrew Jackson*, 10:680–711.
67. *United States Telegraph*, March 4, 1833.
68. Poore, *Reminiscences*, 1:172.
69. Remini, *Andrew Jackson*, 336.

70. *New York Evening Post*, December 3, 1836.
71. Elwyn Burns Robinson, "The Dynamism of American Journalism from 1787 to 1865," *Pennsylvania Magazine of History and Biography* 61 (October 1937): 436. See also Douglas Fermer, *James Gordon Bennett and the "New York Herald"* (New York: St. Martin's Press, 1986), 14–15.
72. The Blair family's brick residence on Pennsylvania Avenue long served as a social, and sometimes political, gathering place in Washington—and later, rechristened Blair House, became an official government residence for visiting dignitaries. President Harry Truman lived there while the White House underwent extensive renovation.
73. William E. Smith, *The Francis Preston Blair Family in Politics*, 2 vols., orig. pub. 1933 (New York: Da Capo Press, 1969), 1:vii.
74. Duff Green to Lincoln, January 7, 1861, Abraham Lincoln Papers, Library of Congress. For the letter Lincoln wrote at Green's request—but which he sent to Senator Lyman Trumbull in Washington—see Lincoln to Green and Lincoln to Trumbull, December 28, 1860, Bastler, *Collected Works of Abraham Lincoln*, 4:162–63.
75. Fletcher M. Green, "Duff Green: Industrial Promoter," *Journal of Southern History* 2 (February 1936): 37.
76. David Dixon Porter, *Incidents and Anecdotes of the Civil War* (New York: D. Appleton, 1886), 307–9. For a less dramatic report of the scene, see William H. Crook, "Lincoln's Last Day; new facts now told for the first time. Compiled and written down by Margarita S. Gerry," *Harper's Monthly Magazine* 115 (September 1907): 520–22.

Chapter Five: Abraham Lincoln

1. Francis B. Carpenter, *Six Months at the White House with Abraham Lincoln: The Story of a Picture* (New York: Hurd & Houghton, 1866), 156.
2. Ibid., 155.
3. *Richmond Examiner*, April 23, 1861, quoted in Robert S. Harper, *Lincoln and the Press* (New York: McGraw-Hill, 1951), 92.
4. *New York Herald*, February 15, 1861.
5. London *Times*, December 4, 1863. Interestingly, a cartoon of the day had likened Lincoln to Don Quixote (with Union General Benjamin Butler portrayed as Sancho Panza). See George McCullough Anderson, *The Work of Adalbert Johann Volck, 1828–1912* . . . (Baltimore: Privately printed by George McCullough Anderson, 1970), 86–87.
6. When the Supreme Court finally ruled (in *Ex Parte Milligan*) against the use of military tribunals to prosecute dissenters—as his administration had occasionally done—Lincoln was dead and the war over.
7. "The Lincoln Nomination Chair," catalog entry, February 2013, http://www.sethkaller.com/item/625-The-Lincoln-Nomination-Chair.
8. Charles H. Ray to Lincoln, July [?] 1858, Abraham Lincoln Papers, Library of Congress.
9. Joseph C. G. Kennedy quoted in Mark E. Neely Jr., *The Boundaries of American Political Culture in the Civil War Era* (Chapel Hill: University of North Carolina Press, 2005), 5.
10. Navy Secretary Welles and Secretary of War Simon Cameron had both been newspaper editors in Connecticut and Pennsylvania, respectively. And Lincoln's running mate, Hannibal Hamlin, bore the nickname of "type sticker" as proudly as Lincoln promoted himself as "the Rail Splitter."
11. Editorial in the *Illinois State Journal*, December 12, 1860, in *The Collected Works of Abraham Lincoln*, 8 vols., ed. Roy P. Basler (New Brunswick, NJ: Rutgers University Press, 1953–55), 4:150 (hereinafter cited as *Collected Works of Lincoln*).
12. Lincoln to Truman Smith, November 10, 1860, ibid., 138.
13. Harold Holzer, *Lincoln President-Elect: Abraham Lincoln and the Great Secession Winter, 1860–1861* (New York; Simon & Schuster, 2008), especially chapters 10 and 11.

14. First Inaugural Address, March 4, 1861, *Collected Works of Lincoln*, 4:271.
15. *Charleston Mercury*, March 9, 1861; *Chicago Daily Times*, March 6, 1861.
16. William O. Stoddard, *Inside the White House in War Times* (New York: Charles L. Webster, 1890), 27.
17. Quoted in James E. Pollard, *Presidents and the Press* (New York: Macmillan, 1947), v.
18. Message to a Special Session of Congress, July 4, 1861, *Collected Works of Lincoln*, 4:426, 430.
19. Holzer, *Lincoln and the Power of the Press*, 338–39.
20. *American Annual Cyclopedia and Register of Important Events of the Year 1861* (New York: D. Appleton, 1868), 329.
21. New York *Daily* News, July 22, 1861; Holzer, *Lincoln and the Power of the Press*, 346–50, 367.
22. Quoted in Michael Hussey, "The Great Censorship Debate," in *Discovering the Civil War* (Washington, DC: Foundation for the National Archives, 2010), 136.
23. Testimony, February 7, 1862.
24. David Homer Bates, *Lincoln in the Telegraph Office: Recollections of the U.S. Telegraph Office During the Civil War* (New York: Century, 1907), 7.
25. General Orders No. 10, February 4, 1862, *The War of the Rebellion: A Compilation of the Official Records of the Union and Confederate Armies,* 128 vols. (Washington, D.C.: U. S. Government Printing Office, 1880-1902), series 3, vol. 1: 879.
26. D. W. Bartlett Testimony to the House Judiciary Committee, February 10, 1862, "Allegations of Government Censorship of Telegraphic Records of the Hearings of the House Judiciary Committee," National Archives, copies of transcripts in the Columbia University Library.
27. Samuel Wilkeson testimony, House Judiciary Committee, January 31, 1862.
28. Ibid.
29. *New York Times*, February 12, 1862.
30. Henry J. Raymond to Secretary of War Simon Cameron, December 13, 1861, copy in Henry J. Raymond Papers, New York Public Library.
31. *Philadelphia Evening Bulletin*, August 20, 21, 23, 24, 1861.
32. *New York Times*, September 6, 1861.
33. *New York Times*, August 20, 1861.
34. Ibid.
35. Mary Lincoln to James Gordon Bennett, October 25, 1861, in Justin G. Turner and Linda Levitt Turner, eds., *Mary Todd Lincoln: Her Life and Letters* (New York: Alfred A. Knopf, 1972), 110–11.
36. In 1862, Congress instead passed a Treason Act that in principle outlawed extreme forms of dissent, though it was not enforced against the press. See Thomas F. Carroll, "Freedom of Speech and of the Press During the Civil War," *Virginia Law Review* 9 (May 1923): 528.
37. Elon Comstock to Lincoln (with "The Rights of the Press," clipping from the *Argus*, June 11, 1863), Abraham Lincoln Papers, Library of Congress. See also *New York Tribune*, June 9, 1863. Horace Greeley served as chairman of the group; his old nemesis Henry Raymond chose not to participate.
38. *Frank Leslie's Illustrated Newspaper*, August 31, 1861.
39. Benjamin Perley Poore recollection in Allen Thorndike Rice, ed., *Reminiscences of Abraham Lincoln by Distinguished Men of His Time* (New York: North American Publishing, 1886), 227.
40. Endorsement on George D. Prentice to Lincoln, September 124, 1861, *Collected Works of Lincoln*, 4:534.
41. When the army destroyed the offices of the *St. Louis Daily Evening News* for criticizing General John C. Frémont, one outraged (but anonymous) correspondent told Postmaster General Montgomery Blair, "We are under a reign of terror," adding: "Will our President countenance such tyranny?" Blair forwarded the letter to Lincoln, but it went unanswered. See letter from unknown correspondent to Blair, September 26, 1861, Abraham Lincoln Papers, Library of Congress.

42. Arguably, as historian Mark E. Neely has demonstrated, state and local elections occurred in the North almost constantly during the Civil War. In fairness, Lincoln's tolerance for campaign-season press freedom extended only to state, congressional, and presidential elections.
43. Stanley Kaplan, "The Miscegenation Issue in the Campaign of 1864," *Journal of Negro History* 34 (July 1949); 316–18. See also, *Miscegenation: The Theory of the Blending of the Races, Applied to the American White Man and Negro* (New York: Croly & Wakeman, 1864); original copy sent to Lincoln in the Stern Collection, Library of Congress. For the full story of the *World*'s "miscegenation" hoax in caricature and print, see Mark E. Neely Jr. and Harold Holzer, *The Union Image: Popular Prints of the Civil War North* (Chapel Hill: University of North Carolina Press, 2000), 152–59.
44. Lincoln's words described as "indecent" in the *New York World*, June 6, 1864. Lincoln was accused of asking his longtime friend Ward Hill Lamon, U. S. Marshall of the District of Columbia, to sing a comic "Negro" song at Antietam. For the draft reply, ca. September 12, 1864, see *Collected Works of Lincoln*, 7:549.
45. Dorothy Lamon, ed., *Recollections of Abraham Lincoln, 1847–1865, by Ward Hill Lamon* (Chicago: A. C. McClurg, 1895), 146.
46. Lyceum Address, January 27, 1838, *Collected Works of Lincoln*, 1:112.
47. *New York World*, May 18, 1864. The anti-administration *New York Journal of Commerce* fell for the forgery as well and suffered similar suppression. Interestingly, the city's pro-Republican dailies instantly recognized the document as a fake and held it until federal authorities could confirm or deny its authenticity.
48. Lincoln to Major General John Adams Dix, May 8, 1864, *Collected Works of Lincoln*, 7:347–48.
49. The man behind the forgery, Joseph Howard Jr., had covered Lincoln's 1861 inaugural journey to Washington for the *New York Times* and later served as city editor of the *New York Tribune*. When they learned of his involvement, federal authorities arrested him and sent him to Fort Lafayette, where he remained incarcerated for months.
50. *Boston Commonwealth*, June 6, 1864.
51. Manton Marble to Abraham Lincoln, *New York World*, May 23, 1864.
52. Lincoln to Erastus Corning and others, June 12, 1863, *Collected Works of Lincoln*, 6:263, 266, 267–69.
53. Jackson had also cracked down on Southern Nullifiers.
54. Lincoln to Corning, *Collected Works of Lincoln*, 6:268.
55. Ibid., 265.
56. Lincoln to Isaac N. Arnold, May 25, 1864, ibid., 7:361.
57. *New York Times*, April 3, April 25, 1861. Lincoln scrawled the heading "Villainous articles" on these newspaper clippings and preserved them in his files; undated originals in the Abraham Lincoln Papers, Library of Congress.
58. See Hawthorne [A Peaceable Man], "Chiefly About War-Matters," *Atlantic Monthly* 10 (July 1862): 43–61. For the unexpurgated text and the letter to the magazine's editor, see Harold Holzer, ed., *The Lincoln Anthology: Great Writers on His Life and Legacy from 1860 to Now* (New York: Library of America, 2009), 32–37.
59. Remarks to a deputation of free African Americans, August 14, 1862, *Collected Works of Lincoln*, 5:370–75. For a modern interpretation of the meeting and the makeup of the visiting delegation see Kate Masur, "The African American Delegation to Abraham Lincoln: A Reappraisal," *Civil War History* 56 (June 2010): 117–44, especially 131.
60. Frederick Douglass, "The President and His Speeches," *Douglass' Monthly*, September 1862.
61. "Prayer of Twenty Millions," *New York Tribune*, August 20, 1862.
62. Quoted in Stefan Lorant, *Lincoln: A Picture Story of His Life* (rev. ed., New York: W. W. Norton, 1969), 159.

63. Lincoln to Horace Greeley, August 22, 1862, *Collected Works of Lincoln*, 5:388–89.
64. *Chicago Times*, September 24, 1862.
65. *Douglass' Monthly*, October 1862.
66. Carpenter, *Six Months at the White House*, 269.
67. Karl Marx, "On Events in North America," *Die Presse* (Vienna, Austria), October 12, 1862, translated and reprinted in Saul K. Padover, *Karl Marx on America and the Civil War* (New York: McGraw-Hill, 1972), 221–22; "historic content" quoted in Mark E. Neely Jr., *The Abraham Lincoln Encyclopedia* (New York: McGraw-Hill, 1982), 104.
68. Lincoln to James C. Conkling, August 26, 1863, *Collected Works of Lincoln*, 6:409.
69. Lincoln to James C. Conkling, September 3, 1863, ibid., 430.
70. Lincoln to Henry J. Raymond, August 15, 1864, ibid., 494. "I have concluded that it is better for *me* to submit, for the time, to the consequences of the false position in which I consider he has placed me," Lincoln complained of Greeley, "than you subject the *country* to the consequences of publishing these discouraging and injurious parts."
71. See Joseph Medill to John Hay, August 10, 1864, in John Taliaferro, *All the Great Prizes: The Life of John Hay* (New York: Simon & Schuster, 2013), 89.
72. Raymond to Lincoln, August 22, 1864, Abraham Lincoln Papers, Library of Congress.
73. Lincoln to Raymond, August 24, 1864, ibid., 517.
74. For details of the arrangement, which even Horace Greeley, by then supporting Lincoln's reelection, enthusiastically endorsed, see Holzer, *Lincoln and the Power of the Press*, 531–37; and A. K. McClure, *Lincoln and Men of War-Times: Some Personal Recollections of War and Politics During the Lincoln Administration* (Philadelphia: Times Publishing, 1892), 80.
75. *Rev. Stuart Robinson to President Lincoln*, pamphlet (Toronto: publisher unknown, 1865), 8.
76. Reply to Stephen A. Douglas in the first Lincoln–Douglas debate, Ottawa, Illinois, August 21, 1858, *Collected Works of Lincoln*, 3:27.
77. Lincoln to John M. Schofield, October 1, 1863, *Collected Works of Lincoln*, 6:492.
78. Lincoln to Schofield, May 27, 1863, ibid., 234.

Chapter Six: Theodore Roosevelt

1. Lincoln Steffens, *The Autobiography of Lincoln Steffens* (New York: Harcourt Brace, 1931), 509.
2. Ibid.; Oscar King Davis, *Released for Publication: Some Inside Political History of Theodore Roosevelt and His Times, 1898–1918* (Boston: Houghton Mifflin, 1925), 138.
3. Steffens, *Autobiography*, 510.
4. Louis Brownlow, *A Passion for Politics: The Autobiography of Louis Brownlow—First Half* (Chicago: University of Chicago Press, 1955), 399. A charming account of the "barber's hour" can be found in Doris Kearns Goodwin, *The Bully Pulpit: Theodore Roosevelt, William Howard Taft, and the Golden Age of Journalism* (New York: Simon & Schuster, 2013), 285–86.
5. Steffens, *Autobiography*, 509–10.
6. David S. Barry, *Forty Years in Washington* (Boston: Little, Brown, 1924), 270.
7. William Allen White, *Masks in a Pageant* (New York: Macmillan, 1928), 303, 326.
8. Ray Stannard Baker, *American Chronicle: The Autobiography of Ray Stannard Baker* (New York: Scribner's, 1945), 171.
9. Steffens, *Autobiography*, 502.
10. Theodore Roosevelt, "Latitude and Longitude Among Reformers," *Century Magazine* 60 (June 1900): 211.
11. Ibid., 216.
12. Ibid.
13. Mark Sullivan, *Our Times*, 6 vols. (New York: Scribner's, 1926–36), 3:72–73.

14. Quoted in William E. Leuchtenburg, *The American President: From Teddy Roosevelt to Bill Clinton* (New York: Oxford University Press, 2015), 25.
15. Barry, *Forty Years in Washington*, 270.
16. Horace Greeley, *Recollections of a Busy Life* (New York: J. B. Ford, 1868), 415. Along with tycoon Cornelius Vanderbilt, abolitionist Gerrit Smith, and others, Greeley signed Davis's bail bond to facilitate his 1867 release from imprisonment at a federal fort. The gesture would come back to haunt Greeley when he tried to resume his political career five years later.
17. Ulysses S. Grant to Robert Bonner [editor of the *New York Ledger*], October 13, 1869, in *The Papers of Ulysses S. Grant*, 32 vols., ed. John Y. Simon (Carbondale: Southern Illinois University Press, 1962–2012), 19:255; for context, see Frederic Hudson, *Journalism in the United States from 1690 to 1872* (New York: Harper & Bros., 1873), 652–53.
18. Warren Harding would later portray himself as an Ohio newspaper editor, but by the time he sought the presidency in 1920, he was a U.S. senator.
19. Stephen Ponder, "The President Makes News: William McKinley and the First Presidential Press Corps, 1897–1901," *Presidential Studies Quarterly* 24 (Fall 1994): 826.
20. "President McKinley in War Times," *McClure's Magazine* 11 (July 1898): 213–14.
21. For "splendid little war," see John M. Hay to Roosevelt, July 27, 1898, in William Roscoe Thayer, *The Life and Letters of John Hay*, 2 vols. (Boston: Houghton-Mifflin, 1915), 2:337. For "blood guilty," see James Creelman, *On the Great Highway: The Wanderings and Adventures of a Special Correspondent* (Boston: Lothrop, 1901), 175–76. For the argument that the "Yellow Press was not solely responsible for driving Americans to war," see David R. Spencer, *The Yellow Journalism: The Press and America's Emergence as a World Power* (Evanston, IL: Northwestern University Press, 2007), chapter 6; and W. Joseph Campbell, *Yellow Journalism: Puncturing the Myths, Defining the Legacies*, orig. pub. 2001 (Westport, CT: Praeger, 2003), chapter 4.
22. Christopher Woolf, "Back in the 1890s, Fake News Helped Start a War," *PRI's The World*, December 8, 2016, https://www.pri.org/stories/2016-12-08/long-and-tawdry-history-yellow-journalism-america.
23. See Clay Risen, *The Crowded Hour: Theodore Roosevelt, the Rough Riders, and the Dawn of the American Century* (New York: Scribner, 2019).
24. See Stephen Ponder, "The President Makes News: William McKinley and the First Presidential Press Corps, 1897–1901," *Presidential Studies Quarterly* 24 (Fall 1994): 827.
25. Quoted in James Bucklin Bishop, *Theodore Roosevelt and His Time Shown in His Own Letters*, 2 vols. (New York: Charles Scribner's Sons, 1922), 1:22.
26. Bishop had started his career at the *Tribune* under founder Greeley, and then worked there with John Hay, who had been Lincoln's private secretary and would later serve as secretary of state under McKinley and Theodore Roosevelt. Bishop went on to become chief editorial writer for the *New York Commercial Advertiser* and a staunch supporter of Roosevelt's gubernatorial administration. For an excellent biography by the journalist's nephew, see Chip Bishop, *The Lion and the Journalist: The Unlikely Friendship of Theodore Roosevelt and Joseph Bucklin Bishop* (New York: Lyons Press, 2011).
27. Edmund Morris, *The Rise of Theodore Roosevelt* (New York: Random House, 1979), 693.
28. Barry, *Forty Years in Washington*, 267–69.
29. Steffens, *Autobiography*, 502–3; White quoted in Goodwin, *Bully Pulpit*, 281.
30. Quoted in James E. Pollard, *Presidents and the Press* (New York: Macmillan, 1947), 571.
31. Acts V: 3–5.
32. J. Frederick Essary, *Covering Washington: Government Reflected to the Public in the Press, 1822–1926* (Boston: Houghton Mifflin, 1927), 88. Essary served as Washington correspondent for the *Baltimore Sun*. For "Oyster Bay atmosphere," see Charles Willis Thompson, *Presidents I've Known and Two Near Presidents* (Indianapolis: Bobbs-Merrill, 1929), 119.
33. Davis, *Released for Publication*, 123–24.

34. Barry, *Forty Years in Washington*, 267–69. The other wire service representatives at the meeting were Charles A. Boynton of the AP and Ed L. Keen of UPI.
35. Essary, *Covering Washington*, 93–94; Barry, *Forty Years in Washington*, 269.
36. Essary, *Covering Washington*, 93.
37. "Individualist" is from "Doyenne in the Drawing Room," *New York Times*, August 23, 1961. For the Wister quote, see Owen Wister, *Roosevelt: The Story of a Friendship, 1880–1919* (New York: Macmillan, 1930), 87.
38. Alice Roosevelt Longworth, *Crowded Hours* (New York: Charles Scribner's Sons, 1933), 60–61. She recalled that, along with the younger Roosevelt children, she "continued to be enjoined not to talk to the 'reporters'" (34).
39. Washington reported he read "too many newspapers" along with "every book and magazine article that has been written about Abraham Lincoln," whom he called "in literature . . . my patron saint." See Booker T. Washington, *Up from Slavery: An Autobiography* (New York: Doubleday, Page, 1901), 253.
40. "The Night Teddy Roosevelt Invited Booker T. Washington to Dinner," *Journal of Blacks in Higher Education* 35 (Spring 2002): 24–25. For a book-length treatment, see Deborah Davis, *Guest of Honor: Booker T. Washington, Theodore Roosevelt, and the White House Dinner That Shocked the Nation* (New York: Atria Books, 2012), especially 179–248.
41. "That Dinner at the White House," *Colored American* (Washington), October 26, 1901.
42. *Memphis Scimitar*, republished in "Booker Washington and Roosevelt," *Scranton Republican*, October 19, 1901. A search on newspapers.com for mentions of "Theodore Roosevelt" and "Booker T. Washington" in October 1901 alone yields three thousand results—and the website by no means covers every American paper.
43. Quoted in Dewey W. Grantham, "Dinner at the White House: Theodore Roosevelt, Booker T. Washington, and the South," *Tennessee Historical Quarterly* 17 (June 1958): 112–130.
44. "Anent the Dining of Booker Washington," *Daily Arkansas (*Little Rock) *Gazette*, October 31, 1901.
45. *Chicago Broad Ax*, October 26, 1901.
46. TR was no integrationist and believed firmly in the superiority of the white race. In 1906, he ordered 167 African American soldiers, among them six Medal of Honor recipients, dishonorably discharged from the U.S. Army following a shooting incident in Brownsville, Texas, even though no indictments were ever brought against any of the soldiers. Although the men were retroactively pardoned in the 1970s, TR's harsh ruling denied all of them pensions. Roosevelt did appoint men of color to lower-level government posts, but after his presidency confessed that he saw no way to achieve full racial equality in America.
47. Thompson, *Presidents I've Known*, 112.
48. Ibid., 112, 119.
49. Essary, *Covering Washington*, 88. Essary made the comments in 1927, comparing TR to Taft, Wilson, Harding, and Coolidge. See also Barry, *Forty Years in Washington*, 271.
50. Isaac F. Marcosson, *Adventures in Interviewing* (New York: Dodd, Mead, 1919), 87–88.
51. William Allen White, *Masks in a Pageant* (New York: Macmillan, 1930), 307.
52. Henry Cabot Lodge, introduction to *Addresses and Presidential Messages of Theodore Roosevelt, 1902–1904* (New York: G. P. Putnam's Sons, 1904), vii; Marcosson, *Adventures in Interviewing*, 85.
53. Steffens, *Autobiography*, 508.
54. Thompson, *Presidents I've Known*, 118–19.
55. Barry, *Forty Years in Washington*, 271.
56. Quoted in George Juergens, "Theodore Roosevelt and the Press," *Daedalus* 111 (Fall 1982): 113; see also William L. Rivers, *The Adversaries: Politics and the Press* (Boston: Beacon Press, 1970), 18.
57. Essary, *Forty Years*, 94–95.

58. Davis, *Released for Publication*, 60–63.
59. *New York Times*, December 16, 1908.
60. Quoted in *Editor and Publisher*, May 8, 1919. Karger later served as chief of publicity officer for the 1912 Republican National Committee—in the race against Roosevelt's comeback presidential campaign.
61. Steffens, *Autobiography*, 505.
62. White, *Masks in a Pageant*, 284–85.
63. John T. McCutcheon, "Roosevelt as Cartoon Material," *New York Evening Post*, March 13, 1901.
64. *The Roosevelts*, 108. The author is indebted to Geoffrey Ward for directing him to these stories.
65. William Henry Harbaugh, *Power and Responsibility: The Life and Times of Theodore Roosevelt* (New York: Farrar, Straus and Cudahy, 1961), 355.
66. Marcosson, *Adventures in Interviewing*, 87.
67. Quoted in David Greenberg, "How Teddy Roosevelt Invented Spin," *Atlantic*, January 24, 2016.
68. "The British Press and Roosevelt," *Syracuse* (NY) *Post-Standard*, November 14, 1904.
69. Essary, *Forty Years*, 95.
70. Theodore Roosevelt, "The Nature Fakers," *Everybody's Magazine* 17 (October 1907): 428, 429.
71. Maurice Garland Fulton, ed., *Roosevelt's Writings: Selections from the Writings of Theodore Roosevelt* (New York: Macmillan, 1920), 177–78.
72. Ibid., 181–82.
73. Ibid., 187.
74. Thompson, *Presidents I've Known*, 160. Thompson claimed he and other reporters at the dinner urged TR to publish his off-the-record address, which the president promptly did.
75. Steffens, *Autobiography*, 581–82; Goodwin, *Bully Pulpit*, 480–87.
76. Theodore Roosevelt, "The Man with the Muck-Rake," *Putnam's New Monthly Magazine* 1 (October 1906): 47.
77. Thompson, *Presidents I've Known*, 122–23.
78. Barry, *Forty Years in Washington*, 270.
79. Davis, *Released for Publication*, 113, 121.
80. Ibid., 121.
81. Ibid., 121–22.
82. Ibid., 128. Lincoln had also seen reporters, and posed for artists, while attending to his correspondence; from reading so many Lincoln biographies, TR must have known this.
83. Ibid., *Released for Publication*, 123–24.
84. Ibid.
85. Tillman remarks before the U.S. Senate, January 17, 1906, *Congressional Record*, 59th Congress, 1st Session, vol. 40, part 2, p. 1181.
86. *New York Times*, December 16, 1908.
87. TR to William D. Foulke, December 1, 1908, quoted in James McGrath Morris, *Pulitzer: A Life in Politics, Print, and Power* (New York: Harper, 2010), 420.
88. Quoted in Ronald G. Shafer, "A newspaper accused the president's family of profiting from a foreign deal. The president sued," *Washington Post*, October 15, 2019.
89. The best book on the subject is Geoffrey Cowan, *Let the People Rule: Theodore Roosevelt and the Birth of the Presidential Primary* (New York: W. W. Norton, 2016).
90. *New York Times*, August 3, 1912.
91. Pollard, *Presidents and the Press*, 589.
92. Theodore Roosevelt, "A Disagreeable Duty," *The Outlook* (June 1913): 316–18.
93. Thompson, *Presidents I've Known*, 129–30, 143.
94. Ibid., 120–21.

95. Ibid., 145–46.
96. *New York Times*, October 15, 1912.
97. Dan Abrams and David Fisher, *Theodore Roosevelt for the Defense: The Courtroom Battle to Save His Legacy* (New York: Hanover Square Press, 2019), 19.
98. Ibid., 130–37.
99. Theodore Roosevelt, *Outlook Editorials* (New York: Outlook Publishing, 1909), 1–2.
100. "Almanac of Theodore Roosevelt," http://www.theodore-roosevelt.com/treditorials.html.
101. Davis, *Forty Years*, 137–39.

Chapter Seven: Woodrow Wilson

1. Isaac F. Marcosson, *Adventures in Interviewing* (New York: John Lane, 1919), 85.
2. Ibid., 79–80, 85. Long associated with the *Saturday Evening Post*, Marcosson was by the dawn of the Wilson-era editor of the popular mass market magazine *Munsey's*.
3. Ray Stannard Baker, *American Chronicle: The Autobiography of Ray Stannard Baker* (New York: Charles Scribner's Sons, 1945), 438.
4. J. Frederick Essary, *Covering Washington: Government Reflected to the Public in the Press, 1822–1926* (Boston: Houghton Mifflin, 1927), 47.
5. David Lawrence of the Associated Press quoted in James E. Pollard, *The Presidents and the Press* (New York: Macmillan, 1947), 615.
6. Marcosson, *Adventures in Interviewing*, 84.
7. Ibid., 87.
8. Charles Willis Thompson, *Presidents I've Known and Two Near Presidents* (Indianapolis: Bobbs-Merrill, 1929), 297.
9. Address to the New York Press Club, September 9, 1912, *Papers of Woodrow Wilson*, 69 vols., ed. Arthur S. Link (Princeton, NJ: Princeton University Press, 1966–94), 25:118 (hereinafter cited as *Wilson Papers*).
10. In fact, reporters acknowledged almost enviously that, among his prodigious skills, Wilson was adept at both shorthand and the typewriter, often spending hours pounding out reflections on his "machine" rather than floating policy ideas among journalists. See Marcosson, *Adventures in Interviewing*, 81, 87.
11. Essary, *Covering Washington*, 99; Thompson, *Presidents I've Known*, 253–54.
12. Speech to the National Press Club, March 20, 1914, *Wilson Papers*, 29:365.
13. Ibid.
14. Thompson, *Presidents I've Known*, 295–96.
15. Eleanor Wilson McAdoo, *The Woodrow Wilsons* (New York: Macmillan, 1937), 168.
16. Esssary, *Covering Washington*, 99.
17. Wilson to Robert Bridges, August 25, 1882, quoted in James D. Startt, *Woodrow Wilson and the Press: Prelude to the Presidency* (New York: Palgrave Macmillan, 2004), 7.
18. Speech of April 26, 1906, *Wilson Papers*, 16:375.
19. The standard autobiography is George Brinton McClellan Harvey, *Women, Etc.: Some Leaves from an Editor's Diary* (New York: Harper & Bros., 1908).
20. *Philadelphia Record*, October 30, 1910, in Startt, *Woodrow Wilson and the Press*, 75.
21. Ray Stannard Baker, *American Chronicle: The Autobiography of Ray Stannard Baker* (New York: Scribner's, 1945), 271–72.
22. *New York Age*, October 20, 1910.
23. W. Dale Nelson, *Who Speaks for the President: The White House Press Secretary from Cleveland to Clinton* (Syracuse, NY: Syracuse University Press, 1998), 27. Tumulty would always address Wilson as "Governor," as if to emphasize their longtime bond.
24. *New York Times*, April 9, 1954, obituary.
25. Speech to the National Press Club, January 31, 1911, *Wilson Papers*, 22:396, 398.

26. Wilson to Josephus Daniels, June 5, June 11, 1912, *Wilson Papers*, 24:461, 471.
27. Address to the New York Press Club, September 9, 1912, *Wilson Papers*, 25:118.
28. Villard was also the grandson of Henry Villard, the reporter who in 1860–61 had covered President-elect Abraham Lincoln in Springfield, Illinois, for the *New York Herald*.
29. Wilson to Oswald Garrison Villard, August 23, 1912, *Wilson Papers*, 24:53.
30. *New York Age*, July 11, 1912.
31. Baltimore *Afro-American*, July 13, August 12, 1912, in Patricia O'Toole, *The Moralist: Woodrow Wilson and the World He Made* (New York: Simon & Schuster, 2018), 56.
32. Arthur S. Link, *Wilson: The Road to the White House*, orig. pub. 1947 (Princeton, NJ: Princeton University Press, 1965), 499.
33. Quoted in Startt, *Woodrow Wilson and the Press*, 187.
34. Quoted in Thompson, *Presidents I've Known*, 168.
35. Josephus Daniels, *The Wilson Era: Years of Peace, 1910–1917* (Chapel Hill: University of North Carolina Press, 1944), 71.
36. Wilson to Mary Allen Hulbert Peck, August 25, 1912, *Wilson Papers*, 25:55–56.
37. Ibid., 56.
38. "Origins of the Political Ad: Woodrow Wilson's 1912 Campaign Film," *PBS NewsHour*, August 28, 2012, https://www.pbs.org/newshour/politics/origins-of-the-political-ad-woodrow-wilsons-1912-campaign-film. The film itself, produced by Universal Film Manufacturing, can be viewed on www.youtube.com/watch?v=jwevrmowCSZ4.
39. Thompson, *Presidents I've Known*, 292, 294.
40. *Owensboro* (KY) *Messenger*, February 25, 1912, quoted in Startt, *Woodrow Wilson and the Press*, xi.
41. *New York Times*, March 16, 1913.
42. Ibid.
43. Edward G. Lowry, *Washington Close-ups: Intimate Views of Some Public Figures* (Boston: Houghton Mifflin, 1921), 19. No written record was made of the first press conference, but subsequent sessions were transcribed.
44. James Kerney, *The Political Education of Woodrow Wilson* (New York: Century, 1926), 345.
45. Joseph P. Tumulty, *Woodrow Wilson as I Know Him* (New York: Doubleday, Page, 1921), 139.
46. Transcript of press conference, March 22, 1913, *Wilson Papers*, 50:3.
47. Ibid.
48. For a longer discussion, see O'Toole, *The Moralist*, 72.
49. Ibid., 3–5.
50. A. Scott Berg, *Wilson* (New York: G. P. Putnam's Sons, 2013), 291.
51. Robert C. Hilderbrand, introductory essay to *Wilson Papers*, 50:vii.
52. Remarks to the National Press Club, March 20, 1914, *Wilson Papers*, 50:363.
53. Press conference, April 21, 1913, ibid., 27:341.
54. Press conference, April 18, 1913, ibid., 27:323.
55. Press conference transcripts, October 16, 1913, ibid., 27:365.
56. Press conference transcript, July 13, 1914, ibid., 30:280. In a more serious vein, Wilson denied that he already had "certain persons in mind." As he told reporters, the late Justice Horace Harmon Lurton, a Confederate veteran, had been "an old friend of my father's." Out of respect, he had no intention of "going very fast in the matter." Not for five more weeks did he nominate James Clark McReynolds.
57. Ray Stannard Baker, memorandum of a conversation with the president, [May 12, 1916], *Wilson Papers*, 37:36.
58. R. V. Oulahan to Joseph Tumulty, July 22, 1913, ibid., 50:x.
59. Press conference transcripts, April 28, 1913, ibid., 27:359; January 18, April 23, June 25, 1914, 29:138, 154; 30:209.

60. Press conference transcript, December 15, 1914, ibid., 31:463.
61. Barry, *Forty Years in Washington*, 309.
62. Press conference transcripts, November 17, 1913, *Wilson Papers*, 27:559; February 26, 1914, 29:291; January 5, 1915, 32:14.
63. Wilson to Oswald Garrison Villard, April 14, 1914, *Wilson Papers*, 29:499.
64. Lincoln Steffens, *The Autobiography of Lincoln Steffens* (New York: Harcourt, Brace, 1931), 736. In defiance of such warnings, Wilson abandoned his "watchful waiting" policy and launched a 1914 military expedition to capture Pancho Villa. See John A. Britton, *Revolution and Ideology: Images of the Mexican Revolution in the United States* (Frankfort: University Press of Kentucky, 1995); for "watchful waiting," see Tumulty, *Woodrow Wilson*, 146–47.
65. *Princeton Alumni Weekly* to Wilson, June 21, 1915, *Wilson Papers*, 33:432–33.
66. Baker, *American Chronicle*, 277.
67. Press conference transcript, September 21, 1914, *Wilson Papers*, 31:63.
68. Press conference transcript, August 17, 1864, ibid., 30:387–88.
69. Wilson to Charles W. Eliot (president of Harvard), June 1, 1914, quoted in Pollard, *Presidents and the Press*, 640.
70. Transcript of press conference, March 19, 1914, *Wilson Papers*, 29:353–54.
71. Ibid.
72. Thompson, *Presidents I've Known*, 170.
73. Ibid., 273–74.
74. Edith Bolling Wilson, *My Memoir* (Indianapolis: Bobbs-Merrill, 1937), 132; Walter Millis, *Road to War—America, 1914–1917* (Boston: Houghton Mifflin, 1935), 430. Among the other publications whose editors received letters or invitations for interviews were the *St. Louis Post-Dispatch*, the *Washington Post*, and the *Springfield* (MA) *Republican*.
75. Oswald Garrison Villard to Wilson, October 30, 1915, *Wilson Papers*, 35:142; see also Villard, "Question of Preparedness," *New York Evening Post*, October 23, 29, 30, November 3, 6, 10, 13, 17, 1915.
76. Remarks at the Princeton Class of '79 Reunion, June 13, 1914, *Wilson Papers*, 30:178.
77. See, for example, Gordon J. Davis, "What Woodrow Wilson Cost My Grandfather," *New York Times* op-ed, November 24, 2015. Davis wrote of his ancestor, who endured demotion and a salary cut at the Government Printing Office: "John Davis, a self-made black man of acknowledged stature in his community by the turn of the 20th century, was, by the end of Wilson's first term, a broken man." See also Eric Yellin, *Racism in the Nation's Service: Government Workers and the Color Line in Woodrow Wilson's America* (Chapel Hill: University of North Carolina Press, 2013).
78. Oswald Garrison Villard to Wilson, August 27, 1913, *Wilson Papers*, 28:240.
79. Oswald Garrison Villard to Wilson, July 21, 1913, August 27, 1913, ibid., 28:60, 240.
80. For a dramatic account of this meeting, see O'Toole, *The Moralist*, 78–80; *Wilson Papers*, 27:442; 28:60–61, 65, 163–65, 202; 239–40. See also Oswald Garrison Villard, "Woodrow Wilson and the Negro," *The Crisis* 45 (December 1938): 384–85.
81. Villard, "Woodrow Wilson and the Negro," 384; Oswald Garrison Villard, *Fighting Years: Memoirs of a Liberal Editor* (New York: Harcourt, Brace, 1939), 240–41.
82. Moorfield Storey, W. E. B. Dubois, and other NAACP officials to Wilson, [August 15, 1913], *Wilson Papers*, 28:164.
83. For a transcript of the November 12, 1914, meeting, see *Wilson Papers*, 31:301–6.
84. Remarks to the Associated Press, New York, April 20, 1915, ibid., 33:40.
85. Ibid., 37:324–28, 332–36, 560–61.
86. Herbert Bayard Swope to Wilson, July 3, 1916, ibid., 37:352.
87. Tumulty, *Woodrow Wilson*, 217, 220, 223.
88. Press conference transcript, January 15, 1917, *Wilson Papers*, 50:767–69.

89. Executive Order no. 2594 identified the committee's members as the secretaries of state, war, and the navy. Press release, April 14, 1917, ibid., 42:59. See also the pamphlet version: George Creel, *Preliminary Statement to the Press of the United States* (Washington, DC: U.S. Government Printing Office, 1917), which began by quoting Wilson: "I can imagine no greater disservice to the country than to establish a system of censorship that would deny to the people of a free Republic like ours the indisputable right to criticize their own public officials" (1).
90. Arthur Ponsonby (Baron of Shulbrede), *Falsehood in War-Time: Containing an Assortment of Lies Circulated Throughout the Nations During the Great War* (New York: E. P. Dutton, 1928), 182.
91. George Creel, *Rebel at Large: Recollections of Fifty Crowded Years* (New York: G. P. Putnam's Sons, 1947), 3–4.
92. See Larry Tye, *The Father of Spin: Edward L. Bernays and the Birth of Public Relations* (New York: Crown, 1998).
93. Alan Axelrod, *Selling the Great War: The Making of American Propaganda* (New York: Palgrave Macmillan, 2009), 44–45.
94. George Creel to Josephus Daniels, March 19, 1917, quoted in Stewart Halsey Ross, *Propaganda for War: How the United States Was Conditioned to Fight the Great War of 1914–1918*, orig. pub. 1996 (Joshua Tree, CA: Progressive Press, 2009), 218; *New York Times* quoted ibid., 223.
95. *San Francisco Examiner*, May 1, 1917; *Washington Post*, May 7, 1917; *New York Times*, May 23, 1917.
96. *New York Times*, May 15, May 23, 1917; Axelrod, *Selling the Great War*, 72–73.
97. George Creel, *How We Advertised America* (New York: Harper & Bros., 1920), 16–18. In reviewing this book, Walter Lippmann condemned its "excruciating title"; see David Greenberg, *Republic of Spin: An Inside History of the American Presidency* (New York: W. W. Norton, 2016), 116.
98. Even the Adams-era Sedition Law limited penalties to five years' imprisonment. See James R. Mock and Cedric Larson, *Words That Won the War: The Story of the Committee on Public Information, 1917–1919* (Princeton, NJ: Princeton University Press, 1939), 42.
99. *Santa Cruz Evening News*, July 5, 1917.
100. Reprinted in the *Catholic Tribune* (St. Joseph, Missouri), April 28, 1917.
101. Mock and Larson, *Words That Won the War*, 66.
102. Creel, *Rebel at Large*, 160; Creel, *How We Advertised America*, 19.
103. Creel, *How We Advertised America*, 72–73; memorandum of April 1917, *Wilson Papers*, 42:39–41.
104. Creel, *Preliminary Statement to the Press*, 11–12.
105. Damon Runyon's report was in the *New York American*, October 13, 1918; see A. Scott Berg, ed., *World War I and America Told by the Americans Who Lived It* (New York: Library of America, 2017), 607–12.
106. Walton Rawls, *Wake Up, America! World War I and the American Poster* (New York: Abbeville Press, 1988), 13, 140–141.
107. Axelrod, *Selling the Great War*, 124–25; Creel, *How We Advertised America*, 7. Millions of Americans went to the movies each week to see stars like Charles Chaplin, who released eight new films in 1917 and 1918, including the World War I comedy *Shoulder Arms*.
108. These efforts are well chronicled in Axelrod, *Selling the Great War*, 90–92; Mock and Larson, *Words That Won the War*, 155.
109. Creel, *How We Advertised America*, 10, 12.
110. Edward Bernays, *Crystallizing Public Opinion*, orig. pub. 1923 (New York: IG Publishing, 2011), 200. His actual quote was the reverse: he defined education first, propaganda second.
111. Rawls, *Wake Up, America!*, 137.

112. See, for example, Creel's address to the North Carolina Press Association, August 1918, in Stephen Vaughn, "First Amendment Liberties and the Committee on Public Information," *American Journal of Legal History* 23 (April 1979): 109, 113.
113. Ronald Steel, *Walter Lippmann and the American Century* (Boston: Little, Brown, 1980), 125–26.
114. Wilson to George Creel, December 29, 1917, *Wilson Papers*, 45:387.
115. Ibid., 45:141–42.
116. Wilson to George Creel, June 18, 1918, *Wilson Papers*, 48:346.
117. Creel, *How We Advertised America*, 401–2.
118. Ibid., 4.
119. Marcosson, *Adventures in Interviewing*, 85.
120. Wilson to Edward House, December 17, 1918, quoted in Baker, *American Chronicle*, 374.
121. O'Toole, *The Moralist*, 344.
122. Creel, *How We Advertised America*, 175, 413.
123. William Allen White, *Woodrow Wilson: The Man, His Times and His Task* (Boston: Houghton Mifflin, 1925), 391, 394–96.
124. Ibid., 387.
125. Quoted in O'Toole, *The Moralist*, 472.
126. Tumulty, *Woodrow Wilson*, 410.
127. Essary, *Covering Washington*, 48; Dr. Cary T. Grayson's health bulletin of October 13, 1919, *Wilson Papers*, 63:569.
128. Essary, *Covering Washington*, 50.
129. Dr. Cary Grayson's health bulletin of October 13, 1919, *Wilson Papers*, 63:569.
130. Essary, *Covering Washington*, 49; O'Toole, *The Moralist*, 428.
131. Essary, *Covering Washington*, 100–101.
132. *New York Tribune*, November 20, 1919.
133. Baker, *American Chronicle*, 204. Baker would spend the next decade and more writing laudatory studies of the Wilson administration.
134. Baker diary entry, February 3, 1920, *Wilson Papers*, 64:360.
135. O'Toole, *The Moralist*, 460–61; *New York World*, June 18, 1920; *Wilson Papers*, 65:415–20. Siebold actually conducted two interviews on two successive days.
136. Notes drafted circa January 21, 1924, *Wilson Papers*, 68:541.
137. Tumulty, *Woodrow Wilson*, ix.
138. Quoted in Berg, *Wilson*, 720.
139. Baker, *American Chronicle*, 486, 496–98.
140. Ibid., 492.
141. Letter to the *Washington Post* (unsent), circa April 15, 1922; to Frank I. Cobb, December 15, 1922, *Wilson Papers*, 68:24, 234.
142. *New York Times*, June 10, 1923; *Wilson Papers*, 68:377.
143. Recorded November 10, 1923, https://www.youtube.com/watch?v=By5nvzsidXO.
144. Ray Stannard Baker to Wilson, November 23, 1923, *Wilson Papers*, 68:482.
145. Wilson to Ray Stannard Baker, December 1, 1923, ibid., 494.
146. Ray Stannard Baker, quoted in O'Toole, *The Moralist*, 478.
147. Lawrence, *True Story of Woodrow Wilson*, 340.
148. Remarks to the National Press Club, March 20, 1914, *Wilson Papers*, 29:362.

Chapter Eight: Franklin D. Roosevelt—I

1. The Sixty-Fifth Street townhouse was a 1908 Christmas present to Franklin and Eleanor from his mother, Sara. The gift came at a price, even if it was not monetary: FDR and his family would live in the eastern half of the six-story building, and his mother, on the western

side—with only interior doors and retractable walls separating the two residences. The house, which FDR sold to Hunter College in 1942, is now the school's Roosevelt House Public Policy Institute.

2. A photograph taken at the scene soon after Roosevelt finished broadcasting, then filming, his statement showed the president-elect seated before the fireplace, surrounded by James, daughter Anna, and mother Sara Delano Roosevelt (original in the collection of the Roosevelt House Public Policy Institute, Hunter College).
3. Franklin D. Roosevelt to Woodrow Wilson, March 31, 1914; Wilson to Roosevelt, April 1, 1914, *Papers of Woodrow Wilson*, 69 vols., ed. Arthur S. Link (Princeton, NJ: Princeton University Press, 1966–94), 29:390, 392.
4. The standard biographies are Lela Stiles, *The Man Behind Roosevelt: The Story of Louis McHenry Howe* (Cleveland: World Publishing, 1954), and Julie M. Fenster, *FDR's Shadow: Louis Howe, the Force That Shaped Franklin and Eleanor Roosevelt* (New York: St. Martin's Griffin, 2009).
5. Elliott Roosevelt and James Brough, *An Untold Story: The Roosevelts of Hyde Park* (New York: G. P. Putnam's Sons, 1973), 258.
6. Arthur Krock, *Memoirs: Sixty Years on the Firing Line* (New York: Funk & Wagnalls, 1968), 154.
7. Speech at Jackson Day dinner, January 7, 1939, Samuel Rosenman, ed., *The Public Papers and Addresses of Franklin D. Roosevelt*, 13 vols. (New York: Random House, Macmillan, Harper & Bros., 1938–50), 8:66 (hereinafter cited as *FDR Papers*).
8. Eleanor Roosevelt, *Autobiography of Eleanor Roosevelt* (New York: Harper & Bros., 1958), 102.
9. "Roosevelt Puts Economic Recovery First in His Acceptance Speech at Convention," *New York Times*, July 3, 1932.
10. Hugh Gregory Gallagher, *FDR's Splendid Deception: The Moving Story of Roosevelt's Massive Disability—and the Intense Efforts to Conceal It from the Public*), 3rd ed. (St. Petersburg, FL: Vandamere Press, 1999), 94.
11. Roosevelt expert and Roosevelt House board member William vanden Heuvel told me, on July 29, 2019, that he had heard this story directly from his onetime boss General William D. "Wild Bill" Donovan, who was a member of Hoover's "Medicine Ball" group.
12. Gallagher, *FDR's Splendid Deception*, 84–85; Geoffrey C. Ward and Ken Burns, *The Roosevelts: An Intimate History* (New York: Alfred A. Knopf, 2014), 276; Earle Looker, "Is Franklin D. Roosevelt Physically Fit to Be President?," *Liberty Magazine* (July 25, 1931): 6–10.
13. Quoted in Gallagher, *FDR's Splendid Deception*, 94.
14. Stephen T. Early quoted in Theo Lipman Jr., *The Squire of Warm Springs: FDR in Georgia, 1924–1945* (Chicago: Playboy Press, 1977), 183. Louis Howe had colorfully warned that, should the public learn of FDR's paralysis, his career would be "kaput." See Stiles, *The Man Behind Roosevelt*, 75–76.
15. Richard Lee Strout, "The President and the Press," in Katie Louchheim, ed. *The Making of the New Deal: The Insiders Speak Out* (Cambridge, MA: Harvard University Press, 1983), 14.
16. Gallagher, *FDR's Splendid Deception*, 93, 101–5. For exceptions to the ban, see "Is FDR Physically Fit to Be President?," *Liberty Magazine*; and a two-part FDR profile in the *New Yorker*, June 16, 23, 1934. For a well-researched argument that the ban has been overstated, see Matthew Pressman, "Ambivalent Accomplices: How the Press Handled FDR's Disability and How FDR Handled the Press," *Journal of the Historical Society* 13 (September 2013): 325–59.
17. John Gunther, *Roosevelt in Retrospect: A Profile in History* (New York: Harper & Bros., 1950), 239.
18. For nearly thirty years, the unpublished original glass plate languished in deep storage. It first appeared in print in Richard Harrity and Ralph G. Martin, *The Human Side of FDR: A Pictorial Biography* (New York: Duell, Sloan and Pearce, 1960), 152. In 2016, editors of the

News discovered the original glass plate in the paper's morgue. To mark his retirement from the paper, *News* editor Arthur Browne had the photo printed in an extra-large format and donated it to Roosevelt House, where it now hangs in the vestibule.

19. Lipman, *Squire of Warm Springs*, 183.
20. Richard Strout, "President's Contact with the Reporters Is Limited While on Campaign Trail," *Editor and Publisher* (October 24, 1936): 5, 40.
21. Carl Mydans's photograph in *Life* magazine, June 15, 1937; Ward and Burns, *The Roosevelts*, 332–33.
22. Dave Reynolds, "Disability Activist Hugh G. Gallagher Dies," *Inclusion Daily Express* (International Disability Rights News Service), July 15, 2004; Gallagher, *FDR's Splendid Deception*, xiv.
23. Merriman A. Smith, *Thank You, Mr. President: A White House Notebook* (New York: Harper & Bros., 1946), 64.
24. Lipman, *Squire of Warm Springs*, 184–85.
25. Quoted in Pressman, "Ambivalent Accomplices," 338.
26. The broadcast and filmed versions differ slightly from the typescript preserved in *Franklin D. Roosevelt—"The Great Communicator": The Master Speech Files, 1898–1945*, Series 1: Franklin D. Roosevelt's Political Ascension, File no. 594a, November 9, 1932, Radio Address of President-Elect Roosevelt from New York, Franklin D. Roosevelt Presidential Library and Museum. See also the text published the next day (November 10, 1932) on the front page of the *New York Times*.
27. *Payment Deferred* stars Charles Laughton as a man so desperate for money he commits murder. *I Am a Fugitive* features Paul Muni as a convict condemned to hard labor under a brutally archaic criminal justice system. Both films opened in November 1932.
28. *New York Times*, November 10, 1933.
29. Frances Perkins, *The Roosevelt I Knew* (orig. pub. 1946, New York: Penguin Books, 2011), 143; Frances Perkins Oral History, 1955, Columbia University, OH 569, http://www.columbia.edu/cu/web/digital/collections/nny/perkinsf/index.html.
30. See, for example, William E. Berchtold, "Press Agents of the New Deal," *New Outlook* (July 1934): 23; and Leo Rosten, "President Roosevelt and the Washington Correspondents," *Public Opinion Quarterly* 1 (January 1937): 41.
31. Lipman, *Squire of Warm Springs*, 178.
32. New York *Daily News*, March 14, 1933; Lipman, *Squire of Warm Springs*, 179–81.
33. New York *Daily News*, March 4, 1933.
34. "Crippled Children Aid Roosevelt Pool," New York *Daily News*, March 19, 1933; Lipman, *Squire of Warm Springs*, 180. Howe thought the pool project "inexpedient"; see Linda Lotridge Levin, *The Making of FDR: The Story of Stephen T. Early, America's First Modern Press Secretary*, orig. pub. 1963 (Amherst, NY: Prometheus Books, 2008), 115.
35. June 15, 1934, *FDR Papers*, 3:329–30.
36. Arthur M. Schlesinger Jr., *The Coming of the New Deal*, vol. 2, *The Age of Roosevelt* (Boston: Houghton Mifflin, 1958), 566.
37. Geoff Manning, "'New Deal' for Press Begins at Once," *Editor and Publisher* (March 11, 1933): 3–4; Richard A. Stokes, "The White House Press Conference: One of Many 'New Deal' Phenomena," *St. Louis Post-Dispatch*, March 7, 1937.
38. Theodore G. Joslin, "President Meets the Press: White House More Important News Center Today Than Ever Before—Vital News Comes from Conferences," *Washington Sunday Star*, March 4, 1934. FDR enjoyed this account so much he had it reprinted in his published papers. See *FDR Papers*, 2:41.
39. Ibid. Estimates for the attendance at FDR's press conferences range from 125 to 200. For one such count, see Samuel Brandt (of the *St. Louis Post-Dispatch*), "The President's Press Conference," *Sunday Graphic* 28 (July 1939): 446.

40. Ibid.; Richard L. Strout (*Christian Science Monitor*), quoted in John Tebbel and Sarah Miles Watts, *The Press and the Presidency from George Washington to Ronald Reagan* (New York: Oxford University Press, 1985), 439.
41. Rosten, "President Roosevelt and the Washington Correspondents," 38; Charles Hurd, *When the New Deal Was Young and Gay: F.D.R. and His Circle* (New York: Hawthorn Books, 1965), 232.
42. Both quotes from the *Chicago Tribune*, March 9, 1933.
43. This and subsequent press conference cites are from "Press Conferences of President Franklin D. Roosevelt (1933–1945)," original typescripts at the Franklin D. Roosevelt Presidential Library and Museum, www.fdrlibrary.marist.edu/archives/collections/franklin/?p=collections/findingaid&id=508.
44. *Chicago Tribune*, March 9, 1933. By other accounts, sons John and Franklin visited the historic session, too, and Eleanor arrived before it got underway to whisper something into her husband's ear.
45. As a United Press correspondent, Early had first met Roosevelt at the 1912 Democratic National Convention in Baltimore. Later, he covered the Navy Department for the AP when FDR served as assistant secretary. Early's papers are in the Franklin D. Roosevelt Presidential Library. James Roosevelt quoted in Levin, *Making of FDR*, 15.
46. FDR memo to Stephen T. Early, June 2, 1942, *FDR Letters*, 2:1327–28.
47. Quoted in Kenneth S. Davis, *FDR: The New Deal Years, 1933–1937—a History* (New York: Random House, 1986), 15.
48. Rosten, "President Roosevelt and the Washington Correspondents," 39.
49. Quoted in ibid.
50. Quoted in Tebbel and Watts, *Press and the Presidency*, 441; Raymond Clapper, "Why Reporters Like Roosevelt," *Review of Reviews* 89 (June 1934): 15. Clapper later joined the staff of the *Washington Post*.
51. For useful biographical sketches, see Berchtold, "Press Agents of the New Deal," 26.
52. Ibid.
53. See E. Pendleton Herring, "Official Publicity Under the New Deal," *Annals of the American Academy of Political Science* 179 (May 1935): 167–75.
54. Gordon Carroll, "Dr. Roosevelt's Propaganda Trust," *American Mercury* 42 (September 1937): 1–31.
55. Herring, "Official Publicity Under the New Deal," 168.
56. Berchtold, "Press Agents of the New Deal," 23.
57. *Los Angeles Times*, September 10, 1937.
58. Kenneth S. Davis, *Invincible Summer: An Intimate Portrait of the Roosevelts Based on the Recollections of Marion Dickerman* (New York: Atheneum, 1974), 132.
59. Clapper, "Why Reporters Like Roosevelt," 15–16.
60. Hurd, *New Deal*, 240.
61. *Atlanta Constitution*, March 14, 1938.
62. Hurd, *New Deal*, 243.
63. Ibid., 241–42.
64. Krock, *Memoirs*, 182–83.
65. Davis, *Invincible Summer*, 131.
66. *Racine* (WI) *Journal-Times*, November 8, 1934.
67. *Decatur* (IL) *Daily Review*, May 9, 1933. See also, "Child Cripples Give Their Friend Roosevelt Help," New York *Daily News*, March 19, 1935.
68. Press conference, June 2, 1944.
69. Press conference, March 10, 1933.
70. Ibid.
71. Hurd, *New Deal*, 234.

72. Ibid., 2, 14–15.
73. Quoted in David Greenberg, *Republic of Spin: An Inside History of the American Presidency* (New York: W. W. Norton, 2016), 193.
74. The administration so scheduled the sessions to give morning papers an advantage at the afternoon sessions, and afternoon papers an opportunity for exclusives at morning sessions.
75. Rosten, "President Roosevelt and the Washington Correspondents," 37.
76. Ashmun Brown, "The Roosevelt Myth," *American Mercury* 148 (April 1936): 390.
77. Press conferences, March 17, 1933, July 17, August 21, 1935.
78. Raymond P. Brandt, "The President's Press Conference," *Survey Graphic* 28 (July 1939): 449.
79. Smith, *Thank You, Mr. President*, 22.
80. San Francisco Press Club Bulletin (*Scoop*), quoted in Graham J. White, *FDR and the Press* (Chicago: University of Chicago Press, 1979), 6.
81. Press conference, July 17, 1935.
82. Press conference, March 17, 1933.
83. Press conference, August 11, 1935.
84. Press conference, July 29, 1936.
85. Press conference, February 18, 1944.
86. Stephen T. Early diary, April 24, 1935, quoted in Betty Houchin Winfield, *FDR and the News Media* (New York: Columbia University Press, 1994), 30.
87. Press conference, March 14, 1944.
88. Hurd, *New Deal*, 231.
89. Rosten, "President Roosevelt and the Washington Correspondents," 38.
90. Press conference, October 11, 1933.
91. Press conference, March 5, 1933. Introduced by protectionist congressman Nelson Dingley Jr. of Maine in the first year of the McKinley administration, the 1897 bill hiked tariffs on many imported goods.
92. Press conference, December 22, 1936.
93. Press conference, March 5, 1933.
94. Press conference, June 29, 1937.
95. Hurd, *New Deal*, 227.
96. Winfield, *FDR and the News Media*, 82, 154. Ironically, the Washington correspondent for the London *Times* had compared the rite at FDR's news conferences to "the British practice of 'question periods' in the House of Commons." See Hurd, *New Deal*, 230.
97. Press conferences, January 25, February 5, 1938.
98. Press conferences, September 4, September 11, 1934, February 5, 1937; Pollard, *Presidents and the Press*, 793, 779.
99. Press conference, September 14, 1937; Clapper, "Why Reporters Like Roosevelt," 16.
100. *Atlanta Constitution*, March 14, 1938.
101. Samuel Rosenman, *Working with Roosevelt* (New York: Harper & Row, 1952), 468–69.
102. Hurd, *New Deal*, 237.
103. Quoted by Raymond Clapper in the *Columbus Citizen*, March 8, 1938. Broun ran as a Socialist in 1930. A veteran journalist who had worked for several newspapers over the years, he became a radio celebrity as well.
104. Joslin quoted in the *Washington Star*, March 4, 1934.
105. Eugene A. Levy, "Distorting the News," *American Mercury* 34 (March 1935): 310–13; Edwin L. James quoted in Hurd, *New Deal*, 11.
106. Davis, *Invincible Summer*, 131–32; *New York Times*, February 4, 1936.
107. Author interview with William vanden Heuvel, July 29, 2019.
108. One magazine profile ranked Clapper as "one of America's ablest and most-respected journalists." See *Life* (March 13, 1944): 34.

109. James Roosevelt with Bill Libby, *My Parents: A Differing View (*Chicago: Playboy Press, 1976), 193. Drew Pearson had previously been married to the daughter of the anti-Roosevelt publisher "Cissy" Patterson, who fired and commenced attacking him in print after their divorce.
110. John Tebbel, *An American Dynasty: The Story of the McCormicks, Medills and Pattersons* (New York: Doubleday, 1947), 157–80.
111. James Roosevelt, *My Parents*, 191.
112. Quoted in Thomas J. Johnson, Wayne Wanta, John T. Byrd, and Cindy Lee, "Exploring FDR's Relationship with the Press: A Historical Agenda-Setting Study," *Political Communications* 12 (1995): 159; James Roosevelt, *My Parents*, 190.
113. Stephen T. Early, "Below the Belt," *Saturday Evening Post* (June 10, 1939): 110.
114. Ibid., 110–11.
115. Elliott Roosevelt, *My Parents*, 189.
116. Ibid.
117. Hurd, *New Deal*, 233–34, 239.
118. Hedley Donovan, *Roosevelt to Reagan: A Reporter's Encounters with Nine Presidents* (New York: Harper & Row, 1985), 18–19.

Chapter Nine: Franklin D. Roosevelt—II

1. Nancy J. Weiss, *Farewell to the Party of Lincoln: Black Politics in the Age of FDR* (Princeton, NJ: Princeton University Press, 1983), 158.
2. To get Social Security passed, for example, the Roosevelt administration had to agree to exclude domestic workers and other job categories mostly filled by African Americans. The Civilian Conservation Corps remained segregated, and the National Recovery Act (NRA) authorized lower pay scales for blacks. For a statistical analysis of black newspaper support for FDR, see George W. Bain, "How Negro Editors Viewed the New Deal," *Journalism Quarterly* 44 (Autumn 1967): 552–54.
3. *New York Age*, November 2, 1940.
4. Grace Tully, *F.D.R., My Boss* (Chicago: Peoples Book Club, 1949), 152–53.
5. Earlier, Bethune had visited FDR's Manhattan home for a visit with the president's mother, Sara, as documented in a surviving photograph in the Roosevelt House Collection, Hunter College.
6. Donald A. Ritchie, *Reporting from Washington: The History of the Washington Press Corps* (New York: Oxford University Press, 2005), 32–33. Today the White House Correspondents' Association awards an annual scholarship named for McAlpin. See Scott Horsley, "Pioneering Black Newsman in the White House Belatedly Gets His Due," transcript of NPR broadcast, April 10, 2014.
7. *Sydney* (Australia) *Morning Herald*, May 29, 1944.
8. "Negro Reporters Charge Bias in Press Seatings," *Pittsburgh Courier*, July 20, 1944.
9. Genevieve Forbes Herrick reported this incident in the *Chicago Tribune*, September 10, 1933.
10. Richard Lowitt and Maurine Beasley, eds., *One Third of a Nation: Lorena Hickok Reports on the Great Depression* (Urbana: University of Illinois Press, 1983), xxix. See also Doris Kearns Goodwin, *No Ordinary Time: Franklin and Eleanor Roosevelt—the Home Front in World War II* (New York: Simon & Schuster, 1994), 26–27. For more on Eleanor's relationship to Lorena Hickok, see Blanche Wiesen Cook, *Eleanor Roosevelt: The War Years and After* (New York: Viking, 2016), 6–8.
11. *Chicago Tribune*, March 10, 1933.
12. Further defying tradition, the First Lady took five women journalists on a March 1934 tour to inspect economic conditions in Puerto Rico and the U.S. Virgin Islands: Lorena Hickok,

Ruby Black of the UPI, Emma Bugbee of the *New York Herald Tribune*, Dorothy Ducas of the International News Service, and Bess Furman of the AP. See Lowitt and Beasley, *One Third of a Nation*, xxxiv.

13. Quoted in Jill Lepore's introduction to Eleanor Roosevelt, *It's Up to the Women*, orig. pub. 1933 (New York: Nation Books, 2017), xii.
14. For the scripts, see Stephen Drury Smith, *The First Lady of Radio: Eleanor Roosevelt's Historic Broadcasts* (New York: New Press, 2014); for the September 4, 1934, broadcast, 42–50. Mrs. Roosevelt said she believed women "could stand the physical strain" but needed more "background in public life" before competing for the nation's highest office. "I do not think that we have yet reached the point," she declared, "where the majority of our people would feel satisfied to follow the leadership and trust the judgment of a woman as president" (48–49).
15. David Witwen, "Who Was Westbrook Pegler: The Original Right-Wing Takedown Artist," *Humanities* 33 (March–April 1932), 8.
16. Smith, *First Lady of Radio*, 10.
17. Raymond Moley, "Heaven or Bust: Five Years of Roosevelt—and After," *Saturday Evening Post* (August 19, 1937): 37.
18. Raymond Moley with Elliot A. Rosen, *After Seven Years* (New York: Harper & Bros., 1939), 337.
19. Quoted in Richard W. Steele, "News of the 'Good War': World War II News Management," *Journalism Quarterly* 62 (Winter 1985): 715; *Newsweek*, September 13, 1943, 79; Oliver Pilat, *Drew Pearson: An Unauthorized Biography* (New York: Harper's Magazine Press, 1973), 173.
20. Quoted in Jean Edward Smith, *FDR* (New York: Random House, 2007), 310.
21. FDR to Stephen Early, September 27, 1937, *F.D.R., His Personal Letters, 1928–1945*, 2 vols., ed. Elliott Roosevelt and Joseph Lash (New York: Duell, Sloan & Pearce, 1950): 2:713 (hereinafter cited as *FDR Letters*).
22. "Press Conferences of President Franklin D. Roosevelt (1933–1945)," Franklin D. Roosevelt Presidential Library and Museum, www.fdrlibrary.marist.edu/archives/collections/franklin/?p=collections/findingaid&id=508; press conference, May 31, 1935.
23. James E. Pollard, *The Presidents and the Press* (New York: Macmillan, 1947), 797.
24. Special press conference for journalism school faculty, December 27, 1935, *FDR Papers*, 4:510, 512.
25. Stephen E. Early memorandum to FDR, September 3, 1937, *FDR Letters*, 1:710–11.
26. A. Merriman Smith, *Merriman Smith's Book of Presidents: A White House Memoir*, ed. Timothy G. Smith (New York: W. W. Norton, 1972), 240.
27. Richard A. Stokes, "The White House Press Conference: One of Many 'New Deal' Phenomena," *St. Louis Post-Dispatch*, March 7, 1937.
28. Leo Rosten, "President Roosevelt and the Washington Correspondents," *Public Opinion Quarterly* 1 (January 1937): 41.
29. *Des Moines Register*, December 31, 1937.
30. Press conference, April 21, 1938; transcript in *FDR Papers*, 7:278, 280, 282.
31. Roosevelt to Thomas D. Schall, Schall to Roosevelt, August 24, 1934; Roosevelt to Schall, [August 25, 1934], *FDR Papers*, 3:384–89. Roosevelt's published papers headlined this heated correspondence as "An Episode of a Type Fortunately Rare."
32. Press conference, December 29, 1936; *New York Times*, December 20, 1944.
33. Merriman A. Smith, *Thank You, Mr. President: A White House Notebook* (New York: Harper & Bros., 1946), 46. For a chronological list of FDR's international trips (including Canada), see Departmental History, Office of the Historian, U.S. Department of State, http://history.state.gov/departmenthistory/travels/president/roosevelt-franklin-d.
34. Quoted in Steven Lomazow and Eric Fettmann, *FDR's Deadly Secret* (New York: Public Affairs, 2009), 61.

35. H. L. Mencken, *Prejudices: Sixth Series* (New York: Alfred A. Knopf, 1927), 14–15, 27; George Wolfskill and John A. Hudson, *All but the People: Franklin D. Roosevelt and His Critics, 1933–39* (New York: Macmillan, 1969), 173.
36. The original is in the collection of the FDR Presidential Library at Hyde Park.
37. "The Light of Democracy Must Be Kept Burning," address before the White House Correspondents' Association, March 15, 1941, *FDR Papers*, 10:60–61.
38. Press conference, December 9, 1941.
39. Press conference, June 6, 1944.
40. Michael G. Carew, *The Power to Persuade: FDR, the Newsmagazines, and Going to War, 1939–1941* (Lanham, MD: University Press of America, 2005), 85.
41. For an excellent survey, see "The Great Debate: Roosevelt, the Media, and the Coming of War, 1940–1941," *Journal of American History* 71 (June 1984): 69–92.
42. Quoted in Richard W. Steele, *Propaganda in an Open Society: The Roosevelt Administration and the Media, 1933–1941* (New York: Praeger, 1985), 108.
43. See Byron Price, *Report on the Office of Censorship* (Washington, DC: U.S. Government Printing Office, 1945); Michael W. Sweeney, *Secrets of Victory: The Office of Censorship and the American Press and Radio in World War II* (Chapel Hill: University of North Carolina Press); Robert J. Hanyok, review of Secrets of Victory, by Michael W. Sweeney, "Intelligence in Recent Public Literature," *Studies in Intelligence* 46 (2002), https://www.cia.gov/library/center-for-the-study-of-intelligence/csi-publications/csi-studies/studies/vol46no3/article10.html.
44. Quoted in Otis L. Graham Jr. and Meghan Robinson Wander, *Franklin D. Roosevelt: His Life and Times—an Encyclopedic View* (Boston: G. K. Hall, 1985), 299. See also *A Report on the Office of Censorship* (Washington, DC: U.S. Government Printing Office, 1945); Byron Price, "The Censor Defends the Censorship," *New York Times Magazine*, February 11, 1945; Byron Price, "Government Censorship in War-Time," *American Political Science Review* 36 (1942): 837–49.
45. Quoted in Allan Winkler, *The Politics of Propaganda: The Office of War Information, 1942–1945* (New Haven, CT: Yale University Press, 1978), 34.
46. The best book is Mark Harris, *Five Came Back: A Story of Hollywood and the Second World War* (New York: Penguin, 2014).
47. Victor Packard, *America's Battle for Media Democracy: The Triumph of Corporate Libertarianism and the Future of Media Reform* (New York: Cambridge University Press, 2014), 144, 146–150.
48. Press conference, December 9, 1941.
49. Press conference, February 21, 1941.
50. *New York Times*, January 24, 1944.
51. Jonathan Daniels to Marvin McIntyre, September 3, 1943, quoted in Steele, "News of the 'Good War,'" *Journalism Quarterly* 62 (Winter 1985): 716.
52. Roy Hoopes, *Ralph Ingersoll* (New York: Atheneum, 1985), 191–92, 260.
53. FDR to Margaret Suckley from the S.S. *Augusta*, August 5, 1941, in Geoffrey C. Ward, ed., *Closest Companion: The Unknown Story of the Intimate Friendship Between Franklin Roosevelt and Margaret Suckley* (New York: Houghton Mifflin Harcourt, 1995), 140; Elliott Roosevelt, *As He Saw It* (New York: Duell, Sloan and Pearce, 1946), 20.
54. David Brinkley, "An Age Less Than Golden: Roosevelt vs. the Wartime Press," *Washington Journalism Review* 10 (June 1988): 44.
55. Ibid.
56. *FDR Papers*, 1:334–38, 521–31, 544–49.
57. Brinkley, "An Age Less Than Golden," 42.
58. *New York Times*, January 5, 1935, quoted in Ashmun Brown, "The Roosevelt Myth," *American Mercury*, 390–94.
59. "Radio's Audience: Huge, Unprecedented," *New York Times*, April 3, 1932.

60. Statistics from Carole E. Scott, "The History of the Radio Industry in the United States to 1940," https://eh.net.encyclopedia/the-history-of-the-radio-industry-in-the-united-states-to-1940/. Among the most useful general sources are Lawrence Wilson Lichty and Malachi C. Topping, *American Broadcasting: A Source Book on the History of Radio and Television* (New York: Hastings House, 1975); and Robert J. Brown, *Manipulating the Ether: The Power of Broadcast Radio in Thirties America* (Jefferson, NC: McFarland, 1998).
61. Waldo W. Braden and Earnest Brandenburg, "Roosevelt's Fireside Chats," *Speech Monographs* (November 1955): 292.
62. Samuel Rosenman, *Working with Roosevelt* (New York: Harper & Bros., 1952), 93.
63. Ibid.
64. Russell D. Buhite and David W. Levy, eds., *FDR's Fireside Chats* (Norman: University of Oklahoma Press, 1992), 12.
65. John Gunther, *Roosevelt in Retrospect: A Profile in History* (New York: Harper & Bros., 1950), 278.
66. Richard Lee Strout, "The President and the Press," in Katie Louchheim, ed., *The Making of the New Deal: The Insiders Speak* (Cambridge, MA: Harvard University Press, 1983), 13.
67. *Chicago Tribune*, June 17, 1934.
68. "Refuses Free Radio Time for 'Fireside Chats,'" *Chicago Tribune*, September 11, 1936; "FDR Banned," *New York World Telegram & The Sun*, September 11, 1936.
69. Lorena Hickok to Harry Hopkins, April 8, 1934, in Lowitt and Beasley, eds., *One Third of a Nation*, 215.
70. Quoted in Geoffrey C. Ward and Ken Burns, *The Roosevelts: An Intimate History* (New York: Alfred A. Knopf, 2014), 331.
71. Frances Perkins, *The Roosevelt I Knew*, orig. pub. 1946 (New York: Penguin Books, 1971), 70.
72. Saul Bellow, "In the Days of Mr. Roosevelt," *Esquire*, December 1983, https://classic.esquire.com/article/1983/12/1/in-the-days-of-mr-roosevelt.
73. Broadcast of December 29, 1940, *FDR's Fireside Chats*, 172.
74. Broadcast of February 23, 1942, ibid., 207; Graham and Wander, *Franklin D. Roosevelt: His Life and Times*, 137.
75. Broadcast of January 11, 1944, *FDR's Fireside Chats*, 292–93.
76. Broadcast of June 5, 1944, ibid., 295, 299.
77. Radio address, June 6, 1944, *FDR Papers, 1944–1945 volume* 152–53; original handwritten manuscript in the FDR Presidential Library, Hyde Park. For painstaking authorship of the prayer, see Nigel Hamilton, *War and Peace: FDR's Final Odyssey—D Day to Yalta, 1943–1945* (New York: Houghton Mifflin Harcourt, 2019).
78. Richard J. Lyons, quoted in the *Chicago Tribune*, October 28, 1938.
79. Charles Michelson, *The Ghost Talks* (New York: G. P. Putnam's Sons, 1944), 56–57.
80. Rosenman, introduction to *FDR Papers*, 10:ix.
81. Rosenman, *Working with Roosevelt*, 5–6.
82. Ibid., 82.
83. Perkins, *The Roosevelt I Knew*, 70.
84. *FDR's Fireside Chats*, 314–15.
85. Smith, *Thank You, Mr. President*, 25.
86. Ibid., 26.
87. Turner Catledge, *My Life and "The Times"* (New York: Harper & Row, 1971), 144.
88. A modern physician has argued that FDR was further wracked by terminal metastatic cancer. See Lomazow and Fettman, *FDR's Deadly Secret*, esp. 63–76.
89. *Franklin D. Roosevelt Day by Day*, July 20, 1944, www.fdrlibrary.marist.edu/daybyday/daylog/july-20th-1944/; photograph in Ward and Burns, *The Roosevelts*.
90. David M. Jordan, *FDR, Dewey, and the Election of 1944* (Bloomington: Indiana University Press, 2011), 267–68.

91. Arthur Krock, *Memoirs: Sixty Years on the Firing Line* (New York: Funk & Wagnalls, 1968), 219.
92. Press conference, February 19, 1945. FDR held another shipboard session four days later.
93. Press and radio conference, March 2, 1945.
94. Press and radio conference, April 5, 1945.
95. Ibid. For a dramatic account, see David B. Woolner, *The Last 100 Days: FDR at War and at Peace* (New York: Basic Books, 2017), 257–58.
96. Smith, *Merriman Smith's Book of Presidents*, 202. For a moving account of FDR's last hours, see Joseph Lelyveld, *His Final Battle: The Last Months of Franklin Roosevelt* (New York: Alfred A. Knopf, 2016).
97. *Chicago Tribune*, October 21, 1933. As early as 1858, the paper's editors had urged Lincoln to emphasize his humble origins and inspiring climb to success—his "trials, disadvantages, &c &c"—rather than his potentially controversial policy positions; see Joseph Medill to Abraham Lincoln, June 23, 1858, and Ray, Medill & Co. to Lincoln, June 29, 1858, Abraham Lincoln Papers, Library of Congress.
98. Smith, *Thank You, Mr. President*, 63.

Chapter Ten: John F. Kennedy

1. Raymond P. Brandt, "The President's Press Conference," *Sunday Graphic*, July 1939, 446.
2. A. Merriman Smith, *Thank You, Mr. President: A White House Notebook* (New York: Harper & Bros., 1946), 221.
3. Quoted in W. Dale Nelson, *Who Speaks for the President* (Syracuse, NY: Syracuse University Press, 1998), 104.
4. Kenneth W. Thompson, ed., *Ten Presidents and the Press* (Lanham, MD: University Press of America, 1983), 46.
5. *Washington Post*, December 6, 1950.
6. Quoted in the *New York Times* obituary for Paul Hume, November 28, 2001.
7. Quoted in the *Washington Post* obituary for Paul Hume, November 28, 2001.
8. C-SPAN video archive at https://www.c-span.org/video/?c4480322/president-eisenhowers-press-conference.
9. Robert H. Ferrell, *The Diary of James C. Haggerty: Eisenhower in Mid-Course, 1954–1955* (Bloomington: Indiana University Press, 1983), 169.
10. Martha Joynt Kumar, "Presidential Press Conferences," lecture at State Department conference "The Kennedy White House and the Press," May 16, 2011, https://www.whitehousehistory.org/presidential-press-conferences. Pathé produced a highlights film for motion picture theaters.
11. See Mark Shanahan, "Pursuing the Parallel Track," in Andrew J. Polsky, ed., *The Eisenhower Presidency: Lessons for the Twenty-First Century* (Lanham, MD: Lexington Books, 2015), 101–7.
12. William Jennings Bryan was only thirty-six when he ran for president in 1896.
13. Robert Dallek, *An Unfinished Life: John F. Kennedy, 1917–1963* (Boston: Little, Brown, 2003), 104.
14. John F. Kennedy, *Profiles in Courage: Decisive Moments in the Lives of Celebrated Americans* (New York: Harper & Row, 1956). Historian Herbert Parmet later deduced that additional writing had been done by Georgetown University history professor Jules Davids. See Wills, *The Kennedy Imprisonment: A Meditation on Power* (Boston: Little, Brown, 1982), 135–36.
15. Arthur Krock, *Memoirs: Sixty Years on the Firing Line* (New York: Funk & Wagnalls, 1968), 375.

16. Eleanor Roosevelt quoted in Robert Dallek, *Camelot's Court: Inside the Kennedy White House* (New York: HarperCollins, 2013), 15. For a lengthy and persuasive analysis of authorship claims, see Wills, *The Kennedy Imprisonment*, 134–36.
17. Ted Sorensen, *Counselor: A Life at the Edge of History* (New York: Harper, 2008), 150.
18. Ibid., 113, 146–47.
19. Krock, *Memoirs*, 355.
20. Herbert Parmet, *Jack: The Struggles of John F. Kennedy* (New York: Dial Press, 1980), 439.
21. Drew Pearson interview with Joe B. Frantz, April 10, 1969, Lyndon Baines Johnson Library Oral History Collection, LBJ Library, Austin, Texas, 8.
22. Bob Schieffer, "John F. Kennedy: Our First Television President," CBS News post on JFK's 100th birthday, May 29, 2017, https://www.cbsnews.com/news/john-f-kennedy-our-first-television-president/.
23. Douglas Brinkley, *American Moonshot: John F. Kennedy and the Great Space Race* (New York: HarperCollins, 2019), 285.
24. Video interview with Imero Fiorentino, n.d., Television Academy Foundation archives, https://interviews.televisionacademy.com/topics/kennedy-nixon-debates.
25. Ted Sorensen, Kennedy (New York: Harper & Row, 1965), 199.
26. Howard K. Smith, video interview for the Television Academy, ibid.
27. Richard M. Nixon, *RN: The Memoirs of Richard Nixon*, 2 vols., orig. pub. 1978 (New York: Warner Paperbacks, 1979), 1:271.
28. Sorensen comment at the *New York Times* headquarters, January 9, 2009. I am grateful to my onetime Mario Cuomo administration colleague Ethan Riegelhaupt, then a *Times* executive, for organizing and including me in that event and for recalling its exact date ten years later.
29. James E. Pollard, *Presidents and the Press: Truman to Johnson* (Washington, DC: Public Affairs Press, 1964), 97.
30. Pierre Salinger, *With Kennedy* (Garden City, NY: Doubleday, 1966), 56.
31. Reston quoted in Jo Ransom, "Pressmen Growl at JFK's Plan," *Radio-TV Daily*, January 17, 1961, 1; Brandt quoted in "'Live' Press Conferences Stir Pro and Con Views," *Editor and Publisher* 7 (January 1961): 9.
32. Sorensen, *Kennedy*, 324.
33. For a good description of these preparations, see David Greenberg, *Republic of Spin: An Inside History of the American Presidency* (New York: W. W. Norton, 2016), 342.
34. JFK news conference #1, January 25, 1961, transcript, *John F. Kennedy: Press Conferences*, John F. Kennedy Presidential Library, http://www.jfklibrary.org/archives/other-resources/john-f-kennedy-press-conferences (hereinafter cited as "JFK news conference").
35. Ibid.
36. Shapiro quoted in "The Kennedy Press Conference: Always Good for a Laugh," New England Historical Society, www.newenglandhistoricalsociety.com/president-john-f-kennedy-gets-laugh-another-another.
37. *New York Times*, January 26, 1961; Greenberg, *Republic of Spin*, 343.
38. Mary Ann Watson, "How Kennedy Invented Political Television: The 35th president's introduction of the televised press conference and his use of the medium during the Cuban Missile Crisis shifted power closer to the White House," *Television Quarterly* 26 (Spring 1991): 62.
39. A. Merriman Smith, "Newsmen Miss Repartee in TV Press Conference," UPI report in the *Columbia Missourian*, January 26, 1961; John Crosby, "The Press Conferences Make Skimpy Repasts," reprinted in the *Washington Post*, May 1, 1961; Donovan quoted in "J.F.K. and the Conference," *Time*, March 24, 1961, all impressively unearthed, assembled, and cited (along with Lisagor) in David R. Davies, "An Industry in Transition: Major Trends in American

Daily Newspapers, 1945–1965," chapter 8, "Kennedy and the Press, 1960–1963" (Ph.D. dissertation, University of Alabama, 1997), http://ocean.otr.usm.edu/~w304644/ch8.html.

40. "The Skill of President Kennedy," *Los Angeles Times*, February 3, 1961, quoted in Brinkley, *American Moonshot*, 288.
41. JFK news conference #2, February 1, 1961.
42. Quoted in Sorensen, *Kennedy*, 324.
43. JFK news conference #15, August 10, 1961.
44. JFK news conference #19, November 29, 1961.
45. Douglas Brinkley, *Cronkite* (New York: HarperCollins, 2012), 229–231.
46. Sorensen, *Kennedy*, 323.
47. JFK news conference #18, November 8, 1961.
48. Helen Thomas, *Front Row at the White House: My Life and Times (*New York: Scribner, 1999), 301.
49. Arthur Schlesinger Jr., *A Thousand Days: John F. Kennedy in the White House* (Boston: Houghton Mifflin, 1965), 261.
50. JFK news conference #10, April 21, 1961.
51. Thomas W. Benson, *Writing JFK: Presidential Rhetoric and the Press in the Bay of Pigs Crisis* (College Station: Texas A&M University Press, 2004), 10.
52. Turner Catledge, *My Life and "The Times"* (New York: Harper & Row, 1971), 264.
53. Salinger, *With Kennedy*, 146.
54. This and additional quotes from "The President and the Press: Address Before the American Newspaper Publishers Association, Waldorf-Astoria Hotel, New York City, April 27, 1961," transcript online from the JFK Library, https://www.jfklibrary.org/archives/other-resources/john-f-kennedy-speeches/american-newspaper-publishers-association-19610427.
55. Schlesinger, *A Thousand Days*, 296.
56. James Reston, "False 'News' from Officials in Cuban Crisis," *New York Times*, May 10, 1961.
57. Sorensen, *Kennedy*, 326.
58. JFK news conference #22, January 31, 1962.
59. JFK news conference #18, November 8, 1961.
60. Elizabeth (May) Craig, recorded interview by Ronald J. Grele, June 2, 1966, John F. Kennedy Library Oral History Program, 15.
61. JFK news conference #19, November 19, 1961.
62. JFK news conference #58, July 17, 1963. For background, see James D. Walsh, "Reaching Mrs. Murphy: A Call for Repeal of the Mrs. Murphy Exemption to the Fair Housing Act," *Harvard Civil Rights–Civil Liberties Law Review* 34 (June 1999): 605–34. For a scholarly appraisal, see Donald C. Lord, "JFK and Civil Rights," *Presidential Studies Quarterly* 8 (Spring 1978): 151–63.
63. "Yes, Sarah McClendon he always hated," said JFK's press office aide Jill Cowan. Recorded interview by William vanden Heuvel, March 16, 1995, John F. Kennedy Library Oral History Program, 5. Cowan and her colleague Priscilla Wear were known as "Fiddle" and "Faddle." Journalist Todd S. Purdham referred to McClendon as "klaxon-voiced" in her obituary in the *New York Times*, January 9, 2003.
64. Godfrey Hodgson, McClendon obituary in the *Guardian*, January 16, 2003. See also Jacob Weisberg, "The White House Beast," *Esquire*, September 1993, https://www.vanityfair.com/magazine/1993/09/presscorps199309.
65. Both the McClendon-Kennedy exchange and Kennedy's admission are from Sorensen, *Kennedy*, 326.
66. Sarah McClendon, *My Eight Presidents* (New York: Wyden Books, 1978), 50.
67. Thomas, *Front Row at the White House*, 57, 58, 301.

68. Sorensen, *Kennedy*, 324.
69. Ibid., 324–25.
70. JFK news conference #46, December 12, 1962.
71. Address before the American Newspaper Publishers Association, April 27, 1961.
72. Salinger, *With Kennedy*, 122.
73. Ibid., 111.
74. Sorensen, *Kennedy*, 312.
75. Salinger, *With Kennedy*, 83.
76. As Jacqueline Bouvier, Mrs. Kennedy had been the "Inquiring Camera Girl" for the *Washington Times-Herald* from fall 1951 to June 1953.
77. Laura Bergquist, "The President and His Son," *Look* 27 (December 3, 1963); Salinger, *With Kennedy*, 119. After Kennedy's death, the *Look* team published a book featuring many of these photographs. See Laura Bergquist and Stanley Tretick, *A Very Special President* (New York: McGraw-Hill, 1975).
78. Sorensen, *Kennedy*, 325.
79. Salinger, *With Kennedy*, 118.
80. Sorensen, *Kennedy*, 316.
81. Salinger, *With Kennedy*, 118–20.
82. Sorensen, *Kennedy*, 311.
83. Schlesinger, *A Thousand Days*, 716.
84. McClendon, *My Eight Presidents*, 50.
85. Pierre E. G. Salinger, recorded interview by Theodore H. White, July 19, 1965, John F. Kennedy Library Oral History Program, 43.
86. Charles Bartlett, recorded interview by Fred Holborn, January 6, 1965, John F. Kennedy Library Oral History Program, 19–21.
87. Sorensen, *Kennedy*, 447; Salinger, *With Kennedy*, 59–60.
88. Bill Lawrence, *Six Presidents, Too Many Wars* (New York: Saturday Review Press, 1972), 4–6, 243.
89. *New York Post*, November 4, 1962, quoted in Davies, "Kennedy and the Press."
90. Ben Bradlee, *Conversations with Kennedy* (New York: Bantam Books, 1976), 49.
91. Jeff Himmelman, *Yours in Truth: A Personal Portrait of Ben Bradlee* (New York: Random House, 2012), 306.
92. Dallek, C-SPAN interview, January 2, 2004, quoted in Brian Lamb and Susan Swain, eds., *The Presidents: Noted Historians Rank America's Best—and Worst—Chief Executives* (New York: PublicAffairs, 2019), 109.
93. Hedley Donovan, *Roosevelt to Reagan: A Reporter's Encounters with Nine Presidents* (New York: Harper & Row, 1985), 71.
94. Ibid., 71–72.
95. Ibid., 71.
96. Seymour Hersh, *The Dark Side of Camelot* (Boston: Little, Brown, 1997), 5–6.
97. Wills, *The Kennedy Imprisonment*, 28.
98. Ibid., 85. In addition to these, Wills named Sander Vanocur, Hayes Gorey, Henry Brandon, Theodore White, Anthony Lewis, Art Buchwald, Pete Hamill, Jack Newfield, Jeff Greenfield, and Roger Mudd.
99. Joseph Alsop, recorded interview by Elspeth Rostow, part 2, June 26, 1964, John F. Kennedy Library Oral History Project 86.
100. Sorensen, *Kennedy*, 311, 314.
101. Alsop, recorded interview, part 1, June 18, 1964, 47–48.
102. Quoted in Davies, "Kennedy and the Press."
103. Sorensen, *Kennedy*, 316–17.

104. Ibid., 317–18.
105. Dallek, *Camelot's Court*, 414, 529; on Baldwin, see also Timothy Naftali, Philip D. Zelikow, and Ernest R. May, eds., *The Presidential Recordings: John F. Kennedy—the Great Crises*, 2 vols. (New York: W. W. Norton, 2001), 2:186–201.
106. Salinger, *With Kennedy*, 129–30.
107. Bartlett, recorded interview, February 20, 1965, 2:162.
108. An excellent scholarly article on the subject is James T. Graham, "Kennedy, Cuba, and the Press," *Journalism History* 24 (1998), https://questia.com/library/journal/1P3-35022156/kennedy-cuba-and-the-press.
109. Quoted in *Sorensen*, Kennedy, 322.
110. Greenberg, *Republic of Spin*, 353–58.
111. Salinger, *With Kennedy*, 296; Graham, "Kennedy, Cuba, and the Press."
112. Salinger, *With Kennedy*, 285, 296.
113. Helen Thomas, *Dateline White House* (New York: Macmillan, 1975), 31.
114. Salinger, *With Kennedy*, 299.
115. Sorensen, *Kennedy*, 322.
116. JFK news conference #50, February 21, 1963. The transcript includes no notations for laughter; for evidence, audio version is on "JFK News Conferences," http://jfk-press-conferences.blogspot.com/2012/06/press-conference-50-february-21-1963.html.
117. Charles Bartlett, recorded interview by Fred Holborn, February 20, 1965, John F. Kennedy Library Oral History Program, 127–30.
118. Graham, "Kennedy, Cuba, and the Press."
119. Samuel L. Becker, "Presidential Power: The Influence of Broadcasting," *Quarterly Journal of Speech* 47 (February 1961): 18.
120. Jimmy Breslin, "Digging the Grave Was His Honor," *New York Herald Tribune*, November 26, 1963.
121. See, for example, "Americans Say Reagan Is the Greatest U.S. President," http://www.gallup.com/poll/146183/Americans-Say-Reagan-Greatest-President.aspx.
122. Lamb and Swain, *The Presidents*, ix–xii.

Chapter Eleven: Lyndon B. Johnson

1. Drew Pearson, interview (with Joe B. Frantz), April 10, 1969, Lyndon Baines Johnson Oral History Collection, LBJ Library, Austin, Texas, 2.
2. Ibid., 3–4. It was later widely conjectured that LBJ had stuffed enough ballots to win that contest, or at least wildly exceeded campaign spending limits to put himself in a position to contend for the seat.
3. Ibid., 4, 6.
4. Ibid., 18, 19, 20.
5. Robert W. Richards, "Where's Lyndon?," Copley News Service, July 24, 1962, quoted in Robert A. Caro, *The Years of Lyndon Johnson: Passage to Power* (New York: Alfred A. Knopf, 2012), 203.
6. Ibid., 176.
7. Sarah McClendon, *My Eight Presidents* (New York: Wyden Books, 1978), 156.
8. Chester R. Huntley interview, October 4, 1974, Lyndon Baines Johnson Oral History Collection, quoted in William C. Spragens, "The Myth of the Johnson 'Credibility Gap,'" *Presidential Studies Quarterly* 10 (Fall 1980): 629–30; Sidey quoting Johnson in Bradlee, *A Good Life*, 273–74.
9. See Robert Dallek, *Lyndon B. Johnson: Portrait of a President* (New York: Oxford University Press, 2004), 366; Clifford Durr quoted in Robert A. Caro, *The Years of Lyndon Johnson: Means of Ascent* (New York: Alfred A. Knopf, 1990), 91–100.

10. Robert A. Caro, *Working: Researching, Interviewing, Writing* (New York: Alfred A. Knopf, 2019), 129–36.
11. Quoted in David Greenberg, *Republic of Spin: An Inside Story of the American Presidency* (New York: W. W. Norton, 2016), 364.
12. Helen Thomas, *Front Row at the White House: My Life and Times* (New York: Scribner, 1999), 75.
13. Quoted in Merle Miller, *Lyndon: An Oral Biography* (New York: G. P. Putnam's Sons, 1980), 375.
14. Charles S. Bartlett interview, November 15, 1978, Lyndon Baines Johnson Oral History Collection, quoted in Spragens, "'Credibility Gap,'" 633.
15. Stewart Alsop interview, June 26, 1978, Lyndon Baines Johnson Library Oral History Collection, quoted in Spragens, "'Credibility Gap,'" 632.
16. Tom Wicker, "Receiving the Johnson Treatment," *New York Times*, May 9, 2012.
17. George E. Reedy, "The President and the Press: Struggle for Dominance," *Annals of the American Academy of Political and Social Science* 417 (September 1976): 70.
18. Quoted in "*American Presidents and the Press Conferences: Kennedy and Johnson*," http://reagan.convio.net/site/DocServer/Dec2011_Reagan_Moments-American_Presidents_and_Press_Con.pdf?docID=446.
19. January 3, 1964, dinner recounted in Kent B. Germany and Robert David Johnson, et al., eds., *The Presidential Recordings of Lyndon Johnson*, 6 vols. (New York: W. W. Norton, 2005–7), 3:124 (hereinafter cited as *Presidential Recordings*).
20. Rowland Evans and Robert Novak, *Lyndon B. Johnson: The Exercise of Power* (New York: New American Library, 1966), 412.
21. Caro, *Passage of Power*, 504, 516–17.
22. A. Merriman Smith, *Merriman Smith's Book of Presidents: A White House Memoir*, ed. Timothy G. Smith (New York: W. W. Norton, 1972), 188–89.
23. *Columbus* (OH) *Dispatch*, May 12, 1964, quoted in James E. Pollard, *The Presidents and the Press: Truman to Johnson* (Washington, DC: Public Affairs Press, 1964), 113.
24. Frank Cormier, *LBJ the Way He Was: A Personal Memoir of the Man and His Presidency* (New York: Doubleday, 1977), 113.
25. Quoted in Pollard, *Presidents and the Press*, 119.
26. Drew Pearson oral history interview, May 16, 1974, Lyndon Baines Johnson Oral History Project, quoted in Spragens, "'Credibility Gap,'" 632.
27. Hedley Donovan, *Roosevelt to Reagan: A Reporter's Encounters with Nine Presidents* (New York: Harper & Row, 1985), 90; for nickname, see Donovan obituary, *New York Times*, August 14, 1990.
28. Reedy, "President and the Press," 67.
29. Ben Bradlee quoted in Van Wynsberghe, "The Most Vulgar American President Ever? It Sure as #$@!%* Isn't Donald Trump," *National Post*, January 26, 2018, https://nationalpost.com/opinion/the-most-vulgar-american-president-ever-it-sure-as-isnt-donald-trump.
30. McGrory and Reedy quoted in George Reedy, interviews with Michael R. Gillette, December 20, 1983, Lyndon Baines Johnson Oral History Collection, 11:49–50.
31. Wicker, "Receiving the Johnson Treatment"; Robert David Johnson and David Shreve, eds., *Presidential Recordings of Lyndon Johnson*, 3:194.
32. Thomas, *Front Row at the White House*, 75, 307.
33. Ibid., 307.
34. For "dearie" reference, see the taped telephone conversation, November 29, 1963, *Presidential Recordings*, 1:351; for Annenberg as "partial," taped telephone conversation, December 31, 1963, *Presidential Recordings* 2:913. Annenberg later became U.S. ambassador to the Court of St. James's (the same post once held by Joseph Kennedy)—for Ronald Reagan, to whom he was indeed "partial."

35. Ronald Steel, *Walter Lippmann and the American Century* (Boston: Little, Brown, 1980), 544.
36. Ibid., 544–47.
37. Ibid., 548.
38. Richard Goodwin, *Remembering America: A Voice from the Sixties* (Boston: Little, Brown, 1988), 267–71; see also Goodwin obituary, *Washington Post*, May 21, 2018. It was said that Lippmann had cribbed his own title from an even earlier book called *Great Society*. See Walter Lippmann, *The Good Society* (Boston: Little, Brown, 1937), and Graham Wallas, *Great Society: A Psychological Analysis* (London: Macmillan, 1914). For an analysis of Lippmann's work, see Frank H. Knight, "Lippmann's Good Society," *Journal of Political Economy* 46 (December 1938): 864–72.
39. *Teaching American History*, https://teachingamericanhistory.org/library/document/great-society-speech/.
40. Rowland Evans and Robert Novak, *Lyndon B. Johnson: Exercise of Power* (London: George Allen & Unwin, 1967), 419–20.
41. Reedy, "President and the Press," 68.
42. Thomas, *Front Row at the White House*, 166.
43. Pierre Salinger, *With Kennedy* (New York: Doubleday, 1966), 331; Ted Sorensen, *Counselor: A Life on the Edge of History* (New York: Harper, 2008), 381.
44. George E. Reedy, *Lyndon B. Johnson: A Memoir* (New York: Andrews & McMeel, 1982), 157.
45. Cormier, *LBJ the Way He Was*, 237–38.
46. Peter Carlson, "LBJ Meets the Press," *American History Magazine*, April 2011, https://www.historynet.com/lbj-meets-the-press.htm.
47. Salinger, *With Kennedy*, 334, 335, 336.
48. Ibid., 339–40.
49. *Columbus Dispatch*, May 22, 1964, quoted in Pollard, *Presidents and the Press: Truman to Johnson*, 120.
50. Dallek, *Lyndon B. Johnson*, 228.
51. Joseph A. Califano Jr., *The Triumph and Tragedy of Lyndon Johnson: The White House Years; a Personal Memoir by President Johnson's Top Domestic Advisor* (New York: Touchstone, 1991), 163.
52. George Christian, *The President Steps Down: A Personal Memoir of the Transfer of Power* (New York: Macmillan, 1970), 7.
53. Ibid., 6.
54. Author interview with Joseph A. Califano Jr., July 10, 2019.
55. Califano, *Triumph and Tragedy*, 163; Christian, *President Steps Down*, 6.
56. Califano, *Triumph and Tragedy*, 163.
57. Ibid., 164.
58. Ibid.
59. Quoted in Miller, *Lyndon*, 375.
60. Thomas, *Front Row at the White House*, 307.
61. Reedy, "President and the Press," 68.
62. Today he may be best remembered as the inspiration for "Pierre Salinger syndrome"—the gullible tendency to believe everything one reads online—which assumed his name when, as an ABC News commentator, he embraced the false report that TWA Flight 800 had been shot over Long Island in 1996. Salinger permanently moved to France, home of his mother's family, after George W. Bush won the 2000 presidential election. There he became a commentator on American affairs for French television.
63. Salinger, *With Kennedy*, 357.
64. *Presidential Recordings*, 3:829–30.
65. Reedy, *Lyndon B. Johnson*, 131.
66. Reedy, "President and the Press," 65, 66.

67. Ibid.; Miller, *Lyndon*, 375; Cormier, *LBJ the Way He Was*, 13.
68. Reedy, "President and the Press," 68, 71; Cormier, *LBJ the Way He Was*, 90.
69. Reedy, *Lyndon B. Johnson*, 168.
70. Ibid., 142.
71. *New York Times*, Lyndon Johnson obituary, January 28, 1973.
72. Michael R. Beschloss, ed., *Taking Charge: The Johnson White House Tapes, 1963–1964* (New York: Simon & Schuster, 1997), 330.
73. Robert S. Allen interview, October 6, 1973, Lyndon Baines Johnson Oral History Collection, quoted in Spragens, "'Credibility Gap,'" 631.
74. McClendon, *My Eight Presidents*, 121; Bobby Baker, *Wheeling and Dealing: Confessions of a Capitol Hill Operative* (New York: W. W. Norton, 1978), 194–96.
75. Recorded telephone conversation with Walter Jenkins, George Reedy, Abe Fortas (with Bill Moyers and Jack Valenti in the Oval Office), January 27, 1964, *Presidential Recordings*, 3:896–909.
76. Theodore H. White, *The Making of the President—1964* (New York: Atheneum, 1965), 319.
77. Quoted in Donovan, *Roosevelt to Reagan*, 101.
78. Smith, *Merriman Smith's Book of Presidents*, 248.
79. Quoted in Charles Roberts, *LBJ's Inner Circle* (New York: Delacorte Press, 1965), 122.
80. Reedy, *Lyndon B. Johnson*, 138–39.
81. Ibid., 139.
82. Ibid.
83. Donovan, *Roosevelt to Reagan*, 99.
84. Ibid., 147.
85. Johnson conversation with Abe Fortas, April 30, 1965, in Michael Beschloss, ed., *Reaching for Glory: Lyndon Johnson's Secret White House Tapes, 1964–1965* (New York: Touchstone, 2001), 305.
86. Johnson phone conversation with George Reedy, May 2, 1965, ibid., 307.
87. Reedy, *Lyndon B. Johnson*, 141.
88. Charles Roberts, *LBJ's Inner Circle* (New York: Delacorte, 1965), 112; George Reedy interview, Lyndon Baines Johnson Oral History Collection, quoted in Joshua Zeitz, *Building the Great Society: Inside Lyndon Johnson's White House* (New York: Viking, 2018), 128.
89. Allen interview, quoted in Spragens, "'Credibility Gap,'" 631.
90. Reedy, *Lyndon B. Johnson*, 158.
91. McClendon, *My Eight Presidents*, 147.
92. George E. Reedy, The *Twilight of the Presidency*, orig. pub. 1970 (New York: New American Library, 1971), 103.
93. Cormier, *LBJ the Way He Was*, 114; Patrick Anderson, "No. 2 Texan in the White House," *New York Times*, April 3, 1966.
94. Christian, *President Steps Down*, 12.
95. Arthur Krock, "In the Nation: The Day LBJ Didn't Broadcast," *New York Times*, September 16, 1965.
96. Bill D. Moyers, "Another Opinion on the Credibility Gap" (adapted from a speech to the New York State Association of Newspaper Editors), *New York Times*, February 11, 1968.
97. Anderson, "No. 2 Texan in the White House."
98. Dallek, *Lyndon B. Johnson*, 228.
99. Allen interview, quoted in Spragens, "'Credibility Gap,'" 631.
100. Robert Dallek, *Flawed Giant: Lyndon B. Johnson and His Times, 1961–1973* (New York: Oxford University Press), 282.
101. For a good account of this development, see David Wise, *The Politics of Lying: Government Deception, Secrecy, and Power* (New York: Random House, 1973), especially 20–25.
102. Bill Lawrence, *Six Presidents: Too Many Wars* (New York: *Saturday Review Press*, 1972), 270.

103. William S. White oral history interview, Lyndon Baines Johnson Oral History Collection, August 6, 1994, quoted in Spragens, "'Credibility Gap,'" 633.
104. Califano, *Triumph and Tragedy*, 170.
105. Moyers, "Another Opinion on the Credibility Gap."
106. Telephone conversation with John Chancellor, March 31, 1965, in Beschloss, *Reaching for Glory*, 262. Henry H. Fowler replaced C. Douglas Dillon as treasury secretary on April 1, 1965, the day after this call.
107. Greenberg, *Republic of Spin*, 374–75.
108. Telephone conversation with Garnett D. "Jack" Horner, February 5, 1968, transcript, *Presidential Recordings Digital Edition*, ed. Kent B. Germany, Nicole Hemmer, Ken Hughes, et al., Miller Center, University of Virginia, https://prde.upress.virginia.edu/conversations/4005941.
109. Telephone conversation with Abe Fortas et al., January 27, 1964, *Presidential Recordings*, 3:905.
110. Reedy, *Lyndon Johnson*, 157; Dobbin quoted in Jeffrey L. Pasley, "Showing the Scars: Presidential Illness and the Press over the Centuries," http://pasleybrothers.com/jeff/writings/showing_the_scars.htm. Bill Moyers was press secretary when Johnson underwent this surgery.
111. Peter Dreier, "An Interview with Bill Moyers," May 8, 2014, https://billmoyers.com/2014/05/08/an-interview-with-bill-moyers/.
112. Allen interview, quoted in Spragens, "'Credibility Gap,'" 631.
113. George Christian obituary, *New York Times*, November 29, 2002. For an early look at LBJ's relationship with the media during this period, see Kathleen J. Turner, *Lyndon Johnson's Dual War: Vietnam and the Press* (Chicago: University of Chicago Press, 1985).
114. Steel, *Walter Lippmann*, 557, 559. The Church-Idaho dam comment has been cited (and paraphrased) in several reminiscences. For one variation, see Thomas, *Front Row at the White House*, 308.
115. Katharine Graham, *Personal History* (New York: Alfred A. Knopf, 1997), 400–401.
116. *New York Times*, November 18, 1967.
117. Tom Wicker, "In the Nation: Johnson on Television," *New York Times*, December 21, 1967.
118. Jack Gould, "Networks Split on Johnson Tape," *New York Times*, December 21, 1967.
119. Jack Gould, "LBJ: To Edit or Not to Edit," *New York Times*, December 31, 1967.
120. For an account on how the media covered the Tet Offensive, see Peter Braestrup, *The Big Story: How the American Press and Television Reported and Interpreted the Crisis of Tet 1968 in Vietnam and Washington* (New York: Anchor Books, 1978).
121. Cronkite editorial quoted in Oliver Lazarus, "50 Years Ago, Americans Finally Got a Look Across the Line of the Vietnam War," *The Take*away, January 9, 2017, http://www.pri.org/stories/2017-01-09/50-years-ago-americans-finally-got-look-across-line-vietnam-war. Among those who attest that Johnson uttered the famous line about Cronkite is Joseph A. Califano Jr. See Califano, *Our Damaged Democracy: We the People Must Act* (New York: Touchstone, 2018), 158.
122. Donovan, *Roosevelt to Reagan*, 103.
123. Lyndon Baines Johnson, *The Vantage Point: Perspectives of the Presidency, 1963–1969* (New York: Holt, Rinehart and Winston, 1971), 43.
124. Ibid., 104.
125. Chester Pach, "Lyndon Johnson's Living Room War," *New York Times*, May 30, 2017.
126. Email interview with Max Frankel, July 21, 2019.
127. Thomas, *Front Row at the White House*, 167–68.
128. "Editors Assert Administration Practices Deceit for Its Own Sake," *New York Times*, April 18, 1968.

129. "News Group Scores Record of Johnson," *New York Times*, November 20, 1968.
130. "Christian Denies He Lied to Press; But White House Aide Says He Withheld Some Data," *New York Times*, January 20, 1969.
131. Reedy, *Lyndon B. Johnson*, 153.
132. Johnson, Civil Rights Symposium Address, December 12, 1972, transcript and video online at *American Rhetoric Online Speech Bank*, www.americanrhetoric.com/speeches/lbjfinalspeech.htm.
133. Quoted in Van Wynsberghe, "The Most Vulgar American President Ever?"
134. Lawrence, *Six Presidents*, 268.
135. Reedy, *Lyndon B. Johnson*, 143.
136. Thomas, *Front Row at the White House*, 307; Donovan, *Roosevelt to Reagan*, 107.
137. Donovan, *Roosevelt to Reagan*, 107.

Chapter Twelve: Richard Nixon

1. Nixon lost to Kennedy nationwide in 1960 by just over 112,000 votes, and to incumbent California governor Edmund G. "Pat" Brown in 1962 by 297,000 votes.
2. Remarks by Richard Nixon, press conference, Los Angeles, November 7, 1962, https://cdn.nixonlibrary.org/01/wp-content/uploads/2017/07/24093803/1962-Last-Press-Conference.pdf.
3. Nixon named as persistently unfair critics, among others, the *Fresno Bee*, the *Sacramento Bee*, and out-of-town dailies like the *New York Post* and *Milwaukee Journal*.
4. Gladwin Hill, "Nixon Denounces Press as Biased," *New York Times*, November 8, 1962.
5. Katharine Graham, *Personal History* (New York: Alfred A. Knopf, 1997), 433.
6. The Nixon Library transcript says, "*won't* have Nixon to kick around anymore," as do many sources, but the surviving videotape clearly indicates that Nixon said, "you *don't*." Video online at www.youtube.com/watch?v=JA1edgjU5E.
7. *Howard K. Smith News and Comment*, ABC-TV, November 11, 1962. See also Howard K. Smith, *Events Leading Up to My Death: The Life of a Twentieth-Century Reporter* (New York: St. Martin's Press, 1996), 291; the transcript is in the Howard K. Smith Papers, Wisconsin Historical Society. Smith had shifted to ABC in 1962 after a long career with CBS.
8. Helen Thomas, *Front Row at the White House: My Life and Times* (New York: Scribner, 1999), 311.
9. Quoted in Helen Thomas, *Dateline White House: A Warm and Revealing Account of American Presidents and Their Families, from the Kennedys to the Fords* (New York: Macmillan, 1975), 145.
10. Quoted in Joseph C. Spear, *Presidents and the Press: The Nixon Legacy* (Cambridge, MA: MIT Press, 1984), 45.
11. Voorhis had his say about Nixon's "ruthless" campaign style (quote from the *New York Times* Voorhis obituary, September 12, 1984) in two books: *Confessions of a Congressman* (1947) and *The Strange Case of Richard Milhous Nixon* (1972).
12. *Washington Post*, August 5, 1948.
13. See Alger Hiss, *In the Court of Public Opinion* (New York: Harper Collins, 1957), and Hiss, *Recollections of a Life* (Boston: Little, Brown, 1988). A valuable recent study is Allen Weinstein, *Perjury: The Hiss-Chambers Case*, rev. ed. (New York: Alfred A. Knopf, 1988).
14. Richard Nixon, *My Six Crises* (New York: Doubleday, 1962), 70.
15. Evan Thomas, *Being Nixon: A Man Divided* (New York: Random House, 2015), 49, 55.
16. Transcript, November 7, 1962, press conference, Los Angeles.
17. The best recent biography of the actress-activist is Sally Denton, *The Pink Lady: The Many Lives of Helen Gahagan Douglas* (New York: Bloomsbury, 2009).

18. In California's then-reigning open-primary system, Boddy was able to run in both parties' primary elections. He finished a distant second in each, but along the way he created unforgettable attacks on both the candidates who defeated him: Republican Nixon and Democrat Douglas.
19. Richard Nixon, *RN: The Memoirs of Richard Nixon*, 2 vols. (New York: Warner Books, 1978), 1:114 (hereinafter cited as *RN*).
20. Katcher, a former *New York Post* city editor who had shot to fame by scoring a jailhouse interview with convicted Lindbergh baby kidnapper Bruno Hauptmann, would be nominated for a best-screenplay Oscar four years later for *The Eddy Duchin Story*. Later, Katcher worked on John Kennedy's 1960 presidential campaign—against Richard Nixon (*New York Times* obituary, March 2, 1991).
21. Jack Anderson with James Boyd, *Confessions of a Muckraker* (New York: Random House, 1979), 325–26. Anderson was Pearson's apprentice, partner, and eventual successor on the "Washington Merry-Go-Round" column.
22. *RN*, 1:116.
23. Roger Morris, *Richard Milhous Nixon: The Rise of an American Politician* (New York: Henry Holt, 1990), 808–52.
24. *Washington Post*, September 25, 1952; Morris, *Richard Milhous Nixon*, 854.
25. Morris, *Richard Milhous Nixon*, 762.
26. Quoted in John A. Farrell, *Richard Nixon: The Life* (New York: Doubleday, 2017), 205. See also Rogers obituary, *Los Angeles Times*, March 26, 2003.
27. Graham, *Personal History*, 223.
28. Bill Lawrence, *Six Presidents: Too Many Wars* (New York: Saturday Review Press, 1972), 236, 239.
29. Ben Bradlee, *A Good Life: Newspapering and Other Adventures* (New York: Simon & Schuster, 1995), 211.
30. Theodore H. White, *The Making of the President—1960*, orig. pub. 1961 (New York: Signet Books, 1977), 377.
31. Ibid., 338.
32. See Joe McGinnis, *The Selling of the President 1968* (New York: Trident/Simon & Schuster, 1969).
33. Jules Witcover, *The Resurrection of Richard Nixon* (New York: G. P. Putnam's Sons, 1970), 150–52.
34. Timothy Crouse, *The Boys on the Bus* (New York: Random House, 1973), 183.
35. John A. Farrell, "Nixon's Vietnam Treachery," *New York Times*, December 31, 2016. Anna Chennault, the GOP "doyenne" who served as a conduit from the Nixon campaign to Saigon, apparently warned the South Vietnamese government that LBJ was attempting to sell them out. The proof that the Nixon campaign tried to scuttle peace talks was eventually unearthed in Nixon aide H. R. Haldeman's long-suppressed private notes.
36. Herbert G. Klein, *Making It Perfectly Clear: An Inside Account of Nixon's Love-Hate Relationship with the Media* (Garden City, NY: Doubleday, 1980), 39–40.
37. Peter Goldman, "Inside the Nixon White House," *Newsweek* (January 21, 1974): 24.
38. Paul *Boller, Presidential Campaigns* (New York: Oxford University Press, 1984), 324; Klein, *Making It Perfectly Clear*, 160–61, 166.
39. Klein, *Making It Perfectly* Clear, 166.
40. Jules Witcover, *Very Strange Bedfellows: The Short and Unhappy Marriage of Richard Nixon and Spiro Agnew (*New York: PublicAffairs, 2007), 47–49.
41. Thomas, *Front Row at the White House*, 313; Graham, *Personal History*, 434.
42. Transcript of Buchanan Q&A interview with Brian Lamb, telecast on C-SPAN May 25, 2017, https://www.c-span.org/video/transcript/?id=55942. A photograph of the memo to

Haldeman was reproduced in Buchanan's memoir, *Nixon's White House Wars: The Battles That Made and Broke a President and Divided America Forever* (New York: Crown, 2017).

43. Reeves, *President Nixon*, 148.
44. Jules Witcover, *White Knight: The Rise of Spiro Agnew* (New York: Random House, 1972), 323–24.
45. Lawrence, *Six Presidents*, 287–88, 293.
46. Graham, *Personal History*, 434.
47. James R. Coyne Jr., *The Impudent Snobs: Agnew vs. the Intellectual Establishment* (New Rochelle: Arlington House, 1974), 274–75; Graham, *Personal History*, 434.
48. Reeves, *President Nixon*, 149.
49. Speech at the Republican state convention, San Diego, September 11, 1970.
50. Norman P. Lewis, "The Myth of Spiro Agnew's 'Nattering Nabobs of Negativism,'" *American Journalism* 27 (Winter 2010): 99.
51. Klein, *Making It Perfectly Clear*, 114, 116–17.
52. Author interview with Brian Lamb, August 1, 2019.
53. Graham, *Personal History*, 435.
54. Thomas, *Being Nixon*, 260–61.
55. Helen Thomas, *Thanks for the Memories, Mr. President: Wit and Wisdom from the Front Row at the White House* (New York: Scribner, 2002), 84–85.
56. *RN*, 2:479.
57. John Anthony Maltese, *Spin Control: The White House Office of Communications and the Management of Presidential News* (Chapel Hill: University of North Carolina Press, 1992), 49.
58. Louis W. Liebovich, *Richard Nixon, Watergate, and the Press: A Historical Perspective* (Westport, CT: Praeger, 2003), 23–25.
59. Klein, *Making It Perfectly Clear*, 124.
60. Memorandum from H. R. Haldeman via Larry Higby to Herbert Klein, September 16, 1970, in Klein, *Making It Perfectly Clear*, 125–28.
61. Nixon memorandum to H. R. Haldeman, May 30, 1970, in Bruce Oudes, ed., *Richard Nixon's Secret Files* (New York: Harper & Row, 1988), 125–26.
62. "Pentagon Papers" became the widely used title for the *Report of the Office of the Secretary of Defense Vietnam Task Force.*
63. Robert S. McNamara, *In Retrospect* (New York: Random House, 1996), 280.
64. Sulzberger made the typically modest comments to me in 1992, when I interviewed with him for the job of communications manager of the Metropolitan Museum of Art, for which Mr. Sulzberger then served as chairman of the Board of Trustees. After asking me about my own career, he asked if I had any questions for him; I inquired about what he considered his proudest moment at the paper.
65. Ben Bradlee, *A Good Life: Newspapering and Other Adventures* (New York: Simon & Schuster, 1995), 310–13.
66. Farrell, *Richard Nixon*, 422.
67. Nixon, recorded White House conversation with H. R. Haldeman and Charles Colson, July 2, 1971, Stanley I. Cutler, ed., *Abuse of Power: The New Nixon Tapes* (New York: Free Press, 1997), 17–18.
68. Nixon's comments to H. R. Haldeman on June 29, 1971 are cited in Carl Bernstein and Bob Woodward, *All the President's Men*, orig. pub. 1974, 40th anniversary edition (New York Simon & Schuster, 2014), 340.
69. Opinion in *New York Times Co. v. United States*, 403 U.S. 713 (1971), http://www.law.cornell.edu.supremecourt/text/403/713.
70. Nixon, recorded Oval Office conversation with Charles Colson, September 14, 1972, Cutler, *Abuse of Power*, 144.

71. Nixon, recorded Oval Office conversation with Secretary of State William Rogers, Secretary of Defense Melvin Laird, National Security Advisor Henry Kissinger, and Admiral Thomas Moorer, February 27, 1971, in David Brinkley and Luke A. Nichter, eds., *The Nixon Tapes: 1971–1972* (Boston: Houghton Mifflin Harcourt, 2014), 35–36; Bernstein and Woodward, *All the President's Men*, 340–41. The author feels compelled to add a bit of personal history. On the day this conversation took place, he was preparing for his wedding in New York.
72. Nixon, recorded Oval Office conversation with H. R. Haldeman and Alexander Haig, May 11, 1973, in Kutler, *Abuse of Power*, 473. That same year, in another ironic development, the Defense Department official who had directed the Pentagon Papers project, Leslie H. Gelb, joined the staff of the *New York Times*.
73. Transcript of office conversation with Nixon, H. R. Haldeman, and Rev. Billy Graham, February 1, 1972, Brinkley and Nichter, *Nixon Tapes*, 359. By this time, Nixon had known for months that Graham was being audited by the IRS, which he attributed to the agency's bias against Republicans—and dominance by Jewish officials. "They've gone after [his friend Bebe] Rebozo. They've gone after John Wayne. . . . [The] IRS is full of Jews," he had complained in September 1971. Why couldn't they investigate "the big Jewish contributors of the Democrats?" Then he instructed H. R. Haldeman, "Could we please investigate some of the cocksuckers?" See Farrell, *Richard Nixon*, 654n. As he had expressed his feelings in front of both H. R. Haldeman and Henry Kissinger (himself a Jew), "the Jewish cabal is out to get me" and "most Jews are disloyal." Quoted in Woodward and Bernstein, *All the President's Men*, 2014 ed., afterword, 340.
74. Mark Feldstein, *Poisoning the Press: Richard Nixon, Jack Anderson, and the Rise of Washington's Scandal Culture* (New York: Farrar, Straus and Giroux, 2010), 278–80.
75. Hunter S. Thompson, *Fear and Loathing on the Campaign Trail '72* (New York: Simon & Schuster, 1973), 377.
76. Ibid., 376.
77. Ibid., 372, 376, 378.
78. Crouse, *Boys on the Bus*, 289.
79. The dinner took place circa 2005 in the Vonneguts' Turtle Bay town house in Manhattan.
80. Liebovich, *Richard Nixon, Watergate, and the Press*, 61.
81. H. R. Haldeman, *The Haldeman Diaries* (New York: G. P. Putnam's Sons), 473.
82. Klein, *All the President's Spokesmen*, 121.
83. For their own account of their backgrounds and fateful assignment, see Woodward and Bernstein, *All the President's Men*, 13–15.
84. Graham, *Personal History*, 560; Bradlee, *A Good Life*, 325.
85. Elizabeth Holtzman email interview with the author, July 29, 2019.
86. Graham, *Personal History*, 465–65.
87. Quoted in Bernstein and Woodward, *All the President's Men*, 57.
88. Bradlee, *A Good Life*, 324, 342–43.
89. *New York Times*, May 1, 1973.
90. See Bob Woodward, *The Secret Man: Watergate's Deep Throat* (New York: Simon & Schuster, 2005).
91. Goldman, "Inside the Nixon White House," 22–23.
92. Ibid., 23–24.
93. Taped Nixon conversation with Henry Kissinger, May 16, 1973, in Kutler, *Abuse of Power*, 503.
94. Klein, *Making It Perfectly Clear*, 152, 351–52.
95. Reeves, *President Nixon*, 297–98.
96. Jordy Yager, "Journalist Recalls the Honor of Being on Nixon's Enemies List," *The Hill*, January 6, 2009, https://thehill.com/capital-living/20243-journalist-recalls-the-honor-of-being-on-nixons-enemies-list.

97. Spear, *Presidents and the Press*, 158.
98. Sam Donaldson, *Hold On, Mr. President*, orig. pub. 1987 (New York: Ballantine Books, 1988), 62. Reagan quote is from a blurb for Donaldson's book.
99. Taped Nixon telephone conversation with Alexander Haig, May 25, 1973, Brinkley and Nichter, *Nixon Tapes, 1973*, 709.
100. Taped Nixon telephone conversation with Rose Mary Woods, July 12, 1973, Brinkley and Nichter, *Nixon Tapes, 1973*, 787. This was the last day his conversations were taped. According to Brinkley and Nichter, General Alexander Haig disabled the taping system while Nixon was in the hospital (787; for "killed me" quote, see 775).
101. Thomas, *Front Row at the White House*, 311, 313.
102. Thomas, *Thank You, Mr. President*, 321.
103. *RN*, 2:493–94.
104. Tom Brokaw, *The Fall of Richard Nixon: A Reporter Remembers Watergate* (New York: Random House, 2019), 81–82.
105. Goldman, "Inside Nixon's White House," 23.
106. Graham, *Personal History*, 494.
107. Sarah McClendon, *My Eight Presidents* (New York: Wyden Books, 1978), 176–77.
108. Dan Rather, *The Camera Never Blinks: Adventures of a TV Journalist* (New York: William Morrow, 1977), 17–18.
109. Theodore H. White, *Breaking the Faith: The Fall of Richard Nixon* (New York: Atheneum, 1975), 297.
110. *Washington Post*, August 6, 1974.
111. *RN*, 2:660.
112. Ibid., 661.
113. Quoted in Woodward and Bernstein, *Final Days*, 450.
114. David Remnick, "Nattering Nabobs," *New Yorker*, July 2, 2006, https://www.newyorker.com/magazine/2006/07/10/nattering-nabobs.
115. John A. Farrell, *Nixon: The Life* (New York: Doubleday, 2017), 551.

Chapter Thirteen: Gerald Ford and Jimmy Carter

1. Helen Thomas, *Front Row at the White House: My Life and Times* (New York: Scribner, 1999), 319.
2. "Gerald R. Ford's Remarks upon Taking the Oath of Office as President," transcript from the Gerald R. Ford Presidential Library and Museum, https://www.fordlibrarymuseum.gov/library/speeches/740001.asp.
3. Kenneth W. Thompson, ed., *Three Press Secretaries on the Presidency and the Press—Jody Powell, George Reedy, Jerry terHorst* (Latham, MD: University Press of America, 1983), 39, 41.
4. Ibid., 53.
5. Jerald terHorst, *Gerald Ford and the Future of the Presidency* (New York: Third Press, 1974), 236.
6. Quoted in William C. Spragens with Carole Ann Terwoord, *From Spokesman to Press Secretary: White House Media Operations* (Washington, DC: University Press of America, 1980), 70.
7. Thomas, *Front Row at the White House*, 321.
8. Helen Thomas, *Dateline: White House*... (New York: Macmillan, 1975), 261; Thomas, *Front Row at the White House*, 318.
9. Gerald Ford, *Humor and the Presidency* (New York: Arbor House, 1987), 16.
10. Marjorie Hunter, "Ford, Teeing Off like Agnew, Hits Spectator in Head with Golf Ball," *New York Times*, June 25, 1974.

11. See, for example, Mark Liebovich, "Chevy Chase as the Klutz in Chief, and a President Who Was in on the Joke," *New York Times*, December 29, 2006.
12. Ford, *Humor and the Presidency*, 19, 47, 48.
13. Kathryn Cramer Brownell, "The Saturday Night Live Episode That Changed American Politics," *Time*, April 15, 2016, https://time.com/4292027/gerald-ford-saturday-night-live/.
14. Ford, *Humor and the Presidency*, 157–58.
15. "Presidential Campaign Debate Between Gerald R. Ford and Jimmy Carter," Gerald R. Ford Presidential Library and Museum, https://www.fordlibrarymuseum.gov/library/speeches/760854.asp.
16. Author interview with Max Frankel, August 5, 2019.
17. Thomas, *Front Row at the White House*, 322.
18. "Jimmy Carter on Politics, Religion, the Press and Sex," *Playboy*, November 1976. (The issue appeared on newsstands a month earlier than its formal date.)
19. Sarah McClendon, *My Eight Presidents* (New York: Weyden Books, 1978), 195.
20. Reprinted in Larry J. Sabato, "Clinton Accused," March 27, 1998, *Washington Post* special report, https://www.washingtonpost.com/wp-srv/politics/special/clinton/frenzy/frenzy.htm. The comment appeared in a posting about Clinton, but in this case referred to Ford.
21. Howard K. Smith, *Events Leading Up to My Death: The Life of a Twentieth-Century Reporter* (New York: St. Martin's Press, 1996), 363.
22. Carter inaugural address, January 20, 1977, Jimmy Carter Presidential Library and Museum, https://www.jimmycarterlibrary.gov/assets/documents/speeches/inaugadd.phtml.
23. Quoted in Martin Schram, *Running for President 1976: The Carter Campaign* (New York: Stein and Day, 1977), 309.
24. Ibid.
25. Douglas Brinkley, *Cronkite* (New York: HarperCollins, 2012), 526; Walter Cronkite, *A Reporter's Life* (New York: Random House, 1996), 226; Sander Vanocur, "The President Carter Show," *Washington Post*, March 13, 1977.
26. McClendon, *My Eight Presidents*, 199.
27. Thomas, *Front Row at the White House*, 329.
28. Sam Donaldson, *Hold On, Mr. President!* (New York: Ballantine, 1987), 169; DeFrank quoted in Spragens with Terwoord, *From Spokesman to Press Secretary*, 82–83.
29. Michael Baruch Grossman and Martha Joynt Kumar, "The White House and the News Media: The Phases of Their Relationship," *Political Science Quarterly* 94 (Spring 1979): 44.
30. Donaldson, *Hold On, Mr. President*, 169.
31. Ibid.
32. Spragens with Terwoord, *From Spokesman to Press Secretary*, 84–85.
33. Quoted in Kenneth W. Thompson, ed., *Ten Presidents and the Press* (Latham, MD: University Press of America, 1983), 88; oral history interview with Jimmy Carter, Plains, Georgia, November 29, 1982, conducted by Richard F. Fenno, Jr., Ernest C. Hargrove, Charles O. Jones, H. Clifton McCleskey, Richard E. Neustadt, Kenneth W. Thompson, David B. Truman, James Sterling Young, final edited transcript at the Carter Presidency Project, Miller Center Foundation, University of Virginia, 63.
34. Donaldson, *Hold On, Mr. President*, 169, 178.
35. Ibid., 108.
36. Many observers have made this comparison, but for a particularly hilarious description, see David Greenberg, *Vast Republic of Spin: An Inside History of the American Presidency* (New York: W. W. Norton, 2016), 404.
37. Thomas Craughwell, "How Carter Lectured, Not Led," *Encyclopedia Britannica* blog, January 14, 2009, http://blogs.britannica.com/2009/01/8-how-carter-lectured-not-led-the-10-worst-decisions-by-us-presidents/.
38. Thomas, *Front Row at the White House*, 325.

39. Katharine Graham, *Personal History* (New York: Alfred A. Knopf, 1997), 610–11.
40. Diary entries for December 19, 1977, and August 9, 1980, in Jimmy Carter, *White House Diary* (New York: Farrar, Straus and Giroux, 2010), 151–52, 456. By the time the ex-president published this book, two of those Georgia staffers—Jody Powell and chief of staff Hamilton Jordan—were dead. Carter dedicated the book to their memory.
41. Donaldson, *Hold On, Mr. President*, 97, 104.
42. Thomas, *Front Row at the White House*, 328.
43. See Kevin M. Kruse, "James E. Carter, Jr., 1977–1981," in James M. Banner Jr., ed., *Presidential Misconduct from George Washington to Today* (New York: New Press, 2019), 395–402.
44. Ibid., 401.
45. Jody Powell, *The Other Side of the Story* (New York: William Morrow, 1984), 105; Cody Combs, "Jimmy Carter Explains 'Rabbit Attack,'" November 21, 2010, based on a report by Howard Kurtz, www.politicalticker.blogs.cnn.com/2010/11/21/jimmy-carter-explains-rabbit/attack.
46. *New York Times*, *Washington Post*, August 30, 1979.
47. Powell, *Other Side of the Story*, 106–7.
48. *Washington Post*, September 4, 1979, in Stuart E. Eizenstat, *President Carter: The White House Years* (New York: St. Martin's Press, 2018), 713.
49. Powell, *Other Side of the Story*, 107–8.
50. Sidney Blumenthal, *The Permanent Campaign: Inside the World of Elite Political Operatives* (Boston: Beacon Press, 1980), 29. Blumenthal analyzed the influential pollster's operating philosophy thusly: "To Caddell, alienation can be roughly defined as a lack of trust in government and politicians" and can be "assuaged by purely political means" (29–30).
51. Howard K. Smith, *Events Leading Up to My Death: The Life of a Twentieth-Century Reporter* (New York: St. Martin's Press, 1996), 392.
52. Quoted in Kevin Mattson, *"What the Heck Are You Up to, Mr. President?": Jimmy Carter, America's "Malaise," and the Speech That Should Have Changed the Country* (New York: Bloomsbury, 2009), 168.
53. Carter-Reagan presidential debate, October 28, 1980, transcript from the Ronald Reagan Presidential Library, https://www.reaganlibrary.gov/10-28-80debate.
54. A third-party candidate, John Anderson, siphoned off enough support, in enough states, from voters tired of Carter but wary of Reagan to guarantee the electoral-vote blowout.
55. Lily Roth and Arpita Aneja, "Eyewitness to a Landslide: Reporting Ronald Reagan's Historic Election," *Time*, November 4, 2015, www.time.com/4090907/time-remembering-ronald-reagan-1980/.
56. Quoted in Rick Perlstein, *The Invisible Bridge: The Fall of Nixon and the Rise of Reagan* (New York: Simon & Schuster, 2014), 602.
57. Jody Powell, "The Relationship of the President and the Press," in Thompson, *Three Press Secretaries on the Presidency and the Press*, 13–16. For the "right to lie," see Powell, *Other Side of the Story*, 223.
58. Powell, "The Relationship of the President and the Press," 17.
59. Carter oral history transcript, 11, 61.
60. Laurence I. Barrett, *Gambling with History: Reagan in the White House* (New York: Doubleday, 1983), 382–83.
61. H. W. Brands, *Reagan: The Life* (New York: Doubleday, 2015), 229.
62. Melinda Beck et al., "Reagan Feeling the Heat: 'Debategate' May Not Be Watergate—but Some Administration Heads Might Roll," *Newsweek* (July 18, 1983): 14–16. See also Tom Morgenthau et al., "The Great Mole Hunt," ibid., 16–17.
63. George Will, "Briefing Book Baloney," *Washington Post*, August 11, 2005; Jimmy Carter, "Putting an End to the 'Briefing Book Baloney,'" *Washington Post*, August 31, 2005; "Feeling

the Heat: The Debategate Plot Thickens—Who's Telling the Truth—and Will Heads Roll?," *Newsweek*, July 18, 1983.

64. Jonathan Friendly, "Columnist Helped Reagan on Debate," *New York Times*, July 9, 1983.
65. Brands, *Reagan*, 232–35.

Chapter Fourteen: Ronald Reagan and George H. W. Bush

1. Ronald Reagan with Richard G. Hubler, *Where's the Rest of Me? The Ronald Reagan Story* (New York: Duell, Sloan and Pearce, 1965).
2. Tony Thomas, *The Films of Ronald Reagan* (New York: Citadel, 1980). This reference book did not appear until the year of Reagan's run for president. Until then, his film career had not rated such a compendium.
3. Reagan made a few other good films, including *Knute Rockne, All American* (1940), and played a supporting role in the Warner Bros. classic *Dark Victory* (1939), a Bette Davis vehicle.
4. In this, his first "presidential" election, the race to lead SAG, Reagan defeated two screen dancers: Gene Kelly and George Murphy, later a Republican U.S. senator.
5. Reagan, *Where's the Rest of Me?*, 139.
6. David Thomson, *The New Biographical Dictionary of Film* (rev. ed., New York: Alfred A. Knopf, 2002), 716.
7. Richard A. Viguerie and David Franke, *America's Right Turn: How Conservatives Used New Alternative Media to Take Power* (Chicago: Bonus Books, 2004), 216.
8. Author interview with former Speaker of the House Newt Gingrich, August 18, 2019.
9. Author interview with Brian Lamb, August 22, 2019; C-SPAN video from February 23, 1983, www.c-span.org/video/?/c4473557/user-clip-president-call-span.
10. Viguerie and Franke, *America's Right Turn*, 217.
11. Gerald R. Ford, *Humor and the Presidency* (New York: Arbor House, 1987), 130–31.
12. Quoted in Mark Hertsgaard, *On Bended Knee: The Press and the Reagan Presidency* (New York: Farrar, Straus & Giroux, 1988), 52.
13. Ibid.
14. Ibid., 52–53.
15. David Greenberg, *Republic of Spin: An Inside History of the American Presidency* (New York: W. W. Norton, 2016), 503n6. See also Martin Schram, *The Great American Video Game: Presidential Politics in the Television Age* (New York: William Morrow, 1987), 24–27.
16. Helen Thomas, *Front Row at the White House: My Life and Times* (New York: Scribner, 1999), 338.
17. Ed Adamczyk, "Flashback: Reagan Jokes About Bombing Soviet Union, 30 Years Ago," UPI, http://www.upi.com/Top_News/World-News/2014/08/11/Flashback-Reagan-jokes-about-bombing-Societ-Union-30-years-ago/7591407784065/.
18. Larry Speakes with Robert Pack, *Speaking Out: The Reagan Presidency from Inside the White House* (New York: Charles Scribner's Sons, 1988), 253.
19. Speakes, *Speaking Out*, 219.
20. Mollie Dickenson, *Thumbs Up: The Life and Courageous Comeback of White House Press Secretary Jim Brady* (New York: William Morrow, 1987), 444–45.
21. Ibid., 57.
22. Thomas, *Front Row at the White House*, 147.
23. Dickenson, *Thumbs Up*, 30.
24. Speakes, *Speaking Out*, 217.
25. Thomas, *Front Row at the White House*, 333.
26. Excerpts from an interview with Walter Cronkite, March 3, 1981, Ronald Reagan Presidential Library archives, www.reaganlibrary.gov/research/speeches/30381c.

27. Hertsgaard, *On Bended Knee*, 75, 151.
28. Haynes Johnson, *Sleepwalking Though History: America in the Reagan Years* (New York: W. W. Norton, 1991), 160–65.
29. For a definitive look at the fortieth president's record, see Sean Wilentz, *The Age of Reagan: A History, 1974–2008* (New York: HarperCollins, 2008).
30. Ibid., 47.
31. *New York Times*, March 30, 1981.
32. "Honey, I forgot to duck" quoted in H. W. Brands, *Reagan: The Life* (New York: Doubleday, 2015), 288; "Republicans" quoted in Del Quentin Wilber, *Rawhide Down: The Near Assassination of Ronald Reagan* (New York: Henry Holt, 2011), 120.
33. Lily Rothman, "President Reagan's Best Jokes About Being Shot," *Time*, March 30, 2015, https://time.com/3752477/reagan-assassination-reaction/. *Time* covered the actual shooting with a cover story depicting Reagan at the instant the bullet struck him. See "Moment of Madness: What Happened—and Why? Can It Never Be Stopped?," April 13, 1981.
34. Laurence I. Barrett, *Gambling with History: Reagan in the White House* (New York: Doubleday, 1983), 120–22.
35. Hertsgaard, *On Bended Knee*, 116.
36. Richard A. Brody, *Assessing the President: The Media, Elite Opinion, and Public Support* (Stanford, CA: Stanford University Press, 1991), 43–44.
37. Thomas, *Front Row at the White House*, 337.
38. Dickenson, *Thumbs Up*, 257–58.
39. Caitlin Greene, "A Disturbing New Glimpse at the Reagan Administration's Indifference to AIDS," *Washington Post*, December 1, 2015; Chris Geidner, "13 Times the Reagan White House Press Briefing Erupted with Laughter over AIDS," Buzzfeed, December 2, 2013, https://www.buzzfeed.com/chrisgeidner/times-the-reagan-white-house-press-briefing-erupted-with#.ImybxqV94w; Dan Amira, "AIDS Was Hilarious to the Reagan White House Press Corps," *New York* magazine, December 2, 2013, http://nymag.com/daily/intelligencer/2013/12/aids-white-house-larry-speakes-joke-press-briefing-1982.html. For more on Kinsolving, see Kathleen Kinsolving, *Gadfly: The Life and Times of Les Kinsolving—White House Watchdog* (Washington, DC: WND Books, 2010).
40. Speakes, *Speaking Out*, 260.
41. Hertsgaard, *On Bended Knee*, 20.
42. Speakes, *Speaking Out*, 111.
43. Sam Donaldson, *Hold On, Mr. President!* (New York: Ballantine, 1987), 180.
44. Diary entry, November 5, 1981, in Ronald Reagan, *The Reagan Diaries*, ed. Douglas Brinkley (New York: HarperCollins, 2007), 47.
45. Stephen Hess, *The Government/Press Connection: Press Officers and Their Offices* (Washington, DC: Brookings Institution, 1984), 91.
46. Speakes, *Speaking Out*, 218.
47. Floyd Abrams, "The New Effort to Control Information," *New York Times Magazine*, September 25, 1983.
48. William Safire, "Question Time," *New York Times*, February 15, 2001.
49. Press Conferences of President Reagan, Reagan Presidential Library, https://www.reaganlibrary.gov/sreference/press-conferences-of-ronald-reagan.
50. Brands, *Reagan*, 278.
51. Donaldson, *Hold On, Mr. President*, 181–82.
52. Ibid., 184–85.
53. Conversations over the years with the governor—for whom I worked as a press aide from 1977 to 1978 and again from 1984 to 1992. Cuomo told the story about his mother many times. The governor also enjoyed telling friends about the day a confused Reagan saw him at an event and remarked, "You're doing a great job, Lee Iacocca."

54. Steven R. Weisman, "The President and the Press," *New York Times Magazine*, October 14, 1984, https://www.nytimes.com/1984/10/14/magazine/the-president-and-the-press.html.
55. October 21, 1984, debate transcript, Commission on Presidential Debates, https://www.debates.org/voter-education/debate-transcripts/october-21-1984-debate-transcript/.
56. Greenberg, *Republic of Spin*, 412.
57. Thomas, *Front Row at the White House*, 335.
58. Diary entry, November 16, 1981, *Reagan Diaries*, 49–50.
59. Barrett, *Gambling with History*, 452.
60. Steven R. Weisman, "Reagan Quoted as Assailing TV Coverage of the Recession," *New York Times*, March 18, 1982, https://www.nytimes.com/1982/03/18/us/reagan-quoted-as-assailing-tv-coverage-of-the-recession.html.
61. Ibid.
62. Remarks at the annual Washington policy meeting of the National Association of Manufacturers, March 18, 1982, Ronald Reagan Presidential Library, https://www.reaganlibary.gov/research/speeches/31882c.
63. Ibid.
64. David Gergen, *Eyewitness to Power: The Essence of Leadership, Nixon to Reagan* (New York: Simon & Schuster, 2000), 224–26.
65. John Anthony Maltese, *Spin Control: The White House Office of Communications and the Management of Presidential News* (Chapel Hill: University of North Carolina Press, 1992), 207. Gergen had quit after learning of the 1984 American invasion of Granada after it began.
66. Bernard Weintraub, "Buchanan Assumes a Powerful Position in the White House," *New York Times*, April 11, 1985.
67. John S. Dermott, "Bernard Kalb's Modest Dissent," *Time*, October 20, 1986, http://www.time.com/time/magazine/article/0,9171,1075205,00.html.
68. William E. Leuchtenburg, *The American President: From Teddy Roosevelt to Bill Clinton* (New York: Oxford University Press, 2015), 646.
69. For Reagan's record-fast descent in public opinion polls, see Richard A. Brody and Catherine R. Shapiro, "Policy Failure and Public Support: The Iran-Contra Affair and Public Assessments of President Reagan," *Political Behavior* 11 (December 1989): 353.
70. Marlin Fitzwater, *Call the Briefing! Reagan and Bush, Sam and Helen: A Decade with Presidents and the Press* (New York: Times Books, 1995), 112–21.
71. Ibid., 121–22.
72. Leuchtenburg, *American President*, 581.
73. Ben Bradlee, *A Good Life: Newspapering and Other Adventures* (New York: Simon & Schuster, 1995), 409.
74. Hertsgaard, *On Bended Knee*, 305.
75. Final report of the Independent Counsel for Iran/Contra Matters, August 4, 1993, https://fas.org/irp/offdocs/walsh/; Jeremi Suri, "Ronald Reagan (1981–1989)," in James M. Banner Jr., ed., *Presidential Misconduct from George Washington to Today* (New York: New Press, 2019), 417.
76. Donaldson, *Hold On, Mr. President*, 184.
77. Lou Cannon, *President Reagan: The Role of a Lifetime* (New York: Simon & Schuster, 1991), 320.
78. Russell Baker, "Sunday Observer: Jimmy Stewart's Best Friend," *New York Times*, January 18, 1981. Several versions of the quote exist. When Reagan himself used the self-deprecating remark at a speech at the University of Virginia in 1988, he remembered that Warner had said, "No, no. Jimmy Stewart for *Governor* [emphasis added]. Reagan for best friend." In fact, Warner died in 1978, two years before Reagan won the presidency—but, on the other hand, had still been alive when Reagan challenged Gerald Ford for the 1976 Republican nomination. The matter will probably never be settled.
79. Speakes, *Speaking Out*, 92.

80. Cannon, *Role of a Lifetime*, 51.
81. Barrett, *Gambling with History*, 9.
82. Hedley Donovan, *Roosevelt to Reagan: A Reporter's Encounters with Nine Presidents* (New York: Harper & Row, 1985), 306.
83. David Gergen, *Eyewitness to Power*, 246–47.
84. Margaret Garrard Warner, "Bush Battles the 'Wimp Factor,'" *Newsweek*, October 19, 1987, https://www.newsweek.com/bush-battles-wimp-factor-207008.
85. Katharine Graham, *Personal History* (New York: Alfred A. Knopf, 1997), 613.
86. Howard K. Smith, *Events Leading Up to My Death: The Life of a Twentieth-Century Reporter* (New York: St. Martin's Press, 1996), 396.
87. *Time*, November 9, 1984, 59.
88. Fitzwater, *Call the Briefing*, 245–46.
89. Remarks at the Republican National Convention, August 18, 1988, video and transcript online at C-SPAN, www.c-span.org/video/?3848-1/george-haw-bush-1988-acceptance-speech.
90. Smith, *Events Leading Up to My Death*, 392.
91. "Top 10 Unfortunate Political One-Liners," *Time*, http://content.time.com/time/specials/packages/completelist/0,29569,1859513,00.html.
92. Larry J. Sabato, *Feeding Frenzy: How Attack Journalism Has Transformed Politics* (New York: Free Press, 1991), 16.
93. Fitzwater, *Call the Briefing*, 352–53.
94. See Susan Page, *The Matriarch: Barbara Bush and the Making of an American Dynasty* (New York: Twelve, 2019).
95. Fitzwater, *Call the Briefing*, 269, 304; Michael Wines, "Bush Collapses at State Dinner with the Japanese," *New York Times*, January 9, 1992.
96. Presidential debate, October 13, 1988. For a transcript, see https://www.debates.org/voter-education/debate-transcripts/october-13-1988/debate-transcript/.
97. Roger Simon, "Questions That Kill Candidates' Careers," April 20, 2007, https://www.politico.com/story/2007/04/questions-that-kill-candidates-careers-003617.
98. David Gergen, "Bush's Start: A Presidency 'On the Edge of a Cliff,'" *Washington Post*, March 5, 1989.
99. William Boot, "The Press Stands Alone," *Columbia Journalism Review* (March–April 1991), 23–24.
100. Andrew Rosenthal, "Bush Encounters the Supermarket, Amazed," *New York Times*, February 5, 1992.
101. For background on Richards's comment and her victim's generous response, see "Bush Sends Critic Her Own Silver Foot," *New York Times*, November 30, 1988.
102. "AP Was There: Bush's Bum Rap on 'Amazing' Barcode Scanner," December 4, 2018, https://apnews.com/61f29d10e27140b0b108d8e12b64b839.
103. Viguerie and Franke, *America's Right Turn*, 177, 183.
104. Thomas, *Front Row at the White House*, 353.
105. Ibid., 356.
106. See Jon Meacham, *Destiny and Power: The American Odyssey of George Herbert Walker Bush* (New York: Random House, 2015).
107. The author, together with the actor Sam Waterston, performed the program "Lincoln Seen and Heard" for the benefit of the George W. Bush Presidential Library in Houston on April 4, 2004.

Chapter Fifteen: Bill Clinton

1. *The Clinton Years*, coproduction of PBS *Frontline* and ABC News *Nightline*, January 7, 2001, DVD edition, scene 3, "The Crisis Playbook."

2. Although the phrase had been used before by others, Mrs. Clinton immortalized it on her appearance with NBC's Matt Lauer on the *Today* show, January 27, 1998 (www.msnbc.com/today/watch/hillary-clinton-speaks-out-on-lewinsky-accusations-44498499720).
3. Kevin Merida, "It's Come to This: A Nickname That's Proven Hard to Slip," *Washington Post*, December 20, 1998. The article attributes the moniker to journalist Paulk Greenberg, who so dubbed Clinton in an editorial for the *Pine Bluff* [Arkansas] *Commercial* on September 27, 1980.
4. Helen Thomas, *Front Row at the White House: My Life and Times* (New York: Scribner, 1999), 360.
5. Neil A. Lewis, "Almost $2 Million Spent in Magazine's Anti-Clinton Project, But on What?" *New York Times*, April 15, 1998.
6. Richard L. "Jake" Siewert Jr. oral history interview, September 22, 2006, Clinton Presidential History Project, Miller Center for Presidential History, University of Virginia, 18, https://millercenter.org/the-presidency/presidential-oral-histories/richard-l-jake-siewert-jr-white-house-press-secretary (hereinafter cited as Siewert Oral History). Siewert served in several White House jobs, including deputy press secretary, before taking over the top job for the last year of the Clinton administration.
7. Siewert Oral History, 21.
8. *The Clinton Years.*
9. Michael Kruse, "The TV Interview That Haunts Hillary Clinton," *Politico*, September 23, 2016, https://www.politico.com/magazine/story/2016/09/hillary-clinton-2016-60-minutes-1992-214275. For "cool and unruffled," see David Maranis, "First Lady Launches Counterattack," *Washington Post*, January 28, 1998; Wayne Glawka et al., "Among the New Words," *American Speech* 75 (2000): 444.
10. Bill Clinton, *My Life* (New York: Alfred A. Knopf, 2004), 386. In her own memoir, Hillary Clinton also denied that theirs was only "a marriage on paper," but acknowledged that many people simply could not comprehend why the couple had stayed together. See Hillary Rodham Clinton, *What Happened* (New York: Simon & Schuster, 2017), 159.
11. Transcript available on *Washington Post* website, "Clinton Accused," https://www.washingtonpost.com/wp-srv/politics/special/clinton/stories/flowers012792.htm.
12. To place the enormous viewership in context, Clinton would receive 44 million votes in the general election.
13. Taylor Branch, *The Clinton Tapes: Wrestling History with the President* (New York: Simon & Schuster, 2009), 90. This curious but invaluable book is based not on the tapes themselves but on Branch's subsequent recollections of what the president had said during each taping; Branch usually wrote down his observations as soon as he left the White House.
14. At the dawn of the "Me Too" movement, Mrs. Clinton faced questioning for indeed standing by her man and assailing the various women who came forward to say he had romanced or even harassed them.
15. Siewert Oral History, 21.
16. Ibid.
17. Larry J. Sabato, *Feeding Frenzy: How Attack Journalism Has Transformed American Politics* (New York: Free Press, 1991), 136, 200. For an opposing view, see Paul J. Maurer, "Media Feeding Frenzies: Press Behavior During Two Clinton Scandals," *Presidential Studies Quarterly* 29 (March 1999): 65–79.
18. Ellen Landowsky, "Bill Clinton Is No Victim of the Press," *New York Times*, March 24, 1992.
19. David Gergen, *Eyewitness to Power: The Essence of Leadership, Nixon to Clinton* (New York: Simon & Schuster, 2000), 254.
20. *The Clinton Years.*
21. Gwen Ifill, "Clinton Goes Eye to Eye with MTV Generation," *New York Times*, June 17, 1992.

22. Sidney Blumenthal, *The Clinton Wars* (New York: Farrar, Straus and Giroux, 2003), 23.
23. For a highly useful summary of this effort, see Joseph Hayden, *Covering Clinton: The President and the Press in the 1990s* (Westport, CT: Praeger, 2002), especially chapter 1, "The Empathy Candidate," 1–22.
24. "The Woman Behind 'The Man from Hope'" (letter to the editor by Linda Bloodworth-Thomason), *New York Times*, September 17, 2017.
25. George Stephanopoulos, *All Too Human: A Political Education* (Boston: Little, Brown, 1999), 90.
26. Clinton, *My Life*, 425.
27. Thomas, *Front Row at the White House*, 363.
28. Clinton, *My Life*, 513.
29. Branch, *Clinton Tapes*, 11.
30. Michael Takiff, *A Complicated Man: The Life of Bill Clinton as Told to Those Who Know Him* (New Haven, CT: Yale University Press, 2010), 165; *Washington Post*, November 15, 1992; *Boston Globe*, January 31, 1992.
31. Thomas, *Front Row at the White House*, 310.
32. By David Gergen's account, Hillary Clinton and her close advisor Susan Thomases originally proposed banishing the entire press corps to the Executive Office Building but agreed to the compromise of having the door to the press secretary's office shut off. See Gergen, *Eyewitness to Power*, 275.
33. Stephanopoulos, *All Too Human*, 112.
34. Kenneth T. Walsh, *Feeding the Beast: The White House Versus the Press* (New York: Random House, 1996), 17.
35. Author interview with former president Bill Clinton, October 25, 2019.
36. Clinton press conference, January 29, 1993, https://millercenter.org/the-presidency/presidential-speeches/january-29-1993-press-conference-gays-military.
37. Branch, *Clinton Tapes*, 7.
38. Clinton, *My Life*, 490–91.
39. Stephen Labaton and Sam Howe Verhovek, "Missteps in Waco: A Raid Re-Examined," *New York Times*, March 28, 1993; Dirk Johnson, "Last Hours in Waco . . . Fire and Terror on Final Day," *New York Times*, April 26, 1993.
40. Gergen, *Eyewitness to Power*, 263.
41. Sally Quinn, "Making Capital Gains: Welcome to Washington but Play by Our Rules," *Washington Post*, November 15, 1992; Takiff, *Complicated Man*, 161.
42. Alter quoted in Takiff, *Complicated Man*, 161.
43. Siewert Oral History, 33.
44. Branch, *Clinton Tapes*, 133.
45. Joseph Lockhart oral history interview, September 19–20, 2005, Clinton Presidential History Project, Miller Center for Presidential History, University of Virginia, 73, https://millercenter.org/the-presidency/presidential-oral-histories/joseph-lockhart-oral-history-white-house-press-secretary (hereinafter cited as Lockhart Oral History).
46. Martha Joynt Kumar, *Managing the President's Message: The White House Communications Operation* (Baltimore: Johns Hopkins University Press, 2007), 35.
47. Thomas, *Front Row at the White House*, 364.
48. Siewert Oral History, 43–44.
49. Ibid.
50. Branch, *Clinton Tapes*, 76.
51. Jann S. Wenner and William Greider, "Bill Clinton: The Rolling Stone Interview—After One Year in Office, the President's Battles with Republicans and the Press Have Put New Wrinkles on His Face," *Rolling Stone*, December 9, 1993, https://www.rollingstone.com/politics/politics-news/bill-clinton-the-rolling-stone-interview-3-178437/.

52. See, for example, "Clinton Slams Media, Then Says Reporter Distorted Comments," *Nashville Tennessean*, November 19, 1993.
53. Ibid.
54. Gergen, *Eyewitness to Power*, 259. Gergen believed that if Myers had "first gained some seasoning as deputy press secretary, the number-two slot, she would have [later] stepped up to number one and been outstanding."
55. Tim Graham, *Pattern of Deception: The Media's Role in the Clinton Presidency* (Alexandria, VA: Media Research Center, 1996), 118.
56. Siewert Oral History, 29.
57. Ibid.
58. Gergen, *Eyewitness to Power*, 263. See also Bob Woodward, *The Agenda: Inside the Clinton White House* (New York: Simon & Schuster, 1994); Elizabeth Drew, *On the Edge: The Clinton Presidency* (New York: Touchstone, 1995).
59. Siewert Oral History, 30, 32.
60. Kumar, *Managing the President's Message*, 60.
61. Gergen, *Eyewitness to Power*, 268.
62. Ibid., 276, 336.
63. W. Dale Nelson, *Who Speaks for the President? The White House Press Secretary from Cleveland to Clinton* (Syracuse, NY: Syracuse University Press, 1998), 250.
64. Gergen, *Eyewitness to Power*, 336.
65. Siewert Oral History, 29. See also Dee Dee Myers, *Why Women Should Rule the World* (New York: Harper, 2008).
66. Author interview with former president Bill Clinton, October 25, 2019.
67. Ben Goddard was the advertising man who created the "Harry and Louise" television advertising campaign; see Russell L. Riley, ed., *Inside the Clinton White House: An Oral History* (New York: Oxford University Press, 2016), 155.
68. Thomas, *Front Row at the White House*, 359.
69. Author interview with former Speaker of the U. S. House of Representatives Newt Gingrich, September 12, 2019.
70. Branch, *Clinton Tapes*, 162.
71. Lars-Erik Nelson, "Whitewater Probe Finds the Clintons in the Clear," New York *Daily News*, December 20, 1995; Blumenthal, *Clinton Wars*, 169.
72. Branch, *Clinton Tapes*, 409.
73. Ibid.
74. Thomas, *Front Row at the White House*, 369.
75. Hillary Clinton, *What Happened*, 160.
76. Ken Gormley, *The Death of American Virtue: Clinton vs. Starr* (New York: Crown, 2010), 72–73, 89–90.
77. Branch, *Clinton Tapes*, 123–24.
78. Ibid., 151.
79. Author interview with former president Bill Clinton, October 25, 2019.
80. Clinton, *My Life*, 589.
81. Richard Lei, "Commander in Briefs," *Washington Post*, April 20, 1994.
82. *Salinas Californian*, June 25, 1994.
83. Ibid.
84. "A Flack Who Uses a Smile," *Baltimore Sun*, May 9, 1996, quoted in Hayden, *Covering Clinton*, 36.
85. Siewert Oral History, 30.
86. Televised address, April 19, 1995.
87. Author interview with Sidney Blumenthal, September 3, 2019.
88. *Booklist* review accompanying Amazon.com listing for *Primary Colors*.

89. Doreen Carvajal, "Columnist's Mea Culpa: I'm Anonymous," *New York Times*, July 18, 1996.
90. William Leuchtenburg, *The American President from Teddy Roosevelt to Bill Clinton* (New York: Oxford University Press, 2015), 770.
91. Lockhart Oral History, 322.
92. Quoted in Woody Klein, *All the Presidents' Spokesmen: Spinning the News—White House Press Secretaries from Franklin D. Roosevelt to George W. Bush* (Westport, CT: Praeger, 2008), 150.
93. McCurry and Donaldson quoted in Takiff, *Complicated Man*, 319.
94. Richard M. Pious, "The Paradox of Clinton Winning and the Presidency Losing," *Political Science Quarterly* 114 (1999–2000): 571. See also Pious, *The American Presidency* (New York: Basic Books), especially 47–84.
95. Clinton, *My Life*, 775.
96. Bill Clinton to the author, February 4, 1998.
97. Author interview with Jim Lehrer, August 28, 2019.
98. Lockhart Oral History, 22.
99. Ibid., 68.
100. Clinton quotes from Olivia B. Waxman and Merrill Fabry, "From an Anonymous Tip to an Impeachment: A Timeline of Key Moments in the Clinton-Lewinsky Scandal," *Time*, May 4, 2018, https://time.com/5120561/bill-clinton-monica-lewinsky-timeline.
101. Leuchtenburg, *American President*, 774–75.
102. Waxman and Fabry, "Timeline."
103. Lyndsey Layton, "The Frenzy over Lewinsky: As the Scandal Unfolded, a Media Storm Swirled in Washington," *Washington Post*, July 27, 2004.
104. Lockhart Oral History, 78.
105. Jeff Gerth, "Clintons Joined S. & L. Operator in an Ozark Real-Estate Venture," *New York Times*, March 8, 1992; Gwenn Ifill, "Hillary Clinton Takes Questions on Whitewater," *New York Times*, April 23, 1994.
106. Lockhart Oral History, 81.
107. See "Conservative Lawmakers Decried Clinton's Attacks Against Osama as 'Wag the Dog,'" *Think Progress*, September 25, 2006, https://thinkprogress.org/flashback-conservative-lawmakers-decried-clintons-attacks-against-osama-as-wag-the-dog-e1ca08cd43ad/.
108. Lockhart Oral History, 100–101.
109. Richard Moran and Claudia Deane, "President's Popularity Hits a High," *Washington Post*, February 1, 1998.
110. Thomas, *Front Row at the White House*, 271, 375.
111. Lockhart Oral History, 46.
112. Siewert Oral History, 61.
113. Gergen, *Eyewitness to Power*, 313.
114. Flynt in Takiff, *Complicated Man*, 370–71. Livingston's memoir is *The Windmill Chaser: Triumph and Loss in American Politics* (Lafayette: University of Louisiana Press, 2018).
115. Gergen, *Eyewitness to Power*, 336.
116. Author interview with Sidney Blumenthal, September 3, 2019.
117. Todd Gitlin, "The Clinton-Lewinsky Obsession: How the Press Made a Scandal of Itself," *Washington Monthly* 30 (December 1998), https://web.archive.org/web/20090315034554/http://www.washingtonmonthly.com/features/1998/9812.gitlin.obsession.html.
118. Lockhart Oral History, 76.
119. Gill worked in the Office of Media Affairs, and Kalil worked for the National Economic Council.
120. Siewert Oral History, 38, 75.
121. Quoted in Gitlin, "Clinton-Lewinsky Obsession."

122. Gloria Steinem, "Why Feminists Support Clinton," *New York Times*, March 22, 1998.
123. Floyd Abrams, "Clinton vs. the First Amendment," *New York Times*, March 30, 1997.
124. "Clinton Vetoes Bill That Would Limit Journalists' Powers," *The Lariat*, November 9, 2000; quoted in Hayden, *Covering Clinton*, 53.
125. Author interview with Sidney Blumenthal, August 21, 2019.
126. This and above quote from *New York Times* in Clinton, *My Life*, 890.
127. Brian Lamb and Susan Swain, eds., *The Presidents: Noted Historians Rank America's Best—and Worst—Chief Executives* (New York: PublicAffairs, 2019), 181.
128. Donaldson in Takiff, *Complicated Man*, 323.
129. Branch, *Clinton Tapes*, 651.
130. Bill Clinton and James Patterson, *The President Is Missing* (New York: Little, Brown and Alfred A. Knopf, 2018), 59–60.
131. Author interview with former president Bill Clinton, October 25, 2019.
132. Interview with Tim Russert, *Meet the* Press, June 10, 2007, quoted in Klein, *All the Presidents' Spokesmen*, 152–53.

Chapter Sixteen: George W. Bush

1. "President Slams Coverage of Errors," *Detroit Free Press*, September 29, 2000.
2. Maureen Dowd, "Liberties; Freudian Face-Off," *New York Times*, June 16, 1999.
3. Evan Thomas, *First: Sandra Day O'Connor* (New York: Random House, 2019), 339.
4. Jean Edward Smith, *Bush* (New York: Simon & Schuster, 2001), 117; Dana Milbank, *Smash-mouth: Two Years in the Gutter with Al Gore and George W. Bush—Notes from the 2000 Campaign Trail* (New York: Basic Books, 2001), 321.
5. Jacob Weisberg, "W.'s Greatest Hits: The Top 25 Bushisms of All Time," *Slate*, January 12, 2009, https://slate.com/news-and-politics/2009/01/the-top-25-bushisms-of-all-time.html.
6. Smith, *Bush*, 82. See also Jacob Weisberg, *The Bush Tragedy* (New York: Random House, 2008), 127–28.
7. Adam Clymer obituary by Sam Roberts, *New York Times*, September 10, 2018.
8. Ari Fleischer, *Taking Heat: The President, the Press, and My Years in the White House* (New York: William Morrow, 2005), 41.
9. Ibid., 100, 102.
10. Ibid., 140, 146–47.
11. *U.S. News & World Report* correspondent Kenneth T. Walsh, who was on the scene covering the Bush visit, remembered it in "George W. Bush's Bullhorn Moment: Three Days After 9/11, Bush Stood Atop the Rubble in New York and Found His Presidency's Cause," *U.S. News*, April 25, 2013, https://www.usnews.com/news/blogs/ken-walshs-washington/2013/04/25/george-w-bushs-bullhorn-moment.
12. Fleischer, *Taking Heat*, 197.
13. Quoted in David Greenberg, *Republic of Spin: An Inside History of the American Presidency* (New York: W. W. Norton, 2016), 433.
14. Smith, *Bush*, 245.
15. Fleischer, *Taking Heat*, 335.
16. Ibid.
17. Ibid., 347.
18. Greenberg, *Republic of Spin*, 436.
19. Fleischer, *Taking Heat*, 348.
20. *New York Times*, October 29, 2003, quoted in Woody Klein, *All the Presidents' Spokesmen: Spinning the News—White House Press Secretaries from Franklin D. Roosevelt to George W. Bush* (Westport, CT: Praeger, 2008), 70.

21. Joseph C. Wilson IV, "What I Didn't Find in Africa," *New York Times*, July 6, 2003.
22. "Washington Merry-Go-Round: Mission to Niger," syndicated column of July 14, 2003.
23. Thomas Mallon, "Washington Scribe: The Diaries of the Ultimate D.C. Insider," *New Yorker*, September 21, 2015, https://www.newyorker.com/magazine/2015/09/28/washington-scribe.
24. James Gordon Meek, "Fleischer Says He Leaked Plame's CIA Employment, New York *Daily News*, January 30, 2007.
25. Kathryn S. Olmsted and Eric Rauchway, "George W. Bush, 2001–2009," in James M. Banner Jr., *Presidential Misconduct: From George Washington to Today* (New York: New Press, 2019), 458.
26. Jack Shafer, "The Novak Report: When the Plame Indictments Come Down, the Columnist Will Have a Lot to Explain," *Slate*, October 27, 2005, https://slate.com/news-and-politics/2005/10/robert-novak-has-a-lot-of-explaining-to-do.html.
27. Sheryl Gay Stolberg, "Red Carpet Spy," *New York Times*, September 24, 2010.
28. Alana Goodman, "Ousted CIA spy Valerie Plame and diplomat husband are divorced," *Washington Examiner*, June 19, 2017; Neil Genzlinger, "Joseph Wilson, Who Challenged Iraq War Neutrality, Dies at 69," *New York Times*, September 27, 2019.
29. See Valerie Plame, *Fair Game: My Life as a Spy, My Betrayal by the White House* (New York: Simon & Schuster, 2007); Joseph Wilson, *The Politics of Truth: A Diplomat's Memoir—Inside the Lies that Led to War and Betrayal of My Wife's CIA Identity* (New York: Carroll & Graf, 2004); Judith Miller, *The Story: A Reporter's Journey* (New York: Simon & Schuster, 2015).
30. Scott McClellan, *What Happened: Inside the Bush White House and Washington's Culture of Deception* (New York: PublicAffairs, 2008), 62–63, 64, 65.
31. Ibid., 165.
32. Ibid., 173.
33. See John O'Neill and Jerome Corsi, *Unfit for Command: Vietnam Veterans Speak Out Against John Kerry* (Washington, D. C.; Regnery, 2004).
34. Fleischer, *Taking Heat*, 259.
35. For context, see the book that inspired the film: Mary Mapes, *Truth and Duty: The Press, the President, and the Privilege of Power* (New York: St. Martin's Press, 2005).
36. Fleischer, *Taking Heat*, 247, 250–51.
37. Ann McFeatters, "Thank 'You,' Ms. Thomas," *Ms. Magazine* (Summer 2006), https://www.msmagazine.com/summer2006/thankyoumsthomas.asp; "Five Minutes With: Helen Thomas," *Campus Progress* (Center for American Progress), February 28, 2006, https://web.archive.org/web/20100613063948/; http://campusprogress.org/features/779/five-minutes-with-helen-thomas?
38. David Stout, "50 Years of Tough Questions and 'Thank You, Mr. President,'" *New York Times*, July 20, 2013.
39. Smith, *Bush*, 488–89.
40. Evan Thomas et al., "How Bush Blew It," *Newsweek* (September 15, 2005): 26–40.
41. McClellan, *What Happened*, 278–79.
42. Ibid., 274.
43. Rove, *The Architect*, cited in McClellan, *What Happened*, 281–82.
44. Quoted in Martha Joynt Kumar, *Managing the President's Message: The White House Communications Operation* (Baltimore: Johns Hopkins University Press, 2007), 297.
45. Draper, *Dead Certain*, 335–36.
46. "Barbara Bush Calls Evacuees Better Off," *New York Times*, September 7, 2005.
47. Siewert Oral History, 18.
48. Ibid., 106.
49. Klein, *All the Presidents' Spokesmen*, 2–3.
50. Steven Lee Myers and Alissa J. Rubin, "Iraqi Journalist Hurls Shoes at Bush and Denounces Him on TV as a 'Dog,'" *New York Times*, December 15, 2008.

51. Lynn Sweet, "Tony Snow: On Lebanon—Not Calling for Cease Fire if It Leaves Status Quo Intact," *Chicago Sun-Times*, July 28, 2006.
52. Press briefing, November 30, 2007, transcript online at Bush Archive, https://www.georgewbush-whitehouse.archives,gov/news/releases/2007/11/2007/1130-5.html.
53. Greg Ip, "Capital Account: Why Bush's Quiet Role in Financial Crisis Deserves Attention Now," *Wall Street Journal*, September 12, 2018.
54. Quotes from Robert Draper, Ari Fleischer, Curtis Sittenfeld, Jacobi Weisberg, Scott McClellan, and Paul Burka in "What I Will Miss About President Bush," *New York Times*, November 1, 2008.
55. Adam Clymer, "Government Openness at Issue as Bush Holds On to Records," *New York Times*, January 3, 2003.

Chapter Seventeen: Barack Obama

1. Roberta Rampton, "Obama Gets His Own Account on Twitter. 'It's Barack. Really!,'" Reuters, May 18, 2015, https://www.reuters.com/article/usa-obama-twitter/obama-gets-his-own-account-on-twitter-its-barack-really-idUSL1N0Y915O20150518.
2. Julie Hirschfield Davis, "Obama's Twitter Debut, @POTUS, Attracts Hate-Filled Posts," *New York Times*, May 21, 2015.
3. Michael D. Shear, "Obama Campaign Taking the Fight to Twitter," *New York Times*, October 4, 2011. See also "The Twitaholic Top 100 Twitterholics Based on Followers," www//twitaholic.com.
4. Eugene Kiely, "Obama, Fox News and the Free Press," FactCheck.org, September 13, 2018, https://www.factcheck.org/2018/09/obama-fox-news-and-the-free-press/.
5. AP report published in *Ft. Myers* (FL) *News Press*, August 15, 2009.
6. L. D. Ingersoll, *The Life of Horace Greeley, Founder of the "New York Tribune" with Extended Notices of Many of His Contemporary Statesmen and Journalists* (New York: Union Publishing, 1873), 103–4.
7. Mark R. Levin, *Unfreedom of the Press* (New York: Threshold Editions, 2019), 21–22; Elspeth Reeve, "Rick Stengel Is at Least the 24th Journalist to Work for the Obama Administration," *Atlantic*, September 12, 2013, https://www.theatlantic.com/politics/archive/2013/09/rick-stengel-least-24-journalist-go-work-obama-administration/310928/.
8. Fredric Hudson, *Journalism in the United States, from 1690 to 1872* (New York: Harper & Bros., 1873), 553–54.
9. Jann S. Wenner, "Obama in Command: The Rolling Stone Interview," *Rolling Stone*, October 10, 2010, www.rollingstone.com/politics/politics-news/obama-in-command-the-rolling-stone-interview-188620/.
10. Albert R. Hunt, "Under Obama, a Chill on Press Freedom," *New York Times*, June 8, 2014.
11. Ken Auletta, "Non-Stop News: With Cable, the Web, and Tweets, Can the President—or the Press—Still Control the Story?," *New Yorker*, January 17, 2010, https://www.newyorker.com/magazine/2010/01/25/non-stop-news.
12. *Chicago Tribune*, August 1, 2004.
13. All quotes from David J. Garrow, *Rising Star: The Making of Barack Obama* (New York: William Morrow, 2017), 999–1000, 1002, 1007. Garrow called the chapter from which these comments are drawn "Disappointment and Destiny." For Lynn Sweet, see Liz Cox Barrett, "Lynn Sweet, The 'Specialist,'" *Columbia Journalism Review*, May 21, 2008, https://archives.cjr.org/the_kicker/lynn_sweet_the_specialist.php.
14. Roy P. Basler, ed., Abraham Lincoln, speech in Springfield, Illinois, June 16, 1858, *The Collected Works of Abraham Lincoln* 8 vols. (New Brunswick, NJ: Rutgers University Press, 1953–55), 2:461.

15. Transcript from CBS News, February 10, 2007, https://www.cbsnews.com/news/transcript-of-barack-obamas-speech.
16. Quoted in David Remnick, *The Bridge: The Life and Rise of Barack Obama* (New York: Alfred A. Knopf, 2010), 518.
17. Ibid., 519, 614n.519.
18. David Corn, "'Black and More Than Black': Obama's Daring and Unique Speech on Race," *Mother Jones*, March 18, 2008 (full text included), https://www.motherjones.com/politics/2008/03/black-and-more-black-obamas-daring-and-unique-speech-race/.
19. *New York Times*, March 19, 2008.
20. Comments on "A More Perfect Union," text from a virtual National Constitution Center exhibit on Obama's speech, https://constitutioncenter.org/amoreperfectunion/.
21. David Axelrod, *Believer: My Forty Years in Politics* (New York: Penguin Press, 2015), 303.
22. Michael Eric Dyson, *The Black Presidency: Barack Obama and the Politics of Race in America* (Boston: Houghton Mifflin, 2016), 94–95.
23. Jonathan Alter, *The Center Holds: Obama and His Enemies* (New York: Simon & Schuster, 2013) 68–69.
24. Bill O'Reilly, *The United States of Trump: How the President Really Sees America* (New York: Henry Holt, 2019), 31.
25. Alter, *Center Holds*, 31.
26. Katharine Q. Seelye and Jeff Zeleny, "On the Defense, Obama Calls His Words Ill-Chosen," *New York Times*, April 13, 2008.
27. Reid Cherlin, "The Presidency and the Press: The White House Distrusts the Media, Reporters Feel Persecuted—a Former Obama Spokesman on the History of the Toxic Relationship," *Rolling Stone*, August 4, 2014, https://www.rollingstone.com/politics/politics-news/the-presidency-and-the-press-74832/.
28. Dyson, *Black Presidency*, 205.
29. Alter, *Center Holds*, 62–63.
30. Alessandra Stanley, "Obama Steps into O'Reilly's 'No Spin Zone,'" *New York Times*, September 5, 2008.
31. Ibid., 68.
32. Becket Adams, "Obama, Whose Administration Prosecuted and Spied on Reporters, Claims Trump Is Very Bad for Criticizing Newsrooms," *Washington Examiner*, September 7, 2018, https://www.washingtonexaminer.com/opinion/obama-whose-administration-prosecuted-and-spied-on-reporters-claims-trump-is-very-bad-for-criticizing-newsrooms.
33. "'How Does Jay Carney Sleep at Night?' Napolitano, Kilmeade Discuss James Rosen," *Fox & Friends*, May 21, 2013, transcript online at *Fox News Insider*, https://insider.foxnews.com/2013/05/21/judge-napolitano-government-has-never-gone-level-against-reporter.
34. Ruth Marcus, "Obama's Dumb War with Fox News," Washington *Post Partisan*, October 19, 2009, http://voices.washingtonpost.com/postpartisan/2009/10/obamas_dumb_war_with_fox_news.html.
35. Quoted in Kiely, "Obama, Fox News and the Free Press."
36. Charlie Savage, *Power Wars: Inside Obama's Post-9/11 Presidency* (Boston: Little, Brown, 2015), 36.
37. Erik Wemple, "Seizing Journalists' Records: An Outrage That Obama 'Normalized' for Trump," *Washington Post*, June 8, 2018.
38. James Risen, "News Analysis: If Donald Trump Targets Journalists, Thank Obama," *New York Times*, December 30, 2016.
39. "Obama's Escalating War on Freedom of the Press," *Huffington Post*, September 21, 2013, https://www.huffpost.com/entry/obamas-escalating-war-on_b_3635370.
40. Quoted in Risen, "News Analysis."

41. For background and text see, for example, Arlen Specter, "The Need to Roll Back Presidential Power Grabs," *New York Review of Books* 56 (May 14, 2009), http://www.nybooks.com/articles/22656.
42. For quotes about both Manning and Assange, see Bill Keller, "Dealing with Assange and the WikiLeaks Secrets," *New York Times*, January 26, 2011.
43. Elizabeth Goitein, "The U.S. Says Julian Assange Is No Journalist. Here's Why That Shouldn't Matter," *Washington Post*, May 25, 2019, https://www.washingtonpost.com/outlook/2019/05/25/us-says-julian-assange-is-no-journalist-heres-why-that-shouldnt-matter/.
44. "Edward Snowden Voted Guardian Person of the Year 2013," *Guardian*, December 9, 2013, https://www.theguardian.com/world/2013/dec/09/edward-snowden-voted-guardian-person-of-year-2013.
45. Leonard Downie Jr. with Sara Rafsky, *The Obama Administration and the Press: Leak Investigations and Surveillance in Post-9/11 America*, Committee to Protect Journalists, October 10, 2013, https://cpj.org/reports/2013/10/obama-and-the-press-us-leaks-surveillance-post-911.php.
46. Ibid.
47. Adams, "Obama, Whose Administration Prosecuted and Spied on Reporters."
48. "Surveillance in the Post-Obama Era," editorial, *New York Times*, October 8, 2016.
49. Steve Frank, "The '47% Tape' and the Man Who Revealed the Real Mitt Romney," *The Ed Show*, MSNBC, March 12, 2013, www.msnbc.com/the-ed-show/the-47-tape-and-the-man-who-revealed-the-real-mitt-romney.
50. Mitt Romney, "Let Detroit Go Bankrupt," *New York Times*, November 18, 2008.
51. Barack Obama interview televised on C-SPAN, August 12, 2010, https://www.c-span.org/video/?295273-1/president-obama-oval-office-interview.
52. Author interview with Brian Lamb, August 22, 2019.
53. As of September 2, 2019, the exact number was 3,024.
54. Alter, *Center Holds*, 113.
55. Ibid.
56. David Greenberg, *Republic of Spin: An Inside History of the American Presidency* (New York: W. W. Norton, 2016), 443–44. Greenberg asserts that unlike his recent predecessors, Obama tried to "spin" news by appearing to disdain spinning.
57. Susan Milligan, "The President and the Press," *Columbia Journalism Review* (March–April 2015), https://www.cjr.org/analysis/the_president_and_the_press.php.
58. Ibid.
59. Julie Mason, "Trump Wages a War on the Press, but Was Obama Much Better to Reporters?," *Variety*, April 24, 2018.
60. Downie with Rafsky, *The Obama Administration and the Press*.
61. "U.S. to Promote Press Freedom," *New York Times*, May 17, 2010.
62. Margaret Talbot, "Obama vs. the Press," *New Yorker*, May 16, 2013, https://www.newyorker.com/news/daily-comment-obama-vs-the-press.
63. Ibid.
64. Jim Vandehei and Mike Allen, "Obama, the Puppet Master," *Politico*, February 19, 2013. Jack Shafer, "How Obama Manipulates the News," *Politico*, May 6, 2016, https://www.politico.com/magazine/styory/2016/05/how-obama-manipulates-the-news-213877.
65. Obama news conference, February 9, 2009, *New York Times*, https://books.google.com/books?id=B_m1zHJQB8IC&ppis=_e&lpg=PA76&dq=%E2%80%9CThis%20is%20my%20inaugural%20moment%20here%20%5BLaughter%5D.%20I%E2%80%99m%20excited.&pg=PA76#v=onepage&q&f=false.
66. Kim LaCapria, "Helen Thomas Calls Obama Administration Out on Social Media Smokescreen," *Inquisitr*, July 2, 2009, https://www.inquisitr.com/28013/helen-thomas-calls-obama-administration-out-on-social-media-smokescreen.

67. Paula Cruickshank, "42 Seconds That Sullied Helen Thomas—and New Media," *Real Clear Politics*, July 31, 2013, https://www.realclearpolitics.com/articles/2013/07/31/42_seconds_that_sullied_helen_thomas_—_and_new_media_119431.html.
68. Melissa Stusinski, "Helen Thomas Remembered by President Obama as 'True Pioneer,'" *Inquisitr*, July 21, 2013, https://www.inquisitr.com/860686/helen-thomas-remembered-by-president-obama-as-true-pioneer.
69. Victoria Dawson, "On the Legacy of Helen Thomas: The White House Correspondent's Career as a Journalist Spanned Ten Presidents and Was Marked by an Unwavering Dedication to the Truth," *Smithsonian* magazine (June 2003), https://www.smithsonianmag.com/history/in-the-legacy-of-helen-thomas-83981220/.
70. Stout, "50 Years of Tough Questions."
71. Ted Bridis, "Obama's Final Year: US Spent $36 Million in Record Lawsuits," AP, March 14, 2017, https://apnews.com/0b27c4d4b23b436d805328694e58c605.
72. Eric Lichtblau, "Report Faults U.S.'s Efforts at Transparency," *New York Times*, March 14, 2010.
73. Ian Bogost, "Obama Was Too Good at Social Media: His 'Cool Dad' Presidency Blinded Him to Technology's Dangers," *Atlantic*, January 6, 2017, https://www.theatlantic.com/technology/archive/2017/01/did-america-need-a-social-media-president/512405/.
74. Gridiron Club transcript, March 9, 2013, https://www.politico.com/story/2013/03/president-obama-gridiron-club-dinner-speech-2013-full-text-transcript-088654.
75. Cherlin, "The Presidency and the Press"; Milligan, "President and the Press."
76. Downie with Rafsky, *The Obama Administration and the Press.*
77. Richard Hofstadter, *The Paranoid Style in American Politics and Other Essays* (Cambridge, MA: Harvard University Press, 1963).
78. See Brian Lamb and Susan Swain, *The Presidents: Noted Historians Rank America's Best—and Worst—Chief Executives* (New York: Public Affairs, 2019).
79. Dana Milbank, "Bill O'Reilly's Interview Showed a Nation Still Divided," *Washington Post*, February 3, 2014.
80. Quoted in Julie Mason, "Trump Wages War on the Press, but Was Obama Much Better to Reporters?," *Variety*, April 24, 2018.
81. Risen, "News Analysis."
82. Barack Obama, speech at the University of Illinois, September 7, 2018, official transcript reprinted by *USA Today*, https://www.usatoday.com/story/news/politics/elections/2018/09/07/president-barack-obamas-speech-transcript-slamming-trump/1225554002/.

Chapter Eighteen: Donald Trump

1. Timothy L. O'Brien, *TrumpNation: The Art of Being the Donald* (New York: Warner Books, 2005); *USA Today* review quoted on Amazon listing for the 2015 revised edition of *TrumpNation.*
2. When in 1990 *Forbes* estimated the Trump fortune at $500 million, Trump dismissed the assessment as part of a "personal vendetta." See Donald Trump, with Charles Leerhsen, *Trump: Surviving at the Top* (New York: Random House, 1990), 29.
3. Donald J. Trump, with Meredith McIver, *Trump—Never Give Up: How I Turned My Biggest Challenges into Success* (Hoboken, NJ: John Wiley & Sons, 2008), 150–51.
4. Ibid., 152, and Robert Slater, *No Such Thing as Over-Exposure: Inside the Life and Celebrity of Donald Trump* (Saddle Brook, NJ: Prentice-Hall, 2005).
5. Donald Trump and Tony Schwartz, *Trump: The Art of the Deal* (New York: Random House, 1997), 18.
6. Joyce Purnick, "Trump Offers to Rebuild Skating Rink," *New York Times*, May 31, 1986; Irwin Kula and Craig Hatkoff, "Donald Trump and the Wollman Rinking of American Politics," *Forbes*, August 24, 2015, online at: https://www.forbes.com/sites/offwhitepapers/2015

/08/24/donald-trump-and-the-wollman-rinking-of-american-politics/#52ff89832fc8. In 2019, the Trump Organization asked the city to remove the family name from the rink. See Liz Cantrell, "The Trump Name Is Removed from NYC Ice Rink," *Town & Country*, October 23, 2019, online at: https://www.townandcountrymag.com/society/politics/a29563404/trump-name-removed-central-park-ice-skating-rinks/.

7. Trump, *Surviving at the Top*, 10.
8. "I was swept up in the scandal of Ivana wanting a decent settlement from Donald," Smith sarcastically recalled years later. See John Leland, "The Rise and Fall of Liz Smith, Celebrity Accomplice," *New York Times*, July 28, 2017.
9. Trump, *Surviving at the Top*, 24, 26, 28, 29, 30.
10. Marc Fisher and Will Hobson, "Donald Trump Masqueraded as Publicist to Brag About Himself," *Financial Times*, May 13, 2016.
11. Trump, *Art of the Deal*, 117. Full disclosure: this writer worked for the Met for twenty-three years but did not start until 1992.
12. *New York Post*, February 14, 1990; Jamie Ross, "The Story Behind Trump's Infamous 'Best Sex I Ever Had' Headline," *Daily Beast*, April 12, 2018, https://www.thedailybeast.com/the-story-behind-trumps-infamous-1990-best-sex-i-ever-had-headline.
13. Omarosa Manigault Newman, *Unhinged: An Insider's Account of the Trump White House* (New York: Gallery Books, 2018).
14. Mark Singer, "Trump Solo," *New Yorker*, May 12, 1987, www.newyorker.com/magazine/1997/05/19/trump-solo.
15. Jane Mayer, "Donald Trump's Ghostwriter Tells All," *New Yorker*, July 18, 2016, https://www.newyorker.com/magazine/2016/07/25/donald-trumps-ghostwriter-tells-all.
16. Tony Schwartz, "Why Trump Can't Change, No Matter What the Consequences Are," *Washington Post*, October 18, 2019.
17. Not only did he republish his harsh condemnation of those writers in two of his own books, *The Art of the Comeback* and *Never Give Up*, but he bragged in the latter that *New York* magazine had judged it "Best Letter of the Year to the New York Times Book Review" (an obscure competition, to be sure). See Trump, *Never Give Up*, 126–27.
18. Mark Singer, *Trump and Me* (New York: Tim Duggan Books, 2016), 26–28, 82–83.
19. Allen Salkin and Aaron Short, *The Method to the Madness: Donald Trump's Ascent as Told by Those Who Were Hired, Fired, Inspired—and Inaugurated* (New York: All Points Books, 2019), 4.
20. Trump, *Surviving at the Top*, 226.
21. Michael Barbaro, "Pithy, Mean and Powerful: How Donald Trump Mastered Twitter for 2016," *New York Times*, October 5, 2015.
22. Peter Costanzo, then director of online marketing for Vanguard Press, quoted in Salkin and Short, *Method to the Madness*, 131.
23. Quotes from Amy B. Wang, "Trump Was Moved at the 2011 White House Correspondents' Dinner. He Insists It's Not Why He Ran," *Washington Post*, February 26, 2017.
24. Barbaro, "Pithy, Mean and Powerful."
25. Tim Alberta, *American Carnage: On the Front Lines of the Republican Civil War and the Rise of President Trump* (New York: HarperCollins, 2019), 306.
26. See Joe Palazzo, Nicole Hong, Michael Rothfeld, Rebecca Davis O'Brien, and Rebecca Ballhaus, "Donald Trump Played Central Role in Hush Payoffs to Stormy Daniels and Karen McDougal," *Wall Street Journal*, November 9, 2018.
27. Ronan Farrow, *Catch and Kill: Lies, Spies, and a Conspiracy to Protect Predators* (New York: Little, Brown, 2019), 342–47.
28. Maureen Callahan, "Trump Card: Behind the Donald's Latest Fake Run for President—and His Weird Embrace of the Birthers," *New York Post*, April 3, 2011; Salkin and Short, *Method to the Madness*, 159–60.

29. Video of Trump's September 16, 2016, statement, www.bbc.com/news/av/world-us-canada/37389180/donald-trump-admits-president-obama-was-born-in-us.
30. Serge F. Kovaleski and Fredrick Kunkle, "Northern New Jersey Draws Probers' Eyes," *Washington Post*, September 18, 2001; see also "Trump's Outrageous Claim That 'Thousands' of New Jersey Muslims Celebrated the 9/11 Attacks," *Washington Post*, November 22, 2015.
31. Singer, *Trump and Me*, 104–5.
32. Robert Mackey, "Beneath Trump's Mockery of a Reporter, a Cascade of Lies Leading Back to 9/11," *The Intercept*, January 9, 2017, https://theintercept.com/2017/01/09/trumps-lie-watching-celebrations-911-lurks-beneath-mockery-reporter. See also Maggie Haberman, "Donald Trump Says His Mocking of New York Times Reporter Was Misread," *New York Times*, November 27, 2015. Two years later, even Meryl Streep joined the chorus of criticism at the Golden Globes ("disrespect invites disrespect"); see Daniel Victor and Giovanni Russonello, "Meryl Streep's Golden Globes Speech," *New York Times*, January 8, 2017.
33. Daniel Arkin, "Donald Trump Criticized After He Appears to Mock Reporter Serge Kovaleski," NBC News, https://www.nbcnews.com/politics/2015-election/new-york-times-slams-donald-trump-after-he-appears-mock-n470016; Victor and Russonello, "Meryl Streep's Golden Globes Speech."
34. Jim Acosta, *The Enemy of the People: A Dangerous Time to Tell the Truth in America* (New York: Harper, 2019), 28–29.
35. Nicholas Confessore and Karen Yourish, "$2 Billion Worth of Free Media for Donald Trump," *New York Times*, March 15, 2016.
36. Paul Farhi, "Megyn Kelly Leaving Fox News for NBC," *Washington Post*, January 3, 2017.
37. Kelly signed with NBC for three years and $69 million, but left that network early, too, departing in January 2019 with a full payout. See Lisa Ryan, "Megyn Kelly Is Officially Walking Away from NBC with $69 Million," *The Cut*, January 11, 2019, https://www.thecut.com/2019/01/megyn-kelly-leaves-nbc-exit-deal-full-contract.html.
38. @RealDonaldTrump, September 5, 2015. Within a few years, whether in response to bullying or genuine political conversion, Hewitt morphed into an enthusiastic Trump admirer.
39. Alberta, *American Carnage*, 237–38.
40. Both quotes in Jeremy Diamond, "Trump: I Could 'Shoot Somebody and I Wouldn't Lose Voters,'" CNN, January 24, 2016, https://www.cnn.com/2016/01/23/politics/donald-trump-shoot-somebody-support/index.html.
41. Rachel Desantis, "Trump's History of Rage and Hostility Toward the Press," New York *Daily News*, June 30, 2018.
42. Alberta, *American Carnage*, 367–69.
43. Trump advisor Stephen K. Bannon later testified that Trump advisor Roger Stone—destined to be convicted for several felonies—had served as the conduit between the campaign and WikiLeaks. See Ashraf Khalil and Michael Balsamo, "Bannon: Trump Team Saw Stone as WikiLeaks Link," AP report in *Chicago Tribune*, November 18, 2019.
44. Trump made further inroads by suggesting online, without evidence, that Clinton was also concealing a serious illness. Bending over backward to be fair, cable networks on both sides of the political spectrum repeatedly aired a brief videotape of Mrs. Clinton appearing to stumble as she headed toward her SUV after attending a 9/11 anniversary ceremony in lower Manhattan. The *Los Angeles Times* (September 15, 2016) dutifully explained that Hillary was recovering from pneumonia, but quoted her doctor as declaring her "healthy and fit" enough to be president. Far less attention had been paid to a bizarrely superlative report provided earlier by Trump's physician claiming he "would be the healthiest individual ever elected to the presidency." See Jessica Taylor report on NPR, September 16, 2019, www.npr.org/2016/09/16/494081537/trump-would-be-the-healthiest-individual-ever-elected-to-the-presidency.
45. Acosta, *Enemy of the People*, 13, 50.

46. Erik Wemple, "Trump Designates Fox Correspondent as a 'Real Reporter,'" *Washington Post*, May 30, 2019. Wemple's story focused on another reporter who had earned Trump's gratitude, Kevin Corke of Fox News.
47. Reid, *The Man Who Sold America*, 37.
48. Michael Goodwin, "The Media's Self-Inflicted Wounds," *New York Post*, August 19, 2018.
49. Barbaro, "Pithy, Mean and Powerful."
50. Tapper made the comment on air on July 25, 2019.
51. The votes of faithless electors made the final count 304–227.
52. Author's conversation with Hillary Clinton at her New York office, February 7, 2018.
53. Bannon quoted in David Remnick, "Trump vs. the Times: Inside an Off-the-Record Meeting," *New Yorker*, January 30, 2018, https://www.newyorker.com/news/news-desk/trump-vs-the-times-inside-an-off-the-record-meeting. For Trump remarks, see transcript of press conference, February 16, 2017, NPR, https://www.npr.org/2017/02/16/515608127/transcript-and-analysis-trump-press-conference-on-labor-secretary-russia.
54. Melissa Quinn, "Hillary Clinton 'Ticked Off' at Matt Lauer After He Questioned Her About Email Scandal," *Los Angeles Times*, September 9, 2017; Acosta, *Enemy of the People*, 30.
55. Julie Hirschfeld Davis and Matthew Rosenberg, "With False Claims, Trump Attacks Media on Turnout and Intelligence Rift," *New York Times*, January 22, 2017. The article attributed the "Nazi" quote to retired CIA analyst Mark M. Lowenthal.
56. Ibid.
57. Ibid.
58. Acosta, *Enemy of the People*, 48.
59. Spicer, *The Briefing*, 130–34.
60. Dave Itzkoff, "Trump Criticizes S.N.L. Writer Who Joked About His Son Barron," *New York Times*, January 26, 2017.
61. Richard Cohen, "Sean Spicer Lied for a Liar. And Then He Wrote a Book About It," *Washington Post*, July 30, 2018.
62. Alberta, *American Carnage*, 428–29.
63. See, for example, Bob Brigham, "George Conway Ridicules Trump for Reportedly Explaining to Red Sox Owner That Abraham Lincoln Lost the Civil War," *RawStory*, May 9, 2019. See also Audrey McNamara, "Kellyanne Conway Threatens Washington Examiner Reporter Who Wrote About Her Husband," *Daily Beast*, October 24, 2019, https://www.thedailybeast.com/kellyanne-conway-threatens-washington-examiner-reporter-who-wrote-about-her-husband.
64. Michael Conway, "Trump's Public Attacks on the 'Enemies of the People' Echo Nixon's Private Press War—and More," NBC News, November 20, 2018, https://www.nbcnews.com/think/opinion/trump-s-public-attacks-enemies-people-echo-nixon-s-private-ncna938481.
65. Sarah Huckabee Sanders quoted in ibid.
66. @realDonaldTrump, Twitter, April 29, 2018, 7:45 a.m.
67. Spicer, *The Briefing*, 178–79.
68. Mollie Ziegler Hemingway, *Trump vs. the Media* (New York: Encounter Books, 2017), 1–2.
69. David Leonhart and Stuart A. Thompson, "Trump's Lies," *New York Times*, updated December 19, 2017, https://www.nytimes.com/interactive/2017/06/23/opinion/trumps/lies.html.
70. Linda Qiu, "Fact-Checking President Trump Through His First 100 Days," *New York Times*, April 29, 2017.
71. Adam Gabbatt, "The 'Exhausting' Work of Factcheckers Who Track Trump's Barrage of Lies," *Guardian*, January 21, 2019, https://www.theguardian.com/us-news/2019/jan/21/donald-trump-lies-factcheckers.

72. Glenn Kessler, Salvador Rizzo, and Meg Kelly, "President Trump Has Made 12,019 False or Misleading Claims over 928 Days," *Washington Post*, August 12, 2019.
73. @realDonaldTrump, July 23, 2018, 8:21 a.m. and 8:35 a.m. See also John Wagner, "Trump Levels False Charges Against the Post and Amazon in a Pair of Tweets," *Washington Post*, July 23, 2018.
74. Jessica Estepa, "Trump Held Only One Press Conference This Year. His Predecessors Had Way More," *USA Today*, December 22, 2017.
75. Gary Shteyngart, "Must See TV? James Poniewozik Traces the Contemporaneous Histories of Donald Trump and Television" (review), *New York Times Book Review*, September 8, 2019. The book in question, Poniewozik's *Audience of One: Donald Trump, Television, and the Fracturing of America* (New York: Liveright, 2019), said of Trump's relationship with cable news: "He pushed the drug, and he got high on it."
76. J. Walker Glassock, "Did the 'Dishonest Media' Really Take on Lincoln, Jefferson, and Jackson?," *Christian Science Monitor*, February 19, 2017, https://www.csmonitor.com/USA/2017/0219/Did-the-dishonest-media-really-take-on-Lincoln-Jefferson-and-Jackson.
77. Spicer, *The Briefing*, 2.
78. Anthony Scaramucci, *Trump: The Blue-Collar President* (New York: Center Street, 2018), 241.
79. Ibid., 249–50.
80. Spicer, *The Briefing*, 2–9.
81. Scaramucci, *Trump: The Blue-Collar President*, 260–63.
82. *New York Post*, August 1, 2017.
83. Amy Siskind, *The List: A Week-by-Week Reckoning of Trump's First Year* (New York: Bloomsbury, 2019), 172.
84. Thomas E. Patterson, "News Coverage of Donald Trump's First 100 Days," Report of the Harvard Kennedy School Shorenstein Center on Media, Politics and Public Policy, May 18, 2017, https://shorensteincenter.org/news-coverage-of-donald-trumps-first-100-days/#introduction_and_Methodology.
85. Joseph D. Lyons, "How Many Times a Day Does Trump Tweet?," *Bustle*, May 21, 2018, https://www.bustle.com/p/how-many-times-does-trump-tweet-a-day-the-president-basically-lives-on-twitter-8909583.
86. Samuel Burke, "How Many Social Followers Does Trump Actually Have?" CNNTech, June 17, 2017, https://money.cnn.com/2017/06/17/technology/trump-social-media-followers/index.html.
87. Joy-Ann Reid, *The Man Who Sold America: Trump and the Unraveling of the American Story* (New York: William Morrow, 2019), 216.
88. Alberta, *American Carnage*, 465–67.
89. Kate Kelly and Maggie Haberman, "Gary Cohn, Trump's Adviser, Said to Have Drafted Resignation Letter After Charlottesville," *New York Times*, August 25, 2017.
90. Emily Cochrane, "'They Can Make Anything Bad': Trump Bashes a Familiar Foe," *New York Times*, August 3, 2018.
91. Jeremy Diamond, "Trump Sides with Putin Over US Intelligence," CNN, July 16, 2028, https://www.cnn.com/2018/07/16/politics/donald-trump-putin-helsinki-summit/index.html.
92. @realDonaldTrump, July 19, 2018.
93. "Trump's History of Rage and Hostility," *Daily News*, June 30, 2018.
94. "Trump Retweets Cartoon of Train Killing CNN Reporter," CNN, August 15, 2017, https://www.thedailybeast.com/trump-retweets-cartoon-of-train-killing-cnn-reporter.
95. Michael Balsamo, "Feds: Coast Guard Lieutenant Compiled Hit List of Lawmakers," AP, February 20, 2019.
96. @realDonaldTrump, July 29, 2018.

97. Philip Rucker, "Trump Accuses 'Very Unpatriotic' Journalists of Putting the 'Lives of Many' in Peril," *Washington Post*, July 29, 2016.
98. Rucker, "Trump Accuses 'Very Unpatriotic' Journalists"; Mark Landler, "Times Publisher and Trump Clash over President's Threats Against Press," *New York Times*, July 30, 2019.
99. Amber Philips, "Sarah Sanders Presents the Official White House Policy: The Media Is the Enemy of the People," *Washington Post*, August 2, 2018.
100. Reprinted in "A Free Press Needs You," *New York Times*, August 16, 2018. The "blitzkrieg" comment came from the Jeffersonville, Indiana, *News and Tribune*.
101. @realDonaldTrump, August 16, 2018.
102. Eileen Sullivan, "President Sees 'Collusion' in Appeals for a Free Press," *New York Times*, August 17, 2018.
103. @realDonaldTrump, August 30, 2018.
104. Reid, *The Man Who Sold America*, 207.
105. Paul Waldman, "Trump Encourages Violence Against Reporters, and His Supporters Cheer," *Washington Post*, October 19, 2018.
106. @realDonaldTrump, October 25, 2018.
107. Emily Cochrane, "'They Can Make Anything Bad': Trump Bashes a Familiar Foe," *New York Times*, August 3, 2018; see also Katie Rogers, "A Trump Who Refuses to Condemn Journalism," *New York Times*, August 3, 2018.
108. Rucker, "Trump Accuses 'Very Unpatriotic' Journalists."
109. @realDonaldTrump, October 29, 2018.
110. John Wagner, "Trump Doubles Down on Blaming Media as Suspicious Packages Continue to Surface," *Washington Post*, October 25, 2018.
111. David Bauder, "Fox's Hannity Speaks Onstage at Trump Campaign Rally," AP, November 6, 2018, https://apnews.com/20f240baf06742c79de711d7e8580eb9. A few months later, the *Daily Caller*, a right-leaning website cofounded by Fox News personality Tucker Carlson, revived a five-year-old story that Carlson had posted an offensive blog post insulting to Jews, the Japanese, and transsexuals. The report had first surfaced when Media Matters criticized Carlson for racist and homophobic comments. See Erik Wemple, "Media Matters President Apologizes for Offensive Statements on Old Blog," *Washington Post*, March 14, 2019.
112. Peter Baker, "Fox Rebukes Sean Hannity's and Jeanine Pirro's Participation in a Trump Rally," *New York Times*, November 6, 2018.
113. Trump and UN experts David Kaye and Edison Lanza, all quoted in Sabrina Siddiqui and David Smith, "Trump's Attacks in Media Raise Threat of Violence Against Reporters, UN Experts Warn," *Guardian*, August 2, 2018, https://www.theguardian.com/us-news/2018/aug/02/donald-trump-un-media-press-freedom-journalist-danger.
114. Mollie Ziegler Hemingway, *Trump vs. the Media* (New York: Encounter Books, 2017), 55.
115. "Six in 10 in U.S. See Partisan Bias in News Media, Gallup Poll," April 5, 2017, https://news.gallup.com/poll/207794/six-partisan-bias-news-media-aspx; Art Swift, "Americans' Trust in Mass Media Sinks to New Low," September 14, 2016, https://news.gallup.com/poll/195542/americans-trust-mass-media-sinks-new-low.aspx.
116. Colbert I. King, "Your Everyday Republican Has Some Galling Views," *Washington Post*, August 10, 2018.
117. Howard Kurtz, *Media Madness: Donald Trump, the Press, and the War over the Truth* (Washington, DC: Regenery, 2018), 181.
118. Michael Conway, "Trump's Public Attacks."
119. Tara John and Brian Stelter, "Press Advocacy Groups Condemn Attack on BBC Cameraman at Trump Rally," CNN, February 12, 2019, https://www.cnn.com/2019/02/12/media/bbc-camera-man-attack-trump-rally-scli/index.html.

120. Bob Woodward, *Fear: Trump in the White House* (New York: Simon & Schuster, 2018), 165, 356.
121. Philip Rucker, Josh Dawsey, and Ashley Parker, "Venting About Press, Trump Has Repeatedly Sought to Ban Reporters over Questions," *Washington Post*, July 7, 2018.
122. This and the previous paragraph quotes Peter Baker, "Trump Bars CNN's Jim Acosta from the White House," *New York Times*, November 8, 2018.
123. Michael M. Grynbaum, "Trump May Blacklist More Reporters Who Don't Show 'Respect,'" *New York Times*, November 10, 2018.
124. @realDonaldTrump, November 26, 2018.
125. Ibid.
126. Acosta, *Enemy of the People*, 289.
127. Ryan W. Miller, "Reporter April Ryan Says She Got Death Threats After Asking If Trump Considered Resigning," *USA Today*, April 11, 2018.
128. Grynbaum, "Trump May Blacklist Reporters." See also Jordan Fabian, "Trump Calls April Ryan a 'Loser,' Threatens to Revoke More Press Credentials," *The Hill*, November 9, 2018, https://thehill.com/homenews/administration/415900-trump-calls-april-ryan-a-loser-threatens-to-revoke-more-press. Later, Ryan, a staunch defender of First Amendment access, was accused of ordering a camera crew removed from a speaking appearance in New Jersey.
129. Dana Milbank, "The White House Revoked My Pass. It's Not Just Me. It's Curtailing Access for All Journalists," *Washington Post*, May 9, 2019.
130. Erik Wemple, "Trump Orders End to New York Times, Washington Post Subscriptions," *Washington Post*, October 24, 2019, https://www.washingtonpost.com/opinions/2019/10/24/trump-orders-end-times-post-subscriptions/.
131. Paul Fahri, "What to Do About Sarah Huckabee Sanders? White House Reporters Have a Few Ideas," *Washington Post*, April 22, 2019; Sullivan comment in *Washington Post*, June 16, 2019; O'Donnell on MSNBC, quoted in the *New York Times*, May 24, 2019.
132. Fahri, "What to Do About Sarah Huckabee Sanders?"
133. Annie Karni, "The Mooch's Gift to Trump Staff: A Taxpayer-Funded Stylist," *Politico*, January 7, 2018, https://www.politico.com/story/2018/01/07/sarah-huckabee-sanders-make-up-anthony-scaramucci-katie-price-327043.
134. Michael Goodwin, "The 2016 Election and the Demise of Journalistic Standards," *Imprimis* 46 (May/June 2017), https://imprimis.hillsdale.edu/2016-election-demise-journalistic-standards/. Disclosure: the author of this book works at Hunter College, whose president is married to Mr. Goodwin.
135. Julia Musto, "Michael Goodwin: The New York Times Has Lost Its Way in Its Hatred for President Trump," Fox News, August 15, 2019, https://www.foxnews.com/media/michael-goodwin-the-times-has-lost-its-way-in-its-hatred-for-president-trump.
136. Woodward, *Fear*, 14.
137. Full transcript of the interviews, *New York Times*, November 23, 2016, April 5, 2017.
138. Michael M. Grynbaum, "Challenge to President and His View of News: Questions About Attacks on the Press for One Who Often Leads the Charge," *New York Times*, February 2, 2019. Partial transcript ("lightly edited") in same issue.
139. Michael M. Grynbaum and Eileen Sullivan, "In Attack, Trump Aims 'Enemy of the People' Directly at the Times," *New York Times*, February 21, 2019. That same week, Trump also used Twitter to urge "retribution" against *Saturday Night Live* for continuing to parody him. And he also applauded a recently filed $250 million libel suit against the *Washington Post*. It had been filed by a Kentucky high school student who alleged felt "bullied" when the *Post* reported the boy's public staring contest with a Native American (while wearing a "Make America Great Again" cap). "Go Get Them," Trump tweeted. ". . . Fake News!"

140. Chris Sommerfeldt, "'Despot' Don Is Under Fire: N.Y. Times Shows Lies, Attack on Free Press," New York *Daily News*, February 21, 2019.
141. Reprinted in "Trump Tweets on Treason," *New York Times*, October 2, 2019.
142. Spicer, *The Briefing*, 241–42.
143. New York *Daily News*, May 27, 2019.
144. Kevin Poulsen, "Far-Right Accounts Retweeted by Trump Keep Getting Suspended," *Daily Beast*, August 7, 2019, https://www.thedailybeast.com/trump-retweet-can-be-a-death-sentence-on-far-right-twitter.
145. *Miami Herald*, January 15, 2019.
146. Kurtz, *Media Madness*, 151, 176–77, 270–71.
147. Mark R. Levin, *Unfreedom of the Press* (New York: Threshold Editions, 2019), 173.
148. Notes to an October 29, 2018, speech at NYU, Floyd Abrams to Harold Holzer, December 3, 2018.
149. Jane Mayer, "Trump TV: Fox News Has Always Been Partisan. But Has It Become Propaganda?," *New Yorker*, March 8, 2009, 51.
150. Woodward, *Fear*, 164–65.
151. Emily Stewart, "Someone in the White House Leaked Trump's Private Schedule. There's a Lot of Executive Time on It," *Vox*, February 4, 2019, https://www.vix.com/policy-and-politics/2019/2/4/18210345/trump-executive-time-axios-private-schedule-leak.
152. Woodward, *Fear*, 195.
153. @realDonaldTrump, January 6, 2018; New York *Daily News*, July 11, 2019.
154. Ryan C. Brooks, "Trump's Latest Racist Comments Included Calling a Majority-Black Area a 'Disgusting, Rat and Rodent Infested Mess," *BuzzFeed News*, July 27, 2019, https://www.buzzfeednews.com/article/ryancbrooks/trump-racist-elijah-cummings-baltimore-tweets.
155. Paul Krugman, "Luckily, Trump Is an Unstable Genius," *New York Times*, October 11, 2019.
156. Erik Wemple, "Sean Hannity and Fox News Have Normalized Media Corruption," *Washington Post*, November 4, 2019; Gabriel Sherman, "'He Thinks Fox Screwed Him': Trump Enraged at Fox, His Impeachment Bulwark," *Vanity Fair Hive*, December 10, 2019, https://www.vanityfair.com/news/2019/12/trump-enraged-at-fox-impeachment-bulwark.
157. Michael M. Grynbaum, "Shepard Smith, Fox New Anchor, Abruptly Departs from Network," *New York Times*, October 11, 2019.
158. Michael M. Grynbaum, "Fox News Anchor Who Broke Away Gives $500,000 to Press Freedom Group," *New York Times*, November 22, 2019.
159. Michael M. Grynbaum and Maggie Haberman, "Fox News, a Presidential Booster, Isn't Exempt from His Reproach," *New York Times*, October 14, 2019; Gabriel Sherman, "'He Thinks Fox Screwed Him': Trump Enraged at Fox, His Impeachment Bulwark," *Vanity Fair Hive*, December 10, 2019, https://www.vanityfair.com/news/2019/12/trump-enraged-at-fox-impeachment-bulwark.
160. John Wagner, "'Crazed Lunatics': Trump Again Attacks the News Media as 'the Enemy of the People,'" *Washington Post*, January 7, 2019.
161. Max Boot, "His Presidents' Day Tweets Showed Why Trump Is Unfit to Be President," *Washington Post*, February 19, 2019.
162. @realDonaldTrump, April 23, 2019.
163. Rich Lowry, "The Don Show: He Better Hope Voters Don't Tire of the Drama," *New York Post*, August 23, 2019.
164. A. G. Sulzberger, "Accusing the New York Times of 'Treason,' Trump Crosses a Line: The Founders Considered It the Gravest of Crimes. Tossing the Charge Around Is Irresponsible and Wrong," *Wall Street Journal*, June 19, 2019.
165. Kenneth P. Vogel and Jeremy W. Peters, "Trump's Allies Scour Internet to Punish Press," *New York Times*, August 26, 2019.

166. Andrew O'Reilly, "Trump Slams Media as 'Crooked as Hell' amid Ukraine Phone Call Controversy," Fox News, September 23, 2019.
167. @realDonaldTrump, August 25, 2019.
168. @realDonaldTrump, September 7, 2019.
169. Peter Baker and Sarah Mervosh, "Trump Storm over Alabama Keeps Raging," *New York Times*, September 7, 2019.
170. Michael M. Grynbaum, "Reporter's Question, Repeated, Kindled Trump's Ire," *New York Times*, October 3, 2019.
171. Michael S. Schmidt and Maggie Haberman, "Fictitious Video of President Shooting Critics and Media Shown at His Resort," *New York Times*, October 14, 2019.
172. Wagner, "'Crazed Lunatics.'"
173. Lifted from a 2014 film called *Kingsman: The Secret Service*, the production was eventually attributed to an online animator who called himself "The GeekzTeam" and boasted that he was "a red blooded American with ZERO tolerance for the liberal agenda." See Annie Karini, Kevin Roose, and Katie Rogers, "Trump's Fans Spice Memes with Violence," *New York Times*, October 16, 2019.
174. Mark Moore, "Trump Says ISIS Leader al-Baghdadi Died 'Whimpering and Crying and Screaming All the Way,'" *New York Post*, October 27, 2019; Peter Baker and Eric Schmitt, "A Whimper That Only Trump Seemed to Hear: Doubts over Story of al-Baghdadi's Death," *New York Times*, November 2, 2019.
175. Exchange between John G. Nicolay and Joseph Medill, June 19, 1863, quoted in Harold Holzer, *Lincoln and the Power of the Press: The War for Public Opinion* (New York: Simon & Schuster, 2015), 467.
176. Michael M. Grynbaum, "Trump Cancels Subscriptions to the New York Times and The Washington Post," *New York Times,* October 25, 2019.
177. Annie Karini, "Trump's Former Chief of Staff Regrets Leaving," *New York Times*, October 27, 2019. See also Elizabeth Williamson, "Turbulent Rise for New Voice of Oval Office," *New York Times*, August 23, 2019.
178. *New York Times*, November 3, 2019.
179. Jack Nicas, "Apple's Award Moment: Trump Takes Credit for a Computer Factory Opened in 2013," *New York Times*, November 22, 2019; Jamie Ross, "Trump Has Now Made Over 15,000 False or Misleading Claims in Office, Says Washington Post," *Daily Beast*, December 16, 2019, https://www.thedailybeast.com/trump-has-now-made-over-15000-false-or-misleading-claims-in-office-says-washington-post.
180. *New York Times*, November 17, 2019.
181. John Avlon, "Fact Check" segment on CNN *New Day*, November 13, 2019, text of speech provided by Avlon to the author.
182. Yochai Benkler, Robert Faris, Hal Roberts, and Ethan Zuckerman, "Study: Breitbart-led right-wing media ecosystem altered broader media agenda," *Columbia Journalism Review*, March 3, 2017, https://www.cjr.org/analysis/breitbart-media-trump-harvard-study.php; Michiko Kakutani, "The End of Normal," *New York Times*, December 29, 2019.
183. Rob Fredericks, "Caving Again on Turkey," *New York Post*, November 27, 2019.
184. Oliver Darcy, "Trump campaign says it will no longer credential Bloomberg News reporters . . . ," CNN online, December 2, 2109, https://www.cnn.com/2019/12/02/media/trump-campaign-bloomberg/index.html.
185. Peter Baker, "Stung in Europe, and Finding No Balm at Home," *New York Times*, December 5, 2019.
186. William Boot, "Woodward & Bernstein: We're Not Fake News: Two of the Greatest Journalists of the 20th Century Have a Message for Political Reports—and for President Trump," *Daily Beast*, April 30, 2017, https://www.thedailybeast.com/woodward-and-bernstein-were-not-fake-news.

187. Mitt Romney, "Trump Is Wrong to Vilify the Press. It's Not the Enemy, It's Critical to Democracy," *USA Today*, November 11, 2018.
188. "Trump's War on Journalism," *Los Angeles Times*, April 5, 2017.
189. An October 2019 Suffolk University poll, however, found that Republicans uniformly trusting Fox News, according to a report on the survey, "compared to the relatively distributed trust Democrats place in various outlets." See Philip Bump, "Another New Poll Shows the Extent of the Overlap Between Fox News and Defenders of Trump," *Washington Post*, October 29, 2019.
190. "Trump unleashed: He's talking more and tweeting more," CNN politics, September 21, 2019, https://www.cnn.com/2019/09/21/politics/trump-unleashed-speaking-tweeting-more/index/html.
191. *List of most-followed Twitter accounts* (as of December 26, 2019), https://en.wikipedia.org/wiki/List_of_most_followed_Twitter_accounts.
192. Transcript of February 16, 2017 news conference, NPR, https://www.npr.org/2017/02/16/515608127/transcript-and-analysis-trump-press-conference-on-labor-secretary-russia.
193. Charles M. Blow, "For Trump, Impeachment is a Show," *New York Times*, November 25, 2019.

INDEX

Note: Page numbers in **bold** indicate main discussion of the text's primary subjects.